DATE DUE

JUN 6 07		
JUL 18 07		

WHEN ISAM WAS SHERIFF

*A True Epic of the Rural
Missouri Ozarks
1945-1955*

Susie Knust

Susie Knust
3/19/07

ABOUT THE BOOK:

When Isam Was Sheriff is an account of law enforcement in a rural Ozarks county run pretty much single-handedly by a colorful, unsophisticated elected sheriff who was close to the people.

But within that account and through history's eyes, **When Isam Was Sheriff** is a rich tapestry about love and lust, passion and failure, rescues, youth, life, illness, murders, birth, death, peace, and war on the home front.

As we read, we begin to detect the gifts and flaws of our ancestors in *us*.

The author skillfully combines the local weekly newspaper archives with the seventy people she interviewed during 2003 and 2004, relating the focus of the book—a true epic of the rural Missouri Ozarks from 1945 to 1955, in its own words and voice.

ABOUT THE AUTHOR:

Susie Essig Knust was born "back east" in Huntington, Indiana, when Isam was Sheriff, in 1948. She taught high school and college English for over fifteen years in Indiana, Illinois, and Missouri, then was a banker in Indiana and Missouri for fifteen years. She moved to Marshfield, "Missourah" to marry Daniel Max Knust in 1998. Together they have four grown children: Scott and Lindsey Moore, and Nathaniel and Ian Knust. In 2001, Susie began writing full-time.

FROM THE BOOK:

[Peg Miller] "Isam was a great big guy, 6'2" maybe. He had a standard uniform. He had some kind of chino pants that he wore with galluses. You wouldn't even call them suspenders, they were galluses. And his badge was on one of them, I assume over his heart. And he kinda wore a gray undershirt kind of thing. He never looked terribly cleaned up. And he wore a hat, a felt hat, that was pooched up, no pleat. I can't remember any occasion on which he replaced it. I can't remember him having a new hat. He always looked the same. But he was just sort of unscrubbed, but not unpleasantly so. I don't think he liked anything but being sheriff. I can't think of anybody talking about anything that Isam did for recreation, once he was sheriff.

I think he was an absolutely heroic character. He was just this kind of big ole raw-boned guy, who was dedicated at what he did. He was absolutely unapproachable. Isam was as honest as the day is long. The people who didn't like him hated him with a passion. And it was mutual!"

"This Thing Called Freedom of the Press—What is it?
It is the reporter, jotting down facts. It is the correspondent,
gathering news of the small community. It is the editor sifting
wheat from chaff. It is the writer, expressing himself clearly.
It is skilled artisans of the mechanical departments,
helping to 'get out the paper.' It is the free American men and
women devoted to the task of keeping America free by keeping
America informed...."

What is a newspaper? A newspaper is many things. It is a record of history. It is a forum. It is a market place. It is a voice. It is a guardian. It is, above all, an institution devoted to the best interests of the community. It is a servant of the people. Its goal---the public be served.

The MARSHFIELD MAIL--Webster County's Newspaper"

[Trooper Gene Tinnin] "I just came out of World War II and I saw death many times...but that was as bad as a war zone.

I remember we formed a group to go to different barns and sheds and scour the countryside. We were afraid the shooter might still be around.

When we stuck our heads up in haylofts, I remember Sheriff Neil Brown saying, 'Gene, let's go up and check. The others have children; we don't.' How's that for being brave? In favor of yielding to someone who might leave a family."

[Afterword: From the Author] "Webster County was a microcosm of rural America in the middle of the 20th century and, because of that, it needs to be remembered and understood as a part of who many of us were and are and who we might become."

WHEN
ISAM
WAS
SHERIFF

A True Epic of

the Rural Missouri Ozarks

1945-1955

Susie Knust

Birch Creek Publishing

Marshfield, Missouri

2005

WHEN ISAM WAS SHERIFF
A True Epic of the Rural Missouri Ozarks
1945-1955
Webster County, Missouri

By Susie Knust

Published by:
Birch Creek Publishing
Post Office Box 777
Marshfield, MO 65706-0777
knust@fidnet.com
Copyright 2005 by Susie Knust

Publisher's Cataloging-in-Publication
(Provided by Quality Books, Inc.)

Knust, Susie.
  When Isam was sheriff : a true epic of the rural
Missouri Ozarks, 1945-1955 / Susie Knust. -- 1st ed.
  p. cm.
  LCCN 2004114587
  ISBN 0-9760004-0-7

  1. Law enforcement--Missouri--Webster County--History
--20th century. 2. Cunningham, Isam. 3. Sheriffs--
Missouri--Webster County--History--20th century.
4. Webster County (Mo.)--History--20th century.
I. Title.

HV8145.M8K68 2005   363.2'09778'8823
                           QBI04-200469

Printed by Litho Printers, Cassville, Missouri, U.S.A. litho@mchsi.com

Contents

Dedication

When Isam Was Sheriff is dedicated with love and gratitude to the people—present and past—of Webster County, Missouri, especially Judge Daniel Max Knust, the person who encouraged me to write the Isam Cunningham stories (and tells them better than anyone I know).

Thanks and Acknowledgments

I want to thank the following individuals and organizations, as well as to acknowledge certain books that were particularly helpful in the course of my research and writing.

Charley and Mary Lou Cunningham
The People Interviewed in 2003 and 2004 (listed in The
                 Preface), their families and ancestors
Webster County's Garst Memorial Library staff
The MARSHFIELD MAIL staff, present and past

Jean Carroll: A Tale of the Ozark Hills,
              John Homer Case (1911)
Take To The Hills: A Chronicle of the Ozarks,
              Marguerite Lyon (1941)
And Green Grass Grows All Around, M. Lyon (1942)
History of Webster County, Floy Watters George (1955)
In Search of History, Theodore H. White (1978)
Across Our Wide Missouri, Bob Priddy (1982, 1984)
A CountryYear:Living the Questions, Sue Hubbell(1986)
Praying for Sheetrock, Melissa Fay Greene (1991)
A Brief History of Webster County and its Families,
              The Webster County Historical Society (1999)
How to Talk Pure Ozark 'Thout Hardly Even Tryin,
              Dale Freeman (2002)
The Gold of Cape Girardeau, Morley Swingle (2002)—
      This book initially inspired me to write Missouri Ozarks history

Huntington City/Township Library, Huntington, Indiana,
            especially the staff from 1948-1970, the years
            I resided in Huntington (as Susie Essig)

Let this be a special recognition of Huntington County's U.S. Rep. J. Edward Roush, known nationwide in 1968 when AT&T unveiled its single emergency 9-1-1 phone system in Roush's and my hometown—Huntington, Indiana—the first city to receive service.
   J. Edward Roush died March 26, 2004, during the writing of this book.

PREFACE: From the Author

Well, you can imagine, I'm sure, the joyous scene when I'd arrive for a pre-arranged interview about Sheriff Isam Cunningham. Though I knew almost no one, initially, we shared a bond with that mutual friend, Ole Isam.

Just before I turned on my tape recorder, I'd remind those involved that Isam was elected in November of 1944, took office in 1945, and died in office in July 1955. I'd also remind them that anything said might be used in my book.

I usually asked, "What do you remember about Isam?"

And the laughter would come easily with still another version of an Isam Story or an Isam-ism.

The interview continued. Eventually, and always, there would be a tumble of unrelated but delightful information about Webster County or other colorful characters, John Hosmer or M.J. Huffman for example.

Yet something I never expected with the interviews were the tears. Nearly fifty years after Isam's death, people remembered not only their Sheriff but their spouses and parents and children and friends who also are gone. Those memories brought tears, theirs and mine, as I listened and tape-recorded their stories, and as I later transcribed the interviews and heard the pauses.

I have included some of their memories in Chapter Three: A Prologue and in Chapter Sixteen: An Epilogue.

However, early on, I realized I needed more local history, the background for their stories: I felt as though I were being swept up and away into a land of another language and was often lost with the places, events, and people being mentioned. So I interrupted my schedule of interviews, located the archives of The MARSHFIELD MAIL in a basement room of our Webster County courthouse, and spent the next three months reading the weekly Webster County newspaper from 1944 through 1955, noting verbatim the references to Isam and law enforcement. Then I sought out and read more history, both local and global, most of which I've acknowledged on the previous page of this book.

But, of course, I was distracted by news about the atomic bomb and the end of World War II, politicians, pictures of famous and infamous people, news about the Korean War and the godless Communists, clever and quaint advertisements, activities of the

Jaycees, the Lions Club, the Fox Hunters, the schools, the B & PW *[Business and Professional Women],* funeral homes, and Route 66. These, and others, I couldn't help but include in my book.

And then, during my note-taking from *The MAIL,* an innocent article in the June 19, 1947 issue grabbed my attention. I remember leaning forward over those massive, bound pages as I read: "B & PW elected new officers, and Carmen Rainey was elected President." I sat back, took some deep breaths, and remembered what I'd heard mentioned in several interviews.

Here I was, with Real Life, and I knew the future. This woman's life would be fully changed in about two years, including an assault on her and a divorce from husband Rex, who even at *this* time was allegedly in the secret relationship with a young switchboard operator named Mary Margaret Evans. These were real people, not characters in a novel. The suspense began!

Also, about this time, the story I'd started to write took on a life of its own and I began to follow, not lead. I'd been warned by other writers that this can happen.

Yes, *When Isam Was Sheriff* is an account of law enforcement in a rural Ozarks county, run pretty much single-handedly by a colorful, unsophisticated, elected sheriff who was close to the people. But within that account and through history's eyes, *When Isam Was Sheriff* is a rich tapestry about love and lust, passion and failure, youth, life, illness, murders, rescues, birth, death, peace and war on the home front.

The real people I interviewed are listed on the following pages, in alphabetical order. I've included a married woman's maiden name, valuable for her genealogy. I've given a brief description of the person relative to the focus of the book: a true epic of the rural Missouri Ozarks, 1945-1955, when Isam Cunningham was Sheriff.

People Interviewed

Janet Sue Letterman Aday...born in 1958; youngest of Mattie Cunningham Letterman's seven children

Billie Galbraith Arthur...born in 1933; native of Marshfield; owned and operated Arthur Funeral Home in Marshfield in addition to working at Sho-Me Power

Joe Arthur...born in 1932; native of Niangua; owned and operated Arthur Funeral Home, including the ambulance service, after working years with other funeral home owners in Marshfield

Warren Beck...born in 1918; Marshfield High School classmate of John Hosmer's and Edna Henderson Cunningham's; elected mayor of Marshfield in 1954; owned and operated a local dairy business

J.E. "Doc" Blinn...came to Marshfield in 1946; became County Doctor in 1952, the doctor called when anything was wrong with prisoners

Patsy Shockley Browning...at age 5 years 11 months, she survived the April 3, 1951 Shockley Family Murders

Shirley Letterman Carrizales...born in 1940; third of Mattie Cunningham Letterman's seven children

Willis Case...born in 1910; auctioneer and businessman; long-time friend of Isam's

Charles "Charley" Cunningham...born in 1933; Isam and Eva's youngest child; moved from Niangua to live in the courthouse with Isam and Eva during Isam's first two terms as Sheriff

David Isom Cunningham...born in 1955, oldest of Helen and William David "Jake" Cunningham's three children

Edna Henderson Cunningham...widow of James "Buster"
Cunningham; she and Buster took over and eventually
purchased the Cunningham family farm in Susanna
near Niangua; a Marshfield schoolmate of Mary Margaret
Evans, and classmate of Warren Beck and John Hosmer

Eldeen Freymiller Cunningham...widow of Wilbur "Red"
Cunningham; mother of Gail, Dennis, Teresa, and Mark

Helen Jones Cunningham...widow of William David "Jake"
Cunningham; mother of David, Marsha, and J.C.

John Calvin "J.C." Cunningham...born in 1960; married Highway
Patrolman Tom Martin's daughter, Debbie; youngest child
of Helen and Jake Cunningham

Mary Bean Cunningham...known as the family historian; married
to Floyd "Snooks" Cunningham, the only other child of
Isam and Eva's still living besides Charley

Mary Lou McNabb Cunningham...born and reared in Elkland;
Charley's wife; helped Isam and Eva as needed, with
meals and other business; mother of Cathy and Todd

Todd Cunningham...born in 1968; Isam and Eva's youngest
grandchild; Mary Lou and Charley's son

Celesta Keeler Davis...telephone operator at Garst Telephone
Company from 1950 to 1955; widow of Orven Davis,
Webster County Clerk for 26 years, beginning in 1948

Marie Letterman Day...born in 1931; oldest of Mildred
Cunningham Letterman's three children and the oldest of
all Isam and Eva's grandchildren

Raymond Day...born in 1918 west of Conway on Starvey Creek
Road; married to May Vestal's daughter Louise; brother
(John) married to Marie Letterman Day

Oliver Evans…Marshfield's first full-time, paid Night
Watchman; a second cousin to Mary Margaret Evans

Alberta Scott Fraker…raised by her grandfather, Willy Scott, and
grandmother, Pearl Cunningham Scott, a half-sister to
Isam; husband Gene Fraker operated a service station on
The Square (and was later elected Webster County
Sheriff)

Marsha Cunningham Gorman…born in 1956; middle child of
Helen and Jake Cunningham; sister to David and J.C.

Paula Case Greer…daughter of Willis Case; a teenager when
Isam was Sheriff, she graduated from Marshfield High
School with Charley Cunningham in 1950

Talt Greer…young man when Isam was Sheriff; now married to
Paula Case Greer

Ruby Childress Hargus…born in 1913; grew up around
Seymour; she and her husband, Clyde "Skeeter" Hargus,
owned and operated the Marshfield Café, on The Square,
from 1947 to 1956; Clyde, a Democrat, was named
Fire Chief of Marshfield in 1951 and was appointed sheriff
immediately after Isam died in 1955

Barbara Dugan Herren…wife of Cline Herren, Jr.; worked for
Roy Miller as a legal secretary; daughter-in-law to Judge
Cline Herren, Magistrate during Isam's tenure as Sheriff

Cline C. Herren, Jr.…his father, Cline Herren, was Webster
County's first Probate Judge and Ex-Officio Magistrate,
which coincided with the entire time Isam was Sheriff

Grace Cunningham Hickman…born in 1908; the daughter of
Isam's half-brother Frank Cunningham

Melba "Mitzi" Douthit Hosmer…former wife of John Hosmer,
Prosecuting Attorney two terms when Isam was
Sheriff; active Democrats, Mitzi and John were founding

members of Webster County Historical Society in 1952

Philip S. Huffman...lawyer in Hartville, county seat of Wright
County; son of Marion (M.J.) Huffman, noted attorney,
Fox Hunter, and Republican Party leader, as well as a
close friend of Isam's

Mary Rosamond "Sally" Day Hyde...born in 1918; graduated in
1935 from Niangua High School; returned to teach; taught
Charley and Wilbur Cunningham at Prospect School; her
father, Luther (M.L.) Day, owned and operated the
Niangua Telephone Company from 1912 until 1951, out of
their residence.

Helen Jackson...went to school with Isam's sons Buster and
Snooks; neighbor of the Isam Cunningham family in
Niangua; a Democrat

Mildred Tindle Jarratt...daughter of local businessman Roy
Tindle; married Jack Jarratt and together they owned and
operated Jarratt's Men and Boy's Store on The Square in
Marshfield for 30 years, beginning in 1952; Democrats

Warren Johnson...son of the Webster County sheriff immediately
before Isam, Johnny Johnson; named Public Relations
person for Sho-Me Power beginning in 1949

Mary Ellen Shockley Kilburn...at age 10 years 3 months, she
survived The Shockley Family Murders of April 3, 1951

Daniel Max Knust...elected Associate Circuit Judge of Webster
County, for seven four-year terms beginning in 1978;
spouse of this book's author; colorful storyteller

Freda Doyle Langston...daughter of Elzie Doyle, deputy and
record keeper of Isam's; when Elzie needed to assist
Isam with female prisoners or female jurors, Freda
helped cover Elzie's job as secretary of Farmers Mutual

Insurance Company of Webster County (elected Nov.10, 1945 and retired Dec.1, 1962); the insurance office was on the second floor of the courthouse

Darrell Letterman...born in 1936; second of Mattie Cunningham Letterman's seven children

Don Letterman...born in 1933; second of Mildred Cunningham Letterman's three children; two weeks *older* than his *Uncle* Charley Cunningham

Fredrick Isom Letterman...born in 1946; youngest of Mildred Cunningham Letterman's three children

Jerry Letterman...born in 1942; fourth of Mattie Cunningham Letterman's seven children

Thomas Dwaine Letterman...born in 1952; sixth of Mattie Cunningham Letterman's seven children

Betty Letterman Marlin...born in 1934; oldest of Mattie Cunningham Letterman's seven children

Margaret Elizabeth McFall "Peg" Miller...wife of Marshfield attorney Roy Miller who served several terms as Prosecuting Attorney with Isam

Mary Lee Day Peck...born and reared in Niangua; niece of Sally Day Hyde

John T. Pierpont...U. S. Marshal for Western Missouri from 1970-1979; sheriff of Greene County from 1981-2000; son of John T. "Tub" Pierpont, sheriff of Greene County twice, once during Isam's first term, 1945-1948

Kerry Proctor...agent for and board member of Farmers Mutual Insurance Company of Webster County, Missouri

Bill Rader...born in 1924 in Niangua; his mother, Velva Letterman Rader, was Mildred Cunningham Letterman's sister-in-law

Jane Hyde Rader...born in Niangua; married to Bill; cousin to Sally Day Hyde's husband, William

Robin Lineberger Rader...granddaughter of Will Lineberger, the man whose report of being robbed spurred Isam to pursue the robber and resulted in Isam's single-car near-tragic wreck on April 1, 1955

Jack I. Rainey...born in 1932, the only child of Carmen and Rex Rainey; grew up in and lived in the family business, Rainey Funeral Home in Marshfield

Maxine "Toots" Shockley Replogle...the oldest child of Bill and Clara Shockley; she and husband Glenn took in and reared three of her surviving siblings after The Shockley Family Murders; she was 22 years old on April 3, 1951

Fred Rost...Webster County farmer; member of the jury that convicted Mary Margaret Evans of felonious assault on Carmen Rainey Oct.19, 1949

Wilma Thomas Ryser...granddaughter of May Cunningham Rader, Isam's half sister; best friends with Jake Cunningham while growing up in Niangua

William "Billy" Shockley...oldest son of Bill and Clara Shockley; he and his wife Lorene took in and reared three of his surviving siblings after The Shockley Family Murders; he was 20 years 9 months old on April 3, 1951

Donald Shockley...at age 8 years 3 months, he survived The Shockley Family Murders on April 3, 1951

James "Jimmy" Shockley...at age 13 years and several months, he survived The Shockley Family Murders on April 3, 1951, and was the oldest and only surviving family member aware of what was occurring at their home that night

Joe Shockley...youngest brother of the murdered Bill Shockley, son of the murdered Mrs. Gus Shockley, he was 32 years old on April 3, 1951; with his wife Mary, then 28 years old, he arrived first on the scene while the murderer [Kenneth Essary] was still present, and shooting; immediately took in the six surviving children after the murders and reared them, for the next nine months, along with Joe and Mary's own six children

Mary Martin Shockley...wife of Joe Shockley; see above entry

Mary Francis "Fran" Thomas Steelman...granddaughter of May Cunningham Rader, Isam's half sister; best friends and schoolmates with Charley Cunningham in Niangua (before Isam was elected and the Cunninghams needed to move into the courthouse in Marshfield)

Francis E. "Tony" Stephens...served in the Missouri State Highway Patrol Troop D from 1947 until 1979; he often came to Marshfield to help Isam

N. E. "Gene" Tinnin...served in the Missouri State Highway Patrol from October 1949 until retiring July 15, 1982; was one of the first law enforcement officers on the scene of The Shockley Family Murders in April, 1951; also helped solve the murder of 11-year-old Jeanette Earnest by her uncle Thurman Priest in November, 1954

Charles Vestal...one of May Vestal's three children; second cousin to and same age as Charley Cunningham; graduated from Niangua High School

May Cain Vestal...born in 1906; from Good Spring, near Niangua; May and husband Herbert took in and cared for his grandmother ("Aunt Eva's" mother) until Mrs. Randolph's death in 1951

Jack Watters...employed by and later owner of the family-owned
The MARSHFIELD MAIL weekly newspaper; former
president of Marshfield's Junior Chamber of Commerce
(Jaycees), among many other volunteer activities

Glen Wilson...while serving in the Missouri State Highway Patrol
Troop D, he often came to Marshfield to help Isam

Gail Cunningham Woody...born in 1952; oldest of Wilbur
Cunningham's four children

David Young...son of Glenn Young who along with Glenn's
brother Carl Young owned several popular retail grocery
stores throughout Webster County for many years

Cathy Cunningham Youngblood...born in 1958; the older of
Charley and Mary Lou Cunningham's two children

"**Evie *[Eva]*** was named the Prettiest Girl at the Pie Supper, when she was
young. She received a plate for that. I have the plate in there, in a cabinet." **[Mary
Bean Cunningham]**

"**Isam** was known in the community, before he was sheriff, as being a
different character than the average farmer would be. He wasn't a leader, he wasn't a
good follower. He was just kind of a unique person. His own person." **[Willis Case]**

Chapter One
Enoch Isam Cunningham,
Isam Stories, and Isam-isms

Sunday, Sept. 12, 1954 Springfield News & Leader

Webster County Sheriff Most Colorful in Ozarks

'Good Old Isam: He's One in a Hundred'

By JOE CLAYTON

For nearly ten years now, a fabled farmer, fondly called everything from "good old Isam" to "that tough bird," has been Mr. Law in Webster County.

Ask any law enforcement officer in the Ozarks—or in many distant points of the nation—if he has ever heard of Sheriff E. I. Cunningham, and you'll get quick results.

"You mean old Isam?"

From then on, you're in for at least an hour of recollections, a mixture of fact and legend, which have entwined themselves with the life of the most colorful sheriff in these hills.

To the thousands of Webster Countians sheltered under his legal wing, Isam Cunningham is a typical country sheriff who talks their language. And they like it.

They have no qualms about coming to him at any hour with a problem—the theft of a gun, a harness; a neighborhood quarrel.

And Cunningham, who knows just about everybody in the county, is quick to pin down the source of the trouble. He gets his man with a mixture of old-fashioned and modern methods of deduction.

* * *

When some out-of-town criminal drifts into Webster County for a few burglaries, he usually learns that the country sheriff isn't the sleeping type. Cunningham can spot a stranger in a second and he has an elephant's memory for auto licenses and other minute data.

In settling family feuds, he usually tries the friendly approach first. When that fails, he quotes the law and turns out to be the most hard-headed man in the bunch.

"And it's a good thing I'm hard headed," he said with a grin the other day. "I've been hit on the head three times by prisoners. I aim to make that third time the last, too."

In his decade of law enforcement, Cunningham has had the dubious honor of nabbing some of the Ozarks' most notorious criminals and he has tangled with many weird cases. Among the most spectacular were the murders of four members of a Conway farm family four years ago, and the strange, nocturnal attempt on the life of Mrs. Carmen Rainey in a Marshfield funeral home a number of years ago.

The sheriff gained his county office in 1945, after two defeats in earlier primaries. He hasn't decided whether or not to seek a fourth term, but if he does there seems to be little doubt that the job will be his.

* * *

Should he run for office again, he'll have to enlarge the cupboard in his office at the Webster County courthouse. It's already overflowing with souvenirs and evidence from countless cases on which he has worked.

There are many guns which were used in slayings, a homemade sock blackjack with which he was bopped on the head in a frustrated jail break, and a narrow strip of gray cloth.

The latter was the only evidence one prisoner left behind when he fled from the sheriff and caught his pants on a barbed wire fence.

The head-bopping episode came close to ending Cunningham's career four years ago. Two men tried to break for freedom from the jail by hitting the sheriff repeatedly with a blackjack made of a shaving lotion bottle in a sock. The holes in the souvenir sock and the splinters of the glass bottle prove the force with which he was struck.

But he gave back almost as much punishment as he took and the prisoners never reached the outside of the jail. A trooper and Cunningham's youngest son heard the commotion and helped him re-jail the pair. The incident hospitalized the sheriff for some time.

* * *

Cunningham shares honors with his wife in presiding over the jail, termed one of the best in the state. Its neat-as-a-pin interior has freshly painted walls and floors, a separate section for juveniles, and offers prisoners home-cooked meals.

Mrs. Cunningham does the cooking in a pastel-painted kitchen and dining room adjacent to the cells.

One of the most notorious characters with whom Isam tangled was Louis "Duke" Petty, the bank robber. During his heyday in the late 1920's Petty robbed the bank of Niangua, had a gun battle with officers, and surrendered only after he was wounded.

Picked up for parole violation in 1947, he broke out of the Lawrence County jail and later selected a Webster County farmhouse for a hideout. Discovering it, Cunningham and two FBI men went there and convinced Petty he was surrounded.

"Don't shoot. I'm not half as bad as you think," Petty called out to the sheriff. Cunningham, made a disbeliever by Petty's past record, took no chances in escorting him to jail.

* * *

The killing of four members of the Shockley family near Conway April 3, 1951, was undoubtedly one of the bloodiest tragedies in Ozarks history, and the worst crime to occur during Cunningham's second term of office.

The orgy had its beginning when shy, thin Kenneth Essary, 23-year-old neighbor of the Shockleys, bought a new rifle and went to their home one night to settle a grudge he mistakenly thought the family held against him.

He shot Bill Shockley, 43, on the back steps, then ran around the house and fired a fusillade through a window, felling Shockley's wife, Clara, 44, and his mother, Mrs. Gus Shockley, 73. Finally, he killed the Shockley couple's daughter, Helen Louise, 16, as she was phoning her aunt for help.

The wild youth, his job still not completed, also fired into an upstairs bedroom but missed five children sleeping there. When the aunt and her husband arrived in a truck, he blasted more than a score of holes in the vehicle.

When other neighbors went into the house to investigate, Essary took parting shots at them before vanishing into the night. He was captured at the farm of his father without incident and eventually was given a multiple life term for the murders.

Sheriff Cunningham, son of James Cunningham, a county judge who also ran a canning factory, sawmill and farm at various times, was born at Susanna community, seven miles east of Niangua, May 28, 1890. Susanna later faded from history when the postoffice folded up and the only store moved.

Since then, the sheriff has acquired much of the land about the old Cunningham homestead, and hopes to keep it in the family. As far back as he can remember, his forebears were born and raised in that part of the county.

* * *

Isam was named for Isham H. Cunningham, one-time Webster County recorder and clerk, but the sheriff decided to drop the H from the name to simplify matters. Folks didn't pronounce it, anyway.

Growing up as a hard working farm boy, he got the itch to travel in his mid-teens and ran away from home. After a brief session as a "sod-buster" in Oklahoma and Texas he backtracked to his old home place and on Feb. 8, 1911, married a neighborhood belle, Eva Randolph.

After a few more years of farming the Cunninghams packed up their two small daughters and headed for the Sooner state in a wagon. They spent a year there on a rented farm, long enough to convince Isam that the Ozarks in general and Webster County in particular was to be his home from then on.

He traded the 1632 bushels of corn he raised that year for a 1915 Ford with brass trimmings, and the family returned to Susanna in high style. By that time they had a new member to introduce to their folks—little Mattie—the only Cunningham born on "foreign" soil, in Oklahoma.

Mattie is a grown woman today with the last name of Letterman and lives north of Springfield. The Cunninghams now have seven children. One daughter, Marie, died when she was seven.

* * *

Charles, youngest of the brood, has a major league baseball contract awaiting him when he returns from his military police duties in Paris. He also was a top scorer when he played basketball at Marshfield High.

Another son, James, lives on the home place near Niangua; Floyd lives in Springfield; David in Marshfield; Wilbur in Rockford, Ill., and Mildred near Niangua.

Isam himself came from a large family of 14 children, some of them half-brothers and sisters. Brothers still living include Fred, employed with the Frisco in Springfield, and Jodie, of Bakersfield, Calif.

Despite the overwhelming unhappiness which often has been laid at Cunningham's doorstep, he still has a sense of humor.

He keeps two ancient iron balls with long chains in his office, just to startle visitors who wonder what medieval torture he uses on prisoners. The chains, long unused, were inherited with his office.

And he's fond of displaying a photograph of himself which was "doctored up" unflatteringly by Springfield police recently. Under his portrait is a prison number and a description which states he is addicted to a weed—"Kools"—carries a hog leg pistol, and is pretty darned desperate.

"You couldn't pull a trick like that on every sheriff and get a laugh out of him," commented Police Chief Troy Cleland. "Isam is one in a hundred."

Isam Stories

[Daniel Max Knust] "The most commonly told story about Isam, from my perspective, was the one about the....

It was early one morning in Niangua before the little café there in town opened, and the lady that ran the café got there, and waiting on her doorstep was Isam, Commodore Smith, and Roy Miller. Commodore didn't work for the sheriff's office fulltime, he was deputized as needed, and Roy Miller was prosecutor at the time. And the lady was kinda surprised to see three people there waitin'. So she unlocked the café, went in and started the coffee, and then came back and directed her question at Isam.

She said, 'Isam, what brings The Law to Niangua so early in the morning?'

Isam said, 'Well, hadn't you heard? It 'pears Old Man Bledsoe shot and killed his wife.'

The lady was just aghast. She said, 'What *happened*, Isam? Did he go *berserk*?'

And Isam said, 'We don't know *where* he went, but we're going to find him!'

Another story: Isam went to serve breakfast to a female inmate. They didn't have many female inmates. He knocked on the door, said 'I've got breakfast, are you decent?'

She said, 'Yeah.'

He unlocks the door, hands her a tray with a bowl of corn flakes and a cup of coffee.

She says, 'Sheriff Cunningham, I'm going to have to have a Kotex.'

And Isam just kinda stared at her and said, 'Missy, you'll have corn flakes just like everybody else!'

Another one you don't hear too often but I heard somebody talking about: It's about Isam and John Hosmer, one of the times that John was Prosecutor. Whenever a Prosecutor would die in office or whatever, John would be appointed by the governor; John was about the only democrat lawyer in the county and the governor was democrat.

Anyway—maybe Gene Fraker told me this story—they'd been to Greene County, Springfield, to testify in a case or something. It was official business. They'd rode up there together and as they came back, they crossed the county line--there was a sign there on the highway, probably on old Route 66, <u>Now Entering Webster County</u>--, and when they crossed that line, there Isam was Sheriff and John Hosmer was Prosecutor, and Isam looked at John Hosmer and said, 'Well, Johnnie, *we're* the stud ducks *now!*'

That's one of the only times I've heard of John Hosmer referred to as Johnnie.

I heard most of my Isam stories from Gene Fraker."

[Cline Herren] "One of the most humorous things I ever happened to have been in on--John Hosmer was Prosecutor and D. Raymond Carter was the defense lawyer.

On what's Banning Street there now, that was just a little gravel road running up the hill there. And there was a vacant house off to the north side of it, set off the road kind 'a ways. There was a professional gambler that came to Marshfield every week, and then every Milk Check Day. He would clean out the local people and then leave. I don't remember his name but it was probably in '51 or '52. Anyway, Isam slipped up on 'em and in that old house the windows came down to about a foot from the floor, like some of the old houses did. And Isam and—I don't know, a deputy or two—and John Hosmer was along, the Prosecutor was along. And Isam looked in the window there, and they were in a semicircle on their knees, right under that window where they could watch.

So in the trial there, where D. Raymond Carter was cross-examining Isam, he said, 'Well, did you *see* them roll the dice?' Isam said, 'No.' He had described that they'd had money in one hand and dice in the other. And Carter said, 'Well, they were on their knees, how do you know they weren't prayin'?' And Isam said, 'You know, maybe they were. They looked up at me and said, 'My God, there's Isam!'

I was there, I was sitting there in that courtroom. It was professional gamblers and local yokels. This had been going on for a long time because there used to be a barn right down at the bottom of the valley there. That valley that runs up parallel with Banning Street.

Well, right there where the fence crossed, there was a barn there. And when I was a kid we used to go sneak up in the woods, on the west side of that, and watch 'em gamble in that barn. So Marshfield had their gambling problem there for a long time. But this was several years after that. This was when Mac Palmer and I walked up there and we both heard that. '51."

Isam-isms

Jack Watters explains: "Everybody realized that he didn't have a college degree by any means, I'm not even sure he went through grade school all the way. I think the way he used the English language was a little bit far out and that, I think, would cause some humor among people that would hear him. He was certainly down to earth.

His English was not good. It might get mispronounced but Isam was Isam. They would laugh about Isam and they would question his intelligence but they never lost respect for him, and people always felt he was doing a pretty good job of being Sheriff of Webster County. That's the thing."

Daniel Max Knust continues: "Gene Fraker, when he was sheriff *[1969-1988]*, he used to talk about **Isam-isms.** Isam would call the Highway Patrol, the Highway *Pee*trol. He'd say, 'Here came the Highway *Pee*trol, their *syringes* a blarin'."

Glen Wilson said "Isam should have gotten graded an E, an excellent, for his ability to see things, to know what was going on. But if he had to spell it, well, that was something else. He had his own way of saying things that showed up more at some times than others."

For example, **Glen** remembers, "Isam had to go to St. Louis about a trucker accident. He had a terrible time trying to tell those attorneys what was going on. He was on the stand and they'd ask him a question. He was obligated to answer. And he'd answer it Isam's way, in his language, and they'd say, 'Well do you mean so-and-so?' and Isam would say, 'No, that's not what I said!'"

Tony Stephens added, "But Isam acted like someone who had a college degree, I mean mentally. He had his own way of thinking about things. He could almost project what somebody in the community was expected to do. I don't know how he could do it. He was really intelligent in his own way. He could remember things! I'd forget things, even back then, but he never forgot anything. You couldn't lead him into an answer! He wouldn't change his mind."

Doc Blinn recalled, "He understood a lot but you didn't think, by the way he talked, that he did. Some people kinda made fun of him because he was not very fluent. Sometimes he'd make a little bit of a problem like that for himself, because he'd try and talk about things he wasn't really fluent in, so he'd kinda put himself on the spot once in a while."

Isam heard much and is remembered as having created words that seemed to be a concoction of actual words, one of which would have a similar meaning to what Isam intended. **Isam-isms** are still used around Webster County, especially among the courthouse employees.

Glen Wilson tells about Isam stopping and searching a car in Fordland, going through the glove compartment, and saying to the passengers, 'Where'd you get those galdarn **binocles**?' (Somehow he knew they'd stolen them from another car in Fordland.) Isam seemed to have created **binocles** from <u>binoculars</u>, <u>monocle</u>, perhaps <u>bifocals</u>, and rhyming his new word with a popular card game called <u>pinochle.</u>

Glen continues: "I remember being at Clyde 'Skeeter' Hargus's Marshfield Café, on The Square, with Isam. Isam and I was eatin' and this woman come over, big ole girl, and you could tell she was mad. 'Course, I was eatin' there and I didn't want to destroy the meal.

Isam wanted to know what she wanted. And she started to givin' him hell, I mean...! And Isam said, 'Hold on there, Miz So and So, you've got the wrong **altitude**!'

I knew what he meant. He didn't need to be an English major."

From **Warren Johnson:** "One story I remember about Isam. He was telling the highway patrol about an accident. 'Now right then at the point of **compact**,' so-and-so happened, and the patrolman said , 'Do you mean at the point of *impact*, Mr. Cunningham?'   'Well, impact, compact, whatever kind of pact you wanna call it, I call it **compact**.' He had his way of sayin' things, his expressions!"

Peg Miller said, "Isam was so quotable!

Isam always referred to the prison up here *[in Jefferson City]* as **Algorey.** Oh, he'd take **juneviles** up to **Algorey**.*[Algora]*

He **conflasticated** something, one time. He meant *confiscated!* That was one of his words.

And of course it was the **Magic Court.** He **arranged** people down in **Magic Court.** *[arraigned...in Magistrate Court]*

When Isam was beaten up in jail, the guy beat him over the head, Isam was just beaten to a pulp. Really, the worst part of his injury was his hand. He broke his hand. What happened was, Isam hauled off to hit him with his fist, the guy ducked, and he hit the wall. Isam described it to *[Roy]* Miller: 'Hell, Miller, I just hauled off and **salivated** the son-of-a bitch!' We never figured out what he meant with that one, but there was some word he was thinking of there we never have figured out.

When we haul off and really miss, on the golf course, we think of Isam **salivating**.

He didn't quite know the words so he would sorta try anything. He had his own vocabulary. And he was sorta consistent. He always said **arranging juneviles in the Magic Court.** Going to **Indiapolis with a furgitive warrant.** *[arraigning juveniles, Indianapolis, fugitive]*

Somebody they'd arrested out by Northview and brought in, Isam had remarked to Miller that these folks were really okay, their main problem was that they were just **igorant as hell.**

He called Niangua **Niangee**."

From **Cline Herren:** "Regarding Isam-isms, I think a lot of them were made up after his death. They're all hearsay, you know. But one of my favorites is when Isam had caught some character from out of state, you know, like he'd do once in a while. And Isam said, 'Well, the Chicago authorities want him but we've already got him **castrated** in our jail.' *[incarcerated]* That was such a joke! I think Ellis Jackson heard him say that and I guess Ellis *[laughing uncontrollably]* just had to go lock himself up.

I think Roy Miller told this one: They were campaigning together before the general election. Isam and Roy Miller and I don't know who else was in the group. And Isam told him, 'Some of the **igerus** people of the county live out here.'*[ignorant-est/ most ignorant]*

When Murray Thompson *[a native of Webster County]* ran for Governor *[in 1948]*, Isam had some of Murray Thompson's cards, and there was a car parked somewhere there in front of Shield's *[Drug Store]* that wasn't a Marshfield car, and Isam went over and give him one of Murray Thompson's cards and said, 'We'd like for you to vote for him, he's from this town,' and this guy in the car said, 'I wouldn't vote for him, he's a prohibitionist.' And Isam said, 'I don't know what he does when he's out of town but he sure doesn't do it around here.'"

Willis Case *[a professional auctioneer]* remembers an Isam-ism. "I had a sale during the time he was Sheriff. I had the Dugans, and Isam was with them. We had bought a new cook stove, in war time. And Isam said, 'Now folks, you know you have to have a **purority** to buy one of these stoves.' He called priority **purority**."

Philip Huffman tells some Isam-isms: "One of the funniest, and I can't remember who this guy was, but he got arrested and they wanted to hire Dad. *[M.J. Huffman]* So Dad came over. And the first thing he would do is go talk to Isam, of course, and see what the guy was in trouble for, you know. And so he asked him. 'What about this?' And Isam said something about the guy wasn't supposed to be drinking, or something. And Isam said, 'I arrested him. He was wearing one of those **macadaw** coats *[Mackinaw,Michigan, probably confused with mackintosh, a raincoat made of rubberized cloth].* And I seen something, there in the pocket. So I retched in there,' he said, 'and out comes a bottle of that **Romie Muscatine** wine.' *[Roma Muscatel wine. Muscatine is a city in East Iowa, one with which Isam was likely familiar].*

I've remembered that one forever."

Pictured above are Isam Cunningham's parents,
James Harme Cunningham and
Alice Williams Shields Cunningham

Parents and Children of
James Harme Cunningham,
Isam's Father

Nathaniel R. Cunningham married Nancy Whittenburg
 1827-1893 in 1848 1834-1881

James Harme Cunningham married Nancy E. Climer
 1850-1915 in 1871 1850-1889
[Nancy's mother was Susanna Epps Climer]

James & Nancy had six children before her death
*[only the grandchildren and great-grandchildren mentioned in interviews for this
book are shown, for easier reference]*

Hulda, Frank, Daily, Leva, May, Pearl
 // \\ //
Grace Hickman Fredah Rader Thomas Walter Scott
 // \\
 Wilma Ryser & Fran Steelman Alberta Fraker

James married Alice Williams Shields
 in 1890 1860-1919
 *[widow of Arnett Shields; had
 two children—Ida & Estell]*

James & Alice had four children

Enoch Isam James Fred Joseph Nathaniel Lucinda
 1891-1955 1893-1964 1899-1973 1902-1953

Children and Grandchildren
of
Enoch Isam Cunningham   May 28,1891-July 31, 1955
and
Eva Belinda Randolph Cunningham   May 25, 1892-July 5, 1969

Marie Cunningham (1912-1919)
Mildred Cunningham Letterman (1913-1992)
Married Fred Letterman
-Marie Letterman Day (3/11/1931)
-Don Letterman (1/17/1933)
-Fredrick Isom Letterman (2/26/1946)
Mattie Cunningham Letterman (1915-1999)
Married Loren Letterman
-Betty Letterman Marlin (10/26/1934)
-Darrell Loren Letterman (5/3/1936)
-Shirley Ann Letterman Carrizales (6/4/1940)
-Jerry Lee Letterman (12/11/1942)
-Linda Jane Letterman Abbett (9/22/1950)
-Thomas Dwaine Letterman (9/2/1952)
-Janet Sue Letterman Aday (8/10/1958)
James A. "Buster" Cunningham (1917-1984)
Married Edna Henderson
Floyd Lee "Snooks" Cunningham (1920-   )
Married Mary L. Bean
-Gary Lee Cunningham (6/18/55)
-Debra L. Cunningham Tarter (4/27/60)
William David "Jake" Cunningham (1925-1994)
Married Helen Jones
-David Isom Cunningham (1/7/1955)
-Marsha Cunningham Gorman (12/11/1956)
-(John Calvin) J.C. Cunningham (6/3/1960)
Wilbur "Red" Cunningham (1928-1993)
Married Eldeen Freymiller
-Gail Woody (4/13/1952)
-Dennis Cunningham (3/5/54)
-Teresa Cunningham Fulton (12/27/57)
-Mark Cunningham (11/20/66)
Charles "Charley" Robert Cunningham (1933-   )
Married Mary Lou McNabb
-Cathy Cunningham Youngblood (10/18/58)
-Todd Cunningham (5/23/68)
An infant son, about whom there is no information

Chapter Two

WEBSTER COUNTY, MISSOURI

Interstate 44 has replaced much of Route 66, which was an adventure more than road according to songs, books, and the television series starring the 1953 Chevy Corvette. However, Historic Route 66 emblems now are displayed everywhere along the old route, from personal mailboxes and yard signs to official roadside markers, challenging all its travelers to take note of its history.

Approximately two-thirds of the way from St. Louis to Joplin, Missouri, on Route 66, is Webster County. The County Seat is Marshfield.

A sign was erected by the State Historical Society of Missouri and the State Highway Commission in 1958, three years after Webster County's spectacular Centennial celebration. It's on the east lawn of the Courthouse, in Marshfield, and reads as follows:

Webster County, organized March 3, 1855, encompasses 590 miles of the highest extensive upland area of Missouri's Ozarks. The judicial seat, Marshfield, lies 1,490 feet above sea level, the highest county seat in Missouri. Pioneer legislator John F. McMahan named the county and county seat for Daniel Webster, and his Marshfield, Mass., home.

Marshfield was laid out in 1856 by R.H. Pitts, on land given by C.F. Dryden and W. T. and B.F.T. Burford. Until a courthouse was built, county business was conducted at Hazelwood where Joseph W. McClurg, later governor of Missouri, operated a general store. Today's Carthage Marble courthouse, built in 1939-41, is the county's third.

During the Civil War, a small force of pro-southern State troops was driven out of Marshfield in February 1862. Ten months later, a body of Confederates was routed east of town. On Jan. 9, 1863, Gen. Joseph O. Shelby's troops burned the stoutly built Union fortifications at Marshfield and at Sand Springs, evacuated earlier. By 1862, the telegraph line passed near Marshfield on a route later called the "Old Wire Road."

In Webster County, straddling the divide between the Missouri and Arkansas rivers, rise the headwaters of the James, Niangua,

Gasconade and Pomme de Terre rivers. A part of the 1808 Osage Indian land cession, the county was settled in the early 1830s by pioneers from Kentucky and Tennessee. An Indian trail crossed southern Webster County and many prehistoric mounds are in the area.

The railroad building boom of the post-Civil War period stimulated county growth as a dairy, poultry and livestock producer.

The Atlantic & Pacific (Frisco) railroad was built through Marshfield in 1872, and by 1883, the Kansas City, Springfield, and Memphis (Frisco) crossed the county. Seymour, Rogersville, Fordland and Niangua grew up along the rail routes. Early schools were Marshfield Academy, chartered 1860; Mt. Dale Academy, opened 1873; and Henderson Academy, 1879.

Astronomer Edwin P. Hubble (1889-1953) was born in Marshfield. The composition 'Marshfield Tornado' by musician John W. (Blind) Boone gave wide publicity to the April 18, 1880, tornado which struck town, killing 65 and doing $1 million worth of damage.

The present-day Webster County Courthouse is a four-level structure which houses county offices, courtrooms, support offices for the court, and the sheriff's department, including the jail which has housing capacity for 15 inmates. The courthouse grounds feature a veterans' war memorial, honoring those soldiers killed in battle, and a scale model of the Hubble Space Telescope, named for the Marshfield native.

The 2000 Census numbers showed Webster County population at 31,045. Based on the census of 1950, the midway point of when Isam was Sheriff, the population of Webster County was 15,072.

[Barbara Herren] "At that time, Marshfield was smaller. You knew everybody. There was no one on The Square on Saturday afternoon or Saturday night or anytime. It was just a different community. Everybody was in church on Sunday. You *noticed* if somebody was not in church on Sunday. And you knew everybody. And it was just different than it is now. Now we're larger but we're such a huge trade area. You do not know who you meet in the car now. And we *did* then. And, course, there were fewer cars. You maybe had one car in the family, you certainly didn't have two or three or four. And so you knew everybody by their vehicle. It just absolutely was different, and simpler. And it was *everywhere*, I guess."

[Cline Herren] "They wanted to put the courthouse and the county seat in Seymour *[southern part of the county]*, back in '39, when they built the new courthouse."

[Barbara] "But they wanted it in the center of the county and that's why it was in Marshfield. Cline went to Seymour on Saturday nights, but my parents wouldn't let me go to Seymour. You wouldn't go to Seymour unless you were gonna fight!"

[Mildred Jarratt] "When I was growing up, that would have been in the early 40's, when I was in high school, I was forbidden to go to south county. My parents wouldn't let me go over there at all, even with a few friends. Too much trouble. No explanations. And back then, you didn't argue with your parents!"

[Warren Johnson] "There was another highway, national highway, running through the south side of the county and we had Fordland, Rogersville, and Seymour on that side. The population of those three towns was equivalent to the population of Marshfield. They had not had as close a law enforcement over there, they had deputies over there but sometimes those deputies were inefficient or unliked or something and didn't get the job done. I don't know, I'm speculating some. It was just further away from law enforcement, from the jail. I don't think the people over there were any meaner or anything. I know my dad *[former sheriff Johnny Johnson]* had most of his trouble over on the south side. Same crimes as anywhere else, robbery or assault, lots of fights, had some bootleggin', but that was more east of town—on the road to Hartville—up and down that-a-road. People were arrested for making it."

[Freda Langston] "I graduated from high school in Fordland. Class of '33. It always seemed to me like it was like a Civil War. The south side was always against the north side. They thought we all was smart alecks and stuff like that. After I was married and I'd go back over there and said I was from Marshfield, they looked at me like I was some kind of wild animal."

[Philip Huffman] "A friend of mine tells me that all we need, that we'd be way better off, if we just had a little '50s morality. And I get to thinking: that may cover the whole problem...that we perceive. There were things going on but not nearly so many, and they certainly weren't publicized. If you were lucky enough to grow up then, well, it was just kinda Utopia!"

Missouri author Marguerite Lyon explains in her 1942 chronicle about life in the Ozarks, <u>And Green Grass Grows All Around</u> :

"As to the war *[WWII]* making great changes in the Ozark way of living...well, I don't think that's possible. If boys have absorbed the get-up-and-go of the outside world, they will stay

36

outside the Ozarks. If they come back to the slow, easy pace of the hills, they will come back because that's the sort of life they prefer.

And it is quite possible the world will find the Ozarkian has been right all along! When the smoke and fury of war clear away, the world may discover that a little cabin of one's own, a patch of beans and 'taters, and a lot of fishin' in a crystal-clear stream, spell quite complete happiness."

During 1945 to 1955, Webster County was discovering that the outside world somehow was making its way in. And that was when Isam was Sheriff.

"Marshfield, Missouri—Just North of the Hot South and Just South of the Cold North"—*The Marshfield Herald,* March 26, 1936

The MARSHFIELD MAIL

[Jack Watters] "After high school I went directly into the army. I was in the army until '45. Went through the back end of WWII. I was in Germany when the war was over. We had just occupied Hitler's hideout. Not me, my group. I was in the 101st Airborne Division. We got there just after the big Battle of the Bulge, so we were replacements for people who either got wounded or killed or captured. I got discharged in April 1946, came home, and went to the university that fall. From '46-'50 I wasn't in Marshfield very much, except sometimes in the summer but I also went to summer school several times. Met my wife there. Boney was her maiden name, French or German. We got married and moved back here in '51 and became part of *The MARSHFIELD MAIL* then.

At that time my dad, T. Ballard Watters, and my uncle, Paul Watters, and my aunt, Faye Lea Watters, were the three principal owners of *The MARSHFIELD MAIL*. I was just kind of a printer as well as a part-time newspaperman. The paper at that time was into job printing—envelopes, statements, letterheads, sale bills, all kinds of things like that. We were busy all the time back then. Of course, now they print letterhead, sale bills, everything on their own computers! Then it was a different story.

My association with covering the courthouse and the sheriff's office and whatever over there, was pretty limited because my dad was still fairly young and my uncle would have been there. So they did most of the news writing at that time. In fact, my major at the university was advertising, so I was more into advertising and plotting along those lines than in the news writing side. What I know about Isam I mostly read in *The MARSHFIELD MAIL* of the stories they wrote!

We divided our week. Monday, Tuesday, Wednesday at a weekly newspaper was all geared around getting the paper out. We printed it Wednesday. Then Thursday, Friday, and Saturday we did job printing--envelopes, letterhead, and so forth. And Monday it was back to the newspaper. Of course there was an intermeshing when there were special things, special times, and we would change that. But mainly it was a split week, one part for newspapering and one part for job printing. And that was it. Kept us busy. Seems like we were always behind. And that was good. Somebody said, 'You're never making money until you're behind.'

My dad's brother, Paul, decided he'd had enough working at The MARSHFIELD MAIL so he sold his portion to my brother and me. Warren Watters and I bought my Uncle Paul's share. There were seven children in that family and he was the next to the youngest one. Dad was the oldest member of the family, the oldest son. There were three boys and four girls. Faye was the second oldest and she was the Linotype operator. She worked at night. She'd come to work late in the afternoon, worked until 2 or 3 in the morning, and then go home, setting type for the paper or setting jobs or setting ads.

And proofreading. You can imagine, the country correspondence we received, those items that would come in, she was very good at interpreting those. Some of that writing was not the best and the handwriting was even worse, so trying to read that was really difficult. And to get it ready for a typesetter to set!

Faye died right after the Centennial. She had previously had a stroke and recovered and had another stroke, and died November 8, 1955. When Faye passed away, we were really in a bind, because she had done all that, so we had, then, to do it. The way I did it, I'd just sit at my typewriter and read it, and if I'd needed to rewrite it, I'd just type it, rather than scribble in little corrections, then send it to the Linotype office. She had just read it at the Linotype machine and set it!

Floy covered outlying areas. She would go to Seymour, Fordland, Rogersville and Niangua, sometimes Elkland and gather news and ads there. She would never say she was part time but it was kinda part time because she did that early in the week and then she didn't have anything really to do until the next Monday and Tuesday. But she was there, and that was her job, to make that trip every week, to go to The South Side, we called it, Seymour-Fordland-Rogersville, she'd do that on Monday. Tuesday she'd go to Niangua and pick up news there. That outlying area.

At the time there were many more businesses in places like Niangua and Fordland than there are now—times have changed—so there was a considerable amount of advertising to pick up. And we, of course, up at the county seat, we weren't really close to that Highway

60 corridor so we had to keep a person over there, so she was more or less our representative down there.

Sometimes I was a little ashamed of us, that we crammed so much advertising in so few pages. Sometimes we wouldn't really leave enough of a news hole, to do *that*, because of our advertising. And the merchants! You had to give them credit because they were very aggressive about getting business into Marshfield or whatever town they were in, they were very aggressive business people.

We were one store north of Jarratt's. Webster Hotel, then a little park, then *The MARSHFIELD MAIL.*

Ed Webb joined the paper, took some pictures, shortly after the war. The university had a linotype school and he went to that. When Ed joined we bought a second linotype machine. He joined in '46, before I did. The linotype training was only about six months long.

We would just go to the courthouse offices, look at their court docket and just write it all down. Write it all down and bring it back to *The MARSHFIELD MAIL.* Either turn it in that way, if our handwriting was good, or type it up and give it to Ed or Faye to set the type. We didn't really dwell on any particular case unless it was something extraordinary. Who did what cases, what was decided, whatever, was a matter of public record. Marriage licenses, land transfers, who sold what.

My dad was responsible for getting information from Isam. Occasionally Isam would come in to *The MARSHFIELD MAIL*, but that wasn't a regular stop. If you wanted to find Isam, you'd go either to the Sheriff's office or stop at Skeeter's Café on the way. If I was hunting Isam, I'd always just go to the café first because I figured he'd be there. He wasn't there all the time, I don't mean that. But, yes, he had his own table and he kinda held court right there. People stopped and visited with him about this or that. And that was probably better than the courthouse, because you'd have to go up two or three flights of stairs to get to his office up there.

Actually we *[Webster County]* only had this newspaper and the newspaper over in Seymour. We didn't have radio in Webster County. At that time Seymour was a bit isolated as far as being part of the county. Seymour people...we've always had a competition between the two of us. Be that as it may well be, *The MARSHFIELD MAIL* was the county seat newspaper and we did have the news from the courthouse. It might be brief and not well written but it was in there somewhere.

Isam wouldn't write much. I don't think Isam spelled very well, but he'd tell you about it and you'd have to keep questioning him about it. What did happen there? Isam was, more than anything else, a stern but fair person. He had an aura of authority, the way he walked, the way he stood.

He was an old-time person. It wouldn't begin to work now. You couldn't be sheriff like Isam was Sheriff. He could chase kids off the streets, he would...not threaten people directly, I don't guess, but when he said something, young people did what he said to do. Clear out, or whatever.

I liked him, I always thought he was fun to be around.

We had some pretty big cases, like the Essary situation, the Shockley murders. There was even one, a week or so later at Niangua, a murder or something, wasn't there?

Early history in Webster County was pretty rough!

Isam might have been afraid—everybody gets afraid—but I certainly never saw it. He was always this huge figure of authority.

Even though we laughed about Isam, we always respected him. There wasn't any doubt who was in charge when he was taking care of something. He was the one.

He was a common man of common men. He was the one! But everybody liked him. I don't know of a person who would ever say they didn't like Isam Cunningham unless it would be some...yes, John Hosmer, later on.

Isam was never the same after that accident as far as being robust. He didn't have a swagger—don't get me wrong—but when he walked, he was very upright. I remember walking out of the courthouse yard, I'd see him walking across The Square, and he was always so straight up. He had that kind of a black hat, not a cowboy hat but kind of a cowboy hat. He looked like a sheriff! He was the man! He always wore a coat and tie. I don't ever remember seeing him in a T-shirt. He always had a coat on and even in the summer time! He always seemed to be dressed like that, always that same way.

Many times our reporters did not go on the scene. Our information came straight from Isam. We wouldn't do that now! You just kind of relied on him to have the information you needed about whatever it was you needed to write the story. You trusted what he said. There was no such thing in our time of investigative reporting as such, we didn't investigate what Isam was doing with all his time and go into backgrounds of why this was like this, or the county commission, how they were spending all the money. We didn't do that! We just took their word that what they were doing...they spent "this thousand dollars for that, that's where it went, this was part of the budget" —or whatever.

There was more trust maybe back then. Maybe we were gullible. You look back and you think about that. Were we? I don't know. 'We' were the newspaper, a typical small town newspaper.

You've got to remember: a small town newspaper didn't have six reporters to send out. Maybe one. So you were not only writing the paper, you were printing the paper. Everybody had two or three jobs. It was a different time, a different time."

[Photo and explanation courtesy of Jack Watters]

"Pictured are some of *The MARSHFIELD MAIL* staff in the early 1950s. From left: Jack Watters, Mary Derry, Hal Derry, Faye E. Lea, Ballard Watters, Jane Watters, and Paul Watters.

Ballard, as senior editor; Faye, as linotype operator; and Paul, as plant foreman and newswriter, were the co-publishers of The MAIL. They were brothers and sister. Jane, Ballard's wife, was bookkeeper and office manager. Hal, former publisher at Buffalo, monitored the tape-operated linotype and worked as a printer. Jack was a part-time printer and part-time newswriter. Mary Derry, Hal's wife, was not employed at The MAIL.

Not pictured members of the staff: Floy Watters George, another sister of the publishers, sold office supplies in addition to collecting news and ads from the county's south side; Mary McKinney worked as a printer; Nadine Rhodes was office girl at the time."

Chapter Three
A Prologue: Before 1945

Janet Sue Letterman Aday…"Mother *[Mattie Cunningham Letterman]* remembered that after Eva lost a baby, she was very distraught and stopped attending church. So Isam would drive Eva to Prospect Church, park under a church window, and let her listen to the service in that way. Then they would drive away before church was let out.

Mother told me about times when Isam would be gone to an auction, and when he returned he would always have fruit or candy or something for the kids.

Mother adored her mother and father. She remembers her father as honest, hard-working, and willing to help a neighbor out with anything."

J.E. "Doc" Blinn… "After medical school I had interned in Springfield, at Ozark Osteopathic Hospital, a privately owned hospital by Dr. Wetzel. He was a surgeon and had established this hospital because, of course, at that time DOs were not welcome at any of the medical hospitals. So he had started this hospital. (Now it's Doctors Hospital.)

I was in Fordland for about two years and then in May of 1944, I went to the Navy. Sold out the clinic in Fordland. Got a doctor from Kirksville *[MO]*, the Osteopathic College, to buy it. Dr.Schultz.

I went into the Navy, spent two years there. 'Course, they weren't commissioning DOs at that time. I was in the medical corp. If I had gone in about two or three months earlier, I would have been given a Chief Pharmacist's rate, commissioned right out of Boot Camp—but at the time I went in, all rates were frozen. They weren't giving anybody any rates. I was sent to a hospital on North Island, an air force naval base in the San Diego Bay, not quite a mile off the coast. I spent the rest of my time there."

Shirley Letterman Carrizales… "Mom *[Mattie Cunningham Letterman]* used to tell me the stories about how compassionate Granddad *[Isam]* was to the two girls in the family. He would always take and warm bricks in the fireplace in the wintertime, and wrap 'em in a blanket or a towel or something, and take 'em up and put it under the covers to keep them warm on cold winter nights. I thought that was really sweet of him. Mom and Mildred were teenagers.

Going back to the farm, when he lived on the farm, I can remember *[when I was]* a little thing about three or four or five years old—something like that—he used to take me up to gather the eggs, and it didn't matter to him that I didn't just take the eggs and place them in the bucket. I threw 'em! So we always had to return back to Grandma with broken eggs and that seemed to be okay with her, too. They both were just such sweet people.

And I can remember back in the days, in that same era, they used to have these huge dinners for all these men on the screened-in porch there at the farmhouse, where they were putting up the hay from the fields and everything, and that was quite exciting, I got to see all these people and things, and all the hustle and bustle of doing the meals.

And we used to play up at the spring. That was so much fun! They had mint growing there, and we would sample the mint. The water was so cool and sweet and everything. Sometimes we'd take it to the house, but mostly we just played down there."

Willis Case..."When I first knew Isam Cunningham, he lived east of Niangua. He lived on his grandfather's homestead. 1878 was the date on their chimney.

And I knew him as a farmer and somewhat of a—we called it back then—a jockey. He traded horses and cows.

Those days they had what was called a Fox Hunters League. The fox hunters would gather, from 8 or 10 counties in southwest Missouri, and he always attended those. Fox Hunters Association, that's what it was called.

You could always see him at most of the funerals. Before he was elected sheriff. I believe he run four times before he was elected.

He didn't necessarily want to be a law officer but was interested in being a man that could help correct wrongdoing in the community.

We had a few sales together; he'd be a partner in the sales. The year he was elected Sheriff, we had a sale at the old homestead down here. Isam did run a little store there once. We made a little talk before the sale. He said, 'Some people have sales because they're changin' jobs. Some people have sales for health reasons or death in the family, or so on. But I'm having a sale to pay my debts.'

It used to be Susanna. There was a post office there. Then they built a brick building, called Prospect. Carl Young built a store there. We'd have monthly sales there at Carl Young's place and Isam would help with that sometimes. Before Isam was elected sheriff."

David Isom Cunningham... "Dad *[William David Cunningham]* got his nickname, Jake, because, maybe it was the malaria or whatever but, apparently Dad walked with a limp as a very young kid. One leg a little shorter than the other, didn't grow up at the same rate or whatever. And there was an Old Timer down there named Jake Delp who had a bum leg. And they named Dad Jake after that! Well, Jake Delp is buried at Shaddy Cemetery in Grovespring where some of our family is also at. And they started callin' Dad Jake when he was grade school. He was Jake everywhere: it's in the phone book, it's on his tombstone."

Edna Henderson Cunningham..."I grew up all around here. Went to high school. Graduated right down here. Marshfield! There were six of us and we all graduated from Marshfield High School. My class of '39 had Warren Beck and John Hosmer.

We got married in '43. I lived with my parents in Marshfield. Buster was the oldest boy. He told me that Porter Rader came by one time, they lived down in there someplace I think, come by to see him when he was just born or real little and said, 'He is really a buster!' And so that's what he went by. Mildred was always called Ollie. I think she was called that on account a she was more like some friend they knew, or some other lady. But Buster said that's how he got his name. My mother used to say, think about, he had such a pretty name *[James]* and then they called him that. She never liked nicknames. There ain't any of us...there's six of us and we didn't any of us have nicknames. But now, there was six of them and they all had nicknames! Ha!

His kids! 'Course they lived down there on the farm. Well, they all slept upstairs. Well, Isam would get up of a mornin' and he'd holler, 'Time to go milk!' So they wouldn't get up, they waited 'til they heard him a comin'. Well, then they'd hide behind the door, you know, and then they'd slip down, if he was in one room or somethin', they'd slip down where he wasn't and go downstairs and go to the barn, real fast. They didn't want to go but when they heard him comin' up the stairs....Oh lord.

I don't know if he was very strict with them or not.

I think Buster was just about as close to one as he was the other. I really do. Charley was the baby, see, and Buster thought a lot of Charley. Whenever we were goin' together, we took him to the movie with us, he wanted to go. Well, Buster told him he couldn't tell a thing that happened, if he went to the movie with us. Well, when we got in there, he went to sleep! And Buster had to carry him out! Here we come carrying that kid out of there, with all those people in the show. I think he was about six years old. When we dated, Charley was on the farm. We dated three or four years. Charley's about fourteen years younger than I am!

When they had that store, in front of their farm, Buster delivered groceries to people, way back in there. (They had got rid of the store before Isam was elected.) They just called in and made the order, and he took it to them. Back then, they just didn't have the transportation.

They all went to school in Niangua, graduated from Niangua, except Charley.

Mildred, the older sister, she lived down there on the farm, and my sister lived up the road from her. And she said every day Mildred went to town about one o'clock and said she might be dark comin' in. *[It might be dark before she came home.]* She went to Niangua every day! She just went to visit and see what was goin' on. The other girl, Mattie, I don't think she done too much of that. 'Course, she got married young and had a family, had several kids. But most of 'em liked to 'go', except Buster.

John Hosmer. That was a smart guy! Too smart! I knew him, sure I knew him! Sat right by him! His name was Hosmer, mine was Henderson, so we were sittin' there. H's. He used to come to school and, mind you, as well fixed as they was and everything--there was four of us in high school at one time--and *he* would borrow from *me* whenever he'd start to take a test! And you'd never get it back! Oh, I'd just hate to know that, when the teacher would say we was going to have a test, you know, and I'd think 'Oh, boy, now I'm gonna have to furnish his paper'...and most the time the pencil too! I'd just hate that he could borrow paper from me 'cause I knew how hard it was for us to get that paper. He never had a sheet of paper, book, nothin'. But, you know, they'd take him on these big trips, someplace. He learned a lot from that. He was smart. My mother used to baby sit for the Hosmers. She just lived down below them. Ava Henderson. They thought she was just 'it', too. I didn't know anything about John Hosmer after he got out of here. I just went to high school with him, it's all I know. And I know he borrowed paper from me!"

Helen Jones Cunningham..."Jake was sorta puny growin' up. Had malaria fever and he was, you know, helped his mom a lot.

"And Jake, the boys always accused him of sittin' across the bridge waitin' 'til the milkin' was done. When they turned the last cow out, he'd come home."

Mary Bean Cunningham..."Nathaniel, then James, then Isam. Nathaniel came from North Carolina. But where? I wish I had asked Isam about all of this. But I didn't.

Isam's mother was Alice and James was his dad.

The farm was patented by Isaac Wittenburg, which was an uncle or something of Nancy Wittenburg. And somewhere along the line it got changed over to the Climers. And Grandma Susie was an Epps, and married Climers. And they tell me that's how it come about.

And that little post office was named after Grandma Susie. Susanna was named after her. Susanna Epps. But I just called her Grandma Susie. I have a postcard in there, two post cards, that have a postal stamp, 'Susanna, Missouri.' I treasure them, because it was a short-lived post office.1892 until 1914.

I believe Isam's birth year is wrong in most reports. I think it was May 28, 1891, not 1890. Otherwise, his mother and daddy would have been married only two days when Isam was born. And if the marriage record is right—and this is the official marriage license—his parents were married in 1890. Her first husband died in July of '89. And I just don't think Isam's birthdate was in 1890. (My daddy's *[birth]* record was *two* years off!) I think Isam was born in '91, but he changed it over the years. Well, if she was pregnant with Isam, when they got married, she would have had to get pregnant on the way home from the funeral of her first husband! I just will not believe that. Even if they were Cunninghams!

Mildred, Mattie, James "Buster," Floyd "Snooks," William "Jake," Wilbur, Charley. Marie, the oldest girl, died. She was 7 or 8. Grandma Evie said she got sores on her. I have no idea what she died of. But she had sores on her. Smallpox? I don't know for sure. That's another thing I should have asked about. But I didn't. And it was their first-born. So sad.

If I remember correctly, Evie said one time if her babies had been born in a hospital, she'd a thought they'd got 'em mixed up, 'cause she didn't know where the red hair came from."

Marie Letterman Day... "We went over, on the 4th of July, all of us kids. We went down to that springhouse. And Grandpa *[Isam]* had pop in the springhouse, where the water was, to keep it cool, and we always tried to see who could drink the most. I don't know who really did but I had thirteen bottles of Grapette RC! I think I won!

This was still when he had a store up in front of the house, and I remember goin' up to the store and he would give me candy bars and stuff like that."

Raymond Day..."I was born in 1918 and I was about ten years old when I'd go to the stockyards in Niangua. It seems to me Isam was there just about every Saturday. He was there with his dad.

My wife tells about going to their country store, when she was young, way before he was Sheriff. He'd give her a candy bar, then all them boys around, they'd give her trouble, tease her. Louise Vestal, that was my wife's name."

Oliver Evans... "I went two years to Marshfield High School. Signed up with the 3 C Camp *[Civil Conservation Corp]*, spent some time there, then come home. The war broke out. I tried to get my mother to sign the papers so I could go with my brother. The draft board got him. But she wouldn't do it. So I waited 'til I got 21 and I went ahead and filed too. Broke her heart but I felt like it was my duty. I was in *[the Army]* 42 months.

I was in the Battle of the Bulge *[a month-long siege that began 12/16/1944]*. *[Later]*, we started moving up, it was Easter Sunday and I didn't pull my shoes off until the 8th of May *[Victory in Europe Day, 1945]*. But I lived through it. We was pushing Germany so fast, they ran out of gas.

Went in August of '42, and got out February of '46."

Alberta Scott Fraker..."He was my half uncle, Uncle Isam. My grandmother Scott was a Cunningham and that's who raised me. He was at my grandparents' a lot, to visit his half sister, my grandma, and I was there because I was raised in the home.

I tell ya, Isam had this bottom farm. And it was the home place. So when all the sisters and brothers would come in, we always went there. And Aunt Eva would cook up a storm. That old hot kitchen. And he was a tease! He was a tease to us kids, see. And that Charley Cunningham! We always had the best time down there. All of Uncle Isam's kids, they'd chase me around, I was young, but not as young as Charley.

He was good to me, Uncle Isam was. I think they had pity on me, because, see, I was raised by my grandma Scott. My mother died giving birth to me. Isn't that a sad story. I never did live with my dad *[Walter Scott]* but I stayed in contact with him and everything. I had a good childhood and Uncle Isam was one of the people we visited a lot.

I grew up here *[in Marshfield]*, moved here when I was three years old and Grandpa was in office. I have friends, cousins in Niangua. My grandpa Scott was circuit clerk and recorder for two terms. I'd run up and down that old hall *[in the old courthouse]*. I called it a horse barn 'cause it was open on one end. My girlfriends would come over every time there was a court case, and we'd run hard up and down it.

I don't think I was proud of him, 'cause, see, my grandpa wasn't his best friend. My Grandpa Scott. They always kinda clashed, even before Uncle Wilber.

We weren't too close to them. My uncle had a bad habit of drinking, my father's brother, and they always clashed but that was my grandfather's fault, partly, my grandpa Scott. They resented each other or something, see, that goes back so far that I don't know what it was all about.

Carmen Rainey taught me Expression, when I was four or five years old. I had a fancy dress and had to speak something, I don't remember what."

Ruby Childress Hargus... "My husband *[Clyde Hargus]* was raised in a large family out on High Prairie. Back then they had no school buses. He had to stay in eighth grade so long. His cousin was a teacher. He walked to town and got a place to work. He worked in a store, then in a filling station out on the Y. Then he worked in Johnny Andrews Café. Then he bought a bus and hauled kids to school. But so many didn't pay him and he had to quit driving the bus.

When we first got married, I was working for Johnny Andrews then. After Clyde got out of high school, he taught school two years. He couldn't teach any more without going back to college. There was just no money for college, you know. I don't know if you know Bob Fyan. He was our representative. He took him to Jefferson City and got him a job at the Honor Camp—Algoa Reform School for Boys. That was his first job away from home, away from Marshfield.

Back then politics played a lot. If you was a Democrat, you got in. Then when the Republicans took over, the Democrats had to get another job and the Republicans got the jobs. But I don't believe it's that way so much now.

I grew up around Seymour, was from a family of twelve. We canned tomatoes. Once we headed out west. Went to Idaho. Took three weeks to get out there. Roads weren't good. We stayed in cabins. One place we went in, it was cold. There was a big stove in the back. Burned cow chips. The woman who rented it explained it to my dad. It didn't have a smell, I don't think. It may have; you know, kids don't remember that.

I went to school and stayed in the eighth grade. I went to high school for one year; we didn't have buses back then. We worked in the truck patches. Then we worked in the evaporators, where they dried apples, pears, fruit. Then I took care of a little baby for a year. Then I worked in Waynesville. My brother had gone to school with a lawyer, and found out about a job. He took me up there and told the lady I wasn't to go out at night. They served meals, 25 cents a meal, and I had to make the salads. They had an all-night café there and wanted a waitress for the evening shift. Then a salesman who sold the café cigarettes and things talked about Crown Drug Store needing somebody. So I worked in Springfield and stayed with an aunt.

My brother, Jason Childress, would take me places. Pie Suppers and things. And we went to this pie supper and there was

Clyde. I asked my cousin, 'Who's that tall good-lookin' guy back there?' And he said, 'That's Skeeter Hargus. His name is Clyde but they call him Skeeter.' Because when he was in high school he played in a play, the character was named Skeeter. So that's how he got his name, after he went to school. He wasn't called that before.

His brother used to come over all the time and said, 'Skeeter wants a date with you.' I said I'm not going alone. So his brother got a date with my sister and we went to the movie.

We'd write. Then when I started working at Andrews Café, he'd come down. We dated.

We all four decided to get married at the same time.*[Norma Rice and Aubrey Phipps were also married when Ruby and Clyde married.]* I caught a ride into Springfield with someone who owned *The MARSHFIELD MAIL.* He had some business and said he'd take me. I bought a pretty blue dress with a big bunch of flowers on the lap part. I kept that dress for years and years.

About nine o'clock one night we all went to get married. While we were waiting for Clyde to get off work at Algoa, he had to serve the boys in the kitchen, one of the fellas from the jail asked if we wanted corsages. He picked a bunch of pansies and made corsages for all of us. At Algoa, they had beautiful gardens and flowers. We got married in May in 1937.

When we was up there, we lived in Jefferson City, then we moved out to Osage City, a little town.

At Osage City, when we lived there, he told me once to get the kids in the house and lock the door. Then he brought some boys from Algoa, along with a horse and plow, and they plowed us up a garden. And they helped keep it, too. Clyde just made friends of some of them. 'Course, they knew which ones they could trust.

Osage City wasn't a mile from the edge of Algoa Farm. It was east of Jeff City."

Cline Herren, Jr... "My dad had polio when he was, like, three, in both legs and both arms. Now, he drove, he did all kinds of things, he played that piano in there. He had braces on both legs. He had a brace all the way to the hip on one leg and to the knee on the other. His hands were oversized from using the cane, from supporting his weight. His hands were so large, and he used his thumb to move his hand back and forth on that rim that's below the keys there. And he could play with about anybody. He'd do both hands that way. And course that was back when there wasn't such a thing as handicapped parking or anything.

I think my folks came to Marshfield in '31, lived out east of town in a little shack. My dad, in his JP*[Justice of the Peace]* days, sold real estate. His office was on Highway 66. It was him and Fred Carpenter.

He taught night school for WPA *[Works Progress—or Work Projects—Administration, 1935-1943]* until they found out he was a Republican! I'm serious! That's the way it worked!"

Grace Cunningham Hickman ..."I wasn't very old, but I was on it *[the covered wagon]*. My family and Uncle Isam and Aunt Evie. And I think Marie. Their oldest kid was Marie, wadn't it? I think she was in there, but I won't say *that* for *sure,* now I'm just gonna tell ya what I really remember. Isam and Evie Cunningham and I think Marie their oldest child was the only ones in *their* wagon. And in *our* wagon it was my mother *[Rosie]* and dad *[Frank]* and my brother *[Lonnie]* and sister *[Effie]* and me.

Well, we went to Oklahoma, was out there about a year, and come back to Springfield 'fore I was old enough to go to school, so I was pretty young and I don't remember too much about it. I don't remember where we run into Uncle Isam and Aunt Evie, but we made part of the trip together. I remember the wagons and we stopped and camped out, you know, and then they went one way and we went the other and I don't know where we went or where they went. I was little! But the thing that impressed me was goin' in that covered wagon, see. We had a lovely team of horses and I liked them. But now, as far as where Uncle Isam and Aunt Evie went after we parted ways, I don't know.

Back when the Cunninghams all got together, it was at Uncle Isam's place, down there. They'd have a kind of reunion and there'd be a whole bunch of them there.

Grandma Alice was wonderful. She was Dad's stepmother but you'd never know it. I think Dad had four sisters and him, by the first set of kids that Grandpa Jim had, with his first wife *[Nancy E. Climer]*. Leva, Pearl, Huldah, Daily, and May. That was the girls. And then Dad. He was the only boy. And then when Grandpa married Grandma Alice *[Alice Williams Shields]*, he had Isam, James, Jodie, and Cindy. *[Alice, then a widow, had two children by her first husband: Ida and Estell.]*

Dad's mother died when he was eight years old, so Grandma Alice more or less raised him.

I went to elementary school here in Springfield. I went to the old Berry School. And then we left here and we moved down there by Prospect and I went to Prospect School, when I was about seven. And then over to Grovesprings and I went to that school. I went to eighth grade, and then I quit. That was typical, *then.*

Dad was either movin' *by* his family or movin' *away* from 'em!

I saw Uncle Isam off and on all my life. I stayed with 'em the summer before David *[Jake]* was born *[1925]*, I stayed with Aunt Evie and helped her.

Evie done the cookin' and I washed dishes and done the laundry, down there by the spring mill. They was a spring in there and they had a place to put their butter and milk on rocks or somethin' and we always had cold milk and fresh butter 'cause they kept it in that spring house, *she* did, and us kids would carry it down there. But that water was so cold, and they had flat rocks...I don't know but they might a been blocks of concrete...but Aunt Evie would cover the milk and we'd take it down there and set it and that cold water would go all around it and it never soured, you'd had good milk all the time and you'd have good butter! See, Mildred and Mattie was home, and Floyd, and Buster.

I think Floyd— Snooks—was a baby then, 'cause he'd get to belly-aching and I'd have to carry him upstairs every night. He was a cute little devil, is all I know. Aunt Evie said, 'Aunt Grace, that kid ain't got the belly ache, he's just doin' you that way.' And I'd carry him upstairs and put him to bed again. Snooks—he was a dandy. I always though he was the cutest little kid I ever saw, with that red curly hair. I stayed 'til about a month before David *[Jake]* was born.

We moved away. We lived down in there and I had worked for Aunt Leva one summer and then Aunt Evie had me come over and help her out, 'cause she was pregnant with David *[Jake]*. That's what I did. I stayed there day and night. I washed dishes and made beds. Aunt Evie had a lot to do and she wasn't physically able to do all of it. I didn't cook! She didn't trust me to cook, I don't guess. But *she* could sure make good biscuits. She made 'em with sweet milk. I never could, I always had to add buttermilk, when I went ta cookin'. Now my sis stayed there one summer before I did and she cooked. 'Course she was older, she was five years older. My sister Effie.

I ate whatever she put on the table. We ate it, we didn't gripe, none of us. You didn't pick and choose when I was a kid! You eat what was put on the table or you done without!

Another thing about Uncle Isam. I think they paid me two and a half a week, and when I got ready to go home he give me a check and he just signed that check, he never filled it out, he just handed me a signed check. And I thought afterwards, I could have added money to that and he'd never said a word. I could have gotten by with that. But I never even thought about getting by with it! I just filled out what they owed me. And my folks was over at Grovesprings then, and I went back over with them. But he trusted me enough to sign the check and I wouldn't have cheated for anything, then!"

"The Cunninghams packed up their two small daughters and headed for the Sooner state in a wagon...the family returned *[to Missouri]* a year later *[1915]* with...little Mattie—the only Cunningham born on 'foreign' soil, in Oklahoma." [Joe Clayton]

Pictured above, in the fall of 1915: Twenty-three-year-old Eva, holding newborn Mattie; 3-year-old Marie, (who was to die four years later), standing between her parents; 24-year-old Isam holding 2-year-old Mildred

Philip Huffman..."My granddad *[F.M. Huffman]* was the pharmacist in Norwood, for years and years and years. Norwood at the time was the important rail head in Wright County, much more important than Mountain Grove, because all the places clear to the Arkansas line and maybe down in Arkansas, that was the closest way when you came by horse and buggy. He not only had a drug store but he supplied them, these stores that they had in every little town, with all the stuff they needed. My dad's dad. *[Philip's dad, M.J., was named after his father, Francis Marion and his mother, Jesse]*

As a youngster my dad *[M.J.Huffman]* didn't get to play sports because of the leg he had, that he nearly lost as a child, to a disease called osteomyelitis. His story was just a miracle. They had him on the kitchen table, at his house in Norwood. They were getting ready, one of the local doctors in Norwood, to saw the leg off, and the other doctor said, 'Let's wait and let me try some of this new ointment, then I'll see what might happen.'

And so it somehow went into remission, but they had dug all through my dad's leg and it was the awfulest looking leg you've ever seen. And he had to learn to walk again! He was about eight, or so, when this happened. But they had had it pinned back under him, or whatever, in bed at home, for six or eight months. So he became interested, and he'd have teams, in these semi-pro leagues, baseball and basketball, and he'd be the manager and coach and stuff. He'd go around and find every good ball player he could find and load 'em up and go around. Big sports fan. Big sports fan. He walked pretty much normally. He didn't limp. He learned to walk again.

Isam was a fox hunter *[like M.J.]*, and a friend of my dad's before he was sheriff."

Mary Rosamond "Sally" Day Hyde... "I was born in '18, and I was in high school in the late twenties and early thirties, graduated from high school in '35.

I was in a class at Niangua of only twenty people, and we counted up one day and almost half of them had a college degree, which was really hard to come by back in those days, because *money* was just hard to come by.

My dad and Isam Cunningham were kinda friends. This is always cute: on Christmas Eve, right after lunch, right after noon, was supposed to be Christmas Eve. One or the other would call and say, 'Christmas Eve Gift!' Every year! They did that for years, for a long time. They'd just pick up the phone and say, 'Christmas Eve Gift!' They used to do that, old timers used to do that. Instead of sending a gift or a card. It was a greeting. It was just a greeting. They didn't say 'Hello' or anything. The first thing they said, 'Christmas Eve Gift!' Like saying, 'Merry Christmas' *[on Christmas Day]*.

They robbed the bank at Niangua over and over and over! That's the time I put a half a cup of butter in my cake. Half a cup! It was kinda rich and fell apart. They robbed the bank and I got real excited.

And then later it was embezzled! The bank disappeared. That was the end of it. Charles Elkins. He just took everybody's money. My dad was so naïve he didn't even keep his check stubs. He trusted the man, didn't even keep them. And then you get a notice that your account is overdrawn and so on. The next thing you knew, the bank was closed. I'd say in '38-'39, along in there.

Snooks was kinda ornery in high school. I didn't have him as a student. I had Wilbur and Charley and Jake. Red—Wilbur—was ornery. Jake was kinda disruptive in class, just mischievous. I never went to the parents. It wasn't that serious. Charley was the cute one. I had Charley at Prospect, the rural school called Prospect, down there. He was in the third grade. He and Carlene Young and Mary Francis Thomas. There were only three third graders down there.

We had a little, rural Pie Supper. I only had eleven students down there, so I'm sure Charley would have been in the program somewhere. Grades one through eight. Didn't have any in seventh grade, only one in second grade. They were really scattered. We supposedly made more money than they had ever made at a Pie Supper in Webster County!

The women would bake this pie, any kind of a pie that they wished. I suppose they were quite fancy, had meringue and all this kind of stuff on them, had spent a lot of time on them I'm sure. And then they would put them in a square box which was lavishly decorated! They used crepe paper, you know...like, if it was close to Valentine's Day it would be red and white and probably a flower or something.

And then, after they got them all assembled, then they'd hold them up—they had an auctioneer—the men would bid on them. On the pie. On the box. They had no idea what they were buying. They just picked one of the boxes that had been brought in and auctioned it and they had no idea what they were buying. So then, whoever was the highest bidder...and I guess they finally cut it off some place...now *sometimes* the person might know whose pie it was and he might run it up a little bit.

But anyway, then you were left to eat the pie--which the idea always turned me off, I never did like it--but you had to eat the pie with the man regardless of who he was. Not the *whole* pie, *some* pie. Maybe the man...maybe *some* of 'em could eat a *whole* pie!

They tried to raise all the money that they could, you know, they'd run up the bid, they'd describe the box, how nice it was, and they didn't even know what kind of pie was in it. But that's the Pie Supper.

I taught there in '39 and '40, just one year. Then I went back to college to get my degree. I taught at another rural school first, and then I moved over to this one. Called Washington. I can't even remember for sure how many rural schools there were. I got my degree from college, and then I taught high school English at Niangua. See, we were interrupted by the war. I taught a full year, and then part of a year, and then I came back and taught another full year, and then I filled in for some. So it was very interrupted. And I was supposed to have been the highest paid teacher in Webster County, at $87.50 a month."

"We had the telephone....Our telephone company was like an information bureau. If there was a fire, if somebody died, if somebody was sick, cr whatever went on, the first thing they did was crank up the phone, you know, and.... I worked at the switchboard, I grew up with the thing, it was in our home. The transmitter hung *down,* instead of wearing it around your neck as you did later on, the transmitter hung *down* right in front of you. That's in the picture. I think he started that up in 1912. He married my mother in 1910 and I think he started that thing about 1912. He had it for thirty-eight years. Luther Day. M.L. Day. Martin Luther Day. My father." [Mary Rosamond "Sally" Day Hyde]

Helen Jackson ..."Isam run a store in Prospect. I went to school with his kids—Buster, Floyd *[Snooks].* Jake was the same age as my little brother.

I'm a first cousin to Ellis Jackson. Our dads were brothers. Uncle Albert. My dad was Jim Jackson, James. He and Isam were good friends.

We milked a big bunch of cattle and I helped. We were just up the creek from Isam's. Daddy and the boys would help each other fill silos.

Isam run a country store. Just a little country store. We always was neighbors. We lived just up the creek from them. Used to have ice cream suppers.

They come up there to play cards. They said us kids could play cards but if we got into fights, that's it, they'd separate us. And they had to separate us a few times!

Evie was a Randolph and I knew all her family. She was a sister to Cory Vestal. Evie was a nice woman. I don't know how she put up with him, I'll tell you that.

Oooh, Isam! He always wanted to be the boss. To run it. We'd have the little to-do's and he'd want to be in charge of everything.

I saw Isam auction several places around in the country. He was a pretty good auctioneer. He auctioned at Pie Suppers when Prospect had them.

He ran the store. At times I didn't trust him, probably 'cause I'd grown up with him. I just knowed too much about him.

He wanted to be sheriff bad. He always wanted to be head of everything! He and Evie owned the store, just an old country store, and when he was elected, they just disbanded the store.

Carl Young had a store down there, in Niangua. He had a ball team, I was on his ball team, and every Saturday afternoon he'd take us girls and go play ball at different places—Rader and all like that, and just leave Glessie with the store and she'd have to run it. Carlene was just a baby. I always had to play in the field."

Mildred Tindle Jarratt... "My grandpa Tindle, Daddy's father, Walter, was the judge when they built the courthouse. My dad had a grocery store, Tindle's, and my grandpa had a hardware store, Tindle Hardware. Daddy was on the school board.

I graduated from high school in '44. I worked for Daddy every summer, all the time I was in high school, through the busy Christmas season when we were out of school."

Warren Johnson..."I didn't live in the courthouse with my mama and daddy, when he *[Johnny Johnson]* was sheriff. I was married and had a little boy then. My boy was about 3 years old and he stayed with his granddad and grandmother quite a lot, enough so that he'd get up in the morning and say 'I'd like to go over with Granddad. We gotta serve some papers today.'

Even when my dad was sheriff I stayed out of the way of the law as much as possible. But I remember one time I saw Dad, across from my filling station, he and another guy got out of the car. Dad grabbed the other fella by the coat collar, and he had his gun in the other hand. And Dad give him a shove. I wondered what was goin' on so I run over there. And when I got over there, Dad kept a sayin', 'Run! You son of a bitch, Run! Run! Take out!'

I run back to the filling station and got behind the concrete wall. I had never seen my father that angry ever before or ever since. He wanted the guy to run so he could shoot him! The guy didn't run! He had slapped Dad or something. And that was the wrong thing to do to my father. Very wrong.

Dad didn't carry his gun very much.

I asked Dad one day, 'What if you get a hurry-up call here and have to jump in the car?' 'Oh, I ain't seen nothin' like that,' he said. What worried me about Dad is that he wasn't afraid. Whatever it took, he was goin' into it. And I think Isam Cunningham was pretty much the same way! He *[Isam]* was mighty rough!"

Freda Doyle Langston..."I graduated from high school in Fordland. Class of '33.

While Paul *[Langston]* was gone *[during WWII]*, I worked all the time in Mary's Variety Store. I got $50 from Paul, that was my allotment, and I don't think I made over 15 or 20 cents an hour working at the Variety Store. I'd have to stand in line no tellin' how long, with my coupon, to get a loaf of bread or a pound of coffee or something after I got off work."

Darrell Letterman..."Back then, we run around the spring and everything, and Charley's a little older than I am, but I still got to run around with him a little bit.

But Dad and Granddad *[Isam]* and myself was up huntin' one time, so, they was huntin' for quail or whatever and I had a little BB gun, I wasn't very old, but anyway they seen a rabbit sittin' back there underneath a bush so Granddad's hollerin', 'Shoot that thing, shoot that thing!' so I started shootin' at it, I probably shot five or six times, nothin' moved. And they was laughin' at me, sayin' 'Well, you can't even hit him!' So, Dad said, 'Well, what's goin' on?' So, anyway, they got him a stick and reached in there and punched him and he was froze dead."

Don Letterman…"I guess the main thing I remember is goin' to the farm and the boys and I would get all the heifers up and ride 'em, play rodeo, or ride the horses, whatever. And go down to the spring. And I remember the store they had out front of the house, Susanna Store, and the concrete is still there today. He would give us stuff out of there, you know.

And I remember he was Constable in the Niangua Township for a long time, before he was Sheriff.

And Grandma. She never did say much but she could really cook. 'Course, I don't remember it. I'm two weeks older than my uncle, Charley. They told that, when Mom wanted to go to Springfield or somethin' like that, well, I nursed Grandma along with Charley! That's what Mom told me, anyways."

Fredrick Isom Letterman…" 'Bout the only thing I can really remember about down there, about *[Grandpa]* Isam, is Mom tellin' me that him and a neighbor, which would be Luther Rader, got into it over the fence line on the creek. Rader went down there and built the fence and Isam thought it was on *him*. So Isam went down there, and tore the fence down, and built a fence where *he* thought it was. Well, they got into it and Isam told him, he said, 'If you come down there in the mornin' and move that fence, I'm gonna *shoot* ya!' Mom said he went down there with his gun but that guy didn't show up! That was back before…I just heard the story…it's older than *me*! What the creek would do, see…over the years, a creek doesn't use the same channel, it moves a little bit here…but both of 'em thought they knew where the line was. I guess that's how it went, anyway."

Betty Letterman Marlin… "When we came back down to the farm, they had this phone down there. At the time the phones didn't have, really, a number, you had a long-short-long, or whatever. Well, we'd talk 'em into letting us go over there and we had really a lot of fun, but we would have to call someone that they knew, to get their long-short-long. We'd have to get us a chair, stand up there, ring that thing.

The spring house on the 4th of July, he *[Grandpa Isam]* had put his drinks down there to cool for the picnic. He came down to get the sodas, to check it out, and there really wasn't much left for anyone else to have, because us kids had already drunk most of the pop, the sodas! But he would just look at us and kinda grin, it wasn't a big deal. That was him."

Bill Rader…"I was born in 1924, at Niangua. My father was Otto and my mother was Velva Rader. I was actually born where my grandfather

Letterman lived. It's one of those Century Farms; the Lettermans have owned it for more than a hundred years.

Isam was kind of a big guy, loud voice. When I used to visit my grandparents, their place was right over there across the creek, it'd get time to milk the cows and you could hear Isam hollering at his kids to get the cows, do this, do that. His voice just carried forever. If he did an auction, my dad probably wouldn't have gone. 'Cause they didn't really have much confidence in Isam. Although the Cunningham farm and my Granddad Rader's farm joined, they were not overly friendly with each other. This happens to a lot of families.

I graduated from high school in Grovespring. 1942. But then, everybody in my age group, you were waiting to be called in the armed forces of some kind. And that happened to me the last day of August, in '44. From '42 to '44 I just waited. We lived on the farm there. You knew your time was coming. Just waited it out. No, we weren't excited about going, but you knew if you were physically able to, that you would be called.

You know what Rader means? It means 'Wheel Maker'. Rademacher. They dropped the ending."

Jane Hyde Rader..."My dad used to tell me about the little store at Susanna. He used to go, he lived down the creek. He said, 'This woman—she was a character.' I think this was Bill's great grandmother, Alice—*[Isam's mother]*. He said he would go up to that little store with his dad and he said she was the first woman he ever heard cuss and he said he just couldn't believe women said words like that! But she stood her ground with all of them, she had all these *step* children and *her* children and *their* children.

Mildred *[Cunningham Letterman]* had a hard childhood. Bill's aunt, who passed away last year at 97, taught the rural school down there...that was Aunt Artie Letterman Shaddy. She taught there at Prospect, that little school, she taught the Cunningham kids. And Mildred had to miss a lot of school 'cause her mother was always having another baby and she just had to stay home and do the washing and everything. And they didn't send her to high school. Isam didn't send either of his daughters to high school. And I think a bus came right by. I think he sent the boys."

Jack I. Rainey..."This has nothin' to do with Isam, but when the Young brothers massacred, just out of Springfield, my dad was the ambulance driver that went out and picked 'em up, while some of the gun fightin' was still goin' on. Shot seven police officers. It's still the most police officers killed in a shoot out. It happened in 1929 or '30. I wasn't born! And then, after they escaped and went to Dallas, Texas, and was *killed* down there, my dad went down and picked 'em up and brought 'em back to Springfield. He and Bill Stearns. They were stopped by, supposedly, Pretty Boy Floyd. He wanted to see the bodies and there was a crowd gathered in Springfield, was gonna take the bodies away from 'em and drag 'em in the streets. And these gangsters supposedly knew that and they said, 'Now don't you let those bodies get taken!' Then, in the meantime, my mother had found out about it, she was callin', and couldn't get a hold of anybody. She was callin' every little police station and every place they could've stayed between here and Dallas. Finally got word to 'em that this crowd was waitin', so they detoured and went to Weir, Kansas. Left the bodies there, and came on in to Springfield. Then a week or so later, they went back and got 'em and buried 'em down in Republic. 'Course the crowd had dissipated by that time. It was all over.

My mother went up to the courthouse and they issued me a social security number when I was about ten years old. They first said they wouldn't issue a social security number to anybody under a certain age and then the Social Security System said if you're gonna draw a wage, you gotta have a social security number. I set pins at the bowling alley. Three cents a line. That's whenever they'd bowl down, knocked the pins down, you'd have to get down, get the ball back on the roll-back alley, set up the pins, get the ones off the alley, each frame you'd have to re-set all the pins. Around 1942. It was because of no labor! All the young men were gone [to the war]! So they had to do whatever they had to do. About four or five of 'em wouldn't come in until about eleven o'clock at night, about the time they wanted to close up, and they'd come in and they'd wanna bowl! They bowled a couple hours. There was one boy just a little bit older 'n me, Dean..., lived out there by Bald Hill, can't think of his name, he kinda looked out for me, kinda see that I got home, 'cause where the bowling alley was, if I went out the back, it was just one long block, a couple streets but one long block home.

My dad made his own caskets at the funeral home. He didn't make any after he moved over to Springfield. He used to buy bolts of material, build 'em,...Now he didn't make *fancy* ones, in other words he could make ones that would be...economy line. That was another one of the things, that you do what you have to do, to make the service affordable.

Back then, a lot of people wouldn't allow to be brought into the funeral home. You'd take your equipment, go to the home, embalm the body, leave it there until it was time for the funeral, go to the home, pick up the casket, go have the service. They'd never come to funeral home at all! Visitation is a relatively new thing, in a funeral home.

'Course, the funeral home was always open. Wasn't locked. I didn't know a locked door. Anytime there was a body in the chapel, it was open for anybody wanted to come in and sign the book. That's my memory. Maybe up at the later end of it, they'd lock it at ten or eleven o'clock at night. It was not scary, not then. Anybody that came there, had business.

The funeral home wasn't morbid. It was *home!* A lot of stories told about me weren't true. There was stories told about me hidin' in a casket and scarin' some of the help. Not true! If I'd ever got in a casket, I'd a never got out! The only time I was in a casket, Dad *[Rex Rainey]* put me there. A couple came in, had lost a child. They didn't know what size casket to get. They said the child was about my size, so to measure, Dad put me in there, to see if it would be right for their child. That's the only time I was in a casket!

The funeral home's an odd deal. It's not now like it used to be. It was…when anybody had a problem, they could come and talk to Dad about it.

I helped Dad with the embalming. The hand pump. That's all part of livin' in a funeral home. 'Course, I was pretty small, but back then it was kind of a one-man operation, and he generally had *some* help, *day* help, but a lot of times he didn't want to call them in after hours. And if a body came in, why, it had to be prepared that night! I remember formaldehyde, I couldn't hardly stand the formaldehyde, I'd go outside and take as deep a breath as I could, go in and do whatever I had to do. The youngest I can remember doin' that, helping, was, oh, probably 7 or 8. But the bodies were covered, the private areas. In other words, he shielded me from *that.* But as far as the embalming procedure, I was there for all of it.

Whenever I was the youngest, before I went to school, that's when I stayed with other people. Except my grandparents, I'd go down there and stay all summer. But by that time they'd *[Rex and Carmen]* got a little better help and I wasn't required as much. "

Maxine "Toots" Shockley Replogle…"Well, back then, you know, we raised chickens and everything. Well, they put the chicken feed out in print sacks. And my mom made us girls a lot of print dresses out of those chicken feed sacks. She'd tell Dad when he'd go to town, 'Now get two alike or three alike so I'll have enough for a dress.' That's a feed sack dress! I wore *many* a feed sack dress!"

Fred Rost…"Beulah, my sister, married Bill Farr. Now I'll tell ya something funny!

Bill Farr was tellin' me this about his brother Jack. He had been working at Rainey Funeral Home, Jack had, Beulah's brother-in-law.

Bill told me that little Jack Rainey was all the time pullin' stunts. Well, Jack Farr, he was up there cleaning all around them caskets and all. Little Jack Rainey crawled in one of them things, shut the lid down, waited 'til Jack got there and was cleanin' up. He lifted the lid real slow, just like a live person was in there! But it was my understandin' now that he quit his job 'cause it scared him so much, he couldn't take it any more.

I'll tell ya, there was lots of things goin' on around here!

Henry King: boy, he pulled stunts on people. Miz Montgomery had some turkeys stolen, and Henry King lied about who took her turkeys. A few days after that some gypsies come by. Henry King owned some land with corn on it. They stopped around there and asked, 'Where could a fella stay for the night?' He sent them down to Henry King's property, told them they could pitch a tent, eat all the corn you want, and it won't cost you a thing!' This was the man that Henry King had accused of stealing the turkeys! He got back at ole Henry King with that one!"

Wilma Thomas Ryser... "He was forever campaigning. 'Course, back then you didn't take a daily shower. Maybe a yearly dip in the creek. And Aunt Evie would follow him to the car with a washcloth, and wash his neck, so he wouldn't have a streak on his white shirt. Before he was sheriff. He always wore a white shirt and dark pants of some kind. I suppose it was surge. That's about all they had back then. And you were dressed up if you have white shirt and overalls on. But I can't remember Uncle Isam in overalls, ever. Just dark pants.

Now Jake   [Cunningham] and I—Helen's husband—was always real close, more like brother and sister than cousins, and I knew to go home and tell Mother whatever I did, when we were out at night, 'cause Jake would come the next morning and tell it. Jake told everything! Nothin' was secret with them!

Jake and I graduated in '44, and the fall of that year I went to Wichita. And somewhere about the same time Jake went to service. So I got married in '46, and Jake and Helen got married in 1950.

I can't remember Uncle Isam ever being in church unless it was a funeral. But he lived his beliefs. He didn't have to go to church, as the old sayin' goes, to get religion."

Mary Francis "Fran" Thomas Steelman..."My mother [Freda Rader Thomas] spent a lot time with them,[Isam and Eva] though. She helped raise all their children.

My grandmother [May Cunningham Rader] was a widow and my mother was an only child so she worked other places besides Uncle Isam's. I've heard Mother say that she spent more time with

Uncle Isam and Aunt Evie than she ever did with her mother. She lived with them. She had a lot to say about Mattie and Mildred. They were ornery! Especially Mildred.

Actually there were three sets of children. What was it Grandma's Daddy said one time? What was his wife's name? Alice? He said, 'Alice, by God, *your* kids and *my* kids are about to kill *our* kids.' Evidently they were fightin' or something.

Charley and I and Carlene Young were the only ones in our class when we were growing up. We went all the way through the seventh grade with just the three of us. We were in the seventh grade when Charley left *[to live in the courthouse in Marshfield]*. And then by the eighth grade Carlene had come up here *[Marshfield]*, and they went to high school together, and I had to go by myself in Niangua. But I think I probably attended more high school functions with them than I did in Niangua, 'cause we stayed close for years.

Here's a picture of Carlene and myself on the steps of the school we went to. Look at the galoshes—we called them—and the rolled down stockings. It was getting warm, I guess, because we had 'em rolled down. Now, she was skinny, hers are bagging at the knees, but I was never skinny.

I still look at that walnut tree down there that my brother used to hang his long underwear on in the summertime, 'cause we couldn't take it off until the elm leaf was as big as a squirrel's foot. We couldn't take our long underwear or our long socks off, and we couldn't go barefoot. So we did it kind of sneaky. And my brother would take his underwear off and hang 'em up in the walnut tree behind the boys' toilet. And that walnut tree is still there. Down in Prospect, where my sister *[Wilma Thomas Ryser]* lives, where Uncle Isam lived.

I remember when I was very small, going to their store and Uncle Isam with his hat on, reared back like this, tellin' some ungodly tale which he could do. 'Course, he elaborated a lot on it and made it a lot funnier. He always gave us kids candy.

Aunt Evie...she was a very quiet person. She was heavy, always wore her hair pulled back. She was very pleasant. I never remember seeing her do anything, but with that many kids, she had to do something some of the time. But she was always sitting in a chair, leaned back, that I can ever remember. And she was a very large woman. And I can't remember the color of her hair!

I just always thought he was dressed up. He didn't look like a workin' man. There's a lot of things he wanted to be, but he wanted to be sheriff more than anything and he finally made it. But I believe he tried more than two times. 'Cause I can remember Mother and Dad saying, 'Well, he's at it again.' And her and Daddy would have a big laugh over it. But I know they voted for him. 'Cause they were Republicans.

A hat and a big nose and he was very loud. You knew where he was at. He wasn't a bit shy.

The last time I remember going to Uncle Isam and Aunt Evie's was when Mother and Daddy bought their piano for me. I was in fourth grade. Charley didn't leave for another three years, when Isam got elected."

Jack Watters... "My mother was a telephone operator in 1916, here. But she married Dad pretty quickly after that. She didn't stay in that profession.

Gene Fraker and I went to school together. He and I were in the same class. He's the one who came by...we were playing football on Maple Street on December 7, 1941, and Gene came by and told us Pearl Harbor had been bombed, and we said, 'Where's Pearl Harbor?' None of us knew, we were just kids, thirteen or fourteen years old, and there he was driving a car! You know, they really had relaxed rules then. Fourteen-year-old driving around and you were supposed to be sixteen even then!"

David Young..."My dad was Glenn Young and was a brother to Carl Young. The Beach store is where it all began, where my grandfather started in business. My dad, and Carl, and another brother were all involved in that store at one time or other. Our grandfather and his brother-in-law, they started it together. Then my grandfather bought him out. They were just together the first year. When it originally opened it was Miller-Young. Miller was my grandfather's brother-in-law. My great uncle. Then my grandfather bought him out and it become W.E Young and Sons. William Ellis. I have a brother Ellis was named after my grandfather.

But Carl and Dad and my uncle Warner were all three involved in that store at different times. My dad and my uncle Warner went to Prospect and had that store before Carl was there. Carl, I assume, bought them out. Went to Prospect, then moved to Marshfield.

Carl and Glessie lived in that house, in Beach, where we grew up. Carlene was born in that house."

64

[James "Buster" next to his father, Isam Cunningham. Eva Randolph Cunningham, Isam's wife. Floyd "Snooks" next to his mother.]

[Bill Rader] "I always remember my mother saying, the last time he run, James was in the army, Floyd was in the army, David *[Jake]* was in the army. When he campaigned he'd shake hands, you know, 'I'm runnin' for Sheriff, I hope you'll vote for me, I've got three boys in the army.' It gave him a different position than the other times he had run."

Chapter Four
The Campaign and Election

Jan. 13, 1944 "Julius L. Uchtman, of near Fordland, became the first announced candidate for office in the coming election in Webster County....for Sheriff in the Republican Primary....August 1st."

April 13, 1944 "Under New Law April 25th Last Date to File for Public Office"

"With the approach of the new April 25 deadline, official filing of candidacies is expected to be accelerated in the next ten days. Neither the Republican nor Democratic tickets have been filled yet in Webster County."

The filing deadline used to be 60 days before the primary election, around June 1, but it was changed in order to make the Soldier Ballot Law effective. There's more about this later.

April 27, 1944 *Isam is announced as a candidate for Sheriff, as part of the entire Republican ticket announcement.*

July 27, 1944 *Campaign travel during World War II was limited by rationing. Farming was difficult with most of the young men gone. It was to be Cunningham against Uchtman in the Republican primary.*

Here's the ad from Isam, presumably in his own words, and signed with his name preference and spelling of Isam:
"TO THE VOTERS OF WEBSTER COUNTY
...I have made every effort to see and talk to all the voters, but on account of rationing of gasoline and tires, and work I have had to do at home, three of my sons now being in the armed services of the United States, it has been and will be impossible for me to see you all, but I believe you will understand the situation....and if nominated and elected Sheriff of Webster County, I will do my best to make you a good Sheriff.
ISAM CUNNINGHAM"

[Bill Rader] "I always remember my mother saying, the last time he run, James *[Buster]* was in the army, Floyd *[Snooks]* was in the army, David *[Jake]* was in the army. When he campaigned he'd shake hands, you know, 'I'm runnin' for Sheriff, I hope you'll vote for me, I've got three boys in the army.' It gave him a different position than the other times he had run."

Isam defeated fellow Republican Uchtman in the August primary and went on to win in the November general election against Democrat Hubert P. Highfill.

Nov. 9, 1944 *Final vote count from the general election, including absentees from those serving in the military:*
Isam Cunningham: 4000   Highfill: 3030

[Jane Rader] "I think people had a lot more confidence and liked him better as a sheriff than they did as Isam Cunningham down on the farm!"

Nov. 23, 1944 "The County Court was in session. W. E. *[Walter]* Letterman was presiding judge, J.H. *[Jake]* Gaupp and Jason Childress, associate judges, J.D. Johnson, sheriff, and C.B. McFadin, county clerk."
[What was called Presiding Judge is now called Presiding Commissioner, and Associate Judges are now called County Commissioners.]

Newly completed Webster County Court House in 1942 **[picture courtesy of Randy Clair]**

Chapter Five
1945

Jan. 1, 1945 "Isam Cunningham assumed his office as Sheriff of Webster County Monday, Jan. 1, succeeding J. D. *[Johnny]* Johnson, who holds the distinction of serving the most number of consecutive years of any of our sheriffs, having held the office since 1937. *[Johnson first was appointed to complete deceased sheriff Condo Evans' term. Then he was elected for one term. Missouri law prohibited a sheriff from serving consecutive elected terms.]* Mr. Cunningham will be the only 'new face' in the courthouse. Jess Cantrell has been appointed deputy by the new Sheriff."

[Charley Cunningham] "We moved in there the first day of the year 1945. That's what they wanted him to do when he was elected Sheriff. My mother cooked all the meals for the jail. What we ate is what they ate. We didn't eat with the prisoners. We stuck it through the hole.

They tell me whenever he was elected Sheriff, that the drunks was all over the streets, that he cleaned it up, pretty quick, I understood. 'Course I was thirteen and don't really remember all that. All I can tell you's what I was told. I was just a kid.

They would urinate on the streets, some of the men would. He cleaned that up right quick. He arrested them. They did it before and they wasn't arrested. That's just what I hear. I hear the old timers talkin' about that. Especially the women. I heard the women talkin' about that.

He made a big difference."

[Todd Cunningham] "Certainly, a courthouse in a small town in the Ozarks in Missouri in the 1940s and early 50s would have been the central hubbub of everything that was going on pertaining to just The Square and the businesses. But *living* down there with the courthouse and the jail as part of your grand house—quite a trip!

From my dad's *[Charley Cunningham]* perspective, you'd see a lot of Isam's business associates--if you want to call them that--highway patrolmen, prosecutors, attorneys, judges, all their personalities and experiences they had. Being a little kid in that situation, having a law enforcement officer pay attention to you, seeing how they dealt with trouble when you were a kid, probably would be a lot of little boys' dreams.

At that age you'd see some very certain responsible, upstanding, law-abiding, take-action kind of men come through all the

68

time, the norm. Given my grandfather's size and height, he would have been like a rock."

[Glen Wilson] "This one businessman, Henry Fellin--a *Democrat,* now--would brag on Isam, and say he did a lot of good for the town. He cleaned up this street up here. There'd be a bunch of drunks hangin' around on the streets—before Isam came—and when Isam came, that was cleaned up."

[Doc Blinn] " I'll tell ya: before he took over as Sheriff, women just didn't want to get out on The Square, especially at night. But anytime after Isam took over—he didn't have any hours, it was all day and all night that he wanted to do it—and he spent a lot of time on that square. He straightened that square out! Just like 'I just tapped him'. That's how he straightened it out! Lot of drunks, some of the younger guys who might be half-way humans. They didn't do anything like rape, I don't think, they just liked to agitate women. Just a lot of messy talk. They'd scare the women, with threats they'd make. Boy, Isam got that stopped. He took a number of them in. They said they used the jail pretty good when he first took over because he'd run them in. It was different back then; you could do a lot of things then as sheriff that you couldn't get away with now."

[Cline Herren] "To begin with, it's hard for anybody now to imagine that era 45, 48 years ago or something, how things were, particularly about the time Isam got elected. You know, that north side of The Square, the east end of it, all except that one building that's across Marshall Street from the bank, was ruins that had brick walls. Those buildings had burned, it had grown up with trees, and people congregated there every day and got drunk and gambled and it was very common to see people on the sidewalk gambling and, not gambling but drunk. It was not quite the same town *before* Isam as it was shortly *after.*

Because Isam did not tolerate things like this happening, here or in other towns, like Seymour. He was actually a good Sheriff as far as enforcing things. Whenever you try and think of what he had working for him, I suppose he had one part-time deputy. And he covered the whole county. And he caught a lot of people doing a lot of things and there was a lot of court going on."

[Joe Arthur] "Oh, when Isam first got elected Sheriff he cleaned up the town! You'd come up here at night, there'd be so many drunks on the street, that women would be afraid to come to town. Everybody used to come to town on Friday night and Saturday night, and get your groceries and go to the show, whatever, The Sweet Shop was open at the time. And I've said Isam's been one of the best sheriffs we've ever had because the drunks did not come out on the street when he was Sheriff because he'd throw them in jail. He was just what we needed at the time! Just what we needed."

[Jack Rainey] "Isam was just a big, raw-boned kind a fella that, on the outside he was very gruff. To meet him the first time you'd think, you don't wanna mess with *him*! But in all reality, he was pretty quiet, laid back. But he meant what he said! He didn't fool around a lot,he didn't joke around a lot. But he'd let a lot of things slide, things that didn't make a lot of difference. If it was gonna disrupt a lot of people, and wasn't gonna help a whole lot...not that he wasn't upholdin' the law! It's just the fact that if it wasn't gonna do a lot of good, he wasn't gonna do nothin' about it. That's the way I read him, I might be way off.

I had trouble understanding Charley being *my* age and *Isam* being as old as my *grandparents*! It just didn't add up to me.

My dad *[Rex Rainey]* and Isam weren't buddies. It was just mainly because of their situations both of them was placed in. They weren't runnin' around people. Actually, my folks didn't...it was just business. And the same way with Isam. When he was Sheriff, he was Sheriff all the time. I don't know of anything he did except bein' Sheriff.

Isam was down at the *[Rainey]* funeral home several times. Webster County had a coroner, but he was from Fordland.*[K.K.Kelley]* So much of the time, they just didn't even want to be bothered with him, because he made more questions than a lot of people wanted to answer. And I'm not sayin' that anything very serious ever got swept under the rug, but a lot of the minor things that they take 'em to jail today for. Just kinda a 'live-and-let-live' situation."

Jan. 4, 1945 "The County Court reconvened Tuesday for the fourth day this week, cleaning up last year's business, with the new Sheriff, Isam Cunningham, attending."

Isam was always listed in attendance at the weekly County Court meeting, unless he had been out of town transporting a prisoner or a mental patient.

March 15, 1945 "Sheriff E.I. Cunningham went to Indianapolis last Thursday *[March 8]* to bring Ralph W. Burks of near Fordland to the jail here on a forgery charge. The Sheriff was accompanied on the trip by Tom Farr."

Isam always took someone with him on his trips to pick up wanted persons who were out of state.

March 22, 1945 "Sheriff E.I. Cunningham and deputy, Jess Cantrell, went to Aurora Sunday night *[March 18]* to bring back William Lusk of Monett, charged with giving a worthless check on The Seymour Bank to Tom Cantrell of Seymour."

April 12, 1945 "Any animal or fowl running loose will be disposed of by the City Marshall. By Order of City Board" *[Donald Bruce was elected City Marshal around April 5, 1945]*

"E.I. Cunningham, Sheriff, and Jess Cantrell, deputy, took Mrs. Edna Black back to the hospital at Fulton Wednesday."

April 19, 1945 *[President]* Franklin Delano Roosevelt dies; Missourian Harry Truman becomes President of the United States and inherits World War as his greatest challenge

April 26, 1945 "An unsuccessful attempt to break jail was made last Friday *[April 20]* by Ralph Burks, 28, of Fordland, charged with forgery. He managed to escape to the roof of the courthouse, but was caught before he could drop to the ground.

While the Sheriff was away from the courthouse that evening Mrs. Cunningham heard Burks prying at something. She went up to the jail, but could not see anything amiss. Later when the Sheriff returned he went up to find Burks gone. A piece of iron was broken off the cells and used as a pry to force a window leading on to the roof of the courthouse.

The Sheriff called Ralph Day, Donald Bruce, and Jess Cantrell. They looked on the roof, but Burks had used a ladder, left by men repairing the roof, to get onto the upper roof of the building, and then pulled the ladder up after him, leaving no trace. As the Sheriff did not know the ladder had been left he did not think about anyone being able to get to the upper roof.

While the officers went out on the highway to search, Wilbur Cunningham, son of the Sheriff, heard a noise on the roof. When the officers came back they saw where some blankets had been tied together on the roof. They then found Burks on the roof. He had a blanket rope fashioned to escape, but had not had time to use it."

[With Isam's family living with him in the courthouse, where the jail was located, the family was a big—unpaid—help for times like these. Eva showed great courage to check out the prying sounds;

Wilbur must have been terrified when he heard the noise on the roof, his dad now gone with the others to look for the escapee!]

May 3, 1945 "Mrs. Doiles Cantrell is in Springfield Baptist Hospital in a serious condition as a result of family trouble Sunday *[April 29]* afternoon in which she is said to have been beaten and stomped by her father-in-law, John Cantrell...it is reported that Mrs. Cantrell, who is separated from her husband, went to the John Cantrell home and got her 14-month-old baby who had been there....John Cantrell was arrested Monday morning by Sheriff E.I. Cunningham on charges of beating and stomping her. He denies having touched her."

May 10, 1945   Victory in Europe! *[May 8]*
"Youth Dies, Another Injured, As Car Overturns—Investigating Officer Learns Auto was Stolen for 'Joyride'. Highway Patrolman investigated the accident near the Eighty Eight Schoolhouse. James Lee McPherson, 19, was killed. Gerald Lee 'Jack'Lawson, 18, was driving and was thrown out...Lawson is in Webster County jail in default of $2000 bond, charged with stealing a car."

May 24, 1945 "Notice: To Whom It May Concern: Greetings. There has been a number of complaints made to the undersigned of the operation of Slot Machines, Punch Boards, and other gambling devices being operated in the County.
We give this notice that on and after the 1st day of June, 1945, anyone operating or letting any gambling device being operated in his, her, or their place of business will be subject to a prosecution, and the gambling device will be confiscated.
So we kindly ask that, remove all gambling devices, and not operate or permit any to be operated in his, her, or their place of business. By so doing will prevent a prosecution.
For which we thank you.
J.P. Smith, Prosecuting Attorney
E. I. Cunningham, Sheriff"

[Bill Rader] "Somebody said, 'Take the hill!'
Now the hills in Okinawa are not like our hills here; for a long time I never could understand it. We look at a hill out here and it's a big rounded hill. But their hills are like this *[straight up]* and maybe the top of the hill would only be fifteen or twenty foot difference between you and the Japanese!

And so *they* were on *that* side of the hill and we were on *this* side of the hill. And I remember this officer, a second lieutenant, telling that we didn't have enough people to take this hill! But somebody else said you're supposed to follow orders. Take the hill!

Well now, I remember the officer telling me and another one or two to go down on the crest of this hill. It turned out that the Japanese were throwing these hand grenades over, like that, and then they'd roll them down. And one, I was close enough from when it went off, it didn't shatter my arm or anything but I have ten holes in my arm, or I did have ten holes, they all grew back together. That was because Japanese hand grenades were a solid mass. *Our* hand grenades were what they call incremented, little squares like this, and when they blew up, they blew up in bigger pieces. But if you were lucky, the Japanese hand grenade could blow out a piece that big and lots of small pieces. But I was fortunate enough that I got all the small pieces. That means that these all went *through* my arm. Went in and went out. But I had an artery hit."

[Jane Rader] "But if he'd been hit in his leg and he couldn't walk, he would have probably died. But he could walk. He could *run!*"

[Bill Rader] "I got to the medics. I have one little piece of shrapnel left. See that right there? Feel it? No, it doesn't hurt. It's just worked its way out there."

[Jane Rader] "He showed that to a little boy one time and he said, 'Why is that there?' and Bill said, 'Oh, I guess they left it so I could show little boys like you.'"

[Bill Rader] "But that *did* send me on the way back and, 'course, I got to the medics and they stopped the artery from pumping blood. And the very next day they put us on a plane—it'll be sixty years ago this fall—to Guam, and then they put us on a ship and we went back to Hawaii. (We'd stopped for thirty days in Hawaii on our way over, to do jungle training.) And then, after Hawaii, on back to Letterman Hospital in San Francisco. No relation!

And then they put us on kind of a hospital train, and kept goin', you didn't know where you was goin', but would you believe I ended up in O'Reilly General Hospital in Springfield! They specialized in treating nerve injuries. See, half my hand doesn't have nerve endings in it. Still. (There's two nerves that run down your hand. One of 'em feeds this half of your hand, which is to right there, and the other one feeds this half of your hand. It's not completely dead, but there's no sense of feel, you can't feel the pain.) And they sent me to O'Reilly Hospital in Springfield, Missouri.

I'd been there about a day and of course everybody back home, by that time, knew where I was. And I was standing in the door of my room, or somewhere, and here came Isam Cunningham! The closer he got to me, he was *crying!* And that surprised me."

[Jane Rader] "It comes through Alice, Bill's grandmother was the same way, she could just...you'd go see her and there'd just be tears. And his sister's kinda like that, Bill's sister is, and one of our daughters. They cried easily."

[Bill Rader] "It was about the 16th or 17th of June, 1945. Isam hadn't been Sheriff very long."

July 12, 1945 "Women Fined On Charges of Peace Disturbance. Following the complaint of Mr. and Mrs. Harry Bowman, residing at the place formerly known as the Irish Inn, on Hwy 66, of a disturbance of the peace, Sheriff E.I. Cunningham and deputies arrested two women and placed them in jail here Friday night. The women are said to have put up resistance, especially one, and the officers are said to have had to take no little abuse and had some trouble getting them into cells.

The women are said to have been guilty of a peace disturbance at Andrews Café in addition to that at the Bowmans'. They were reported considerably under the influence of liquor." *[One woman was from Kansas City and the other was from Chicago. Both were fined $1 and costs after pleading guilty to charges of disturbing the peace.]*

[Charley Cunningham] "I come in one night. My dad had three women they were gettin' ready to put in jail. They picked them up down here below the golf course. Used to be Irish Inn, a beer joint. So I come in one night, from high school, from a basketball game or something, and he had three women up there.

And I'd been up there before, got up in the night and come in, when the highway patrol or Dad would bring somebody in. I used to get up and run in there as a kid.

They throwed some women in jail so Mom had to go up there. Dad would go up, after the highway patrol was leavin', and make sure they was all right, and the women would say, 'Dad, throw him in here with us, we'll take care of him!' They meant *me!*

I learned a lot of things while I was in high school!"

[Don Letterman] "I stayed lots of times...well, the first time I went to the jailhouse he locked me in. The jail. Isam did! Just a joke. He just took us in there, you know, walked in there with us, then he'd just walk out and shut the door! It was all just in fun.

Grandpa had one boy in jail almost all the time. He didn't have nowhere to go! He was a trustee, an artist. He used to draw. He stayed in the woman's cell. And he never did lock him up, the old boy would just go up there, go to sleep of a night, and he'd sit out on the front of a daytime, and he'd go to the restaurant and get something for the prisoners, if they needed it to eat, or whatever, and I remember he was the best artist I'd seen. Sit down and draw anything. But if they turned him out, he'd just go do somethin', a little somethin' so they'd throw him back in! He didn't have nowhere to stay!"

[Darrell Letterman] "Granddad locked me up in the jailhouse too, and kinda pointed to the guys and said, 'Be good', to the prisoners that was in there, and he took off, went downstairs! Come back up a little later, unlocked the door, and said, 'How do ya like jail?' and I told him I didn't, you know, and he said, ' Well, now, see, now you'll know whether you wanna be in here later on in your life, or not!' And I said, 'I'm not bein' in no jail!' The prisoners were just sittin' around talkin' to me like I was one of them! They were good to me, but he told 'em to be good. I was somewhere around twelve. But anyways, that was my last time in jail!"

July 19, 1945 "Businessmen Request Hiring of Nightwatch After They Learn Marshal's Change to Daytime—The City Board has employed Porter Rader as nightwatchman *[on July 16]* and he has gone to work. After the first of the year when merchant's licenses will be due again, the license will probably be increased to take care of a part of the expense of employing a nightwatchman. The city marshal is needed, according to city authorities, to enforce traffic regulations, auto licenses, and city ordinances. It is expected that the dog ordinance will also be enforced shortly." *[see April 12, 1945]*

[A city employee--the marshal Donald Bruce--helped   Isam during nighttime problems. When it was announced that the marshal would move to days, the businessmen seemed to have raised a ruckus that got results.   But the source of this new nightwatchman's ongoing salary was a gentle threat back at them. And had the dogs all been running wild since April?]

August 2, 1945 "Pvt. James H.*[Buster]* Cunningham, son of Sheriff and Mrs. E.I. Cunningham of this city, arrived in the United States

Friday *[July 27]*. He landed in Boston and sent a telegram home. Then Saturday morning he called his parents. He said he might be sent to O'Reilly General Hospital, Springfield. Pvt. Cunningham has been in the hospital the last three months."

August 6, 1945 ATOMIC BOMB DROPPED ON HIROSHIMA, JAPAN *[The first military use of an atomic bomb]*

August 9, 1945 SECOND ATOMIC BOMB DROPPED, ON NAGASAKI, JAPAN

August 9, 1945 "County Court Proceedings and Warrants issued:
E.I. Cunningham, service and board of prisoners $125.90
E.I. Cunningham, circuit court service $9.00

[Though the amount varied, each time the county court met there were two checks issued to Isam. One was for feeding the prisons at the rate of 75 cents per day per prisoner, set by the county court. The other amount was for serving papers to various Webster County citizens, for the circuit court, such as divorce papers.]

August 16, 1945 JAPAN SURRENDERS!

August 23, 1945 "Cunningham Brothers Unknowingly Helped in Capture of Same City: James A.*[Buster]* Cunningham and William David *[Jake]* Cunningham, two of Sheriff and Mrs. Cunningham's sons, are home after serving overseas. They discovered after they got home that they both helped in the capture of Metz, Germany, and entered the city on the same day. They also found that they were both in the same hospital at the same time. They were that close together without getting together."

[Wilma Ryser] "They always had cows and the farm had crops...corn and so forth....And they usually had a hired hand to help. Paul Bowden and his family lived down there, until Buster got out of service, when Isam was elected Sheriff and they had to move into the courthouse."

[Fran Steelman] "I remember that, because Grandma *[May Cunningham]* Rader was upset, because there had never been anybody *[living on the farm]* but a *relative*."

September 20, 1945 "Prosecuting Attorney J.P. Smith and Sheriff E.I. Cunningham left Wednesday morning *[Sept.19]* for Los Angeles, Calif., to bring back John Collins, sentenced to two years for stealing a car and who has broke his parole. The officers will go by way of Sacramento, Calif., the state capital."
[Extradition papers had to be completed and issued at the state capital.]

October 18, 1945 *[A feature story about J.P. Smith, prosecuting attorney of Webster County describes his 52 years in law business. Called "Uncle Porter," he was elected 6 times as prosecuting attorney. First elected in 1900, he was re-elected 1902, elected again in 1920, again in 1940, then '42, then '44. It seems reasonable to say Smith was over 70 years old at this time.]*

November 15, 1945 "Sgt. Floyd L.*[Snooks]* Cunningham discharged from Army Air Forces."

November 29, 1945 "Sheriff Frustrates Jailbreaks, After Man Attacks Him....Richard Hewson, Greenfield, Indiana, who was arrested November 15 at Strafford *[for stealing a car in St. Louis],* hit the sheriff in the side of the head with a piece of iron and attempted to get away, but the Sheriff parried the blow and after knocking the man down, hit him over the head with his gun. The prisoner suffered a gash that required a doctor's attention and about nine stitches and some clips....The piece of iron raised a lump on the side of the officer's head, but the Sheriff parried the blow sufficiently to prevent being seriously hurt."

Chapter Six
1946

January 3, 1946 "J.P. Smith, prosecuting attorney, filed first degree murder charges against Charles Bruce, 45, Seymour auctioneer and stock dealer. His preliminary hearing will be held today, Jan. 3. Bruce was arrested by Sheriff E.I. Cunningham, Sheriff John T. Pierpont of Springfield, and a highway patrolman. Bruce, who did not attend the *[coroner's]* inquest, is being held without bond in the county jail here.

[Tom] Cantrell *[café and night club operator of Seymour]* was killed by a bullet fired from outside his café December 24, after an alleged 'racket' he and Bruce had inside the building and the latter had left, according to reports. Bruce is said to have received a head injury and entered a Springfield hospital that night.

An open verdict was reached by a coroner's jury at an inquest investigating the death of Tom Cantrell…conducted nearly all day last Friday *[12/28]* in the Seymour high school gymnasium. The jury agreed after deliberating about 15 minutes that Cantrell 'came to his death by a gunshot wound fired by parties unknown.'

Proceedings began at 10 a.m. and ended at 3:15 p.m. Friday *[12/28]* and were witnessed by approximately 250 spectators, Coroner K.K. Kelley of Seymour reported."

[John T. Pierpont] "I was at the Fair Grove Festival when Isam was Sheriff. He was sitting on the curb when I walked by. He called me by name. I recognized his name. He told me about when my dad was sheriff of Greene County, during 1945-1948, Isam could pick up the phone and ask Dad for anything and Dad would be right there. And Isam Cunningham would do the same for my dad. They worked like that back then. My dad was *also* John T. Pierpont but they called him 'Tub'. He was a big man, like Isam."

January 10, 1946 "A change of venue was granted from the court of Justice of Peace T.C. Clayton to Justice of Peace J.G. McKinney. The date of the preliminary is now Jan.18. Cantrell was killed by a bullet from a small caliber rifle thrust through a window at the Cantrell place of business a few minutes after an altercation in which it is alleged that Cantrell struck Bruce over the head with a piece of iron."

"Richard Hewson, found guilty of grand larceny *[given 5 years]* and also of felonious assault *[given 2 years]* was taken to state penitentiary, Jefferson City, Sunday *[1/6]* by Sheriff E. I. Cunningham and Marshal Don Bruce." *[See Nov. 29, 1945]*

January 17, 1946 "Sheriff E.I. Cunningham took Miss Rosa Gravin to Buffalo Monday. The county court there ordered her admitted to the State Hospital at Fulton. She has been in this county taking medical treatment."

January 24, 1946 "Circuit Court In Session This Week Here; Divorce Cases Becoming More Numerous at Each Term"

January 31, 1946 "Sheriff E. I. Cunningham returned Tuesday *[1/29]* from San Antonio, Tex., where he went to pick up Roy Marlow. While on the trip he visited his son, Pfc. Wm. David Cunningham *[Jake],* at Camp Swift, Tex." *[Circuit Court notes from Friday Jan. 25]* "State of Mo. vs. Roy Marlow, operating motor vehicle while intoxicated; bond forfeited; capias ordered."

[Helen Cunningham] "When Jake was in the service—he was down in Camp Hood, Texas, and at one closer to Austin, Swift, it's no longer there, but, anyway—a bunch of 'em had gone into town that night. They were in a hotel, I think he said, and they were shootin' craps.
'You know,' Jake said, 'I was down on the floor havin' a good time, looked up, and there stood my dad!' He had brought a prisoner, or came after one. He said, 'I said "Oh my god." But shoot, Dad never said a word about it.' Jake was in the service, down in Texas, and Isam appeared!"

February 7, 1946 "Carl Young Sells Prospect Store to Charity Man—A deal involving one of the best country stores in Webster County took place this week when Carl Young sold his store at Prospect to O.N. Maddux & Son of Charity."

February 14, 1946 "Car Stealing Shows Folly of Leaving Keys in Ignition—A car stolen Sunday night and an attempt to take a car Monday night should give warning here to auto owners to be sure and not leave their keys in their cars.
The car belonging to Buddy Potter was taken Sunday night and was found Monday afternoon near Waynesville *[MO]* out of gas.

Monday night a party was taking Jake Burchfield's car at this place when he was frightened away.

As Elston Miller was passing he saw a car apparently stalled at the Burchfield place. He stopped to help, thinking it was Mr. Burchfield. The man ran when Elston stopped and Mr. Miller chased him but was unable to catch up with him. Sheriff Cunningham was called but no trace could be found of the person.

The Sheriff warns that everyone should be sure that keys are not left in cars."

February 21, 1946 "Notice, Car Owners! Notice has been given by Wilson Bell, Secretary of State, that the deadline for securing Missouri Auto License tags is February 25th.

This is to give notice that Webster County officers will follow instructions of the Secretary of State and enforce the law. All Webster County cars and trucks should have 1946 tags by next Monday or their operators will be subject to arrest.

J.P. Smith, Prosecuting Attorney
E.I. Cunningham, Sheriff"

March 7, 1946 "County Court, having been informed that there are certain ballots stored in county clerk's office that are more than a year old and required by law to be destroyed, ordered E.I. Cunningham, Sheriff, to destroy said ballots by burning."

March 14, 1946 "Roy C. Miller announces Candidacy for Webster County Prosecuting Attorney."

[Peg Miller] "When we first arrived in town, Roy had been in the Navy. We were married and then he went back out to sea. He came back for some training in communications. He was on a fleet oiler the first half of the war and then on an attack staff ship later. While he was back doing his training, he was in the states, and we were married. When he came back, we hit Marshfield and there was literally no place to live. The town...there had been no building for five years. There was no place to live! Was '46, we would have come back.

He was from Norwood: it's north of Ava, between Mansfield and Mountain Grove *[all towns in southwest Missouri]*. Went to Norwood High School, then MU and MU Law School, and then into the navy.

We managed to talk Lester and Nanny Garst into letting us stay in their upstairs. Of course, Miller chain-smoked and he *[Lester Garst]* made him go outside and smoke. They were perfectly marvelous people. They lived right next to the telephone company.

Quite early on, Roy ran for Prosecutor, at the first opportunity, and won."

March 28, 1946 "Sheriff E. I. Cunningham took Shelby Eliott to Boonville to place him in the Missouri Training School for Boys."

[Noted in Circuit Court minutes, Judge C. H. Jackson presiding]: "State of Mo. vs. Shelby Eliott and Dorsey Osborne, burglary and larceny. Ellsworth Haymes and Roy Miller appointed attorneys for defendant Shelby Eliott. Shelby Eliott, age 15, appeared and his case transferred to the Juvenile Division. He enters a plea of guilty and is adjudged guilty. Punishment assessed at imprisonment and detention in Missouri Training School for Boys at Boonville for 18 months. Dorsey Osborne, age 13, punishment same as with Eliott, defendant paroled."

[Doc Blinn] "I came to Webster County in 1946, straight out of the Navy. I got out, was discharged, February of 1946. A classmate of mine who had been practicing here in Marshfield wanted to leave, Spencer Macauley, and so he got in touch with me and wanted to know if I'd be interested in buying his practice. We'd been classmates, and he had been practicing here in Marshfield while I went to Fordland. He stayed and practiced while I was in the service.

I was interested because I loved Webster County! I wanted to come back here. So we got our arrangements made and I came then in March of 1946 and took over the practice. Of course at that time we were doing Obstetrics in the clinic. We'd have women come in, we'd deliver them, keep them about eight to ten hours after delivery, then send them home by ambulance. We were doing that—and that was back in '46, in the 40's—and they just found out some years ago in Springfield that you could do that! But we did that way way back. And everybody liked it real well.

We know now that was The Baby Boom. And I did Obstetrics for 26 years, the first 26 years. I did Obstetrics when I worked in Fordland but I did it in the home there, I delivered babies in the home.

I had a General Practice, too, but I would average ten or twelve babies a month. I delivered something just under 4,000 babies."

[Jack Rainey] "I drove the ambulance, after I got my license, but not on a regular basis. Back then, there was two places in Marshfield where they'd go to have their babies. Well, if they had the baby in the morning, they were sent home that afternoon but they had to go in an ambulance. So I'd go with my dad [Rex Rainey]. Put the lady on the cot and I'd carry the baby, hold the baby in a basket and take it home. We made a lot of trips like that. Long before Doc Blinn there was doctors in the same building that Blinn came in, they all had their clinics in the same house, right across from the old Lutheran Church, kitty-corner from the Masonic Lodge. So they were just a block from the funeral home. We'd go around, pick 'em up, take 'em home, five miles or so out. I held the baby most of the time, because there really wasn't a good place to…my daddy would buy a big four-door car, cut the post out of the side of it so that they could load a cot into the side of it, and then had, like, barn door latches top to bottom, so that back door would shut. Front door worked just like it always did, but the back door would open without that post in it."

[Edna Cunningham] "In '46, when Buster came home from the service, we went to the farm. Paul Bowden and his wife ran it after Isam became Sheriff, until Buster got out. He was the oldest boy and he always worked a lot down there anyway. I mean, they run the store and he done a lot of that, before he went to the service. So that's how it came about.

I'd lived on a farm when I was a child. Well, you know, you can always learn! I enjoyed it, as long as he was able to do, you know. We worked together. We didn't have a family, but anyhow, I got out and baled hay and raked hay and picked hay and done everything. Milked cows.

Every Memorial Day…they was all buried at Prospect. Well, here they came! And they stopped at my house for coffee and cake, whatever I had, you know. Yeah, I had them down there a lot! And Isam and Evie would come down, too, on a Sunday, and then *my* folks would come and maybe I'd have the whole, both sides, of the family. I enjoyed it, 'cause I was young then. Couldn't do it now, though.

Isam would come to the farm whenever he took a notion to come! He'd just show up. He give Buster full responsibility. He didn't try to run it or anything. Buster run it before he left [for the service], because, I'll tell ya, Isam was gone a lot. He liked to run around. And Buster'd stay there and do the work. He [Isam] didn't have any doubt that Buster couldn't take care of the farm. Or I don't think he did.

It was just the two of us. At harvest time the neighbors, we'd all pitch in. Like filling silos, we had help. When you put up hay, you hired somebody to help haul it in. But I've got out and baled hay and done all of that and helped get it in, too. We had hired hands then, boys, but that was the way it was.

We didn't do anything for *fun*. We just worked. We'd go to church on Sunday. And we'd come to the 4th of July. We didn't do much runnin' around. Oh, we went on some trips, I'll have to say that. We went to Connecticut, my sister was livin' there then. And we went to Seattle, Washington. Well, I know that was two long trips that we took. But see, whenever you did that, you had to get somebody to milk the cows! And they didn't nobody wanted to milk cows! Well, he had a cousin, Herbert Vestal, he did it one time, I know. And then I think one of the Dudley boys done our milkin' one time when we was gone. Herbert and Herman *[Vestal]* lived down there real close. They were full-time bus drivers.

I mowed all that yard all the way to the barn, every week. A riding mower. He *[Buster]* would help if he had time. But he had to work out in the field, there was plenty to do out there. And I would mow this yard. I mowed it from the highway all the way to the barn. And then I'd trim, with scissors, not electric trimmers. I enjoyed doin' that, but, boy, I told somebody, when I'd get off of that mower I'd feel like I was deaf, dumb, and blind. I'd ride about three hours.

We built two barns and we remodeled the house and built a new storage house in the yard. We built a grade A barn, we built a hay barn, we done all that, and then we moved. They had just got electricity before we got there. There wasn't a bathroom. There wasn't water in the house. I carried many a bucket of water from that spring down there. Just drank it straight from the spring."

April 18, 1946 "Circuit Court in Short Session 4/11—Clyde Raymond Schildtkneck of St. Joseph, charged with stealing a $35 diamond ring from B.T. Bruton, Niangua, pled guilty and was sentenced to serve two years in the penitentiary. Sheriff Cunningham, accompanied by Bill Spriggs, took Schildtkneck to Jefferson City Friday *[4/12]*. Schildtkneck was serving a three months jail sentence for shoplifting from the Rathbun Drug store recently."

April 25, 1946 "Township Offices have been abolished by the new state constitution—those of Justice of Peace and Constable."

[from Bob Priddy's Across Our Wide Missouri, vol 1, 1982]
"In 1946 the legislature pushed a bill through which provided not only for the institution of magistrate courts, but the transition from the 140-year old system of Justices of the Peace to the new system of magistrates. Justices of the Peace were allowed to serve in that position until their terms ran out. The first Magistrates to succeed them were elected later that year....Today you have to go a long way to find a kindly man in a white frame house to perform the marriage ceremony while his wife plays that convenient organ in the corner. He hasn't

existed in this state since Governor Donnelly signed the bill creating Magistrate Courts in Missouri on…March 11, 1946."

May 2, 1946 "Virgil Looney, 29, who was the object of one of the greatest manhunts ever witnessed in south Missouri last week after shooting a state patrolman at Lebanon, on April 22, committed suicide Friday morning at his father's home at Grove Spring, Wright county. He shot himself through the head with the revolver that he had taken off Patrolman Joe E. Brummell when he made his escape.

Looney said he walked to his father's home from near Eldridge, where he abandoned the state patrol car in which he made his escape from Lebanon after shooting the patrolman. He told his father, who urged him to surrender, that he would rather die than give himself up.

Looney shot the officer through the chest and arm after he had been arrested on a pick-up order from St. Louis. He took the patrol car and guns. Then the chase was on. Planes, bloodhounds, neighboring peace officers and many of the state patrolmen were used, but Looney escaped.

The patrolman is expected to recover from his wounds.

E.I. Cunningham and Donald Bruce of Marshfield were among the officers that joined in the pursuit of Looney. The fugitive, said to have a previous police record in many places, lost himself in the wooded hills south of Hahatonka, where he was said to have several relatives and friends."

[This ad began in the May 5 paper and continued almost weekly throughout the rest of 1946.]

[Willis Case] "He was an auctioneer, well, he was *called* an auctioneer, he called sales for people, but he never had much of a chant."

[Warren Beck] "Isam was expected to be at all the Pie Suppers, to auctioneer, and to keep order. At the rural schools. The Sheriff was always asked to auctioneer. All the girls and their mothers, mostly the girls, would bring pies, and then they'd bid on them and they'd have contests—The Man With the Dirtiest Feet, Most Love-Sick Couple, various things.

Some of those Pie Suppers had rowdy people there who insisted on comin' drunk, havin' trouble. I can remember Isam takin' out one of the Price boys. Alvin. He's dead now. Alvin and Elvin, they were twins. Alvin grabbed ahold of the door, where it was open, at the hinges on the side of it, and he just took the door right with him. At Black Oak School, out past the Scout Camp. That's where I grew up."

May 9, 1946 "Catch Wanted Man—Patrolman Wallace and Sheriff E.I. Cunningham apprehended Edward Bruce McIntuff of Riverside, Calif., at Buffalo Saturday night. The man was wanted for taking a car, a large convertible coupe, which he was driving."

"Circuit Court to Convene Here Monday *[5/13]*—About twenty criminal cases, among them the murder case of the State vs. Charles Bruce of Seymour, charged with the shooting of Tom Cantrell at the Cantrell place east of Seymour on Christmas eve, is on the docket for the regular May term of Circuit Court starting here next Monday. There are also about fifty civil suits on the docket to come before Judge Chas. H. Jackson."

"Niangua Café Man Victim of 'Stick-Up'—Dwight Cantrell, café man at Niangua, was held up by two men Saturday night *[5/4]* when he stepped out on the back porch of his home about one o'clock. The thieves took about $300 off of him, after putting a gun into his ribs. No arrests have been made as yet."

May 16, 1946 "Pick Up Runaways—Betty Lowe, 14, and Eleanor Berri, 12, both of Springfield, were picked up at the west side of Marshfield on Highway 66 Wednesday *[5/15]* by Webster County officers. The fathers were called and it was found that they had run away from home and started to St. Louis. The fathers came after the girls Wednesday evening."

"Charles Bruce is Acquitted at Trial—Scenes reminiscent of famous murder trials of former years were enacted here Tuesday and Wednesday *[5/14-5/15]* as the crowded court room listened tensely to the trial of Charles Bruce of Seymour charged with the killing of Tom Cantrell at the Cantrell roadhouse east of Seymour on last Christmas Eve....Motion to disqualify Sheriff filed and sustained. Noah Compton appointed. Arguments presented for plaintiff by J.P. Smith, John C. Pope and Edwin Douglas. For defendant by D.R.Carter and M.J. Huffman....The jury came in with a verdict of 'Not Guilty,' after an hour and fifteen minutes deliberation. There had been much conjecture breathed in the halls of the courthouse the two days as to what the verdict would be....Defendant discharged."

Here's a list of some other cases in court that session, and the judged outcome:
1. violation of commercial feed law—guilty, $100 fine
2. dynamiting fish—guilty, 6 months in county jail
3. selling mortgaged property—guilty, $100 fine and 6 mos. in county jail
4. operating motor vehicle while intoxicated—guilty, $100 fine
5. rape—trial by jury, guilty, 2 years in the penitentiary
6. 17 divorces—all granted

May 23, 1946 "County Court Proceedings from session Monday, May 20—Sheriff E. I. Cunningham authorized to cause all persons who have been convicted and sentenced by a court of competent jurisdiction in this county for a crime for punishment which is defined by law to be a fine or by imprisonment in the county jail for any length of time, or by both such fine and imprisonment, or until such fine be paid, to work on the public roads, highways, or other public works or buildings of such county, or to break rock for a macadamizing purpose. Said order not to be applicable to females or other persons incapable of performing manual labor due to physical disability."

June 20, 1946 "Officers Here Catch Reformatory Escaper—John McGee, who broke away from Algoa Reformatory at Jefferson City Sunday, was caught here Tuesday evening *[6/18]* by Webster County officers and state patrolmen. He was lodged in jail here awaiting return to Algoa, according to Sheriff E. I. Cunningham. McGee was sent to Algoa from Springfield April 16, for two years, on a charge of stealing a car in Texas, according to the Sheriff."

July 4, 1946 "Office of City Marshal vacant caused by the moving of Don Bruce outside of the city limits. Candidates are H.E. Cheek, W.E. George, and Owen Claxton."

July 11, 1946 *[H.E. Cheek was elected New City Marshal.]*

"Smaller Crowd Than Usual at 4th of July Celebration and Homecoming...presumably caused by the fact that rumors were circulating saying the celebration had been called off as a result of the infantile paralysis epidemic *[polio]* in the nearby town of Lebanon."

July 18, 1946 "Pledge Motorist to Drive Safely. Mayor F.L. Stockton takes the lead....Sheriff E.I. Cunningham was the second to sign the small cards....containing six safe driving agreements which, if adhered to, are designed to reduce the toll of traffic accidents. The agreements are: 'I'll not drive while drinking. I'll not pass cars on hills or curves. I'll signal before making a turn or stop. I'll keep alert while driving. I'll drive within the speed limit. I'll drive with both hands.'

Among others signing the pledge cards were Ellis Jackson; J.G. McKinney, police judge; Oscar L. Carter, county superintendent of schools; B.F. Julian; and E. L. Struble, local agent of the MFA Mutual Insurance Co., who is making the cards available for distribution to motorists."

July 25, 1946 "Many Arrests After Seymour Disturbance; Warrants Issued For 27 Persons on Complaint of Eli Davis

A disturbance between the streetcar and the Davis Service Station in Seymour has resulted in the issuing of warrants for the arrest of 27 persons charged with disturbing the peace. Many of them have been brought to Marshfield, but some are still to be arrested by the officers. Most of those brought here have been released on $500 bond for appearance in Circuit Court.

The crowd, which is said to have gathered after midnight Saturday night or early Sunday, July 14, disturbed the peace of Mr. and Mrs. Eli Davis 'by cursing and swearing and loud and indecent conversation and by threatening, challenging, and fighting.' Most of those charged are said to reside outside of Seymour."

August 1, 1946 "Fordland's Exchange Robbed—Thieves broke into the Fordland Farmers Exchange Saturday night *[7/27]*, blowed the iron safe and escaped with $1,862.91 in cash. The checks in the safe were not taken. The theft was discovered Sunday morning about 8 o'clock. The safe had been opened with nitroglycerine.

The guilty party or parties broke into the rear of the building and seemed to know the place, according to Sheriff E. I. Cunningham. He stated that the Patrol and he were called and are now working on the case. No arrests have been made, and the officers do not divulge clues they have, if any."

[Jack Watters] "I don't think Isam ever held back on anything we'd ask him about, or Dad *[Ballard Watters]* would ask him about. He was forthright, he didn't try to hide anything from anybody. He might have said, 'Well, I can't tell you that.' But he was straightforward."

"Woman Sues Sheriff for Damages—Katherine Emmerson has filed an action for damages against E. I. Cunningham, Sheriff, asking for $5,000 actual damages and $3,000 punitive damages.

She charges that he held her under arrest and confined her in jail for two days and nights without legal process of any kind having been issued against or served upon her, about July 6th of this year.

It is reported that the officer was called by her husband and that it was at the husband's request that she was confined."

August 8, 1946 *[from Circuit Court notes]* "Eight of the 27 persons charged with disturbing the peace at Seymour on or about the 14th of July appeared and plead guilty. *[Four were]* fined $5 and sentenced to six months in the county jail."

"Carl Young Opening Wholesale Supply Here"

August 15, 1946 "As a result of a ruckus on the east side of the square Monday morning *[8/12]* Hugh King is charged with 'assault on E. M. Bumgarner by striking and beating him with his fist.' He made bond for $500 and the case will be heard in circuit court."

August 22, 1946 "Theft Epidemic Breaks Out through County—Five places were robbed Saturday *[8/17]* in the east part of the county and Sheriff E.I. Cunningham announces that he will give $25 reward for the arrest and conviction of anyone connected with any one of the robberies....

The robberies took place between 10 a.m. and 4 p.m. and while the folks were not at home. It would seem that someone who knew that the people were gone from home and the places is guilty."

September 5, 1946 *[from Editor's column]* "The Editor Is Thinking by T.B.*[Ballard]* W.*[Watters]*....One of the meanest, most contemptible and littlest acts we have heard of in a long time is the stealing of a watch and chain from the room of Byron Fross recently. The chain had just been given him as a present a week or two before it was stolen. Anyone who would steal from a blind person is a rat of the lowest order."

September 12, 1946 "First Jury Duty Served By Women—New State Constitution Now Allows Women to Serve As Jurors—For the first time in the history of Webster County women are serving as petit jurors in Circuit Court in session here this week....When some of the regularly selected petit jurors for this term of court were not present, Judge Chas. H. Jackson ordered Sheriff E. I. Cunningham to subpoena women to fill the places....

Judge Jackson states that he believes that with women serving there is more likelihood of having better qualified juries."

[Peg Miller] "I can remember the first woman on a jury. It was Nellie...from 'Niangee'...*[Peg is pronouncing Niangua as Isam did, described earlier in Chapter One's Isam-isms]* one of the definitely single-minded broads of the county. She was a pushy one. Wonderful gal. And it was a drunk-driving case. And the poor ole defendant was scared out of his wits. And she was made foreman in honor of the occasion. And they were out for a little while, then came in, and rendered a very just and temperate verdict. And the town immediately accepted women on the jury. And *[Roy]* Miller said it was the best thing that ever happened because for the first time they listened! The women made 'em listen! He said it was wonderful!"

[Freda Langston] "I was in my 30's when Isam was Sheriff. My mama *[Elzie Doyle]* worked at Farmers Mutual Insurance Company, on the same floor that Isam and Evie lived on. Evie and Isam had their living quarters there too. Evie had to go up on the third floor to cook the meals for the prisoners.

I helped, too. They had Assessment Time once a year and I always made out all the assessment cards. Then I helped my mother when they came in to pay. I helped my mother at the courthouse after I worked part of the day for Mary *[Mary's Variety]* and then I'd work the rest of the day with my mother. But I'd work there other times, too, when she needed help."

[Kerry Proctor] "Farmers Mutual was originally organized in 1907 in Webster County to write the fire and lightning coverage for the farmers and people who had homes in the rural areas. That was all that they wrote, the fire and lightning coverage. It was because the large companies that wrote in the large cities like Kansas City and St. Louis and Springfield would not come out and write in rural areas. So the farmers organized a mutual company which means the policyholders own the company. As a policyholder you become an owner of the company, a member like the Webster Electric Coop. It's the same situation.

The way it was originally organized, you had a township agent that covered that area, because transportation was such that, now, I cover the whole county but then you were lucky to be able to cover a whole... voting township, is actually what it was. They continued that for a number of years. Then they added what is called reinsurance, which was a larger company providing coverage for the farm mutual so they could write more coverage. The farm mutual could write a limited amount of coverage because they didn't have enough capital. So they went to a larger company that provided either above a set amount or a portion of each loss.

Reinsurance has been in existence for hundreds of years. So that they can withstand catastrophes, like hurricanes, they have other companies that come in. Lots of times it's a pooling of a number of companies.

The mutual agent would collect a premium at the time they wrote the policy, as I understand it. Then they would bill out each year and if the losses were higher in a given year, they would mail out an assessment to the policyholders to cover over and above what they had collected on the basic premium. They called it assessments. Well, come to the middle of the year, they might have had a number of fires that winter or something like that, and they didn't have enough money to pay the claims, or they were getting close, then they would send out notices to all the policy holders that "We're going to have to assess you an additional twenty cents a hundred on your insurance to pay the claims that have been submitted to us, to keep us in solid condition." The rates that you originally wrote the policy for basically stayed the same for years and years, but if they had to have more money, they'd run an assessment. And they might run two or three during the year!

Reinsurance stepped in Webster County, probably about 1949, when a fella came down from the Grinnell Mutual Reinsurance Company and talked about the reinsurance program to the board. Sometime, I would say, in the 50s, they signed up for the reinsurance. Sometime prior to 1955. From information in those Board Minutes. They still only wrote fire and lightning."

[Freda Langston] "My mother was a deputy for Isam, for a while. If they had women on a jury, they didn't let them go home at night if it was a very serious trial. Mama would bring some of the women home with her to stay all night, you know, for Evie and for Isam.

I'd go up and work on her insurance job while she took care of those women jurors. They'd have to go out and eat at night, or they'd have to go to the bathroom and all that stuff.

She took care of the women part, with the female prisoners, not with the cooking or anything. There weren't very many women ever arrested. Some woman got in jail, lived on Panther Creek, for makin' White Lightning.

Evie, she cooked all the prisoners' meals--up on the third floor, that's where their kitchen was--and boy, she fed them so good. She'd give them chicken and dumplins' and beans and everything like that. She'd always have a dessert of some kind for them.

It was kinda funny. She'd get 'em all fed at noon, do the dishes all up, and then here she'd come. She'd sit in there with my mom, in Mama's office, and they'd visit. Oh, they'd just enjoy each other...Evie giggled a lot."

September 19, 1946 *[Circuit Court notes]* "State of MO vs. Hugh King, common assault. Defendant enters a plea of not guilty. Trial by jury. Jury returned verdict as follows: 'We the Jury find the defendant not guilty.' Defendant discharged."

October 10, 1946 "Max Laverne Kleier, 2-year-old son of Mrs. Gladys Kleier, Marshfield, was burned to death when caught in a blaze in an outbuilding at the farm home of his grandparents....The child was playing with his three-year-old uncle, Rex Yates, in the building when it suddenly blazed. Relatives opined that the children had found some matches and set the building on fire.

Young Yates ran to summon his mother, but she returned too late.

Sheriff E. I. Cunningham investigated the accident and said there would probably be no inquest."

"Negro Reported To Have Admitted Robberies—A Negro, giving the name of J. D. Halls, Chicago, but probably of Plumerville, Ark., and recently in the Tulsa, Okla. jail, was caught in the woods near Sampson Tuesday morning by Sheriff Cunningham. Others taking part in the search were Deputy H. E. Cheek, I. Fred King, and two Perryman men.

The Negro was charged with breaking into and robbing the homes of Bill Deckard, near Northview Sunday, and Jim Brashear, near Niangua Monday. The suitcases, clothing, watches, jewelry and other items taken were found with his capture. He was trying to cook some corn when found.

He admitted to the highway patrol to breaking into houses from Seneca to Springfield. It later developed that he broke into the Dr. J. H. Day milkhouse at Niangua, taking milk and some tools.

In the articles taken from the Brashear home was the Purple Heart won by Ralph Kleier who was killed in Italy. The Negro had it on him.

He is being held in jail here pending preliminary."

October 17, 1946 *[Circuit Court Notes from 10/10 & 10/11 session]*
"State of MO. vs. Judge Hall, charged with burglary and larceny in two cases after breaking into the homes of Bill Deckard and Jim Brashear last week. Defendant…will be 18 years of age 10/23/46 *[so]* the court proceeds with the case. Plea of guilty to burglary and larceny….Punishment 6 years…in the intermediate reformatory at Algoa. Sheriff allowed one guard to take Hall to Algoa, near Jefferson City."

November 21, 1946 "Notice—there has been lots of complaints made to us of parties hauling tin cans, bottles, and other refuse out and dumping the same along, and on the public highways and roads, or on lands not their own, which is a violation of Section 4729 of Revised Statutes of Missouri, 1939, and which provides a punishment of a fine not less than ten dollars, nor more than fifty dollars, and if the same is not removed within three days thereafter it shall be deemed second offense against the provisions of this section.

We, the undersigned, …notify…there will be a case filed, arrest made, and a prosecution.

Please comply with the law.

This November 20th, 1946

J.P. Smith, Prosecuting Attorney

E. I. Cunningham, Sheriff"

"Mayor F.L. Stockton stated that the city board has decided to have two or three clean-ups a year instead of the usual annual spring clean-up in the past. It is hoped that this move will halt the dumping of unsightly trash on rural roads and by-ways."

December 5, 1946 "Sheriff E. I. Cunningham returned November 24 from a trip to Visalia, Calif., where he went to bring back Darrell Yates wanted for embezzlement. Sheriff Cunningham saw a large number of Webster County people at Visalia and Ivanhoe, Calif. He says most of the town of Ivanhoe is composed of people from this county. He also visited his brother Joe at Bakersfield, Calif., one day."

[Fran Steelman] "I remember Uncle Isam, one time after he got in office, I was in high school, and me and three more girls skipped school. We come to Marshfield to watch a ball game play. And Uncle Isam saw us, and he wanted to know what we were doin'. And the only thing we could think of, was, we'd come to get our driver's license. So we went in and bought our driver's license for a quarter and none of us had a car!"
[Wilma Ryser] "You had to go to the Justice of the Peace, that's who sold driver's licenses."
[Fran Steelman] "But it cost a quarter. I was about fourteen, fifteen years old. But he caught us and we had to think up something! 'Course, that's the first thing I thought of. He said, 'Well, come on! I'll show you girls exactly where to go!' I'm sure he knew we were skippin' school, 'cause it was through the week, you know. We did have to buy a driver's license. I'm surprised any of us had a quarter. Back in those days we didn't have much money."

December 12, 1946 "The Sheriff has been holding in jail here for federal officers Robert J. Aubut who is said to be AWOL from his army post at Roswell, NM. Aubut was picked up here Monday right after he began to act suspicious when questioned by officers."

December 26, 1946 "Under the New Constitution the combined office of the probate judge and ex-officio magistrate will start its duties on January 1. This will be one of the busiest and most responsible offices in the county since, in addition to the present duties of the probate judge court, this office will handle juvenile matters, all sanity proceedings, and all work now being done by the justice courts in the county (jurisdiction in civil matters being doubled to $500 over the justice jurisdiction of $250)....Cline C. Herren was elected to this important office at the November election."

Chapter Seven
1947

January 2, 1947 "County Court proceedings:
  E.I. Cunningham, salary $175.93 *[monthly]*
  E.I. Cunningham, board prisoners & postage $13.60
  E.I. Cunningham, mileage $6.80"

January 9, 1947 "It is believed that 1946 set a record in number of divorces granted in the circuit court here. According to W.L. Burks, circuit clerk and ex-officio recorder, there were 106 divorces granted in this county and there were only 127 marriages recorded for the year. Thus the number of marriages barely kept ahead of the number of divorces."

January 23, 1947 *[sample of the]* "Cases heard in Magistrate Court and Circuit Court:
  1. common assault
  2. giving weapon to a minor
  3. disturbing the peace of an individual
  4. operating motor vehicle while in intoxicating condition
  5. destroying public property
  6. selling intoxicating liquor on Sunday
  7. forgery
  8. giving intoxicating liquor to a minor
  9. burglary and larceny
  10. failing to send children to school"

"John Hosmer married Melba Douthit on January 16 at Jeff City. Both returned to Columbia where they are students."

February 6, 1947 "County Court proceedings:
  E.I. Cunningham, court service and boarding prisoners $212.30
  E.I. Cunningham, salary $175.93
  E.I. Cunningham, serving notices, mileage, and assistant
                              $35.00
  E.I. Cunningham, feeding jury $12.75
  E.I. Cunningham, mileage and equipt., and exp. to Boonville
                              $83.40

E.I. Cunningham, board advanced for George Alexander
$36.00"

March 27, 1947 "The two candidates for city marshal are H.E. Cheek and Commodore Smith." *[Elections will be on April 1]*

"Investigate Small 'Flurry' of Break-ins—Sheriff E. I. Cunningham and state patrolmen are investigating robberies committed here. Last Friday the Burchfield Mill was broken into and about five dollars in change was taken....Burchfield Produce broken into, nothing taken....the home of Clifton Dugan...loss included clothing and foodstuffs, mainly sugar."

April 3, 1947 "County Court proceedings
E.I. Cunningham, salary $179.93 *[looks like a $4/month raise]*
E.I. Cunningham, postage, mileage, deputies $49.50
E.I. Cunningham, mileage, serving notice and 2 trips to Nevada
$73.40"

April 10, 1947 "Cases Heard In Magistrate Court—State of MO vs. Norman Garner, manslaughter; set for April 16; bond fixed at $3,000 (Sheriff Cunningham went to O'Reilly Veterans Hospital Monday and brought Garner here.")

"Two more thefts are reported, both on Monday night of this week.*[4/7]* Webster County officers and the state patrol are working on the cases. The Marshfield school was broken into by way of a window and money taken....A bicycle was stolen from the home of Kelly Robertson who resides near Oak Grove Lodge west of Marshfield. It belonged to his grandson and was purchased new at Christmas."

April 24, 1947 "The offices of Dr. C.R. Macdonnell, Dr. L.T. Melton and Dr. George Melton were robbed last Thursday *[4/17]* during the noon hour. The guilty party or parties apparently knew the hours of the doctors and operated accordingly.
     A little morphine and $27 in cash was taken from the office of Dr. Macdonnell. Some gold used by the dentist was taken from the office of Drs. Melton and Melton, valued possibly as much as $35 or $40. A small amount of the gold was in plate and some was in bridges, inlays, fillings, etc."

May 1, 1947 "Man Asks Sheriff For 'Push' But Only Lands In Jail Here—About three a.m. Monday [4/28] Bill Rigg, operator of a café at the west side of town, saw a man rolling out a car from the F.C. Tucker and Son Station on to the highway. He tried to call Mr. Tucker, but being unable to get him, called the Sheriff.

Sheriff Cunningham went out and came up behind the man taking the car near the junction of West Jackson Street and the Highway. The man asked the sheriff for a 'push' as he had not started the engine of the car. The sheriff gave him a 'push' by pushing a gun into his face and ordering him to get his hands up.

It was found that the man had attempted to take the car belonging to Edward L. Webb, who resides in a trailer at the Tucker Camp, but gave it up and rolled out the Tucker car.

Hodge had no means of identification on him and gave the names and stories, finally settling on the name of Hodge. He says he has no home and has been 'here' and 'there.'"

"The Better Business Bureau of St. Louis has just issued its annual warning to local citizens against rackets that flourish in the spring and summer months. According to the Bureau, the same wonderful weather that lures the householder into the yard or garden, lures the racketeer into the open to search for victims. Perhaps at no time of the year are people more gullible than when spring fills them with the joy of living and good will toward their fellow creatures.

[Examples of said racketeers]
1. Unknown nursery solicitor may not be so co-operative after he has got your signature and deposit.
2. Unknown itinerant describing himself as a tree surgeon
3. By the time you learn your bulb will not grow, the bulb peddler will be seeking suckers in more distant fields
4. Where will you find Mr. Itinerant Roofer—who told you he just happened to be passing and noticed your roof needed fixing—when you want to invoke the 'guarantee'?
5. Last, but not least, some magazine subscription services are employing discharged service men, knowing they will profit as a result of increased orders because people will be sympathetic and want to help out an ex-service man. Do not let sympathy mislead you."

May 8, 1947 "Small 'Building Boom' In Progress In and Near City....Carl Young is building a store room in front of the Young wholesale building for use as a retail grocery store."

"Circuit Court will convene here next Monday May 12, in regular May Term with Judge C.H. Jackson on the bench....For the first time several women were drawn in the panel of petit jurors. In the last year several women have served as jurors but they were summoned by the Sheriff at the request of Judge Jackson to fill vacancies on the regular panel."

"Dial Phone System Gets Start Here—the rural lines out of Marshfield will be turned to dial system just as fast as Mr. Garst *[manager of the Webster County Telephone company]* can rebuild them metallically. He does not expect to put Marshfield city on dial unless he is forced to do so.

Dial is being installed 'to improve rural service if they want it,' says Mr. Garst."

May 15, 1947 "Sheriff Outsmarts 'Rustler' To Foil Cattle Theft—With some quick detective work Sheriff E.I. Cunningham apprehended a cattle thief last Thursday *[5/8]* the same day the theft was reported.

Lyman Skates, Route 2, Conway, reported that morning that he had 4 Jersey heifers missing. The Sheriff went out to the field where the cattle had been and found only one clue, a piece of rope.

The Sheriff came to town and found the heifers had been sold to Oscar Stever ....Stever had sold 3 of them to Lonnie Wilson and one to Mr. Chapman....Mr. Skates identified the heifers.

The Sheriff, from a description of the man given him by Stever, went to Phillipsburg, Conway, and other places seeking James Wilhelm of near St. Louis, who had been visiting his aunt, residing on route 2, Conway. He finally found him at Forkners Hill store. Before going into the store, the Sheriff looked into the car and found the other end of the rope matching the piece of rope found in the field from which the cattle were stolen. He knew that he had the right party.

Wilhelm admitted the theft. It was found that he had cashed one check at the Roper Store, one at the H.E. Fellin store, and one at the Burchfield Produce.

The Sheriff had the highway patrol check on the car and it was found that it had been stolen from Bern Riesenbeck, St. Louis, on about March 20. Riesenbeck came and got the car Sunday *[5/11].*

Wilhelm pled guilty in circuit court here Monday *[5/12]* before Judge C.H. Jackson, and was sentenced to two years at Algoa on three charges, a total of 6 years. He told the judge he was 20 years of age, but the Sheriff says that Wilhelm stated he was 24 years old the other day."

[Cline Herren, Jr.] "He *[Isam]* actually did some pretty darn good detective work. I remember one time he caught some people, I think at the stockyards, selling the cattle. 'Course, they denied all knowledge and that was when they weren't branded or earmarked. They still had rope there in the car, and there was one of them that got away. Still had the lariat around their neck, but they'd broken the lariat rope—the cow did—and they got that and the strands matched perfectly. It was pretty good detective work!"

May 22, 1947 "Circuit Court Proceedings--Jury returned verdict finding the defendant Norman Garner guilty as charged of manslaughter, assess his punishment at 2 years in the penitentiary."

"Sheriff E.I. Cunningham made two trips to Algoa Reformatory near Jefferson City this week taking prisoners. Monday *[5/19]* he took Donald E. Martin who was sentenced to two years for attempting to steal the car belonging to F.C. Tucker recently. Windsor Cunningham of Rogersville and Neal Manary of Duncan accompanied the Sheriff.

Wednesday *[5/21]* the Sheriff took James W. Wilhelm.... Accompanying the Sheriff were John Cologna, Jr., David *[Jake]* Cunningham and Jeff Smith of Niangua."

May 29, 1947 "Mary Louise Bean marries Floyd Lee *[Snooks]* Cunningham, son of Mr. & Mrs. E.I. Cunningham, on May 20."

June 5, 1947 "Nab Pair On Charges of Robbing Home—Homer Fleetwood, of Fordland, and a woman giving the name of Elnora Johnson, 23, of Searcy and Little Rock, Ark., were arrested Tuesday by Commodore Smith and Harold Cheek, deputies of Sheriff E.I. Cunningham, at a woodland camp on the Knapp farm, 2 1/2 miles northwest of Fordland, on charges of robbing the home of Levi Burks, 1 1/2 miles northwest of Fordland. Articles of clothing, shirts, sweaters, flour, canned goods, and flashlight were found that were later identified by Mr. Burks as items stolen from his home on three different Saturdays. Last Saturday was the third time that his place had been robbed.

The woman drew a gun on the officers when they made the arrest, but they got the drop on her, and made her drop the revolver. The pair had been living in a tent, it is thought, for the past four weeks in a dense thicket.

They were brought to the jail here and are being held (Wednesday evening) in default of $2,000 bond."

"County Court proceedings, warrants issued:
E.I. Cunningham, summoning of jury $33.40
E.I. Cunningham, waiting on court $37.00
E.I. Cunningham, salary $175.93"
[no raise after all; it must have been a typo]

"St. of Mo. vs. Elenor Johnson
St. of Mo vs. Eleanor Johnson and Homer Fleetwood"
[Elnora, Elenor, or Eleanor: How is her name spelled? An Isam-ism?]

June 26, 1947 "Gate Disappears In A Hurry—It takes a bold and brazen thief in the daytime but that is the way it happened at Lloyd Burchfield's home Wednesday morning *[6/25]*. A gate, right in front of his house, was there when he went to work before 7 o'clock but was gone when his sister came along before 8:00. Lloyd checked with the neighbors but none of them had seen the thief in action. However, he says he is out 'to get him.'"

"Marshfield Café is opened under new management."*[Ruby and Clyde Hargus]*

[Ruby Hargus] "Clyde always wanted a restaurant. We had it for eight years. George Barnes owned it one time, before us. That and Johnny Andrews' were the only restaurants. Yes, we competed with Andrews Café.

My husband knew everybody, he had a photographic memory. He just remembered so much, especially to locate where people were. He would get information. Highway patrolmen, or anyone, would come in and drink coffee. It was kind of a big place, lots of room.

Men would come in there and drink coffee, and do their business, you know, on that phone, on our phone. It'd ring, and I bet I walked 4,000 miles answering the phone for them. They'd be in there and they'd know where they would look. There was always someone in there. It was real interesting.

So many of the businessmen didn't have offices like they do nowadays and the restaurant's where they did their business, contact people, use the phone. Realtors like Miley Dugan.

We stayed open Sunday. Seven days a week and as late at night as anyone wanted to stay.

Isam came in real often, every day. He ate in there a lot. Sometimes they'd bring a prisoner in there. We fed them—I don't know how many years—we'd send the food over from the restaurant. I fixed just lunch for the prisoners. Not breakfast or supper.

Evie cooked for them, yes.

One time I remember, my husband was gone and Isam was gone. So I took the food over there and Mrs. Cunningham—that's before she was sick—we took it up there and she'd unlock one door. Then there was a window ledge, she'd put it in this window, she was setting the plates in there, and this one prisoner was there taking them out. He reached in and he grabs her hand. She starts saying some pretty strong words! She had a gun in her apron pocket. She said, 'I'll take the butt of this gun and, boy, just bash your head in!' Boy, he backed off real fast, you know, his eyes got real big. He backed off. She said, 'Just stand back!' And she set the rest of the plates up there on the window there.

It scared me! So I told my husband, 'I'm never going over there again.' So then he would deliver them or send some of the older help over there. That was quite exciting.

Everyone was friendly to my children; they thought that was wonderful. 'Course you know how people pay attention to kids.

My children, they thought a lot of Isam. He would talk to them, take them with him sometimes. My kids liked to go to his table, sit down and talk to him unless he was with a group of businessmen or other officers. He'd come in on a break or wait to get a call or come to do business over a cup of coffee. People didn't call here for the Sheriff. They probably called his office first and she, Mrs. Cunningham, would say he was here. She would know where he was. Or else he was at Johnny Andrews's [café] or else he was at Seymour.

My daughter, Clydine, was nine. Julian was seven. They went to work in that restaurant right with us, you know. Right away I was pregnant again when he was eight, and I had this other boy, Stanley. Raised him in the restaurant. Then a few years after that I had a girl,

Rebecca, we called her Becky. They were both raised in the restaurant.

I had this old-time wooden baby buggy and I'd put my kids in that buggy and they'd go to sleep. I'd give them a bottle. I just went ahead and worked. They loved it. I kinda run the front part, did a lot of the buying and stuff, you know. My children were small.

There were so many high school kids that worked there, after school, or come up at noon.

Becky was about four years old when we got out of the restaurant business. I guess we would have kept the restaurant longer, but a teenager, just sixteen years old, she'd driven the car for the first day. My son and I, and Lorna Day, was loading some apples in the trunk of the car. I was buying a bushel of apples from a boy. And the [teenage] driver saw the kids at The Sweet Shop, she waved, lost control of her car and plowed into us. Shoved me up into my trunk of my car and I thought it was going to kill me. But it just tore up one of my legs completely. I had to go to the hospital and had to stay three months. Back then, you know, first they had to do two operations on it so I could have movement. I had to wear a brace for a long time; then I had a walker. That's why I walk with a cane now today.

We saved up a little money in that restaurant and...my husband was so trusting...he was raised in the country and believed your word was bond. So we wound up having to pay all the bills. I think we got $4,000 out of it. It just took every dime we had, we just got in debt so bad, trying to get all the hospital bills paid and everything else.

When we first moved to town we looked at a house Clay McVay had built, but they hadn't got the kitchen finished yet. They had the water pipes sticking up in the kitchen. We talked them in to letting us live there because we all ate at the restaurant so I didn't really need a kitchen. They had the bath in and everything else except the kitchen. I moved my stove and refrigerator there. I think we lived there about a year. Then we moved here and have lived here ever since.

Well, I called up my son, Julian, and said, 'Son, can't you remember something about Isam?' He said one thing.

There was five or six boys. They had gathered at the café and Isam took them all out on Niangua Creek, close to Isam's homeplace. There was a soft drink truck, and while Isam was showing the driver around his farm, the boys stole some bottles of soft drink off that truck and put them in the creek, to get cold.

The thing is, Isam had already paid the driver for enough bottles for the boys to have some. But the boys didn't know that.

There those kids were scared to death, they thought they were all gonna go to jail. But Isam had paid the soft drink man for it and when he found out the boys thought they had stolen the bottles, he laughed and laughed.

But then he gave them a lecture, I guess that was it. Instead of going through court and having them arrested. He was real good with kids. I bet not a one of those boys never stole another thing, because I never saw such a frightened bunch of kids in my life. They had just thought that was something smart to do, a few boys were real daring, my son kinda followed, he was always a year younger than the other boys in his class. He was about ten years old when that happened, he was born in 1940. Most sheriffs would have talked to the parents but Isam knew it would do more good to talk to the kids. He didn't tell the parents. My son told us about it later. It might have been a 4-H group. I tried to keep the kids occupied and had them in different things.

Clyde didn't get paid by *[Oral]* Edwards, for driving an ambulance. He just liked the excitement. He'd drop everything and go. Yes, there I'd be, with the babies and with the café. During the daytime we had help. There'd be the cook back there and lots of times I'd be the only one up front. Clyde would be the cook; that's what he did at Johnny Andrews's. He loved to cook. He had a main cook, Elsie Yates, and she could make pies out of this world.

John Hosmer was running for something. When we was politicking, 'course they had this big van and we'd get our families together and we'd go out politicking. We went down by Fordland and Rogersville, down around there. We were all in a restaurant there; the kids were with us and we'd always have to take them in and get ice cream or something, you know, that was the thrill of the trip. Well, they put human feces from an outside toilet in his van. There we had babies, Mitzi had little ones, I had little ones. And we had to sit in that restaurant and they kept it open for us while they took the van and sprayed it down to get it washed down. They never did find out who did it. 'Way down in there they had some pretty rough characters, around Fordland."

July 10, 1947 "Five Arrested At Same Place, Time By Patrol—Five arrests for reckless driving were made at one place and time by a state highway patrolman on the Northview Hill Tuesday *[7/8]*. The five arrests were made as a result of cars and trucks passing a truck on the hill. The parties were brought here, pleaded guilty, and were fined in magistrate court.

We want to compliment the patrol on any work they do in enforcing traffic laws on the highways. We venture a lot of arrests could be made in just one day's patrol of the Northview Hill alone.

There is a national campaign going on now to reduce highway accidents. The MAIL and a large number of the leading business firms of the county are taking an active part in this campaign....Last year a test campaign in New Jersey resulted in traffic accidents being reduced 50 per cent.

Everyone should get behind the officers and help enforce traffic laws and reduce accidents."

[In the previous months of The MARSHFIELD MAIL, there have been numerous articles and ads related to increased traffic accidents and tips for safe driving. There are many more cars and drivers on the road than before and during WWII.]

"Resigns As Seymour Mayor—E. F. Gorman has resigned as mayor of Seymour. This is said to have been caused by the Board of Aldermen granting a beer license to Marguerite Carter. W. E. Robison, mayor pro-tem, has taken over the duties of mayor. Mayor Robison has abolished the nine o'clock curfew siren at Seymour."

"No Disorders Mar Day--The Fourth was a big success in Marshfield with a large crowd present to enjoy the day. There was no disorder of any kind and the officers report that for the first time in many years there was not a single arrest. No automobile accidents are reported although there was heavy traffic."

"County Court proceedings: Marguerite Carter granted license to sell intoxicating liquor, same being 5 % beer, she having paid the fee of $17.50."

"Editor's Note: ...Judge Herren is saving the county some money. *[A]* new law provides that the county court shall select a regular panel of jurors to serve in magistrate court. In smaller populated counties a provision was made that the magistrate could set this aside and permit the sheriff to pick up a jury when a case requires a jury. This saves considerable money to the county."

July 31, 1947 "The Webster County Court has had an electric clock installed on the first floor of the courthouse."

August 7, 1947 *[an ad]* "DIGGINS 47TH ANNUAL PICNIC
August 14-15-16
Plenty of Entertainment, Contests, and Midway
Attractions
For Stand Rights, etc.,
See John Rudolph, Diggins, Mo."

[Oliver Evans] "They used to have what they called Diggins Picnic. I'd just got out of school, single boy, wild as a buck I guess. I went over to Diggins Picnic one night. Just as I walked in the gate I seen somebody get the hell knocked out of 'em. So I just got in the car and come back to Marshfield! I didn't have no backup!

They always was a little....Well, anybody from the northside go over there, you'd better have somebody with ya. Same way with Seymour, if they come over here, they'd better have a reason or somebody would whup 'em. Kinda feudin', you know. Probably didn't even know why!"

August 14, 1947 "Sheriff E.I. Cunningham went to Fayetteville, Ark., last Thursday and his son, Wilbur Cunningham, who has been in the veterans' hospital there, accompanied him home on Friday. Wilbur may return to the hospital later."

"Arrests Ava Men—Six Ava men were arrested at Diggins about 3 a.m. Sunday morning *[8/10]* by Sheriff E.I. Cunningham on charges of disturbing the peace."

[Magistrate court notes later report State of Mo. vs. six men, disturbing the peace, most all plead guilty, fined $25.]

"This is the week of the annual Diggins Picnic."

"Sheriff E.I. Cunningham arrested Hiram Henson Monday night at Seymour on charges of disturbing the peace of Gene Carter and Marguerite Carter, two counts. The case is set for September 3rd before the County Magistrate."

"Eugene White, charged with writing worthless checks, had his bond forfeited and is in jail here awaiting trial. Sheriff Cunningham reports that White is also wanted in Greene county on the same charge."

"Sheriff E.I. Cunningham, accompanied by Tom Farr, Jr., and Freddy Layman, took Rolland Barton to the State Training School for Boys at Boonville August 4th. The parole of young Barton was recently revoked."

September 4, 1947 "Robbers Escape After Holding Up Highway Store—Officers are searching for two men who robbed the Highway Tobacco and Liquor Store, at the west side of Marshfield, Saturday night *[8/30]* at about 8:50 o'clock. They escaped in an old model car. The Sheriff notified the highway patrol of the robbery only ten minutes after it occurred and said the car headed west. As yet no trace has been found of them.

According to Sheriff Cunningham, one of the men went into the store and asked for a fifth of whiskey. When Bill Ash turned to get it, the thief jumped over the counter and pointed a .38 or .45 caliber revolver at Ash, and ordered him to open the cash drawer.

The thief grabbed the currency out of the drawer and ran out the back door. His companion was waiting in the car and they drove off.

The Sheriff said Ash was unable to describe the robber, and did not see what kind of a car it was. Thus the officers have had little to go on. The amount taken is said to have been about $140."

"County Court Proceedings—"H.E. Cheek makes claim in sum of $528 for services as Deputy Sheriff of Webster County, from August 8, 1946 to August 2, 1947. The court, hearing the evidence and giving consideration, ordered the claim be disallowed. "
[A Deputy Sheriff claim turned down? What is this all about?]

October 9, 1947 "Two Burglaries Reported To Officers—The George Burks home, one mile east of Northview, was broken into Tuesday and all his clothes were taken. Officers have been working on the case.

The Sheriff was notified Wednesday morning *[10/8]* that the Anderson Schoolhouse was broken into Tuesday night and went out to investigate."

"Intruder Found in Home, Puts Up A Scuffle—An intruder was discovered in the kitchen of Paris Anderson home Saturday night about 8 o'clock. The man was hiding behind the kitchen stove and refused to come out. Help was called and Melvin Bell and Otto Schikowski, from neighboring service stations, responded immediately.

It was found that the intruder was a soldier, apparently drunk. He attacked Mr. Schikowski and it was quite a fight before Sheriff Cunningham arrived. The soldier was placed in jail, gave his name as Billy J. Easter. He said his mother resided four miles from Waynesville and his father, Joe Easter, resides at Houston, Texas. The soldier was on furlough from a camp in California. Sheriff Cunningham says that the boy's father formerly resided near Niangua.

Young Easter was released Sunday *[10/5]* and left for California to return to camp Monday.

The doors of the Anderson home were locked and Mr. Anderson is puzzled how the man got into the house."

October 16, 1947 "Springfield Officers Arrest Three Men and Nab Stacks of Loot—Springfield Officers believe they have broken up a series of large-scale robberies with the apprehension of John R. Nokes, 39, unemployed welder; Archie Willard Haeflinger, 34, a welder; and James R. Green, 37, furniture factory employee.

Several truckloads of furniture and miscellaneous articles were found in a house in Springfield. Hundreds of people have been going by the Springfield jail to attempt to identify stolen articles.

Sheriff E.I. Cunningham of this county says that anyone in Webster County who has had stuff stolen in recent months should go by the office of the sheriff in Springfield and look over the stolen goods. Should any stuff be identified, it would help the officers clear up robbery cases."

"Robbers Take Food, Other Items, From Two Schools—The Northview school was robbed Tuesday night *[10/7]* of last week and a large amount of food used in the school lunchroom meals and other articles were taken according to Sheriff E.I. Cunningham. About 65 cans of fruit and other food were taken by an intruder who made his entry through a window on the north side of the school superintendent's office and ransacked it.

The same night the Anderson school two miles southwest of Marshfield was broken into but the only missing item was a gramophone, according to the Sheriff.

The same day the George Burks home, 1 mile east of Northview, was broken into and clothing taken. No arrests have been made as yet."

November 6, 1947 "Woman Held After Liquor Cargo Disclosed—As a result of a collision on Highway 60 about a mile and a half east of Rogersville last Thursday night, Mrs. Cleo Mae Epps of Sapulpa, Okla., was held by officials. She was driving a truck with stock-rack body which smashed in the side of a car belonging to a West Plains man. She was held by the driver of the car until Highway Patrol arrived and brought her to Marshfield.

The truck was loaded with 223 cases of liquor which has since been valued at $9,556.67. The cargo was hidden by tin roofing on the sides and covered on top. She made bond Friday *[10/31]* and the truck was held on an attachment suit, according to Sheriff E.I. Cunningham.

The Sheriff states that she was taking the load of liquor from Cairo, Ill., through Missouri. As Oklahoma is a dry state in which it is illegal to sell liquor, it is not known what the destination of the cargo was to be.

Wednesday morning *[11/5]* two charges against Mrs. Epps were dismissed after a preliminary hearing in the Magistrate Court here by Judge Cline C. Herren. The prosecuting attorney *[Roy Miller]* stated he would file another charge."

[Raymond Day] "I don't know how many times he run for sheriff before he got it, but after he got it, he didn't have no trouble getting elected sheriff. He had trouble getting elected at first! He just wasn't well known in the south part of the county.

When I got in from the Navy, he kinda had to talk to *me*. I'm not telling *why* he was talking to me. We just got in from the Navy, you can imagine, we was out pretty late, 2 or 3 o'clock in the morning, sittin' up on The Square. Everything was quiet except when we got on The Square. He had to tell us—in a nice way—what we could and couldn't do. We remembered that. He spoke with authority, especially with the younger group

He kinda cultivated that after he got into being Sheriff. Some people he had to talk kinda loud to. And he wasn't afraid of nothin'. Anybody ever tell you that? Well, I was wondering....He knowed it was his job. Maybe he was a little afraid. But he knowed it was his duty.

I remember he had some time off, not very much, and my father-in-law Herbert Vestal and I took him fishin'. We had a good time.

One time, right before we was married, right after I got back from the Navy, '47, we was going into Marshfield one time to eat. We were off the highway, in town, and I was driving pretty fast. There was a guy standing right beside the road and about the time I got even with him, he just fell over and went to kickin'. I decided I could get Isam about as quick as I could stop and help him. I got to the courthouse and I could hear some banging around upstairs. See, this was Sunday afternoon, after a typical Saturday night.

I went up the stairs, down the hall where I could hear the banging going on. He was in there, in that room, the holding pen I think they call it, with about a dozen guys, by himself! The deputy on the outside, he was kinda a frail old man, he had a gun. Homer Alexander. I seen that he was in there, in the middle of them, and I just stood there a little bit. One guy give him a lot of trouble. He kinda made him sit down. And when he turned his back to walk out, he got up, like he was going to hit Isam in the back.

Isam turned around and sat him down, like he would a little kid, and he said, 'Now you git up again and when I set you down, you'll stay down!' He turned around and walked out, and he stayed set down.

Isam was bound to have been pretty afraid, but he knowed he had to not *appear* afraid.

Isam's wife, she was a good ole lady. She fed all those prisoners. I never ate there. I never got in any trouble! The only ticket I ever got was in Colorado, for stopping past the stop sign.

When Isam was Sheriff, you didn't have to have speed limits. They had 'careless and reckless driving'. Those patrolmen, they liked that, and they knew the sheriff and the judge would back them.

Most of Isam's laws was common sense. If somebody done something they wasn't supposed to, they got in trouble. Isam was all business, to me."*[I have no idea about what happened to the guy on the side of the road.]*

November 13, 1947 *[re: Mrs. Cleo Mae Epps]* "Both of the charges of leaving the scene of an accident and carrying concealed weapons were dismissed in the Webster County magistrate court and there seemed to be no law against hauling liquor across Missouri....The new charges were filed in circuit court. She is charged with reckless and careless driving (the highway patrol reported that she was on the wrong side of the highway when the accident occurred), and she is charged with unlawful possession of intoxicating liquor. The truckload of liquor was released to Mrs. Epps last week when she posted a cash bond of $1000 to appear in circuit court here in January.

Officers here expected her to be arrested when she entered Oklahoma with the truckload of liquor, *[because Oklahoma is a dry state]* but no report has been made if she was."

"JAMES PETTY ARRESTED ON CHARGES OF DOG THEFT, DENIES STEALING—James Petty, 50-year-old brother of long sought ex-convict Louis 'Duke' Petty was arrested by Springfield police Saturday night *[11/8]* and Sunday was turned over to Webster County authorities seeking him on a felony warrant.

According to officers, Petty is wanted here for grand larceny in connection with the theft of a dog from a farmer.

However, police reported following Petty's arrest at the Met hotel in Springfield about 7 p.m., Saturday, he denied the dog theft accusation.

'That's just something Duke and his mob are trying to frame on me,' he was quoted as saying.

Petty's younger brother, 40-year-old Louis, broke from the Lawrence county jail at Mt.Vernon last June and disappeared. Since then authorities have been kept busy tracking down tips to his whereabouts, but to date he hasn't been found."

"Late bulletin!...LONE BANDIT ROBS BANK AT SEYMOUR—Escapes After Herding Employees and Cashier Into Vault—A lone bandit robbed the Bank of Seymour at Seymour Wednesday morning of this week at about 11:20 *[11/12]*. At press time the highway patrol is using several patrolmen on the case. Sheriff Cunningham was out of the county, having taken some prisoners to Jefferson City.

The armed robber is said to have held a gun on E. R. Mayfield while he ordered M. E. Cochran and sister, Anna Cochran, and Mrs. Jessie Hargus, the other employees of the bank, to sack the money. He then herded the group into the bank vault and made his escape.

As it happened no customers were in the bank or entered the bank during the robbery."

November 20, 1947 "DUKE PETTY CAPTURED EAST OF MARSHFIELD TUESDAY"

"Louis A. 'Duke' Petty as he appeared in the sheriff's office Tuesday night *[11/18]* to the right of Sheriff E.I. Cunningham. It will be noted that a patrolman was holding a gun on him as he was photographed by Morris Moody by the Photon Studio for the MAIL."

"A second pose of Duke Petty in the office of Sheriff E. I. Cunningham in the Webster County courthouse Tuesday night after his capture east of Marshfield. He was later taken to Springfield where he is held in close custody."

"And I wasn't even 16 years old. They let me have the key to the car because whenever they—I had a walkie-talkie radio—whenever they called me, I was supposed to come back to the courthouse and call Springfield, call the Highway Patrol and tell them they got him. And that's what I done. Duke Petty. Local boy. Marshfield."

[Warren Johnson] "Duke Petty was one of my dad's main people, one my dad *[former Webster County sheriff Johnny Johnson]* was after. He was a mean boy. He wasn't afraid of my dad, he wasn't afraid of Isam Cunningham. But neither one of them was afraid of Duke, either. And that makes a difference. Duke was just a mean boy, that's all you can say about that. Bootleggin' whiskey and robbing the Bank of Niangua, for some."

"Identified as Seymour Bank Robber—OFFICERS DISGUISED AS HUNTERS TO APPROACH HOUSE –

Louis A. 'Duke' Petty, 40, object of a man-hunt for the past five months, and an intensive search since the robbery of the Seymour Bank a week ago Wednesday, was captured without the firing of a shot Tuesday afternoon about 4:15 at a home 6 miles east of Marshfield on highway 38.

He was taken at the home of Emma Holcomb, the former wife of Jim Petty, Duke's brother, and brought to the Marshfield jail where he was questioned and taken on to Springfield for safe-keeping about 10 p.m.

He was identified by E.R. Mayfield, cashier of The Seymour Bank and other bank employees as the robber who held a gun on them last week, took about $3,600 and escaped after forcing them into the bank vault. He was also identified by the manager of the liquor store at Conway which was robbed a few weeks ago. He is also said to have been identified as the robber of the liquor store at the west side of Marshfield which was robbed some time ago.

Petty is said to have admitted orally and then signed a written statement admitting the robbery of The Seymour Bank, according to Sheriff E.I. Cunningham who has been working with highway patrolmen, the FBI and Springfield police to apprehend the man. It was generally believed that he was hiding in this county, sheltered by friends, but not until Tuesday were the officers able to catch him.

Officers, dressed as hunters, made their plans here with Sheriff Cunningham and Prosecuting Attorney Roy Miller, in the courthouse

Tuesday afternoon, and went out and surrounded the Holcomb home and another place at the same time. The officers who were sent to the Holcomb place went into the house and knocked down the bedroom door. There Petty was standing with his hands in the air. He came out meekly and said 'Don't shoot me. I am not as bad a boy as they told you I am.'

He had his shoes off and had been laying on the bed. His coat was on a chair and in it was some of the money. There under the pillow was the .45 caliber gun which had been taken from the Lawrence county sheriff at Mt. Vernon when Petty escaped jail there. Petty made no attempt to use it.

FBI agents and the other officers indicated they had anticipated a battle with the cornered ex-convict, who once before had engaged Webster County officers in a gun battle following the robbery of The Niangua Bank of $3,692. October 31, 1928. Sheriff Cunningham took part in that fight."

[Cline Herren, Jr.] "Isam was a Constable at Niangua. This is unofficial but I think Isam got shot in the foot when Duke Petty was robbing the Bank of Niangua, way back there.

When Duke robbed The Seymour Bank, when Isam was Sheriff, the FBI was in on it, but Isam actually located him."

"Petty was wounded in the heel then, but escaped. He arranged for a surrender through friends a week later, and early in 1929 he was sentenced to 45 years in the state penitentiary for the robbery."

[Oliver Evans] "The Petty boys lived right there next to my folks, by Good Hope Church. Duke was older than me. I had a soft spot in my heart for him. I jumped in the creek over there, when I was about 6 years old. I went down for about the last time and ole Duke, he reached down and pulled me out. I've got a soft spot in my heart for him.

I don't believe them boys did half the stuff they was accused of. Jack Bumgarner, he was the instigator of the bank robbery in Niangua.

Those poor boys, they didn't have much of an education. They talked them into it, Duke and his brother, they went in the bank and got the money, I guess. But Jack Bumgarner, he was the one that did it. But the Petty boys done the time for it. Bumgarner got out of it, they didn't charge him. Everybody said he had it buried some place. They never did find the money. He lived over there around Crown Store, Friendship Church, James River, south of Marshfield."

[Details of the 1928 robbery in Niangua are in The MARSHFIELD MAIL issues dated November 15 and November 22, 1928, and January 24, 1929. Here is a short excerpt from November 15: "Louis Petty confessed Sunday morning to the robbing of the Citizens State Bank of Niangua of about $3600 on Wednesday afternoon, October 31. He told the entire story first to Deputy John McDaniel and later to Sheriff King. He implicated E.M. (Jack) Bumgarner and Lawrence Bumgarner, who was declared innocent last week and released....Monday night Jack Bumgarner at Lebanon offered to confess to E. I. Cunningham and Constable Will Muse if the officers would return him to Marshfield....The officers apparently took little stock in Bumgarner's story as they left him in Lebanon and brought Petty back to Marshfield."]

"--In January, 1943, Petty was paroled."--

[Paula Case Greer] "When he got out of prison, he got off the bus there at the Webster Hotel and we were coming up from school. He got off the bus. We got awfully excited, that's about all, 'cause we got to see Duke Petty come home from prison."

"--and in February of this year Petty was arrested at Mt. Vernon and charged with shoplifting. Application was made to revoke his parole and he was awaiting a hearing on the question when he broke from the Lawrence county jail under cover of a thunderstorm June 30th. Authorities had traced him about the Ozarks since then, and came within minutes of catching him at the homes of various friends several times.

Following the robbery of The Seymour Bank last week, Cashier E.R. Mayfield identified photos of Petty as the hold-up man and agents of the Federal Bureau of Investigation entered the case, since the bank was federally insured.

Roadblocks were placed at several points in this county and a patrol plane was dispatched to the area to comb the wooded area long familiar to Petty, who has spent most of his life in this county."

[Willis Case] "Duke Petty was supposed to be in the woods over by High Prairie. So Isam went over there to hunt him. And Isam was walking down through the woods and stepped on a dead limb, and it popped! And I said, 'What ya do, Isam?' He said, 'I just took out my ole revolver and shot right into the ground! I thought Duke had got close to me!'

Oh, Isam, he was a funny ole feller."

"The plane spotted a stolen car on the old Seymour-Marshfield road about three miles southeast of Marshfield and it was thought to have been the car used by Petty to make his get-away from Seymour. (The car was found to have been stolen at Hartville.) The plane didn't spot Petty, but it kept him from attempting to leave the Marshfield area. Officers who talked to Petty Tuesday evening said that the bank robber told them that he had seen the plane and had hidden in the dense brush.

Sheriff Cunningham called the Springfield police department Tuesday morning and asked for three officers and a supply of tear gas. The officers came to Marshfield accompanied by six state patrol officers, and three federal agents. They with Sheriff Cunningham, Prosecuting Attorney Roy C. Miller and Commodore Smith, deputy sheriff, went east. As Petty was suspected of being in one of two houses, the officers divided forces and surrounded both places. A few minutes after 4 o'clock one group of officers rushed the Holcomb house armed with machine guns, shotguns, rifles, pistols, gas hand grenades and a gas shotgun.

Officers said Petty was haggard looking as he walked out. He has apparently dyed his normally gray hair a jet black, probably in an attempt to disguise his appearance somewhat, but the hair over his temples was still gray. He was wearing a brown sport shirt, blue jean trousers and white socks.

The other house surrounded was the Mutt Casteel place.

Other arrests have been made in connection with the Petty case. Mrs. Emma Holcomb signed a statement admitting that Petty had been at her house several times and she is said to have also had some of the stolen money.

Casteel was arrested. He had some of the dollar bills on him and he is said to have admitted that Duke gave him about $50.

Others held by the officers are Roy Graves, William James Hunt, and Jake Thompson. Thompson has been in the Springfield jail since Monday charged with harboring a criminal.

These different parties are expected to be arraigned before Cline C. Herren, Magistrate, here this Wednesday afternoon as the MAIL goes to press. *[11/19]*

November 27, 1947 "CHARGED WITH AIDING PETTY IN HIDING—Arrests Made During Past Week In Connection With Capture—Following the capture of Louis A. 'Duke' Petty Tuesday of last week, several other arrests have been made by officers in connection with the case. Officers have not revealed whether or not there still may be other arrests.

Most of those taken into custody have been charged with being 'accessory after the fact' in connection with The Seymour Bank robbery. In addition to those named in this issue of the MAIL in the proceedings of the Magistrate Court, a warrant was issued Monday for a Wilbur Frank Clark, charged with being an 'accessory after the fact' to The Seymour Bank robbery.

All those arraigned before Cline C. Herren, Magistrate, have been placed under $5,000 bond. Roy Graves, charged in two cases, has made $7,500 bond. Others making their bond up to Monday were Basil Rice and Jim Robinson, in the state cases.

Reliable information received here by local officials indicated that federal warrants had been issued for Wilbur Frank Clark, Jim Robinson, James 'Mutt' Casteel, Mrs. Ema Holcomb and her daughter Mrs. Flora Filbeck.

Duke Petty is still held by the FBI in Springfield. His preliminary hearing will be there November 28th.

It has been reported that a suitcase, said to have been purchased with money stolen from The Seymour Bank, was found under a bed in the Jim Robinson home."

December 4, 1947 "DUKE PETTY IS TRANSFERRED TO KANSAS CITY—Duke Petty, who has confessed to the robbery of The Seymour Bank, was taken from Springfield to Kansas City by agents of the U.S. Marshal's office Tuesday. He is being held in the twelfth story 'escape proof' Jackson County jail. No reasons have been given for the removal of Petty from Springfield.

The office of U.S. Marshal Fred Canfield refused to reveal any information regarding the move. Efforts by a Springfield newspaper photographer to take pictures of Petty precipitated an argument last week in which Canfield was quoted as saying, 'The constitution be damned.'

Petty waived hearing before Commissioner Roy Arnold at Springfield Friday and was bound over for trial in the April term of Federal court at Springfield, unless a special session is held earlier. He was returned to jail in lieu of $25,000 bond on federal bank robbery charges.

James Robinson, 38, Webster County farmer, and Flora Mae Filbeck, 16, also waived hearing on charges of accepting from Petty some of the money he admitted taking from The Seymour Bank. Petty and the Filbeck girl do not have a lawyer. Robinson was represented at the hearing by attorney Seth V. Conrad of Marshfield.

Robinson made $2500 bond and the girl was released on a $1000 recognizance bond. She is the daughter of Mrs. Ema Holcomb, at whose home Petty was captured November 12. Several from this county attended the hearing in Springfield.

It is reported that Robinson was arrested again here Saturday on another charge and made bond.

A charge against William Hunt and two charges against Roy Graves of 'accessory after the fact' were dismissed in the magistrate court, by the Webster County prosecutor, Roy C. Miller.

On Friday night officers, including Sheriff Cunningham, FBI and state patrol officers, acting on a tip went out and found $360.25 more of the money reportedly stolen from The Seymour Bank. The money consisted of coins and currency and had been hidden in the woods about five miles east of Marshfield."

"SAFE TAKEN FROM EXCHANGE AT ROGERSVILLE—Thieves broke into the Rogersville Exchange after midnight Friday night *[11/28]* and spirited away the safe by way of a back door. The safe contained not only an unestimated amount of cash, but also checks, money orders, and account records.

It was reported the electricity was turned off at Rogersville for almost two hours after midnight that night, and it was thought the burglars did their work during that time.

Webster County officers and the highway patrol are reported to be making an investigation."

[Glen Wilson] "When we'd *[Highway Patrol]* go on duty, we'd always go by the Sheriff's office over there, see what was goin' on in the county. We'd go around The Square and he'd be down there wavin' at us when we went around the second time. And first he'd ask us, 'Where ya goin'?' Then he'd tell ya, 'I've got some papers to deliver over there.' Don't make any difference which way you'd go, he'd have some papers! So we killed two birds with one stone there."

[Tony Stephens] "Isam would be in the front seat and you'd get the car out of second gear and Isam would be asleep! Ole Isam would go to sleep, just like that.

Drunken drivers. You'd take a drunken driver in over there at the jail and ole Isam would set 'em down and say, 'My good buddy, I own this jail and you're not going to disrupt it in any way. And whenever I lock that door, you're going to stay there. You be a good fella.' And he stayed there 'til court time! I remember him tellin' that so many times.

They didn't think about escapin' except that one time, Kenneth Kile.

Most of the problems back then were domestic violence. 'Course, Isam handled most of them. I'd been with him on a few domestic violence, where the husband would be beatin' up his wife. And I'd always let Isam do all the talkin'. I'd just back him up, you know.

He could talk anybody out of anything!

If he had somebody who was a little belligerent, you know, he'd just had a knack about him. He could calm that person down. He could talk to 'em. He never raised his voice, hardly ever. He had an act about him that could calm that person down. He'd go over and pat him on the back a little bit, lead him right out the door. He'd arrest him, yes.

Nine times out of ten they wouldn't file charges the next day.

They broke into the MFA down in Fordland, four or five times. They'd wait for the train to go through, makin' lots of noise. So me and Al Leslie, we looked all over the place and everything. Then called ole Isam to come over there and he said, 'I tell ya, fellers, I know who done that. That gang out of Carthage.' The Crow Gang, that was their name. So we picked them up and they admitted it! Ninety-nine times out of a hundred they'd confess! And they got credit for them! But I just wonder if they done all those jobs. Ole Isam, he had a mind!

He was on call 24 hours a day, 7 days a week."

[Glen Wilson] "I'll tell you what, if every county in the state of Missouri had a sheriff as conscious of everything goin' on as he was, this would have been a hell of a lot cleaner state. We wouldn't have had people from Kansas City comin' down here."

[Tony Stephens] "Everybody liked Isam, except the criminals or anybody who committed a crime. He told me one time when he couldn't diagnose a crime or decide who was in it, he'd go to Whittlers' Den and he'd find out...there on The Square...people sittin' on the bench whittlin', tellin' tales.   That'd work most of the time. Everybody knows somethin'.

When Duke Petty robbed The Seymour Bank, I was over there in Webster County all day and all night, 'til the next day. Me and Al Leslie. Isam come by. We had a roadblock set up north of Seymour. About 10 or 11 o'clock in the morning, somebody come by and said they'd found out where he is, in an old abandoned house. And the FBI we all gathered around, you know, we surrounded that house. Isam was beside the door over here, I was on that side of the door, and the FBI agent went through the door, the front door. Me and Isam was standin' there at the door. And he was lyin' there on the bed and had one of those thumb-buster pistols--I don't know if it'd shoot or not but that's what he'd robbed the bank with--under his pillow.

So we got ole Petty out of bed and got him outside, and that FBI agent kept tellin' him to get his hands up! He had 'em up, like this. The FBI had that .45 automatic machine gun under that arm, kept hittin' under Petty's arm to get em' up higher, and dern if he didn't throw the trigger and a bullet went off and just missed me and ole Isam!

Because of that, Isam decided he wasn't going to support the FBI anymore until they made some changes! Boy, that made ole Isam mad! Me, too!

Me and Isam went to huntin' somebody, wanted him for breakin' in someplace. We went up to the house. I told Isam, 'Go around back.' Isam said, 'I ain't goin' back there, there's dogs back there!'

Isam used to say, when those guys would get into fist fights, 'That's their entertainment on Saturday nights.' Ava, Seymour, and Mansfield. South Webster County.

He was something else, boy. He knew everybody in Webster County and all the surrounding counties. He knew every convict and anybody that done any problems.

We'd work a burglary and call ole   Isam and Isam would say, 'You go and get so-and-so, he done that.' We'd go get him and he'd say, 'Yeah, I been there.'

He'd knew everybody, and what they were doin' and what they were going to be up to. That's the derndest guy I ever saw in my life. He really knew what was goin' on.

He was kinda hard to describe, really. You'd have to be around him a little bit to figure out what he was thinkin' and what he was gonna do.

We went in that Skyline Café over there in Seymour one time, me and Isam, and sit down to have our food, and everybody come by slappin' ole Isam on the back and tellin' him what a good fella he was, and he'd get in there and wouldn't have time to eat his lunch! Things like that."

"ARREST 13 FOR GAME LAW VIOLATIONS—Road blocks were placed under direction of the Conservation Department agents at the junction of highway 60 and route C and highway 38 and route C, in this county Sunday. Thirteen arrests were made for violation of the game laws.

The game found in the cars of the game law violators were confiscated and delivered to the Webster County Farm by H.A. Roehrs, game warden, and E.I. Cunningham, Sheriff.

These road blocks have been set in various parts of the state and many violators have been found." *[Listings from Magistrate Notes: hunting without license, plead guilty, fined $5; hunting with an illegal gun; hunting without license, etc.]*

December 11, 1947 "James Casteel Held in Lieu of Bond on Federal Charge—James Casteel, 32, of Marshfield, was held in the Greene county jail Tuesday night for lack of $2500 bond after he waived preliminary hearing that day before U.S. Commissioner Roy Arnold there.

Casteel is charged by the federal government with having received from Louis 'Duke' Petty fifty $1 bills, knowing them to have been stolen.

Casteel was represented by Attorney John C. Pope. He was picked up at the Webster County jail Tuesday morning. He was out on bond here on charges by county officers."

" 'Red' Hollis Trial Opens Wednesday—The murder trial of John Ellis 'Red' Hollis, 51, former Webster Countian, was scheduled to open Wednesday morning of this week *[12/10]* in circuit court in Springfield and will be tried by a jury.

Hollis is said to have admitted the fatal shooting of Elston Orel 'Bus' Adams, 30-year-old cab driver September 7. The shooting occurred at the Hollis home in Springfield. Indications are that Hollis, reported to be a friend of 'Duke' Petty, held in Kansas City on charges of bank robbery, will claim self defense."

"Thieves Crack School's Safe At Strafford—Highway patrolmen are investigating a safe-cracking at the Strafford

Consolidated school, which occurred sometime Monday night *[12/08]* and which netted apparently expert thieves $215.76 in cash.

Lawrence Ghan, superintendent of the school, said $114 of the money was in roll packages of coins.

Ghan said the thieves apparently entered the school building through a loosely- latched classroom window on the ground floor, and 'jimmied' the lock on the upstairs office door.

The office faces on a Strafford street, and the thieves placed a desk lamp on the floor and shaded it with a typewriter cover while they worked.

After an unsuccessful attempt to knock the hinges off the 'medium sized' safe, the men turned it over, drilled holes in the bottom, and blew it open, apparently with nitro-glycerin, Ghan related.

'They seemed to know their safe construction,' he said.

About $50 in checks, in the same envelope with the cash, was left by the thieves. Also overlooked were several class rings and a stopwatch.

The office files were thoroughly ransacked, and Ghan figured the thieves were searching for the safe combination."

December 18, 1947 "Atty. Seth V. Conrad, Sheriff E. I. Cunningham, Guy Dugan, Don King, and LeRoy Brinkley were in St. Louis the first part of last week attending federal court. They were there for a damage suit for $15,000 brought by the 5-year-old child of William Knossel, who was killed in a collision at the Rader bridge east of Marshfield on Highway 66, December 10, of last year."

Chapter Eight
1948

January 1, 1948 "Petty Given 25-Year Sentence in Federal Court—Louis Alfred (Duke) Petty was sentenced December 23, to 25 years
in federal prison by Federal District Judge Albert A. Ridge after he pleaded guilty to the robbery of the Seymour, Mo., bank on November 2.

Petty, 44, showed no emotion when the maximum sentence was assessed. Petty, more than six foot tall, showed little physical sign that he had spent 23 years of his life in various prisons.

He was born and reared near Marshfield, and, except for his trips to prison, has not been away from this vicinity. It was at a farmhouse east of here that he was captured November 18, by a large number of federal, state, and county officers, who expected him to put up a bloody battle.

The federal sentence brought to 72 years the total sentences which have been passed against him.

When asked by Judge Ridge if he had anything to say, Petty replied in the negative.

In the Seymour robbery he took about $3600, most of which has been recovered. It was his second bank robbery term. In 1929 he was sentenced to 45 years for the robbery of the Niangua bank. Practically all of the money was recovered from that robbery."

"Arrests Made After Two Safes Found—Warrants charging burglary and larceny were issued by Webster County authorities in mid-December for three Springfield youths wanted in connection with a safe burglary at the Rogersville Farmers Exchange, it was revealed Tuesday *[12/30/47]*.

One of the youths, Carl Roger Gregory, 17, address listed as 502 S. Broadway, is already in custody. Springfield police arrested him Saturday afternoon and turned him over to Webster County authorities.

Webster County Prosecutor Roy Miller said Gregory was arraigned Tuesday and committed to the Webster County jail in default of $5,000 bond pending a preliminary hearing January 7 before Magistrate Cline C. Herren, at Marshfield.

Gregory is a mailing room employee of Springfield Newspapers, Inc.

The other two, listed by officers as Ralph Gregory, brother of the youth in custody, and Coy Miller, both about 25 years old, are object of a systematic search by Springfield policemen and state troopers. Another youth, Russell Pogue of Springfield was arrested Monday in connection with the robbery in Rogersville. He is being held in the Webster County jail charged with burglary and larceny.

Prosecutor Miller said a safe containing about $1800 in cash and checks was removed from the Rogersville Exchange November 28.

About a week later, officers received a tip which led to a probe made by police, patrolmen, and Webster County authorities--and eventually lead to issuance of the warrants.

Although no charges have been filed against them in connection with a subsequent safe burglary at the Diggins Farmers Exchange, officers will question them about the robbery since safes from the two exchanges were found lying within 50 feet of each other in the James River.

The Diggins burglary, which included a loot of about $1500 in cash and checks was discovered the day after Christmas.

The safe from the Diggins Exchange was found Friday *[12/26]* by Lee George, Springfield fisherman. He immediately notified Sheriff Cunningham who went to the scene with Prosecutor Miller and highway patrolmen. The safe from the Rogersville Exchange was found later nearby and both were tugged out by a wrecker Saturday *[12/27]*.

Sheriff Cunningham said the building at Diggins had been entered by breaking the back door glass. The anchored safe was yanked loose from the concrete floor."

[an ad from Isam]

"To The Citizens of Webster County—I note in the following article printed in the Marshfield Mail, 'H.E. Cheek offers to compromise claim for $250, and the court being of the opinion it will be to the best interest of the County, the offer be accepted. It was ordered that H.E. Cheek be allowed said amount and that suit now pending in the Circuit Court, be dismissed with prejudice at cost of H.E. Cheek.' As this article does not explain the full facts of the case, I desire to say that the claim referred to was first filed in the County Court for the sum of $535, by Mr. Cheek, which he claimed was due him from the County for services as Deputy Sheriff. The facts are, while Mr. Cheek was my deputy, he was paid in full for all his services as such deputy, by me, and the County owed him nothing as such deputy, which I showed to the satisfaction of the Court when the Claim was up for hearing, and the Court at the time did allow the whole claim, which was later appealed to the Circuit Court. I am at a loss to know why the Court considered it to be to the best interest of the County to pay on the claim as compromise the sum of $250 when it owed Mr. Cheek nothing; I at all times stood willing, without cost, to prove to the Circuit Court that nothing was due Mr. Cheek, but was not given a chance. Therefore the County Court paid Mr. Cheek $250 of the taxpayers money, when nothing was due him from the County. I feel it my duty to make this statement and explanation, in view of the fact that Mr. Cheek was my deputy, and was paid in full for all the services he rendered as such, and the County owed him nothing.

E. I. Cunningham, Sheriff of Webster County, Missouri."

"Warren Beck Enters Dairy Business Here—Warren Beck has acquired the Bertoldie Dairy and announces the delivery of milk starting with the first of the year." *[Beck's Milky Way Dairy is in a subsequent ad.]*

He has been planning the establishment of a pasteurizing plant here for some time. As soon as he can, he expects to see pasteurized milk."

[Warren Beck] "January 1,1948, I started my milk route. I had four years at the University of Missouri. Then I had Advanced ROTC. They cut out summer camp. I had to go to OCS. Had to spend 39 months. Returned from WWII in 1946. Then I had a Veteran's Class, on-the-job-training, they called it.

At that time I had a 1939 Buick, I lived 6_, 7 miles east of Marshfield, but you wouldn't have thought about driving and it was 12 miles to Elkland. I roomed and boarded at Elkland at Willis Case's parents and his younger brother, Loren. So I got well acquainted with all the people at Elkland and all of Willis's brothers and sisters. I lived over there from January to July.

At that time I was corresponding with Freda. She lived in Texarkana, Arkansas. We got married the 2nd of July.

There was a County Extension Agent then, but I did something like that, with the GIs. I did that for 6 months while I tried to decide about a job. H.H. McNabb, my former high school superintendent, was at Elkland, talked with me about a milk bottling plant. I had a building built, bought used equipment. Joe Hyde, Dale's brother, worked for me for a little while. Virgil Young worked 4 or 5 years for me. Dale Hyde worked for us until he was drafted *[in 1952]* for the Korean War."

January 15, 1948 "Atty. D. Raymond Carter became the first to file for county office in this county by filing last Thursday for the nomination on the Republican ticket for prosecuting attorney. Others filing since have been: E.I. Cunningham for Sheriff and Jason Childress for associate judge of the county court."

January 22, 1948 "Officers Clear Rogersville and Other Robberies—Officers are clearing up the Rogersville Farmers Exchange robbery on November 28, and possibly other robberies in this county with the arrest of certain parties and confessions already secured from them.

Ralph Gregory formerly of Springfield is being held by Los Angeles, Calif., police and Sheriff E. I. Cunningham, accompanied by A.L. Drumright, left this Wednesday to bring him back to face charges of robbing the Farmers Exchange at Rogersville. Gregory's wife, also picked up by Los Angeles police, has been released.

Coy Miller of near Coday, is held in jail here and has confessed his part in the Rogersville robbery. He was picked up by police in St. Louis Tuesday night of last week and Sheriff Cunningham went to St. Louis the next day to bring him here.

He made his confession here Monday night *[1/19]* to state highway patrol officers, Prosecutor Roy C. Miller and Sheriff Cunningham.

Mrs. Ruth Lyons, also of Springfield, was picked up and questioned last Wednesday. She confessed to her part in the robbery and told of others who helped take the large safe from the Rogersville Exchange, dynamiting it, and dumping it into James River just above the Kinser bridge in Greene county. She is now out under bond."

January 29, 1948 "Convicted for Not Sending Tots To School—Two very important cases were tried in Webster County Circuit Court at Marshfield last Thursday *[1/22]* when County Attendance Officer Oscar Carter filed charges against Pansy Newcomb of the Seymour School District, and Christopher Durbin of the Pack District north of Marshfield, for failing to send their children to school.

Mrs. Newcomb was tried before a jury of eleven women and one man, and was found guilty and fined $25 and costs.

Mr. Durbin pleaded guilty before Circuit Judge C. H. Jackson and was fined $25 and costs.

The State Laws of Missouri makes it mandatory on parents or guardians to send children between the ages of 7 and 16 to school regularly and Mr. Carter is making every effort possible to enforce this attendance law."

[It is interesting to see eleven women on the jury because it was only the previous year that the State Constitution was changed, allowing women to be selected jurors.]

"Faces Charges in Rogersville Robbery—*[in connection with the Rogersville Farmers Exchange November 28]*—Three other persons, Coy Miller, of Coday; Mrs. Ruth Line, Springfield; and Ralph Gregory, are under arrest in connection with Exchange burglary. Sheriff E.I. Cunningham left Friday for California to bring back Gregory, who was apprehended by Los Angeles police. The Sheriff had to go by Sacramento, Calif., to get proper extradition papers....

Some more of the records taken from the Rogersville Farmers Exchange safe, which was hauled off, dynamited and dumped into the James River near the Kinser bridge in Greene county, were found by a farmer Saturday evening. Only a portion of the records have been recovered, and it is believed that a number of the records were destroyed. None of the checks have been recovered and it is believed that they were destroyed. There were about $800 in checks in the safe when it was taken.

Ralph Gregory, who is being brought back from California, was sentenced to two years at Algoa for burglary in 1936. In 1931 he was sentenced to a 6-year-sentence in the state penitentiary at Jefferson City for burglary and larceny from Christian county."

February 5, 1948 "John D. Johnson Files Candidacy for Sheriff Nomination--Johnny Johnson needs little introduction to the people of Webster County as he has lived here all his life. He is 62 years and well and favorably known. He has held the office of sheriff filling out the term of Condo Evans and then being elected to a four-year-term in 1940. He established a reputation as a fearless law enforcement officer when sheriff before and states that if he is nominated and elected this year, he will enforce the laws impartially and to the satisfaction of the law-abiding people of this county. He is making the race only after requested to do so by friends in all parts of the county."

February 12, 1948 "E. I. Cunningham Asks Re-Election as Webster County Sheriff—Sheriff E.I. Cunningham, who was elected Sheriff of Webster County four years ago, and who will be the first sheriff to serve full term and run for re-election due to the change in the State Constitution adopted since he entered office, announces his candidacy in this issue. He makes a statement as follows: TO THE CITIZENS OF WEBSTER COUNTY:

In announcing myself as a candidate for the office of Sheriff of Webster County, I want to thank the citizens of Webster County for their support and co-operation in assisting me in the enforcement of the laws in this county. During my term of office I have to the best of my ability endeavored to do my duty as Sheriff of your county, fairly and impartially, without fear or favor. If again nominated and elected to the office of Sheriff of Webster County I will continue to carry out the same policy, and do my duty as your Sheriff. Your vote and support is earnestly solicited and will be greatly appreciated, in the coming Primary Election. E. I. CUNNINGHAM"

February 26, 1948 "Armed Robbers Hold Up Niangua Man, Getting $1100—Two armed robbers held up Hugh Arthur at his home in Niangua Monday night *[2/23]*, taking $1120 in cash and some checks. Mr. Arthur, who had closed his feed store about 7:30, was sitting in his home reading the paper, when he heard a knock on the door about 9:30. When he opened the door a well dressed man, about 30, in dark suit and hat, and wearing horn rimmed glasses, inquired the way to 'Spring Grove.'

Mr. Arthur told him he knew of no 'Spring Grove' but of a 'Grovespring.' He stepped outside the door to give directions and was told to 'Put 'em up!' Another man, in khaki colored clothes or a uniform, stepped from the shadows and struck Mr. Arthur's hand with his gun, telling him to hurry. They stripped his billfold from his pockets and a paper sack with loose change from which the bottom fell out and scattered the change on the porch. They left the change and ordered Mr. Arthur to get behind the house until they got out of sight. They hurried to a car standing in front of the house.

Mr. Arthur went to the home of Josh Hamilton, his next door neighbor, and they notified the Sheriff's office. The Sheriff was out of town, so officers did not get on the case until Tuesday morning but are making extensive investigations.

Later that night Mr. Arthur and his neighbors found a half pint whiskey bottle wrapped in an army shirt and a carton of Camel cigarettes in the road where the car had been parked which the thieves evidently had lost out."

"Thieves Enter Several Places At Rogersville—Several business places in Rogersville were broken into Tuesday night by thieves, but at only one place was anything taken so far as has been discovered. At all places, cash registers, drawers, and desks were ransacked indicating that the thieves were searching for money or other valuables.

The Underwood Motor Co. was broken into and robbed of $4,735 in cash, a 22-caliber pistol and two 6:50x16 tires.

The following places were broken into, but nothing taken so far discovered: Tydol Filling Station, George Dunn, operator; Phillips '66' Station, operated by Billy Collison; Rogersville Motor Co; F.M. Kessinger Hardware.

In each case entrance into the places of business was gained by breaking a glass in a window or door.

The Highway Patrol was called and they with Webster County officers are working on the case."

"Chas. Tower Asks Nomination for Office of County Sheriff—Chas. F. Tower of Marshfield makes his announcement this week as a candidate for sheriff, subject to the Republican primary. He was a candidate four years ago but withdrew on account of ill health. Mr. Tower makes the following statement: ...I have decided to do so at the request of my many friends and acquaintances.... I was born near Rogersville in 1890...have been a life-long resident of Webster County...a veteran of World War I....I do not believe in machine politics, nor do I think it right or just for any person to stay in public office until he feels like he is indispensable....I assure you I will perform my duties...show no favors to one more than another, but be honest and truthful in all dealings."

April 1, 1948 "ONE OF ESCAPED PRISONERS OF WEBSTER COUNTY JAIL GIVES SELF UP TO HIGHWAY PATROL OFFICERS—Pair Freed Themselves Last Friday Night By Breaking Out, Climbing Down Blankets—

Two prisoners in the Webster County jail escaped Friday night *[3/26]* from a west window of the third floor of the courthouse. They tore up an iron bunk in their jail cell and used part of it to force open their cell door, and then to pry loose an iron bar in the window. They tied blankets together and swung down to the ground. The prisoners are Ralph Gregory, 30, of Springfield, and Coy Miller, 27, of near Rogersville, who have been in jail charged with the robbery of the Rogersville Farmers Exchange on November 28. Another prisoner in the jail did not take the escape route.

Coy Miller gave himself up Tuesday *[3/30]* in Springfield to the State Highway Patrol. He walked into troop headquarters in company with his brother Wayne Miller. He was returned to Marshfield and placed in the Webster County jail again. Gregory, last seen at Joplin, is the subject of a search by state and federal officers in Arkansas, Oklahoma, Kansas, and Missouri.

The search for the two men began Saturday morning *[3/27]* when the jailbreak was discovered. It was learned that a Black and White Cab from Springfield came to Northview Hill and picked them up and took them to Joplin, after stopping in Springfield. The State Patrol and other officers have notified the Oklahoma State Police to be on the lookout for the two men who may have taken to the hills in that state.

The two men are reported to have called the cab to Northview about 8 a.m. Saturday morning. Clyde Ash, a dispatcher for the cab company, rode 'for the ride' to Northview Hill with Johnny Fender, the cab driver. Ash recognized 'Barney' Gregory, a former Black and White cab driver. He didn't recognize Miller, but identified him later from a picture officers showed him.

In route to Joplin the men stopped at the Ash home and made a couple of telephone calls. Ash made the trip to Joplin and said that Fender let the pair out at what appeared to be the middle of the business district shortly after noon Saturday. Ash said Gregory paid Fender with a $20 bill and five $1 bills and the police so far do not know where the pair got the money.

Gregory and Miller were both arrested in January: the former in California and the latter in St. Louis. In addition to the burglary charges, the pair now face federal charges of violation of the Dyer stolen car act, filed following the escape. The charges, filed so the FBI can join in the search, are in connection with a stolen car the men allegedly transported interstate from Kansas City before their arrest on burglary charges."

"SLAYER OF JUDGE C.H. JACKSON SURRENDERS—Well Known Jurist Fatally Shot by Douglas County Man Who Later Slays Own Wife"

"Webster Countians Shocked By Judge's Murder...Webster County citizens were shocked when they learned Tuesday morning of the murder of C. H. Jackson. While he resided in Wright county, the people of Webster County thought of him as belonging to this county. In the years he has been the Circuit Judge here his knowledge of the law, decisions and fairness gained him the respect of most all citizens. He was praised as a fine judge.

His chair in the circuit court room is covered with crepe in mourning for his passing.

Meantime, there has been conjecture as to who Governor Donnelly would appoint to the place. Whoever is appointed will serve out the balance of this year as there is time for candidates to file for the office before April 27, the last day for filing. There will be four years to serve to fill out the remainder of the year term. Judge Jackson was re-elected in 1946."

"Sheriff James Baker of Wright county was informed that Ernest Afton Scott, 48, a farmer from Douglas county, bore a grudge against Judge Jackson as the result of a lawsuit over property in Mountain Grove against his brother-in-law and sister, Mr. and Mrs. Elmer Moore of Mountain Grove....

Judge Jackson, who had only one arm, had been judge of the circuit. The circuit is comprised of Camden, Dallas, Hickory, Polk, Webster, and Wright counties. During World War II he served for Sam C. Blair while the former was in the army. He had still nearly five years of his present term to serve.

It was said that he lost his right arm when a child, by a horse throwing him, and the injury resulted in an infection which necessitated its amputation....

Scott's 13-year-old daughter, Alice, related to officers how her 43-year-old mother was shot to death a short time after Judge Jackson was fatally wounded at a farm where he had gone to buy cattle.

'Mother and Daddy had been quarreling for a long time,' Alice said. She is one of the ten children in the family...."

Mrs. Rainey *[Carmen]*...said the daughter *[Alice]* told her Scott had 'run' the family away from the farm Sunday and at that time had expressed jealousy of a friendship he believed existed between Judge Jackson and Mrs. Scott."

[Philip Huffman] "We can start with there *[the murder of Judge Jackson]* because Charlie Jackson was from Mountain Grove, which is where my mother is from. My dad *[M.J. Huffman]* was from Norwood.

He was affectionately known as One-Armed Jackson, by the populace who elected him. And people thought he was a good judge. And I guess he probably was.

It's hard for me to remember exactly, because the families kinda got crossways.

My dad very much respected Charlie's legal skills. Of course, he was a 'runner.' A Circuit Judge and a womanizer! And that didn't suit my father. Absolutely, he was a womanizer! And there's no question that he was caught with this guy's wife. And he killed him. Well, the guy got away and he hunted his wife down like a dog. He killed Charlie down in Douglas County and he killed her in Wright County...I believe. They had a hunt on to find him. Afton Scott. His son is still alive as far as I know. Lives in Mountain Grove. I have never talked with him, the son, about the situation. But he *[Afton Scott]* got the death penalty.

My dad told me about Bill Robinett. He was a lawyer in Mountain Grove, later State Senator, and something else.

But they didn't have enough law enforcement to catch the guy. I'm not sure that my dad didn't have a gun. So did Mr. Robinett and other people went out, caught him, wherever it was. Jim Baker was for sure the sheriff. He was sheriff of Wright County...."

April 8, 1948 "Ralph Gregory Nabbed, Returned To Jail—Ralph Glenn Gregory, 30, who escaped... March 26, was captured peacefully in the Hoff Hotel, Springfield, by city police. He was turned over to Sheriff E.I. Cunningham Thursday *[4/1]* and brought back to the jail in the top floor of the courthouse here.

He rejoined Coy Miller, 27, who surrendered last week....They now have additional charges against them.

Police of Springfield received a tip Wednesday night of last week that Gregory was in Springfield and had gone to the hotel in a Black and White cab. They found him registered under the name of Bill Watson. His arms and legs were covered with scratches inflicted by briars through which he fled....

Gregory said they paid the driver of the cab with money he claimed he and Miller had been allowed to keep in jail."

"Judge Sam C. Blair of the Fourteenth Judicial Circuit whose home is in Jefferson City, has been assigned temporarily to this Judicial Circuit by the Missouri Supreme Court. He will serve this circuit until Governor Donnelly appoints a judge to serve the period....which ends with 1952....Now the Supreme Court can transfer judges as needs require to various parts of the state."

"Prosecuting Attorney Roy C. Miller and Sheriff E.I. Cunningham are in Springfield this week attending Federal Court. Among the cases before the court are some from Webster County charged with accessory after fact in connection with the robbery of the Seymour bank."

"Officers Hold Man—Webster County officers were requested Wednesday to hold Floyd Knowlton until McAlester [Oklahoma] officers could come and get him. Knowlton is charged with stealing a motor scooter at McAlester and was riding it when taken by Sheriff E.I. Cunningham on Highway 66 near Marshfield about 3 a.m. Tuesday [4/6]." [3 A.M.!]

[Tony Stephens] "We [of the Highway Patrol] were assigned to the Springfield area, when Isam was the Sheriff. He was able to be called on any time, night or day. He even gave Glen a key to the courthouse. Glen would go and unlock the courthouse."

[Glen Wilson] "The lights would go on and Isam would be coming down the stairs, trying to put his shoes on, not tied up yet, and pulling his suspenders over his shoulders. And he'd say, 'What's a goin' on?' We would get the call. We never worried about Isam. If he was capable of being there, he was there."

[Tony Stephens] "The one thing I know about Isam Cunningham was the fact that whenever he come out on a call, at 2 or 3 o'clock in the mornin', he had his suit on, his tie, everything. We accused him of sleeping in his clothes.

We were chasin' a stolen car in Springfield, me and Wallace, we couldn't catch him so we had the office call Isam. Isam come out there and he stopped that car. He had his full suit on but his tie was way around here. I said, 'Did you sleep in your clothes, Isam?' and he said, 'Mostly.'"

[Charley Cunningham] "Dad wore a fresh shirt every day but he would go to bed with that day's shirt and tie on, over his long-handled underwear, in case he'd get called during the night."

[Don Letterman] "Well, we *couldn't* get in no trouble, he was awake all night!"

[Marie Day] "He slept I don't know when, but you could go in that office sometime and he'd be settin' there, his head would be down in there, and he'd be snortin' and snorin', sittin' up, leaned back in the chair!"

[Helen Cunningham] "Another story: Isam rode with the Highway Patrol a lot. He always wore suspenders. And the Cunninghams can fall asleep just like that. He'd get in the car and fall asleep and they'd undo his suspenders. Then they'd stop real fast, like there was a wreck or something, and he'd get out and...."

"Thieves Enter Baptist Church, Take Collection—The Marshfield Baptist church was broken into by a thief or thieves Wednesday night *[3/31]*. About $15 was taken from the birthday collection box which was in the pastor's study. A straw hat believed to belong to the thief was left as possible evidence."

[an ad] "NOW! Air Ambulance Service Phone 29
Rainey Funeral Home, Marshfield, Mo."

[Jack Rainey] "Rainey's Air Ambulance Service? No, that wasn't my dad's *[Rex Rainey's]* plane. He may have had *access* to air service. I think they fixed a plane that my uncle *[Roscoe Prescott]* had at the Springfield Airport to accept a cot, and they did fly. He may have been associated with promotin' it or makin' it available, but he never owned it or was a pilot, as far as I know.

About the only thing he *[his dad, Rex Rainey]* ever had so far as a hobby was concerned—his business was his hobby as far as that goes—he dealt in a little real estate. He liked to buy and sell real estate.

He had an airplane for awhile and he liked that. That was during the war, he was never in the service, but my mother's brother *[his uncle, Roscoe Prescott]* had come back from the service and opened a flight school but in Springfield. He was in old Springfield downtown, for just a short time, and then they finished the airport where it is now and they moved it out there. And there was an association...I say an association...it was Doc Cardwell, Oren Pierce, I *wanna* say Earl Shields, there was about seven business people, went together and bought an airplane, and they kept it in a hangar out there about where the golf course is now, only it was on the side where the clubhouse is. Used to be an airstrip up there and a nine-hole golf course. Well, later on they moved the golf course off that site but they kept the clubhouse. But they used to have a hangar out there and they kept the plane in the hangar

And each one of 'em was supposed to been able to use it certain times. And I guess that got a little too congested and my dad bought him his *own* plane and had it for a while.

We went to Kansas City to pick up this plane. I went with my dad and I wasn't real crazy about flyin' *anyway.* And I had a little...they used to dress me up...had a little hat and overcoat on and everything. So the plane wasn't ready when we got up there, and we went to the administration building, I had a big ole juicy hamburger. I was probably fourteen or fifteen years old. We started home and it was obvious I wasn't gonna make it home without getting sick. Dad was flyin', bubble top, we were side by side. And I told him I was gonna be sick and they hadn't made *any* provisions for it at all, so he said, 'Well, just use your hat.' And I used the hat! And that's one of those situations where, if you're airsick and you throw up, then you're fine!

I'm not much on flyin'. I don't travel. I just don't travel at all."

[In County Court Notes] "Elzie Doyle *[deputy]* salary, \$25"

April 15, 1948

"Among those passing the bar exam last February is John Hosmer."

"Tonnie H. Doyle, 60, a retired salesman collapsed and died in the Fellin Cash Store....He is survived by his wife, Elzie, and one daughter Mrs. Freda Langston...."

"Morgan M. Moulder, Camdenton attorney, was appointed by Governor Phil M. Donnelly Monday to the 18th Judicial District Circuit Bench. Moulder, a Democrat, succeeds Circuit Judge Chas. H. Jackson of Mountain Grove, who was shot and killed March 29 by a farmer residing in Douglas county.

Moulder will serve until a new judge is elected at the coming November election to serve the remaining four years of the term. He ran for this office in 1935 against the late Judge C.H. Skinker.

Two Republicans have filed for the unexpired term—Atty. Lieutellus 'Lieu' Cunningham of Camdenton and James P. Hawkins of Buffalo."

"Two Plead Guilty in Federal Court to Charges of Accepting Money from Duke Petty--....Some extremely damaging confessions made by James Casteel to FBI officers at Marshfield last November were admitted as evidence in the case.

Here are the statements offered in the first two confessions signed by Casteel, dated November 19 and November 23 (the robbery was November 12 and Petty's arrest November 18):

July I heard Petty escaped from jail...Petty came to Casteel's farmhome mid-July and had been there off and on ever since, Casteel having known him all his life...

In October Casteel rented a car at a drive-it-yourself place in Springfield, picked up Petty and drove to Seymour. Petty got out there, but Casteel didn't know he was looking over the bank. Petty got back in, they drove to Mansfield and got whiskey. A few days later they drove to Lebanon.

After bank robbery, Casteel received $50 in $1 bills from Petty, said Petty told him to keep his mouth shut. Casteel thought this money came from the Seymour Bank...he had read in the paper about the bank robbery and that Petty was suspected...

On November 17 Petty came out of the woods to the Casteel farm, gave Casteel $80 with instructions to buy him some clothes in Springfield. Casteel went to Highway 38 south of his home, got a ride with James Robinson and a milk truck driver to Springfield. In Springfield they bought clothes for Petty, also bought a $46 suitcase and $2 change back to Petty, leaving them in the woods.

A glass jar containing $360 in bills and coins from the Seymour bank robbery was introduced as evidence.

It was dug up from a farm about five miles east of Marshfield by a party consisting of Prosecutor Miller, Casteel, Trooper William Owens of the highway patrol, Sheriff Cunningham, and Robert W. Conn, an FBI agent, upon Casteel's direction, Miller testified.

Sheriff E.I. Cunningham declared that Casteel told him that Petty divided the money with him and Jim Robinson. Trooper Owen also testified as to the finding of the money.

A plea of guilty by James Casteel, 32-year-old farmer of near Marshfield, came suddenly in federal court Wednesday afternoon *[4/14]* after two hours of testimony, and Judge Albert A. Ridge handed him a two-year sentence.

Casteel had been charged with knowingly accepting money stolen in the robbery of the bank at Seymour November 12.

Prosecutor Roy Miller of Webster County said he was not sure what action would be taken on state charges against Casteel for harboring 'Duke Petty,' robber of the Seymour Bank.

Disposition of the state's case possibly will await Casteel's release from the two-year sentence received in Federal Court."

April 22, 1948 "Next Tuesday, April 27, will be the last day that candidates for public office either county or state may file. In former years candidates could file up to 60 days before the primary election. Now the law sets the filing date for the fourth Tuesday in April. This earlier date permits the printing and mailing of soldier ballots for the primary. If there are no candidates filed for office on a party ticket, the place cannot be filled by the county committee of that political party. This makes it important that all places be filed for by the fourth Tuesday in April."

"State of Mo. vs. John C. Pope, driving while intoxicated. Application for change of venue filed by defendant. Change of venue granted."

[Mitzi Hosmer] "John Pope and John *[Hosmer]* had an office together in Springfield. John Pope was arrested for driving while intoxicated. So was John Hosmer!"

[Cline Herren, Jr.] "John Pope and my dad were very very very good friends. My dad didn't graduate from law school; he passed The Bar. He and John Pope studied together. Dad worked in a law office in Springfield, and there was a period of time you had to be in training, and Dad took The Bar and passed it.

Fact is, somewhere, Pope got the liquor. John had a drinking problem. All of those Popes had more brass. Whether it was right or wrong, they'd try to 'drive it home'. They had it in their genes, I think. They were all tough like that. And they all died young."

"Another Anniversary of Famous 1880 Tornado Passes—Only a few of the older citizens of Marshfield remembers that Sunday, April 18, was the 68th anniversary of the storm so widely called the Marshfield Cyclone. Such storms are now called tornadoes.

The tornado in 1880 that swept most of this city which had a population then of 750 people came on a Sunday afternoon. 93 persons were killed and 250 injured, which was a large percentage of the population. Because of the fact that it was the most devastating and the most deadly of any such storms recorded up to that time, it received widespread publicity.

There have been tornadoes since that have killed as many but not in so small an area. Most Marshfieldians would rather not remember the Marshfield Cyclone."

[Apparently there was confusion about whether it should be called a cyclone or a tornado. This appears to want to settle that debate. However, some around Marshfield still refer to it as the Marshfield Cyclone.]

"Circuit Judge Morgan Moulder, Camdenton, held his first session of court in Marshfield Friday, April 16. He was appointed April 12 to fill the office until a circuit judge is elected in November and qualifies."

[an ad]
"You Can Join the Coffee Gulpers Club…Coffee time is anytime at Andrews, but if you drop in around 10 each morning you'll see local business men gulping and discussing. Join them and you'll be a member of the Coffee Gulpers Club. Andrews Café, over 26 years in same location. It may be a cup of coffee to you but it's a reputation for us. Open 5 a.m.—Close 8 p.m."

April 29, 1948 "Lively Contests Seen As Several Candidates File for County Office…primary election August 3…Prosecuting Attorney—Republicans Roy C. Miller, Marshfield; John C. Pope, Marshfield; Democrat John Hosmer, North Grant township.

For Sheriff—Republican E.I. Cunningham, Niangua; J.D. Johnson, Marshfield; Carl J. Pittman, Marshfield; Charley F. Tower, Marshfield; Tom Woodruff, Fordland; Democrat Ralph H. Day, Marshfield; William H. Hume, High Prairie township."

May 6, 1948   "Sheriff, Patrol Pick Up Man on Notice from Janesville, Wis.—Sheriff E.I. Cunningham received a telegram Monday night *[5/3]* from Janesville, Wis., requesting him to arrest Clarence Ellett on a felony warrant. The Sheriff with highway patrol officers took the young man into custody Tuesday afternoon *[5/4]* south of Dogwood in Douglas county, and he was taken to Ava.

The Sheriff stated that they found some watches, a compass and a pawn ticket for a diamond ring thought to have been stolen in Wisconsin in the car belonging to Ellett. It was reported that he was getting ready to leave for California in the next day or so."

"We try to be careful but we still make mistakes ever so often. Last week we listed Tom Woodruff of Fordland as having filed for sheriff....His name should have been listed under those filed for Assessor."

May 13, 1948 "Marion J. Huffman Announces for Office of Circuit Judge—In this issue Marion J. Huffman of Hartville announces his candidacy for Judge of the 18th Judicial Circuit, unexpired term, subject to the Republican primary.

Atty. Huffman, present Representative in the state legislature from Wright county, has served five terms as prosecuting attorney of that county. He is 41 years of age, attended SMS three years and received his LLD degree from Cumberland University, Lebanon, Tenn. He passed the Missouri Bar in 1929 and has practiced law in Wright county since.

A staunch Republican, Atty. Huffman has served on the Republican State committee two years. He is married and has a son and daughter. He is a member of the Masonic and IOOF Lodges and a member of the Methodist church. He is president of the Board of Education at Hartville and is a member of the Chamber of Commerce. He takes an active interest in civic affairs.

He feels that he is qualified to fill the position of Circuit Judge of this circuit and will appreciate the support of the voters."

[Philip Huffman] "This is interesting. You know, my mother never saw my dad try a case until way late and she went once, and I think she was appalled, at the closing argument.

My dad would cry real tears. His voice would get...oh my goodness. And he would, if he had a second chair lawyer, when he finished his argument, he would walk out the door of the courtroom, if he was defending a criminal case, and never listen to the prosecution. He would tell the other lawyer what to object to. And never listen to the prosecutor's proposal part of the prosecutor's closing argument. 'Course, he had learned that. He did that, because, as if...when they got done listening to him, there wasn't much more for them to listen to. He was one of best prosecutors there ever was, for years.

He always told me that more people had been sent to the pen in the last part of the state's closing argument, that was more important than anything else, with these country juries and the way things used to be, and the way the facts and the charges came about, than anything. And that you had, if you were defending, to minimize that *someway*. And one of the ways he chose to minimize it was to walk out the door when he finished his...if he had someone else helping him. I saw him do it more than once. I've done it a time or two myself.

No, I don't think he was just acting. He usually would not be too interested in a case unless he thought there was something to it. That was my dad.

Jean Paul *[Bradshaw]* used to say about him, 'You know, you would just think, if you were on the other side, that you were just slaughtering him. Just getting him. And all the time he'd just been letting you be out there getting your neck out--further and further and further and further. And then he'd have some little issue that didn't seem that important until he brought in about two witnesses. And it would just nail what really was the heart of the case. And then he might not even take great attention as he examined the witnesses, just get the real facts out. And *[Jean Paul]* said you'd soon find out where you were!

My dad was not terribly emotional except in the courtroom. Passionate. He was a soft-hearted guy. He was viewed by the public as being this mean, big Kingfish. That's the nickname they called him."

[Charley Cunningham] "Ole Marion Huffman, he was full of stories. He was my dad's lawyer, back years ago.

Anybody who'd had a child out of wedlock was a 'wood's colt'.

He was a fox hunter, coon hunter, everything.

Back when my dad was elected Sheriff, Huffman was a young lawyer. Jean Paul Bradshaw in Springfield, he was a young lawyer, Judge Hawkins from Buffalo, used to be Circuit Judge, he was a young lawyer.*[Read on to see how this happens.]* When I come to Marshfield, Charley Jackson was the Circuit Judge. A one-armed Circuit Judge. I think he got killed by a woman's husband. I think that's what happened, I'm not sure. He was dating somebody's wife and her husband killed him."

[Mitzi Hosmer] "M.J. Huffman—he was the ultimate politician. He could talk politics. I think that was just *in* him. And he was kind of The Old School lawyer. He didn't worry too much about the decisions. He got up and he knew his people, he knew the juries. He was a fun guy to listen to.

M.J. always called his wife Miz Lylian. He was just funny. He had that big smile on his face.

M. J. was a storyteller and a half! John*[Hosmer]* just knew M.J. after we moved back here. They didn't grow up together. He *[M.J.]* liked to talk; John liked to talk.

John always liked M.J. He used to come up to the house, the hill *[Bald Hill]*. He was so much fun. Every kid would be seated around him. He would talk to them, look right in their face. And he'd say, 'Now you really are a kind of Republican, aren't you?' And they'd say, 'No, we're Democrats!' He'd end up, before he left, giving them all quarters after they'd say they'd vote Republican! Craig *[Hosmer. later elected State Representative as a Democrat]* was one of them! He would just spend hours doing that. He was a character."

[Peg Miller] "M.J. Huffman! *[Roy]* Miller was in tight with all these because they were Wright County guys. When Hawkins ran against M.J., of course Miller was for M.J. And the *[Ellsworth]* Haymes crew were all for Hawkins because they had gone to school together. And were just buddies anyway. And that took some settin' in.

Roy was related to M.J., 'Boss', Huffman! And he did smoke. He had a cigar that was never out of his mouth. He was just a character. And Phil looks just like him."

[Philip Huffman] "When Isam was Sheriff, one of the largest fox hunts held in America was right down here at the fairgrounds. I've been to it many times.

Fox Hunting, in England, they ride to the hounds, on horses, and they kill the fox. Every time, if they can. They ride, and run, until they catch him. Fox Hunting in Rural Ozarks, Missouri, the *last* thing you want to do is kill a big, fine red dog fox that you can turn the dogs loose two nights later and listen to 'em run. And they sat around campfires and they told stories and listened to their dogs. Some of them drank, not all of them. And every fox hunter worth a dern, and the others after a while, could identify which dog was in front by its bark, and who it belonged to. If there were *forty* in the pack, they could do that! They'd stay all night, if the dogs were game enough to run the fox, one that would stay away from them all night. I've spent all night in the woods many a night, with my dad. Other people at times. Fox hounds, if they're any good, will almost always come back to the place where you turned them loose, unlike a bird dog. A fox hound will come home, too, if you're not there to get it. There are myriads of stories about that. A deer doesn't do like a fox. A dog fox runs a big circle and will lead the dogs around. A deer just takes off and runs as hard as it can run. Coon hunting is a different sport entirely. You intend to kill the coon, after the dog trees it.

I fed fifty, as a child, more than once. My dad...we had a dog named...Highgrade Hornet. He finally decided it was too expensive for him to run, back then. Sold it to an evangelist down in Fort Smith, Arkansas. He was the third best stud dog in the Walker breed, for years and years and years. Hornet was a wonderful dog, and a wonderful pet. But wanted to hunt. Most show dogs, Dad just hated being in shows with dogs that hadn't completed the field trials. If they haven't changed, the Missouri State Fox Hunters Association *still* will not let you show your dog in an event show unless it's completed the field run. Doesn't have to win, but it's got to complete the three days of going out there and running. For years, at least, it was that way. Missouri was considered to be crazy.

But Dad was the President of it for some years. Gene Hamilton, a Judge up in Columbia, I knew Gene well before we went to law school, I was behind him a year or two. But our dads were friends, they were fox hunters. And Gene is a show dog judge now. And his dad never was as hot as my dad on *[his dog]* being able to run and still be pretty. Even so, Gene judges at the National Fox Hunter show now. These people were in every county, and their grandfathers were fox hunters and it has gone on ever since people moved here! Walker Fox Hound's one of the best breeds.

And those folks had a bond. They stayed into it with the Conservation Commission because they wanted them to buy a license. They said, 'We're not killing anything! We don't *intend* to kill anything! We're not out hunting, we're out listening to our dogs.' And it was a running battle that the Fox Hunters won for years and finally.... I remember going to Conservation Federation Meetings and everything where Dad would go, and represent the Fox Hunters, for years. Dad always told them that if they would recognize what it was....But finally voluntarily they started buying hunting licenses. Because the Federation started to do something to protect the red fox. They were just letting people kill every one of them, you know, encourage it actually, tracking and everything. And there were no red foxes, almost, for years. And when the Conservation Commission agreed that they would try to preserve that and put a season on, and stop the trapping, then all the fox hunters agreed and bought their hunting licenses. That happened after '55, but not *much* after.

There are some great articles in the Springfield paper archives about my dad. Dale Freeman wrote some of 'em. About being able to run foxes all night and try cases all day. And in his prime he did that! That was really his passion. And the law. And politics. But he had vast interests. He was an avid reader."

[Jack Rainey] "Dad *[Rex Rainey]* didn't have any connection to the Fox Hound Association In fact, he was at odds at one time with 'em because the fox hunters run through the place and spread out fifty some head of cattle all over the country, run 'em through the fences. On his property! Back then, fox hunters assumed they had the right to go anywhere. Fences didn't mean anything.

They'd just got a fresh load of cattle in out of St. Louis and had unloaded 'em, and either that night or the next night fox hunters come through, those cattle didn't have any idea what fox dogs were, and they run through the fences, and they went in every direction that there was around there, and they like to never got them caught up. So we had a little round with the fox hunters. When I was a teenager."

"Ralph Glenn Gregory, who pled guilty to charges in connection with the Rogersville Farmers Exchange robbery, was sentenced to a total of ten years in the penitentiary the first of the week *[5/10]*. Bulletin: the jury brought in a verdict of guilty in the case of Coy Miller on the charge of burglary only of the Rogersville Farmers Exchange and for two years in the penitentiary." (Coy Miller had been charged with burglary and larceny of the Rogersville Farmers Exchange on November 28.)

"State of Mo. vs. Cleo Mae Epps, unlawfully possessing intoxicating liquor. Defendant discharged. Sheriff ordered to refund $500 deposited with Sheriff for bond. State Highway Patrol ordered to return revolver seized and taken from defendant at time of her arrest."

County court proceedings: "E.I. Cunningham salary, $181.03"
[Looks as though this time Isam got a raise!]

May 20, 1948 "Matters Before the Magistrate Court May 15, 1948—Hold Sanity Hearing—A sanity hearing was held Monday before Cline C. Herren, Judge of Probate and Ex-Officio Magistrate. It was ordered that Elva Brandenburg of Seymour be admitted to the State Hospital No. 3 at Nevada. Sheriff and Mrs. E.I. Cunningham accompanied by Mrs. Will Scott *[Pearl, Isam's half-sister]* and John James took Mrs. Brandenburg to Nevada Tuesday morning."

"Carl Pittman has announced candidacy for office of sheriff. Carl Pittman, 31-year-old farmer and grocer, is announcing his candidacy in this week's MAIL for the office of Webster County Sheriff, subject to the Republican Primary on August 3.

A lifelong Republican, Mr. Pittman was reared on a farm, but entered the grocery when he grew to manhood.

He feels that he is qualified for sheriff and pledges a square deal for everybody if elected."

June 3, 1948 "James P. Hawkins of Buffalo Announces for Circuit Judge—To the voters of Webster County: I hereby announce my candidacy for the Republican nomination for Circuit Judge of the 18th Judicial Circuit (unexpired term due to the death of Judge Jackson)."

June 10, 1948 "Man Found Dead On River West Of Here—The body of a man was found on the Pomme de Terre Creek a quarter of a mile north and a quarter of a mile east of Cap Pamplin's station four miles west of Marshfield last Thursday night *[6/3]* about 8:30. Wayne Collier, who lives on the Pamplin place, while going along the creek with his dogs, came upon the body and notified Sheriff E. I. Cunningham.

The Sheriff, accompanied by Bob George, Shirley Hogan, James Hogan, W. L. Grier, Wayne Collier, Howard Hobson, Rex Rainey, and Gordon Connor went out and brought the body to the Rainey Funeral Home. Up in the day Friday officers found that the man was Andrew Jackson Harris, 53 or 54 years old, who owned a home and resided at 610 Market St., Springfield. He was not married and his sister, Mrs. Mittlebrook, resided there with him.

Mr. Harris formerly worked for the Springfield Water Co., but had 'had the call to preach,' and left home May 25. His sister had heard nothing from him since that date.

The body was found lying on the creek bank with his head in the stream, in a position which suggested that he had started to drink and suffered a heart attack. All he had with him was a Bible and a Bible dictionary. He had no wallet or any identification papers on him. The only clue was a glasses case stamped with the name of Dr. J. R. Hawver, a Springfield optometrist.

K. K. Kelley, Webster County Coroner, viewed the body and visited the scene Friday. He found no marks of violence on the man or no sign of violence at the spot where the body was found. He decided that no inquest was necessary. He evidently died from exposure and a heart attack.

Leaves on a ledge on a nearby cliff indicated that the man might have slept there and ashes of a fire indicated that he may have stayed there a day or two. It is believed that he had been dead since Sunday before the body was found.

The body was taken to Little Rock overland for burial Saturday morning. Funeral services were held at a cemetery there at 10 a.m."

"Warrant to E. I. Cunningham, summon jury, mileage, waiting on court, postage jury board $292.62"
["Warrant" used to mean payment to the person naming the expenses.]

June 17, 1948   "The Trial of Ernest Afton Scott, 48-year-old Douglas county farmer charged with the slaying of his wife, Verla, last March 29, has been postponed until June 23....The prosecution is expected to ask the death penalty for Scott, who also faces murder charges in Douglas county in connection with the shooting of Judge Jackson on the same day Scott's wife was slain."

July 1, 1948   "Scott Trial Underway in Hartville—Ernest Afton Scott, 48-year-old Douglas county farmer went on trial Monday *[6/28]* at Hartville for the shooting of his wife Verla on March 29....The defense attorneys announced as the evidence began that Scott would plead innocent by reason of insanity. The courtroom has been packed for every session.

Allie Mae Scott, 15, proved a star witness for the state. She told how she saw her father kill her mother in the yard of her grandmother in Mountain Grove.

She told of how her father whipped the older sister until her back was bloody and how the family feared him. She said if he was crazy he had been crazy all the time (for many years). She said they lived in constant fear of her father as far back as she could remember.

When Scott surrendered to officers last March 31, he said he believed Judge Charles H. Jackson, who was killed at a farm in Douglas county by Scott before he went into Mountain Grove and shot his wife, was the father of his youngest boy, age 2. Allie Mae introduced the accusation as evidence –then dismissed it with the statement that her father had made it up. 'It wasn't true and he knew it,' she said."

July 8, 1948 "Jury Finds Scott Guilty of Murder—Assesses Punishment of Death In Gas Chamber For Man. The jury hearing the case of Earnest Afton Scott, charged with the murder of his wife, Verla, on March 29, found him guilty on the fourth ballot at Hartville last Thursday, July 1, after four days trial. They assessed the penalty at death in the gas chamber at Jefferson City….

First-degree murder charges are pending at Ava. Douglas county Prosecutor J. Bernie Lewis was a spectator at Hartville. His comment as the verdict was read by Circuit Clerk Burke Dennis: 'Well, that saves us a job.'"

July 22, 1948 "Senate Bill 307 became a law July 18. This new school law creates in each county in Missouri a county Board of Education composed of six members, who shall make a comprehensive study of the county school problems and prepare a plan of reorganization.

Within sixty days each county superintendent of schools shall call a meeting of the members of the school boards in the county to elect a county board of education. Oscar L. Carter, county superintendent of schools of Webster County, has tentatively set Sept. 10 as the date for the election of a county board in Webster County."*[This idea of county-wide school reorganization and consolidation was to be very controversial, but not while Isam was Sheriff.]*

July 29, 1948 *[an ad]* "To The Voters of Webster County….Thanking you for the favors shown me in the past, and kindly asking you to support me in the coming election, I beg to remain your humble servant.   E.I. CUNNINGHAM"

August 5, 1948   *E. I. Cunningham   1440 votes*

J. D. Johnson   1240 votes
Ralph Day was the Democrat candidate for sheriff.

August 12, 1948   *Hawkins 1407 votes   Huffman 1071 votes*
[Webster County tally—Hawkins won by only 76 votes
in the six-county circuit]
Roy Miller defeated John C. Pope for Prosecuting Attorney

"Officers Probe Six Business Places Robbed—Six Marshfield business places were found robbed Monday morning *[8/9]*. Officers know that three of the places were broken into Sunday night and assume that all six were entered that night and probably by the same person or persons as the method of entry was similar in each case.

At all six places windows were broken. No safes were open, but at the Producers Exchange the cash drawer was broken open.

The greatest loss was at the MFA Service Station. $64.75 in cash was taken. The Producers Exchange next door had about $6.50 stolen.

No cash was taken from the Wayne Biggs Service Station but 10 inner tubes were gone.

J.H. Robertson reported $5 in dimes taken from his place of business and at the Firestone Store $36 in cash was stolen. O. M. Lane states that $7 or $8 was taken from the Sinclair station operated by W.A. Wingo.

The robberies are being investigated by Sheriff E.I. Cunningham and the highway patrol.

These may have been committed by those guilty of a wave of robberies reported in Springfield, Buffalo, Willow Springs, and other places. At Springfield the weekend robberies reported totaled nearly a dozen."

"Ernest Afton Scott...was locked in a death row cell at the Missouri penitentiary in Jefferson City Monday evening.

Scott's execution in the prison's lethal gas chamber was set for Sept. 21, but it will be delayed. The Missouri Supreme Court has permitted Scott to appeal his first-degree murder conviction.

Scott also was accused of killing the late Circuit Judge Chas. H. Jackson south of Mountain Grove the same day. He has not been tried on that charge."

August 19, 1948 "….Last Wednesday *[8/11]* James P. Hawkins filed a charge of vote fraud in the Wright county circuit court. His petition cited several instances where he claimed votes were added to the Huffman total. He made the following accusations with regard to the conduct and count of the primary election in Wright county, and demanded a recount of the ballots….

Two election judges in the Mountain Grove precincts had large sums of money bet on Huffman's nomination, Hawkins charged…. Huffman trailed Hawkins 76 votes in the official election count, and Judge Blair agreed with Bradshaw's argument that the 'winner' in an official count could not bring a contest against the loser….

Before leaving the bench and turning the case over to Judge Blair, Judge Moulder declared: 'In view of the charges made and filed, and the countercharges, I consider it my duty as a judge to order the prosecuting attorney of this county to make a thorough investigation of charges of election irregularities, fraud, intimidation, and any other violations of laws of this state. He should call to his assistance the attorney general's office and such other assistance as he may need, and prosecute each and every guilty person, whoever he may be.'

…Sixty-three residents of Wright county had been subpoenaed to testify Monday for James P. Hawkins, the official count Republican nominee for circuit judge. But none were needed after Judge Blair sustained a motion to dismiss Mr. Hawkins's petition, the motion having been made by Jean Paul Bradshaw of Lebanon, counsel for Mr. Huffman."

August 26, 1948 "Taken To Hospital After Car Strikes Culvert East of Here. S. G. Farmer of St. Louis, employed by the American Stove Co., working out of Lebanon, struck the end of a culvert on Highway 38 about 5 miles east of Marshfield Monday morning, and his car turned over about twice. He was bruised and cut.

Mrs. Rex Rainey and Sheriff E.I. Cunningham took him to the Lebanon hospital by ambulance.

He said a truck crowded him over on the road to cause his accident."

"Arrested On Charge Of Robbing Man—Russell Pogue, 22, and Martin Bruce Reed, 17, both of Springfield, were arrested at their homes there by Springfield police Wednesday afternoon, August 18, on charges that they had robbed Ralph Bailey of Seymour. The two men were turned over to Webster County Sheriff E.I. Cunningham, and committed to jail here.

Bailey, 35, gave this story: Bailey, Pogue, and Reed were drinking together at Seymour Tuesday, August 17, and Bailey said the pair forced him to enter Pogue's 1935 Ford to drive to Springfield. They had a flat tire near Rogersville, and when he refused to lend the pair money to get it repaired, Bailey said he was slugged. When he awakened, Bailey claimed, he found his wallet and his shoes and the $60 they contained, gone. A Springfield truck driver, Nolan E. Cross, picked up Bailey early Wednesday morning, August 18, and took him to Fordland to report the incident.

The preliminary for Pogue and Reed has been set for August 30, according to Prosecuting Attorney Roy Miller. Pogue has been released on $1500 bond. Reed is being held in lieu of bond."

September 2, 1948 "Serious charges continued to stack up Friday against a 22-year-old Springfield youth as Springfield police jailed him for the third time in less than a year for his alleged activities in Webster County.

Russell Pogue...was arrested at his home late Friday in connection with the theft of a valuable fur coat from the home of a Webster County couple living south of Seymour about a week ago.

Charged with burglary and larceny in connection with the theft, Pogue was released to Webster County Sheriff E. I. Cunningham Saturday morning for further action.

Cunningham knows the prisoner well. At the time of this last arrest, Pogue was free on bond on another burglary and larceny charge, as well as a robbery count, both filed in Marshfield.

The former charge is in connection with the theft of a safe from the Rogersville Farmers Exchange last November 27. The robbery complaint was filed a week ago after Ralph Bailey, 35-year-old Seymour resident, claimed that Pogue and another man had taken $85 from him in a roadside incident.

The $200 fur coat, stolen from the home of Mr. and Mrs. Charles Burks near Seymour August 17, was found that night beside a road near Rogersville, at the same spot Bailey claimed he had been robbed.

Sheriff Cunningham said he believed Pogue had left the stolen coat there 'on purpose,' but declined to elaborate further.

At present, Pogue, a Springfield painter and ex-bartender, is facing trial next month on the burglary charges connected with the Rogersville Exchange. Two other men convicted of complicity in the safe theft, Coy Miller and Ralph Gregory, are now serving penitentiary terms.

Another man, Martin Bruce Reed, 17, ...was identified by Ralph Bailey as a companion of Pogue at the time Bailey was allegedly robbed near Rogersville a week ago, and Reed already has been turned over to Webster County authorities on that count."

September 16, 1948 "Prosecuting Attorney Frank C. Collier of Wright county has requested Circuit Judge Morgan M. Moulder of Camdenton to call a grand jury to investigate alleged irregularities in the recent primary election in Wright County."

September 23, 1948 "President Harry S. Truman will make a seven-minute stop the evening of Wednesday, September 29. His special train is scheduled to arrive here at 10:25 p.m."

"The Missouri Supreme Court Wednesday of last week *[9/15]* dismissed as outside its jurisdiction a case by which M.J. Huffman of Hartville had hoped to be declared winner of the Republican primary nomination for judge of the 18th judicial circuit....In its opinion...the court said it had no jurisdiction if arguments showed the case was an election contest. Election contests, the opinion added, were the jurisdiction of the circuit court.

The action leaves Hawkins apparent winner in the contest by 76 votes as certified to Secretary of State Edgar C. Nelson as the official count in the six counties comprising the circuit....Possibly the Supreme Court's dismissal leaves open the door for Huffman to file a petition for a recount in the Webster County circuit court, an action apparently previously avoided by seeking a *writ of mandamus* in the high court to obtain a different vote certification from that county. But it is not certain that the circuit court would grant such petition, since the law provides that a petition for a recount should occur five days after the official canvass of votes, and this deadline was passed on August 11. Should it grant such petition, however, it is expected it would also entertain a petition in Wright county by Hawkins for a recount in this county as previously asked by Hawkins."

[Philip Huffman] "Of course, they had the trial and then they had the election. The circuit was Wright County, Webster County, Camden County, Dallas County, and Polk County. I think.

It's important about my dad, because in 1948 if you were elected circuit judge in that circuit, your salary was $6,000. That's what it paid per year. And that was lots of money back then but it still wasn't that much money because my dad always told me, as far as making money, that it was the best thing in the world that ever happened to him when he got beat. Though he probably didn't!

It's an interesting story about my dad and Jim Hawkins, because they became bosum buddies as the years went on. Jim was a good judge, and we had a judge who was a problem. Couldn't even get a default divorce. Almost all the Wright county divorces were filed over here *[in Webster County]*. Waived venue. They were filed, defaults were filed, in front of Jim Hawkins, over in Marshfield *for years.* As I grew up and even afterwards. After Webster and Wright split. *[from being in the same circuit]*

I don't think the people voted. I just think when the total came in, they needed a few more so they probably did some ballots and threw 'em in there and totaled it up and went on. It was counted out in rural places.

Dad started to file *[a petition for a recount]*, and then withdrew.

My folks kinda sheltered me from that election business. It was a mean, close race, that everybody since that time, most everybody, said Dad won. It happened right here. East Ozark? Was that the one that came in late? They knew enough to know what they needed, and they got them. All the township votes came in, but East Ozark held out until they saw the votes around the circuit. Then they tallied an extra hundred and Hawkins won."

[Peg Miller] "Election night was always something! The politics were something down there. East Ozark was always bigger than West and the results always came in last."

[Philip Huffman] "The only thing that I know about, you know…I remember going with my dad afterwards to a guy named Perry Reno, up in Hickory County. Dad was a Fox Hunter, so he had votes. They never expected him to be in the race, I don't think, but he had votes in Polk County and Dallas County and Camden County and Hickory County that those folks never had any idea until people started talking to folks. Because they were Fox Hunting buddies of Dad's. If he hadn't been by then, he later was President of Missouri State Fox Hunters, two or three times."

September 30, 1948 "President Here Soon!—No estimate can be made of the crowd expected to be at the Frisco station tonight, Wednesday, to see President Harry S. Truman. His special train is expected to stop here seven minutes while his engine takes on water. The President is expected to talk from the rear platform of the train....

There has been some conjecture here as to whether the train would stop at the depot or at the water tower east of here. Frisco officials have had no information as to a train stop at the station, but have been told the train would stop here for water.

However, since those in charge of Mr. Truman's trip have scheduled him for a talk here, it is believed that the special will stop at the station, while the engine goes to take water, or that the train will stop at the station and again at the water tower."

October 7, 1948 "The crowd of over 2,000 people gathered at the Frisco station Wednesday night of last week to see and hear President Harry S Truman during his scheduled seven-minute campaign stop here. The President's 17-car train was twenty minutes late, arriving at approximately 11:05....

An interesting sidelight to the Presidential visit was the arrival a few minutes before the train of state patrolmen and (presumably) secret service men, who worked with local officers in keeping the crowd back when the train pulled in. The officers also appeared to be inspecting the track and general conditions in the neighborhood before the train's arrival."

[Charley Cunningham] "Dad was directing traffic the whole time. After Truman left, Dad told me, 'He didn't even say thank you.'"

October 21, 1948 "Woman Struck By 'Hit-Run' Driver Reported Better—Mrs. Martha Butts, 78, of near Marshfield, ...was injured by a hit-and-run driver near her home Saturday night....The elderly woman...suffered a broken left leg and her 77-year-old husband, Sam Butts, received a hip injury and head lacerations when an auto sped past them on Highway 38, southeast of Marshfield, knocking the couple several feet in to a muddy driveway....A daughter, Mrs. Ethel Mullin, of Cabool, was walking to church with the elderly couple at the time of the accident but did not get hit.

Webster County Sheriff E.I. Cunningham said an extensive search had failed to net the missing motorist—'but we've got a few clues to his identity,' he said."

"Ralph H. (Baldy) Day is candidate for sheriff on the Democrat ticket, running in the General Election November 2."

November 4, 1948 "Isam Cunningham won his race for re-election as Sheriff, receiving 3,905 votes. Ralph H. Day received 2,776 votes. The race was never in doubt."

[Marie Day] "I don't know if he *[John Day]* was my boyfriend or my husband, it was one or the other, but we turned him into a Republican 'cause he went to vote for him *[Marie's Grandfather Isam]*, who needed his vote! So *John* voted for *Isam*. And I don't know if I'd got married yet or not. Anyway, because John's family and all of them was Democrats, I think...I *think*, anyway, it turned John into a Republican!"

"Harry S Truman was elected President. Forrest Smith was named Governor. All other Democrat state candidates win in the Truman landslide. *[Murray Thompson, 52 years old, was Republican candidate for Governor and a native of Webster County. Retired from the furniture business, he was elected to the State Legislature 8 years prior. He was serving his fourth two-year term. In the Legislature he was currently Speaker of the House.]* Webster County went all Republican....except for Silvey, associate judge of the county court....Rain over the state is thought to have hurt the Republicans, as the farm vote is usually Republican, but this could not account for the Democrat landslide. In north Missouri there was a five-inch rain Tuesday, while other parts of the state had rain either the night before or during the day, causing muddy roads....It was the out-state vote that was expected to go Republican, that changed over and gave the Democrats their huge lead."

"The election in Webster County passed without disturbance, according to Sheriff E.I. Cunningham. Quiet and orderly voting proceeded at all voting places.

The only disturbance Tuesday was at Seymour and it was not connected with the election, according to the Sheriff. Gene Carter was arrested that night by the state highway patrol and is charged with setting fire to the dwelling of Margaret *[Marguerite]* Carter, his former wife.

He was brought to the jail here by the patrol but was suffering injuries said to have been inflicted by two men after the fire. Sheriff

Cunningham called Dr. Blinn who took Carter to the Baptist hospital about 2 a.m. Wednesday morning."

[Willis Case] "Isam Cunningham was a People's Sheriff. He wanted everyone to have the same lawful and legal treatment. They thought he would be this strong Republican but he was a People's Sheriff. I was on the jury a time or two, and I think we can say Isam Cunningham wasn't prejudiced against any political party in particular. He wanted votes from everybody and he wanted everybody treated alike. That's what made him a good sheriff. I think he was one of the best peace officers that we've had in my time, as sheriff.

Isam was a positive fellow. They say pipe smokers are never sure about anything. There'll be two dogs fightin' out here in the middle of the road and a pipe smoker would always say, '*Apparently* them dogs are fightin'.' They're never sure about nothin'! But Isam wasn't that kind of fellow. He was *sure* about what he was doin'.

I went with Isam on some trips, when he was Sheriff. He'd say 'Come, go with me, I'm going down to Conway, there's a wreck down there.'

Then they had one down here on the corner, a man turned his cream truck over and there was an old felt hat lyin' there, his hat, and it had some odd lookin' fluid in it and Isam said, 'Looky there, there's his brains!'

He learned politics by experience. He was not diplomatic about very many things but he was a pretty sharp sheriff.

He smoked anything. If he didn't have a cigarette, he'd bum one or he'd smoke a cigar. He'd smoke anything.

He was a well-liked fellow, after you got acquainted with him. Some people hated him but he was a pretty good fellow.

He wore his hat full-bloom, no crease. Wore a brown hat that had a wide brim.

Isam would want me to go along sometimes for company, but I didn't want him to make me a deputy. Why? Because in the auction business there'd be enough people that won't hire you because you're Republican. So you don't want to create any more. That's the most hated law office in the county, the sheriff. "

[Don Letterman] "He was a Law Officer but the only thing he had that showed he was a law officer was his badge. He never wore his gun on the outside, he never wore uniforms or nothin', he always had a suit on, and he had his star on his vest. He wore his gun on his hip, underneath his pants. That's where it was at. You never seen it."

[Charley Cunningham] "He was always in a suit, not a uniform, which was typical for sheriffs of his time. He wore suspenders and carried his pistol stuck inside his pants. I don't remember that Isam ever used his pistol. When he took hold of you, you knew it. You knew he was in charge when he came up to you.

I was with him one night in Seymour. We was just over there serving warrants, divorce papers, stuff like that.

And some drunk—I forgot who it was now—was there on The Square in Seymour and he got out of his car, got up on the sidewalk, pulled out a fake gun, he was bad-mouthin' Dad.

And Dad just punched him (smack), knocked him back on the hood of the car, with his hand, hit him in the chest, knocked him back.

'Course that guy just dropped that ole gun. Just a mold, is all it was. I was right there, well, back there at the restaurant door, the sidewalk was just so wide.

He wasn't much on sports or anything, but every once in a while when I was in high school, we'd be playin' a basketball game or something, and you could look up at the door where people were comin' in the gym and there'd stand Dad and a highway patrolman. That could've been at Conway, that could've been at Rogersville, at Lebanon, just wherever they wanted to go, they went!

But Elzie Doyle, Freda Langston's mother, would answer the phone during the day. I don't know what she'd tell 'em. She knew he was gone.

My mother was involved in a lot of my dad's life. See, my dad didn't have any radios. As far as my mother went, if someone would call in for the Sheriff, she'd always know where he'd be. She could get a hold of him within thirty minutes, just using telephones. If he was in Seymour, she knew who to call...Fordland, Rogersville, anyplace, Mom always knew who to call."

[Freda Langston] "Isam—he was a character! One time he come down here to visit, one evening, with my husband. And they was visitin', and Paul said, 'Isam, why is it that you never wear a pistol?' He looked at Paul and said, 'I don't want the little children to make an image of me a havin' a big ole pistol on my hip.' And he reached down his pant leg and brought it up, brought it up, the string! And on the end of that string he had his ole pistol hangin'. Why, kid, if he'd had to draw it up to shoot somebody, he'd a never done it!

On a string! It was funny, I'll tell you!

He always wore an old black hat. He never did splurge and make a show of himself. He was a big man, what we used to call a burly man. He was a nice person and nearly everybody liked him. If he found out that anybody was doing something that was wrong, he was on to 'em right now! He didn't waste no time getting 'em. He was pretty good at gettin' those guys who was stealin' stuff.

Him and Evie lived up there on that second story, I guess until he died. She would just laugh and go on. She always wore an apron.

She wasn't afraid!

Those old guys would be out on the benches, whittlin' and spittin' tobacco juice, and Isam would worm information out of them.

I never heard of Isam Cunningham takin' a drink.

All I can remember was that he just done his job and went on, and if they liked it, all right, and if they didn't, all right. He didn't care if you were Democrat or Republican or Negro."

[Oliver Evans] "Isam was a poor man's Sheriff, I'd say. He would respect a person, no matter if you were high up or low down. You were all the same in Isam's eye. He was kinda jolly but he was a pretty serious ole boy.

Most of the problems was liquor, drunks. They'd buy it there, Burley Hutchens run a liquor store there, where Connie's [Portraits] is at now, they'd buy it there, then they'd slip off someplace and drink it, then they'd pass out on the street. Isam would bring 'em along, wake them up. One of the boys got a little mouthy with him, he split his head open with a blackjack. Most of that happened during the daytime. They'd drink during the day. Isam'd take'em upstairs, sober them up, then send them home.

Isam was overworked, had a lot of stress. Isam was the best Sheriff that Webster County had, because he cleaned the county up. The others just didn't have the guts, I'd say. Ole Isam, he wasn't scared of the Devil."

[Charley Vestal] "I didn't spend the night with Charley. It was too close to the jail! We'd been to the show, The Ritz across the street, and got about to his room and I said, 'Charley, I believe I'll just go home.' He wanted to know why, and I said 'I don't like it in here.' So I went back out and people were getting out of the second show and I caught me a ride home! I was about 14 or 15, something like that. I went to Niangua High School. That's where Charley would have gone if Isam hadn't been elected Sheriff. Charley is my second cousin."

[May Vestal] "When we went to visit them, it was like going into their home. I wasn't afraid of the jail and I never saw the jail much.   I just went into their rooms and visited them. It had their furniture in there. Eva stayed there all the time, they lived there, next to the jail.

She always did the cooking for them but she'd never say anything about it. She had cooked a lot on the farm, for her family and for people who came to visit, when they lived on the farm. Cooking wasn't any problem for her.

She was a nice person. 'Course, he was too.

I went to her house, ate dinner with them and all, but we was just a nephew of hers visiting his uncle and aunt. My husband *[Herbert Vestal]* never helped Isam, as a deputy or anything.

Isam always seemed like a businessperson to me. He was a good Sheriff."

[Edna Cunningham] "Evie was kinda quiet. She was a nice person. She didn't like to keep house much; she didn't like that. But she did cook. She was a good cook. We came once in a while, we'd come up on Saturdays or sometime. No, no, we didn't go to the courthouse and eat with them. She had all she could do to feed the prisoners and everything. We might have eaten a time or two, but we didn't always go there. We never stayed over in the courthouse. I always figured there wasn't enough room, and we didn't really have any reason *to* stay all night. We just lived down there on the farm. We could always come if anything happened.

Isam was awful good, though, I'll tell ya. One time I come to town on Saturday and he said, 'Edna, I've got somethin' for ya,' and I said, 'Okay,' and he said 'I'll put it in the pocket of your truck.' We was in the truck, and when I went out there he had butcher knives, and I guess I've still got 'em. That he got at a sale, somewhere where he'd been to a sale."

[Alberta Fraker] "Evie Cunningham—she was a heavy woman, cooked all the time, fed all those highway patrolmen and deputies and the whole courthouse. She made pie every day!

Isam made the jailbirds make garden over there where the post office is. They grew most of what they ate. I don't remember who oversaw it.

People thought Isam was kinda hard-headed, then they'd turn around and say he had a heart of gold. So, see, you don't know what characteristics they thought of him having.

We weren't too close to them. My uncle had a bad habit of drinking, my father's brother. Uncle Wilber got real intoxicated one night, Wilber Scott, and I think Uncle Isam had to fight Uncle Wilber to get him up the steps. He arrested him. And he really kind of hurt him, is what I *heard*. He used a blackjack on him, or something. Oh, it made my grandpa and my dad furious, see. And it never did quiet down. Everybody in the family didn't like that.

Uncle Isam would come down to the house and visit his half sister, my Grandmother Scott, see, and I was there because I was raised in the home. And he was good to me. I don't know anymore about it than that."

[Glen Wilson] "Eva: she was a very attentive housewife. She didn't get in any of his business, as far as I know. They had a good family. She cooked all the meals for the prisoners. I got to eat there once in a while. If you were up there at noon, it was kinda hard to get out of there. Isam wouldn't let you go. He'd given her orders to dish us up something."

December 9, 1948 "A 22-year-old Springfield Army veteran was arrested Tuesday morning *[12/7]* on a Webster County warrant charging him with defrauding an aged Seymour widow $440. 25 on an allegedly fraudulent termite extermination contract....E. J. Crawford was said to have frightened Mrs. Lida Vanderbilt into paying him for the 'extermination' by telling her the termites would 'carry her away.' The 'extermination' was said to have been unsuccessful....Sheriff E.I. Cunningham brought young Crawford here Tuesday. The warrant against him had been issued several weeks ago but Springfield officers did not pick him up until Tuesday."

December 30, 1948 "Fifty-Three Thursdays In Year 1948, MAIL Notes—For the first time in several years there were fifty-three Thursdays in the year just closing. Thus in 1948 all MAIL subscribers will receive an extra issue. While we do not expect our readers to rush in and pay us for the extra paper, we are calling attention to the extra reading they are receiving this year in this newspaper.

In earlier years it was customary for many weekly newspapers to take a vacation on such an occasion when there was an extra week in the year."

"Sanity Hearings—...Trial by court and judgment of insanity...commitment ordered ...Pearl Manar taken to Nevada Tuesday *[12/28]* by Sheriff E.I. Cunningham."

Chapter Nine
1949

January 13, 1949 "Short Session of Circuit Court Held Saturday... Judge James P. Hawkins was here Saturday for a session of court. One case was heard: State of Mo. vs. James P. Conn, charged with driving while intoxicated. Defendant arraigned and enters a plea of guilty. Judgment and sentence that the defendant serve a term of one year in jail and that he be fined a $100. Defendant paroled as to his jail sentence on condition that he abstain from use of intoxicating liquors.

Conn, who gave his address as Harrisonville, Mo., when he secured his driver's license, is said to have had several brushes with the law. Sheriff Cunningham says that Conn 'gave him the worst time' of any prisoner he had handled."

January 27, 1949 "Webster County Coon Hunters Assn. held their post season meeting in the circuit courtroom Thursday night, Jan. 20. About forty members and Sheriff Cunningham were present."

"On Saturday night, a traffic accident resulted in injuries to four persons and considerable damage to five cars, and possibly minor damage to others. According to Sheriff E.I. Cunningham, an eastbound Buick, when attempting to pass a car, collided with a Ford coupe west bound. As a result of the accident, 2_ miles west of Marshfield on Highway 66, other cars began to jam up to the west and three cars were considerably damaged....Several other cars on behind them also bumped before the traffic line could be stopped, but the latter caused but minor damage and all drove on when traffic was open."

February 17, 1949 "Joe E. Graves, Route 3, Rogersville, was arrested by Sheriff E.I. Cunningham last week at the request of Greene county officers. According to proceedings of the Magistrate Court in Springfield, Graves, 46, was committed to jail there in default of $2,000 bond pending preliminary hearing February 21 in Magistrate Gideon's court, on charges of obtaining money under false pretenses. Allegedly mortgaged cattle he pretended to own, obtaining $343.53."

March 3, 1949 "Ernest Groves of Norwood broke into the Rogersville Motor Co. office Monday night *[2/28]* and is said to have broken show cases and messed things up generally. Just what the idea was is not known. At any rate, he was taken in charge by Mayor Vircil Burks, City Marshal Carl Smith, and Ralph Smith of Rogersville.

Sheriff E.I. Cunningham was called about midnight and when he arrived at Rogersville they had Davis (?) in custody. He was brought to the jail here."

[There seems to be an error—about the person in custody. Who is Davis? What happened to Groves?]

March 10, 1949 "D. Wayne Rowland, Willow Springs...purchased *The Seymour Citizen* a few weeks ago....Mr. and Mrs. Maurice Darnell, who have been owners of the Seymour paper, have not announced their future plans."

March 17, 1949 "A thief or thieves broke into the Wee Dug Inn at the north side of Marshfield Saturday night *[3/12]*, according to Sheriff E. I. Cunningham. Some candy and cigarettes were taken. The lock was broken on a gas pump and some gasoline was taken. Entrance to the building was gained by prying open a door."

[an ad] "This is to announce my candidacy for City Marshal, election Tuesday April 5. I will appreciate your vote. PORTER RADER"

"Assailants In Cruel And Brutal Robbery Attack. An elderly spinster living near Strafford is slowly recovering from a terrifying and brutal robbery which occurred at her small farm home Tuesday night, March 8.

The victim, Miss Ruth Caldwell, about 85, who lives two and a half miles southeast of Strafford near the Webster County line, was severely bruised by assailants who took her entire savings of $100 after ransacking her two-room house....She was alone in the house when someone knocked at the door. She asked them what they wanted, and two or three men—she isn't sure how many, she was scared so badly—ripped down the door and stepped into the house, a neighbor Mrs. Tom Burwell reported.

One of the men quickly tossed a piece of cloth over the woman's head—evidently to prevent being identified—while the other one or two men began ransacking chests of drawers and closets in a search for money.

Several times, Miss Caldwell told her neighbor *[Mrs. Burwell]*, the man twisted her arms in futile attempts to force her to reveal the hiding place of her money.

'Her arms were blue with bruises,' Mrs. Burwell said, 'but 'Aunt Ruth' said she'd die before she'd tell them anything. They finally had to almost turn the house upside down to find the $100—that's all she had in the world.'

After the men left, Miss Caldwell sat in the broken doorway of her home—and was found there next morning by Mrs. Burwell's son, Louie, who lives on his mother's farm.

'It was raining on the poor old soul—and she was just scared to death,' Mrs. Burwell said. 'The men had threatened to come back and hang her and burn her house and barn if she told anyone about the robbery.'

Mrs. Burwell said she believed the robbers were men who knew the elderly woman lived alone—and knew she recently had sold one of her cows for $100.

'She lost several chickens several times in the past. Every time she tried to start a flock, someone stole them,' Mrs. Burwell said.

Miss Caldwell, who was born on the same farm and has lived there her entire life, recently was forced to quit milking cows because of her infirmities.

'She pointed to the family cemetery on the farm after telling me about the robbery, and said she was afraid she'd be there before long,' Mrs. Burwell said.

'She said, "I'm afraid this is just about going to get me." ' "

"The landscaping and beautifying of the courthouse lawn is assured by the raising of sufficient money the past week to pay the initial cost. This project sponsored by the Marshfield Lions Club, was recently placed before the county court for approval....John Hosmer and O.L Carter, two of the prime movers and leading members of the Bore's Nest, wish to make it plain that any organization, group, or individual may still donate to this fund. Those desiring to do so may contact Rex Rainey, drive chairman for the Bore's Nest.

The shrubbery will be placed around the large fine courthouse building and at needed places elsewhere on the lawn."

[Jack Watters] "The Lions Club was *the* chamber of commerce. There was no Rotary Club or no Optimist Club or no Chamber of Commerce. I don't think I got into the Lions Club until 1960 or so, after I'd run out of time in the Junior Chamber of Commerce, the Jaycees as we called it. Others may have been members of both, some were, but that didn't seem to work very well. The Lions Club had the elder statesmen, you might say, of the town. They were the people who made it happen, they made things move. "

[Doc Blinn] "Lions Club got Webster County out of the mud. Literally. We hadn't had very good roads. The Lions Club put pressure on the county court. We got a Roads Committee that was very very active. C.R. *[Macdonnell]* was chairman of that committee for years.

Lions Club just was active in a lot of things like that. There was a number of years there, anything that was good for the community, the Lions Club was backing it. It was the only thing. There was no civic club or anything of that kind. We'd take over! Usually they assigned the committees we were on.

I was here about five years before I was invited to join, you had to be invited to join. They were kind of apologetic about it. One of them finally told me, he said, 'We were just afraid if we invited you, that C.R. would black ball you.' So finally somebody had the nerve to go and ask him. 'What would you think about asking Doc Blinn to join Lions Club?' He said, "Fine! I think he's a good man, I just think he's a hell of a poor doctor!" C.R. eventually got to where he talked to me. I got a kick out of some of the things he said. He told somebody, 'DO is like going hunting with a fishing license.'

'Course, that was true of the medics back then, the MDs. They just didn't accept DOs for a long time. Now they're on the staff of many hospitals.

We had a few in Lions Club who were out a little way into the county, but it was mostly businessmen. 'Course, there were no women."

March 24, 1949 "A reward of at least $400 has been pledged by residents in and near Strafford for information leading to the arrest and conviction of the attackers March 8 of 'Aunt Ruth' Caldwell, about 85, from whom $100 was stolen that night. Miss Caldwell lives on a farm 2 1/2 miles southeast of Strafford.

Dan Hokanson, operator of a general store at Strafford, said feeling about the manhandling and robbery of the beloved woman is so high in the neighborhood that he believes pledges to increase the reward can be attained....

Meanwhile, the congregation of Woodland Heights Presbyterian Church in Springfield has started a fund toward replacing the $100 stolen from Miss Caldwell. She had obtained the money through the sale of a cow."

"Rollive Day of this city was severely injured Saturday night. He was found between the Rathbun Store and Walter's Style Shop severely beaten and unconscious. According to Sheriff Cunningham, Loren Bledsoe of Niangua, who recently was discharged from the army, is held under two charges: 'assault upon Rollive Day with a deadly weapon with intent to kill or murder,' and with 'assault to rob Rollive Day of the sum of $2.40.'

It is said that Day had been stuck with a screwdriver in the face and in the mouth and throat.

Sheriff Cunningham says that two others may have been connected with this altercation which took place about 12:30 or 1:00 Saturday night *[3/19]*.

Day has been under treatment by a local physician."

"Matters Before the Magistrate Court—March 21   State of Mo. vs. Loren Bledsoe, felonious assault. Bond fixed at $1,500....robbery. Bond fixed at $1500. Hearing set for April 1."

"Sheriff E.I. Cunningham arrested Kenneth Johns of Seymour Saturday night *[3/19]* at the request of the sheriff of Christian County. The Christian county sheriff came here Sunday and took Johns to Ozark. It is reported that Johns is charged with issuing 'check with no funds.'"

"Sheriff E.I. Cunningham reports the arrest of Leford Willis of the Northview Hill vicinity on a charge of assault on his wife, Lottie Willis, one day last week. She said he knocked a tooth out and gave her a black eye."

[Freda Langston]   "It always made me feel so sad and kinda sick in my stomach to see a woman come in all beat up. They'd have to make a record of it."

"The burglary of the MFA Farmers Exchange at Seymour February 15 was believed cleared up with the arrest last Thursday night *[3/17]* of two Seymour teen-agers by Sheriff E.I. Cunningham and Jason Kennemer, Seymour City Marshal.

The two youths—Fred Cook, 17, and Wayne Matney, 16— were arraigned before Magistrate Cline C. Herren Saturday, charged with robbery, and their preliminary hearings were set for March 30.

Bond was set at $2,000 which neither youth was able to make and both are held in the county jail here.

The arrests followed considerable sleuthing on the part of the Sheriff. Loot from the store was mostly clothing and cigarettes. Sheriff Cunningham said the youths had disposed of part of the clothing to a man living near Seymour.

'The man, as far as we have been able to determine, bought it in good faith,' he said, and he 'willingly turned it over to us as soon as he found out how the boys had acquired it.'

One of the youths is said to have confessed."

[Oliver Evans] " Isam almost *always* got a confession!"

"Sheriff E.I. Cunningham was called south of Diggins Thursday night of last week *[3/17]* to take in charge Delbert Fye, about 32, who is charged with 'wandering from place to place with no visible means of support.' It is said he had built a large fire in an empty garage building on the Grandma Hale place and was in danger of burning himself when he was found and taken to his father's place.

He was brought to the jail here."

"State of Mo. vs. Delbert Fye, vagrancy. Plea of guilty. Defendant sentenced to one year in jail."

March 31, 1949 "Frank Thomas Hicks, 25, was arrested at Northview last Friday *[3/25]*, and placed in jail here by Sheriff E.I. Cunningham. Hicks, an employee of Harry Bridwell, is charged with the theft of a cow from Bridwell. The cow is said to have been taken to Springfield and sold to the MFA Stockyards for $110."

[an ad] "This is to announce my candidacy for City Marshal, election Tuesday April 5. I will appreciate your vote. HOMER ALEXANDER"

April 7, 1949 "Matters Before the Magistrate Court—April 4. State of Mo. vs. Leford Willis, common assault, dismissed at cost of defendant."

"Robinson Freed—Last of the Duke Petty bank robbery money cases were disposed of today as James Robinson of Marshfield was released from a complaint that he accepted from Petty money stolen in

1947 from the Bank of Seymour....U.S. Attorney Sam Wear told a reporter that there was 'no case against Robinson' without the testimony of Petty, currently serving a 15-year sentence at Leavenworth. And he said that Petty 'has weakened' in his story as to Robinson.

Wear also said that the prosecution didn't want to bring Petty here to testify because it would be 'dangerous.'

John C. Pope, Robinson's attorney, described the case to a reporter as one that had been founded 'on pure suspicion.'

Judge Reeves *[Federal Judge Albert Reeves]*, at attorney William Sanford's request, ordered returned to the bank $360.25 which has been held as evidence by Sheriff Cunningham at Marshfield.

It was pointed out that the money had not been taken from Robinson but from James Casteel, already under sentence. Attorney Pope said, there was 'no objection' to its being returned to the bank."

"Not a great interest was shown in the city election Tuesday *[4/5]* as less than four hundred out of about a thousand voters cast their ballots....Porter Rader was an easy winner for City Marshal, receiving 225 votes to Commodore Smith 107, his nearest competitor. Homer Alexander, the third candidate received 52 votes....In the race for Police Judge, John Hosmer easily defeated Harold Cheek by a vote of 275 to 103."

April 21, 1949 "Man's Body Found On Tracks Near Here—An ex-serviceman identified as Eli Edmund Posey, about 35, of Pittsburg, Pa., was found lying alongside the Frisco tracks one and a half miles east of Marshfield Saturday afternoon. He had apparently fallen from a train or tried to catch a train just north of the crossing east of this city. He was taken by Rainey ambulance to the Niangua hospital.

The injured man was transferred from the Niangua hospital to the O'Reilly Veterans hospital Sunday and received treatment for a basal skull fracture and multiple lacerations.

He had been hospitalized at O'Reilly for two days last week for treatment of a skin rash and was released about 1 p.m. Saturday *[4/16]*. Before going to O'Reilly Thursday, Posey had applied for money from the Red Cross to help him hitchhike to St. Louis to contact a skin specialist, officials said.

Authorities believe Posey was hitchhiking cross-country from a Veterans hospital at Van Nuys, Calif., to his home when the accident occurred. His wife has been notified and is expected to arrive soon.

The injured man was found by Margaret Garten, Kathreen Garten, and Donna McDonald. Other young people arriving soon were Bonnie Henderson, Bobby Henderson, Howard Henderson, Norma Henderson, James Evans, and Freeman Nease. They called Sheriff E.I. Cunningham, who went to the scene of the accident."

[It seems likely that Isam insisted the newspaper print the names of all the teenagers who showed up, whether or not they were initially involved. People said he had a way with teenagers!]

May 12, 1949 "By custom this next Sunday, May 15, is Straw Hat Day, when all the men who want to be in style throw away their felt hats and start wearing their straws. In some cities the mayors have issued an official proclamation designating May 15 as Straw Hat Day."

June 2, 1949 "A Cessna 170 four-seater airplane crashed in a field about ten miles east of Marshfield on the Lane farm near High Prairie Saturday afternoon *[5/28]*, but none of the six persons in the plane were injured, according to Sheriff E.I. Cunningham....

The Paul A. Hart family of Lincoln, Nebr., had left Lincoln on the 389-mile trip at 9:40 Saturday morning and the flight had gone smoothly until Mr. Hart became uncertain as to where he was and decided to land....He decided to land in this county to make sure he was going in the right direction. He 'hit a down-draft,' according to his daughter, as he was coming down. This caused him to brush a wire fence, upsetting the plane. The landing gear was torn up.

Charles Hamilton picked up the Nebraska family in a car and brought them to Marshfield where they contacted a brother at Mountain View by telephone and waited his arrival here to get them."

June 9, 1949 "Warren Johnson has joined the staff of Sho-Me Power Corporation as public relations and power use department head effective last week, according to S.E. Roberts, general manager. Mr. Johnson has been associated with his father-in-law, Robert Florance, in the Marshfield Oil Co."

[Warren Johnson] "I was gone two years, three months, and five days during World War II. I didn't count the hours. I think I came back in

'46. The war was over. I came back to my wife and son. I had a filling station, the building right next to the *[Ritz]* theater. The day after I came back, I went to work at the filling station, for several years. Gene Fraker bought that filling station. It's in that picture. 'Saturday Night at the Ritz,' by Jerry Rice. I took that picture and he painted it. *[Jerry Rice of Marshfield has painted scenes mostly of the 1950s, and nearly all of these depict scenes along Route 66.]*

I worked at the station, same as before the war. Lot of people came in there that had gone to other stations before the war. My father-in-law owned the station and I was an operator.

S.E. Roberts came over one day—he was general manager of Sho-Me Power—and he said, 'I want you to go to work for me.' I said, 'I don't want to go to work for you. I've got a business of my own here.'

He said, 'You're tired of this.' (And I was.)

I said, 'What do you need me for?'

He said, 'I want you to put out the bullshit just like you do with Lions Club, around among the towns we operate in.'

Exactly what he said!

I said, 'I don't know what you mean by that.'

He said, 'You don't? You know just exactly. You just go into town and tell them what a good job Sho-Me does. All the rest of it, you take it from there, 'cause you know more about it than I do.'

I didn't know what he was talkin' about!

He said, 'I'll give you $150 a month. In six months if I like you, I'll give you another $50 a month. In six months again if I still like you, I'll give you another $50.'

So I said, 'I'll try it.' And I loved the job.

All I had done in Lions Club was get up and give little talks about something we'd done.

We *[Sho-Me Power]* had about 50 different towns we were serving in and I was going to these different towns, to Lions Clubs and other clubs. If we were going to change anything or the town had something they wanted, more streetlights or something, they'd talk with me. I'm the one they'd ask, to see who they needed to ask. That job was just suited to me. Part of it was to get the right people to the right people. S.E. Roberts had to make the commitment. Then Charlie Boulson replaced Mr. Roberts as general manager, when S.E. retired *[in December 1953]*."

"Sheriff E.I. Cunningham went to Springfield to bring here a farmer, listed on jail records as Irwin S. White of Route 2, Springfield, wanted here on a charge of issuing a check to Blackwell Sales Co. without funds in the bank to cover it. He pleaded guilty in Magistrate court here and was fined $1, with him making good on the check.

When he was released here he was taken in custody by Greene county officers on a charge said to have been connected with giving a mortgage on property that was already mortgaged."

June 16, 1949 "The following is taken from the May 10, 1949 Newsletter sent out by the Democrat State Committee, Jefferson City:

MARSHFIELD—John Hosmer is a staunch Democrat and an attorney in Republican Webster County. To make matters worse, Webster County is in the Seventh Congressional District which is represented by the lone Missouri Republican Congressman, Dewey Short. But Hosmer has a system to prove to all of his neighbors his allegiance to the Democratic Party. He has taught his small daughter that the name Dewey Short is a naughty word and when she hears Short's name mentioned, she naturally assumes that people are cursing."

"Two youths from Evansville, Ind., were arrested at Lebanon Tuesday morning *[6/14]* by the State Highway Patrol charged with stealing a car here the night before. According to Sheriff E.I. Cunningham, the boys were Donald Massie and Donald Dill. Massie is said to have been out under parole from Evansville on a charge of stealing a car.

According to the Webster County Sheriff the car was taken about 7 o'clock Monday evening from the McFadin & Lilley Motor Co. at the west side of Marshfield. It was found ditched about a mile and a half north of Conway when the patrol got after them. They hid in a barn but were found Tuesday morning. Sheriff Cunningham went to Lebanon and brought them here."

"Jefferson County voters have approved school district reorganization—the first county in the state to take advantage of a 1948 law."

June 30, 1949 "City employees have been busy this week putting up fences to protect the new shrubbery on the courthouse lawn from being trampled on the Fourth. It is hoped that Marshfield visitors will use care of the shrubbery Monday *[7/4]* in order that the lawn may retain its beauty."

[Don Letterman] "And I was drivin' one night there in Marshfield, and back then, four times is all you could drive around The Square without goin' off one block, then comin' back on. And *[after he]* went *five* times around it, *[Grandpa Isam]* stepped out from behind a car and he stopped me, and he said, 'Now you *know* better'n that!'

You could just about see him any time you wanted to after dark. He'd step out from behind a building or somethin'. He was around there."

July 7, 1949 "Alonzo Freeman Turner, familiarly known as Lon or Dangit, died Sunday morning about 4 o'clock after a ten-day serious illness. He was nearly 89 years old....Dangit was widely known as a fisherman, and his old fishing buddy, Wilbur Wise of Springfield, 93, attended the funeral services Monday. Dangit took pride each year in securing fishing license No. 1 here. Mr. Turner had been a member of the Masonic Lodge for more than 50 years.

Since the death of Mrs. Turner *[in 1944]* Mr. Turner continued to reside in the old Turner place, and Mr. and Mrs. Ben Case, who resided there, had taken care of him."

"Circuit Court Notes: State of Mo. vs. Loren Bledsoe, robbery. Defendant enters plea of not guilty. Jury selected. Jury brings in verdict of guilty after 34 minutes' deliberation. Punishment assessed at five years in the state penitentiary. Sheriff allowed one extra guard."

July 14, 1949 "Thomas J. Adams, 22, giving his home address as Twin Rocks, Pa., was arrested at Bland Saturday by the State Highway Patrol. It is claimed that he and a man by the name of Jack Steward, both connected with the carnival that was at Seymour last Thursday, Friday and Saturday, took the proceeds of one stand at the carnival and some articles and left on Thursday night or early Friday morning.

The men are said to have taken $17 in money, 4 microscopes, a hunting knife, and a pocket watch. Sheriff Cunningham has Adams in jail here, but Stewart *[Steward?]* has not been apprehended."

"Arrest Reported Soon After Release From State Penitentiary—Ralph W. Burks of Fordland, who is reported to have been released from the penitentiary May 30, was arrested Saturday night *[7/9]* by Springfield officers and Sheriff Cunningham went there for him Sunday morning. Burks is charged with forging two checks for $30 and passing them at Fordland."

168

[Burks attempted jailbreak from Isam back on April 26, 1945, soon after Isam entered office. They meet again.]

"Stolen Truck Is Found—A truck, property of the construction company building the REA lines here, was stolen early Wednesday morning *[7/13]* from in front of the John D. Johnson residence. It was found about 9:00 o'clock Wednesday morning by Sheriff E.I. Cunningham in an alley near the Leo Blades home. The guilty party has not been apprehended."

[In the 1930s and 40s, big electric companies found it wasn't economically feasible to their bottom line to expand into sparsely populated areas. This lack of investment left many rural communities across the country without electricity. With no one else to turn to, these communities banded together to form electric cooperatives in order to bring electricity to their farms, homes, and businesses. Around 1946, the Rural Electrification Act—REA—created Webster Electric Cooperative which by 1951 had almost completely electrified Webster County farms. Also, Sho-Me Power began providing electricity to a 25-county area of Missouri which includes 9 other distribution cooperatives, in addition to Webster Electric Cooperative.]

[Peg Miller] "On the first night in Marshfield, we stayed in the old hotel. I told *[Roy]* Miller I might be heading home if we couldn't find something better than this! We'd lived in New Jersey, right outside New York. It was definitely a culture shock. I couldn't believe when I got here, for instance, that there were no lights between towns! The REA came in during the late 40's and early 50's. The local Republicans thought it was terrible, this socialist plot…absolutely crazy…it was freeing the women, for heaven's sake! Which it did! They were hauling water. Not to mention roasting! I can remember somebody out on High Prairie whose light bill was just awful, when it came in the first couple of times in the summer. The REA went out to investigate and found that when everyone else had left, she was in the habit of opening the refrigerator door and sitting in front of it—to cool off! Ha!"

"Charley W. Burks, Jr., and Lloyd J. Privett, both of Route 2, Seymour, were arrested Monday *[7/11]* by Sheriff Prock of Ava and Sheriff E.I. Cunningham of this county. The men are charged with stealing two calves from Fred Miller Saturday night, and are in jail here.

Sheriff Cunningham says the calves were taken to the Burks place first and then taken to the Privett place Sunday where they were found by the officers Monday. While the theft was in Webster County, the men lived over the line in Douglas County."

July 21, 1949 "Strafford Recluse Found In Ditch Near Her Home—An elderly spinster known to her neighbors near Strafford as 'Aunt Ruth' Caldwell remains semi-conscious and in a fair condition at Burge Hospital, where she was taken early Monday afternoon after being found in a water-filled ditch on her farm.

The elderly woman, believed to be in her 80's or 90's, rallied enough to tell neighbors she had fallen Saturday noon while walking to her mailbox.

Marks near the ditch indicated she had vainly attempted to crawl to her small clapboard cabin, two miles southeast of Strafford.

Miss Caldwell has lived in the cabin all her life and has been alone since the death of her mother 25 years ago.

Early last March Miss Caldwell was brutally beaten and robbed by three still-unidentified men.

Members of Woodland Heights Presbyterian Church in Springfield later initiated a fund of $100 which was presented to 'Aunt Ruth' to replace money taken by the intruders.

The money, obtained from the sale of a cow, was her entire savings."

July 28, 1949 "Funeral Services Held Near Strafford for 'Aunt Ruth' Caldwell—Funeral services for 'Aunt Ruth' Caldwell, 86-year-old last surviving member of a pioneer Ozarks family, who died Friday at Burge Hospital in Springfield, were held at her home near Strafford at 2 p.m. Sunday....

A week ago last Monday 'Aunt Ruth' was found lying in a water-filled ditch near the clapboard cabin in which she had lived alone for 25 years. She rallied from her state of exposure long enough to tell friends she had fallen while walking to the mail box two days earlier. A physician said she apparently had suffered a stroke.

'Aunt Ruth' was the last surviving member of a pioneer Ozarks family and still used primitive methods of cooking over a fireplace. She wore ankle-length dresses with high necks and long sleeves, like those worn during the Civil War period, and still carried spring water a half mile to her cabin.

Her family came to this vicinity from Tennessee in the 1830's and settled at the present home site on Route 1, 2 miles southeast of Strafford. Her father died shortly before the Civil War, and her mother passed away 25 years ago. Every Saturday, 'Aunt Ruth' walked two miles to Strafford to sell cream and butter from her small herd of cows.

After robbers twisted her arms and stole $100 from her last March, members of the Woodland Heights Church in Springfield reimbursed her to restore her faith in the Ozarks.

Recently, she had requested that she be buried in clothing similar to her mother's, the old-fashioned type she had worn all her life.

The only remaining close survivors are three second cousins, Mrs. J. D. Foster of Route 2; Mrs. S.E. Thomas of Milk Rover, Canada, and Mrs. Ed Deeds of Sparta."

"Oliver Evans was elected Commander of Webster County Post 142 of the American Legion...."

August 4, 1949 "According to Oscar 'Bud' Kasten, Conservation Agent for this District, 11,700 multiflora rose seedlings supplied by the Missouri Conservation Commission were planted in Webster County this spring. Some 7,000 plants were purchased and planted by individual farmers and landowners. An additional 4,700 were sent out by commission personnel as demonstration plantings....

Landowners desiring the low cost living fence, should make application early to be assured of delivery, and are urged to prepare their ground this fall. Those who now have multiflora rose plantings are urged to cultivate for the first two years to insure successful fence."

[Writes Missouri author Sue Hubbell in her A Country Year, *published in 1983: "Years ago the multiflora rose, an exotic, was touted as a Miracle Plant. Its fruits are eaten by birds and its habit of thick, rapid, tangled and thorny growth could turn it into what the nursery catalogs used to call a Living Fence, one that even cattle will not go through.*

In the early 1940s the Missouri Conservation Department grew the plants and encouraged landowners to set them out. Birds did indeed like the fruit, but the seeds passed through their digestive systems fully fertile, and so birds planted new multiflora roses with their droppings. Instead of staying in tidy fencerows, the multiflora rose spread rapidly over pastures where it was not wanted. It could not be dug out because the broken roots, hydralike, sprouted new plants.

*Recently strong herbicides have been developed that kill
the rose, but they may contaminate water supplies and ponds. Brush-
hogging multiflora roses at least keeps them from spreading…They
[were] put on the official state noxious weed list, and most farmers
were pouring on the herbicides and were paid for doing so by the
Conservation Department, which was trying to make up for its past
sins."]*

"Webster County people are keeping their 'fingers crossed' as
no new cases of polio have been reported in the County up to
Wednesday morning *[8/3]*. Health officials are urging cleanliness and
spraying by farmers and town people as a preventative to the dread
disease.

Over the nation there have been more than 8,000 cases reported.
California has the most with 794. Missouri had 302 cases reported up
to Tuesday. Oklahoma had 498, Arkansas 492, Illinois 376….

Volunteer workers under five captains appointed by Mayor
Frank Stockton sprayed all sections of Marshfield Friday afternoon
[7/29] with DDT as a prevention to polio here. An effort was made to
spray all feeding and breeding places of flies and mosquitoes….Every
citizen should do everything possible to prevent polio striking here."

[The agricultural use of DDT was prohibited from use in 1973.]

August 25, 1949 from Magistrate Court notes: State of Missouri vs.____
A sample of crimes: " disturbing peace of a family;
selling mortgaged property;
driving while intoxicated;
grand larceny;
exhibiting deadly weapon while intoxicated."

"The service station operated by Al Hanna on Highway 60 east
of Fordland, was broken into August 1, and the cash register and some
merchandise were taken. The total loss was estimated by Mr. Hanna at
about $200. Entrance was gained by breaking a window, and the thief
or thieves left by way of the door."

September 1, 1949 "Burchfield Appliances stores has been the scene
during the past week of the first television broadcasts received in
Marshfield. The General Electric set installed by the owner, Calvin
Burchfield, is able, with the aid of a high antenna, to bring in programs
from St. Louis over station KSD-TV."

"Three Webster County men were arrested Monday evening *[8/29]* by federal officers on charges of possession of mash in process of making liquor. Troy S. Cleland of Springfield and Mr. Baker of Joplin, Federal Investigators, Alcohol Tax Unit Department of Revenue, accompanied by Sheriff E.I. Cunningham, arrested Arthur Mott and sons, Pearl Mott and Sye Mott, near their home about three miles from Fordland.

The officers had previously located a barrel of mash which was carefully hidden in the brush and left to 'season.' They lay all Monday afternoon near the barrel of mash and were waiting when the three men came to it. They had apparently come to take it somewhere in a car. The place is rented by the Motts from John Relaford.

The men were taken to Springfield and lodged in jail. Tuesday morning they were arraigned and their bond set at $3,500 each. Their preliminary hearing has been set for Sept.9.

Sye Mott is said to be under bond on other charges including a charge of rape, in the Webster County Circuit Court."

September 22, 1949 "Merchants and businessmen held a meeting Monday evening *[9/19]* at the courthouse to discuss means of securing the services of a full-time night watchman. In the past the duties have been combined in the City Marshal and he has not been able to work all night and day-times too.

Mayor Stockton, who presided at the meeting, read the city financial statement and showed that the city could not pay more out on a night watchman than at present.

It was decided that Marshfield should have a good, full-time night watchman and that it would need to be financed by contributions of $2 per month from each merchant. A committee was appointed consisting of John Brooks, Ralph Gander, and Dave Roper to contact the business firms and see what a good man with a car can be hired for.

Another meeting will be held this Wednesday night when all business people are asked to attend and make final decisions."

September 29, 1949 "As a result of a merchants' mass meeting held Wednesday night *[9/21]*, the city board has employed Oliver Evans as a full-time night watchman. The appointment was made at a meeting of the board Tuesday night *[9/27]*.

The night watchman's hours will be from 9 p.m. until daylight. The city marshal is expected to be on duty during the daytime. Mr. Evans will be a city officer with power to arrest.

At the merchants' mass meeting last week it was decided that the city should have a full-time night watchman with a car in order that he might patrol the streets of the city. It was also decided that he should be appointed by the city board rather than by a merchants' committee in order that he might be a city officer.

The city, not being able to finance the additional man, the merchants voted that the extra money should be raised by an increase in the city merchants' licenses $9.00 each six months. This is considered by most as cheap insurance against burglaries and fire losses.

Mr. Evans, the new night watchman, is an ex-service man, and is now Commander of the local American Legion Post."

[Oliver Evans] "I got out of the service in 1946. They wanted a Night Watchman and Isam brought my name up. The City Men, the Mayor, they considered me. I took the job. Yes, I got paid but they didn't overload me or nothin'.

It was a full-time job. I carried a Deputy Card up until after Isam died. I didn't get no money for that, but I was deputized and had the power to arrest people. The Deputy Card was signed by the Sheriff, Isam signed it.

I carried a gun and a blackjack. I got paid a salary, I think it was about $175 a month, close to that, but I wasn't getting rich or anything.

I went on at 9 p.m. and got off at daylight. I worked every night. I was the only one for Marshfield.

Ole Isam, when he signed my card, he said, 'You got a gun?' I said, Yeah, I got one. He said, 'I've got something else I'm going to give you.' He called it The Persuader. He give me the blackjack. He said 'That'll take care of you.' It did. I never had to use it, but I had it. Isam said, 'Now that'll protect you.'

I've seen Isam use his. He wasn't too gentle with it either.

Isam told me—I was workin' full time every night, I was married, just had come back from the service—he said 'Now Son, if you need off any night, you let me know, I'll carry on.' But I didn't make him do it. Oh, once in a while I took off.

Anytime I needed help—I guess Isam slept with a window open—anytime I'd holler, Isam was down there, he'd have his necktie on.

Commodore Smith took over after I left. Porter Rader was before me.

I was the Marshfield Police Department *[before it was officially started]*. Isam took care of things during the daytime. I took the night. The first thing of an evening, I'd have to rattle the doors of every business in town, see that they were locked.

I never did have any problems. I'd let my presence be known.

That's another thing about poor ole Isam. On the west side of the street there, where Connie's Photo store is now, they used to have a liquor store in there, just sold it in bottles. Women wasn't hardly allowed to walk up and down it. Ole Isam cleaned that up. Isam would walk down there and they'd scatter like waves. Drunks!

That ole boy wasn't scared of the Devil!

Isam was pretty rough on those drunks. I never had to arrest anybody for drunkenness. Mostly for traffic around The Square. Back then we didn't even have a curfew for teenagers, but we didn't have no trouble with them. They just had a racetrack around The Square, especially on Friday and Saturday night. I'd just stop them and tell them I'd have to take them upstairs *[to the jail]* if they didn't get on home, and that would take care of it.

The jail was not in my jurisdiction.

Telephone Company used to be there where Mary's Variety Store is now. They had a night operator, stayed there all night.

You'd go in the door and before you get into the office they had a phone. If I needed anybody, I could go up there and call from there and the operator would get 'em. If I found a door open someplace and needed to contact the owner, I'd go in there and she'd call 'em and get them to come in.

She didn't care what hour of the night, if I needed somebody, she'd answer. Her and my wife was good friends, before we was married, and my wife would go up there and spend the night with her. Jo Alexander was her name, married to Cecil Alexander. She was Coleen Meyers' mother.

My way to communicate with Isam? My voice. I'd run up to the window there, holler, and ole Isam was down. The Square was more or less my headquarters but every hour, hour and a half, I'd make a round around the buildings, rattle the doors. I was just in the city limits. I just yelled if I needed Isam. Didn't have no walkie-talkie.

The Highway Patrol was in and out. They didn't have a patrolman in Marshfield at the time. They was based in Springfield.

See, Isam give me a key to get in over there but I could run to the window and get him quicker than I could run in up the stairs through the door.

I wasn't responsible for the prisoners, just seein' that everything was under control. I was the Night Marshal. My badge said City Marshal.

I didn't know much of what went on during the day with Isam. I'd just go down there at 9 o'clock *[p.m.]*, check in, let him know I was on duty. The rest of the time I was, more or less, on my own.

I never had to arrest any of 'em. I'd talk to 'em, straighten things out. As Isam said, 'Give 'em a little leeway,' but he give me that blackjack and said, ' Now that's The Persuader.' I never used the blackjack but I let them know I had it. My gun? I had one but I don't even know if it shot or not. I had it loaded.

I never was scared. Just walkin' the streets, nobody ever attacked me, not even dogs. I always figured if someone was up that time of the night, they was up to no good.

If he was goin' over on the southside or something, he'd let me know he was goin' to be gone. He was over there quite a bit. Seymour and Diggins, they was across the river. *[the James River]*"

"Earnest Afton Scott, 49-year-old Ozarks farmer, must die in Missouri's lethal gas chamber November 4, for killing his estranged wife.

The Missouri Supreme Court set the date Monday *[9/26]*, upholding a death sentence by the Wright county circuit court.

Scott shot his wife in Mountain Grove March 29, 1948. The state charged he attacked her after killing Circuit Judge Charles H. Jackson. He has not been tried in the Jackson case."

"Thieves broke into a window of the McFadin and Lilley Motor Co. last Wednesday night and took 80 cents in change. They attempted to take a car by wiring around the ignition. They backed the car down an incline against an outside roof support and abandoned it there, evidently unable to get it started.

A small quantity of cigarettes, tobacco, and candy was taken from the Wee Dug Inn just north of Marshfield the same night. Sheriff Cunningham says that an investigation is being continued."

"Sheriff E.I. Cunningham was in Kansas City Monday *[9/26]* to appear before a Federal Grand Jury which was investigating liquor charges against the Motts, three Webster County men charged with operating an illegal still."

October 6, 1949 "Ervin 'Sonny' Graves was arrested Saturday, charged with arson and felonious assault on his wife, Marie. He is also facing charges on drunken driving and writing a check with no funds.

According to Sheriff E.I. Cunningham, Graves had an argument with his wife Friday afternoon and 'chased' her and the children from the dwelling. The house, which is located north of Marshfield, was destroyed by fire a short time later. The place is owned by J. D. Pitman of Borger, Texas.

The drunken driving charge resulted from his driving Friday afternoon and he is said to have written the check that night, according to Roy C. Miller, prosecuting attorney."

[Peg Miller] "We were Republicans. Isam and Roy just hit it off fine. They were soul mates.

Isam was kind of puritanical in many ways and he didn't approve of John [*Hosmer*].

I don't remember what Evie did at all. I'd see her, when I was there, and if she wasn't cooking or cleaning up, she'd be sitting around fanning and looking exhausted.

Isam was a great big guy, 6'2" maybe. He had a standard uniform. He had some kind of chino pants that he wore with galluses. You wouldn't even call them suspenders, they were galluses. And his badge was on one of them, I assume over his heart. And he kinda wore a gray undershirt kind of thing. He never looked terribly cleaned up. And he wore a hat, a felt hat, that was pooched up, no pleat. I can't remember any occasion on which he replaced it. I can't remember him having a new hat. He always looked the same. But he was just sort of unscrubbed, but not unpleasantly so. I don't think he liked anything but being sheriff. I can't think of anybody talking about anything that Isam did for recreation, once he was Sheriff.

I think he was an absolutely heroic character. He was just this kind of big ole raw-boned guy, who was dedicated at what he did. He was absolutely unapproachable, Isam was as honest as the day is long. The people who didn't like him hated him with a passion. And it was mutual!

Miller's descriptions of traveling with Isam: they'd walk in somewhere and here would be this character, dressed the way he was, who never changed. It was priceless. He wore a gun stuck in his pants. He insisted that Miller should have a gun and he brought it home one day and I said, 'Get that thing out of my house!' So he took it out and hid it in his office. I wasn't about to have a gun here with all our babies!

He [*Isam*] liked kids. Fourth of July was just his big day. Riding on his horse at the head of the parade which he did, as far as I know, as long as he was able. And the Marshfield High School Band would play right behind him.

There was not a dumb bone in his body. He just didn't know things. But he would bluff it out. He wasn't about to ask! He didn't give an inch on anything. He was either right or wrong.

He did once—honestly—say to Miller, Miller was talking about somebody that they had just charged with something. And Isam was discussing their guilt, and Miller said, 'Well, you know Isam, they haven't been tried yet.' And Isam says—the classic!—'Hell, Miller, you know we don't file on 'em unless they're guilty!' That is priceless! And he believed it sincerely. The court process was...*[a formality]*.

That just was Isam's philosophy of life in a nutshell. The important thing was the accusation, and...'we wouldn't do that if it weren't so'! That's just the way it was. A simplistic attitude."

October 13, 1949 "A new state law requiring motorists to stop when meeting or overtaking a school bus which has stopped on the highway to load or unload passengers is effective Friday *[10/14]*....Many other states have had this kind of a law for some time."

October 20, 1949 "MRS. RAINEY ATTACK VICTIM. Warrant Issued For Mary Margaret Evans After Complaint Filed Wednesday."

[Mary Lou Cunningham] "Oliver Evans will know all about this. But, supposedly, Miss Evans—maybe she's some relation to Oliver—was having an affair with Rex Rainey, the undertaker here in town. And someway she decided she was going to get rid of the wife, Rex Rainey's wife. She tried to kill the wife, the wife struggled.

Isam caught her and put her in prison."

"A brutal attack was made on Mrs. Carmen Rainey Tuesday night *[10/18]* about 3:00 o'clock by a person, who Mrs. Rainey said was a woman, at her basement apartment in the Rainey Funeral Home. Rex Rainey, her husband, had gone to the American Royal in Kansas City and she was alone.

According to reports her assailant attempted to chloroform her and then beat her on the head and face with a toy pistol and a flashlight. She escaped out of the building screaming and went to the home of neighbors, Mr. and Mrs. Howard Minor. She said her assailant had on rubber gloves and that she bit one of her *[assailant's]* fingers.

Mrs. Rainey was taken to Burge Hospital, Springfield, but was expected to be released this Wednesday afternoon, according to reports.

Up to press time Wednesday afternoon neither Roy C. Miller, prosecuting attorney, or E.I. Cunningham, Sheriff, were available for an interview as they were in Springfield working on the case.

However, Wednesday morning a complaint was filed in magistrate court by Prosecuting Attorney Miller charging 'Mary Margaret Evans, in and on one Carmen Rainey, feloniously and of her malice aforethought, did make an assault, and did then and there with a deadly weapon, to-wit: a toy revolving pistol of the length of eight inches and a flashlight of the length of ten inches, her, the said Carmen Rainey, did then and there feloniously, on purpose and of her malice aforethought, strike, beat and wound, with intent then and there her, the said Carmen Rainey, feloniously, on purpose and of her malice aforethought, to kill and murder.' A warrant was issued for her arrest based upon the complaint so filed.

The Springfield radio news broadcast at 12:30 noon Wednesday stated that 'a woman was being held in Springfield while a check of fingerprints, found on a chloroform bottle found in the basement of the Rainey funeral home, was being checked.'"

[The picture on the next page and this information is from History and Families, Webster County, Missouri, but was originally written by Billie Arthur.]

Arthur's Colonial Chapel, formerly Barber-Edwards-Arthur Funeral Home, located just one block east of *[The Square in Marshfield]* was built in the 1930s by Rex and Carmen Rainey and was the Rainey Funeral Home. The building is constructed of rock obtained from Webster County. The Raineys, along with their son Jack, operated the business until about 1950 when it was sold and became the Roller-Bruce Funeral Home.

In 1951, Russell and Emma Barber and Mary Barto bought the business which became known as Barber-Barto. Mary Barto soon sold her interest and it was later purchased by Oral and Wilma Edwards, who were managing the business at that time. In 1970, Joe and Billie Arthur purchased an interest and in 1980, they bought the entire business. Joe had been an employee since 1951 and *[was]* a licensed embalmer and funeral director.

....In 1988, the business was sold to Equity Corporation International and became a part of the Colonial Funeral Home group of Lebanon....Thus, Arthur's Colonial Chapel came into being. James Lea Day *[Jim]* had been employed since 1989 *[and became manager]. [Now the building is a private residence.]*

[Jack Rainey] "Where was I the night Mary Margaret Evans attacked my mom? I had moved. I had left Marshfield School, because of the whole situation. Well, it had gotten to where something was gonna happen someway or another. I'd left home. With my mother's support, I had moved to Springfield and was tryin' to go to school at Central High School, and was stayin' with my granddaddy up there. Prescott.

That particular night, they brought her *[his mother, Carmen]* by the house, I was still stayin' at Granddad's at that time, they brought her on the cot, by the house, before they took her to the hospital. She didn't want me to find out about it any other way.

I'd been away from home but I was back one night and I was sleepin' or gittin' ready to go to sleep, in my bedroom, which was downstairs, and I knew there was somebody outside the window. I didn't know who, but I knew somebody was out there. And I suspected who it was. Anyway, I went in and told my dad, 'Somebody's outside the window!'

And I *guess* he was nervous enough about it, that, there was an area in the funeral home, between the kitchen and the bedrooms, where you'd be in there and not be seen, from any window in the house. He got my mother up, he told us to stay in that room, he went outside, then came back. And it wasn't a long time after that, that this happened.

Mother knew something was gonna happen one way or another. She was thinkin' about leavin' him. But, thinkin' back on it, I don't know why she put up with it. I thought a lot of my dad, but at the same time, it went on for a long time.

Well, in all reality, I wouldn't want it in my thoughts that she stayed in that situation for *me*.

See, you can remember what you want to remember and you can block out what you want to block out, and while I have a generality about a lot of those things, *specifics*, that I *know* I was there and I can dwell on them and recall some of 'em…you don't *want* to remember. So you block out.…

I do remember a conversation when John William Brooks came down. It was before they ever got divorced.

John William was talkin' then, to my mom and dad, and I happened to be there. And he was sayin' some things that were probably a little inappropriate for a fifteen year old. So finally he said…and I was just standin', I wadn't doin' *anything*, I wadn't hiding, I was just *there*, and the conversation got around to some things that he probably thought wadn't appropriate…so he finally said, 'Here's fifteen cents'—or something, whatever it was—'go get me a pack of cigarettes' and all it was, was to get me gone so they could carry on their conversation, is what it amounted to. John William was a good friend of Dad's.

My mother went out to California to stay with her brother, to get away from here. I went out there to see what her feelings was about whether they would ever get back together. I was out there for two weeks, came home, I never did leave home after that. Stayed with Frieda and Paul. I was datin' Anne *[Cardwell]* the whole time.

I just went to talk to her, then came back. I had living expenses, but I didn't have any money to buy a train ticket. And I sold…I can't remember if I sold one cow or two…to Lester Garton, a cattle jockey, and I got $327. And that's what got me the money to go to California. I got to Kansas City…I don't even remember how I got to Kansas City now…I had to catch the train out of Kansas City. And it was not an awful long time before that, that my dad had bought that heifer, *[a prize-winning Angus heifer that cost Rex $8,000]* and I had a newspaper clippin' with me and I showed it to somebody on the train.

I went out there. My uncle lived in Pasadena. I'd get up, just walk around the neighborhood, and went often to this little pet store. And they had a monkey. And I come home talkin' about the monkey. Well, my mother went over there and *bought* it. And I didn't even know she'd bought it. We kept it in a cage that my uncle built. It's sittin' out there in the back yard right now, used for cats. That's the monkey cage! We finally took *him* to the zoo, in Springfield.

You probably know my folks went through a messy situation. And then, it resolved.

What happened to Jack Rainey? I was on my own. Because I wouldn't take sides. Isam stopped me down there, I'd come around the corner of The Square and I saw him, I guess it was about where Haymes Law Office was, right in there somewheres, and he got down a little ways and parked. Came on down and said, 'I've got a subpoena for ya, to appear in court.'

I said, 'I'm not a goin'.'

He said, 'Well, I'll have to take ya to jail.'

So I said, 'Well, let's just go, 'cause I'm not going. I won't be in court.'

He said, 'Well, I'll see ya later' or something like that. And that's the last I heard. He was doin' what he had to do. Somebody…either my mother or my dad, one, wanted me as a witness. If he gave me a subpoena, I didn't take it.

I put my time in, in school, didn't cause any trouble, and they let me slide right on through. The only thing I ever got out of school was arithmetic. And I wasn't good at it *then*, but I got enough basics that I use it to estimate stuff. But I couldn't sit down and write a letter. I can read! My oldest son's wife is a schoolteacher and I've told her several times, 'There's something wrong with my brain that I can *read* but I can't *write*.' I can write little notes and things, but my spelling and grammar is so far off, I couldn't correspond with anyone. And I never *did* finish school. When I dropped out of high school in Springfield….I didn't even want to take the GED. The kind of jobs that I did, it wasn't necessary. Labor-type jobs. While they…if I made application, they'd have a place on there for it *[high school diploma]*, it wasn't anything to me, for the kind of work I did."

[Doc Blinn] "Yes, I treated Mary Margaret Evans's finger. That was quite a deal, quite a deal. It was so stupid, really, you know. 'Course, they tried to use a cloth, I think chloroform, that they tried to put over her face and she *[Carmen]* bit them, she really bit down on the finger. It was indented pretty bad, bruised, the skin was broken, so I put some antibiotic ointment on it until it healed. She really wasn't hurt otherwise. Carmen went to Springfield to be treated."

[Willis Case] "Me and Rex Rainey, we bought and sold houses together. He had the money and I had the guts.

She *[Mary Margaret Evans]* put some cayenne pepper in her slippers. Supposed to keep the bloodhounds from trailing her. She's kinda smart. She came to this window in the funeral home, the old funeral home. She put this paper over her *[Carmen's]* face. It was supposed to be attempted murder. That's what they charged her with.

Rex and I were good friends. He came over here one night and told me all about it."

[Oliver Evans] "I usually took a suppertime break around 11:30 or 12:00 *[midnight]* and pulled in that old Conoco Station there on the Square, Gene Fraker run it, where Lurvey's is now. It had a lane you could pull in off the street.

And I'd pulled in there to eat my lunch, and I could hear 'em a squallin' down there. So I jumped in the car and run down there. And Mrs. Rainey and Howard Minor and his wife was out in the street. And she said, 'They're tryin' to kill me, they're tryin' to kill me!' So I made a circle around the funeral home, didn't see anything, so I went up and got Isam, to help, to come with me. Boy, he was down there like that [snap], with his necktie on!

The Rainey case was the biggest one I was involved with. When I went around the funeral home, this girl that'd done the damage, she was hidin' under the bushes there. She seen me, but I didn't see her. I heard about it later.

She had her car parked down there, across from the Lutheran Church. The doctor had a hospital in there. I didn't think nothin' about the car. The night before there was a baby case and they'd had a car parked down there.

She parked down there, I guess, walked up and attacked Miz Rainey. When she heard me a'comin', she hid under the spirea bush and after I left, she walked and got in the car. I never saw her!

Miz Evans, her dad and my dad were first cousins. I went to school with her. In a way I was surprised she did that. I had an indication something was goin' on with Rex Rainey, but I didn't think it was that serious. But I understood afterwards, she thought she'd get shed of Miz Rainey and Rex would take her."

[Peg Miller] "When Sarah was born, in '49, you had to stay in the hospital for five days and then you'd come home by ambulance. Can you believe that? When Marge was born, in '56, it was three days and Doc got me up the first day. And it was night and day between my recovery from her and the other two children, in a span of seven years.

But, anyway, Miller and Isam were off somewhere, chasing… oh, one of his favorites, he *[Isam]* called fugitives, they were *fugitives*.

Anyway, Miller was tied up, and called up *[to the hospital]* and asked if I would mind, just 'cause it was a problem, if Rex Rainey, then the funeral director of note, came and got me. So, it didn't bother me, I said, 'No, that'd be fine.' And Rex showed up, and 'course I didn't have any money, so Rex wrote a check for my bill. I was at Burge,[Hospital] now Cox, to have my second child. And going home in the ambulance, as I remember, I sat and rode with him. We had a jolly talk. At which point he announced he was off for the American Royal.

The next morning here are the headlines of the newspaper, the story about Mary Margaret Evans sneaking in the back of the funeral home and clobbering Carmen, who then proceeded to get a hold of her finger and almost bite it off. Anyway, here Miller is the prosecutor and all this is going on. And Rex has picked me up at the hospital, written a check for my expenses and taken off for the American Royal.

When Miller brought charges against Mary Margaret, ohhhh. It caused a great amount of hurt feeling in the town. It just did. Everybody kinda took sides.

My brother-in-law was going through Chicago at the time and said his eye sort of strayed to the *Chicago Tribune* in a bank of newspapers, which, as he said, he would not have bought, because it didn't always suit his political philosophies--of which he has entirely too many. But he saw a headline in it which said something about 'The Ozarks: Two Women Battle For Love Of An Embalmer.' Which he bought and read. And here was the whole story about 'Mary Margaret Evans said I didn't mean to hurt her, Carmen said something or other, and Embalmer Rainey said nothing.'

The trial was sort of traumatic for the community. Of course, Rex was the only undertaker in town. And, anyway, the check didn't clear! And it didn't clear. And it didn't clear. And Roy would say something to him, and Rex'd say, Yeah, he'd deposit it. And I don't know, it may have been after the trial or something, but it was a long time. Roy came home one day and had his bank statement and he said, 'Guess what? Rex's check finally cleared.' It was all fascinating."

[Warren Johnson] "Rex Rainey, he was just as guilty as she was. That was our opinion, my opinion.

Carmen Rainey, she went to Springfield to live. I lost track of her. Carmen was a lot better woman than Rex was a man, in my opinion. And it is an opinion."

[Edna Cunningham] "I knew Mary Margaret real well. As I said, I went to church with her, went to school with her. She went to grade school where I did, then she went to high school. We went to Good Hope Church together. Bible School. I've got a picture of all of us in Bible School. I knew about her and Rex Rainey. I think a lot of people knew it. I wouldn't know *[whether Rex encouraged her to attack Carmen]*, but it looks like it could be.

Didn't that take nerve to go in the funeral home of a night and do all that she done and then take out on A highway and go up on 60 or whatever she done? I understood she went out on A highway instead of going up 66. She went out A highway, hit 60, went into Springfield. That's what I was *told* that she did.

He went to these big...well, what do you call them... stock meetings they have in Kansas City and around,*[like the American Royal]*. She went with him to that."

"Victims Identity Still Unknown. Webster County authorities are still trying to locate relatives of a 75-year-old hitchhiker who was killed Monday night *[10/16]* when struck by a truck.

Sheriff E.I. Cunningham said the man had been identified through papers in his possession as Sam Busy, probably of Waynesville. He was instantly killed about 11 p.m. on Highway 66 a mile east of the Niangua junction.

Cunningham said Busy was walking on the wrong side of the pavement when he was struck by a Jones Truck Line vehicle from Springdale, Ark., driven by Eugene Eidson, 32, of Springfield.

Eidson told officers he was heading east from Springfield to St. Louis when he dimmed his lights at the approach of another truck and two cars. After he passed one machine he saw something on the road and struck it before he could stop.

Sheriff Cunningham said he had checked at Waynesville and Rolla in an attempt to learn more about Busy but found no one who knew him. A paper in the elderly man's possession said that he was a 'friend of Thomas Easter of Rolla.'

The man was fairly well dressed with a black hat, blue shirt, an Army jacket, dark pants, and a pair of mule-skin shoes. In his billfold were a penny, key, and an identity card. He weighed about 170 pounds, was six feet tall, had gray hair, and had only one upper tooth. He had no baggage.

Webster County Coroner K.K. Kelley said no inquest would be held. The body is being held at Rainey funeral home in Marshfield."

October 27, 1949 "Two AWOL Youths Nabbed After Filling Station Holdup—Slug Owner After Asking For Gas; Take Cash.

Two youths, AWOL from the marines, were brought here this Wednesday morning *[10/26]* from Springfield and lodged in jail by

Sheriff E.I. Cunningham. They were arrested by the Highway Patrol Tuesday evening after they had held up John N. Taylor of the Wee Dug Inn station just north of this city. They admitted the charge.

Taylor said he filled up the gas tank of the pair's auto shortly before 7 p.m. and was still holding the cap to the gas tank when one of them slugged him with a blunt instrument. He was felled with the blow and escaped with a scalp laceration.

'The guy waited until my back was turned to hit me,' Taylor said. 'He asked me for five gallons of gas and I had just finished filling the tank when he let me have it. I didn't see any gun, but he kept his left hand in his pocket and threatened to shoot me. From the look in his eye I thought sure he was going to do it, too. He forced me to go inside the station and empty the cash register—there was between $18 and $20 in it—I never keep much there. After I gave him the cash he seemed to be debating whether or not to kill me.'

Their car, a 1949 Chevrolet sedan, was headed east when it pulled into the station, but turned around and headed toward Springfield on Highway 66. The second man stayed in the car. Both were clad in khaki clothing.

Mr. Taylor quickly notified the State Patrol, and a trooper started toward Marshfield to look for the robbery suspects. He spotted them and stopped them as they neared Springfield. They offered no resistance and were taken to patrol headquarters for questioning.

There they admitted going AWOL from the marine corps base at Cherry Point, N.C., October 13, and stealing the sedan from a taxi company there. The car had only about a thousand miles on the speedometer when they took it, but when arrested it had about 6,000 miles on it.

They had only $35 in pay with them so they headed for Houston, Texas, obtained $25 from the parents of one youth, and drove to Chicago and got another $25 from the parents of the other young marine. They said they were going back to Texas when they got into trouble here.

When arrested they had $22 in their possession, and a blackjack made from a bicycle handlebar grip. No gun was found.

The two youths, identified as Douglas McMurray McAfee, 20, of Chicago, and John Kermit Rice, 18, of Houston, Texas, were arraigned this Wednesday morning before Cline C. Herren, magistrate here, on charges of robbery. They were each bound over to circuit court and bond fixed at $5,000 each."

"Man Arrested On Non-Support Charge. Basil Wallace Loveland was arrested Tuesday night *[10/25]* by Sheriff E.I. Cunningham of this county and George F. Spencer and Rock McKown, deputy sheriffs of Greene county, at the home of his mother, about four miles southeast of Rogersville. He is charged with non-support of his 13-months-old child in Springfield. It is reported that he was arrested some months ago on the same charge.

Mr. Loveland, who worked some time in Detroit, Mich., admitted after his arrest that he was wanted in Michigan and in St. Louis for passing forged or bogus checks. He said he and Lloyd Douglas and Earl Shoebridge passed $7, 800 in bad checks in Michigan the last of August and first of September, and he and Douglas $1,000 in bad checks in St. Louis during September. Douglas and Shoebridge are said to be in custody in Detroit now.

When arrested he had no money on him. The officers went to his mother's home and found a small printing press, some safety check paper and ink which he is said to have used in printing the bad checks.

Loveland was placed in the Greene county jail."

"A 75-year-old hitchhiker killed by a truck, October 17, near Marshfield, has been identified positively as Sam Bucy, by Walter McKemon of Route 2, Dixon, Sheriff E.I. Cunningham says.

Bucy, an old age pensioner, had been staying with the McKemon family most of the time for the past eight years.

His body was taken to Dixon Saturday for burial.

McKemon says the old man ate dinner there the Saturday before, and told Mrs. McKemon he was going up in the pasture to look after some horses. He never returned. Eight people from that community came here to identify the deceased. Mr. Bucy had no relatives so far as known."

"Search is being made for a Mrs. Wilbur Johnson of Carlsbad, N.M., daughter of Mr. and Mrs. Walter Barker of Route 1, Niangua, who reside just over the line in Wright county, southeast of Radertown. Sheriff E.I. Cunningham received a telegram Saturday evening *[10/22]* from Sheriff Elmbaker of Carlsbad asking him to check up with her folks on whether they had heard from her lately.

Sheriff Cunningham says that he found that Patsy was home about the time of the Webster County Fair and they received a telegram

September 16 saying she had arrived back at her home at Carlsbad all right. They had a letter dated September 26 saying that everything was fine. Then on October 3, they received a telegram from her husband that she had left. They have not heard from her since."

[still October 27, 1949]
"MISS EVANS ARRAIGNED ON ASSAULT CHARGE
Admits Attack on Mrs. Rex Rainey; Says She and Mr. Rainey were
'Intimately Acquainted.'

Mary Margaret Evans, charged with felonious assault with intent to kill, following an assault on Mrs. Carmen Rainey the early morning of October 19, in the basement apartment of the Rainey Funeral Home, was arraigned Saturday morning before Cline C. Herren, magistrate here. She waived preliminary, was bound over to circuit court. She was released on a $2,000 bond which was signed by her parents, Mr. and Mrs. Doug Evans, and herself.

The story of this case as told by Sheriff E.I. Cunningham is as follows: Oliver Evans, night watchman, was sitting in his car on the square, eating his lunch, when he heard screams in the direction of the funeral home. He called up to the windows of the Sheriff's living quarters in the courthouse. The Sheriff came to the window and also heard the screams. They went to the home of Mr. and Mrs. Howard Minor where Mrs. Rainey had gone for help. They found Mrs. Rainey covered with blood.

Mrs. Rainey had a toy pistol in her hand which she said she had taken from her assailant. Mrs. Rainey is reported to have said, 'I took the gun away from her' and named Mary Margaret Evans. 'She was trying to shoot me,' evidently not knowing the gun was a toy.

The Sheriff and Mr. Evans made a circle of the city in Mr. Evans's car and not finding anyone, went to the home of Doug Evans. They had not seen their daughter. The Sheriff then called the Springfield police to watch for her.

The Sheriff made a thorough search of the Rainey apartment and found everything a mess with blood all around the place. He found some cotton, one rubber glove torn badly, a chloroform bottle, and a flashlight there. Mrs. Rainey is said to have told the officers that when she was awakened she had a towel over her face. She then fought with her assailant, biting her fingers.

Night watchman Evans got Homer Frick, Rainey ambulance driver, who with Bill Kleier, a neighbor, took Mrs. Rainey to the Burge Hospital, Springfield.

Wednesday morning Sheriff Cunningham and Prosecuting Attorney Roy C. Miller had a warrant issued and went to Springfield. They located Miss Evans about 11 o'clock at the Harry Cooper Supply Co., where she has been employed as a telephone girl, and took her to the police station where she was questioned.

Meanwhile, about the middle of the morning the police received a telephone call from a person who told them to meet her, that she had valuable information. When they met her, she told them Miss Evans has come to her apartment and left bloody clothing and that she had lent Miss Evans some of her clothes.

Miss Evans at first denied knowing anything about the attack, but when confronted with her bloodstained clothing, she admitted it and made a statement. She said she became intimately acquainted with Mr. Rainey about five years ago—and accompanied him on trips to horse shows. She said, Mrs. Rainey had written her notes back in 1944 asking her to quit seeing her husband. More recently she had received telephone calls from Mrs. Rainey. And not long ago Miss Evans said Mr. Rainey told her his wife had removed a pistol from the glove compartment of an ambulance and intended to kill Miss Evans.

Fear that Mrs. Rainey would follow up her alleged threat lead Miss Evans to devise a scheme to find the gun, she said in her statement. Over and over again that day and since, she has said, 'I didn't intend to kill her.' (Mrs. Rainey).

Knowing that Mr. Rainey had gone to the American Royal Livestock Show in Kansas City Tuesday and that Mrs. Rainey would be alone at the funeral home Tuesday night, Miss Evans after work that day gathered equipment for her trip to Marshfield. She bought a bottle of chloroform, a stomach pump at a surgical supply house. Taking several sleeping tablets she possessed, she dissolved them in a small vial of water. She packed a box of red pepper, a pair of rubber gloves, some cotton, a pink shawl, and a toy pistol.

She said her plan was to clap a wad of chloroform cotton over Mrs. Rainey's face. Then she planned to pour the sleeping tablet solution through the stomach pump tube to make certain Mrs. Rainey slept soundly during her search for the gun. About dark Tuesday she rented a car from the Dugan Drive It Yourself company, giving the name of Inez N. Davis of St. Louis. She said she drove to Marshfield and parked east of the Rainey Funeral Home. Then she entered by a rear door to the basement apartment.

When Mrs. Rainey awakened, a terrific struggle was carried on over several rooms. Mrs. Rainey was battered repeatedly over the face and head with the metal toy pistol. Miss Evans suffered bitten fingers on both hands, but her left-hand forefinger and middle finger was worst injured. After she was brought here the Sheriff said he took her to a doctor to have an X-ray made of one hand to see if the forefinger was broken and to have the fingers dressed. The middle fingernail was practically off.

Miss Evans denied that anyone was with her.

Miss Evans was brought to the jail here that Wednesday afternoon about 6 o'clock, where she remained until Saturday morning.

Meantime Rex Rainey returned here from Kansas City where he had gone to attend the American Royal and then went to Springfield to be with Mrs. Rainey, who was released from the hospital and went to the home of her parents, Mr. and Mrs. G. R. Prescott. They returned here to their funeral home Saturday evening."

Mary Margaret At Jail

—Courtesy of Springfield Leader-Press
Mary Margaret Evans, 31-year-old Springfield woman, who last Wednesday admitted assault upon Mrs. Rex Rainey, well known Marshfield business woman, photographed in the office of E. I. Cunningham, Webster county sheriff, in the courthouse here last Thursday. Pictured are Sheriff Cunningham, her father, Doug Evans of Route 3, and Miss Evans. As she was brought down the steps from the county jail to the sheriff's office, she wept and said: "I didn't intend to kill her."

November 3, 1949 "Name of Firm To Be Roller-Bruce Funeral Home—The Rainey Funeral Home has been sold to Denver Roller of Mountain Home, Ark., and Arthur Bruce of Mountain Grove. The funeral home has been operated here by Mr. and Mrs. Rex Rainey since 1930....

Mr. Rainey has not revealed his future plans."

"Michigan authorities came to Springfield last week to obtain custody of Basil Wallace Loveland, 22-year-old former Rogersville boy, who faces charges of participating in a bogus check ring in Detroit."

"A rusty cash register-adding machine fished from James River Friday *[10/28]* has been identified as one stolen from the Al Hanna Service Station west of Fordland last August 1.

The machine was found near the bank of the river by Jim Williams of Route 3, Springfield, as he was fishing near Highway 65 south of Galloway. He notified deputies, who found the $165 machine badly damaged, but partly in working order.

How much money was in the register at the time wasn't known, but officers said the thieves evidently decided the machine would be difficult to pawn and threw it into the river.

It had apparently been swept up to the bank by recent heavy rains which flooded the river."

"The days are growing short for Ernest Afton Scott.

He's scheduled to be executed in the gas chamber at Jefferson City, Nov.4, for the murder March 29, 1948, of his wife, Verla, in Mountain Grove.

About an hour before that, he had shot to death Circuit Judge Charles H. Jackson. Scott was not tried in that killing.

After a four-day jury hearing at Hartville in June, 1948, the death recommendation was returned by the jurors after about 50 minutes of study.

The 50-year-old Douglas county farmer's appeal was rejected by the state Supreme court which set the execution date as November 4.

One of Afton Scott's numerous children was a star prosecution witness. She is Willa Mae Scott, 15, whose scornful testimony cancelled her father's accusations against Judge Jackson as the 'father' of one or more of the Scott children.

Evidence as to the shooting of Judge Jackson was permitted in the trial—although it was another crime and committed in another county—at the insistence of the defense because of the insanity plea.

Scott never did deny that he shot Judge Jackson in the back, about a quarter of a mile from the Scott farm in Douglas county just over the Wright-Douglas county line, then jumped into his car, drove to Mountain Grove and stalked his wife at her mother's home until he had her in position for the rifle bullet that slew her instantly.

Unless a reprieve is given by Governor Forrest Smith, Scott will go to the gas chamber Friday at the prison in Jefferson City."

"Mrs. Rex Rainey Asks Divorce. Mrs. Carmen P. Rainey, wife of Rex Rainey, Marshfield undertaker, filed suit for divorce last Thursday afternoon in the Greene county circuit court at Springfield.

In her petition, Mrs. Rainey identified herself as a resident of Greene county. Her attorney, Flavius B. Freeman, said she was living with her father, G. R. Prescott, at 1423 Benton, Springfield, and that after a conference with her husband following an attack made on her at the Rainey Funeral Home October 19 by a woman assailant, she had decided to sever her connection with the funeral home.

Mrs. Rainey asks in addition to the divorce decree, custody of their son, Jack, 17; a monthly sum for his support; a reasonable settlement of alimony in gross; and attorney's fees.

She charges her husband with mental cruelty and adultery.

In detail, she says he quarreled, fussed, and nagged; pointed a gun at her in the presence of their child and threatened to kill her; was close and stingy with money, making himself the judge of what she should spend for clothes; was domineering; often went on trips without her; was guilty of reprehensible conduct.

The name of Miss Mary Margaret Evans, 31, of Springfield, who now faces felonious assault charges in Webster County for her admitted attack on Mrs. Rainey at the funeral home October 19, does not appear in the petition.

However, a paragraph reads as follows: 'While the defendant was away on a trip, the plaintiff's home was entered and she was assaulted by a woman who has since admitted that she and the defendant have been intimate for more than five years.'

That much, according to the petition, satisfied Mrs. Rainey that her husband was guilty of adultery.

Mr. and Mrs. Rainey were married January 1, 1930, according to the petition. It goes on to state that they both entered the marriage state without much wealth, but that through the efforts of both they now owned property which Mrs. Rainey had reason to believe might amount to more than $100,000."

November 10, 1949 "Joe Trent of Springfield and Harlin Burks of this city were arrested Friday night *[11/4]* by Sheriff E.I. Cunningham on a charge of breaking into the house owned by Mr. and Mrs. Alfred Bumgarner, south of Shockey schoolhouse the latter part of October and taking shoes, canned goods, lard, flashlight and other items.

They were taken to Prosecuting Attorney Roy C. Miller's office and admitted the theft. The value of the items taken amounted to about $32. The officers went to the home of Burks's mother here and found the stolen articles, except the food that had already been eaten.

Sheriff Cunningham saw the youth enter the picture show with Burks wearing one of the pairs of stolen shoes, and then made the arrest."
        [Read the previous sentence again. Ole Isam.]

"K.K. Kelley, H. C. Ferrell, and Robert Bergman, who have operated funeral homes at Seymour, Fordland, and Rogersville for several years, have acquired the large A.L.Drumright residence on W. Jackson street and will open a funeral home here. The announcement is given in this issue of the MAIL."

"Jess McPherson was arrested at his home Saturday evening *[11/5]*, according to Sheriff E.I. Cunningham, after he was said to have driven his car into the residence of Mrs. Nannie Robertson in the north part of the city that evening. The Sheriff said he left his car and went on home.

The car smashed through the porch and into the side of the house doing considerable damage."

"November 7 Magistrate Court notes: State of Mo. vs. Jeff McPherson, driving while intoxicated; hearing set for Nov. 21. Bond fixed at $2,000 and approved."

November 17, 1949 "A news release...says that H. Dean Mack *[a Webster County boy]* has composed and has had printed a new song,

'I'll Betcha I Letcha'…."*[The author has tried and can find nothing about this song or its author.]*

"Roy E. Lamb, held in the jail at Ava, was identified Monday by Mr. Bay of the Bay Shoe Store at Seymour, as the man who cashed a worthless check last June at his store at Seymour. Officers had been looking for the man since June 4, when worthless checks were cashed at the Bay store and at the lumberyard at Seymour, according to Sheriff E.I. Cunningham.

Sheriff Cunningham accompanied by Mrs. Cunningham and Mr. Bay went to Ava Monday to check on Lamb, who will be brought here when papers have been issued."

"Lela Fern Casteel, 20, whose husband lives on Route 3, Marshfield, was picked up at her mother's home on Route 4, Springfield, last Thursday and turned over to Sheriff E I. Cunningham of this county.

She is charged with abandoning two children. The warrant was issued the first of October. She filed bond for appearance on November 23, before Cline C. Herren, Magistrate."

"A petition was presented to the County Court by a committee representing the Marshfield Business and Professional Women's club, the Lions club, the Junior Chamber of Commerce, and the Webster County Health Council, regarding the 'bad, unsanitary conditions existing in the courthouse.'

The petition made two suggestions as follows: first, arrange at once for hot water to be available in the basement or first floor for janitor services and that a capable and competent person be appointed by the court to keep the courthouse in 'such condition that we can point to it with pride.' And second, that when the court is absent or not in session (as there seems to be a decided lack of janitorial supervision), the court should consider 'an appointment of a building representative who will have jurisdiction over the janitors or other maintenance personnel.' The court has not yet acted upon the petition."

[Charley Cunningham is showing up as a leading scorer for the Marshfield High School basketball Blue Jays.]

November 24, 1949 "Twin calves born 17 days apart is reported by John Price, Route 2, Conway. A Jersey cow owned by him gave birth to heifer calves in August, which is unusual, but to make it more unusual, the calves arrived 17 days apart. He says both are living and doing well."

December 8, 1949 "Leroy King of Niangua was arrested at Springfield Monday for taking 11 spools of barb wire and 2 rolls of chicken wire from the Niangua Farmers Exchange last July. Sheriff E.I. Cunningham obtained a search warrant and found the wire in a granary on King's farm. The granary was locked. King waived preliminary and is being held in jail here.

Howard Boyce was arrested Tuesday and is in the Springfield jail charged with helping King rob the Niangua Exchange. He was picked up by the Highway Patrol at the request of Sheriff Cunningham."

December 15, 1949 "Webster County officers believe that they have solved several robberies of recent months, with the arrests of Leroy King and Howard Boyce of Niangua, and the finding of considerable stolen goods at the King place. After securing a search warrant last week, the officers found barb wire, woven wire, school books, brick siding, oil stove and cooking utensils and other items at the King home. Items found are said to have been taken from the Niangua Farmers Exchange last July, '88' school building early part of November, Osage school building middle part of November, bunch of stuff from the Joe Coonce place, some stuff taken from the Dewey Rowden (Shook place), and other places.

It is reported that King has admitted the thefts and also that Boyce has admitted accompanying King in several of these robberies."

Chapter Ten
1950

January 5, 1950 "The night watchman proved his value early Saturday morning when he discovered a motor burning in the rear of the Marshfield Café about 2:00 a.m. The back window of the café was burned and a serious fire averted when the blaze was extinguished. The motor was on an air compressor, and was thought to have burned out due to lack of oiling.

The city, due to lack of finances, is discontinuing the night watchman, unless the business people of the city make up the necessary finances. The fire at the cafe shows how much a night watchman is worth, not counting the possible losses from burglary that may ensue with no one to be on guard nights."

"The body of an 18-year-old Marshfield youth was found huddled in the back seat of his car in a wooded area about two miles east of Rogersville late last Thursday afternoon.

Sheriff E.I. Cunningham said the young victim, Jimmie W. Haggard, son of Mr. and Mrs. Hubert Haggard, died of a bullet wound in the middle of his forehead. He evidently had been dead about two days.

Officers quickly investigated the possibility of murder. An inquest will be held at 1:00 this Wednesday afternoon at the courthouse in Marshfield to try to determine if death was caused by accident. Coroner K. K. Kelley has already had a jury examine the body.

Young Haggard was last seen alive between 9:30 and 10 p.m. Tuesday of last week when he drove two friends, Luther Detherow, 15, and Dorsey Tannehill, 16, to the former's home and then left in his car.

Questioned by Sheriff Cunningham the boys said they and Haggard had driven to Conway, Mo., Tuesday, had returned to Marshfield, driven to Conway again and met two girlfriends. They drove around for a while, then left the girls at their homes, returned to Marshfield, and 'just drove around country roads before heading homeward.'

When Haggard left his companions at Detherow's home, he told them he had to hurry home because his folks would worry if he stayed out later, they said.

When the youth failed to appear at his home the next morning, the parents contacted Cunningham, who issued a pickup order.

The boys said Haggard had his .22 caliber bolt action rifle in the car when they left him. The weapon was found lying beside the youth's body when he was found.

A farmer living near Rogersville saw Haggard's 1933 Dodge sedan parked in woods 100 yards from Highway 60 early Wednesday but didn't investigate. Later he told two neighbors of seeing the auto, and they drove to the isolated spot two miles east of Rogersville about 4 p.m. Thursday.

The men, Sam Delzell and Ira Roller, found all the doors locked except the right rear one. The youth was lying on his right side in the rear seat with a quilt pulled over him. The rifle beside him had been fired once, and the empty cartridge lay on the floor.

There were powder burns around the wound, indicating the weapon was almost against the youth's head when it was fired. Officers said there was nothing to indicate he had been injured otherwise. His billfold and watch were intact, and he was clothed in two pairs of overalls and a leather jacket. The keys were still in the ignition.

Coroner K.K. Kelley said Haggard had been dead since Tuesday night.

Cunningham said the car appeared to have been driven into the woods, then turned around and headed back toward the highway.

The boy's tragic death was the second to occur in the Haggard family within a year.

About 12 months ago, a younger brother of Jimmie fatally injured himself when a sawed-off shotgun he was playing with discharged accidentally. The Haggards, who have three other children, lived in a house trailer at that time.

Young Haggard had been doing general work at Marshfield, often helping his father, a city employee.

Funeral services were held at 2 o'clock Saturday afternoon at the Roller-Bruce funeral chapel with the Rev. Herbert Davis of the Christian Church officiating. Burial was in the Marshfield cemetery."

"Mrs. Rainey Files Denial of Allegations—A denial that she forgave her husband allegations mentioned in her suit for divorce was filed in circuit court Saturday morning in Springfield by attorneys for Mrs. Carmen Rainey, wife of former Marshfield funeral director Rex I. Rainey.

Mrs. Rainey sued for divorce on October 27, little more than a week after being attacked in her Marshfield home by a former Marshfield woman, confessed paramour of Rainey.

In answering the suit, Rainey claimed his wife forgave him of all the charges included in her petition and lived with him nine days after the incident. (from the Springfield Leader-Press, Jan. 1 issue)"

January 12, 1950 "Sheriff E. I. Cunningham, accompanied by Mrs. Ted Stuber and Mrs. Fred Letterman *[Isam's daughter, Mildred]*, took Bernice Ryan to the State Hospital at Nevada Tuesday. He brought back two from the hospital, Fred Holcomb and Mr. Bennett."

"In this issue of the MAIL will be found the announcement of Judge Cline C. Herren as a candidate for re-election. He is completing his first term in the combined office of Probate Judge and Ex-Officio Magistrate.

Three years ago it was necessary to set up a complete set of Magistrate record books, blanks and fee records to comply with the law making the change from the old Justice of the Peace system. This change was made by Judge Herren with a minimum of confusion, and the state auditors, who have just completed a complete audit of this office, have no criticism to offer on the records thus established...."

[Cline Herren, Jr.] "Initially my dad was Probate Judge from '42 to '46. And then that's when they added the Magistrate and wiped out the JP system *[Justice of the Peace]*, in '46. That's when the people ran for election in '46. I suppose it was '47 when it actually came into effect. They had Ex Officio Magistrate. They'd had a JP for every township, and a Constable."

[When Daniel Max Knust was elected in 1978, he was the last Probate Judge and Ex-Officio Magistrate. The title and duties were for January 1, 1979 only. On January 2, 1979, Knust became Webster County's first Associate Circuit Judge, with greatly expanded jurisdiction over that of the Probate Judge and Ex-Officio Magistrate.]

"Mrs. Herman Tade, who was appointed by the Webster County court last month to janitor at the courthouse, has been doing a fine job and has gotten the building into fairly good shape. There was quite a lot of cleaning to be done.

She says that she has heard about how people are inconsiderate about keeping public toilets and public buildings clean, but she says she has faith in the people of this county helping keep the courthouse clean.

She expects the cooperation of all those that use the courthouse, not only in keeping toilets clean, but in not spitting or throwing trash on the floors.

The people should take pride in their nice county building and help in keeping it clean."

"James Haggard, 18, of Marshfield, 'came to his death by gunshot wound from a .22 caliber rifle, accidentally self-inflicted,' a coroner's jury here decided Friday afternoon....Dorsey Tannehill and Luther Detherow told of the last trip in young Haggard's car they had made with him to Conway and back.

Both boys were somewhat nervous and Tannehill couldn't remember the date, but Luther established it as Tuesday, Dec. 27.

The boys testified they had all three gone hunting, with Haggard carrying the rifle and the other two shotguns.

They left for Conway about 10 a.m. and there located the two girls *[Ruth Wilkerson and Bonnie Terry, 14]*. Then they went to see a man named Tucker, then went to a bridge Jimmy had helped build last summer, then to a cave, where Luther said they 'messed around.' Then back to Conway, where they picked the girls up and drove around.

While driving around they looked at a 'haunted house,' where the Terry girl said Jimmy fired his gun twice—not at anything, however. They let the girls out, drove around some more, looked in on the scout camp, then went back to Conway and picked up the Terry girl again. *[According to the testimony, both Tannehill and Haggard had dated Ruth Wilkerson, while the Detherow boy had dates with the Terry girl.]*

Prosecutor Roy Miller questioned all the young people closely as to whether Jimmy was upset about Dorsey having a date that day with the Wilkerson girl whom he also dated. They all said no.

Ruth Wilkerson testified, however, that Jimmy, 'talked a lot when he was mad, and that he talked plenty that day.'

Through his questioning, Miller found that, in the early stages of their acquaintance, Jimmy who owned the only 'ride' the three had, made Dorsey and Luther walk home from a date one night. One other time, however, he had turned over the car to Luther and walked back to Marshfield from the Conway date himself.

None of the four young people said there had been any quarreling just before the disappearance. The two boys said they were let out at the Detherow residence in Marshfield about 8:30 p.m. December 27, and that Jimmy had said he had to get home or his family would worry.

Hubert Haggard, the father, last saw his son at 7:30 a.m. that day. The boy was supposed to get some meat ground and had promised to have it back at 1:30 or 2 o'clock But his car never showed up the rest of the day, and when his father went to work at 4 a.m. the next day, there was still no sign of the car....

Attorney Miller asked each witness if he had made any trips to the Rogersville-Fordland vicinity with young Haggard, or knew why he should go there.

Homer McCormick, who does some wiring for homes, said about a month ago he and young Haggard had wired a house a mile east and six miles south of Rogersville. He also testified young Haggard told him he had slightly overdrawn his bank account, which resulted in two or three small checks being up for payment.

At the close of all testimony, Coroner Kelley addressed the packed courtroom and asked if anyone else could contribute any evidence. Silence followed, and soon after the greater part of about 200 persons left the room—Taken from Springfield Daily News."

January 19, 1950 "About fifty business people attended a meeting held at the courthouse Friday night *[1/13]*. An effort was made to invite all the business firms to be represented for the purpose of discussing hiring a night watchman. The city, being short of funds, had decided that January 15 would end the employment of the night watchman unless some method of financing was worked out.

There was no question among the business people but that a night watchman is essential and that some means should be worked out to pay him. The consensus of opinion was that the current night watchman is doing a good job and everyone seemed satisfied with his work....

It was recommended to the board that the city estimate the extra money necessary to employ a night watchman....that a city ordinance be passed levying the extra cost to city business licenses, taking into consideration the size of different business firms."

February 2, 1950 "Announcement is made of the engagement and approaching marriage of Miss Eldean Marie Freymiller, daughter of Mrs. Marie Freymiller of Lancaster, Wis., to Wilbur Cunningham, son of Mr. and Mrs. E.I. Cunningham of Marshfield. The wedding will take place March 25, at the Winnebago Street Methodist church,

Rockford, Illinois.

Mr. Cunningham and Miss Freymiller are both employed in Rockford and will make their home there after the wedding."

[Edna Cunningham] "Wilbur has the nicest wife. He worked in the same factory as she did. That's how they met."

"*[Marshfield Blue]* Jays Conquer Norwood 69-37…There was a range of scores. 'Red' *[Charley]* Cunningham was high with 14.…"

February 9, 1950 "The separation of Mrs. Carmen Rainey and Rex I. Rainey, former Marshfield funeral home director, became a legal divorce Friday morning in Springfield.

Appearing with her attorney, Flavius Freeman, Mrs. Rainey filed an amended petition for divorce and took the stand in Circuit Judge William R. Collison's court.

Her former husband was present at the hearing, taking a seat toward the rear of the courtroom. He was represented by his attorney, John Hosmer.

Tearful testimony of Mrs. Rainey consisted mostly of answers of 'yes' to questions worded by her lawyer. The decree was not contested in any way.

With an occasional teardrop fallen onto the lay of her conservative wine-colored suit, Mrs. Rainey affirmed the fact that she was married to the 41-year-old ex-undertaker in Springfield on New Year's Day in 1930. She said they separated in the month of October 1949.

Mrs. Rainey's original petition was filed October 27, less than a week after she was attacked by Rainey's confessed paramour, Miss Mary Margaret Evans, 31-year-old Springfield telephone operator.

In the original document, Mrs. Rainey's charges included specific instances of indignities. It read that Rainey had pointed a gun at her and threatened to kill her in the presence of their 17-year-old son, that he was stingy in regard to allowing her money, domineering, and that she was attacked by a woman admitted being intimate with Rainey for more than five years.

The amended petition mentioned only general indignities.

Following Mrs. Rainey's testimony that she had been subjected to general indignities, Judge Collison called for 'a little more specific account of such acts' for the record.

Going back to the original petition, Attorney Freeman asked

Mrs. Rainey if it were true that Rainey had quarreled and fussed with her for a period of time with no just causes and if he would stay away from home without explanation.

Mrs. Rainey's affirmative answers to the two additional queries brought an end to the establishment of grounds to divorce in testimony....Mrs. Rainey said the youth is living with friends in Marshfield and is employed by International Harvester there. He has one-half year of high school to attend for a diploma....The divorce decree granted Mrs. Rainey the custody of their son and the agreed $75 monthly support. Rainey was allowed visitation rights."

[Jack Rainey] "My dad was the business end of it, he was the funeral director and he prepared the bodies, but my *mother* was the one that held it together. She done *all* the bookwork, filled out *all* the death certificates, if there was *any* correspondence that needed taken care of, she done that. She could put an obituary together. She would gather the information and then put an obituary together that would be factual as well as flattering. She'd call them in to Springfield and they would print 'em word for word.

Overall, how do I feel, what do I think about it? The disappointment, for that to ever happen, because it was...*somebody* has to take blame and my mother was absolutely blameless. She was a victim. She had to put up with *so* much that a *lot* of people *probably* didn't even *know* about. Just for the fact that, I guess, he was pretty discreet about his situations, up to a point, and then, while I don't even know Mary Margaret, and even for the things she did, she wouldn't a done it if she hadn't loved him. 'Course, Mother had to love him to put up with it! But for her *[Mary Margaret]* to go to those extremes, she was probably a victim too.

My dad, I got closer to him later on, but actually all the time I was growin' up, he was rather strict, pretty strict. He didn't have to say anything twice; whatever he said is what I did. Actually, I guess, my upbringing was influenced a lot more by the people that I stayed with, probably, than it was my mom and dad.

Lookin' back on it, and I guess it was because of respect for my folks, everybody that I stayed with, I could do no wrong. I was treated like royalty! But, I was a little bit like John Hosmer was: I didn't *want* to be and I *hope* I didn't take advantage of the situation that other people was put in because they was lookin' after me. I accepted how they lived and was proud to be with them. But I remember goin' out and stayin' at Alexanders'. Their kids were enough older than me, I wasn't even in school, and I'd gone to stay with them and school started, school was goin' on, at Black Oak School, and I went with 'em one time and they took egg sandwiches for lunch. Well, before dinnertime I got hungry! And there was probably ten kids in the school, all different ages, and the teacher was Bill...he was probably just out of high school. But I guess I was fussin', I went with the two girls, Eloise was the oldest and Shorty or Ernestine, they always called her Shorty, and they were tryin' to keep me quiet, and I guess I was causing enough of a problem, the teacher said, 'Go ahead and let him have his lunch!' and I had that egg sandwich for lunch. And why I can remember that when I was five years old....I just got in all kinds of situations where other people were not equipped...in other words, they shouldn't have been responsible for me, but they took on responsibility.

My folks were too busy to have a kid.

They'd adapt to whatever they had to do, rather than spend the money to...because they needed the money to go into the business, they didn't slough off any money. My dad was as tight as I am, but at the same time he'd splurge on...he'd *save* money so he *could* splurge. Nobody else in Marshfield had an airplane.

They went somewheres... My mother didn't like to fly, but, just because, she had to do it. They went someplace and got fuel. It had two tanks on it and for whatever reason, one of the tanks got turned off. The only way...you weren't *supposed* to be able to get to the switch, the valve, except from the outside. But they were flying, I think from Kansas City but I'm not sure about that, and it was about to run out on this one tank and they thought they was gonna switch it over to the other tank.

It didn't switch. So they decided...and the glide on it, it was a metal plane, underwing plane, no glide to it, you run out of power, you run out of *flyin'*, a lot of those lightweight planes, they could glide in sometimes, but this one didn't glide—so they decided that was the end of it, they were gonna crash right there. And he started sayin', 'Well, the valve is in such-and-such a place!' and they had to tear the seats out of the thing, get back behind seats to get to a valve, and she got around and got that valve turned on! This was before the divorce, because actually through the divorce she wound up with the plane! Dad was through with it. But she wound up with the plane and sold it to the company that delivered semen to the farms, the stud farms, and dropped it in little parachutes. The inseminator would call in and say, 'Well, I'm gonna be at a certain place and you get semen and drop it,' and they'd fly over and drop it. It was fresh semen! It wasn't frozen! They didn't have the technology, it was fresh. And they called it The Flyin' Bull. "

February 16, 1950 "Marshfield Seniors to present the play 'You Can't

Take It With You.' Donald, Negro butler, is played by Charles *[Charley]* Cunningham."

March 9, 1950 "County Court Warrants Issued *[checks]:*
    E.I. Cunningham   Salary.........$181.03
                 Board bill............ $180.25
                 Expense and attending court.....$47.10
                 Transporting prisoners to Jefferson City...$226.40
                 Deputies, mileage, transporting prisoners to
                                Jefferson City..$386.40"

[Did Isam pay all this out of his own pocket, then file for reimbursement? His expenses here total over $840.]

[from *Springfield News Leader and Press* March 22, 1950]
    "Mary Margaret Evans, 31, a native of Marshfield and former Springfield switchboard operator, was convicted of assault with intent to kill Mrs. Carmen Rainey, then the wife of her clandestine sweetheart for the past five years, Rex Rainey, former funeral home owner in Marshfield. The Raineys had held the funeral home property jointly. Mrs. Rainey divorced Mr. Rainey in February.
    Spectators had packed the courtroom for every minute of the lengthy trial. At least 400 were seated in the room and in the final sessions half again found standing room. Doors of the courtroom were left open so persons in the corridors outside could hear the testimony.
    The jury of 11 men and one woman began deliberations in the case at 8:20 p.m. At 10:33 p.m. Circuit Judge James P. Hawkins ordered the jury to return to the courtroom for a progress report. 'Has the jury reached a verdict?' he asked. 'Well, your honor,' answered Foreman W.W. Denny, 'we've agreed on a decision but can't decide the punishment.'
    That tip-off to a guilty verdict caused a ripple through the courtroom which was suddenly hushed as Judge Hawkins ordered the jury to resume deliberations.
    Judge Hawkins finally had to fix the punishment: four years in the state penitentiary because she had been found guilty by the jury of assault with intent and purpose to kill.
    'I figured she'd get fined about a $100 dollars or at the most get six months in jail,' one spectator said.
    Mrs. Carmen Rainey was almost exhausted from the strain of testifying and sitting in the courtroom during nine hours of testimony

from other witnesses. She had been the first witness for the state. She 'told of being awakened about 3 o'clock on the morning of October 19 *[1949]* by the acrid odor of chloroform in her bedroom. She lunged from her bed, stumbled into the living room and there grappled with her assailant. The two women struggled through three rooms of the dark apartment in the funeral home basement. They traded blows with a flashlight and heavy toy pistol until blood streaming from their wounds splashed floors and walls. Mrs. Rainey said she clamped her teeth down on Miss Evans' fingers and retained her hold throughout the struggle. She testified that she finally wrenched away from the other woman and fled to a neighbor's *[Howard Minor]* home.'

Rex Rainey, the former prominent funeral director, gave surprise testimony that aided in convicting his lover in attacking his ex-wife. He admitted he had communicated his wife's threats to Miss Evans during the years of their courtship. But he flatly denied suggesting that Miss Evans go to his house to look for a gun or that he aided her in her preparations.

Webster County's Prosecutor at the time was Roy Miller and its Sheriff was E.I. Cunningham.

The Sheriff testified that even before he had been summoned to the funeral home the morning of the attack he heard a woman 'squealing and hollering.' When he arrived on the scene and saw Mrs. Rainey at the neighbor's home 'she was so bloody you couldn't have told who she was.' He said he found furniture overturned and torn up in the Rainey apartment. The floor and rug were bloody and he found blood-stained handprints over the walls. Cunningham said the smell of chloroform was strong in the house and that he had to air out Mrs. Rainey's bedroom before he would enter. 'That chloroform would about kick you off.'"

March 23, 1950 "MARY MARGARET EVANS CONVICTED—Prosecutor Files Charges Against Rex Rainey (2 photos, one of Carmen Rainey, one of Mary Margaret Evans, courtesy of Springfield Newspapers, Inc.)

As a result of the testimony in the trial of Mary Margaret Evans here this week, a warrant was issued this Wednesday morning for the arrest of Rex Rainey. He is charged with felonious assault with intent to kill, the same charge upon which Miss Evans was convicted Tuesday.

It has not been learned at press time Wednesday noon *[3/22]* whether the warrant had been served upon Mr. Rainey or not.

Court set sentence at four years: Mary Margaret Evans was found guilty of felonious assault with intent to kill as a result of her attack on Mrs. Carmen Rainey in the early morning hours of last October 19. Following two days of the trial Monday and Tuesday, the case finally went to the jury shortly after 7:00 o'clock Tuesday night. The final verdict was rendered to the court at 11:47 p.m.

Since the jury was unable to agree upon the amount of punishment, Judge James P. Hawkins immediately set the penalty at four years in the state penitentiary.

(The jury foreman, Walter Denney, upon inquiry by the court stated that the jury had agreed early upon guilt but could not agree on the amount of punishment when 11 jurors were in favor of four years against the opinion of one juror who would not go above two years. The judge had previously instructed the jury that in case of deadlock on the penalty, it would become the duty of the court to set punishment.)

Miss Evans' attorneys immediately asked for permission to make bond, and Judge Hawkins immediately set the bond at $4,000. Written bond was made Tuesday night by her father, Doug Evans, of east of Marshfield, and several others. Bond was made subject to an appeal of the case.

If an appeal is ruled out, Miss Evans is to be taken to the penitentiary by the Sheriff at once.

The verdict came as a climax to an exciting two-day trial which was attended by hundreds of people who jammed the courtroom from morning until night. Lunches were taken by those who were cautious enough to make sure they would hold their seats. Aisles, corridors, doorways and even the front of the courtroom behind the railing were tightly packed constantly.

The state ended its testimony Monday evening at shortly after 6:00 o'clock, with Mrs. Rainey as the chief witness. Mrs. Rainey (who since the attack has divorced Rex, her former husband and the admitted paramour of Mary Margaret) told of the wild and bloody struggle which ensued when Miss Evans entered the Rainey's funeral home and attacked her (Mrs. Rainey) with a toy pistol and a flashlight. Other state testimony included Dr. C. R. Macdonnell's story of the extent of the wounds inflicted upon Mrs. Rainey. He testified he had treated the head cuts and bruises she suffered and then sent her to a Springfield hospital. Her neighbors, it was brought out, were unable to recognize her when she escaped and ran to them for help.

The case grew more sensational Tuesday morning when the defendant went on the witness stand to testify that Rex Rainey had urged and encouraged her to enter his home, and according to her claim, secure a gun which Mrs. Rainey was supposed to have taken from a funeral home vehicle. The defense had announced in its opening statement to the jury that morning that it would prove that the fight between the two women was in self-defense upon the part of Mary Margaret, who merely sought the gun when she entered Mrs. Rainey's bedroom. Mary Margaret also testified that she had received threats of bodily injury from Mrs. Rainey in the form of two letters in 1945 and by Mrs. Rainey following her around in Springfield. Her testimony further was that Rex Rainey had transmitted threats to her, telling her that his wife had threatened the girl's life. In cross-examination Prosecuting Attorney Roy C. Miller sought to establish that no threats had been made in recent years or immediately before that attack of October 19, 1949. Miss Evans claimed that Rex told her about the pistol taken by his wife, told her of his wife's sleeping habits, furnished part of the bizarre array of equipment consisting of a sleeping medicine, stomach pump, chloroform, etc., which she claimed were to be used to keep Mrs. Rainey asleep while she, the defendant, sought gun.

The prosecutor's cross-examination also sought to tear down the defense's contention that Mary Margaret tried to escape when Mrs. Rainey awakened and struggled with her.

When defense attorney Harold T. Lincoln of Springfield announced that the defense was completed early Tuesday afternoon, Prosecutor Miller caused a ripple of excitement to pass through the crowd by asking the court to subpoena Rex Rainey. Mr. Miller told a reporter he intended to use Rex as a rebuttal witness for the state.

In spite of whispered murmurs, heard by this reporter, that 'they'd never catch him,' Mr. Rainey appeared on his own account within a few minutes and testified readily. He was accompanied by his attorney, John Hosmer.

In testimony the former funeral home director denied aiding, urging, or encouraging Mary Margaret's entry into the Rainey living quarters in the basement of the funeral establishment, or furnishing any of the aforementioned array of drugs, etc. He admitted transmitting to Mary Margaret threats made upon her by his wife, Carmen. He admitted upon questioning that he had told the defendant that Mrs. Rainey had 'taken the gun and was liable to kill her' (Miss Evans).

Attorney Haseltine of Springfield made the opening defense plea to the jury. The chief defense attorney, Mr. Lincoln, made an impassioned plea in which he described Miss Evans as a meek but brave woman who could not, he seemed to be trying to impress the jury, have had killing in her heart, a timid woman who had been an easy prey for Rainey's attentions. Because a past mistake had precluded her chances for a 'normal life.' He told the jury that she should not be imprisoned and taken away from her son.

In his argument, Roy C. Miller told the jury that 'Miss Evans had tried to take Mrs. Rainey away from her son, Jack' and that if the jury found Mary Margaret not guilty 'it would be the same as telling every teen-aged girl and every woman in Webster County that it was all right to run around with married men, and that it was all right to have illegitimate children.' He implied that if Mrs. Rainey had made threats about Mary Margaret that it was only natural that she would, under the circumstances, hold little love for her husband's paramour. Roy told the jury, furthermore (in connection with these alleged threats of Carmen's) that it was not Mrs. Rainey who drove 25 miles to Springfield in a rented car and under an assumed name, to attack Mary Margaret, but that it was Mary Margaret, the defendant, who did those things and entered the bedroom of Mrs. Rainey's home and attacked her. He showed the jury the evidence of the stained clothes Miss Evans wore at that time, the toy pistol and the flashlight allegedly used by her in the attack.

Mrs. Rainey was present in court most of the trial. Rex Rainey was not in court until subpoenaed, but after finishing testimony, returned, and was present when the arguments were made.

Mary Margaret apparently was calm when the verdict and sentence were rendered. Her father was her faithful companion throughout the trial.

All reports were that never had such crowds attended a trial in recent Marshfield history."

[Edna Cunningham] "The trial: I was up there a few times but, you know, I just don't hardly remember much about it. I remember the mother and dad sittin' there and the dad cryin', and her there, but I've just forgot about it. I didn't want to remember it, anyway."

[Celesta Davis] "The Rex Rainey thing, that was before my time at the phone company, but I went to the trial, a lot of it. He sat up on the

208

stage just as calm as a cucumber while she was being sentenced. She certainly paid the price. She just got off on the wrong track.

After she came out, her friends rallied around her pretty much. She shouldn't have done it, but I don't feel like she planned it. I feel like she was used. I don't know just how it happened, but I guess Carmen was just strong enough to get away.

Carmen was a lovely person, she really was, and they were wonderful operators of the funeral home. They worked together and they just couldn't have been better.

That was the talk of the town for years."

[Members of the jury that decided the fate of Mary Margaret Evans: Ivan Ewing of Fordland; H.C. Crowe of Fordland; Edgar Miller of Marshfield; Floyd Davison of Elkland; Clint Snider of Marshfield; W.W. Denney of Seymour; Audie Criger of Northview; Ed Glaubitz of Rogersville; **Fred Rost of Marshfield**; Bill Bellinger of Seymour; Warren Davis of Niangua; Opal Mayfield of Seymour, the only woman juror. *Elzie Doyle, Webster County Deputy Sheriff, was in charge of the jury, March 20 and 21, 1950.]*

[Fred Rost] "Ya see, there was a lady on the jury, too, just one lady. I can't think what her name was. She just wanted to turn her loose, turn her loose. All the rest of us wanted to do something about it. So it went on from there.

Oh, that courthouse was full up. They had to stop people from comin' up because it was so full, they was afraid the courthouse wouldn't hold 'em up, that it would collapse! Oh, they was the awfulest crowd I ever saw.

They kept us all night and I *do* know that, 'long that evening, someone said something to the Sheriff, Cunningham, said, 'What are you gonna take us to?' Well, it was down at what we called The Y, down at the end of Jackson Street, where the highway come up through, there was a bunch of cabins at that time. The Old 66 come up through in there.

They said, 'Well, we can't sleep!' Well, he said, 'I'll tell ya, if you get the permit now, from the old judge, I'll take every one of you to the picture show and I'll pay every one of your way.' Well, someone talked to the judge and he said, 'Well,' he said, 'It's alright now--if you (Sheriff Isam) stay with them.' The lady, you see, had to stay with this one other lady.' *[Elzie Doyle]*

Well, we was sitting in there eatin' at Andrews Café, the Sheriff come in and said, 'Well, it's time to go to the show.' So we went to the show.

And I'll bet you we wasn't in there fifteen minutes and he *[Isam]* was sittin' there right behind us—sound asleep!! And he didn't know whether we was there or had walked out! He wouldn't have even known! He was just that tired!

[According to The MARSHFIELD MAIL, the movie playing on Monday, March 20, 1950 was Top O' the Morning, *starring Bing Crosby and Barry Fitzgerald, with Ann Blyth and Hume Cronyn.]*

But now, he did make a good Sheriff, I'll tell you right now. They couldn't get by with that speedin' like they do today!

But anyway, the next day the judge said, 'You fellas are getting tired of settin' here. You get out and walk around The Square. But you keep that Sheriff right behind! But be back in an hour. Well, we started around The Square and we got ahead of the Sheriff, you know, just goin' down the sidewalk there. And he had to holler at us. 'Hey! You wait a minute!'

I'll tell ya, we had a time! The next morning—oh, I don't know whether I oughta tell it or not....Well, they took us all night to that bunch of cabins. Me and another feller—Glaubitz was the ole boy, lived over here toward Fordland—we roomed together and we was gonna take a bath. But them others used up all the warm water! But anyway, we tried our best to take a bath. We had that darn cold water.

Them boys of ours, they had the chicken pox, both of them. There I was sittin' out there, I didn't know how them kids were getting along.

So the next morning we got up and went up there.

One feller said, 'I can't serve on this, I just can't do this.' Sheriff said, 'Well Man, you have to! You already started on it. There ain't any way you're gonna get out of it,' he said, 'even if a fella went sick, we'd have to go get him and bring him up here. That's my job.'

Now that'd be pitiful, wouldn't it. He said, 'What's the matter, why can't you serve?' And the fella said, 'I've got the scours!'

Rest of us couldn't laugh at him. I felt sorry for him.

Sheriff said, 'Well, I'll have to bring the judge around, to tell him.' And the fella said , 'You better,' before he ever called us in there. So Isam brought the judge around, and the judge said, 'Now, I'll tell ya,' he said, 'Whenever I call ya in, you see that front seat down there? You get down there on that end, and you stay there. You be the first one in!' Well, that's where he got.

I'll bet we wadn't in there fifteen minutes when the ole judge hollered, 'Fifteen minutes recess, boys!' and that ole boy he took off out that door! We couldn't hardly keep from laughing, but we didn't want to laugh at him, either. But, you know, he had good luck the rest of the day up until around 11 o'clock that night. But, boy, I'll tell you right now, we had a time.

They was both guilty. Well, now, he was guilty of goin' to see her, is what I mean.

They tried to find Rex Rainey, finally went and got him. He was right there, in just a little while. Rex owned up to it! They asked him if he'd been goin' out there and seein' her, and he said, 'Yes.' He owned up to it.

But I believe Carmen was a good lady, I sure do.

I always liked Rex. You couldn't help but like him. He made a good undertaker.

I believe he wanted to treat people right. But, I don't know, I guess he just, you know, had that on his mind, goin' out there to see her. I could show you the very place he went. Out past the golf course, on the way to Niangua. She worked in Springfield but she lived around here.

The jury took a vote, we sentenced her. The lady was the main one who didn't want anything to happen to her. The jury vote was 11-1. She was a lady, you see, she didn't want to sentence a lady.

They had me on four or five different juries.

There was two of 'em, down at Niangee, went and stole cars. When Isam was Sheriff. Now one of these boys, he kinda got shell-shocked over there, in World War II. These brothers had another boy with them. They stole tires down by Niangua.

They got him up there [in the courtroom] and, boy, you could tell, oh, man, his mind wasn't good.

I'd been to a Box Supper at the old school house—Pie Supper, they used to call it—and he was over there. And they used to put these pretty girls up there, to get the cake, you know. Well, they put one up there and they had me on a Board...Oak Hill School...and they had me on the Board. But that old boy, he didn't know what he was doin'. He pulled a $20 bill out and said, 'Take this up there and put it on this girl.'

I said, ' You don't want to give all that,' and he said, 'Yeah, yeah, just put it all.' I went up there and, I don't know, I think I spent a dollar or two on it, and I took him back the change.

Now, they had *him* arrested for that tire deal! But we cured him. The judge told us—we was undecided what to do—we knowed he was guilty, but we didn't know what to do, you know. And the judge came back and told us, 'Now I know you fellas are up against it there. But I'll tell ya, if you clear him, we'll send him down south to the hospital.' And I guess they did, 'cause he got over it.

The only time I had to spend the night was the Evans trial. They furnished the eats. We went to Johnny Andrews Café. 'Just order anything you want to eat,' they said. Then he *[Sheriff Isam]* said, 'Let's go to the picture show now. The judge gave you consent,' so we went.

I'll tell you, oh I was glad to get away from there! I'll tell you right now. That jury is something."

[Wilma Ryser] "My grandmother had no use for Rex Rainey after all that happened. She made the remark that 'When I die, if you don't have any undertaker but Rex Rainey, throw me in the ditch.' I remember her saying that! She had definite opinions about everything!"

March 30, 1950 "Sam Fleetwood, 19, of near Seymour, was arrested in Wichita, Kan., Monday where he was found in possession of the red 1948 2-ton truck belonging to the city of Seymour, which was stolen early Sunday morning.

Word was received in Seymour that Fleetwood had the truck in Wichita and he was apprehended only a short time later. Since two men reportedly were seen in the truck, a pick-up order is still in effect for another Seymour resident listed as a suspect.

Fleetwood probably will be returned to Webster County, officers said. Sheriff Cunningham has gone to Jefferson City to try to get extradition papers from the governor.

The truck was stolen from the city garage early Sunday morning. It was reported the thieves gained entrance by breaking a rear window. The large double doors were locked and chained from the outside, so they rammed the truck through the wooden doors. One door, badly splintered, was ripped loose from its hinges, and the doors toppled to the ground, still chained together.

Neighboring residents who heard the crash about 6 a.m. reported seeing the truck drive away, occupied by two men. Taken with the truck were several picks and shovels which were carried in the bed."

"During the trial last week of Mary Margaret Evans, charged with felonious assault, the Springfield newspapers ran a short story on how near Sheriff came to having to go out and milk the cows for Clint Snider, one of the jury. The jury had to stay together on Monday night. However, a neighbor milked the cows and the Sheriff said, 'Don't you go getting the Sheriff any milking jobs.'

A radio program known as the Rex Allen Radio Program in

212

Oklahoma City picked up this story as interesting...and told Clint Snider that he was awarded a milking machine worth over $200 and other prizes given by the Rex Allen Program, which is a cowboy 'give-away program.'"

[Eldeen Cunningham] "I first met Wilbur's parents the morning of our wedding day *[3/25/50]*. Being by nature shy and quiet, I was at first very intimidated by Isam. He was a big man with a rather rough, booming voice and I was at a loss about how to react to him. As time passed I soon realized he was simply a wonderful man who cared deeply for his family, loved being Sheriff of Webster County, and was a pushover for little children."

[In the middle of everything else, especially his friends' trial, Isam's son Wilbur—Red— gets married. Life goes on.]

April 6, 1950 "Sheriff E.I. Cunningham and B. F. Yeubanks of Niangua, returned Saturday from Wichita, Kan., with Sam Fleetwood, 29, of Seymour, charged with stealing a Seymour city truck. Bill Blankenship, charged the same offense, returned from Kansas the Tuesday before."

County Court Proceedings--"The court met with a representative of the State Auditor's Office....Sheriff E.I. Cunningham was shown to owe the County $923.50 for overcharges on board of prisoners, fees and mileage."

April 20, 1950 "To Whom It May Concern—Inasmuch as there has been rumors and misrepresentations spread throughout the County concerning the Sheriff's Office as a result of a recent article published in the Marshfield Mail concerning a recent audit made in Webster County by the State Auditor's Office, it is my desire to publish this statement in order to clarify any misunderstanding that may arise and to present the true facts.

By way of introduction I quote from the letter of transmittal accompanying the State Auditor's Report which will explain the policy of the State Auditor's Office. Quote:

'Any person or persons examining this report for the purpose of obtaining information for the general public as to the results of this examination, should remember:

That it takes years for a man to build a reputation. Ungrounded charges may destroy that reputation overnight.

That it is one of the purposes of these examinations to protect the honest, well-meaning official, who has made a 'Mistake of the head and not of the heart.'

That the summary of findings, as found in the front of this report only shows bare cold figures.

This summary is indexed so by turning to the page so indicated you can see just what the examiner really has to say in connection with his findings. If this course is pursued, the general public, whose servant the official is, will receive an unbiased report as to just what their officials are doing.' End quote.

In view of the above explanation, I feel that it would be unfair to any county official to publish any part of the report without any explanation or any further details. In order to prevent the further spread of any malicious rumors and to avoid any further implications which may arise, the following statements are made for the information of the general public. Some of the discrepancies as shown by this report was the result of clerical errors in the County Clerk's office, some through the misinterpretation of statutes and new laws, and others through clerical errors, etc.

The Constitution of 1945, which went into effect July 1, 1946, changed many of the laws pertaining to County Government. The fees which were formerly retained by the Sheriff are now turned into the County Treasurer and the Sheriff receives mileage and other compensation in lieu of the fees.

The State pays the Sheriff for the transportation of prisoners to the State Penitentiary. The Attorney General and the State Auditor has ruled that the Sheriff must pay these fees over to the County. The County Court then pays the Sheriff for mileage and also the Deputy Sheriff's salary and mileage. The amount of these State fees earned by the Sheriff since July 1, 1946, was $646. The County Court allowed $226.40 for the Sheriff's mileage and $386.40 for Deputy hire and mileage, in lieu of these fees.

The Sheriff's Office made settlement with County Court for these fees as soon as the State Auditor completed the audit and ruled that these were accountable fees which was March 1, 1950.

The balance of all shortages and discrepancies as shown by the State Auditor's Report has been satisfactorily settled with the County Court on April 12. The amount due the County was $277.50 and the amount due to the Sheriff's Office was $202.10. Therefore, after all errors were corrected through the County Court it was found that the Sheriff owed the County only $75.40, on account of the clerical errors, aforesaid.

It is hoped that this brief explanation will serve to inform the public of the true facts concerning the conduct of the Sheriff's Office and to further present a fair and unbiased report of the settlement of the Sheriff's Accounts with the County Court. You are invited to inspect the County records for verification of any statement made by me.

Respectfully yours,
E.I. Cunningham, Sheriff,
Webster County, Missouri."

"County Court Proceedings—Agreement was made with Sheriff E.I. Cunningham on boarding prisoners. It was agreed that the court would furnish the Sheriff two rooms on the second floor of the courthouse as living quarters together with all utilities furnished without charge to the Sheriff. The Sheriff is to feed each prisoner confined in the county jail at a cost of not more than $1.50 per day per prisoner. This agreement to be for six months from April 15, 1950.

Settlement was made with Sheriff E.I. Cunningham on overcharges as shown in the recent state audit."

April 27, 1950 "In weather more suitable for an ice hockey game, the Blue Jays lost a heartbreaker to Buffalo High School in a baseball contest at Buffalo last Thursday.... 'Red' *[Charley]* Cunningham pitched a fine game for Marshfield."

May 11, 1950 "State of Mo. vs. Rex Rainey, felonious assault. Motion to quash information filed, considered and overruled....State of Mo. vs. Mary Margaret Evans, felonious assault. Motion for new jury argued, considered, and overruled. Judgment and sentence that defendant serve a term of four years in the state penitentiary. Sheriff allowed one extra guard."

[While I was reading about and taking notes on the Mary Margaret Evans/Carmen Rainey/Rex Rainey events—especially the trial in March of 1950—the obituary of Mary Margaret appeared in the current MARSHFIELD MAIL. She died at age 85 in Marshfield on March 15, 2003, in Webco Manor Nursing Home, apparently from cancer, someone told me later. The article described Mary as a homemaker and long-time member of the Good Hope Baptist Church.

It explained that Mary especially enjoyed her home and flowers, and her fellowship with her church family. She loved being with her Wal-Mart friends where she worked as an associate for a number of years before her retirement; that she is survived by one son, Larry Evans; that she is buried in the Marshfield Cemetery as Mary Oedekoven, having been preceded in death by her husband William Oedekoven and her parents.

I couldn't help but contrast all I'd been reading in October 1949 and early 1950 about the paramour Mary Margaret Evans, the attack on Carmen Rainey, the trial, the prison sentence. None of this was alluded to in her obituary.

And I was reminded: we all have our secret life stories.]

"Circuit Judge James P. Hawkins Monday overruled a motion at Marshfield by attorneys for Rex Rainey, former undertaker, to quash the information charging Rainey with felonious assault.

The undertaker was charged last March by Prosecutor Roy Miller following testimony by Miss Mary Margaret Evans, of Springfield, concerning her love affair with Rainey and concerning her struggle with Mrs. Rainey last October after she had entered the Rainey home at night. Miss Evans was convicted and sentenced to four years in prison.

On April 29, Mr. and Mrs. Rainey, who had been divorced, were remarried.

At noon Wednesday *[5/10]* MAIL press time, Judge Hawkins had not set the date for the Rainey trial."

[Mitzi Hosmer] "Rex Rainey was absolutely the most charming man ...a wonderful smile. I mean, everybody just loved him.

Bess *[John Hosmer's mother, owner of Hosmer and Hosmer Insurance]* adored him. I mean, she absolutely adored him. When all that happened she didn't believe a bit of it. She thought that Mary Margaret was so in love with him and wanted him to leave, that she concocted all this herself. She was trying some way, because she thought Rex would leave her in a minute. Rex denied it all. He denied that he ever had anything to do with it, with the breaking in. He admitted he had had an affair. She *[Mary Margaret]* was a beautiful young woman. And her parents were just sweet.

So it was really a small area, much smaller than it is now, and everybody knew everything. Everybody.

Everybody that I was with, we were all on Rex's side. Because he had eaten with us, he'd been Bess's friend. Carmen was a sophisticated...probably more education than Rex had. She taught kids reading, plays, drama. John *[Hosmer]* took classes under her. Elocution.

She was a lovely lady. Really accomplished. And just worked along with him, like a perfect pair, at the funeral home. They were sincere and loved people. You didn't think of them as being the typical funeral home persons.

Bess had Rex with her for a few weeks *[when Carmen was in the hospital]* because she wanted to comfort him. He could do no wrong. Rex stayed with Bess because she was worried to death about him. She thought, 'He'll do something crazy.' She just kept him there, like a kid, huddled over him.

She got him back with Carmen.

Bess arranged with Carmen to be at some restaurant in Springfield. Then she took Rex, she got in there and worked it out. I have no idea what she said but she took him up there and they talked. And they got back together. That was always her high point. She was so proud when she got that done because she thought they had had such a good life. The community loved them. And this one woman doing this crazy thing. He shouldn't have had an affair but I don't think she ever mentioned that, she didn't even care. It was like, he had had that affair but he was sorry and he really still loved Carmen. It was obvious he did. He always seemed to just adore her.

Bess died in 1957 and he was the funeral home operator. In Springfield. Because she always said she wanted Rex, she wanted to go to that funeral home.

Carmen's aunt was raised by my grandmother in Odessa, Missouri. Her name was Marianna Thanne and her dad was an alcoholic. The mother died. So my grandmother raised Marianna and somebody else raised another one of the children, like somebody else raised Carmen's father. Nobody had said a word to me about this. But one time I was reading in *The MARSHFIELD MAIL* that Marianna Thanne was visiting Carmen Rainey. I was thinking, 'How does she know Carmen Rainey?' I grew up knowing her, then she taught school while I was in Odessa High School. And I asked Carmen. And I thought, 'Gosh, my grandmother had raised a member of her family.'

Carmen and I were friends mainly through Bess. How did Bess get so close to Rex Rainey? Well, you know, Bess was in business and she probably sold insurance to the funeral home. Rex came and she just adored him, so just got attached to him. He came, maybe borrowed money from them, I have no idea. She just always simply adored him.

What's my take on it? My take was that Bess felt that here was a girl who was just crazy about him and she did a stupid thing. She was jealous and she wanted him. Maybe he made some silly statement to her but Bess didn't ever confront that, as I remember.

Of course, Mary Margaret grew up here in Marshfield.

I think they *[Carmen and Rex, after they remarried]* were as happy as could be. Of course, I'm sure he bent over backwards trying to make up because from then on, they seemed happy.

Carmen was so energetic, she worked so hard. Maybe he was a little tight. He dressed flashy, he dressed beautifully. And she did too. But she stayed with it every minute. I think she was a workhorse. I heard Bess tell her, 'You need to do things!' but they didn't really get out any and do things. They just stayed stuck in their house.

We all knew the Raineys, but it was Bess."

[Jack Rainey] "I was afraid of Bess Hosmer! She was authoritative, if that's a word. Her voice...you would have had to heard her voice to understand. She was so above everybody. She just had that aura about her. Being a kid you're easily influenced.

John Hosmer, the older one, John's dad, Bess's husband, he teased me to no end. When I'd be goin' to school, he'd be comin' out of Johnny Andrews's Café, and he'd holler across the road at me...and he done it to other kids too, not just me...John's dad was a whole different character than John. He wasn't liberal, he was for *John*. But he'd holler across the road at me and he'd say, 'Well there goes that rainy weather Rainey!' He was as bald-headed as he could be, and he'd pull his hat off and slap his head and say, 'When I was born, they said all they had was red hair, and I just turned it down, I didn't want any of it!' I was red-headed, see. He'd be goin' right by the MAIL office, it was just almost straight across from Andrews's Café, and he'd say, 'Here's fifteen cents. Go in there and get you a bottle of ink and dye that red hair! I wouldn't have that red hair on my head!' My mother told him one time, 'If he ever goes ahead and dyes his hair, puts any ink on it, I'm gonna be after you!'

They were both characters but entirely separate. John was nothin' like his dad. Almost like John wasn't even his dad. Both Johns were pretty much of cut-ups, but at the same time, John Junior was so radical, and his dad wasn't radical like that at all. Not that I know of. At one time I think they'd had some money, but times had changed on 'em and they had to go into the insurance business to survive, and Bess was the one that was the salesperson. John, just, was *there. My* view of it anyway.

Later on, I wound up buying insurance from her, when I got old enough to have insurance, I bought it from Bess. But I bought it just because my folks had done business with her and I didn't have to go through a lot. Could go in there, buy the insurance, and be out. She didn't have to ask a lot of questions. She knew she was gonna get her money, and if she didn't get it from me, she'd get it from somebody else."

"An application for a parole will be filed in circuit court today, Wednesday, in behalf of Miss Mary Margaret Evans, Horace Haseltine, a member of her defense staff said. And Haseltine indicated that if the parole is denied, an appeal to a higher court may be asked.

Miss Evans was committed to the Webster County jail here about 5 o'clock Monday afternoon after Judge James P. Hawkins had denied her motion for a new trial.

Miss Evans was convicted of felonious assault on Mrs. Rex Rainey and was sentenced to four years in prison."

"City Appointments--Night Watchman: Commodore Smith"

[Oliver Evans] "After I quit to work for MFA, I was still available to be a deputy. But he *[Isam]* never called for me."

[Oliver Evans, Night Watchman, was related to Mary Margaret Evans and needed to be a key witness—against her—at her trial.]

May 18, 1950 "Circuit Judge James P. Hawkins refused to grant Mary Margaret Evans a parole from her four-year prison sentence at the hearing Wednesday of last week. The judge turned down her plea despite these efforts in her behalf:

a statement by Mrs. Rex Rainey in court that the public interest would best be served by paroling Miss Evans (she was the victim of an attack by Miss Evans.)

a petition signed by 240 citizens, including many prominent persons in Marshfield, requesting the parole.

another petition signed by 11 of the jurors that convicted Miss Evans.

The trial of Rex Rainey on felonious assault charges, which charge was brought as a result of the trial of Miss Evans, was continued to next regular (September) term of circuit court by Judge Hawkins last week.

Rainey is charged in connection with the mysterious night attack on his wife, Mrs. Carmen Rainey, made last October by Miss Mary Margaret Evans, 31-year-old former switchboard operator. Miss Evans admitted scuffling with Mrs. Rainey and received four years in prison for felonious assault with intent to kill.

John C. Pope and John Hosmer, Rainey's attorneys, indicated they would probably seek a change of venue in his case. They made their comments after Judge Hawkins had uttered a scathing denunciation of Rainey in turning down Miss Evans' application for parole.

Mr. and Mrs. Rainey, divorced after the October attack, were remarried April 29."

"Sheriff E.I. Cunningham, accompanied by Paul Mitchell of Fordland, took Sam Fleetwood and Wayne Jinks to the penitentiary at Jefferson City Monday. Fleetwood was convicted last week in circuit court here on charge of grand larceny, and Jinks was convicted on a bogus check charge.

Sheriff Cunningham is taking Ralph W. Woods to the penitentiary today, Thursday. Wood [s?] was convicted on a charge of forgery."

"Ralph Bridwell is the new mayor of Marshfield."

"from COLUMBIA, MO. The average Missourian lives nine months longer than the average American, according to a bulletin, 'The First Hundred Years Are The Hardest.'....It explains that out of 100 babies born in Missouri, 96 will reach school age, 93 will reach high school age, 92 will become legal voters, 60 will live to the retirement age of 65, and 22 will probably celebrate an 80th birthday."

May 25, 1950 "Population Numbers from Early Census Figures—Webster County drops some 2,205 since 1940 census, when the population was 17, 226.

Seymour   1,011 a gain of 260, a better showing than any other town in County

Fordland   299, a loss of 32
Rogersville 323, a loss of 107
Niangua   343, a gain of 50
Diggins   125, a loss of 3
Marshfield 1,913, a gain of 149

The final analysis will come from Washington, D.C., men and women in the armed services, persons in hospitals, and travelers will be added."

June 1, 1950 "Homer Clarence Montgomery, a 25-year-old garage worker at Conway, was found dead in an old model pickup truck parked just east of the Roller-Bruce Funeral Home on East Washington Avenue here about 8 o'clock Monday morning *[5/29]*.

He had apparently placed the barrel of a .12-gauge shotgun under his chin and pulled the trigger. Death came instantly.

Sheriff Cunningham said this is apparently what happened:

Montgomery drove to Marshfield Sunday night—he was seen on the highway near here about 11:30—and parked near the funeral home.

He rolled up the glasses on the truck, owned by his father, and fired the fatal blast. Time of the deed was fixed at about midnight.

The body was discovered by Mrs. Eula Singer, who noticed blood running from under the left door of the truck. Earlier passersby did not note anything wrong because the body was slumped over on the seat of the car.

Cunningham said two notes were found. One merely said to 'Notify Luther Bell at Conway.'

The other note, dated Sunday May 28, was addressed to his 4-year-old daughter, Elaine Louise Montgomery. It read:

'In regard to you, honey, I love you so much I can't live without you. I lost my nerves from not being able to be with you. I tried so hard, Sissy. Make a nice woman, Sissy. I tried to be a nice daddy but I failed to keep your mother, Floe. I love you, Sissy, more than anything. No one knows. You can't understand how much I love you.'

The note was signed 'Homer C. Montgomery.'

Coroner K.K. Kelley viewed the body Monday at Roller-Bruce Funeral Home and decided no inquest was necessary. Montgomery, crippled by polio, is said to have been despondent recently.

Montgomery, who worked in his father's garage, is survived by his wife, Floe; the daughter Elaine; three step-children, Norma, Mary, and Joe Bill; his parents, Mr. and Mrs. Roy Montgomery of Conway; and three brothers....

Funeral services were held Tuesday afternoon, May 30, at 3 p.m. at the Conway Baptist church with the Rev. Hobbs officiating. Burial was in the Conway cemetery."

[There were times when I discovered tears running down my cheeks as I read about people in The MARSHFIELD MAIL. Reading Homer's note for his daughter Elaine was one of those times.]

June 29, 1950 "The new Seymour marshal seems to mean business. Saturday night *[6/24]* two men were hospitalized after they were reported to have attacked David Coots. Admitted to O'Reilly Veterans hospital was Hiram L. Henson, 27, of Mansfield. (He is said to reside south of Cedar Gap.) He had a bullet wound in his left thigh. Taken to Springfield Baptist Hospital was Bill Blankenship, 26, of Seymour, who was shot in the right ankle.

Sheriff E.I. Cunningham, who was standing on The *[Seymour]* Square, heard the shots, but did not see the scuffle. The Sheriff said Henson was intoxicated and causing a disturbance. He was arrested at the northwest corner of The Square by Marshal Coots. As they started to the jail Blankenship is said to have followed, cursing the marshal. The marshal invited Blankenship to go to jail, too. At that, Blankenship is said to have struck at Coots. The marshal ducked and Henson is said to have hit him with a wine bottle, knocking him against a barber shop window.

As they advanced upon him, Marshal Coots is said to have fired two shots with his .32-caliber revolver, with each bullet stopping a man. The men were bandaged up by a local physician and sent to Springfield by ambulance."

July 6, 1950 "For the past week the United States has been moving troops into South Korea and July 5th the American forces went into action on the ground. Previously air forces had been in action bombing troop and tank columns, installations, etc. The naval forces have also been in action, with several ships reported sunk....

Whether this war will spread into another worldwide conflagration cannot be foretold. Russian propaganda has been that the Imperialistic United States is on a war of aggression against the Korean people. Russia has demanded that the United Nations order the U.S. to withdraw troops from Korea.

That the high army and navy men of this country do not expect a global war at this time is indicated by the fact that the Reserves are not being called as yet, nor is the draft act being used. However Congress has continued the draft law, in order that it might be used if necessary."

4th of July, 1950 [Freda Langston] "You should have saw Isam! Kid, he rode up there, just as straight as a stick, holdin' the American flag, leaning the pole against his foot. Then he had his horse and he was riding at the head of the parade. He was so proud. I thought that was so pretty. He was quite a character."

[Warren Johnson] "I helped set up the 4th of July parades for years. When my dad [Johnny Johnson] was sheriff, he rode in the parade. The sheriff has always led the parade and carried the American flag, as far back as I can remember. That's a long tradition."

[July 6, 1950 con'd.]

"Allen Bledsoe, 57, of Niangua, is being held without bond in the Webster County jail pending a preliminary hearing on charges that he murdered his wife, Altie, 51.

Bledsoe, arraigned last Thursday afternoon before Magistrate Judge Cline C. Herren, is to have a preliminary hearing July 14, on first degree murder charges.

The fatal shooting occurred shortly after noon last Wednesday at the Bledsoe's cottage at the south edge of Niangua. It apparently stemmed from an argument over when Mrs. Bledsoe should go to a doctor. It is reported that she and her husband have had previous quarrels.

The woman died in an ambulance as it prepared to leave for a Springfield hospital. She suffered a .22 caliber bullet wound in her abdomen.

Bledsoe fled from the house before learning the seriousness of the wound. He was found Thursday at the home of his eldest son's mother-in-law.

Bledsoe claimed he didn't know the gun was loaded, and that it went off while his 12-year-old daughter tried to take it away from him.

Following the shooting Wednesday, Highway Patrolmen, Sheriff Cunningham, Prosecuting Attorney Miller and other officers conducted an all-night search in the east part of the county. He was found a few minutes before 5 a.m. the next morning. Bledsoe quietly surrendered at the farm home of Mrs. John Crumm, about two miles north of Marshfield (Mrs. Crumm's daughter is married to the eldest Bledsoe son, Carless, 25). The officers surrounded the Crumm residence and shouted for him to come out. He came out quietly.

It is reported that a neighbor of Mrs. Crumm called officers to tell them where the man was. While awaiting the arrival of the posse Mrs. Crumm said they talked very little of the shooting.

Authorities reconstructed the slaying in this manner:

The couple's son, 17-year-old Floyd Bledsoe, said his mother had been in ill health for some time, and that after lunch Wednesday she asked her husband to take her to a doctor. Bledsoe became angry and in the ensuing argument grabbed up a rifle.

Floyd said he first tried to wrench the gun away from his father and then ran to a neighbor's home to borrow a rifle.

As he returned to the house, officers said, he heard a shot and saw his father run from the house still carrying the rifle.

When the youth entered the home he found his mother lying on a bed bleeding profusely from a wound in the abdomen. Two younger children, ages 8 and 10 years, had witnessed the shooting.

Mrs. Bledsoe was placed in a Roller-Bruce ambulance which headed for a Springfield hospital, but she died before the ambulance left Niangua.

Coroner K.K. Kelley said the bullet completely penetrated the woman's body and she lived only about 20 minutes after being wounded.

Within a short time after Mrs. Bledsoe's death Sheriff Cunningham had organized the posse. The searchers were later joined by C. M. Hutchens, Springfield, and his two bloodhounds.

They followed Bledsoe's trail through the heavily wooded farm area throughout the night and about dawn received word—by radio from highway patrol—that Bledsoe could be found at the farm home of Mrs. John Crumm, a widow, about two miles north of Marshfield.

A coroner's jury viewed the body at the Roller-Bruce Funeral Home here Saturday, but the inquest is not being held until this Wednesday [7/7] by Coroner K.K. Kelley.

Funeral services were held Sunday afternoon at 2 o'clock with the Rev. L.L. Rodgers officiating, at the Roller-Bruce Funeral Chapel. Burial was in the Timber Ridge cemetery.

Mrs. Bledsoe is survived by five sons, Carless, Floyd, Fay, Leaman and Loren, all of Niangua; three daughters, Mrs. Inas Witten of Memphis, Tenn., Miss Nola Bledsoe of Moline, Ill., and Miss Clyda Bledsoe of the home; two brothers, ...four sisters....and two grandchildren."

[Edna Cunningham] "I remember Bledsoe shot his wife. That happened one Saturday afternoon we were in town, in Niangua!

One of Bledsoe's sons was goin' to GI school, and after Buster got out *[of the service]* he went to GI school. You've heard of that. GI school? Training for the boys? So this Bledsoe boy said to Buster one day, Buster said he come up to him and he says, 'What are they gonna do with my dad?' And Buster says, 'Well I have no idea, I don't know anything about it.' 'Oh,' he says, 'you know all about it!' he said to Buster like that. Well we didn't! Isam didn't tell us things that was goin' on. He wasn't supposed to and we didn't ask! And he *[Buster]* didn't know nothin' about that!

Oh he got mad at Buster! 'Oh, you know all about it!' But that just hurt Buster so bad, 'cause he said that to him. He come home and tell me, he says, 'I didn't know nothin' about it. Dad never has said what they are going to do with him.'

We didn't ask! We had all we could do to take care of the farm. We didn't go to Marshfield very often. We traded in Niangua. Other than emergencies, we didn't know every time they put in a prisoner. And we didn't care!"

July 13, 1950 "Magistrate Court Notes from July 10—State of Mo. vs. Clifford Nunn and Lowell Nunn, disturbing the peace."

[It's been stated that these men were arrested by the new night watchman, Tom Nunn, and that arresting these relatives were in fact his first arrests made in office!]

"Correction: In the article last week regarding the shooting of Mrs. Altie Bledsoe by her husband, Allen Bledsoe, it was stated that 'While awaiting the arrival of the posse Mrs. Crumm said they talked very little of the shooting.' (Mrs. John Crumm's home is where the officers found Mr. Bledsoe after an all-night search.)

The MAIL has been informed by a friend of Mrs. Crumm that she was not at home when Mr. Bledsoe came there. That she had gone to Crocker on Tuesday morning and did not return home until Thursday evening at 7:30 p.m. (Bledsoe was found at the Crumm home early Thursday morning.)

The MAIL is informed that three of Mrs. Crumm's children, John, Melvin, Sallie and Shirley Crumm, and Derrell Dudley, a 17-year-old boy, were the only ones at the house when Mr. Bledsoe arrived there. Mrs. Crumm and son, Jack, were gone to Crocker where she was working for Dr. W. F. Schlicht."

[This is the same Dr. W.F. Schlicht who was indicted June 21, 1935, for the first-degree horrible torch murder of Robert Robinson of Marshfield. Also indicted were Mrs. Robinson and the son, Lloyd Robinson. Both the wife and son were found guilty and sentenced to life in the state penitentiary. Dr. Schlicht's trial ended with a hung jury—with seven for conviction and five for acquittal.]

"What might have been a destructive fire was prevented Sunday night *[7/9]* by Tom Nunn, night watchman, when he discovered smoke pouring from the transom over the back door of Letterman's Market. He went and got Sheriff E.I. Cunningham, who broke into the store. They found a compressor on fire, but the flames had not spread. The time was about 11:30 p.m."

July 20, 1950 "The 50th annual Diggins picnic and homecoming is to be held Thursday, Friday and Saturday, August 3, 4, and 5. A splendid program is being planned to entertain all visitors. The Starr Amusement Co., has been secured to present a carnival, shows, and varieties. There will be numerous concessions. Everyone is welcome."

"....People, remembering the last war, have been buying up sugar, tires, refrigerators, washing machines, etc., causing temporary shortages and rising prices. Most of the fears of shortages are unjustified. Warehouses have been full of sugar and there will be plenty. Standby plants for making synthetic rubber are beginning operations and there is not likely to be the shortage of rubber as in the last war. Things are different this time than they were ten years ago....Webster County's quota for the first draft is 2 men. The total for the nation is 20,000."

"Magistrate Court Notes from July 14—State of Mo. vs. Allen L. Bledsoe, charged with murder. Application for change of venue filed by defendant and change of venue granted to Judge of Magistrate Court of Wright county.
Judge E. L. Calton of Hartville was here that day and held the hearing. After preliminary examination the defendant was ordered held for trial by the Webster County circuit court at its next regular term, without bail."

July 27, 1950 "Two Springfieldians joined a couple of Niangua youths in the Webster County jail Monday night in connection with a house burglary near Niangua the night of July 4....Sheriff Cunningham said Elvin Wayne Dudley, 19, and Roger William Brown, 20, went to the Jesse Reese home (Route 2, Niangua) to steal some gasoline, then entered the unlocked house while the Reese family was celebrating the Fourth in Marshfield. They allegedly stole a watch valued at $30, $1.75 in cash, and five gallons of oil.
About ten days ago Brown swapped (Elbert Gene) Crawford, 19, the watch, who sold it to Charles Marsh, a farmer living on Route 2, Niangua. Officers recovered the watch from Marsh and then tracked down the accused four. (The fourth was Virginia Lee Benenie, 23.) Brown and Crawford are from Niangua. Dudley is formerly of Niangua. (from the Springfield Leader, July 25)"

"State of Mo. vs. Lowell Nunn, disturbing the peace. Plea of guilty and fined $15. State of Mo. vs. Clifford Nunn, disturbing the peace. Plea of guilty and fined $15."

August 3, 1950 "Sheriff E. I. Cunningham had as a 'guest' at his boarding house Monday night Elza McCovey, Negro, of Mansfield, O. He was being taken back to Ohio from Oklahoma City by J. E. Graves, U.S. Marshal, who stopped here to stay the night. The man was wanted back at Mansfield on a charge of rape."

"Cornelius Van Ness, 53, maintenance man for the Sugar Creek Creamery Co. here for more than a year, was arrested last week by Sheriff E.I. Cunningham on charges of larceny of tools and equipment from the creamery. Sheriff Cunningham says the man admitted the theft.

Tools and equipment valued at nearly $200, including hoisting jacks, and wide pulley belts, were found at the Van Ness farm, 6 miles south of Hartville. The Sheriff said the man told him he had accumulated the articles over a period of time, but didn't explain why.

Van Ness now is said to have a burglary and larceny charge against him in Wright county. He is charged with robbery of a dwelling house."

"The Fordland Farmers Exchange was robbed last Thursday night and among the items taken were 175 cartons of cigarettes, shotgun shells, 2 cases of lard, cigars, etc. The thieves broke in the back door and pried the center door open. The robbery was discovered Friday morning. No arrests have been made as yet."

"Harry Gilbert Gann, 16, one of three youths who escaped from the State Training School at Boonville July 17, was picked up by Sheriff E.I. Cunningham and Tom Nunn last Thursday night at the home of his father, Fred Gann, 5 miles northeast of Elkland. The guard from Boonville, accompanied by his wife, came Sunday for the youth. Gann's two companions in the escape were captured the next day near Boonville. Since then Gann said he had visited relatives in Springfield and Webster County."

"Primary Election Results....The closest race was between Roy C. Miller and Raymond Carter for prosecuting attorney. When the complete unofficial returns were in, Carter had 95 votes majority. There are about 50 absentee votes to be counted, but it is not likely that the final count will change the result."

August 31, 1950 "A search is being made for Elvie Carroll, Marshfield, who, according to Sheriff E.I. Cunningham, stole a taxicab belonging to Raymond Rost, Marshfield, about 12:30 Monday *[8/28].*

Sheriff Cunningham said that Carroll hired the taxi to take him to the Roy Graves place north of town. When they got there, Carroll threatened Rost with a shotgun and told him to get out of the car. Carroll then drove away in the car and was last reported getting gas at Niangua junction."

September 7, 1950 *[Noting the following man's names, I asked myself: is this for real?]* "L.B. (Elby) Carroll, Marshfield man, sought by officers from Monday noon, Aug. 28, when he held up a Marshfield taxi driver and took his cab, was shot and fatally wounded in Seymour on Friday night, Sept. 1, by Marshal D. A. Coots. He died a few minutes after being taken to O'Reilly Veterans Hospital, Springfield.

Carroll, 29, an ex-convict, had held up Raymond Rost with a shotgun after hiring him to take him to the Roy Graves place north of town. Carroll went in and got the gun and then ordered Rost out of the car, and then drove it off.

On Friday night the Seymour marshal saw a car run a stop sign in Seymour and then go around The Square. The car then stopped on the west side of The Square. Marshal Coots noted the license and saw the description fitted the stolen taxi, for which he had been asked by Sheriff E. I. Cunningham to be on the watch for.

Carroll was accompanied by a woman. He left her in the car and went into the Burnett Drug Store, apparently to buy a pint of whiskey. As he came out, he was arrested by Marshal Coots.

Mr. Coots took the man into a café about three doors down the street and asked the woman in charge to telephone Sheriff Cunningham. As she called, Mr. Coots took his eyes off Carroll for a moment. When he looked back he was looking down the barrel of a revolver.

Coots said Carroll was crowding him back into a corner of the room, the gun only about 18 inches from his face. He did not know what to do or what Carroll was going to do. Taking a chance he grabbed quickly at the gun and caught Carroll's wrist. In the scuffle the gun was discharged, the bullet going close by Coots's head.

Meantime the Seymour marshal was trying to get his gun out. When he did, he shot Carroll in the abdomen. He fell to the floor and lay there until the Kelley-Ferrell-Bergman ambulance arrived. He was rushed to the hospital.

The woman with Carroll was Lawanda Jenkins, 26, of Ava, said to be a divorced mother of two children. She was brought to the jail here but was released Saturday afternoon. She said that she first met Carroll the Friday afternoon of his death in a beer joint at Ava.

According to the woman Carroll told her he was a silo builder, and was building some silos in Taney county. She said that she did not know the car was stolen.

Officers have not yet found where Carroll disposed of the shotgun with which he held up Raymond Rost, or where he secured a .32-caliber German-made revolver that he drew on Marshal Coots. The man is said to have sold the wheel, spare tire, tire chains, etc., from the stolen car. At least they are gone.

As Carroll died in Greene county the coroner at Springfield was asked by Prosecuting Attorney Roy Miller to hold an inquest, but the Greene county official refused as he did not believe that an inquest was necessary. The doctor at O'Reilly Hospital signed the death certificate as 'homicide in self-defense.'

Marshal Coots desires an inquest in order that he may be entirely cleared of any blame in the death of the wanted man.

Funeral services were held here at the Roller-Bruce Funeral Chapel with the Rev. W. W. Yoder officiating Monday afternoon at 2 o'clock. Burial was in Marshfield cemetery. The deceased is survived by his mother...three sisters...all of Marshfield.

Carroll was an army veteran of World War II and had served in the Pacific area."

September 14, 1950 "Circuit Court Notes—State of Mo. vs. Allen L. Bledsoe, murder, defendant formally arraigned, and enters a plea of not guilty. Set for trial Nov. 16. State of Mo. vs. Rex Rainey, felonious assault, set for trial Nov. 15."

September 21, 1950 "Last week was Perfect Attendance Week for Lions. The Marshfield Lions Club enlisted the services of Sheriff E. I. Cunningham to make several 'arrests' to bring the club up to near perfect attendance. He, with the chairman of the attendance committee, John Hosmer, went out and brought several members in.

The club authorized the Sheriff to be employed again in bringing the absent Lions to the meeting.

Last Thursday evening one Lion had to wear handcuffs for nearly an hour while a search was being made for keys to unlock them.

The Perfect Attendance Week was the start of an attendance contest by the Marshfield club. The membership has been divided into six teams with members of the Attendance Committee as captains. The six captains are Ernie Vestal, Tom Farr, Norman Lundh, Ralph Gander, John Hosmer, and Carl Young.

The winning team each week will receive their meal free. The winning team the first week was that of Norman Lundh."

"In the Webster County jail at Marshfield Friday night were David Leroy Hedger, 17, of Alex, Okla., and Tony Kenneth Jones, also 17, of Olney, Okla., who have admitted stealing from several homes in various states since they left their base, Fort Monmouth, N.J., Sept. 5.

Sheriff E. I. Cunningham nabbed the youths just south of the Webster-Laclede County Line Friday. He said they probably will be released to army authorities for prosecution.

In addition to four burglaries, they are accused of stealing a station wagon at Norristown, Pa.

The soldiers were arrested Friday morning after several Webster Countians became suspicious of the youths and their loot-laden vehicle and asked Sheriff Cunningham to investigate.

He found them camping near Highway 66, and said they refused to give their names at first. Later, they were identified through papers found in the stolen car. After being jailed in Marshfield, they made statements detailing their cross-country trip.

They said they departed from Fort Monmouth, N.J., a week ago last Tuesday, slipping away at night. Hitchhiking to Norristown, Pa., they stole a 1940 station wagon and drove to Clear Springs, Md.

They broke into a home there, taking a quantity of articles, including a .22-caliber rifle, gas, oil, a shotgun, hunting coat, shoes, cigarettes, bed clothes, clothing, and some change.

Then they headed for Wheeling, W.Va., where they said they entered another house and took about $11 or $12 by breaking open half a dozen small saving banks, towels, clothing, wash clothes, pillows, cooking utensils, and food.

Their next stop was Brazil, Ind., where another house burglary netted them shotgun shells, a coat, bedspread, two pairs of slippers, cigarettes, rings and other items.

Thursday morning they drove their well-loaded vehicle through

St. Louis. About 25 miles southwest of the city near Highway 39, they said they broke into a fourth house and carted off a suitcase full of clothes, blankets, dishes, canned goods and silverware.

Thursday night they stopped in northern Webster County, set up a small camp near the highway, and about noon Friday went to a nearby service station to purchase some hamburger, milk, and other food.

They were busy eating their lunch when Sheriff Cunningham dropped in on their camp after receiving calls from nearby residents asking him to check on the vehicle and the youths.

All the money the soldiers had left was a handful of pennies stashed away in an old sock. They said they were going to Springdale, Ark., where Jones's mother is said to own a 40-acre chicken farm.

Federal agents came Tuesday and took Jones and Hedger to Springfield where they will face trial for stealing the car. The car and stolen articles are still held by the Sheriff here."

September 28, 1950 "Stevens Bros. Circus which showed here Monday, was a disappointment to most people who remember the circuses that made Marshfield in years long ago. To the younger people, who have seen a large circus in Springfield, or other city, it did not measure up.

Travelling with the circus were some gambling booths that caused a little trouble here. Prosecuting Attorney Roy C. Miller made the operators of a wheel gambling device give back one man's money and close up the game.

It seems that one man became involved and let the gambling fever take hold of him to such an extent that he borrowed some money and made two trips to the bank to get money, and then went back to the bank to borrow some more. On this last trip he tried to borrow some money from the prosecuting attorney after he failed to get it from the bank. Atty. Miller made inquiry as to why he had to have it so quickly. When he found out that the man had been losing it at the circus grounds, the prosecutor went there and made the operators of the wheel give back nearly $1,400 they had taken from the man. He ordered the game closed.

The man is said to have lost the money he had on him, borrowed some, then went to the bank and drew out $500. Later he went to the bank again and drew out $900, which was all he had on deposit. When he went back to borrow $1,000 more, Attorney Miller happened to be in the bank."

October 5, 1950 "Harvey J. Kulp, Route 2, Pottstown, Pa., came last Thursday to claim the station wagon held by Sheriff Cunningham here since the arrests of David Leroy Hedger and Tony Kenneth Jones, both 17-year-old lads AWOL from Fort Monmouth, N.J. The Sheriff picked up the youths in the north part of this county after being informed by people in that area of their suspicions. The station wagon was filled with loot that the youths admitted taking from several places on their trip across country.

The young men were taken to Springfield in federal custody and the Sheriff has been waiting for someone to claim the car. Kulp was accompanied by his father, Harvey B. Kulp, who operates a garage repair shop at Pottstown. They said the car was parked at Limerick, Pa., near a school, while young Kulp was attending church services. It was a 1941 model and they did not think about anyone stealing it. Kulp also claimed a blanket that was found in the car."

"Two Wright county lads, residing on Route 1, Seymour, and three men with the carnival connected with Steven Bros. Circus, were arrested last week by Sheriff Cunningham and State Patrolmen on charges of robbery. The Wright county boys met up with the carnival men in a beer joint at Mansfield on Tuesday night while the circus was at Mansfield.

After their arrest, Mickey Herl Weish, 17, and Lonnie Edward Borders, 14, both of Route 1, Seymour, were brought to the jail here. James W. Simmons, 25, Harrisville, W.V., William Paul Nease, Louistown, Tenn., and Sam Sondergaard, 23, Columbus, Ind., were taken to the jail at Hartville. The two brought to Marshfield made bond last Thursday *[9/28].*

The men are said to be charged with robbing the Street Car filling station west of Mansfield Tuesday night of last week *[9/27]* and then a filling station a mile and a half west of there. They then went to the circus grounds and unloaded their loot. Wm. Paul Nease is said to have remained there.

About 2:30 a.m., just after the rain, the other four are said to have robbed the Earl Ellis service station at Seymour. The stolen articles consisted of oil, cartons of cigarettes, candy, gum and chewing tobacco.

Most of the stolen articles have been recovered. Some were

found in a barrel on a circus truck covered with barley. Some was found in the car owned by Weish."

"Magistrate Court Notes, Sept. 28, State of Mo. vs. Mickey Herl Weiks, burglary and larceny....Bond fixed at $2,000 and approved."

[Sometimes a name is spelled several ways, even in the same issue of the paper. Not sure where the fault lies. Certainly not with Ole Isam!]

October 19, 1950 "It is believed that the war in Korea is nearing an end, although guerilla fighting is expected to continue indefinitely."

"Hundreds of people have been coming and going this week from the Webster-Wright Counties Fox Hunters Ass'n. Between 250 and 300 dogs have been brought here for the bench show and field trials. More than 75 dogs were in the bench show and between 160 and 170 dogs took part in the field trials run Tuesday morning *[10/17]* from the Hubble Farm, west of this city....Methodist ladies have been serving food to the visitors from a stand at the city park grounds. Rides and concessions have been set up by the VFW and Junior Chamber of Commerce...."

[Peg Miller] "Heart of the Ozarks Fox and Coon Hunters Association! And the Methodist Church fed these guys. For days! They stayed up all night! I think the booth they used was kept in our garage."

November 2, 1950 "The Strafford schools continue to have financial troubles. After failing to get their levy voted and needing every penny that could be found to operate, the school's safe was robbed last Friday night. About $320 was taken.

The money, most of it in currency, was taken from a large safe in the office of the Superintendent Lawrence Ghan after burglars had 'torn it asunder,' reported Sheriff Glenn Hendrix of Springfield.

A state patrol sergeant said $10 of the loot was stamp money and the remainder receipts from the carnival held Friday night. Most of the carnival money had been taken home for bank deposit, however.

Entry apparently was made through an unlocked window on the second floor—which burglars could have unlatched from the inside during the carnival—because a ladder inside the building at the time of the carnival was found on a coal pile outside the window.

Sheriff Hendrix said thieves must have spent 'two or three hours' knocking off the safe's combination, 'peeling' its metal covering, and pounding through its inner wall. A janitor found the burglary Saturday."

" Next Tuesday is Election Day.
With the Communist menace to the world everyone will surely want to vote....The third ballot will be the Official Ballot and on it will be found seven parties—Democrat, Republican, Progressive, Socialist, Socialist-Labor, Prohibition, and Christian Nationalist, in the order named. Only the Democrat and Republican parties have candidates for county offices.

The voting is secret. A black patch is put on over the number on each ballot, so that no one can tell how anyone votes. The voter will fold his ballots and hand them to the judges of election.

Next Tuesday should be the most important date in the year for every citizen. He or she should go vote even if they have to crawl on their hands and knees.

It cannot be emphasized too much.

Be Sure to Go Vote Tuesday."

"Two Marshfield business firms changed ownership in deals which became effective the first of this week.

Walter's Style Shop was sold by Mr. and Mrs. Dean Walter to Mrs. Bob Abbott and Mrs. Paul Beckerdite, who will operate the women's ready-to-wear business under the name of The Style Shop.

Mr. Walter acquired the Maytag and Crosley agencies from Mr. and Mrs. Orin Pearce and will operate this firm under the name of Maytag Sales and Service...."

[Mary Lou Cunningham] "He always had a way with the younger generation, Isam did. He knew how to tease 'em but yet they knew he was serious.

One night some guy that hauled hay had brought a big load of hay onto The Square, so it would be safe, I guess. They allowed him to park it there. Well, this bunch of boys decided, 'Wouldn't that be fun to unload all that hay out there?'

So they were unloading it and Isam just happened to notice it so he just goes out. He said, 'Boys, I'm going to help you unload all this hay. But when we get through, we're going to load it *all back* on the truck.'

And that's how he did! He helped them finish unloading it! And then he made sure they put it back where it belonged.

He just had a way about him, you know, that he would have fun with them but they also knew he was in control.

A young man in the late 40s or early 50s loved cars and would speed down the country road and in town. One evening was no different and he caught the eye of Isam. The young people hung out at Pete and Red's Café in Marshfield and Isam stopped unexpected many evenings, having coffee or drinking cokes with them. This evening one of the young men told on The Speeder (who chooses to remain anonymous) so Isam and a highway patrolman went in pursuit. The Speeder had hurried home by way of the back roads and his car was parked behind a small house he lived in next to his parents. Isam and the patrolman talked with his parents and his dad said that he must go with Isam because he had done wrong. The patrolman wanted to handcuff The Speeder but Isam said no, that if he had wanted to run away he would have long been gone. They all got in the car and headed for the Webster County jail. The Speeder's dad did not go with them. When they arrived, Isam told The Speeder to 'go over there in the Sheriff's office and lay on the cot.' The Speeder spent the night there and was not put in jail."

[Charley Cunningham and Mary Lou kindly drove me to several interviews that they had arranged. I asked questions and took notes as Charley drove. Here is my rendition of one story Charley told on himself .]

One Halloween evening, teenager Charley and four or five of his buddies decided Sheriff Isam would be around Seymour, always the trouble spot in Webster County, especially on a night like tonight.

Even Charley, the Sheriff's son, wanted desperately to play a trick. It was Halloween, after all!

One of them, probably Charley, announced he'd seen a pile of car tires behind the service station at the stop sign. *[In the 2/8/45 MARSHFIELD MAIL there's an ad for Carpenter Service Station and Garage, north of Depot, that says "See us for tire repair, tire vulcanizing and recapping."]* He thought it would be terrific if they could fling those tires over the privacy fence around the station and stack them in a tremendous pile on one of the side streets leading into The Square from Highway 38.

That's a great idea, the friends must have said, and they raced—quietly—over to the spot. All but one jumped the fence to begin the mighty task of transferring the discarded tires from their heap to the street.

They determined the best way to do this was to fling them over the fence to the one guy on the other side, who would roll or drag it to a growing stack in the dead center of the street. They began, trying not to make any noise whatsoever but surely so excited that suppressed, victorious laughter slipped out occasionally.

The plan was working so well!

The pile behind the station was nearly gone, when, suddenly, a tire came flying back over the fence and nearly hit one of the pitchers. They each and every one froze in place.

Unknown to them, their outside buddy had spotted...oh no...Sheriff Isam coming down the street and took off running as fast as he could the other way. There was no time or desire for a warning to his jolly partners behind the fence.

Charley and the other pitchers heard a too-familiar voice calmly but firmly speak from next to the fence. "You boys come on out here now and put ever' one of them tires right back where you shucked them from."

They could hardly see each other but they knew this was not a decision to be discussed.

They climbed the fence and felt Isam's hard stare, saw his straight back, knew that posture.

Isam patiently watched the much slower, much harder task of hauling dirty tires back over a splintering fence into a dark, dank refuse yard.

Nothing was ever said about it to anyone else, as far as Charley knows.

And Charley decided once and for all that the old timers and others were right: *nobody ever* could be sure where Sheriff Isam might be—even Isam's son.

November 9, 1950 *[results of election from Tuesday, Nov. 7]* "Attorney John Hosmer of Marshfield was the only Democrat candidate to carry Webster County Tuesday. Hosmer defeated Atty. D. Raymond Carter, R., of Seymour by 487 majority *[for prosecuting attorney]* while most of the Republican candidates went over by 700 majority. Hosmer had 3,270 votes. Carter had 2,783 votes."

"Although Mrs. John C. Pope entered the race for Representative in the State Legislature only about two weeks ago, she won by a majority of 807 over Evan McMahan, Mayor of Seymour. She was placed on the Republican ticket when Capt. Lewis Childress was called into active service...."

"To the Voters of Webster County—Thank you for your votes

and messages of good will. I am deeply conscious that your memory of John C. Pope has brought me your support. Let us hope that I can show the same faith and loyalty as he would have done.

Gratefully yours,
ICIE MAE POPE"

[Mitzi Hosmer] "Icie Mae, it was after John *[Pope, her attorney husband]* died, she came up to the house and she was grieving. She came up to the house and we talked her into running. She was a Republican, I know, but she'd always been a close friend. John *[Hosmer]* would say to her, 'Now Icie Mae, you can do it!' She had always been real quiet

You know, she never came out of her shell or really became who she was until John Pope died. She became a teacher—went on to finish college after she was state representative. I think she ran two terms. Everybody loved her. They said she was ineffective but they loved her. She got the Dogwood named as our State Tree. That was her one big bill.

She was a smart lady. But John Pope, he drank, he was gregarious, he talked, he took over, he never *saw* her. She sat quietly, like a full woman is supposed to do. The Icie Mae I later knew, I thought, 'My gosh!'"

November 16, 1950 "Sheriff E. I. Cunningham performed some detective work that caused the arrest of a youth named Clark in Indianapolis Monday.

According to report the Sheriff was in a Marshfield café Friday night when Clark approached him and inquired about a place to spend the night. The Sheriff replied that he could not put him up in the jail as it was full.

About 11 o'clock that night, Curtis Davis of this city returned home and found the dwelling had been ransacked by someone who left the front door open. The thief had removed his own clothes and put on a $60 suit owned by Mr. Davis. It was found that about $15 in cash, some rings and other items were gone.

Sheriff Cunningham went to the Davis home and recognized the clothing left there as those worn by the stranger he had talked to at the café. He recalled the youth had told him he was hitchhiking to Indiana and immediately notified the patrol to be on the watch for him.

The pickup notice caused the Indianapolis police to nab the youth Monday. They said he admitted the robbery and waived extradition.

The Sheriff was to go to Indianapolis this Wednesday, after taking Jimmy Joe Trent to Boonville, and bring back Clark."

"Judge James P. Hawkins was here Monday and Tuesday holding circuit court....State of Mo. vs. Allen L. Bledsoe, murder; continued to next regular term on application of defendant....State of Mo. vs. Rex Rainey, felonious assault. Application for change of venue on account of bias and prejudice of inhabitants of Webster County, filed by defendant. Change of venue granted. Cause transferred to circuit court of Wright county and John Hosmer recognized in sum of $2,000. (Hosmer has been Rainey's attorney and will become prosecuting attorney Jan. 1. He will no longer be able to represent Mr. Rainey.)...State of Mo. vs. Jimmie Joe Trent, burglary and larceny. Parole revoked and terminated. Clerk ordered to issue and deliver to Sheriff a certified copy of sentence and judgment, together with certificate that defendant was paroled and his parole terminated."

"A Springfield couple escaped possible death by inches Sunday morning when their truck was smashed by a train in Niangua.
Sheriff E. I. Cunningham identified them as Mr. and Mrs. Ralph Reed, former operators of a café in Springfield.
The couple was headed east across the main street railroad crossing in Niangua when their Dodge pickup truck stalled as it started across the tracks.
Cunningham said a witness told him the Reeds evidently didn't hear a warning bell until it was too late. However, they heard a Springfield-bound Frisco passenger roaring toward them, and both jumped out of the stalled vehicle.
Seconds later, the left front part of the truck was smashed by the diesel locomotive, which carried the machine about 40 feet down the tracks.
Neither of the Reeds was hurt. Mrs. Reed lost her purse in her race with death, but she found it a short time later near the wrecked truck."

"State of Mo. vs. Jimmie Joe Trent, burglary and larceny. Defendant appears. Judgment and sentence that Jimmy Joe Trent serve an indeterminate term in the State Training School for Boys at Boonville. Sheriff allowed one extra guard."

[An "indeterminate term" was a typical juvenile sentence back then.]

"Revenge was sweet Tuesday night *[11/14]* as the power-studded heavy laden Alumni fell before the 1950-51 crop of *[Marshfield]* Blue Jays, 65-50. Play was fast and furious....Line score, for the Alumni, 'Red *[Charley]* Cunningham' scored 9 points....The game was closely called with 53 personal fouls being called on both sides and the Alumni, coached by Jim Trantham, lost five men via the foul route...."

[I suspect Isam found a reason to check security at this game, with son Charley playing.]

November 30, 1950 "SHERIFF VICTIM OF ATTACK—Prisoners Turn On Him Suddenly.

Sheriff E. I. Cunningham was the victim of a murderous attack Sunday afternoon about 5 o'clock *[11/26]* when two prisoners apparently attempted a jail-break. But for a State Highway Patrolman and Charles Cunningham, the Sheriff's 17-year-old son, who were in the Sheriff's office at the time of the attack, Sheriff Cunningham might have been killed.

The Sheriff and state trooper had been questioning Kenneth Wayne Kile, 26, of Avilla, who was arrested near Marshfield early Sunday on suspicion of stealing a 1937 Ford from in front of the home of Walter Gladden of Springfield Saturday night *[11/25]*. Officers said that Kile apparently ran out of gas. Troopers spotted the car at the north side of Marshfield and began searching the area for the thief.

Sheriff Cunningham joined them and nabbed Kile nearby a short time later. The prisoner had been in jail all day Sunday and had been removed only long enough for the questioning session Sunday afternoon.

The Sheriff was placing Kile in the same cell with Nathan Lyle Clark, 17-year-old soldier with the Air Force in Great Falls, Mont., arrested recently for burglary of the Curtis Davis residence here. As he opened the door of the cell Clark suddenly pulled a homemade blackjack made by placing a bottle in his sock. He hit the Sheriff over the head. The blow knocked Mr. Cunningham to the floor, but he rose again before the men could run. Kile then held him while Clark smashed the bottle across the Sheriff's mouth virtually cutting his lip in two. Clark, while only 17, is said to be about 6 feet tall and weigh 180 pounds.

The brutal attack was interrupted when the State Trooper and Charles Cunningham heard the disturbance upstairs and rushed to the jail. They yanked both men from the Sheriff and subdued them. They were apparently trying to get the Sheriff's gun, but he rolled over on it so they could not reach it.

They summoned a Roller-Bruce ambulance which took the injured man to Burge Hospital in Springfield. 42 stitches were taken in sewing up the wounds Mr. Cunningham suffered. He remained in the hospital overnight and had X-rays made. He was brought home Monday.

Officers believe that Kile and Clark apparently decided upon the double assault on the Sheriff while they were jailed together earlier in the day, and probably intended to escape from the building.

Clark was arrested in Indiana November 14, through the request of Sheriff Cunningham who identified the youth as a house burglar because of some clothing he left behind in the home of Curtis Davis. The youth had approached the Sheriff in a Marshfield café the night of the burglary, seeking a place to stay the night. Later when the Sheriff was called to the Davis home to investigate the break-in he recognized clothing left by the thief as that worn by Clark. The youth is accused of stealing a $60 suit, about $15 in cash, a ring and a necklace. Returned from Indianapolis Clark was to be held for trial on burglary and larceny charges.

The attackers will be charged with felonious assault according to Roy C. Miller, prosecuting attorney."

[Charley Cunningham] "I never saw my dad afraid. I was afraid *for* him—on jailbreaks, bringing somebody down to the jail, when he was by hisself, no highway patrolman was around. But he was all the time havin' to do that. And I was always scared to death that someone would try to knock him in the head. And they tried to, two or three times. They didn't get away with it, though.

Mumford was here, highway patrolman. [*Actually it was Patrolman Tony Stephens.*] They fingerprinted this feller, and took him back upstairs—I guess they thought the highway patrolman was gone—so when Dad took him up, they knocked him in the head, another boy in jail, a young boy, that we'd been to Indiana to get, I'd went with Dad to Indiana to get him in Indiana and bring him back here, and he had a Woodsbury After Shaving Lotion bottle inside a sock. And those after-shaving lotion bottles were real thick. He hit him over the head with that. Mom opened the door, started up to fix the dinner meal, I heard him holler, so we went up there.

The night before there was a guy that had robbed a bank name of Kenneth Kile. They'd got after him on Saturday night. He got away from them on Old 66 here, just jumped out down below old Cunningham's Grocery, that was all woods, he jumped out of the car and went up to the woods, they never did get him.

The next morning my dad come to my bedroom, in the courthouse, we lived in the courthouse, where the courtroom is was my dad's bedroom. The next morning my dad come in before daylight and said 'Come on and go with me, let's go down there and see if we can catch that guy.' So we go down there. Dad had a piece of pant leg that the guy had tore on the barbed wire fence. And we pulled in down here in the City Park, on Marshall Street, there was an old skating rink where those apartments are now.

There stood the guy. Dad said 'That's him!' Of course Dad had Sheriff of Webster County writing, had Sheriff of Webster County written on the trunk lid but nothin' on the doors. So Dad said 'That's him.' Well, he said, 'Don't pull the car up or the back end will show.' So the man just stopped, we stopped, I was drivin', he said to the guy, 'Where ya headed?' and he said 'I'm headed to St. Louis' and Dad says 'Well, we're goin' to Rolla,' he says, 'You want a ride to Rolla?'

So he said, 'Yeah' and jumped in the back seat. We drove up to Pine Street here.

Dad said, 'I know a fella right over here in town I'd like to see here a minute. Do you care?' 'No.'

So we drove up Pine Street over here, turned there on Jackson Street, I drove up there. There was a Night Watchman name of Commodore Smith lived there. So we pulled in the driveway, I honked the horn, and Commodore came out. My dad just reached over and told me more or less with his hand, Sit still. So Commodore came out and they got to talkin' and Dad got out and was talking, they shook hands, one went around one side and the other went around to the other, and they got him out of the car and handcuffed him. Ha. This was a little past daylight, on a Sunday morning.

I was scared. Yes! The guy was sittin' right behind me.

See, he was the one that was in jail that they'd brought down to fingerprint, but the other boy, me and my daddy brought back—oh, probably a week earlier—from Indianapolis, Indiana, getting' him because he'd robbed a house here in town, and they caught him and brought him back. And he was only about 17 years old, 16, but anyway he's the one that hit my daddy over the head with the sock that had the lotion bottle in it.

They done that just about the time my mother opened the door and we heard him scream and rescued him. He split his head down through here, was in the hospital for two or three weeks. He was on the floor.

Me and the highway patrolman— I took the 17-year-old boy and *[Stephens]* he hit the other guy across the face with the barrel of his pistol, knocked his teeth out.

Kenneth Kile was that guy's name, and he was from over here around Brighton, someplace near by. But later on he got out of the penitentiary. He'd always made the statement he was going to come back and kill my dad. But they caught him over here at Cody, other side of Rogersville, and I don't know whatever happened to him. I think they sent him back to prison because I think he done something, he robbed somebody down in Arkansas. But I never did know what happened to him after that. Back then he was a man probably 30, 35.

But Tony Stephens could tell you all about that, too, 'cause he was in on catchin' him over at Cody. He was in on it the night they were chasin' stolen cars out here."

[Tony Stephens] "I'd just come into the courthouse over there and went up to the jail when Isam went upstairs to check on the jail. He didn't come back. Charley hollered at me, as I come in the door, and said 'They're attemptin' to jailbreak!'

So I went up them stairs to the jail. Charley was in the way so I throwed him clear to the side, and they'd hit Isam up the side of the head with a after-shave lotion bottle wrapped in a sock. He was bleedin' out the side of his mouth. I hit ole Kile up the side of the head with my fist and, boy, he went in that cell in a hurry. My fist was still tinglin' a few minutes after. I 'bout broke my wrist.

Charley had this young kid on the floor and I was puttin' ole Kile in the cell."

[Helen Cunningham] "'Course, the night he got beat up there in jail, Jake and I's the one who took him to the hospital. He'd got hit in the mouth with a bottle and of course it broke. And I forget how many stitches it took to sew him up that night. He wouldn't go in an ambulance, of course. We went in the car. He probably was afraid he would have choked on blood. Anyway, we took him to the hospital. It took quite a while to get the car cleaned up, from all that blood. But, no, he wouldn't go in an ambulance. And it was probably a good thing.

The only thing he complained about was his   knuckles. He started to hit the guy, the guy moved, and he hit the concrete wall.

'Course, Charley was there but he come downstairs and, clunk, passed out. Fell flat on the floor."

"Magistrate Court—Nov. 27—State of Mo. vs. Kenneth W. Kile, felonious assault. Defendant arraigned and hearing set for Dec. 8. Bond fixed at $3,000. Commitment ordered.... State of Mo. vs. Kenneth W. Kile, stealing motor car. Defendant arraigned and hearing set for Dec. 8. Bond fixed at $3,000. Commitment ordered."

"County court proceedings...Drs. W. F. Schlicht and Sherman Schlicht appointed county doctors for year beginning Jan. 1, 1951, at a salary of $80 per month."

December 7, 1950

[picture on the next page]

"...shows part of the injuries suffered by the Sheriff....

He was struck in the face, in the head, and had his hand smashed with a blackjack made by putting a bottle in a sock. The bottle broke at the first blow. *[Isam said he started to hit the guy, the guy moved, and he hit the concrete wall, with his hand.]*

The Sheriff was brought home after an overnight stay in the hospital. He was immediately up and around although he was still weak from the loss of blood.

Mrs. Herman Tade, janitor at the courthouse, said it was 'awful the amount of blood that the Sheriff lost before the ambulance could come to take him to Springfield.' She had the job of cleaning it up from the floor."

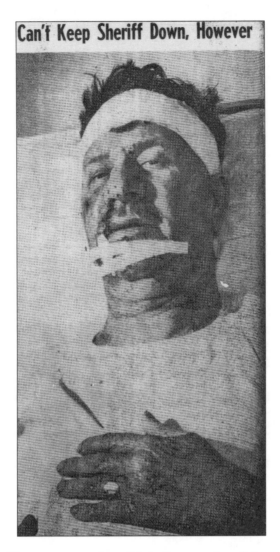

Can't Keep Sheriff Down, However

"After days of hasty retreat in which thousands of American soldiers have been trapped by red Chinese forces there is discussion in Washington of a withdrawal of United Nations forces from Korea. The Chinese hordes have overwhelmed the U.N. forces in bitter cold weather of North Korea.

When the Chinese broke through the lines held by South Korean troops the retreat became necessary to save an entire army from being trapped. It is the most disastrous defeat ever suffered by American forces....

It is estimated that China has thrown a million men into the

Korean war....

Should the U.N. retire from Korea and turn it over to the Reds, leading the South Koreans to their mercy, it means the death of the United Nations. It was not working anyway....

Apparently the United States is not prepared to fight a war against China, much less Russia. Americans must face the fact that this country is getting licked."

December 14, 1950 "Three Marshfield men are charged with burglary and larceny in connection with the breaking in and taking 33 second-hand batteries from the Stanley McVay Salvage building Thursday night of last week *[12/7]*. They are Bill Ward, Kenneth Daniels, and Wayne Casteel.

According to Sheriff Cunningham, the McVay building was entered by breaking a glass in the door, the batteries hauled to Springfield and sold to Jim Sheppard. The Sheriff says Sheppard would not buy them that night, so the batteries were unloaded at the home of Simmie 'Curley' Pine. The batteries were hauled over to Sheppard's the next day.

Part of the batteries, valued at $125, have been recovered. Sheppard paid $66 for them according to the Sheriff.

Pine was released here Tuesday afternoon, but charges are expected to be filed against him in Greene county, according to the Sheriff."

"Circuit court notes: State of Mo. vs. Nathan Lyle Clark, felonious assault. Defendant appears in custody of Sheriff and without an attorney. Defendant appraised of his rights. Raymond Carter appointed attorney for defendant. Defendant waives formal arraignment and enters a plea of guilty. Punishment assessed at imprisonment in the state penitentiary of ten years.

State of Mo. vs. Nathan Lyle Clark, burglary and larceny. Defendant appears in custody of Sheriff without an attorney....Defendant waives formal arraignment and enters a plea of guilty. Punishment assessed at imprisonment...for a term of two years for burglary and a further term of two years for larceny. Sheriff allowed one extra guard."

December 21, 1950 "A business deal was consummated this past week in which the Roller-Bruce Funeral Home here was traded for the

Barber-Barto Funeral Home at Mountain Home, Ark. Before Mr. Roller came here he sold the funeral home at Mountain Home to Barber-Barto. The deal will be effective as of January 1, 1951.

Russell Barber, Mountain Grove, and Mary Barto of Lebanon, new owners of the funeral home here, will operate the business under the name of the Barber-Barto Funeral Home, the same as they operate under at Mountain Grove and Norwood, Mo.

John Davis of Poplar Bluff will be manager here and Jack McCarty of Mountain Grove, will be assistant.

Arthur Bruce, who has been connected with Denver Roller here in the business, will go to Muskogee, Okla."

"A teen-age boy recently paroled from Algoa Reformatory after serving a sentence for burglary was back in the Webster County jail Sunday night. This time he is accused of two burglaries.

The youth, identified by Sheriff E.I. Cunningham as Wayne Matney, 18, of Seymour, was nabbed less than 24 hours after he burglarized the Marlin Milling Co. and White's Department Store in Seymour.

Most of the loot was recovered from an old house near Cedar Gap, five miles east of Seymour, where Matney had hidden it.

Cunningham said the youth admitted entering both places after midnight Saturday night. He got into the mill by forcing open the front door, but it hasn't been determined what, if any, loot was taken there.

Matney said he crawled through a transom over the front door of the department store and departed through the rear door. At the store he stole an automatic rifle, two boxes of shells (500 shells to box) and some gloves.

Cunningham and troopers picked up Matney at his home Sunday afternoon and obtained the confession from him a short time later.

The youth had been paroled from Algoa last May after serving 14 months for burglarizing the Farmers Exchange at Seymour."

Chapter Eleven
1951

January 4, 1951 "….Another new Webster County official sworn in Saturday *[12/30]* is John Hosmer, Prosecuting Attorney, who succeeds Atty. Roy C. Miller. Mr. Hosmer does not expect to use the regular office rooms of the Prosecuting Attorney in the courthouse, except while Circuit Court is in session and for interviewing prisoners. He will continue to be in his office in the Hosmer Building on the west side of The Square."

[Peg Miller] "Isam was Sheriff the entire time Miller was Prosecutor.

He and Miller were a great team, because Miller just thought he was the derndest thing he'd ever seen. He had a real instinct for law enforcement which, I suppose, was different back then. It wasn't quite so wild and awful. There wasn't the drug business.

John *[Hosmer]* and Miller had a rather acrimonious race, when they ran against each other. And Miller was Isam's friend! And I think that was part of Isam's problem with John. He beat Miller! And they were sort of a team. *[Isam and Miller]*

Prosecuting Attorney was not a pleasant job. It took a lot of time. But it was a rite of passage in many ways."

January 11, 1951 "Two Farmers Exchanges were burglarized on successive nights last week. Largest loot was at the Fordland Farmers Exchange where thieves must have needed a truck to haul away enough merchandise to start a store of their own.

State Troopers called to the scene Wednesday, Jan. 3, by Webster County Sheriff E.I. Cunningham, said Manager Raymond Crowe listed the following items as missing:

Fifteen to 20 pairs of overalls and overall pants, 15 to 20 cartons of cigarettes, 20 cartons of pipe tobacco, 30 cartons of chewing tobacco, 10 to 12 cartons of chewing gum, 5 boxes of cigars, 12 to 15 60-pound sacks of sugar, 5 cases of washing powder, 3 50-pound stands of lard and 4 bundles of coffee.

Thieves apparently broke in and out of the building. Entry was gained by prying a board off a window and exit was through a feed room door opening onto a loading dock. Thieves had to break an inside padlock to open the door.

The second burglary occurred that night at the Crane Farmers Exchange.

Stone county sheriff T. J. Walker reported thieves broke a glass panel in the back door to the feed room and took about $2 in cash, 3 electric irons, a table model radio, and a portable radio."

January 18, 1951 "Circuit Court Notes: State of Mo. vs. Kenneth W. Kile, felonious assault. Application for change of venue on account of bias and prejudice…change of venue granted. Clerk ordered to notify the Chief Justice of the Missouri Supreme Court to transfer a judge to hear case. Set for Jan. 20."

January 25, 1951 "Circuit Court Notes: Under a change of venue, the Missouri Supreme Court, Lawrence M. Hyde, Chief Justice, sent Judge Tom R. Moore of Ozark here Saturday to hear the case of State of Mo. vs. Kenneth W. Kile.

(Kile was charged with felonious assault following an attack upon Sheriff E. I. Cunningham in the jail here back in November.)

The defendant was arraigned and entered a plea of guilty. Punishment assessed at imprisonment in the Missouri State Penitentiary for a term of 15 years. Prisoner sentenced. Sheriff allowed one guard.

(Nathan Lyle Clark, another prisoner at the time, was charged in the same attack on the Sheriff. He was sentenced to 10 years in the penitentiary Dec. 7 on the assault charge.)"

February 8, 1951 "Seymour's colorful City Marshal, D. A. (Dave) Coots has been given his 'walking papers' by the Seymour City Board. At a special meeting of the aldermen Monday *[2/5]* the vote was unanimous to uphold Mayor R. E. McMahan, who suspended Marshal Coots on January 27. One alderman was not present.

The hearing was attended by a group of citizens. Atty. Seth V. Conrad of Marshfield represented Marshal Coots and after the action of the Seymour City Board, said that an appeal would be taken, presumably to the Circuit Court. There is also a rumor that Mr. Coots will run for City Marshal at the city election this April.

There has been much criticism of the Seymour marshal by the manner in which he has been enforcing the laws in that community. Many citizens believe he has been doing a good job, while others thought he was too stringent in his law enforcement."

"The third burglary in three months at the F. M. Kessinger & Son Hardware in Rogersville early Tuesday resulted in the loss of varied items.

Charles Kessinger, who operates the store with his father, listed the loot as 75 pennies, a 'handful of mills,' some shotgun shells, cigarettes, and pipe tobacco.

He said thieves broke a side door glass, but the door was double-locked so they made an opening large enough to crawl through.

Kessinger said the burglary occurred sometime after midnight. He passed the store at that time en route home from a basketball game, and it was all right then.

Because of previous burglaries, the cash register and safe had been left open. Webster County Sheriff E. I. Cunningham reported the burglary to the State Patrol at 7:50 a.m. Tuesday."

"Isaac Frank Cunningham died Saturday following a long illness *[2/3]*. One of his brothers is Webster County Sheriff E.I. Cunningham."

[Grace Hickman] "But, I remember Uncle Isam always, when we had trouble, when my sister's baby was born dead, why, we got a hold of Uncle Isam! And he went up to Prospect and got them a lot for this little baby.

Then when my dad *[Isaac Frank Cunningham]* died, Uncle Isam and David *[Jake]* was there that night. 'Course, that was after I was married, quite a long time. He died in '51. He was awful bad and Uncle Isam and David come that night. (Now, everybody called him Jake but to me he was David) They was there when he died.

And Uncle Isam went down to Prospect and he picked out the place for him to be buried. My brother, I think, went with him. But we always called on Uncle Isam to go to the cemetery. And I don't know how he did it, but he done it: he'd go over there and make arrangements, get the grave dug. He always done it. He helped us every time! I can tell you *that* for sure, I know *that*! And he always did, and he did it for everybody I *suppose*, now *that* I don't *know,* but I know personally what he done for *us*. He always came. When we had to have help, he showed up."

February 15, 1951 "The Missouri Supreme Court held Monday that Mary Margaret Evans of Springfield was properly convicted and sentenced to four years in prison for assaulting Carmen Rainey.

Miss Evans was convicted of assault with intent to kill for attacking Mrs. Rainey at the Rainey Funeral Home in Marshfield the night of October 19, 1949. Mrs. Rainey was beaten severely with a flashlight and a toy cap pistol.

In her appeal, Miss Evans said the Webster County Circuit Court erred in admitting into evidence some sleeping tablets, a stomach pump, a jar of Vaseline and other articles which she took from Springfield to Marshfield.

She testified that Mr. Rainey, whom she had been dating, had her go to the funeral home to get a gun his wife was supposed to have.

Under the circumstances, the Supreme Court said, the evidence was properly admitted. It was ruled that the jury had not been prejudiced by the introduction in evidence of the clothing Miss Evans wore that night.

Sheriff E. I. Cunningham was notified Monday to take Miss Evans into custody. She is being held for the marshal of the court.

Mr. Rainey, charged in connection with the assault on Mrs. Rainey, took a change of venue from Webster County, and the case is supposed to come up at Hartville February 26."

"An unusual situation existed the first of the week when Sheriff E. I. Cunningham had two fathers and sons in jail here. Among 14 prisoners in the jail were Joe Stapp, charged with non-support, and his son, 'Buddy' Stapp, charged in connection with the robbery of the Kessinger Store at Rogersville. Also in jail were Allen Bledsoe, charged with first degree murder, and his son, Lloyd, charged with forgery."

"Four recent robberies in the Rogersville community have been solved with the arrest of Clifford Thomas Prine, 16; George Herman Stepp, 17, and Junior Eugene Phelps, 16, all of Rogersville. *[Which is it: Stapp or Stepp?]*

According to Sheriff E. I. Cunningham, the first three named were arrested for burglarizing the Kessinger Store, taking meat, pencils, books, and other merchandise. Some of the articles are said to have been recovered.

Stepp is also said to have admitted burglarizing the Rogersville Skating Rink last month, taking cigarettes, candy, and confessed to taking a dozen knives from the Kessinger Store. Four of the knives have been recovered. Also last month it is reported that Prine and

Stepp took a radio from the home of Mrs. Fancher. They were frightened off when Mrs. Fancher came down stairs while they were still in the house."

"Three persons were held in the Hartville jail the first of the week for robbery of a grocery store on Highway 5, near Hartville, last Wednesday night. They are James Henry McCracken, 23; Robert Capps, 27, and his wife, Frances Capps, 17. They were captured by the Highway Patrol east of Lebanon Friday when he spotted their car on Highway 66. They had allegedly stolen the 1950 Ford near Savannah, Ga. In the car were two pistols, a large dog, a .22 caliber rifle, a shotgun, ammunition, new clothing and a quantity of cigarettes.

The rifle, shotgun, ammunition and cigarettes, plus about $35 in cash were taken Wednesday night when the two men allegedly held up the grocery. It was the victim's description of the stolen car, and the dog inside, that tripped up the trio. They had forgotten to remove a travel tag from the rear of the car, and it was spotted by the officers.

Gene Carter's place between Fordland and Rogersville was held up the same night about a quarter to twelve. Gene and Murl Pierce had gone to Seymour. Maude Hoyt, at the Carter's Store, said she was robbed of about $40 and some whiskey by the armed pair.

She viewed the men, with others at the Hartville jail Sunday morning, and identified Capps and McCracken as the men who held up the Carter Store. They didn't admit the holdup. Sheriff Cunningham says that a pistol in their possession at the time of their arrest has been identified as one stolen from under the pillow of Gene Carter, owner of the liquor store. The pistol was owned by Murl Pierce, who has identified it.

Warrants were issued here Monday for the trio on charges of robbery with firearms.

It is reported that the two are wanted on various charges in other states."

"Lloyd Arthur Bledsoe, 18, and Howard David Boyce, 19, both of Niangua, and Jack Crumm, 16, of Marshfield, were arrested Saturday evening [2/10] by Sheriff E.I. Cunningham on forgery charges. Bledsoe is charged with forging Dr. Schlicht's name to three checks and with passing one to J. C. Needy Grocery for $22 on January 27, and another one at the same store for $11 on February 3, then passing one at Riggs place for $16 Friday.

They have admitted taking part in the forgery, according to Sheriff E.I. Cunningham. The youths said Bledsoe wrote and cashed the checks while all of them were present."

February 22, 1951 "The Webster County Court, in session Tuesday, *[2/20]* inspected the county jail and decided to have some plumbing done in the cells...."

March 1, 1951 "Atty. Seth V. Conrad, Atty. John Hosmer and Sheriff E. I. Cunningham were attending Circuit Court in Hartville Monday.*[2/26]*...After the filing of a motion by the defense asking for the disqualification of Circuit Judge Hawkins, Judge Hawkins disqualified himself in the Rex Rainey case at Hartville. The State Supreme Court is being notified and the Chief Justice will appoint a judge to hear the case. The date for the hearing of the case is expected to be set at Hartville this Thursday."

March 8, 1951 "Governor Forrest Smith remained silent yet Monday about the Kefauver Crime Investigating Report issued last week.

He told his news conference he still had not read the report and did not plan to ask the Senate investigators for a copy.

He said last week he might have something to say when he reads the report. It charged gamblers helped elect him in 1948. It has been shown time after time that he had the backing of the gamblers in St. Louis and Kansas City.

The Kefauver committee set up by the U.S. Senate to investigate crime conditions has especially castigated Missouri and Florida on the hook-up between politics and criminals."

[Estes Kefauver, American lawyer, and U. S. senator from 1949-1963, became chairman in 1950 of the newly created Special Committee to Investigate Organized Crime in Interstate Commerce, popularly known as the Kefauver Committee.]

Circuit Court Notes from Tuesday, March 6: "*Judge Upholds Seymour Board in Coots Case* D. A. Coots vs. R. E. McMahan, et.al., petition for <u>writ of certiorari</u>, proceedings of Board of Aldermen sustained."

[A <u>writ of certiorari</u> is issued from a superior court calling up the record of a proceeding in an inferior court for review.]

"A continuance was granted last Thursday *[3/1]* in the trial of Rex Rainey, former Marshfield undertaker who is charged with felonious assault and the case was re-scheduled to be heard in the June term of Wright County Circuit Court.

Mr. Rainey is accused of complicity in planning an attack on his wife, Carmen, in October of 1949.

Judge Tom Moore of Ozark was appointed by the Supreme Court to hear the case after Circuit Judge James P. Hawkins disqualified himself. Judge Moore has appointed Ellsworth Haymes, Marshfield attorney, as Special Prosecutor.

A jury last March found Mary Margaret Evans, former Springfield switchboard operator, guilty of the assault and she was sentenced to four years in the state penitentiary."

March 15, 1951 "Charley Cunningham, son of Sheriff and Mrs. E.I. Cunningham, left early this Wednesday morning *[3/14]* by train for Sanford, Fla., where he will try out with the New York Giants organization. He will have all expenses paid. He decided to make the try-out after being contacted by Ray Mang of Springfield and Mr. Martin of St. Louis, Scouts for the Giants.

Charley, a graduate of Marshfield High School, has been recognized for his pitching ability. He has been invited to try out with the New York Yankee organization at Branson or Brownsville, Tex., and with the Chicago Cubs training camp at Shreveport, La. He decided to make the try-out with the Giants."

"Sheriff E. I. Cunningham took Bill Ward and Kenneth (Jr.) Daniels to Algoa Reformatory near Jefferson City last Thursday *[3/8]*. He was accompanied by Fred Byrd of Fordland."

March 22, 1951 Circuit Court Notes: "State of Mo. vs. Allen L. Bledsoe, murder, application for a change of venue filed by defendant, alleging bias and prejudice of the inhabitants of Webster County. Change of venue granted and cause ordered transferred to Circuit Court of Dallas County. Sheriff ordered to remove defendant to the jail in Dallas County."

March 29, 1951 "Charley Cunningham, son of Sheriff and Mrs. E.I. Cunningham, returned Tuesday night *[3/27]* from Sanford, Fla., where he had a try-out with the New York Giants. The Giants offered him a contract in their organization. However, Charley will go to Branson tomorrow (Thursday) *[3/29]* to try out with the New York Yankees. This try-out was arranged by Tom Greenwade of Springfield, a scout in the Yankee organization."

"Two Springfield youths, residing near the old airport, Carl N. Schultz and Clarence D. Johns, were sentenced to terms of 10 to 21 years in the Kansas Reformatory at Yates Center, Kan., Tuesday. They pleaded guilty to charges of armed robbery of a Yates Center filling station.

Sheriff E.I. Cunningham, accompanied by two Springfield officers, went to Yates Center Monday, and secured admission from the youths of the robbery of places in Webster County. He said they admitted robbing the McMahan station near Diggins at the junction of Highway 60 and Route A on March 11, taking about $225 worth of tires and other merchandise. The Sheriff has recovered the tires.

On March 18 they are said to have admitted robbing the Ralph Foster and Bill Turner homes two miles north of Seymour, taking five guns and a lot of sacks. They are said to have admitted stealing 800 sacks in robberies since the first of the year at places between Lebanon and Seymour. They also are said to have admitted robbing three places in Springfield.

Some of the merchandise recovered was found at the homes of the youths, and others were found at Walnut Grove and other places where they had sold or traded it."

"The Marshfield City Elections will be held next Tuesday....A spirited race for City Marshal is in the making with three candidates already filed: George Duren, Homer Alexander, and A. O. Hutchinson. Porter Rader, the incumbent, has not made any statement regarding *[whether]* he will run for re-election or not."

[David Young] "This happened when I was a little kid, about 6. I don't remember the exact dates. But I was born in '45. So probably this happened about '51. When Isam was Sheriff.

My dad had a country store *[the Glenn Young Store at Beach]* and there were two phone lines. One was a local Beach telephone line with the old crank wall phone, and the other was a Marshfield line with one of the old rotary phones.

So we were at the store, the folks were gone, we had a hired man there helping us. But my oldest brother was kind of in charge.

And I was being a nuisance and giving him a lot of problems. So this man my dad had hired told me if I did not leave my brother alone he was gonna call the Sheriff and have him come and get me.

So, you know, I knew he was pullin' my leg. I kept harassing my older brother. This guy went to the telephone but he went to the crank phone, the old Beach line which just encompassed the area, and acted like he was talking to the Sheriff, and I knew he wasn't because you'd call the Sheriff on the *other* phone. I was smart enough to know he was pulling my leg!

But it wasn't fifteen minutes later that the Sheriff pulled up. No big deal because the Sheriff come by there a lot. He'd just come by to visit my dad, they were good friends. But it did kind of make me nervous, so I just went over and sat down in a chair and was being really good. And Isam come in, walked in to where we were at. And before he ever said a word, he put his hand down on top of my head and said, 'Is this the boy I come after?'

And, I'll be darn, so help me, he did not know anything that had just happened. He wasn't even aware of it. He didn't know there had been a phone call. But it scared me to death. So I took off running, and ran out of the store. Our house was just across the yard there. I went up and got under my bed! And Isam came up, and two or three other people, and tried to get me to come out. But I never did come out from under that bed!

And he felt really bad about that. He didn't know anything about the circumstances. But I learned a real lesson from that and have remembered it to this day!

That was 50 years ago!

After that he always wanted to buy me ice cream and stuff. He was trying to make up for that little deal."

April 5, 1951 City Marshal election results: "Homer Alexander won by a huge margin."
[Porter Rader didn't run.]

"Dave A. Coots failed in his attempted come-back Tuesday when the voters of Seymour defeated him 248 to 114 for City Marshal. James Hamblin was elected to the office. County officers were called to Seymour that afternoon when election judges refused to let Mr. Coots and his wife vote either at the city election or the school election without signing an affidavit that they had been citizens of Missouri for a year.

The officials investigated the incidence but no charges were filed. It is reported that it has not been a year since Mr. and Mrs. Coots returned to Webster County from California."

"YOUTH HELD IN JAIL AFTER FOUR SLAIN!"

[Charley Cunningham] "What happened here, Essary wanted to date this young girl, and the parents wouldn't let him date her.

So he sells a bunch of hogs, goes to Conway and sells them, goes back to Conway and buys a rifle, a 22-automatic rifle, went back and killed them.

Yes, including the girl he wanted to date."

"In a most horrible mass murder, four members of the William T. Shockley family were shot to death Tuesday night at their farm home in the north part of Webster County. The dead are: William Thomas Shockley, 43; his wife, Clara Emma Shockley, 44; his mother, Mrs. Martha Ellen Shockley, 73, and the daughter, Helen Louise, 16.

The killer was Kenneth Essary, 23, who lived on a rented farm nearby the Shockley home. He has admitted the killing and the only excuse or reason that he is reported to have given is that he 'didn't think them people liked him.' He had not been in trouble before.

Essary is in jail here and first-degree murder charges are to be filed against him today, Wednesday *[4/4]*.

Mr. and Mrs. Wm. T. Shockley, parents of nine children, are survived by eight, six of whom were in the house, upstairs asleep at the time of the crime. The surviving children are Mrs. Glen Replogle, 22, Marshfield; Billy Joe Shockley, 20, Conway; Donald Dean, 8; Jimmy Lee, 14; Mary Ellen, 10; Patsy Ann, 5; Carol Francis, 2; and Robert L., age 10 months.

Essary purchased the .22 rifle, a Savage automatic, and four boxes of shells at a hardware store in Conway Tuesday. He also bought more shells at another store.

Between 8 and 9 o'clock Essary is said to have opened fire on the family as they were at home, from an east window.

The bodies of Wm. Shockley's mother and wife were found lying close together on the floor. Shockley had apparently run out the front door and was shot down in the yard. The daughter, Helen, ran to the telephone and called Luke O'Connor, a neighbor, to 'come quick, we have trouble, bad trouble.' She was shot as she telephoned and she then apparently tried to run upstairs, but fell back down the steps.

Mr. and Mrs. Luke O'Connor drove to the Shockley place and into the yard. There they were fired upon by the killer. Both were cut by glass, but not hurt critically as they hurriedly drove away for help. (13 bullet holes were found in their pickup, including holes shot through the windshield, according to Sheriff Cunningham. It is a miracle they were not shot.) Mr. O'Connor said that about 30 shots were fired at them.

Meantime, Jack Shockley, Joe Shockley and wife Marie, and Fred Shockley, brothers of the dead man, had come to the aid of the stricken family. (One of them had overheard the telephone call to the O'Connors.) When they went into the room where the bodies were, Essary opened fire on them. They put out the light and lay on the floor until officers arrived quite some time later.

Sheriff Cunningham and Commodore Smith went from here, Sheriff Neil Brown of Lebanon and Trooper Taylor, were the first officers on the scene and to begin the search for the killer. They were soon joined by many others. The search was carried on until 2:30 Wednesday morning when the man was found at the home of his father, Bill Essary, in the south part of Conway.

Essary surrendered peaceably and admitted the crime. He said he went to the Howard Latimer house and told them to call the officers and bring an ambulance to the Shockley home. (This has not been verified by officers.) Essary is said to have reached his father's place about 11:30 Tuesday night.

K. K. Kelley, Fordland, County Coroner in Marshfield Wednesday morning, said that he would probably hold an inquest in order that a coroner's jury might bring a verdict.

The Shockley family is one of the most highly respected in Webster County."

[from Springfield Daily News dated 4/6/51, Springfield Leader-Press dated 4/4/51, and Marshfield Mail dated 4/12/51]

[Gene Tinnin] "Trooper Marvin Taylor and I were the first people there. I don't know why; we happened to be in Conway, I guess, when the call came in. We asked directions, somebody on the radio gave us directions, and when we appeared, to me it looked like a war zone.

Mr. and Mrs. Shockley were lying on the porch, dead. We went inside and the young lady was at the foot of the stairs, she was dead. We went further in the house using flashlights. Mrs. Grandma Shockley was lying there. There was a baby.

I just came out of World War II and I saw death many times…but that was as bad as a war zone.

The house was not only on a county line—Laclede and Webster—but it was on a troop line. Back then it didn't make much difference. We were trained that our badge said Missouri, not a county. So troopers came from both counties.

Apparently she *[Helen]* had been shot while standing and talking to Luke on the phone. Evidently she started up the stairs, then fell back down the stairs. I remember a little boy up the stairs. We were afraid the shooter might still be around.

Sheriff Brown came down, from Lebanon, Neil Brown. He and Isam got along. He was maybe a little further along in training than Isam was. I remember we formed a group to go to different barns and sheds and scour the countryside.

When we stuck our heads up in haylofts, I remember Neil saying, 'Gene, let's go up and check. The others have children; we don't.' How's that for being brave? In favor of yielding to someone who might leave a family.

Somewhere along the line, someone had called someone in town and said Kenneth was at his dad's. We got there and Essary was standing behind a heater. His weapon was real close to him. We got the weapon right away.

In the meantime we called the coroner, ambulances/hearses… they were the same vehicle back then.

I believe Mr. Shockley had fallen off the porch."

[Newspaper Headlines sketched the story over the next several days]
"Ozarks Maniac Slays 4 Persons: Posses Searching Four-County Area For Mystery Killer

Girls Last Words a Frantic Plea for Her Uncle to Come

Kenneth Essary, 23, Taken Six Hours After Unexplained Fusillade Into Farmhouse

Farm Youth's Savage Gunfire Kills Four In One Family: Two Neighbors Wounded

Hastily-Called Inquest Puts Blame on Essary

No Indication of Why Youth Killed Friends

Solemn Crowd of Neighbors, Relatives Visit Murder Scene

Essary Waives Preliminary *[on April 11, after admitting the killing of the four Shockley family members]*

Timid Farm Youth Feeling Better Today: Essary Still Refuses to Tell Motive for Murdering Family

Killer in Better Mood: Essary Expected To Give Motive

Shockley Rites Attended by Large Crowd

Benefit Fund Started For Shockley Children"

[Various articles provided the following information]
"Sheriff Cunningham summoned Webster County Coroner K.K. Kelley, and troopers from Springfield, Lebanon, and Marshfield to assist in the investigation. Early the next morning, bloodhounds had been ordered sent from Jefferson City *[the state penitentiary]* by the patrol. And Conservation Agents—familiar with the wooded region surrounding the scene—were asked to assist in the search.

The killing of four members of the Shockley family near Conway April 3, 1951, was undoubtedly one of the bloodiest tragedies in Ozarks history, and the worst crime to occur during Cunningham's second term of office....

Victims shot dead by Essary were William Shockley, 43, shot several times in the head, once near the right eye, once in right side; his wife Clara, 44, shot in the chest; their daughter Helen Louise, 16, shot in the chest and neck, and twice in her right wrist while she was telephoning neighbors for help; and William's mother, Martha Ellen (Mrs. Gus) Shockley, 73, shot in left neck, right side, left side, right hip, and left shoulder. Though Essary shot into the upstairs where 6 other children were asleep, ranging in age from 10 months to 14 years, they survived unharmed. Two other surviving children were not living at home....

Sheriff Cunningham and Commodore Smith went from here *[Marshfield]*, Sheriff Neil Brown of Lebanon *[Laclede County]* and Trooper Taylor *[Missouri Highway Patrol]* were the first officers on the scene and to begin the search for the killer....

The officers were told that Essary had bought a gun the previous day. He became an immediate suspect....

Sheriff Cunningham approached the youth *[at his father's home after the murders]*. He had known the boy since he was knee-high to a grasshopper. 'Why did you do it, Kenny?' the Sheriff asked. Kenneth Essary replied promptly—if a bit incoherently, 'They were good neighbors,' he said, 'but they didn't like me.'

'It looks like the whole thing happened because of a grudge Essary thought the Shockleys had against him,' the Sheriff pointed out."

April 12, 1951 "A coroner's inquest was held by K. K. Kelley, coroner, in the office of Sheriff E.I. Cunningham Friday morning *[4/6]* at which Kenneth Essary was blamed for the death of four members of the Wm. Shockley family Tuesday night of last week *[4/3]*. The verdict was brought in after an hour-long hearing at which Essary, a bachelor farmer, was the only one to testify.

When he was told of the scheduled hearing for that afternoon Essary asked Sheriff Cunningham if he could 'talk to the jury now while I'm in my right mind.' He agreed only to talk to the jury and Coroner Kelley. The coroner got the jury together as soon as he heard of Essary's request.

The jury was composed of Clyde Hargus, Lorance Hamilton, Herschel Davis, Hermon Pearce, Bill Bertoldie and Eph Rader.

[Each jury member was paid $1 by the county for this task, shown in the May 3rd MARSHFIELD MAIL. K. K. Kelley, Coroner, was paid $17.09.]

According to Sheriff Cunningham, Essary said he 'went up to the Shockley home Tuesday night to talk to them and apologize if there was anything between them.' He said he 'bought the gun (a .22 caliber rifle) with the purpose of straightening up the matter.' However, the Sheriff said Essary told the jury that he did not go to the Shockley house with the intention of killing them.

'I thought the gun would make them hear me out better,' he is quoted as saying. Essary said he thought the Shockleys had been 'sore' at him the past two years, ever since he rented a farm nearby the Shockley farm south of Conway.

The Sheriff said Essary told the jury that he got 'rattled' at the back door of the house and shot Wm. Shockley. He later admitted killing three other members of the family, Helen Shockley, her mother, and grandmother. Essary said he 'liked the Shockleys.'

Although he had told the Sheriff after his arrest he'd give the motive for the slaying 'when I'm rested up', he did not give the coroner's jury anything new as to his motive. He said after his arrest that his reason for the killing was because he thought the Shockleys did not like him.

Four separate charges of first degree murder have been filed against Essary, one for each of the family he admitted killing.

Due to reports being made to the Sheriff that there might be an effort made to take *[Essary]* from the jail here by friends of the stricken, Sheriff Cunningham took the man to the Springfield jail Friday.

The Sheriff reported that he and the Prosecuting Attorney *[John Hosmer]* were at the Shockley place Monday and counted the following bullet holes:

6 holes in the window on the north side of the house and one through an upstairs window

3 holes north side of porch

5 holes through south window on the west side of the house.

2 through the window on the east half of the west side where the telephone was.

2 holes in southwest corner of screened in back porch.

1 hole through screen door in back porch.

4 more in walls of back porch, a total of 24 bullet holes.

18 holes or marks were found on the pick-up belonging to Luke O'Conner.

The five younger children were asleep upstairs and Jimmy Lee, 14, was reading upstairs. When Essary shot through the upstairs' window, Jimmy Lee put out the light and hid in a closet, according to the Sheriff.

Essary is said to have kept very much to himself and did not visit or mix with anyone. He lived alone and is said to have spent much time reading love stories and western stories, according to officers."

[Jim Shockley] "Well, it was a night out on the farm when kids didn't have anything to do like they do now and we all went to bed, seemed like about eight o'clock. Five of us was upstairs in bed and Carol, our baby sister, was downstairs in the bedroom, on Mom and Dad's bed.

I was laying in bed with a lantern, reading a comic book and all of a sudden I heard a knock on the front door, and that don't happen when you live out in the country in that particular time in history, very often, without a car driving up or something.

My mother went to the front door and she says, 'You'll have to go around to the back door because we've got the front door locked and we don't know where the key is.'

There was a short period of time when I didn't hear anything and then my dad went to the back door and the screen door squeaked, actually, as he opened the door, I heard him open the door, and then he said, 'Well, hi!' he says, 'Come on in!' and I heard the door open, and my dad always kinda chuckled a little bit after he said something, and then that's the last words I heard until I heard a gunshot.

And my mom ran out on the back porch and she said, 'Oh, he shot him!'

And I don't   *know* what happened down there except for the account that *seemed* like it happened. He said—and I believe he did—he shot my mom on the back porch as she ran out. And she ran to the bedroom, to protect Carol I'm assuming, and she ran in there and she was shot in the heart, I suppose.

And then Helen—they were doing dishes, she was at the cabinet putting dishes up, a corner cabinet that we had, I believe—he shot through the window into the kitchen, I'm pretty sure. There was a bullet hole in that cabinet, I believe, and some blood on her arm from that. And she ran into the dining room. And we had one of these old crank-type telephones and our neighbor, our Uncle Luke O'Connor's number was four shorts. And she rang those four shorts very erratically and she said, 'Luke,' she said, 'get over here just as fast as you can!'

And honestly, I couldn't say just exactly what happened but he must have shot her through the dining room window while she was standing at the phone.

At the same time my grandmother went through the dining room and he shot her several times as she went through the dining room, I think in the stomach and in the abdomen area, as she went on into the bedroom.

And then Helen ran from the telephone over to the stairwell to come upstairs.

And I had heard all this start and we had an old rocking chair sitting beside our bed there, and I thought, 'What can I do?' And so I jumped up out of bed, and there was an arm hanging loose on that rocking chair and I grabbed that arm off of that chair and I ran over and I started to go downstairs, then I thought, 'No, I can't do that.' And I had it in my hand, you know, to use as a weapon.

Then about that time the door come open in the stairwell and I was standing in my bedroom and I thought, 'Well, I'll wait right here because that must be him—or whoever—coming up the steps.'

And as I thought he was coming up the steps—this is the part I haven't told very many people—as she [*Helen*] got up to the top of the steps, I'd stepped out with my chair arm drawn back and almost hit her with it, I didn't but I almost did, and we stood there for just, it seemed like a long time, face to face, and stared at each other.

And this is the part I can hardly stand: I didn't even reach out my arms, or anything, to help.

She fell backwards, all the way down the steps, and she just kinda...you know how a doll would just fall down the steps and go just one step at a time, sorta,...until she come in contact with the door.

And at that point I got scared. I went back in the bedroom and sat down on the floor. And I listened to what was going on. And I heard Luke come. And I heard him shooting at Luke. And I couldn't tell you what was happening, history only knows.

Apparently he [Essary] followed him down to the creek as Luke drove across the creek. He [Luke] said almost anytime he would've hit the creek as hard as he did that time, it would have drowned his truck out and he would've had to stop, but this time he went right on across.

And during that time, Edgar as we call him—his name is James, some call him Jack—my dad's oldest brother, come in the house, and my dad was laying at the back steps and he went right past him and he thought, 'Well, there's an old rug or something laying there,' and he come on in. And he went in to the living room and we had a light—I don't remember whether we had the gas light on in the kitchen or not, but we had a white gas light—but he had just one of those lamps in his hand and he was in the living room.

And by that time he [Essary] had come back up, from the creek I suppose, from running after Luke. And Joe and Mary come at that particular time...she [Helen] must have been so erratic on the phone that everybody—it was a party line phone—that everybody must have picked it up and listened in.

And when they come in, he started shooting at them. Only they can tell you what happened as they come in the door, but I heard bullets hit all around them. Anyhow, as they come on in the door, Edgar was in the living room and Joe told him, he said, 'Get in here and get down in this room, there's somebody out there trying to kill everyone!' And I don't know whether he dropped the lamp or whether it was shot out of his hand, whatever, anyhow, it was broken, and normally it would probably have caught on fire but it didn't.

But, anyway, during that time they were down in there.

And getting back...this is gory...it's something that's sorta haunted me...because...as she fell down those steps and I sat down beside the wall and listened, I could hear her breath, hear her breathing. And it sounded like gurgling. And I listened...and was scared. I guess I knew what was going on. But she kept breathing harder...and harder...finally she breathed her last.

From there on I remember seeing lights coming from a long way off and I don't know what happened, Billy will have to fill you in on that, but when they got there—I don't know what happened between the time I seen that and by the time they got in the house—but they come in the house and he [Billy] opened the door.

And I had walked down the steps because I knew that help was there at that time. I walked down the steps and as I did, I straddled Helen. She was laying there on her back, with a wound in her neck and one in her stomach, I believe, and her arm was bleeding, or had been bleeding at least. And I knocked on the door and I think that's when you *[Bill]* opened it. And then the State Highway Patrol and a deputy or it could have been the Sheriff, I don't know, I don't remember, they had their guns, both guns was pointed at me.

Then they realized...I stood there...I don't know if you *[Bill]* remember...I was pointing down at her, and everybody focused on her, then, and from there on, they can tell you better what happened."

[Joe Shockley] "My brother, her *[Mary's]* sister and her husband was at our place, I lived on the old home place, where I was born, about two miles southwest of where that happened, and the telephone rang. 'Course, it was a party line, the whole neighborhood was on the same line, she *[Mary]* picked up the receiver and listened, and she said, 'Joe, there's somethin' wrong down at Bill's!'"

[Mary Shockley] "Helen was on the phone and she said, 'Fay, tell Luke to come quick!' and then there was just a terrible noise. And that was all I heard."

[Joe] "So I said, 'Well, maybe we'd better go down there,' and we got in the car, went down there, drove up on the north side of the house, she got out and I forgot to turn the lights off...I'd got out of the car, walked around, and noticed I hadn't turned my lights off, and I went back and turned my lights off, and just after I done that, why, they was a gun fired behind this building north of the house and I think the bullet went right through the doorway beside a where she was a goin' in.

And I hurried back in the house then. She had gone on in the house. In the kitchen, there was just an old-fashioned one-wick lamp sittin' there, kerosene lamp. Electricity had been put in, wired up in that neighborhood, but the power wasn't turned on yet. And they had this old lamp and I think they called 'em Aladdin Lights, they had some kind of a lamp with a round burner on it, that really put out a good light. Both of them lamps were sittin' on the table. Well, I went on through into the other room and we were lookin' around, and Mom and Clara was both a layin' on the floor. And I went to 'em and...."

[Mary] "Carol was layin' between 'em."

[Joe] "Yeah. They were layin' on the floor."

[Mary] "We figured probably that Clara grabbed her *[Carol]* and she was layin' on the bed asleep. She was dressed, had her coat on, like she had been when they'd come home that day. They had been to a school election."

[Joe] "So after we saw that, found them and they were both dead, why, we stayed out of sight. We got down on the floor there, a layin', and in a little while Jack—that's my oldest brother, he's the oldest in the family and I was the youngest—he come in and he, I think he picked up the little one and I said, 'Jack! You better....'"

[Mary] "He went through the door, into the bedroom, and when he did, why, he *[Essary]* shot again through the windows. Joe knocked the lamp outta Jack's hand, said, 'Jack, you're gonna get shot! Get that light out!' And so, there was a little vanity settin' in there, and I pulled it out and set him behind it, and Joe set down before me and Jack set down at the other end of that vanity, and we set there for quite a while. And finally Fred came.

Well, *after* Fred came, Joe went after the telephone. Fred came in...."

[Joe] "We told him to get down outta sight."

[Mary] "We told him to get down outta sight, that Mama and Clara had been killed, that we hadn't seen nothin' of Bill."

[Joe] "Bill was outside the door and it was dark and we had walked right by him and never noticed him, so we went in."

[Mary] "And Fred said, 'I'll bet you that Bill is out here by the steps,' he said, 'I thought I seen something there and I thought it was a rug rolled up, layin' there.'"

[Joe] "Fred is another brother. He was just younger than Bill. He come in, and he got down on the floor with us, and we were in there a little while and I said, 'Well, I believe I'll crawl over to the telephone and see if I can learn anything,' and so I just rang the phone, and—'course, in them days we all had just regular wall telephones and they was a lady workin' in central office in Conway, someone there twenty-four hours a day—and she answered and I started, said something about Bill's, and she said, 'Yes, it's already been reported and The Law will be there in a little while.' And I said, 'Well, I'm just gonna stay quiet then.'

In a little while, why, The Law come. I believe they was three come in. 'Course, they had to search all of us. And we was standin' there talkin' to 'em.

And I was standin' right there by the stairway door, I reached over and opened the door, and Helen's head slid down. She had slid backwards, I guess, down the steps, her head against the door, and when I opened the door, her head come on down over the edge of the step where she'd been layin.'"

[Mary] "During the time we was settin' there, we heard Bob cry out one time. And then he went back to sleep. We never heard no more. 'Course, we knew some of the kids was upstairs, you know about that."

[Don Shockley] "How long was this, from the time you arrived until the police came?"

[Joe] "Oh, I guess around an hour, wasn't it?"

[Mary] "Every bit of an hour."

[Joe] "See, they didn't know anything about it until *[Essary]* had walked...I'd say it was at *least* two miles, he just probably walked up the creek 'til he got on that road and walked on and come up and had them call the Sheriff.

That night, why, they took him in, and after he'd been in jail for a while I said, 'Well, I'm gonna go talk to him.' Of course, they wanted to know if I was gonna try to do anything and I said, 'No, I just wanna talk to him. I've known the boy a lot of his life.' So I went in, where he was at in jail, I said, 'What in the world did you do that for?' He said, 'Well, I went down to Bill's, knocked on the door,' said 'he come to the door and told me to come in,' he said, 'I had set my rifle around outside of the door. I picked it up and,' he said, 'when I picked it up, he grabbed me and we got strugglin' and,' he said, 'that's when he got shot.' He said, 'If my own mother and dad would've come in there, then, I would have...' he said, 'I shot at anything I could see a movin'.'

That's the only thing he ever said about it, that him and Billy got to scufflin' over the rifle. But I said why did he take the rifle with him the night it happened. Well, a fella that knew him in Conway and worked at the Exchange there told me that he come to the store, Larson Feed that day, and he had been to the hardware and bought a new rifle. Some of 'em that knew him well said that boy could shoot a rabbit runnin' and kill it with a rifle. 'Course my brother claimed he'd heard some of 'em claimed they'd seen him do it.

But he got up in the barn loft, that night, after we all got in there, and shot out of the barn loft through the upstairs windows, two or three or four times. I guess he just give up and left."

[Mary] "Maybe he seen Helen get in the stairway and thought maybe she might be up there, that he could get her up there."

[Joe] "They said the bullets he shot up there that went right over the bed, would've been over a foot or two above where some of 'em was layin'."

Missouri State Highway Patrol
Rolla, Missouri
April 4, 1951

From: Trooper M.E. Taylor
Subject: Murder – Shockley family, Webster County, Missouri
To: Commanding Officer, Troop I
    Missouri State Highway Patrol, Rolla, Missouri

1. About 9:20 p.m., April 3, 1951, Trooper M. E. Taylor received a phone call from BILL WILKERSON, CONWAY, MISSOURI, requesting officers come down and investigate a shooting. He stated that LUKE O'CONNOR and his wife had driven up to the BILL SHOCKLEY farm, located in WEBSTER County, just south of the LACLEDE County Line and about four miles southeast of CONWAY, in response to a telephone call for aid, and someone had riddled O'CONNOR'S pickup truck with bullets and Mr. and Mrs. O'CONNOR'S hands were bloody. Trooper TAYLOR immediately called Sheriff NEIL BROWN and started to CONWAY. Upon arriving in CONWAY, WILKERSON was picked up. Sheriff CUNNINGHAM, of WEBSTER County, was at the HARRIS CAFÉ with LUKE O'CONNOR. O'CONNOR was very excited. His 49 OR 50 Ford pickup truck showed 14 bullet holes in the windshield and right side and hood. He said he and his wife, FAY, drove to the SHOCKLEY farm when one of the children called them saying, "Bill, get here quick as you can". Screaming was heard over the phone. When they drove up to the SHOCKLEY farm in the pickup, some men opened up on them with a rifle. They got out of there as quick as they could and went to CONWAY for help.

2. While officers were talking to O'CONNOR, a local call came to the HARRIS CAFÉ. Sheriff CUNNINGHAM answered it and was informed that two people had been killed at the farm. Sheriff CUNNINGHAM and his deputy, COMMODORE SMITH, Sheriff BROWN and Trooper TAYLOR went to the home in Patrol Car 273. SHOCKLEY'S son, BILLY JOE SHOCKLEY, age 20, married and living in CONWAY, accompanied us as a guide. Enroute, we asked for additional officers.

3. Arriving at the farm home, we called on those inside to come out. Several people were there. Three SHOCKLEY brothers were there, huddled on the floor. They were JACK, JOE, AND FRED. Found in the yard, just off of the back steps, was the body of WILLIAM THOMAS SHOCKLEY, age 43. Later, two long rifle Super X, fired cartridge cases were located by this body. Inside the house, on the steps leading to the second story, was found the body of HELEN SHOCKLEY, age 16. She was lying headfirst, down the stairs. In the southwest bedroom were the bodies of Mrs. CLARA SHOCKLEY, age 44, and Mrs. MARTHA ELLEN SHOCKLEY, age 73. Asleep between these two bodies, was a little ten month old baby SHOCKLEY girl. Numerous window panes were full of bullet holes, plainly caused by rifle or pistol fire from outside. The telephone receiver was off of the hook. We searched the house. Four small SHOCKLEY children were asleep upstairs. JIMMY, age 13, could give us a pretty good story of what happened because he was reading a funny book upstairs when all the shooting started. He put out the lamp upstairs during the melee."

[Bill Shockley] "When I opened the stairway door, she was against it, and she just kinda slid down. This *[Inside Detective magazine article]* don't tell it right, but that's the way it was.

The first thing I knew about it, they came to my house. I was married, we lived in Conway, we'd been married eight or nine months. They came there, *Luke* came there. He came on into town—he had to get away from him *[Essary]*! And one of the first things he said to me, he said, 'Bill, it's your dad, shooting at us!' He made that word, he told me that thing, said 'It's your dad!'

Well, what would you think, if you drive up to somebody's house, somebody run out in the dark and start shootin' at ya? He said, 'It's your dad!'

And, 'course, Isam got there and so did Taylor, the trooper from Lebanon, and I think the Lebanon sheriff, which was Brown, his name was Brown. They got there and they said, 'You go with us!' They said, 'You know the layout of this place.' They said, 'If we have to have somebody to show us the layout, you'll know the layout.'

So we got in the car and we got out there, and the fence that comed up in front of the barn, which was probably a hundred foot from the back door or more...they stopped right there.

Well, it's only natural they was scared to go. They stood there hesitant to go up there, everybody did. Isam. We all stood there.

Well, all at once a highway patrol reached in the car and pulled out a rifle. I think they had it up over their head at that time, some how, some way. And he walked just as straight as he could walk by *himself* to that back door. He didn't try to hide behind anything. He walked right up to the back door. Then the rest of us kinda went up there. But he was the one who went up by himself!

That's when I went in the house. After a while we went in the house with Joe, and the rest of them was in the house. Mary came to the back door. Well, I got in and opened the stairway door like he *[Jim]* was telling you about and she did slide on down, when I opened the door.

But there was a player piano sittin' in the front room and he shot through so many...well, he shot through the window upstairs and my brother Don was laying with his head, you could see exactly where his head was laying and the back of the bed was up against that window, he shot through that window, it went through that headboard, missed him *that* much *[about three inches]*.

He shot through the living room windows, it come through her picture, her wedding picture, my wife's wedding picture was up on the piano, it went just as direct a hit as it could through the picture, in her chest, through the picture. Then another one went through the player part of the piano, we still have it, you know where the roll goes on it, it went into that.

So we stayed there. People started gatherin' in. We didn't know who it was or what it was. 'Course, it was scary there. Well, he *[Essary]* had left then, there was too many around. He left.

But—in the meantime—now, he loaded this gun after the pickup went down to the creek. Well, when the pickup pulled up in the yard he shot eighteen holes in that truck. He shot the windows and never hit either one of them. The only thing they got out of it was a flying piece of glass that flew against her arm, I believe. Eighteen shots in that truck and never hit 'em.

And...so he went directly across two miles, he didn't follow the roads, I know almost the way he had to go. And he stopped at Howard Latimer's house on the way to town. He was going to his dad's, his dad lived in Conway, that's where he was headed.

And he stopped there *[at Latimer's]*, still with his gun. And her husband had heard this on the phone like—well I suppose the rest of 'em had started callin'—and he left to go down there, he left her and her family there in the house and their son had just got married and he had his new wife there at this house and they had, what, three or four kids besides that.

He said, 'You call The Law and have them pick me up at my dad's house,' and she said she was so scared that she was hesitating. And he said, 'I said you call The Law or I'll do the same thing here I did at Shockleys!' She said she started cranking the old type telephone and that satisfied him and he left. He still had about a mile, a mile and a half to go, to get to his dad's.

So when he went to his dad's house...I guess she'd got the word out someway for The Law and that's where they went, and when they went to the house, his dad said, 'He told me that he'd shot Bill Shockley.' His dad said, 'Well, you just shot the best neighbor you had.'

So that's about it..."

[Jim Shockley] "Everybody knows that I have a special relationship with Joe and Mary. And one of the reasons for that is, uh, that night, that particular night...well, he kept shooting at the house, I mean, it just seemed like hours, every once in a while a bullet would hit somewhere on the house, and all of a sudden our old dog let out a loud yelp, at the time he shot, and I thought, 'Well, he's killed the dog now.'

But, anyhow, during this time, Joe must have crawled into the dining room and he got on the phone and called Central. And when he got a hold of him, he told him what was going on out there and had 'em to send the Sheriff, or send Law, I don't remember whether he said to send an ambulance or not, but I could hear him talking to them on the phone and....that's...that's always been...."

[Maxine Replogle] "Did he reach up and get the phone? You know, the phone would have been hanging up high, wasn't it...up on the wall!"

[Jim] "The phone was probably five foot in the air.

And...anyhow...Joe has really been special. Maybe for no reason, but it took a lot of courage, to be able to do that."

[Maxine] "...See, the telephone was by *the window*, a double window."

[Bill Shockley] "Kenneth Essary? He was a loner. We had went to grade school with him. He had more brothers that was older but there was three of 'em in school when I went, I didn't go with any of them. And his mother and father had separated years ago and his dad had raised these boys without a mother. Or did she die? Maybe she died and left them."

[Maxine] "I think she finally died, didn't she? She died and left them, I think she did."

[Highway Patrol reports states Father: Wm. Albert Essary, age 82, Conway, Missouri. Mother: Matilda Jane Ikerd, age 65, Springfield, Missouri].

[Bill] "Anyway, he was left alone with these boys. He was a fine fella, the older fella, was a fine fella. And, uh, just like you *[Jim]* said, he told him, he said, 'You killed the best neighbor you ever had.'

And the only thing that he denied after this was, we thought he fell for Helen, as a girlfriend. We even had heard—I don't know how true—but when she'd go get the cows of the evening, he'd be hid somewhere behind her and maybe he'd jump out. Had you ever heard that *[to Maxine and Jim]*? Maybe these things happened more than we knew about.

Another boy had brought her *[Helen]* and Shirley Jo *[Shockley]* home from school, and they met him *[Kenneth Essary]*. So we figured maybe that might have set it off, I don't know. But he denied that."

[Jim] "I can say something that would sorta support what he's sayin' and...I didn't know what was going on at that time and it must have been something like that, but I can remember at night I'd hear Mom and Dad downstairs and Dad would go outside, Mom would tell him 'You'd better go out and look,' and he'd go outside and look all around and I got curious about what was going on one night and I asked 'em, 'What's going on out there?' and she said, 'Oh, there's a dog out there, got some puppies and he's going out to see about 'em.'

And I really never thought much about it at that particular time but I'm pretty sure after I thought about that, because...well...this is another thing that maybe boys do that they shouldn't be too proud of. Helen was a little bit older than me but she was a nice lookin' girl. And she slept in this bedroom and I slept in that bedroom. And back then when you took a bath, you took a washtub or whatever, and you took it into your room and then you stripped down and you washed. Well, a couple of times when she done that...it's terrible to say...but ...boys will look, you know.

And anyhow, I'm sure that during that time is when he might have been out, he probably knew that went on, and he was watching. I don't know that but I believe that happened because during one of those incidents is when the puppy incident come to light.

And anyway, that particular day—I wanted to tell this too—they had a school election, or it might have been another election, I don't know if it was a school election or what, but they had the election at school on Tuesday, this was Tuesday April 3rd. We left home to go to the school election and when we went by his house...'course our school was already out, we got out in March, we only went eight months out of the year in grade school up through the eighth grade, Reed School...and anyway he was out and he had one of these hand saws, you know, that you saw up wood with, and he was out there sawing wood, he was out of wood and he had some full-length stuff there in his yard and he was just sawing up wood.

And we stopped, my dad stopped and hollered at him *[Kenneth Essary]*. He come over to the car and he *[Dad]* said, 'Why don't you go to the school election and vote with us?' And he said, 'Nah, I better stay around here, I've got some wood I've gotta cut.' And he said, 'Well, just let that go. Just cut enough for today.' And he *[Dad]* said, 'Me and the boys will be up there tomorrow and we'll bring our buzz saw and our tractor and we'll buzz up a bunch of wood for ya.' And he said, 'OK, I'll think about it.' We went on.

And I don't remember whether it was *that* time but I did hear my dad say one time...I don't remember...it probably wasn't that day...but I heard him remark to Mom, 'You know, that guy is gonna kill somebody one of these days and it might just be some of us.' And why he said that, I don't have any idea. I heard that remark.

What kind of person was he *[Kenneth Essary]?* He was mine and Don's idol, you might say, sort of, if you will! We were young, we liked to hunt, we thought we liked guns. He had a lot of guns! He had some guns that was high-powered rifles. We'd go up there and he'd show us his guns. He'd show us how good 'a shot he was. And there was trees out there, seemed to me they was *that* big around, and he'd say, 'I've got a rifle that'll shoot through those trees,' and he'd show us. We went up there, Don and I—and I don't know if Don remembers this or not, 'cause he's enough younger than me that he might not—but we used to go up there and see him, not often but once in a while, and he'd show us his guns and how good 'a shot he was.

And we liked him! Well, I don't know that anybody *dis*liked him. He, I guess, was weird, a little different because...don't you think he was a squatter? I don't think he paid any rent, I think he just moved in. The old house is still standing, that he lived in."

[Maxine] "Well, he was rentin' from Penders, they owned the place up there. They said, when The Law went to investigate everything, the upstairs was just full of detective magazines. You boys have heard that, haven't you?

And another thing, when we went to school with him, you remember how he would...the teacher...you know, used to, if you didn't get your work done in grade school, you're gonna stay after school and get it done. Well, she told him to stay one time and he said, 'I'm not gonna do it!' and he'd sass her back and say, 'I'm goin' home, I've got work to do,' and he wouldn't do it either, he'd sass the teacher back and he wouldn't stay, he'd leave. He was still that kind of a guy.

But back to a lot of this talkin' about him roaming around and things. I know, me and Glenn lived on a farm, we lived probably—Billy, a mile and a half from Mom and Dad?—and they'd been many a night that we'd lay there and we'd hear our dog barking. And we've often wondered since that happened if he [Kenneth Essary] wasn't peeking in windows back then too. I'd wake up and say, 'Glenn, the dog's barkin'.'

But, anyway, that was just our theory, we wondered if he hadn't been…because the dogs would go to barkin' and then in a little while they'd hush. See, his brother just lived above where we lived on the farm and he might have been comin' up there and goin' home, I don't know what he was doin', but we just always wondered about that."

[Bill] "Don't know if you remember or not but there had been *two* dogs. We had two dogs. The other was a little old collie lookin' dog, barked a awful lot. If you remember, that dog disappeared about a month before this happened. He completely disappeared. The little dog, that barked so much. Cattle, stock dog, more or less.

Also, his brother lived, probably, a mile and a half, two miles away. Lived on the Bates place. When he heard this, he was enough afraid of his own brother that they started carrying whatever they could. They blocked stuff against the doors. Said, 'He'll come up here!'"

[Jim] "One of the reasons that Kenneth could have been coming by your house, if he was at Lonnie's [Kenneth's brother, Lonnie Essary] house, there was an old trail down through the woods, and that was the only route that you could go to get to Kenneth's house at that particular time, from Lonnie's house, is down through the woods."

[Maxine] "See, we had just moved to Marshfield about three weeks before this happened. We lived on a farm down there."

[Jim] "He had a old Hupmobile one time that he drove, that had gasoline lights or kerosene lights or something on it, you remember they had them alongside the windshield on a car? And one night we was leavin' your place, I don't remember who I was with, and we went up through there and we went up, and he almost run over us, we didn't see him, back then the road went down like that, and he didn't have a light of any kind on that car, it was a moonlight night, and we almost hit him head on in the woods out there because we couldn't see him. I don't know what it was!"

[Bill] "I remember it as a Model T with no top on it. It didn't have a windshield on it! It was a Model T, had lights on the side, and he'd pull up there at Conway at the service station and the joke...Virgil Rennen come out and the Model T gas tank was right in the middle of the top up there, by the dash, on the outside, and he'd fill up with gas and he'd get his rag out and he'd just...like he was washing the windshield. But there was no windshield on that Model T! That made Kenneth perturbed! He told me once about that. He said, boy he didn't like that! Thought they was makin' fun of his vehicle. I guess."

[Jim] "Whether I thought I heard this, or whether it was said, or whether it might have been written in print somewhere, that they asked him one time why he done this and he said, 'Well,' he said, 'they refused to take me in the Korean War so I thought I might as well start killin' people here.'...but I heard lots of things said during and before the trial, from a lot of people."

[Maxine] "I know that was the worst nightmare of my life because I had, well, I had a baby about three weeks old, and I know Glenn's brother and his wife come to get us, and I thought, 'This is not true, you're just tellin' us this,' I said, ' this is just a nightmare.'

And we got in the car. They said, 'Well, just come on, get in the car with us and we'll take you down there.' And I kept tellin' Glenn—we was sittin' in the back seat—I said, 'This is not true, I'm not going to believe it.'

Well, we got just outside of Conway and we met the ambulances and I said, 'Well,' that's when I said 'I guess it's true.' See, I didn't get there before they...."

[Bill] "They just had loaded them and had started in. I got there before anyone got to the house; I was with Isam."

[Jim] "I'll never forget that as long as I live, what it looked like to have them two guns pointed right at me, when they opened that door."

[Bill] "But they didn't know what maybe...they couldn't find him!"

[Jim] "I know, I know that. That's the reason I knocked on the door and...and...nobody said anything, everybody just seemed to....well, when— Billy said he opened the door, and I guess he did 'cause I don't know who opened the door— but when he opened the door, everybody just kinda standin' around a little bit and then two guns were pointed right on me."

[Bill] "Well, another thing I might add to what you said a while ago: my brother Bob was in there on the bed, too."

[Maxine] "Yeah Billy, I always thought it was Bob, and they say it was Carol."

[Jim] "It *was* Carol. I *know* it was."

[Maxine] "I didn't know that 'til just recently. I always thought it was Bob that was laying between Grandma and....See, our Grandmother was with them. She had come to stay all night with 'em. See, she'd lost her husband in September *[Gus Shockely died 9/27/1950]* before this happened and she had never stayed by herself so she came home with them to spend the night and she just happened to be there."

[Jim] "Well, they were taking her to Niangua to the doctor the next day."

[Maxine] "And, you know, she'd spent time with her kids and everything, she just happened to be there."

[Bill] "Carol was more of a problem baby than almost any of them. She cried a lot. You remember that? She cried quite a bit and I guess she needed special attention or something."

[Maxine] "See, Mom had put Bob on the bottle and they probably sent him on upstairs to go to bed."

[Jim] "One time, during all that, I heard Bob kinda like he was gonna wake up and wanna get up, or something, and then he kinda settled back down and went to sleep."

[Maxine] "See, he was just eight months old. Eight months old.
 And I'll tell ya, when we got down there—I don't remember how long it took us to get down there—but anyway, 'time we got down there, why, my uncles was there and they said, 'Squat down! They haven't caught him yet. We can't have no lights on in there.' I had the baby with me—it was that boy right there, he was the baby, he was three weeks old, the one sittin' down, that's my son Jack—and he said, 'I want to see your baby,' he said, ' but I can't hold the light over him,' but he held the light down to look at the baby, and he said, 'Let's keep the lights on the floor,' 'cause, see, we didn't know he was caught yet when we got down there. So we was all just still on pins and needles when we got in the house."

[Jim] "If I remember right, when I got downstairs...they talked about who they thought it might be. And they had decided they thought it was him. I heard them talking about who they thought it was and I thought to myself, 'Surely it can't be him. He surely wouldn't do something like this.'"

[Conclusion of Trooper M.E. Taylor's report]

8. Sheriff CUNNINGHAM told us today that HELEN was shot three times, BILL, 5 times, CLARA, once, MARTHA ELLEN, 6 times. The bodies are all at the BARTO-BARBER FUNERAL HOME, MARSHFIELD, MISSOURI. Inquest time is set for 1:00 p.m., April 6. Pictures were taken by Sergeant BURNUM and Trooper GIBSON of SPRINGFIELD, MISSOURI."

[pictured left to right at the Shockley home: the back of an unknown friend, Sheriff Isam, Edgar "Jack" Shockley, Bill Shockley]

This was taken of the surviving Shockley children, shortly after their family tragedy April 3, 1951. (left to right) Patsy Ann, 5; Carol Francis, 2; Mary Ellen, 10; Donald Dean, 8; Robert Lawrence, 10 mos.; Bill Joe, 20; James Lee, 13; Gloria Maxine Replogle, 22.

[from April 5, 1951]
"Sheriff Cunningham approached the youth [at his father's home after the murders]. He had known the boy since he was knee-high to a grasshopper. 'Why did you do it, Kenny?' the Sheriff asked. Kenneth Essary replied promptly—if a bit incoherently, 'They were good neighbors,' he said, 'but they didn't like me.' "

April 12, 1951 cont'd. "Five persons were killed or died from injuries in a car collision on Highway 66 about 10 miles northeast of Marshfield Sunday morning about 10:30....

With the four members of the Shockley family murdered, this made nine tragic deaths in the north part of this County within five days."

[Bill Shockley] "Do you remember that, within two days probably, the accident on that curve there, that killed five people? Wasn't it within two days?"

[Maxine Replogle] "Well, we'd just buried 'em—hadn't we, Billy?—on Saturday, and that happened on Sunday night or Monday."

[Bill] "Troops from Fort *[Leonard]* Wood going back to Fort from Springfield, run off a curve there, just this side of Conway, hit a light pole, wadn't it? The other side of Sampson turn off."

[Maxine] "Old 66 Highway. Elkhorn Road, there's a sharp curve there, that's where they got killed. Five soldier boys. And it come out in the paper, didn't it, said, 'Forty-eight hours before they just buried four people.'"

[Celestia Davis] "During the Shockley murders, Helen would have called into the Niangua Phone Company. They would have called the Sheriff directly.

And I also worked at the telephone office when there were five boys killed in Elkland, in a car wreck. They had a station in Elkland but all their calls came through our switchboard, long distance calls and all. Oh, that was the most dreadful thing I've ever gone through in my life. Everyone called, you know, and we had a payphone outside the telephone office, in the lobby, and one lady came up from Elkland and she just used it constantly and we had to kinda watch it. We finally told her to keep her calls down and pay later, because we couldn't mess with her. But it was terrible. It was a car wreck and they were all killed. Teenagers."

"Kenneth Essary was brought here from the Springfield jail Wednesday morning and shortly after eight o'clock he waived preliminary hearing before Cline C. Herren, Magistrate Judge. He is charged with first-degree murder in four cases as a result of his admitting the killing of four members of the Shockley family in the north part of this county on Tuesday evening, April 3.

He was immediately returned to Springfield."

"While hunting some goats with his brother, Dr. W.L. Fisk, N.H. Fisk, who was visiting here from Iowa, and unacquainted with the country, became lost Saturday afternoon *[4/7]*. The goats were on the John W. Brooks farm north of Marshfield. A search party with Sheriff Cunningham and possibly as many as 25 persons searched the area from about 5 p.m. to 7:30 when Mr. Fisk came to the home of Seth Steward. He had wandered from about 3 o'clock until that time before coming to the Steward place."

"Three auto wheels and tires and two rims, believed to have been stolen, have been found and turned over to Sheriff E.I. Cunningham. Parties who may have lost these items, should identify them at the Sheriff's office."

"Ralph Wommack of Seymour was arrested Saturday night *[4/7]* on a charge of stealing chickens in the night time, according to Sheriff E.I. Cunningham. Bond was set at $2,000 but he failed to make bond.
Kenneth Matney, reported held in the Seymour jail on a city charge, will be served a warrant charging him with stealing chickens in the nighttime, on his release by Seymour, according to the Sheriff. Officers have recovered some of the chickens."

"Sheriff and Mrs. E.I. Cunningham, accompanied by their grandson, Don Letterman, were in Branson Sunday to see their son Charles pitch for the Quincy, Ill., team against Joplin. He pitched the first five innings, allowed 2 hits and was ahead 6 to 2 when another pitcher was tried out. Charles is trying out with the Yankee organization."

April 26, 1951 "The trial of Allen Bledsoe, 58, of Niangua, charged with the fatal shooting of his wife, Altie, 51, last June, is being held before Judge James P. Hawkins at Buffalo. Change of venue was taken from the Webster County Circuit Court.
The examination and selection of the jury began Tuesday morning at Buffalo. Defense attorneys are E. C. Curtis of Springfield and Frank Collier of Mountain Grove. Special Prosecutor is Roy C. Miller of Marshfield, who was Prosecuting Attorney at the time of the shooting.

Mrs. Bledsoe died June 28 of a bullet wound in her abdomen. Her husband was arrested early the next morning. He claimed the shooting was accidental. He said the gun went off while his oldest daughter (12 years old) was wrestling with him for possession of the gun. Bledsoe claimed that an argument had developed about whether or not his wife should go to the doctor."

May 3, 1951 "Charley Cunningham, son of Sheriff and Mrs. E.I. Cunningham, has signed a year's contract to play ball with Giants baseball organization. He left Sunday morning for Jenkins, Ky., to report. When the weather warms up he will go to Oshkosh, Wisc.

Charley first tried out with the Giants in Florida and later with the Yankees in Branson. He decided to go with the Giants. He was signed by Scout Martin with the Giants organization of St. Louis."

"It only required the jury 10 or 15 minutes to bring in a guilty verdict in the Bledsoe case held in Buffalo last week. Allen Bledsoe, 58, was found guilty of murder and sentenced to 12 years in the state penitentiary.

The case went to the jury about 3 p.m. last Wednesday afternoon *[4/25]*. After defense attorneys made no closing arguments, only three defense witnesses were called. They were Bledsoe, his son, Lloyd 18, and daughter, Cleta, 12.

Bledsoe was convicted of the fatal shooting of his wife, Altie, 51, last June 28 at their home near Niangua. The case was before Judge James P. Hawkins, Circuit Judge."

"A sanity hearing was held Friday, April 27, before Cline C. Herren, Probate Judge, in matter of alleged insanity of Clarence E. Hale of Fordland. Seth V. Conrad was appointed attorney for defendant, answer filed, jury waived and trial by court. Ordered defendant be committed to State Hospital No. 3. Attorney fee of $5 allowed Seth V. Conrad. L. S. Brooks appointed guardian and curator. Bond fixed at $25,000 and approved.

Sheriff E. I. Cunningham, accompanied by Tom Nunn, took Mr. Hale to Nevada Friday."

[Whereas the guardian is responsible for the person, the curator is responsible for the assets and income. The bond guaranteed that the curator didn't misappropriate the assets; evidently Clarence Hale had assets worth $25,000.]

May 10, 1951

"Joins New York Giants Organization"

[pictured above] **"Charley Cunningham, Marshfield ball player, has signed a contract to play ball with the New York Giants organization. He will go to Oshkosh, Wis., from Jenkins, Ky., as soon as the weather warms up."**

"New City Council is Organized—Mayor Ralph Bridwell presiding...Willis Case was elected Chairman of the Board."

May 17, 1951 "Three Mexicans, giving the names of Gumersindo Vasquez, Fidel Rodriguez Medellin, and Thomas Garcia Franco from Texas were arrested Monday evening *[5/14]* after stealing some gas from the Harry Bowman store east of Marshfield on Highway 66. They were lodged in jail here.

When Mr. Bowman put the gas in their car, one of the men is said to have struck at him and when Bowman went into the store to get a gun they drove off. He shot at the car and the .22 rifle bullet entered the back of the car and nearly struck one of the three men. Highway Patrolmen Wallace and Mumford were at the Skyline *[Café]* and being notified of the affair caught the men at the Top-O-The-Ozarks station near Conway."

"Magistrate Court Notes--- State of Mo. vs.   *[the three Mexicans named above]*, petit larceny, *[all]* plead guilty and were fined $10, except for Franco who was fined $25."
[I suspect Franco was identified as the one who swung at Mr. Bowman!]

"Circuit Court Notes—State of Mo. vs. Lloyd Bledsoe, forgery. Defendant waives formal arraignment and enters a plea of guilty. Punishment assessed at imprisonment in state penitentiary for a term of three years. Due to defendant being only 18 years of age, his sentence is commuted to two years in Algoa Reformatory. Application for parole filed....

State of Mo. vs. Kenneth Essary, murder. Roy C. Miller appointed attorney for defendant in all four cases in which he is charged with murder. Set for trial July 2, 1951, at 9 a.m."

May 24, 1951 "Preparations have started here for holding the State Fox Hunters Association meeting in Marshfield next October 3, 4, 5, and 6 when hundreds and even thousands of visitors are expected to be on hand. The big event of Missouri fox hunters, held annually, is being held this year by the Marshfield Lions Club...."

"The 1950 census reports that the number of farms in Webster County has decreased from 2,848 in 1945 to 2,573 in 1950, or 275 in five years. This is a greater percentage of drop than was shown by the state. In Missouri the number of farms dropped 242,900 in 1945 to 230,000 in 1950. This is a 10 % drop from 1940 when there were 256,000 farms in the state.

For the United States the decrease in the number of farms in the last decade is as follows: In 1950 there were 5,400,000 farms reported. In 1945 there were 5,800,000. In 1940 there were over six million farms in this country."

"Circuit Court Notes—State of Mo. vs. Kenneth Essary, murder. Reset for July 9. All four cases."

"....The Marshfield Cemetery has filled up and it has been necessary to acquire more land....With the larger cemetery the present City Tax for the care of the cemetery will not be sufficient, and it is only just, that people who have relatives buried here should contribute some to the expense of the cemetery care, as they do not pay the city tax that citizens of Marshfield pay each year.

We are soliciting you for a donation to the cemetery maintenance fund, or if you desire to acquire a lot sometime, would appreciate your buying it now.

You may contact the committee or Frank Francis, the City Clerk.

Cemetery Committee: George Barnes, George Dailey, John Andrews"

June 7, 1951 "Some excitement was created in the Niangua community when it was learned that Oral Wayne Evans, 22, who lives north of Long Lane, had walked out the back door of the Niangua Hospital Saturday night *[6/2]* clad only in shorts and undershirt. The young man, said to have been suffering a mental disorder, had been admitted to the hospital earlier.

A search conducted by Sheriff E. I. Cunningham, Dallas county sheriff Lonnie Pitts and about twenty-five other persons continued through Saturday night and Sunday.

Monday morning about eight o'clock the youth was found in the garage at the McDonald Café, three miles northeast of Marshfield, where he had found some quilts to protect himself from the cold weather. He had been about frozen from exposure. *[Sounds untypically cold for June in Webster County.]* His underclothes were in rags and his face was bruised and scratched from going through the woods.

Officers were called from here but when Tom Nunn and Homer Alexander went to the McDonald Café they found Dr. Will Schlicht had already arrived and was giving Evans some coffee. He was taken back to the hospital for treatment and then taken to Buffalo that evening."

"John Edward Krugel, 35, of Grand Rapids, Minn., or Fessenden, N. D., was killed in a three-car collision Tuesday near Elk Horn Lodge on Highway 66 near the north part of Webster County. He was killed outright as a result of a skull fracture.

Another man, Harry Paul Breber, 55, of Tulsa, was taken to the Niangua Hospital, severely injured. Slightly hurt were Archie Thompson, driver of a Patton Creamery truck and Clarence Copsey of Steelville, driver of a MFA truck. Both men were badly bruised.

The accident occurred, according to Sheriff E.I. Cunningham, when the 1949 Cadillac in which Krugel and Breber were riding, sideswiped the creamery truck and then crashed into the MFA truck. The Sheriff said the Cadillac attempted to take a curve at a high rate of speed. The Cadillac, owned by Breber, was demolished, and the MFA truck was badly damaged. The creamery truck was able to continue on its trip.

K.K. Kelley, Coroner, said that no inquest would be necessary. The body of Mr. Krugel was brought to the Barber-Barto Funeral Home here. Papers found on him indicated he traveled for a circus side show.

Breber denied to Highway Patrolmen that anyone was riding with him at the time of the accident. Breber, a paraplegic, suffering concussion and lacerations, could not recall having the accident when questioned at the Niangua Hospital Tuesday, and denied having a hitchhiker with him. He explained that since he is a cripple and forced to use braces and crutches, he never picks up anyone because he would be unable to defend himself against possible violence.

The troopers said they were fairly certain Krugel was riding in Breber's car since his luggage was also found in it. They believe that Breber was still suffering from a concussion and unable to recall picking up Krugel."

[A hitchhiking circus side show employee and a paraplegic driver of a Cadillac—and Sheriff Isam in the middle of it all.]

"Gene Fraker has leased the Marshfield Service Station from Bob Florance and assumed operation Monday *[6/4]*. He will be assisted by Gardner Thomas.

Walter Florance, who has been associated with the station, has indefinite plans."

"Circuit Court Notes—State of Mo. vs. Lloyd Bledsoe, forgery. Application for parole sustained. Defendant paroled. Defendant and Carless Bledsoe recognized in sum of $1,000. Case assigned to probation officer."

June 14, 1951 "State Highway Patrolmen picked up two Oklahoma boys at Mtn.Grove after they were charged with stealing a battery from a pickup east of Rogersville Saturday evening on Highway 60. Sheriff E.I. Cunningham went to Mtn. Grove Sunday and brought them here.

Monday Clifford Laramore was arraigned in Magistrate Court, pled guilty to petit larceny, and was fined $100.00. His brother, Irvin Laramore, charged with the same offense, was arraigned and being only 16 years of age was transferred to the Juvenile Division of Webster County Circuit Court."

"It is reported that Judge Tom R. Moore of Ozark has been appointed to preside over the felonious assault trial of Rex Rainey, former Marshfield undertaker, scheduled to get underway in Circuit Court in Hartville June 25.

The action followed the disqualification of Circuit Judge James P. Hawkins of Buffalo to hear the case. The case was taken to Hartville on a change of venue from Webster County.

Rainey is charged with complicity in a nighttime attack on his wife, Carmen, in October, 1949. Miss Mary Margaret Evans, former Springfield telephone operator, is serving a four-year prison term in connection with the case.

The Raineys, divorced shortly after the attack, were re-married more than a year ago."

"Sheriff E.I. Cunningham is investigating four break-ins reported in Rogersville Wednesday night, June 6. The only store reporting a loss was the Rogersville Drug where $10 in change was taken. At two firms, Underwood Motor Co. and Rogersville Motor Co., the thieves damaged the safes considerably trying to pry them open. At the fourth place, Ewing Hardware, the safe was left open and was undamaged."

[It appears that merchants were beginning to leave their safes open so they wouldn't get damaged when a thief tried to break in. Seems the cost to replace their safes exceeded potential losses from theft.]

June 21, 1951 "Gene Terrill and Joe Trent, an escapee from the Boys Training School at Boonville, were arrested at Parsons, Kan., recently. They are charged with robbing a store of $500 in Springfield, and stealing a car from a garage there. The car was said to have been left at Pittsburg, Kan. They were charged with holding up a garage and filling station at Parsons, but as more serious charges were held against them in Springfield, the Parsons officers turned them over to Springfield police, according to Sheriff E. I. Cunningham."

"Arrest Webster County Men Charged With Robbery of Aged Recluse—Deputies of Sheriff E. I. Cunningham arrested Glenn Willis of Northview and Harlin Burks of Marshfield last Thursday evening and turned them over to the sheriff and prosecuting attorney of Greene county. Officers at Springfield arrested Willis, Burks, Leaford Willis and Gene Terrill, who is in jail at Springfield. They are said to have signed a confession to the robbery of Mrs.*[Aunt Ruth]* Caldwell, aged Strafford woman January 9, 1949. She died a short time after the robbery."

"Officers are in search of Gerald Layne, 24, of north of Rogersville, according to Sheriff E.I. Cunningham. He is charged with stealing a calf from A.F. Patton of Christian county, south of Rogersville, Friday night *[6/15]*. The calf is reported to have been sold to Bill Wright at the Union Stockyards Saturday morning for $30. The calf was identified Sunday morning by Sheriff Clay Hodge of Christian county, the Patrol and Mr. Patton.

Layne was also charged with stealing a tire and wheel, and 1952 license tag from Jim Graves, a neighbor of Patton. It is reported that Layne wrecked his car Saturday evening near Oakland Park, Kan., south of Kansas City. He sold the car to a garage there."

June 28, 1951 "REX RAINEY 'NOT GUILTY'—The jury brought in a verdict of 'Not Guilty' in the trial of Rex Rainey of this city at Hartville Tuesday afternoon *[6/26]* about 4 o'clock. He was charged with complicity in the felonious attack in the early morning of October

19, 1949, on his wife, Carmen, by his paramour, Mary Margaret Evans, in the living quarters of the then Rainey Funeral Home here.

The testimony of Mrs. Rainey, who has since remarried the undertaker after divorcing him soon after the attack on her by Miss Evans, was not admitted in the trial.

Miss Evans, who was a telephone operator in Springfield at the time of the attack, was taken to Hartville to testify from Jefferson City where she is serving a four-year term in the state penitentiary on a felonious assault charge. It was her testimony at her trial here that resulted in charges being brought against Mr. Rainey.

Judge Tom C. Moore of Ozark presided over trial taken to the Wright County Circuit Court on a change of venue from Webster County and the disqualification of Judge James P. Hawkins. Jean Paul Bradshaw of Lebanon, M.J. Huffman of Hartville, and John Hosmer of Marshfield defended Mr. Rainey. Ellsworth Haymes was appointed special prosecutor by the state after John Hosmer disqualified himself. Roy C. Miller, who was prosecutor at the trial of Miss Evans, was employed to assist Mr. Haymes in the trial at Hartville."

July 5, 1951 "A 21-year-old colored soldier was apprehended here late Saturday in the late model Buick sedan he had stolen only a short time before at Fort Leonard Wood.

Turned over to military police at the Fort last night was Pvt. Billy R. C. Duncan.

Sheriff E. I. Cunningham said Duncan was picked up by a state patrol trooper Saturday *[6/30]* on Highway 66 near Marshfield. Only a few minutes before, the car driven by Duncan was involved in a minor accident with a vehicle driven by Dewey Redden, 52, of Lanesville, Ind., near Conway.

Neither car was damaged heavily, and Duncan was said to have fled from the accident scene in the stolen auto. The car is owned by another Fort Wood soldier, the Sheriff reported."

"Earl Haye Brake and Kelly Eugene Brake, who have been working around Fordland, were arrested Thursday and are held in jail here on charges of grand larceny according to Sheriff E.I. Cunningham.

The Brakes are charged with stealing four radiators, a tire and tube, from the junkyard at the old Hanna place west of Fordland. The Sheriff reports that they have admitted *[stealing]* two radiators which they sold to a junkyard in Springfield."

July 12, 1951 "The first degree murder case of Kenneth Essary, Webster County farmer, began here Monday before Judge James P. Hawkins, circuit judge, with the selection of a jury taking all day and into a night session. Essary was charged with the killing of William Thomas Shockley, 43, farmer and neighbor, on April 3.

Essary is also charged with first degree murder for the shooting to death of each, Mrs. Wm. T. Shockley, 44, Helen Louise, their 16-year-old daughter, and Shockley's mother, Mrs. Gus Shockley, 73, the same night.

Tuesday night, after only 37 minutes of deliberation the jury brought in a verdict of guilty of first-degree murder and assessed his punishment at life imprisonment in the state penitentiary. Defense Council Roy C. Miller was given 30 days to make a motion for a new trial by Judge Hawkins.

Essary still faces charges of first degree murder in the other three cases.

It required all day Monday to secure the necessary panel of 30 jurors from which 12 men were selected. 85 were questioned and 55 were disqualified either because they objected to capital punishment or they did not believe in temporary insanity.

Tuesday morning the jury was sworn, defendant waived formal arraignment, and entered a plea of not guilty. Prosecuting Attorney John Hosmer asked for the death penalty. Attorney Miller countered with a request for a verdict of not guilty by reason of insanity. As witness after witness testified, the courtroom was crowded to its fullest all day despite the heat. The jury went out originally at 6:52 p.m. after hearing stirring closing arguments by Prosecutor Hosmer and Brady Duncan, an assistant state's attorney general and Attorney Miller. The jury recessed for supper and actual deliberation was held up until 7:55 p.m.

Judge James P. Hawkins told the jury they could return four different verdicts: First degree murder with a punishment of life imprisonment or death; second degree murder with a penalty of not less than 10 years in prison; not guilty by reason of insanity with a belief that Essary is entirely recovered; or not guilty by reason of insanity with belief that he is still insane.

Most damaging testimony for the state was the written confession of Essary made two days after he had killed the four members of the Shockley family.

The defense used two doctors, John Sartin of Springfield, and Paul Barone, superintendent of the state mental hospital at Nevada. They had examined Essary in Springfield and they testified that Essary's confession showed signs that the timid bachelor farmer was mentally ill.

Witnesses included Shirley Shockley, teen-age daughter of Fred Shockley and niece of William Shockley. She told of seeing Essary that afternoon near the Shockley mailbox.

Charles Bilderback said that he had paid Essary $120 for 12 pigs the morning of April 3 and Charles Warren, clerk in Brooks Hardware store at Conway, related that Essary had purchased a .22 rifle and four boxes of shells.

Jimmy Shockley, son of Bill Shockley, testified that 'someone come to the front door and Mother told him to come around to the back. Daddy told him to come in and he started shooting.'

Luke O'Connor, brother-in-law of Bill Shockley, described being summoned to the Shockley home by a frantic telephone call from Helen Shockley (who subsequently was shot). He recounted that when he and his wife arrived at the Shockley place in his pickup truck, somebody shot into the truck numerous times before they could drive away to escape.

Testimony revealed a tale of horror the night of the tragic shootings as relatives finally entered the house and saw the bodies of the victims.

Joe Shockley told of shots that were fired from outside after he and his brother Jack had gone into the terror-stricken house. They dived to the floor, he said, and then he crawled to the telephone and called central in Conway.

'Then we stayed on the floor until the patrol and the Sheriff arrived.'"

July 26, 1951 "Clyde Hargus, Marshfield Café owner, has been named Marshfield fire chief effective this week, succeeding Roy C. Tindle, whose recent retirement from the grocery business makes him not so readily accessible. Mr. Hargus is experienced in fire fighting work, and has already announced he is planning a refresher course for volunteer fire men of the city as well as a training course for some new men...."

[Ruby Hargus] "He helped organize the fire department. He would have their meetings in our restaurant at night. Furnish them coffee. He was so civic minded. He just wanted to do everything. He would drive the ambulance for Edwards Funeral Home. If Mr. Edwards didn't have help, he'd call on Clyde, Clyde would take out. Especially if it wasn't around mealtime, the afternoon or something, we wouldn't be that busy.

The fire department, it was all volunteer. They asked Clyde to try and get a fire truck. There was a company out of St. Louis that had a used one. He contacted them. They brought one down, the rest of them looked it over, and they approved it. The City bought it."

[Joe Arthur] "Clyde Hargus would help us *[at Edwards Funeral Home]* sometimes whenever we were busy, go with us on *[ambulance]* calls. I knew Clyde real well...and Ruby."

"....Regardless of whether the China and North Korea Reds agree to truce terms with the UN, no let-up is expected to preparedness in the United States. Further outbreaks in other parts of the world by the Soviet Communists are expected."

August 30, 1951 "Tuesday night *[8/28]* about 2:30 Mrs. Arthur R. Riggs, just west of Marshfield, saw a man starting their car and start off west. They called Sheriff E.I. Cunningham and the State Patrol. The Sheriff started west and the troopers east. The troopers, Lindsey and Wilson, headed off the car near Strafford. The car turned around and raced east. The troopers fired two shots (one of them striking a bumper of the fleeing car).

The car overturned east of the Ranch Hotel at Holman. The man jumped out and ran over the railroad track with the troopers firing several shots at him. One of the bullets struck the man in the right shoulder, which stopped him.

It was found that the man was a soldier from Fort Leonard Wood, identified as Pvt. Robert Adams. He was seriously hurt and was taken to O'Reilley hospital in a Barber-Barto ambulance which was called from here.

Sheriff Cunningham who arrived just after the man was shot said he ran about 200 yards from the car.

Tuesday night Sam Fleetwood of Seymour had a car wreck east of Seymour and was brought to the jail here on a charge of drunken and careless and reckless driving by Trooper Tapmeyer of the Highway Patrol.

Also Tuesday night Troopers *[Glen]* Wilson and Lindsey of the State Patrol brought Delbert Frye of south of Diggins to the jail here on a charge of drunken and careless and reckless driving. Sheriff Cunningham states that Frye was driving a car with another state license and wrecked it east of Rogersville near the intersection of the White Oak road with Highway 60 when he ran into a culvert.

Officers are checking on the ownership of the car. The Sheriff says that Frye has been in jail here before."

"Thieves broke into the Twin Pines Café *[in Rogersville]* about 4:30 Monday morning *[8/27]* by forcing open the back door. Mrs. Wanda Bowers, owner of the café, reported $4.00 taken in change from the cash register. Also the coffee was turned on ready to drink. The Taystee Bread men heard the back door slam as they entered the front door and upon investigation discovered the break-in although they failed to find the thieves. The Webster County Sheriff's office is conducting an investigation."

September 13, 1951 "At a night session of Circuit Court Tuesday *[9/11]* Kenneth Essary, 23, charged with the murder of the Shockley family, his neighbors, last April, pleaded guilty to murder in the second degree. He was sentenced to life imprisonment by Judge James P. Hawkins in each of the three cases, reduced to second degree from first degree murder, in the deaths of Mrs. Clara Shockley, 44; her daughter, Helen, 16; and her mother-in-law, Mrs. Gus Shockley, 73.

In the May term of court Essary had entered a plea of guilty to the slaying of William Shockley, 43, husband of Clara Shockley. All were shot to death at their farm home south of Conway on the night of April 3. The jury set his new punishment at life imprisonment in the state penitentiary.s

Sheriff E.I. Cunningham said he would take Essary to the penitentiary at Jefferson City as soon as possible, to begin serving his four terms of life imprisonment.

The trial of Essary was set for this Wednesday morning *[9/12]* and fifty special jurors had been summoned by Sheriff Cunningham....

Essary was accused of shooting the Shockleys the night of April 3 when he appeared at their home with a rifle. He resided alone on a farm nearby and afterwards said he went to the Shockley home because he thought they had it in for him.

After shooting Mr. Shockley at the back door of the home, he fired through a window at the other members of the family that were downstairs, killing Helen as she was telephoning relatives for help, Mrs. Shockley and the mother of Mr. Shockley.

Later he fired into the pickup truck of Mr. and Mrs. Luke O'Connor when they drove to the Shockley home after receiving the telephone call from Helen. Over twenty bullets were shot into the pickup before the O'Connors could get away.

Essary, after buying the rifle and plenty of shells at Conway that day, had gone to the Shockley home. The man was arrested a few hours later at Conway. He was a quiet sort, and has not had much to say since the killings. He said nothing when sentence was pronounced.

Many other cases were before the circuit court Monday and Tuesday...."

[Mary Shockley] "We just let the kids stay in bed until *[the ambulances]* picked them up. Then we got the kids up and took them along with us. They was with us for nine months."

[Don Shockley] "There's one thing I remember very well. Mary took us out, we sat in the back seat of...I don't know whose car it was...all of us kids were in the back seat and Mary sat there and talked to us."

[Mary] "We had those six and we had six of our own. Jimmy Lee was 13, he was the oldest, and our baby was 5 months old, and their baby was 10 months, and we had twins and everything else."

[Don] "I'll tell you one story: Joe always did what he thought Dad would want to do. One time he sent me to gather eggs. I said I did. And I lied to him. And then he went out and gathered eggs and come back and, I never will forget it, Joe said, 'I hate to do this to you, but if your dad was here and you told a lie, your dad would whip you, so I have to give you a whippin'" so I got a whippin'. I was eight.

We used to sit around the table, we'd play cards at night, we had a lot of fun. Mary always treated us like a mom, Joe like a dad. Toots *[Maxine Replogle]* used to do the same, whenever she'd give me a whippin' she'd say, 'If Mom and Dad were here—I hate this—but they'd do the same,' so they took over where Joe left off."

[Joe Shockley] "There was never two better people than your mom and dad. Bill was the second boy. Jack was the oldest, then Bill, then Fred, then Ray, then me. I was the baby in the family. I've always said that Bill was the best one of that nine in every respect. Whatever you was a doin' and whoever you was a dealin' with, you was supposed to do what you knowed was right. He didn't believe in makin' any excuses for anything."

[Jim Shockley] "But, you know, kids really see things a lot different than adults, and after this all happened and we ended up in Marshfield, I was with *[Bill Shockley]* for a while and then I was with *[Maxine]*, most of the time. But, I used to go into the courthouse and just visit—kid stuff, I guess. But Isam would be in there and I'd kinda look for him, you know, because I knew I was going to get a nickel! A nickel would buy a lot back then."

[Maxine Replogle] "I'll tell ya, he was a good ole Sheriff, you know it? Wasn't he, boys? He was really a good Sheriff."

[Jim] "I can tell you one thing, that if it hadn't been for the willingness of Bill and Maxine....I can't say enough about how much I appreciate what they both done for us. We didn't always see things the same way."

[Maxine] " Well, they were just like our kids."

[Bill Shockley] "Actually the two, like Lorene *[Bill's wife]* and Glenn *[Maxine's husband]*, were the outsiders and it might have been more of a chore for them than it was for us, as far as a highlight in their life, for them to...."

[Jim] "They both *willingly*...I never, ever heard either one of them complain about one thing. I know, Lorene used to set and try to keep me from wantin' to go out on Saturday nights and say, 'Well, we'll just sit and listen to the Grand Ole Opry' or something like that, and I didn't much like country music, and...."

[Bill] "She sat at the sewing machine for many many days making clothes for those kids.

And another thing we didn't bring out here—I don't know if you know it or not—whenever they went through...the estate was settled, they give us $25 a kid a *month*, that's all we got, $25 *each kid*. We went to the Welfare Office to try to get some help, 'cause I was makin' probably a dollar an hour.

And I remember that: 'No! no, you're not qualified for welfare, to help these kids. No! no!' They wouldn't do *nothin'*, Webster County wouldn't do *nothin'* to help us, in the Welfare Department."

[Maxine] "Yeah, like he said, there's been times that we didn't have very many pennies in our pockets but we managed. We put out gardens."

[Bill] " Well, the Essary family, the boys, gave $100 each, to go on the funeral expenses. $100 each. $600. Lot a money at that time.

'Course, it was a big expense. One of the biggest funerals ever in all of Conway. They were stretched down the street, high school building, people and all that, across the yard at the high school. Remember that?"

[Maxine] "Well, the school was right across from the church."

[Jim] "It said in one of the newspapers I read, there was a two-hour procession, to view the bodies."

[Patsy Browning] "Well, let me ask you this: they had Mom's funeral separate from the others?"

[Maxine] "Yeah, she was a Lutheran. The others was Catholics."

[Patsy] "The other, did they have it in the gymnasium or at the church?"

[Bill and Maxine] "The church."

[Patsy] "All those caskets…was Mom there too?"

[Maxine] "She was in back, and when they viewed 'em, at the cemetery, sometimes they do that, they don't do that anymore but they used to, and one of the papers, it tells how long that funeral procession was."

[Mary Ellen Kilburn] "Well, they always told me there's over three thousand people there."

[Bill] "And then the grave, they put them all in one three-way grave. Remember that? One hole, not just small graves. The three were buried in one hole. They buried 'em there, and they got one name wrong. So where my mother is, my dad is, just opposite of what it says. The tombstone's wrong. They had the caskets there, so we knew which one was where, but it was all one hole. And when we came back, saw the tombstone, we knew it was wrong.

In years ago, people came out, the neighbors gathered in with picks and shovels. They didn't hire anybody. They came in and dug the graves. That went on for years and years."

[Maxine] "Well, that's my mom and dad, but I thought they was the best people in the world. Like I said, when we was going out there I just didn't believe it, and I didn't believe it until we got to the ambulance, and I thought, 'Well, how are we gonna make it without them?' because we were young. I was 22 and Glenn was 23. He [Bill] was 20. We were really just newlyweds. I just had the two kids and he [Bill] didn't have any yet. We was kids that took kids. I just thought we couldn't live without them, but we had to learn."

[Bill] "But they had the farm. Times were tough when they bought the farm. I remember what they gave for it. The payments was $120 a year when they bought it. They built a nice-looking new barn, new house, new grade-A barn, new tractor, new equipment, sold grade-A milk. They lacked $1500 of having it paid for. Everything. They lacked $1500. And they had enough fat hogs down there on the lot, they sold them in two weeks and we paid the farm off. After this happened. Two weeks."

[Maxine] "They were just fixin' to get electricity. And they had all the new appliances sittin' on the back porch, and they'd bought'em up here—Chevrolet Rod used to handle appliances, Frigidare—and they took every one of them back, for us. See, they'd never been hooked up or anything. They took them all back...."

[Jim] "When you think about what he accomplished in those thirteen years, especially given the fact that it was during a time in history when stuff like that just wasn't happening, you know, you can imagine what things would have been like had he been able to continue on."

[Maxine] "We just had to go ahead and do the best we could. We had our own family to raise, and those kids, and I know there's been times they probably done without things they shouldn't have, we didn't have the money to do it, but I think they all turned out pretty good."

[Jim] "Billy had a special relationship...I think you'd have to say this...with Lee and Fern, our dad's brother."

[Maxine] "And I think I kinda looked to Edgar. Isn't that weird? He [Bill] kinda looked to Lee, and Jimmy to Joe, and if I wanted to know anything, I always went to Edgar, Edwin's dad. My dad's three brothers. That's weird that one of us looked to one, and one looked to the other, but if I wanted to know anything, I would go and ask Edgar. He told me a lot of stuff about family history. He knew; he was the oldest of Grandpa's."

[Bill] "We could have went on the farm, probably, and took the farm over, and if we could have been managers, *half* of the manager my dad was, we could've had a good livin' and kept the kids *all right there.* But I didn't want that farm, I didn't want to live there!

   We rented it for three years, I guess, or more, then sold it in 1955, four years, to people who lived there until four years ago."

[Maxine] "Sold it to these people who live in Lebanon now, Robert and Juanita Schultz. And we could go down there anytime we wanted to and visit them and we was welcome just like we was kinfolk."

[Bill] "It was a really good farm, and we had such a terrible drought in the '50s, early '50s, for about five years. '51 was the flood, flooded Kansas City, then there was about five years of a *terrible* drought. And, we sold the farm in 1955 for ten thousand five hundred...wasn't it?

   After this fella *really* built it up, finished the house, brought the soil up, and everything—it was one of the best farms in the country—he got ready to sell it, to get off the farm, due to health he had to retire, he priced the thing to me....It wasn't long before it sold."

[Jim] "He contacted each one of us and asked us if we was interested in buying it, before he put it on the market. He *[Bill]* thought a lot about it, he thought a lot about it.

   I think that our dad was kinda the glue to help keep the Shockley family together. Because when you talk real serious with any of the others, when they needed advice on money or whatever, they always come to our dad. We traded work, let's see, 70-30, I think, with an uncle we had, because he had more farm than we did, and Dad had Billy and me and Don, whoever, when we traded with him. We had all the equipment and he depended on us. The whole family come to him when they were in need.

   In '47, in his bank account, he had a balance of $1200 and something. And that was a lot for that day and time, for them. And he managed *everything* and he really managed close; had to. Came near out of debt in thirteen years! Can you imagine, building a house and a barn and hiring help and doin' all that, in thirteen years!"

[Maxine] "After Glenn and me got married, she'd *[her mother, Clara]* write me letters. We lived here in Marshfield. Talkin' about 'I'm sorry we won't get to come up Saturday night to see you' or something, and 'You try to get down here and see us', you know. Fifteen miles apart. You see, you didn't run back and forth then like people do nowadays.

Well, the biggest thing I'd say, I hope anybody don't *ever* have to go through it. And if they do, you just have to do the best you can, look to God for help…that's all you *can* do."

[Bill] "It's a learning experience."

[Maxine] "Yeah, and we growed up in a hurry, didn't we.

[Bill] "Yeah."

[Maxine] "We was real young but we had to grow up."

[Jim] "I think one of the most important things that you can tell people about this is, make s*ure* you keep the family intact, don't let 'em be scattered out amongst, because at that particular time we had letter after letter after letter of people who wanted one or two of the kids, to take, you know. 'Course, they *[Maxine and Bill]* heard more about that than I did."

[Maxine] "Well, they wanted to adopt the two little ones, mostly, because they were the younger ones."

[Bill] "We had a prominent businessman in Marshfield, who had money, who wanted the two littlest ones. And I'm sure they would have been well taken care of and well set up in life, because he was a businessman. But I think Family was more important to us."

[Maxine] "We didn't even talk about it, did we. We just said no to begin with."

[Bill] "No. And they were fine people."

[Maxine] "They lived right here in town, but we said no, we didn't want to separate them.

And *these* kids just grew up with *my* kids, and if they had little fusses, they had their little fusses. They got along real good. Of course kids will have little spats once in a while, but they got along just fine!

I know, Jimmy was with you *[Bill]* for a while and Glenn said, 'I think I want Jimmy for a while.' He put in a sawmill, didn't he, and he said 'Let's take Jimmy'. So he was going to put Jimmy to work! How old were you then? You'd been about 15? 16?"

[Jim] "Fifteen. Don't tell your husband *[my husband, a state court judge]* but he had a '36 Chevy truck and we had a saw-mill out in the country and I wasn't old enough to drive but I drove that pickup. In fact, after he got the sawmill, I don't know whether he decided it was too hard or he wasn't making enough money or what, but he ran off and started driving a truck and left me and Walter Brixey and Don in charge of a sawmill!

Well, Don and I wasn't in charge. Walter Brixey *[around 60 years old at the time, according to historical records]* took care of it.

Anyhow, we worked at the sawmill, sawed ties. They took ties over to Mansfield, wasn't it. They used to have a tie lot over there where they brought railroad ties. And we sawed them, kinda, and then we took the slabs that we cut off of that and we cut it up for wood and we sold it for wood.

There was lots of little ways to get by."

[Maxine] "Like Billy said, he worked for a dollar an hour for a while and I worked for fifty cents an hour, up at Sho-Me's Café, at one time. The first week I took it home I bought me a new dress for five dollars, at a dress shop here in town.

I tell my kids, 'That was the good old days.' So you see, I'm old-fashioned.

And I'll always be that way I guess."

[Bill] "We'd had the sale—sold equipment, cattle, whatever. We had an auction. Three weeks after.

I remember Willis Case talkin' about me carrying Bob around all the time. See, Bob just clung to me like a father, almost, 'cause he was only ten months old. He was a real good lookin' boy, really good lookin' boy. Everybody...can you imagine...how they took him up in their arms, everybody.

'Course, it was such a chore for us to milk by hand, to continue this until the sale. And we had a neighbor to the north, name is Clyde Stevens, and his son came over there and helped us, we finally got them to come and help us, and they helped us all through this until the sale, back and forth, morning and night, without any charge or anything."

[Jim] "Well, Clyde Stevens, the son that helped us, was Kenneth's *[Essary]* cousin."

[Bill] "Yeah! I believe they were cousins. And he come and donated their time to help us. 'Cause that's a job, for somebody to run in, because, even though I was familiar with the place, to take over the milking and do it by hand, sixteen cows, twice a day, and I had a job, too, with the Frisco Railroad, see."

[Maxine] "And I guess there was a lot of chickens around the place to feed, too."

[Jim] "This, uh, it's kinda strange, but I heard Dad say that once he got to a point in life where he didn't owe anybody anything, it would probably be his time to go. And it turned out that way.
     So I try to stay in debt."

[Maxine] "I think he *[Kenneth]* just stayed up there and read so many magazines, and kinda lost it."

[Bill] "I think there's a possibility he was crazy about Helen."

[Jim] "I really believe that too. And one of the reasons I believe that, Shirley Jo and Helen were about the same age. They were best of friends and went to school together. Shirley Jo Shockley. First cousins."

[Bill] "She lived on the next farm up."

[Jim] "Her and Helen, wherever you seen one, you seen the other one. That particular day, Carl *[Buck, now Shirley's husband]* happened to have one of his friends from Hartville, Missouri, was with him there, and they picked Helen and Shirley Jo up at school and brought them home. And north of our place, on the road, as they come home from school, they met Kenneth Essary with his team. He was on a wagon.
     This is just me thinking that—and maybe Shirley has kinda supported this a little bit with what she said—but they kinda waved to him in sort of a, in *his* mind, was making, like Virgil Vernon washing a windshield that wasn't there, had sorta poked fun at him just a little bit, you know, and not bad, not bad, but enough to irritate him to a point to where, 'she is with a guy here, and I wanted her for myself, and if I can't have her, nobody else is gonna get her.'"

[Bill] "Another thing, too, though. I don't know how many days were between these two things. He took them hogs, he had a few pigs that he had ranged, and sold 'em and went to the hardware store in Conway and bought this gun, brand new, it was a brand-new gun, automatic 22 rifle. And he'd sold enough hogs, he went to loot. He'd sold them pigs to loot, didn't he. And he'd sold them pigs for enough money ahead of time to buy this rifle, so he may have the plan ahead of time that, 'If I ever need it, I'll have it' or something. I don't know."

[Jim] "Joe and Mary Shockley lived up on Grandpa and Grandma's place, which was about a mile and a half away. Several times, when they'd go away, they would have Kenneth Essary come and milk their cows and do their chores. And I stayed with them one time when they were gone, and he come up and helped us with our chores. So Joe had a relationship with him that was a little different, maybe, than some of the others. But Lonnie, Kenneth's brother, lived less than 500 yards, probably, well, actually a quarter of a mile, from where Joe and Mary lived.

He *[Joe]* actually went and visited Kenneth. He's talked to us about that. I don't remember if it was after the trial or during the time before the trial. But I know Joe went and talked to him."

[Maxine] "Well, you was talkin' about Lonnie. You know, he just lived, what, a quarter of a mile from us, and he was one of the best neighbors we had when we lived on the farm. His brother, Lonnie. Couldn't ask for anybody to be any nicer to us."

[A few days from when this interview took place, I read this in The MARSHFIELD MAIL obituaries: "Lonnie Edward Essary departed this life Aug.22, 2003 in his home at the age of eighty-nine years, five months, and twenty-six days... Preceding him in death were...two brothers, Luther and Kenneth Essary...."]

[Don] "The only thing I remember...in fact, I don't think they woke us up until about 6 o'clock the next morning...I remember wakin' up and goin' downstairs and I needed a pin for my overalls. But I remember, Billy, when I come downstairs, *everybody* was there. It must have been pretty late into the night or early in the morning, because I remember people sittin' around in the living room. It was completely packed when we come down.

I looked for a pin, and I asked, 'Mom, where's a pin?' 'cause I needed a pin, to hook the strap. *[Of course his mother was dead, but Don didn't know any of what had happened, yet.]*

And I remember Fay, my aunt Fay, took us out to the car and we all sat in the back seat of the car and my aunt come out and talked to us. Remember that? Aunt Fay. Well, Mary talked to us first, then Aunt Fay come out and talked to us as well."

[Bill] "It's hard to remember who all was there, but Henry Smith's wife said that Henry was there, and he went in and got Carol, and washed her and cleaned her up. And I said, 'No I don't think so, 'cause I don't ever remember Henry bein' there.' Well, I talked to Dorothy the other day and she said, 'Yes he was! He was there. And him and Bill Replogle and Clyde came down to the house. And he was there.' But I don't remember him being there."

[Patsy] "I always heard Grandma Shockley put [Carol] under the bed, that's what I've always *heard*. I don't *know*."

[Jim] "I don't know if anybody knows that, because Mom was shot on the back porch and she, I could hear her running through the house, and also Grandma running through the house, and so they both got in the bedroom about the same time, the best I could hear. 'Course, I don't know what they were doing, I couldn't know, but one or the other of 'em probably checked Carol, and maybe picked her up and held her, I don't know, that's something I really don't know.

A 22 rifle doesn't make much noise. Just like a...I don't know...how would you describe the sound? You could hear them hit the house. I don't know that I heard any windows break, but it just seemed like he was out there for a long time and it seemed like everything was all over and then all of a sudden there would be another barrage of shots, and you could hear 'em hittin' the house. I don't know where he was shooting, or if he was shooting in a window, or what, but it was a while before he quit shooting completely."

[Mary Ellen] "My first recollection was, I believe it was Lloyd Hendricks come up the steps, wrapped me in a blanket, took me and put me in the car with Joe and Mary Shockley. Or Mary Shockley. And, then eventually, we all wound up in the same car and she said, 'Well kids, I've got something to tell you. Everything's gonna be okay, we'll take care of ya, but you don't have a Mom or a Dad. And Grandma and Helen are gone and we don't know who done it.'

And I don't know where we went. I thought we went to my Grandma Shockley's house, which my Uncle Joe had just moved into. We were in the side bedroom, squatted down on the floor, and hid for a long time with flashlights, scared because we didn't know who was doin' what. And after that I just remember our lives changed forever.

Joe, somebody, had a farm, it was my Grandma's farm, they had a house across the field, a canning factory house, probably three hundred yards. My uncle was milkin' cows so he wanted to be close to the barn, and Grandma's house was close to the barn, so they moved her in the other house. So my dad said to her, that day on the way back, you know, after we went by, 'Go home with us and spend the night, because if you don't, you'll straighten up all night, and Clara and the kids'll help you *later.*' That's what *I* remember."

[Mary Ellen] "Well, I don't know if anybody else ever did, but I know me and Don and maybe her [*Patsy*], but anyway, me and Don used to go down to Kenneth's and talk to him. He showed us how to make a rabbit gum, didn't he—a rabbit gum, to trap a rabbit, they call 'em rabbit gums—we knew how to make a rabbit gum, isn't that right, Don?"

[Jim] "I didn't know about that, but...he was...we liked him!"

[Don] "I just remember goin' down with you [*Jim*] one time and he had this high powered gun that he showed us he could shoot through a little tree. 'Cause I was a little boy, you remember something like that."

[Jim] "Yeah, we was impressed."

[Mary Ellen] "Does anybody remember this? I remember this: Dad got throwed from a horse down by the spring, Kenneth Essary came down, he said, 'Let me help with the work.' He came down and he helped do the work. We'd feed him but he wouldn't come in the house. He'd take his food out, he'd sit out under a tree, and eat his food with the dogs. I never knew him to come in the house. Never knew him to come in the house. He was an odd one but likable, for some cause. And Helen never knew that he liked her, but we've always heard that's why he did what he done.

Now, I talked to Mary Shockley on the phone one day and I was tellin' her about this paper I saw, and she kinda confirmed some of the stuff in there. And she said that Joe went to see Kenneth and he said, 'Did I get the girl?' and he said, 'Yes, you did.' That seemed to be his main concern, that he wanted to, that if *he* couldn't have her, nobody else could. And she [*Mary Shockley*] pretty much confirmed that."

[Jim] "Yes, Joe was the only one who ever talked to Kenneth [*after the murders*].

You won't know what a Doodlebug is, but a Doodlebug was a tractor made out of a car frame and a truck transmission and truck rear end. And that was our tractors, and we had to pull a wagon to feed hay, and we was tryin' to start that Doodlebug and it wouldn't start. And so we pushed it off down the hill. Helen was guidin' it—I don't think she would have known what to do if it had started anyways—but it run through a big trash pile down there and *[Kenneth Essary]* come down and helped us get it started and come up and hooked on the wagon and we fed hay. And I don't know if it was *that* winter, I think it was probably in the winter of '50 and '51, but it *was* in the wintertime, or we wouldn't have been feedin' hay if it wasn't."

[Patsy] "Well, have I been told right? Have they said before, that Grandpa Stogsdill just grieved himself to death over this?"

[Maxine] "Well, I'm the one that started that. Because he thought so much of Mom and Dad. See, Grandpa never did have a car and Mom and Dad kinda waited on him, went to town and seen about him and done everything for him. (That's my mother's father.) He died the next summer, and everybody said, I've always heard, that he grieved hisself to death. 1952, when he died."

[Don] "I don't remember much at home, but one thing that always sticks in my mind, I say it all the time: one of the best places I can always remember setting is on my mom's lap. And then I set on Mary's lap afterwards. I can remember that. But there's *no* place like sittin' on your mom's lap. Isn't that right?"

(September 13, 1951 continued)

"A joint meeting of Webster County Fox Hunters and Marshfield Lions Club members was held Monday night to complete plans for the State Foxhunters Association annual hunt which is to be held here October 3rd, 4th, 5th, and 6th. The Webster County Fairgrounds is to be the headquarters for the hunt.

Fox hunters present were Hugh King, Bob Dugan, Fred Cantrell, Clifford Burchfield, George Caine, Ronnie Clair, Frank Fellin, Si Price, Glenn King, Ralph Davis, Bob George, Del Massey, Herschel McClanahan, George Toliver, and Alva Hutchins....

It was decided to reserve all cabins available on Highway 66 between Conway and Strafford. It may be necessary to secure cabins as far as Springfield.

In addition it was decided to ask that all Marshfield people, who will give sleeping accommodations for the visitors during the four days, Oct. 3-6, call Frank Stockton, chairman of the *[housing]* committee, and list their rooms.

The committee thought that it would be a good idea to set a price on these private rooms at $1.50 per person, or two to a room, $2 per night."

"Clifford Earl Wheeler, 37, apparently committed suicide Tuesday morning [9/11] by hanging himself in a shed at his home on route 1, Marshfield.

According to his wife, Georgia, he went to the barn about 5:00 a.m. to put the cows up. When he failed to return she went out to look for him and found him in the shed. He had put the cows in the barn, but did not feed or milk them. He had apparently placed a rope around his neck and dropped off a stanchion.

Mr. Wheeler was recovering from an operation and had returned home from a hospital about two weeks ago. Mrs. Wheeler is reported to have said he told her he was going to kill himself last week, but no reason is known why he should.

Mrs. Wheeler called neighbors and Wes Twyman, Fred McNabb, and Cleland Hunt came immediately. They called the officers and Sheriff E.I. Cunningham and Prosecuting Attorney John Hosmer went out, and soon a large number of neighbors and friends gathered. Coroner K. K. Kelley of Fordland was called and he decided death was by suicide and no inquest was necessary.

Mr. Wheeler is survived by his wife, Georgia; two daughters, Rosemary and Annette; one son, Dale; his parents, Mr. and Mrs. Joe Wheeler; and one brother, Clyde Wheeler, of Springfield.

Funeral services will be held this Thursday afternoon at 2:00 o'clock at St. Luke with burial in the cemetery there."

September 27, 1951 "Citizens representing Rogersville, Fordland, Seymour, Diggins, Elkland, and Marshfield attended the Civilian Defense meeting held at the court house here last Thursday evening [9/20]. Discussion and plans to make the Civilian Defense organization countywide were discussed.

….Nurses in the county are working on a program to set up first aid classes in order to be prepared for atomic attack. Classes will be held in the various parts of the county where requested."

"This Thing Called Freedom of the Press—What is it? It is the reporter, jotting down facts. It is the correspondent, gathering news of the small community. It is the editor sifting wheat from chaff. It is the writer, expressing himself clearly. It is skilled artisans of the mechanical departments, helping to 'get out the paper.' It is the free American men and women devoted to the task of keeping America free by keeping America informed.

THE MARSHFIELD MAIL

Webster County's Newspaper

NATIONAL NEWSPAPER WEEK, OCT. 1—8."

"Everything is all set for Missouri State Fox Hunters Association to be held at the Webster County Fairgrounds October 3, 4, 5, and 6....The program starts Wednesday evening, October 3rd, at 7:30 with opening remarks by Rev. Selph Jones of Aldrich. Then will come old time singing and quartets and other numbers.

On Thursday night, starting at 7:30, Paul Beckerdite, Marshfield, magician and entertainer, will be the main feature. There will also be special singing numbers.

Friday evening square dancing and a fiddling contest will be features.

Then on Saturday night the Bench Show will be held.

The Missouri Conservation Commission will show movies each evening...."

October 4, 1951 "What is a newspaper? A newspaper is many things. It is a record of history. It is a forum. It is a market place. It is a voice. It is a guardian. It is, above all, an institution devoted to the best interests of the community. It is a servant of the people. Its goal—the public be served.

THE MARSHFIELD MAIL

Webster County's Newspaper

NATIONAL NEWSPAPER WEEK, Oct. 1-8."

"The car of Atty. Roy C. Miller was stolen from in front of his office last Thursday [9/27]. It was later found damaged and abandoned in a ditch beside Highway 60 2 1/2 miles east of its junction with Highway 63 near Willow Springs by the Highway Patrol.

The Patrol picked up Davis Newman of Detroit, a 15-year-old youth, a short time later and placed him in jail at West Plains.

The boy was brought here Friday by Sheriff E.I. Cunningham and is held to appear in Juvenile court next week before Judge James P. Hawkins.

It is reported that the boy arrived in Marshfield Thursday morning and was seen at a service station about 9 a.m. and later at a store where he asked for a job. The car was stolen about noon. Atty. Miller, former Webster County Prosecutor, has been embarrassed by his friends ribbing him about leaving the keys in the car.

The car, a 1949 Ford coach, had the front end damaged, as if it had been run into something."

October 11, 1951 "Following the blowing of a safe at Cabool Sunday evening *[10/7]*, county officers and patrolmen of all this area were out throwing up road blocks on all highways. Sheriff E. I. Cunningham and deputy, Commodore Smith, of this city were up all night on this work. However, the car of the robbers was not caught."

"Rex Rainey of Marshfield and John Rush of Springfield, former Marshfieldian, were elected directors of the Ozark Empire Aberdeen-Angus Association in Springfield last week...."

"The meeting of the State Fox Hunters Association was held here last week sponsored by the Marshfield Lions Club. Although an anticipated crowd of 2,500 to 3,000 estimated by the state association did not materialize, approximately six to seven hundred attended the meet. Registration totaled 275 dogs and more than 500 dogs were here.

The meeting generated considerable interest in Marshfield and vicinity and large crowds attended the programs held each night. Large crowds were also present for the early morning casts...."

October 18, 1951 "Mrs. Fay Bryant of Seymour is entitled to keep the $1000 she found over a year ago in the 600 block South Main, Springfield, Magistrate Gideon of Greene county has decided.

Mrs. Daisy Shipman, 626 South Douglas, Springfield, thought the money might have been part of $1400 she lost on April 22, 1950. She believed she lost it at about noon that day, at Kresge's Store.

Judge Gideon ruled that the money Mrs. Bryant found didn't match the description of the money Mrs. Shipman lost.

In attempting to find the owner, Mrs. Bryant followed the law, the judge held. She posted a notice in five different places in Springfield, and ran a legal ad in the *Marshfield Mail*."

"Mr. and Mrs. Wilbur Cunningham of Rockford, Ill., came last Friday night *[10/12]* and visited until Sunday with his parents, Sheriff and Mrs. E.I. Cunningham. They attended the funeral of Wilbur's grandmother, Mrs. Clara Randolph, Saturday."

"Funeral services for Mrs. Clara C. Randolph, 83, of Niangua, who died in the home of her grandson, Herbert Vestal there early Thursday following several months' illness, were held at 1 p.m. in Eureka Church, with the Rev. Selph Jones officiating. Pall bearers were Charles Cunningham of Marshfield....Surviving are two daughters, Mrs. E.I. Cunningham, wife of Webster County's Sheriff, of Marshfield,...."

[May Vestal] "Isam was always nice to me. He was the one that asked me if we could take her, if I could keep Mrs. Randolph. She was Herbert's grandmother, Eva's mother. Eva couldn't take care of her.

We kept her 'til her death. I don't remember how long she lived with us, a year or more.

She stayed with Eva and Isam a little bit. In the jailhouse, close to the jail, she didn't like to stay there. And Eva didn't have the time because she cooked for the jail. Nothing was especially wrong with her mother, just age."

[Raymond Day] "I remember Isam's mother-in-law. Shirley lived at home with them, when Mrs. Randolph stayed with them. Mrs. Randolph, she wouldn't take her medicine. Shirley would say something, fool around, trick Mrs. Randolph, and then stick it in Mrs. Randolph's mouth."

[Edna Cunningham] "Evie's mother, Mrs. Randolph, she was the sweetest thing. She used to come to our house and we'd have gooseberries, and she'd sit out there and stem the gooseberries. She used to come to our house and stay with us after we moved to the farm. Grandma Randolph. See, we had a porch swing out there and she just loved that porch swing. We'd go get her, any of 'em would go get her, 'cause they liked Grandma. She didn't live too far down the way.

May and them just said they would take care of her. But we all went up and took a night, when she got bad, we had to set up with her. So we all went and took our times, settin' up. They lived in Niangua, right there where the post office is, just west of the post office."

October 25, 1951 "Three Webster County teenagers, arrested last Thursday *[10/18]*, have admitted the theft of a $5 bill in the burglary of a farm home early this month.

Held in the jail here pending a hearing on juvenile delinquency charges were two brothers, 14 and 16 years old, who moved here this summer from California, and a 17-year-old neighbor boy. All three live southwest of here.

The boys were picked up Thursday by a state trooper and Sheriff E.I. Cunningham, who said the boys entered the unlocked farm home of Wesley Anderson, proprietor of the Marshfield Cleaners, about October 5 and took the $5."

"Charges of milk adulteration will be filed this afternoon *[10/25]* against 12 independent Greene county farmers, Milton Kirby, Greene county Prosecuting Attorney said today.

The farmers are accused of adding water to milk they sold to dairies here this summer, and if convicted, face maximum penalties of a year in the county jail or $1000 fines, or both. The charges, which will be filed directly in Circuit Court, according to Kirby, are misdemeanors...."

November 1, 1951 "Fortune tellers, reported to be gypsies, set up a tent behind the Highfill Grocery last week. Saturday afternoon *[10/27]* two of the women were arrested on a charge of Grand Larceny. They were charged with having taken $231 out of the billfold of Marion Kesterson at the tent.

When Prosecuting Attorney John Hosmer and Sheriff E. I. Cunningham went to the tent it is reported they found $200 of the money on the ground in the tent. The women said the man must have lost it out of the billfold.

The women, Mary Costello and Rosie Urich, were arraigned and hearing set for Nov. 5 before Judge Cline C. Herren. They made bond."

November 22, 1951 "Fannie Cunningham returned to her home in Long Beach, Calif., last Thursday *[11/15]* after a two weeks' visit here with her nephew, E.I. Cunningham, and family, and other relatives."

[Isham H. Cunningham (1868-1941) married Harriet "Fannie" Dollarhide, who owned oil wells in Oklahoma and later lived in both Texas and California. Isham was a brother to Sheriff Isam's father, James Harme Cunningham.]

November 29, 1951 "The big rat and mice banquet is being prepared all over Webster County for the week starting November 30, according to Karl Wickstrom, County Extension Agent. It is hoped that every farmer and town resident of the county will join in providing feed (poison) at this time…. 'These rats do approximately $80,000 worth of damage in a year, without considering the mice. We can save two-thirds of this at a cost of approximately 5 cents per rat, which would certainly be a big help. We want to try and kill as many of the rats and mice in the County beginning November 30 as is possible' states Wickstrom."

December 6, 1951 "When P.G. Lindsay of Joplin was brought before Magistrate Judge Cline C. Herren here November 30, charged with careless and reckless driving, he admitted drinking a half pint of whiskey.

The judge, surprised at the admission—the first man to admit drinking whiskey and driving on the highway since he had been Magistrate—fined him $50.00 instead of the usual $100.00 in such cases. He told the defendant that his honesty had made him $50.

Usually defendants in such cases claim they had only been drinking a beer or two."

"Officers are in search of a man giving the name of Harry Henson of Springfield. According to Sheriff E. I. Cunningham, the man went to Pyatt Motor Co., at Seymour Saturday evening *[12/1]* and bought a 1951 Chevrolet and another used car, giving Mr. Pyatt a check for $2500.00 on the Union National Bank of Springfield. The man took the 1951 Chevrolet with him.

Monday Mr. Pyatt was notified by the Union National Bank that there was no money deposited there under the name of Harry Henson, nor had there been.

Monday afternoon a man giving the name of Harry Henson deposited checks to the amount of $2,000.00 in the Pleasant Hope Bank and drew $200.00 in cash. Sheriff Cunningham says that the checks deposited were no good, but that it indicated the man was still around in these parts."

December 13, 1951 "Sgt. Howard Closton Lee, about 30, soldier at Fort Leonard Wood, was instantly killed last Friday evening about 8:30

o'clock when his automobile rammed into a large tractor-trailer truck on Highway 66, almost exactly in front of the Skyline Café.

Riding with Lee, whose home was Washington, D. C., was Bob Ruiz, 17-year-old hitchhiker of Toledo, Ohio, who told Sheriff E.I. Cunningham he was a run-away. Ruiz suffered a fractured arm and severe facial lacerations, and was taken to Burge Hospital, Springfield.

The driver of the large truck was not injured. He said the car driven by Lee was on the wrong side of the highway. The car was going west and came over the hill on a curve to meet the truck, which was going east. The car was almost demolished by the impact. According to Mr. and Mrs. George Barnes, of the Skyline, the smash seemed like a big explosion.

Mr. and Mrs. Rex Rainey and a bridge party at the café were immediately on the scene.

Editorial comment: Sheriff Cunningham called attention to the fact that five people have been killed in Webster County on the highways within ten days, three young men at Diggins, Mrs. Fannie Slicer near her home, and this accident. He might have added that while two of the deaths were on what some newspapers like to call Bloody 66, three of the deaths in the county were on another highway. It might well be said that all of the highways are bloody."

"James Alvin Casteel, Wilbur Casteel, and Lewis Osborn are held in jail here charged with breaking in and entering the Producers Exchange, Ritz Theatre, Marshfield School building, and the Skating Rink here. These break-ins were during the last part of November or first of December, except the Skating Rink is said to have been entered during the Fox Hunt or cattle sale.

Reported taken were 10,000 22-shells, a half case of cigarettes and gloves from the Exchange, two rolls of tickets from the theatre, a suitcase and money sack (no money) from the school building, several pairs of roller skates from the skating rink. It has not been determined if anything else was taken.

Most of the stolen articles have been recovered, according to Sheriff E. I. Cunningham."

December 20, 1951 "When Dale Ivie returned home from Springfield last Thursday evening *[12/13]*, he followed his family down to the home of his father-in-law, Mitchell Hightower, east of Niangua. It is reported that he drew a gun and as Hightower turned, shot him. The bullet struck him inside and glanced off a rib.

Officers were called and Hightower was taken to a doctor while Ivie was brought to the jail here. According to Sheriff E.I. Cunningham, Ivie was apparently drunk.

Mr. Hightower was not critically wounded, and Ivie is charged with felonious assault. His bond was set at $3,000."

[Edna Cunningham] "Isam gave us all a brand-new five dollar bill for Christmas one year. At that time it would be about like $50. My husband carried that bill and never did spend it, and had it in his billfold when he died in 1984.

I looked at it the other day. It was 1951. He gave us all one. I couldn't wait to spend mine, but my husband... 'course, he was that way. He had put it in his billfold, folded up, flat. Because it was from his dad! He never had spent it. Well, I never either! I spent *mine* but I haven't spent *his*! I think all the rest of 'em spent theirs, too, I don't think they saved 'em. I was always likin' new shoes and I put mine on a pair of shoes.

He gave us all one! He went to the bank. Brand-new bills. To the in-laws and all the kids."

Chapter Twelve
1952

January 3, 1952 "Dave Coots, former marshal of Seymour, has sued Bonnie Payton and D. Wayne Rowland, editor and publisher of *The Seymour Citizen*, for a total of $80,000, charging four libelous statements were printed about him.

Coots asks $10,000 actual and $10,000 punitive damages on each count. The suit was filed in Marshfield Thursday.

Through his attorneys, Seth V. Conrad, John Hosmer, and John Newberry, Coots charges the newspaper published statements that were 'false, defamatory, malicious, and libelous' on August 24, 1950, December 14, 1950, December 21, 1950, and August 31, 1951.—from *Springfield News and Leader,* Dec. 30."

January 10, 1952 "Weekly Publishers Select Top Ten Stories—Top ten news stories of 1951, selected by a representative panel of weekly newspaper publishers polled by The Publishers' Auxiliary are:
1. MacArthur ouster
2. Korean cease-fire talks
3. Churchill's return to power
4. Iran's nationalization of oil
5. Dismissal of 90 West Point cadets
6. Kansas floods
7. Senate crime committee revelations
8. Signing of Japanese peace treaty
9. Placing of two-term limit on presidential tenure
10. Hearings on irregularities in internal revenue department."

January 17, 1952 "Three teen-age boys on parole from an Indiana juvenile institution were picked up last Friday by Sheriff E.I. Cunningham at Seymour in connection with a service station burglary.

The trio, J. Allen Burkholder, 14; Charles Preston Spillers, 14, and Oliver Lee Myers, 13, all of Hammond, Ind., have admitted a break-in last Thursday night *[1/10]* at a Sinclair service station in Seymour.

Officers reported the youths broke a restroom window at the station owned by Gordon Heckendorn and took $11.75 from an unlocked cash register. *[Unlocked to save Heckendorn the money*

needed to repair/ replace a cash register damaged by burglars?]
The station is located on Highway 60.

The youths admitted being runaways and on parole from Indiana, where they had been serving terms previously on burglary and car theft. They also admitted breaking into a filling station in Indiana Monday night a week ago and taking about one hundred dollars.

They took a room at a Seymour hotel about 3 a.m. Friday morning and stayed there until about 1:00 p.m. when they appeared on the streets and were apprehended by Sheriff Cunningham.

After admitting their past escapades to the Sheriff and Highway Patrol, the trio were brought to the Webster County jail here."

"The political pot is boiling right along for so early in the year. Five Republicans have filed for nomination for office according to County Clerk Orven E. Davis. Two or three others have indicated that they had 'the bug.'

Those filed are: Mrs. John C. Pope, for county representative; Walter Ray, for county assessor; J. H. Gaupp for associate judge of the county court from the western district; W. A. McDonald for associate judge of the county court from the western district, and E.I. Cunningham for Sheriff."

January 24, 1952 "Circuit Court notes—State of Mo. vs. Mary Costello and Rosa Urich, grand larceny. Information charging vagrancy filed by state. Defendants waive formal arraignments and enter pleas of guilty. Punishment of each assessed at fines of $395. Fines and costs paid."
[These are the two gypsies who had raised a tent behind Highfill's grocery.]

February 14, 1952 "Circuit Court notes—Warren Beck *[among others]* served on jury. One case was grand larceny; jury found man not guilty. Other case was rape; jury found defendant guilty and assessed punishment as imprisonment in state penitentiary for term of four years."

[Warren Beck] "When Isam was Sheriff, it was the first time I was ever called for jury duty. It was a change of venue from Polk County. We called it The John Aberdan Cattle Rustling Case. We were sequestered in the Marshfield Courts, out by where US Bank is now. There's office buildings now, but there were little motel courts. I was running the milk route at that time and had to have somebody else run it. I had to serve on the jury duty.

Isam played rook with us that night, and the next morning he was up and gone, then came back and informed us we'd have to behave, take care of ourselves, because a businessman had committed suicide. It was Herb Ellis. He lived down on North Clay Street.

After it was over, we acquitted the fella who was accused of it! He was accused of shooting the bull that got into his pasture. He had registered Jerseys, registered cattle, and a different kind of bull got in. And afterwards I can remember John *[Hosmer]* pinning us and said, 'We as attorneys need to know what we done wrong. How come you ruled in favor of the defendant?' That was around 1952."

"Herbert E. Ellis, well-known Marshfield man, killed himself Friday morning about 7:15 at his home on North Clay Street. In ill health for some time he had evidently spent a sleepless night. He got up that morning and penned a lengthy note to his family, and listed his poor health as the principal reason for taking his life.

He had placed a sofa pillow on the kitchen floor, lay down on his back and shot himself in the head. He had placed his left hand on his chest and held a .32-caliber pistol to his right temple. The bullet went through the skull and stopped inside the skin on the left side of the head. He apparently died instantly.

His wife, who was just getting up at the time, heard the shot and immediately called Dr. C. R. Macdonnell and Sheriff E.I. Cunningham, who went to the home immediately.

William Ferrell of the Kelley-Ferrell-Bergman funeral home at Fordland investigated in the absence of K.K. Kelley, Webster County coroner, and said no inquest would be held.

Funeral services were held Tuesday afternoon at 3:00 o'clock in the Barber-Barto Chapel with the Rev. Herbert Davis officiating. Burial was in the Marshfield Cemetery with military services at the graveside.

Survivors include his widow...two daughters...a son...two sisters...and three brothers...."

"Blaming ill health for his despondency, Jeff McDaniel, 59-year-old farmer, shot himself fatally at his home on Route 1, Seymour, Sunday morning *[2/11]*....

McDaniel used a .22 caliber rifle to shoot himself behind the right ear. Relatives said he had been in ill health for a number of years. He had operated a farm near Seymour most of his life.

Surviving are his wife...three sons...three sisters...three brothers...and three grandchildren.

K.K. Kelley, Fordland, viewed the body and decided that no inquest would be necessary...."

February 21, 1952 "A county-wide meeting of those interested in forming a Webster County Historical Society will be held at the Circuit Court room next Thursday evening, Feb. 28. The meeting, which has been called by a Lions Club committee, will start at 8:00 o'clock.

The committee, John Hosmer, chairman, was appointed some time ago to take the lead in forming a county organization to preserve historical material, in order that future generations may have some history of this section.

It is hoped that there will be folks present from every part of the county."

February 28, 1952 "The Brentlinger Miller Garage at Fordland was broken into Saturday night *[2/23]* and about $90 stolen. Entrance was gained by breaking a back window and prying open the door of the office. The money was taken from the cash register and a desk. No merchandise was missing but it appeared that the guilty party or parties started to take a few cans of oil and then left them setting in the floor.

Sheriff E.I. Cunningham and the State Patrol were called Sunday morning when the theft was discovered. An investigation was started and fingerprints taken."

March 20, 1952 Lonnie Wilson announces his plans to run for nomination of Sheriff of Webster County.

[Willis Case] "One thing I never told about Isam: I never voted for him when he ran against a friend of mine name of Lonnie Wilson. Me and Lonnie traded together, traded cows and so on. And Lonnie said, 'I just sure want you to vote for me.' That was for the nomination, the primary. But I voted for Isam the next time he run."

" A new law recently signed by the Governor affects the 18th Judicial Circuit. Wright and Camden counties are taken out of this circuit...This will leave Hickory, Polk, Dallas, and Webster counties in the 18th Judicial Circuit.

The bill also changes the regular terms of Webster County Circuit Court. The regular terms now open on the first Monday in February, the fourth Monday in May, and the first Monday in November."

April 3, 1952 "Seymour's most controversial figure—ex-marshal Dave Coots—almost became the target of a gunman here last night *[4/2]*.

Webster County Sheriff E.I. Cunningham said Coots narrowly missed injury about 6 p.m. when a man identified as William Willard Blankenship, 28, of Seymour, fired a double-barreled shotgun blast at the former officer.

Cunningham said Blankenship, an ex-convict, was injured about a year ago by a shot fired by Coots who was city marshal at that time.

Last night's incident began when Blankenship and two other men listed by the Sheriff as Ira Hyden and Harold Davis, both about 30, drove up in front of Coots' home and Blankenship got out of their car.

Coots said he was sitting in the house reading the newspaper when Blankenship yelled for him to step outside. The ex-marshal said the sun was shining in his eyes when he stepped out of the house and he couldn't see who the men were until he was almost upon them.

Then he quoted Blankenship as telling him he was going to kill him.

Seeing Blankenship was armed with a gun, Coots turned and ran back in the house just as the man fired. The blast struck the siding of the house only inches over Coots' head, but he escaped injury.

Blankenship got in the car and left, but Hyder and Davis remained behind. Coots obtained a revolver in the house, went outside again, and took Hyder and Davis into custody. They were picked up by Cunningham last night to be taken to the Webster County jail at Marshfield.

Meanwhile, authorities continued their search for Blankenship, believed to be driving a 1940 black Chevrolet coach.

Blankenship and another man were wounded in the leg and foot about a year ago by Coots following a fray in Seymour.

Coots had arrested the pair for creating a disturbance while drinking, and one of the men struck the officer on the shoulder with a bottle. When they tried to escape, he shot them.

Cunningham said the three men involved in last night's episode also had been drinking.

Coots was removed from the office of city marshal a year ago following his declaration of a liberal policy of arrests, and also following several shooting incidences.—*The Springfield Daily News*, Monday, March 31.

Then Tuesday former marshal Coots was arrested on a charge of exhibiting a deadly weapon. It is reported that when Mayor R. E. McMahan met Mr. Coots on the street at Seymour and asked him if they had caught the fellow who shot at him Sunday night, Mr. Coots became enraged and drew out a gun on the mayor.

Mr. Coots was brought to Marshfield and faced charges before Magistrate Judge Cline C. Herren. He demanded hearing on the charges and the date for the hearing was set for April 16."

"Lester Garton of Niangua has filed for nomination for Sheriff in the Democrat primary...."

April 10, 1952 "H. O. (Dick) Rader announces candidacy for nomination for Sheriff on the Republican ticket."

April 24, 1952 "Bill Blankenship, 28, of Seymour, wanted in Webster County on a warrant charging felonious assault, surrendered to a Springfield policeman there last Wednesday *[4/16]*.

Officers said Blankenship is accused of firing a shotgun at Dave Coots, Seymour's colorful former shooting marshal, on March 31. Coots, who wasn't hit, detained two companions, but Blankenship drove away.

He approached Officer Roy Craig at 12:50 a.m. last Wednesday in the Union Bus depot and told him he was wanted. He was turned over to Webster County Sheriff E.I. Cunningham. He was arraigned last Wednesday and preliminary hearing has been set for May 2nd. Bond was fixed at $5000."

May 1, 1952 "Sheriff E.I. Cunningham and his bonding company were named defendants in a $10,000 'false arrest' damage suit filed in Marshfield Circuit Court last week.

Freeman Lea of Marshfield charges that Cunningham last December placed him under arrest and turned him over to an Oklahoma county officer without 'valid legal process.'

The petition, filed April 21, by H. T. Lincoln and Wallace Springer, Springfield attorneys, claims that Cunningham arrested Lea on December 15 of last year and turned him over to 'Slim' Weaver, Mayes County, Okla., constable.

Lea was taken from his home, the petition states, by Cunningham, and when he attempted to protest the arrest, Cunningham allegedly closed a car door on his leg, forcing him to go with him. Why Lea was wanted by the Oklahoma officer, the petition does not state.

The petition claims that Lea, when arrested, objected to being placed under arrest without any formal legal process, but that Cunningham ignored his protests."

"John Hosmer has filed for Democrat candidate for Congressman from Missouri...."

May 8, 1952 "Two masked men entered the V.P. Robinson home Saturday night *[5/3]* about midnight and tied up Mr. and Mrs. Robinson with bed sheets. They held a gun and flashlight on them while they securely tied them up.

The men then tore up the house searching for money, turning things out into the floor. They then went to the Forkner's Hill store, which the Robinsons operate, some distance from the house, and took money and merchandise, including 18 cartons of cigarettes, sox, earrings, etc.

Before going to the store they took Mr. Robinson's billfold and keys to the store from his pants. The billfold had money, driver's license and other papers. Altogether, the thieves got more than $500 in money from the billfold, home, and store.

Mrs. Robinson worked her feet loose and then was able to untie Mr. Robinson. He then finished untying her. They had just got free when their daughter, Helen, arrived home. Sheriff Cunningham was called about 12:20 a.m. and he called the State Patrol. The Sheriff and two patrolmen arrived at Forkner's Hill about 1:00 p.m. *[probably should be 1:00 a.m.]* No arrests have been made but it is believed that the guilty parties were familiar with the store.

According to the Sheriff, the men were in a Buick and possibly had a third person with them in the car while they ransacked the house and store."

"Astounding Total of 104 Candidates Running for 11 Seats in Congress—With all congressmen in Missouri having to run at large this year, the astounding total of 103 candidates for congress have been filed. There are 54 Republican and 49 Democrat candidates.

This condition was brought about by the unfair gerrymander of the state by the Democrat controlled legislature. When the census showed Missouri would have only 11 congressman instead of 13 as formerly, the legislature was required to re-district the state.

The senate committee which had charge of this job turned in a bill said to have been drawn up by Jim Pendergast and henchmen. No public hearings were held on the bill before it was put into the legislative hopper. It gave the Republicans two congressman and the Democrats nine.

The Republicans considered this unfair and when the Democrats refused to compromise, petitions were secured over the state which puts the redistricting law to a referendum, and it will be voted on at the General Election in November. Meantime, it makes all candidates for Congress run at large. They will be elected by the voters of the entire state instead of by districts as formerly.

At the August primary Republican voters will find the names of 54 candidates for Congress, and they must vote for only 11. They will be required to place an X before eleven candidates of their choice. They must be careful to not vote for more than eleven or they will lose their vote for all candidates for Congress. The Democrats must pick eleven out of 49 on the ticket.

Then in November there will be eleven candidates on each the Republican and Democrat tickets. The voters will vote for eleven. It will be possible for all eleven Congressman from Missouri to be Democrats or it is possible that all eleven will be Republicans."

"Man Taken to 'Pen'—Sheriff E.I. Cunningham, accompanied by Homer Alexander, city marshal, took Lyman Edward Tibbetts to the penitentiary at Jefferson City Monday. Tibbetts, charged with the robbery of the Jack Morris store at Diggins, was sentenced to serve four years. He was formerly in the reform school."

"Magistrate Court Notes—April 30—State of Mo. vs. Dave Coots, exhibiting dangerous and deadly weapon. Preliminary held and defendant bound over to Circuit Court. Bond fixed at $1000 and approved."

"NOTICE—The office of the Webster County Farmers Mutual Fire Insurance Co. will be closed at 12 o'clock on Saturdays until further notice.

John L. Alcorn, President
Elzie Doyle, Secretary"

[It seems there were many fires, destroying not only private homes but also well-known businesses. It was usually noted in the story reporting the fires whether or not the owners were adequately insured.]

"NOTICE! There is a City Ordinance against DOGS running at large. If dogs are mutilating or in any way destroying your property, CALL THE CITY MARSHAL.

R. T. BRIDWELL, Mayor"

May 22, 1952 "The robbery of Mr. and Mrs. V. Price Robinson home and store at Forkners Hill on the night of May 3, has been solved, according to Sheriff E I. Cunningham. Four men, picked up by the State Highway Patrol near Rolla Friday morning have admitted a series of armed robberies throughout Missouri in recent days.

The four—described as being 'pretty rough'—were taken into custody after two cars in which they were riding were stopped by troopers in a routine check on Highway 66, west of Rolla. The men were taken for questioning after the troopers spotted a large quantity of loot in the cars.

The four men were identified as Irvin M. Ostrowski, 24, Aaron W. Burgett, 22, both of St. Louis; and James W. Wilhelm, 25, and Jess A. Taylor, 39, both of Kimble, Mo. (Sheriff Cunningham says that Wilhelm was sentenced to the penitentiary from this county some time ago on charges of stealing cattle.)

Troopers said that the victims of an armed robbery at a café near DeSoto Thursday night have identified the men as the robbers, and also identified some of the loot—some of which had not been removed from wallets and billfolds taken from the café customers. This robbery was at the Etta K. Café on Highway 21, one mile south of DeSoto in which $500 cash, $380 in checks, were taken from the café operator and wallets and watches were taken from the patrons.

Other robberies reported were:

Holdup of a combined post office and general store in Banner, Mo., May 8, in which about $300 worth of clothing, cash, and merchandise was taken;

Robbery of E.J Johnson Service Station near Fletcher, Mo., May 12, in which $150 cash, and $150 in checks, and other merchandise;

And a robbery of the Lake Side Hotel in East St. Louis May 13 in which about $500 in cash and other property was taken.

Troopers said that a large portion of the loot taken in the Thursday robbery was recovered in the thieves' two cars and that a major part of the loot taken in the post office and general store robbery was recovered at the home of Taylor and Wilhelm in Kimble.

The wives of Ostrowski and Burgett were picked up in St. Louis Friday also, troopers said, and a quantity of loot was also found at those homes. What the loot is has not yet been determined, they added. Wives of three of the men—Ostrowski, Burgett, and Kimble—are suspected of being involved in some of the robberies, for some witnesses have said that women were along in some of the hold-ups.

Two of the men, Burgett and Kimble, are said to have past criminal records.

When the Robinson store was robbed, two men held a gun on Mr. and Mrs. V.P. Robinson and tied them up in bed sheets. They ransacked the house and took money and the keys to the store from Mr. Robinson's trousers. They then robbed the store of money and merchandise. It was thought that another person might be in the car while this was going on.

Mr. and Mrs. Robinson had just freed themselves when their daughter, Helen, returned home. More than $500 in money besides merchandise was taken.

Mr. Robinson had identified some of his property in the loot recovered, including a $2 bill, according to Sheriff Cunningham. Troopers say all four men deny the Robinson robbery. Mr. and Mrs. Robinson viewed the men at Rolla. They recognized one as a former resident of the Ozarks, but couldn't identify any of the robbers."

June 5, 1952 "John Hosmer, Prosecuting Attorney of Webster County, this week issued a warning to all persons who have been dumping trash indiscriminately within the county. Hosmer stated he has received many complaints of unauthorized dumping and warned that violators are subject to arrest and prosecution.

A great deal of rubbish, tin cans, and garbage is being thrown out along highways and roads, littering up the countryside. And some is being dumped on private property, generally in lonely spots. Both acts are against the law, Hosmer stated."

[Fred Letterman] "I remember goin' down, when I was little they *lived* in the jail, upstairs, and we'd go visit them and I'd run through the courthouse. Go in there where, I guess, they had court, and they had seats up there, and the judge would sit, and I'd get up in his chair and bang that gavel. 'Course, there wasn't anybody in there. I used to think that was the biggest room in the world.

I can remember *[Granddad]* Isam's office there, and we went by, and he was settin' in that chair if he happened to be in. He had a door behind where he kept all the guns and stuff that he got from the prisoners. And he always gave me a pair of brass knuckles. He'd get'em out and let me play and put'em on me...and I'd run around and beat on stuff, just whatever.

And I can remember Charley's brother Jake. If he was hangin' around there he would always get me a *cee*gar and set me on the steps...seemed like they were wide enough on the side that you could get up there and slide down them concrete things...well, he'd get me up there, set me up, and get me that *cee*gar and get me smokin' it and my mom *[Isam's daughter Mildred]* would come around and see me doin' that and he'd just think that was the funniest thing in the world.

I can remember doin' that. And runnin' around the courthouse. And him givin' me them brass knucks."

[Jerry Letterman] "During summer vacations, when we'd go down and stay with him, of a night he would put us in the movie to get rid of us. You know, it seemed like the movie ran every night for a week and we always spent at least two or three nights at the same movie, I guess to get us out of the way. But it was fun, too. We got anything we wanted from the snack bar. The nights that he didn't put us in the movie, why, I spent the night setting out on The Square in the park benches with Grandma and Granddad.*[Eva and Isam]*

There was a lot of times I wanted to walk his beat with him, of a night, so to speak, but he never would let us go. During the daytime he would, but not of a night. I remember those quite well.

Another thing: Grandma used to send us up to the kitchen, to get something out of the kitchen, and the jail was up there by the kitchen—she cooked for 'em, the inmates—and so I would sneak up the stairs, get to the open door at the landing up there, and peek and make sure there was no jail inmates there and run across in the kitchen and turn the light on and I was okay. But still there was no door on it or anything. Then I would get what she wanted and I would do the same thing runnin' back, so, it was real scary to me. I was between five and ten years old.

One time I remember, we were out one evening ridin' around, 'course in the Sheriff's car, and *[somehow]* he got a call and I guess we were too far from Marshfield to get back there, and he turned the lights on and the siren and we ended up in Seymour in front of a pool hall or beer joint, tavern, and he told me, he said, 'You stay in this car and don't unlock this door for *nobody* but me 'til I get back!' So I was pretty nervous! But he came out in a little bit and we went on. And that was it. I don't know what had happened but I do remember that!

There was times when, one year that I was down, and he was up for re-election, he took me out with him and we'd tack up signs all over the fence and fence posts and stuff like that. 'Course I got to hand out cards and stuff like that.

Another thing I'll always remember is whenever we were up by Niangua, on old Route 66, there was a gas station right there on the corner, I don't know the name of it, but we always stopped there and had a Brown Cow ice cream cone. So anytime we got close to that area, we always went by there. Brown Cow was an ice cream bar with chocolate icing, basically all it was.

Just spending time with Granddad was great.

Most of the time Grandma was around the house *[in the courthouse]*, and I was out with Isam, Granddad, walkin' around, doin' things with him."

[Shirley Carrizales] "We thought that was really neat that we got to stay there and actually stay all night in the courthouse, because that's where they were living, on the second floor.

There was never a time would go by that troopers didn't come in. Well, they're all dressed up and I'm a sucker for uniforms so that was just awesome to see these troopers come in there, take their hats off, and spend some time with us."

"And Grandpa had this wonderful office. To children it was everything! He had all these things you could play with, things he'd collected from his prisoners that they never were able to find the owners, who these things belonged to. We'd play with the typewriters, look at the watches, different articles that he had."

[Shirley] "And then Jerry and I would go in the courtroom, and he would be the judge banging the gavel, and I would be the person at the piano playing and singing. I couldn't play a note on the piano, still can't, but we had so much fun. And we'd make all this racket. 'Course, court wasn't in session, but, later years, Mom *[Isam's daughter Mattie]* and Helen *[Isam's daughter-in-law, Jake's wife]* and all of 'em told us they could hear us all over that entire courthouse! We were embarrassed then, but not when we were doing this.

We liked to play in the jail cells. 'Course, the men's jail was never empty, but occasionally the women's was empty. He'd give us the key, we would go lock ourselves in. Well, one time Jerry got locked in and he couldn't get out! He couldn't get that key to work, puttin' his hands through the bars, so he was in there yellin' 'Help! Help! I can't get out of here!' so after awhile we finally went and let him out. That was pretty good.

All of us girls helped feed the prisoners. We'd help Grandma with fixing meals and getting the trays ready. I can remember one time one of 'em got *[cousin]* Marie's hand. Well, after that I was *shoving* those trays in there! I wasn't placing *my* hand in there!

One time Granddad decided that it was okay for Grandma and I to go to another town with him in the Sheriff's car to pick up a prisoner who had been in a fight the night before, and he said, 'He's okay, he just had a little fight last night, I just have to go pick him up, it's a formality.' So we got in the car and we went with him. We picked up the prisoner from the little local jail, I don't remember what town. We started home. Somewhere on that trip home, hands started flying, feet started kicking, and the head started jerking, and I didn't know what was wrong with this guy! Scared me to death! So, Grandpa pulled over real fast, and—he used to tell the story after that—that I was out of that car, in the front seat, sitting on Grandma's lap before the car stopped rolling. Well, it turned out, Grandpa knew what to do. The man was having an epileptic seizure. So Grandpa got him under control. But he made me go back to the back seat and set the rest of the way into town with him! So I was quite concerned. He dropped us off and he was looking for medical attention and everything. That was really scary!

He always took us to the movies. This one night—I was probably about eleven—and this little boy came and sit by me. I didn't like that, so I moved. He followed me, sat down by me again, this happened three or four times, and I kept moving from him. Well, finally that movie was over— I thought it'd never get over and I knew not to go out 'cause Granddad wouldn't be there until the movie was over—I ran outside, grabbed him *[Isam]* around the leg, and stood there, and he was talkin' to some people and I kept my eye on the door and this boy came out and he saw me over there with the Sheriff and boy, did he run! He made tracks in the other direction!

Granddad used to sneak up to our house. Someway he could always sneak up, get in that driveway, and hit that siren on that car before we even knew he was there, and that was excitement, just unreal what he could do with that!"

[Marie Day] "When he was the Sheriff, I was feedin' one of the prisoners one day and he caught my hand, and Granddad said, in no uncertain terms, he was to turn my hand loose!

I remember Grandma was cookin' for 'em, but when she got a headache, she tied this tea towel around her head. She just made a band out of it and tied it around her head real tight. That way, she said, it helped her head and she didn't have the headache as bad.

And I remember goin' down there and all the patrolmen and everything comin' into the office. And, like Shirley said, I'd go into the courtroom and play the piano. And my mom *[Isam's daughter Mildred]* would be up there too. And I would go in there and they'd want me to play it and I would play, just ring it out, 'How Beautiful Heaven Must Be' 'cause my mom, she loved it."

[Betty Marlin] "In the summertimes—I think I was probably about ten when he came into office, 'cause when he passed away I was nineteen, so I was probably about ten, I guess—but I'd come down and stay, and I spent a lot of my time with Grandma when I came down. 'Course, they stayed on the same floor as the office there, and Granddad was pretty busy during the day. He had the highway patrolmen comin' in and he was out takin' care of his county. But on days that he wasn't there, there was times I'd go in there and it was really fun to be in the office and look at all the things that was in the office, and just neat bein' down there.

Granddad sorta insisted that we feed the prisoners after Grandma had fixed the meals. And she fixed all the meals. He would insist that we put them over. Well, I would go in there and I knew that opening wasn't very big but I just knew one of 'em was going to grab me. So I would set there and watch, and shove it in real quick. But that was one thing he kinda insisted, had us to do. Not to scare us, but just to help Grandma. She was a wonderful Grandma.

'Course, he would take us to the movies and put us in the movies and stuff like that, on Sundays. And, as I got older though, as to a teenager, Charley and I are just a couple years apart, age, and he'd always take me to The Sweet Shop. So I got to go over there with all his friends. Jerry came over to the Sweet Shop one day, to get his ice cream, and he came back and they said, 'Well, what's goin' on over

328

there?' and he said, 'Oh, Betty and Charley are settin' in the caboose over there.' Instead of *booth*, Jerry said *caboose!*"

[Darrell Letterman] "We used to go down and spend a week, you know. Sometimes maybe a whole week, maybe sometimes not quite, but anyway I guess I was old enough that he let me just go to The Sweet Shop or the movies by myself. I didn't have to have company. I usually made a couple trips a day...to The Sweet Shop. But other times I would run around with Charley.

And sometimes I'd go out when they had a call, a wreck or something, I'd go out with him, and go to the wrecks, you know, in the police car and stuff. But one day I went over to Seymour with him and they had this little filling station-café thing. So everything was real nice 'til we got there, and then when we got out, he said, 'Now, you stay close to me, something may go on!' So I kinda got next to his pant leg and stayed there! But anyway, he went in and talked to everybody, we did, and I probably had a pop or somethin' or other, but he talked to all of 'em and then turned around and came back out, so there wasn't nothin' goin' on. I think he was lookin' for somebody and he wasn't there.

I got to go on a trip with him and Grandma once. Charley was playin' ball down in Kentucky or Tennessee or somewhere. I got to go along—I was sixteen—to help drive. We come off this big hill or up over this little hill, a little dip there, and Grandpa was doin' the speed limit or better I guess, but anyway we hit those railroad tracks, and, I mean, it threw me plumb up against—I was in the back seat—up against the roof and everything else, and Grandma, she got after him pretty much, you know, and he said, 'Well, I didn't see the...blankety-blank...thing!' I can't say the right word! But we had a pretty good trip, enjoyed it and everything, got to run around with Charley and his ball team and stuff like that. So I enjoyed that trip very much with 'em, and I always remember that 'cause I was sixteen.

He was a fun guy to be around. Grandma was a little quieter to me than he was, but she was a very good cook, you can't deny that."

[Charley Cunningham] "One time I was playing minor league baseball, they came down in Tennessee, they came down there, just took a vacation. The county was without a Sheriff that time. Nobody knew he was gone, that's the thing about it." *[except Elzie Doyle]*

[Eldeen Cunningham] "I recall driving to Marshfield the summer of 1952 with our first child *[Gail]* when she was three months old. We carried her into the courthouse in her bassinet with Isam alongside just waiting to pick her up. Luckily she woke in a good mood and cooed and gurgled her way into his heart.

At this time the 500 miles of highway between Rockford *[Illinois]* and Marshfield was all two-lane. That was a long exhausting trip so one or two trips a year were all we could manage. However, whenever we got in, daylight or dark, Isam was always on The Square waiting for us."

July 3, 1952 "The opening last week of 30 miles of new cement pavement on Highway 66 through Webster County calls to mind that it was just 26 years ago that the first concrete highway across the county was constructed. The highway was then known as Highway 14 and was later designated as Highway 66....

When the first pavement was finished through Webster County, Marshfield was elated because this county was the first on the route from St. Louis to Joplin to have the concrete pavement built across it.

There was no elation in Marshfield, Strafford, Conway, or Niangua when the new Highway 66 was opened last week due to the fact that the highway leaves these towns and goes on a more direct route. This will cause considerable financial loss to those owning business property on the old route. Many of these business firms will probably close. It is doubtful that much tourist business will come in to any of these towns.

The new highway should be safer because the pavement is 24 feet wide instead of 18 as on the old road, and because there are no sharp curves and few hills....

It is hoped that the savings in lives will make up for the financial loss suffered by the business firms along the old highway. If it does, it will be well worth while."

"Several new businesses are opening on new Highway 66 which was opened to traffic last week. Among them are the following:

Mr. and Mrs. Kermit Lowery announce the opening of a café and Service Station about halfway between Marshfield and Conway....

Jim and Velma Lichtenberger announce the opening of the Illini Café one-fourth mile east of the Marshfield spur on July 5....

Jimmie O'Brien just recently opened the Jimmie O'Brien Tobacco Store at the junction of the Marshfield spur to new Highway 66."

July 10, 1952 "T. Ballard Watters of Marshfield is running for Secretary of State of Missouri. He has been editor and publisher of the *Marshfield Mail* for the past 30 years."

[Jack Watters] "I was here when my dad ran for Secretary of State. We helped plan his campaign and to his credit...Missouri was a huge Democrat state, so statewide offices, Republicans never won them. He did lead the Republican ticket, he got more votes on the Republican ticket than any other Republican in the state, but he got beat. He didn't get more votes than Eisenhower in Missouri.

He was kind of campaigning for that office. He had worked for the state highway department during the war years. He was a district governor of the Lions Club. He loved to go to Missouri Press Association Meetings or Ozark Press Association Meetings. He loved that type of thing. I assume his connections with the Press Association allowed him to get that job with the highway department to work in publicity, back in the war years. I don't know, he just had a hankering, he just wanted to be a state official.

Historically the Secretary of State in Missouri had been a newspaperman, up 'til that point in time. I don't know why that was, but at some point I had a conversation with him and he told me the Secretary of State was supposed to be a newspaperman. The Missouri Press Association always pushed on that, too.

I helped work on his ads that he sent out. Paul *[Watters]* ran the paper when he was gone. I was green and could have helped more but I wanted to play softball in the evenings!"

July 17, 1952 "....It was a dramatic moment Friday evening when Dwight D. Eisenhower, smiling his famous, broad grin, strode into the Republican national convention hall to accept the party's nomination for the presidency of the United States and to pledge himself to lead it on a crusade—'a great crusade for freedom in America and freedom in the world.'

The man who went from Abilene, Kan., to lead a great military crusade in World War II threw his arms wide in acknowledgement of the applause, wild cheers and shouts of the delegates who had nominated him for the first political office he had ever sought....The next day Senator Richard Nixon, 39-year-old navy veteran of World War II, was named the Republican nominee for vice-president with no other name being placed before the convention...."

"Ballard Watters for Secretary of State...New in Politics, Old in Experience...He has never been a candidate for public office."

[There seemed to be a backlash going on in the upcoming election against the Old Politicians. Political Experience is portrayed as a <u>negative</u>.]

August 7, 1952 "Ballard Watters won the Republican nomination for Secretary of State..."

"The three civic clubs of Marshfield will begin a drive for funds within the next few days to pay for a large electric sign to be erected on new Highway 66 at the Marshfield spur, pointing the way into the city. As the situation now stands, Marshfield does not have a very prominent place in the directional signs on the highway, so the three clubs decided to erect the more prominent sign.

Committees from the local JCC *[Junior Chamber of Commerce or Jaycees]*, B & PW *[Business and Professional Women]*, and Lions Clubs will work on the solicitation of funds, which has already started among merchants within the groups....

Webster Electric Cooperative has offered to wire the sign and furnish the electricity free of charge. The sign as being constructed will be large enough to be easily seen and is neon lighted."

[Jack Watters] "Sometime after World War II, the Junior Chamber of Commerce was started. Boy, that was a growing organization. I think the age bracket was 21 to 35 year-olds. We had a lot of 21 to 35 year-olds back then; a great number of veterans of World War II came back, liked Marshfield, they'd grown up here. We had a lot of young people around, like me in a way, coming back from the war, going to school, getting out of college and I was 25 years old. I wanted to live here; I liked it here. It was a good place to live. I don't know if it, really, was from homesickness when you were in the Army or whatever.

The Junior Chamber of Commerce was formed before I came from college, right in the mid-to-late 40's. I got involved with it, of course. I think, at the time, everybody took a term being president of the Jaycees. As you grew older, you joined the Lions Club."

"Sheriff E.I. Cunningham and Lonnie Wilson of Marshfield won the Republican and Democrat nominations for Sheriff of Webster

County in warmly contested races in the primary elections Tuesday and will face each other in the November general election....

Only about 3360 ballots were cast by both parties out of a possible 8000 or more voters in the county....Of the total vote cast in Webster County Tuesday, about 2000 were Republican and 1360 or so Democrat....Unopposed county candidates on the Republican ticket were...Clyde G. Meise for Prosecuting Attorney....Democrat unopposed candidates in the primary were Seth V. Conrad for Prosecuting Attorney...."

[Warren Beck] "They used to flip coins as to who would be Prosecuting Attorney. They said all the job was, was airing people's dirty laundry in public. It was a community duty to do Prosecuting Attorney. Nobody wanted to do it. Yes, it was an elected position but they kinda decided who was going to run."

August 14, 1952 "E.I. Cunningham received 1255 votes and H.O. Rader received 1,041 votes."

August 21, 1952 "Two Highway Patrolmen from Springfield will be stationed at Marshfield beginning September 1, Patrol Capt. George Kahler said today.

The two are C. F Stone, transferred to Springfield recently from Mount Vernon, and D.R. Turpin, a probationary patrolman just out of training school.

Kahler said the two will ride together in one car until Turpin is checked out on patrol procedures; then each will operate the car on separate shifts.

Kahler said Marshfield citizens have been asking for a trooper to be assigned there for the past two or three years. The captain said the Marshfield men will be able to patrol much of new Highway 66, leaving Springfield cars free to check other Springfield highways besides east 66.

With no troopers at Marshfield, Springfield men have had to drive nearly to Conway to check accidents on occasion."

[Mildred Jarratt] "Highway 66, it was just a highway. It wasn't an interstate yet. Our business did not fall off when the new 66 opened.

We were married in '46. Jack was recalled in *[to military service]* and we went to Fort Riley, Kansas and we were out there 'til the fall of '51. Our two boys were little, there's just twenty months difference in their ages. It was a little bit hard right at first, with both of them as small as they were, and that's when Jack got recalled, but I didn't have a lot to do. I just went to Fort Riley and stayed with him. Jack was an officer, and he taught in the officers' candidate school out there. And that was wonderful. They took *some* officers over to Korea but they didn't take them like they did the *other* ones.

So I was gone during part of Isam's time. And my parents were not real politically minded, or they didn't talk it anyway, because my father *[Roy Tindle]* run a grocery store—Tindle's—and he felt like you should keep it to yourself.

He sold the store when Jack was recalled because he says 'I can't go through another war with just women help.' That's all he had had in World War II, was women help. Well, he had two or three older men, but he couldn't get young men 'cause they was all taking them to fight. So he sold the grocery store and when we came back we had to do something! So we opened a clothing store. And I guess the reason we opened it, we had two boys of our own! And we were thinking about where they might need clothes and there wasn't very much for boys in town. Now we had another men's store that was all right but we didn't have a good *boys'* market in town.

My husband and I knew absolutely nothing about clothing stores. And the salesmen would just drop their mouth open, you know, when he'd tell them we were going to open a clothing store and they wanted to know where we had worked. And Jack said, 'Well, the only place I've worked is a grocery store and the military.'

You can learn! If you want to. And we enjoyed it so. We really did.

We sold Men's and Boys' clothes. Started at age two and I think the largest suit I can remember we sold was maybe a 54 chest size. We gradually added, got up into the 50s. I think the largest was 54.

I worked at my daddy's store, but grocery was a far cry...because you saw the same people two or three times a week buying groceries. You didn't see the same people buying a shirt or underwear two or three times a week. You saw them maybe once every two or three *months.* That was one of our biggest adjustments, not seeing the same people come into your store often.

Dr. Oren Cardwell owned the land. He built that building there, for us. He built it all, just rented us the building, never raised the rent but one time in forty years. Bernice *[Dr. Cardwell's wife]* liked Jack. Bernice thought Jack was the smartest pupil she'd ever had in the fourth grade. She's told me that more than once! And Oren just kinda went along with what Bernice wanted. And she wanted us in there.

I can remember night watchmen. They never did call us, but they walked the streets and checked the fronts of the buildings and checked the door and checked the back of the store buildings.

We had a regular wine ghetto back behind our store all the time! They'd come from the liquor store—not a tavern, they didn't serve drinks—a package liquor store. The winos would go buy their bottle of wine and they'd come down and sit behind our store and lean against the gas tank. But you know, I was never afraid of them. I think if I had needed help, all I would have had to do was run to the back door and yell. I do! I really feel that way! That may not have been what would have happened. But they would always get their feet out of the way for me to walk through; I really think they would have helped!

Who were the winos? Oh, unemployed, mostly. Or they'd do yard work. Or help do some job that someone needed. They were just the city winos, is what I called them! They were pretty regular. I know some of their names but I don't think I need to tell.

You know, most little towns have a few people that, you know, don't feel very energetic. And they'd take them off to jail and they'd stay a day or two. Then they'd let 'em out and then they'd be back out again!

Really, I didn't consider the winos too much of a problem except I had to pick up their bottles and throw it in the trash. I finally had the city put a barrel back there, and they did, and you would be surprised how fast that barrel would fill up with wine bottles.

But I ran into a problem I didn't think about. (And I'd *asked* for the city to put the barrel back there, because I was tired of picking up the wine bottles, you know.) The school kids would come down through the back and I'd hear this jingle, jingle of these bottles, you know. And they'd go through 'em to see if there was any wine in them. Sometimes there'd be a little dab. Ohhh!

So finally I went and I said, 'Boys, do you have   *any idea* who you're drinking after? Do you have *any idea* whose mouth has been on that bottle?'   'No,' and off they'd go! They'd be junior high and high school age. Every two or three days, you'd hear them down there, going through the bottles, drinking that last sip out of 'em!

Seems like we finally got rid of that barrel. It was like we decided it wasn't as much a help as we thought it would be, you know, because that was dangerous.

Our store was opened every day except Sunday from 7:30 a.m. until 5:30 p.m. We were just a little bit earlier than some of the other businesses on The Square, but that's what Jack wanted to do. And you'd be surprised. Someone would need something overnight that they didn't know they were going to need. And then Jack was the janitor along with everything else so he would always do the mopping of the floor of the morning. Sometimes we had to go back Sunday afternoon and re-stock the store. It was not easy.

Most of our customers were local, but also Niangua, Hartville, south county, we had lots of south county people come over because they would come to the courthouse and they'd maybe come down and trade, especially people who had boys. I think we drew in the out-of-town people by having boys' clothing. But some were from Springfield. Maybe they'd lived here before and knew what we had and they'd come back and forth.

Back to school, cold weather, Christmas. That's your big selling time. You'd always have a sale in early January that would help. February, March, part of April, were bad. Nobody wanted anything. They'd spent all their money. Now if it was an early Easter, it might help a little bit. We took very few vacations.

Jack and I took turns eating lunch. Jack usually ate at Andrews. Sometimes I'd go there, sometimes I'd go home, and sometimes I'd go to the Davis Café, a little café behind our store, on East Jackson.

I thought the secret was to have what people wanted. You had to invest quite a bit in order to have a variety for people.

We wanted people to have value for their money. I say we had medium-priced clothes. We had ladies that came in afternoons and did alterations. I did some, too."

September 4, 1952 "Ballard Watters, Marshfield publisher, had a majority of 33,260 over his nearest opponent for the Republican nomination for Secretary of State at the August 5th primary, according to the official figures released last week by the office of Secretary of State of Missouri....John Hosmer, Marshfield attorney, received a total of 12, 211 votes to win the Democrat nomination for Representative in Congress from the Seventh District from his opponent, Rex B. Mealey, of Carthage...."

"Webster County Sheriff E.I. Cunningham reports that he arrested Hiram Franklin Nease of east Niangua Tuesday morning *[9/2]* on a charge of assaulting a 9-year-old girl.

The Sheriff says that Nease is accused of coaxing his niece into a wooded area near his home Sunday afternoon and attacking her. She ran away and later told her parents, who were visiting at the Nease home. Examination by physicians is said to have verified the fact that the child had been assaulted, the Sheriff said.

Nease, whose driver's license shows him 18 years old, claims he is 17 years old according to the Sheriff. It is reported that his sister says he is only 16 years old. Investigation was being made this Wednesday by Webster County officers. The age of the youth will determine whether the charges will be filed in Magistrate court or in the Juvenile division of Circuit Court."

"New, Expanded Burge Hospital To Be Opened To Ozarks Sunday....Lester E. Cox, Springfield industrialist and civic leader whose gifts started the hospital on its way to greatness, will preside over the ceremonies....Mr. Cox first became interested in Burge Hospital when his mother, Mrs. Amanda Bell Cox, canned fruit and vegetables, made quilts, sheets and pillow cases for Burge. The Cox family lived in Republic, but Mrs. Cox worked long and tirelessly for Burge....

As Mr. Cox grew to greater stature in the Ozarks, became the great industrialist and the civic leader of the area, he gave more and more help to Burge, to Drury College and other worthwhile projects."

[Two separate Classified Ads, one beneath the other]
" STRAYED"
"Strayed—one pig at our farm. Owner may have by identifying and paying for this ad and feed bill.
Luther M. Thompson,
Route 3, Seymour, Mo.

Strayed—From my place about 10 days ago, a black pig with white spots. If found, notify Richard Fowler,
Phone 2502, Niangua, Mo."

[If this was the same pig, it traveled almost 20 miles.]

September 11, 1952 *[Luther Thompson's Classified Ad is again in the paper but not Richard Fowler's.]*

[Joe Arthur] "What I remember about Isam was in 1952 when Billie and I got married—the first thing I *really* remember about him is—they give us, Billie and I, a shivaree. This was right behind the funeral home. I worked at the funeral home at the time. At Barber-Barto. So they give us our shivaree about a week and a half after we got married, we got married on August 30, 1952, and then about a week and a half after that, why, they had a shivaree.

'Course, it was unbeknownst to us that they had this plan that Isam and Charley and a bunch of 'em had, oh, I think there was 35 or 40 people there, and Oral Edwards was in on it and Wilma, they'd been in on it, that was my boss and his wife, they's in on it, 'course we didn't know it, but we *did* have the cigars and candy, we was *kinda* expectin' it, we wasn't sure *when*.

So Isam come down and they blocked the streets. We'd just finished eating supper, they come pretty early, we really wasn't planning on this thing comin' this quick. But anyway, they give us our shivaree and everything, and I thought everything was over, so here come Isam and his deputy and he said, 'Now Joe, here's a big wheelbarrow. We want Billie to set in it and we want you to push her around The Square.' So his deputies held off *all* the cars around The Square! And that was the *only* time in my life that I've ever went around the middle of The Square with a wheelbarrow!

Yes, I went the right direction."

September 18, 1952 "The new electric sign to direct people traveling on Highway 66 into Marshfield has been installed and is now in use. The sign was erected under the direction of a joint committee appointed from the Business and Professional Women's club, Junior Chamber of Commerce, and the Marshfield Lions Club.

The money, about $650, was raised by the three organizations from business people and contributions from the three clubs. Electricity is being furnished by the Webster Electric Cooperative.

At night people wanting to come in to Marshfield, if they were unfamiliar with the highway, had trouble finding the spur leading into the city. Even in the day time the small highway sign indicating the road into Marshfield was not too easily noted. The new sign should help out this situation a great deal."

"A Wright county mother of five children died in Ozark Osteopathic Hospital Monday night *[9/15]*—nearly 14 hours after she made a human torch of herself at her home in Cedar Gap.

Coroner Dr. E. Allen Pickens of Springfield identified the victim as Mrs. Alvina Cobb, 41, and said her death evidently was suicide.

She died at 7:30 p.m. of burns over half her body and from inhaled flames and fumes.

Acquaintances said Mrs. Cobb had been in poor health for several months and was receiving treatment for a nervous condition.

She arose early Monday, and about 5 a.m. carried a container full of kerosene into the yard in front of her home at Cedar Gap, east of Seymour. Soaking her clothing with the fuel, she touched a match to herself.

A neighbor woman across the street, who saw the fire and smoke, thought the Cobb house was ablaze. She wakened her husband who ran outside and discovered the woman rolling on the ground.

Mrs. Cobb's 15-year-old daughter, Ethel, heard her mother's screams and ran outside also, tearing the flaming clothing from the woman. She managed to beat out the fire. Mrs.Cobb was first taken by neighbors to a doctor in Mansfield for emergency treatment.

The most severe burns were on her legs and the lower part of her body, attendants said. The injured woman is quoted as saying that if she had known the fire wouldn't have killed her immediately, she would have 'used a gun.'

In addition to her daughter, Ethel, she is survived by her husband, Bedford; another daughter, Bonnie, about 7; and three sons, Guy of Lawrence, Kan., Elmer of Topeka, Kan., and Louise, about 5.

Funeral services will be held this afternoon at 2 o'clock in the Baptist Church at Cedar Gap with the Rev. Bob Martin officiating. Burial was in Cedar Gap Cemetery under direction of Kelley-Ferrell-Bergman of Seymour."

"Atty. Ellsworth Haymes was named by the Republican Central Committee to go on the Republican ticket for Prosecuting Attorney at a meeting held at the courthouse here last Thursday evening *[9/11]*. He takes the place of Clyde Meise of Seymour, who is now employed in Kansas City. Mr. Meise did not desire to leave his position to make the race....Mr. Haymes served one term as Prosecuting Attorney in 1939-1940...."

October 2, 1952 *[a political ad]* "To The Voters of Webster County....After thinking the matter over, I have decided to remain on the Democratic Ticket for the November Election. I have always believed that a party offering himself for office, if known by the people of the county should not be required to travel and campaign for the office, and furthermore I feel that the voters should choose their officers without solicitation or any attempt to use any kind of influence by the candidates. I will have been a resident of Webster County for 41 years on the 17th day of October, 1952, and believe the people of the county pretty well know me or have heard of me, and will know what my attitude would be in the Prosecuting Attorney's office, as I have previously served two terms as such officer, in Webster County. I do not intend to campaign for this office, and the only money I will spend will be to pay the *Marshfield Mail*, for printing this article. So if the voters want me for Prosecuting Attorney, I will very much appreciate your votes, and should the voters not want me for the office, I do not understand why I should want the office.   SETH V. CONRAD"

October 9, 1952 "Another tragic highway accident happened at 1:20 early Sunday morning on Highway 66 near Oak Grove Lodge, 8 miles west of Marshfield, when Mrs. Barbara Jean Raiford, 19, of Wichita, Tex., was killed instantly. Her husband, James W. Raiford, 21, a soldier in the Air Forces, was badly injured and was taken to Burge Hospital, Springfield. He suffered a broken hip and other injuries. His condition was reported improved Tuesday.

They were en route from a Texas air base to an air base in Illinois. The Texas car, a 1939 Chevrolet, driven by Raiford, was struck by a car driven by a colored soldier, John House of Fort Leonard Wood, on a curve. With him was another soldier identified by officers as Frank Howard, also of Fort Leonard Wood. After the accident, someone picked up Howard and officers have not been able to contact him. House was injured and taken to Burge Hospital.

Sheriff E.I. Cunningham, Highway Patrolmen Turpin and Stone were called from Marshfield and went to the scene with two Barber-Barto ambulances. The two injured persons were taken to the hospital by ambulance....

According to Sheriff Cunningham, both cars in the accident were total wrecks."

[Joe Arthur]   "I worked at the funeral home, Barber-Barto. I didn't work for Rainey. Raineys was there, but then it was Roller-Bruce. Then Oral Edwards came up and I started working when I was 18 years old. September of 1951.

We worked on the wreck calls. 'Course then, the coroner wasn't so prominent. The Sheriff did a lot of the coroner work. So we worked with Isam on numerous occasions. With wrecks and fires and this sort of thing.

The first death call I went on was with Lee Mason, a man who lived at the funeral home at the time. And I was in high school and they went somewhere and I just set in for 'em, where they could go. And while I was there I got a death call down at the *old* County Farm, it's right on the corner where Mary Ruth Brooks's house is now. A big old two-story building, and they called it The County Farm then, they don't call it that now. And I know there was stairs we had to go up and I almost fell comin' down 'cause I wasn't familiar with all the stuff. Never will forget the very first one, the very first death call!

This person did *not* have a doctor, as I remember, and so Isam came down, of course K.K. Kelley asked him to, come down and kinda act as coroner, just to be sure their death was proper and everything was done the way it should be done and that sort of thing. We've always laughed about the stairway, you know. There was no elevator in that time. You had to carry the cot up and they had this very short bend, and it was a pretty heavy person.

We were the first ones on the scene a lot of times. If they didn't have a doctor, you had to have somebody to sign the death certificate so we'd have to get the coroner or the deputy coroner, and Isam would sometime act as deputy. Like, if Mr. Kelley was gone or on a funeral or busy. Isam did, for several cases. If the coroner was busy.

We'd get an ambulance call and they'd say, 'Well send Joe, because I live the second yard light from' so-and-so. They didn't have addresses like they do now. They just had the road name. 'Road' so-and-so. 'There's a pole light, I'll turn the pole light on.' Or 'I'll turn the porch light on and this'll be where you're comin'.'

The country was just a route! Route 1, Route 2, Route 3. So, if you didn't know where you were going, their country miles was sometimes, it'd be like, *two* miles instead of *one* mile. I was pretty familiar with the county at that time."

[Billie Arthur] "But you didn't have to have the training *then* that you have to *now*. It was a lot different. It was a matter of just *getting* them there." *[to the hospital]*

[Jack Rainey] "I know that Isam relied on Dad *[Rex Rainey]*, Dad relied on him, a lot of times because, what happens, Dad was involved in going out to these situations where they were shootin' each other, knifings, wrecks, a lot of wrecks. They'd regularly go to Northview Hill, that was Old Bloody Hill.

I don't know whether this happened while Isam was Sheriff; I don't remember the time frame on it, but there was a gasoline truck come down Northview Hill, and where that crossing is now, was either just this side or just the other side, turned over, burned, and the driver was burned terribly bad, but he was still alive. And he had run down the road from the wreck and they were trying to get him up, take him to the hospital, and he was beggin' the highway patrol to shoot him. 'Course, they couldn't do it. Because *he* even realized that he was burned beyond getting help. They did take him into Springfield, he later died. Dad went there, got the body, brought him down. Pretty difficult case to embalm....That's exactly the type of thing Dad was involved in.

One night in particular there was an attorney in Buffalo...it was a real foggy night, I don't remember why my folks wasn't available, they were somewhere. They called the funeral home, somebody had to take these people in to the hospital. The man was hurt, well, *both* of them were hurt. A man and a woman. They shouldn't have been together, is what it amounts to. But they'd run into the front end of a Greyhound Bus, about where the Wee Dug Inn is. About right there, where that road turns off. They'd tore the car all to pieces. Herman Pierce, he had the Ford dealership here for a number of years, I don't even know why he was there, but I think I was sixteen years old and there wasn't anybody else to drive the ambulance, so I took the ambulance out there, and they helped me load this feller. Herman said, 'Are you takin' him in?' And I said, 'Yes, there's nobody else!' And it was so foggy you couldn't see from here to the front door. And Dad had always impressed on me, if somebody was hurt bad, even though you need to get them there as soon as possible, you don't want to do it to where you're going to injure them worse getting them there, because a lot of times they're not going to do an awful lot for them, once you get there. Herman said, 'Well, I'll go with you.' So we took him to Springfield. And he died the next day. It wasn't because we didn't get him there in a timely fashion. There just wasn't anything they could do.

That's just one of the things that I did. Most of the time I was left there to answer the phone. Somebody had to always be there to answer the phone.

Back then, you weren't expected, the doctors didn't even *want* you to do anything *[regarding first aid in the ambulance]*. Anything you would do was wrong. Transport only.

See, the funeral directors *reluctantly* were ambulance people. They didn't *want* it, it was forced on them, because they had the equipment. When I took that fella in, it was in a *hearse*. It wasn't in a regular car. They *[Carmen and Rex Rainey]* used the hearse when it was necessary, but he designed this little...what I call an ambulance, primarily for convenience.

Another thing: people that just needed transportation, they didn't particularly *like* riding in a *hearse*. Before he got this car and designed it, he used what they called a paneled delivery, because the whole back door would open, and he had a cot hooked to the side of it. But *it* was all enclosed and they didn't like *it* too well, either! But still, it was better than riding in a hearse, because so many people associated riding in a hearse with 'the last time around'. And they don't particularly like it. That's the last thing you wanna be thinkin' about, coming home from the hospital; you want to be thinking that life is *startin'* rather than life is *endin'*.

As soon as it got profitable enough for somebody to run an ambulance service only, all the funeral directors *pushed* it.   They *wanted* to get out of the ambulance business. In other words, it was just a 'have to' situation. Actually, it *cost* money to perform that service. They'd make a call to Springfield, go to the hospital, pick up somebody, bring 'em back, because...*used* to, they wanted 'em out of the hospital as quickly as they could, they didn't want anybody stayin' in the hospital. Then later on it went through the situation where they wanted *everyone* to stay in the hospital whether they was sick or *not*. Now, it's reversed *again*; they've got all this outpatient stuff and all, and you go to the hospital as a last resort. Even back then, you'd go to Springfield to pick up a patient they would release, you'd come home but couldn't ride in a car, then it was five dollars. We couldn't make the trip for five dollars, even back at *that* time!

So it was a public service, and all the funeral directors got pushed into it and didn't want it. They did get paid, but it wasn't enough to pay for the time to go. It was priority. As soon as the phone rang, you had to go."

"Mrs. E.I. Cunningham and son, Charles, and her granddaughter, Betty Lou Letterman left Monday morning for Rockford, Ill., to visit her son, Wilbur, wife, and baby for three or four days. They were accompanied by Mrs. Vern Bailey who is visiting her son in Illinois."

[I wonder who did the cooking for the prisoners...and Isam...when Eva was gone. Is this when Marshfield Café and Ruby Hargus were enlisted?]

October 16, 1952 "Pictured *[on the next page]* **is the electrically lighted sign which points the way to Marshfield from Highway 66 at Marshfield Spur northwest of the city. The sign was erected this summer with funds raised by local civic clubs. Hugh Bennett, manager of Webster Electric Cooperative, is shown looking at the sign in the photo. The Cooperative furnished the electricity to light the neon sign free of charge as a donation to the public."**

"Two Webster Countians, Mrs. Pansy Newcomb and Andy Lageare, were wounded late Saturday following a shooting at a farm home three miles east of Seymour. Held in jail at Marshfield is Mrs. Newcomb's son, 18-year-old Donald Newcomb.

Taken to Springfield Baptist Hospital in Springfield at 10:25 p.m., Mrs. Newcomb was found to have suffered minor wounds about the head from shotgun pellets. Lageare was admitted to the hospital about a half hour later. He was treated for serious wounds about the left hip, back, and abdomen. He was reported in fair condition.

Donald Newcomb, who reportedly fired the gun which wounded both his mother and Lageare, is being held pending further investigation.

Sheriff E.I. Cunningham said he had received two or three versions of the incident, which occurred after all three had evidently been drinking at the Newcomb home. The Sheriff said the youth told him he picked up a 410-gauge shotgun, ordered Lageare to leave the house, then fired twice.

Later, Newcomb claimed he thought the weapon was not loaded. Sheriff said the house was spattered with blood and the gun was found in the yard about 10 feet from the rear of the house.

Cunningham attempted to question Lageare at the hospital Sunday but he was unable to talk.

Mrs. Newcomb told attendants at the hospital that her son was cleaning the gun when it discharged accidentally. She was released from the hospital Sunday.

Sheriff Cunningham said that he had previously been summoned to quiet the boy for shooting around the neighborhood. He said that Newcomb has previously become 'trigger-happy' from drinking.

The youth has been on parole from a previous sentence, and that parole was revoked Sunday at the request of Judge James P. Hawkins."

October 30, 1952 *[an ad]* "To the Voters of Webster County—Most newspapers in the Seventh District have already conceded my defeat by my friend, Dewey Short, in his eleventh campaign for congress.

I will need every vote I can get (and probably 20,000 more).

Your support will be appreciated by everyone on the Bald Hill.
JOHN HOSMER"

[Don Letterman]   "And I remember when [Granddad] moved to Marshfield and was Sheriff, why, I got to be old enough while he was there that when an election would come up, I'd go haul votes in Niangua Township. People who didn't have no car to get to the polls, I'd go get 'em. They was three or four that, every year he run, I had to go get them, they wouldn't go with nobody else."

November 6, 1952 *[results of elections]*
"IKE AND DICK WIN....GOP TAKES ALL OFFICES IN THIS COUNTY...JOHN HOSMER BEHIND SHORT...BALLARD WATTERS, EDITOR OF THE MAIL, LOST TO INCUMBENT TOBERMAN...ELLSWORTH HAYMES WINS PROSECUTING ATTORNEY OVER SETH CONRAD...SHERIFF CUNNINGHAM DEFEATED LONNIE WILSON, 3767 TO 3282."

November 13, 1952 *[photo caption]* "Jaycees Promote Safety...Dr. J.E. *[Doc]* Blinn, Jaycee president, installing reflective tape on the Sheriff's car; Mayor Ralph Bridwell, whose car had just received the tape, and Sheriff E.I. Cunningham....

The tape embodies several safety features. It can be seen two to three times farther than a taillight. In the event of failure of lights, it offers protection. It is guaranteed to remain on bumpers for a period of two years. It greatly reduces the danger from rear-end collisions at night...."

[Doc Blinn] "I became the County Physician November 1952. If any of the prisoners got sick in jail, I took care of them. Some of them made a effort to get sick, you know. Usually there was something, though.

One night, about 9:30 in the evening I got called up there, Isam had a young fellow but he was a big fellow.

Isam was a pretty good size man himself. Another thing, he wore pants with no belt and suspenders. And they were about three or four sizes bigger, and he wore his gun down inside. We had a preacher here who used to say, 'It's the first Sheriff I ever knew who had to drop his pants to draw his gun!'

Anyway, he called me up there that evening and still had this fella in the office, they hadn't booked him yet, because he'd started to resist. And Isam had a little blackjack, about that long—six inches—and it had a handle and there was a leather pouch that had shot in it, like beebee shot or shotgun shot. It wasn't full but it was full enough, that it didn't shift much, but it gave a good weight, you just had to flick it a little bit. And that's what he'd done. This guy had started to give him some trouble and he just picked this thing up. The guy had three deals, about two or three inches long, where that thing had whop-whop-whopped on the prisoner's head. They told me when they called to bring some things along, that I'd probably need to do some sewing.

I looked it over and I said, 'Sheriff, you really got his attention, didn't you?' and Isam said, 'I just tapped him.'

Isam would call me on the phone and say he needed someone examined, like from a fall or something like that. Every once in a while they'd have someone sick, but they didn't use the jail as much as they do now. There wasn't too often they had that many people.

I never treated Eva and I didn't treat Isam too much.

The one thing I've never forgotten: he called me one evening, it was about six or six thirty. He was having a lot of pain in the rectal area. He said it started suddenly, it came on, it was giving him a lot of difficulty. So we went back in my examining room, I did a digital examination first and I felt something long and narrow on the posterior surface of the sigmoid, the rectum. So I put a speculum in there, and it was a fishbone! About that long! Instead of making the little curve there to come out, it had stuck right into the edge of where the rectum rolls in. So I lifted that out of there. It was a good 2_ inches long.

I said, 'How in the hell did you ever swallow that, Sheriff?' and he said, 'I don't know,' and I said, 'Man, I hope I never get that hungry!' Anyway, that took care of that situation. It wouldn't have passed. It just was buried in there. It came out fairly easily. I just took a forceps and kinda pulled it back. I'd say there was that much of it—at least an inch—stuck in the wall of the rectum there.

We got along real well. Every once in a while we'd have to go up to the jail, to see somebody, and I'd sit around and talk to the Sheriff a little while. We had a good relationship. He didn't seem to resent anything I'd suggest to him. I didn't have a lot of suggestions to make because he was doing a pretty good job. But if I'd suggest something, he was open to it.

He was just a good fella, a good good fella."

"Circuit Court Notes: Carmen P. Rainey, vs. Jack Rainey, partition. Trial by court. Decree in partition. Land ordered sold for cash." *[Jack Rainey said when his mother, Carmen, divorced his dad, Rex, she added him, their only child, to her share of the property settlement. Then after they remarried and began making plans for the future funeral home business in Springfield, she wanted to sell the property and needed to clear the title. This decree in partition was a formality, no contention whatsoever.]*

"Mr. and Mrs. Rex Rainey, formerly of Marshfield, have purchased a landmark house and tract of land on South Glenstone, Springfield, from Mrs. Louise C. Martin.

The price paid was $75,000, according to Charles Martin, son of Mrs. Martin, who said that the Raineys, now living near Strafford, bought the tract for 'investment and holding purposes.'

The residence is to be used as a home for the foreseeable future and some of the 635 frontage on Glenstone is expected to be opened for restricted commercial usage, with lots to be sold on the western part of the tract for home sites.

Recently the city council authorized the rezoning of the property to 'E' commercial."

[Jack Rainey] "See, they remarried, moved into...they had converted the barn that I milked in, into a little house, out on the dairy. In the meantime, we'd gotten married and we bought...I was tryin' to farm, that's all I ever wanted to do, and in the settlement I got a little lump sum. I bought a tractor and a baler, and a truck. My dad found out this place up at Strafford was for sale, it was Leroy Blunt's old place. I would never have got it bought without my dad's connections. I had about $2,000. It had a little grade A barn.

We lived on the Arkansas side of Texarkana. That's where Dean was born.

She *[his wife, Anne Cardwell Rainey]* was 17 years old, first time she'd ever spent a night away from home, with a new baby, I was working ten hours a day, seven days a week. So, she decided she wanted to come back. Well, in the process, my folks had *started* to build a funeral home in Springfield. I had that place there in Strafford, they had this place down here *[in Marshfield]*, and this was gonna be a more livable place, they let us have this house down here, *they* moved into the grade A barn in Strafford *[which they had earlier remodeled into a little house]* and lived *there* while they were getting the funeral home far enough along that they could move into *it*.

That's kinda what they did all their life. They'd adapt to whatever they had to do, rather than spend the money to...because they needed the money to go into the business, they didn't slough off any money. My dad was as tight as I am."

November 20, 1952 "Two attempts at suicide were made last week by James D. Major, alias J. W. Harvey of Springfield, held in jail here for the sheriff of Laclede county, charged with blowing a safe at Camdenton. On Thursday, while at the upstairs office of Dr. Levitan, he tried to jump out a window, but was caught by the feet by an officer as he hung out the window.

Then on Saturday night he cut his wrist with a dull cake knife, which wound required sewing up by Dr. Blinn. The cake knife was hidden in a loaf of bread said to have been brought with him when he was lodged here in charge of Sheriff Cunningham.

The man has acted queerly while in jail according to the Sheriff, who says 'Harvey or Major has walked the floor all the time like a caged lion.'"

"Population of Bald Hill Increases. Miss Jane Hosmer was born at 6:33 p.m. Sunday, Nov. 16, at Burge Hospital. The young lady weighed 9 lbs. 13 oz. Atty. and Mrs. John *[Mitzi]* Hosmer now have four children."

[Doc Blinn] "A number of times I was called up to Bald Hill, maybe to see one of the kids, I couldn't get away, I'd sit there for an hour, it was a most interesting thing! That was a family!

They had a table that looked like an army table, they'd all get around that and John would teach. They'd have readings. They'd read some book, some of the classics. Those kids grew up pretty smart! A lot of stuff like that they learned at the table. They didn't just eat, they had discussions about things. I think they all had to participate too...as they got old enough to.

I always just felt real good after I came back from there. Because they got along so well. That whole family was all for one and one for all, you know.

John Hosmer. He was just a really disturbed sort of a guy. His growing up was not a pleasant time for him, I don't think. I understand his mother *[Bess Hosmer]* dressed him in Little Lord Fauntleroy suits, things like that, and sent him to school. Kids picked on him, I think. Then he had this eye problem, blind in one eye. People used to say he was the best one-eyed lawyer in southwest Missouri! He was a character. I guess he was a good lawyer but he just didn't...well...he'd get something going and do things that didn't help his case. He'd do things just for spite, lots of times. He dressed like a tramp, he'd buy his clothes from these rummage sales. You know, he had thirteen kids. And that was the best bunch of kids you ever saw!

His wife Mitzi was a wonderful person, I don't know how she put up with him. He would do just anything to get a laugh, get something going, stir things up. That's what he loved to do, stir things up. I delivered four or five of the Hosmer kids. I think Tommy delivered some, C.R. first and then Tommy, and then they got mad at the Macdonnells so they came over to me. Looked like he was waiting to stir up trouble.

We'd be out somewhere, like in a restaurant. I'd walk in and John would be in there and shout, 'There's my baby doctor!' Real loud! He was just a character. But he was a real likeable sort of guy."

"Circuit Court notes: Carmen P. Rainey vs. Jack Rainey, partition. Judgment of Nov. 3, 1952, set aside. Seth V. Conrad appointed guardian ad litum for defendant, Jack Rainey, a minor, and his answer filed. Trial by court. Decree in partition. Land ordered sold for cash...."

" Marshfield is closing one of the greatest building years in its history. 1952 has seen the construction of a large factory building, new business buildings and many new homes in and near the city...."

"Two Fordland youths, arrested by the state patrol and Webster County authorities have admitted the theft of enough liquor to open their own business.

Held in the Webster County jail at Marshfield are 19-year-old James Hardy Hoyt and Earl Haze Brake, 18, both of Fordland.

Most of the spirits they stole from a Fordland liquor store earlier this month were found hidden in a groundhog hole.

Troopers C. F. Stone and D. R. Turpin of Marshfield and

Webster County Sheriff E.I. Cunningham, who made the arrests, said the pair has admitted burglarizing the Carpenter Liquor Store in Fordland the night of November 7.

The youths shattered a north window to unlatch it and enter, taking $6 in change, 24 pints of lime, 114 half-pints of whiskey, 25 cartons of cigarettes, 12 half-pints of gin, 23 fifths and nine pints of whiskey.

The youths were arrested Friday night and admitted the theft Sunday night after being questioned several times at the Marshfield jail.

Much of the whiskey and cigarettes was found in the groundhog hole before the pair admitted the burglary, but the officers wouldn't disclose how they found the spot.

The loot was hidden near Panther Creek north of Fordland, and more of the merchandise is expected to be recovered."

"The Webster County Court, in session Monday *[11/17]*, employed Dr. J. E. Blinn, D.O., as county doctor. Drs. Schlicht and Schlicht resigned effective the first of November...."

[Doc Blinn] "I billed the county, when I did something for Isam, and they paid me at the next county court. When I was County Doctor, I had a stipend. I didn't make any money doing that. That was something the county court could consider a public service. C.R. Macdonnell recommended me, but because he and Dr. Schlicht didn't get along worth a darn."

November 27, 1952 "Magistrate Court Notes from Nov. 21...State of Mo. vs. Dave Coots, exhibiting dangerous and deadly weapons. Dismissed for want of prosecution...."*["Want of prosecution" means lack of prosecution; the State (represented by the Prosecuting Attorney) chose not to proceed.]*

December 4, 1952 "....This year marked the 13th consecutive time Missouri has been on the side of the winning presidential candidate—ever since 1904.

And this year's vote was a record turnout by Missourians. The total vote this year for president was 1,892,062, or 58,333 more than the previous record, established in 1940....There were six splinter parties that had presidential slates in the election this year. They collected this smattering of votes....Progressive Party 987, Socialist

227, Socialist-Labor 169, Prohibition 885, Christian Nationalist 302, and America First 223...."

December 18, 1952 "Circuit Court Notes from Dec. 12...State of Mo. vs. James Harvey Hoyt and Haze Brake, burglary and larceny. Defendant James Harvey Hoyt appraised of his rights, and upon his request, Roy C. Miller appointed as his attorney. Defendant waives formal arraignment and enters a plea of guilty. Punishment assessed at imprisonment in state penitentiary for a term of two years for burglary and a further term of two years for larceny. Defendant being only 20 years of age, his sentence is commuted to imprisonment in the Intermediate Reformatory at Algoa for a term of two years for burglary and a further term of two years for larceny. Application for parole filed....

Carmen P. Rainey vs. Jack Rainey, partition. Report of sale filed and approved. Deed ordered executed. Deed acknowledged in open court. Seth Conrad allowed a fee of $10 as guardian ad litem. John Hosmer allowed a fee of $50 as attorney. Distribution ordered."

"William Ried, 16, Collinsville, Ill., and William Thomas Birch, 16, Maryville, Ill., were arrested this Wednesday morning on new Highway 66, about a mile north of this city, charged with breaking into the Producers Exchange Tuesday night. They were lodged in jail after their arrest by Trooper Turpin, Sheriff E.I. Cunningham, and Commodore Smith.

According to the officers, the youths entered the Producers Exchange by breaking a glass in the back door. They took clothing, cigarettes, pipe, tobacco, flashlight, knife, candy, purse, comb and other items including food. They are reported to have built up a fire in the stove in the rear of the Exchange and ate cheese, candy, etc. Later they built a fire in a shed at the U.S. Poindexter place and stayed the rest of the night.

According to the story told by the boys, they had been at Fort Worth, Tex., after leaving home about two weeks ago. They were hitchhiking back home."

December 25, 1952 "Judge James P. Hawkins was here Friday *[12/19]* and heard some juvenile matters. The boys who broke into the Producers Exchange last week were sentenced and paroled to their parents in Illinois."

Chapter Thirteen
1953

January 1, 1953 "A youth from Michigan was caught Saturday afternoon in a Webster County house which he burglarized.

He is listed as Charles Albert Hauser, Jr., by Webster County Sheriff E.I. Cunningham, who said the youth appears to be in his twenties, but had been drinking and told officers he is 109 years old.

Cunningham said he was caught about 4 p.m. by Jimmy Popejoy, in his farm home three miles north of here on Highway 66.

Popejoy grabbed a .22 caliber rifle, said the Sheriff, and marched the youth to a relative's nearby house where he called officers.

Cunningham said the boy had broken a window to gain entry while the family was in Marshfield, ransacked the house and took about $1 and a wrist watch.

Because of his evident intoxication, officers couldn't understand what community in Michigan he is from.

Hauser was booked at the county jail here."

"New county officials take office today, January 1….Ellsworth Haymes is the new Prosecuting Attorney, succeeding John Hosmer…."

[Cline Herren, Jr.] "Ellsworth and Roy were both good prosecutors. I don't think John Hosmer was a good prosecutor, because John Hosmer would not take care of business. He just would not take care of business. A brilliant person, but a lousy paper man. Always had something else to do, on his mind, or something."

"Roy Morris, of near Niangua, was wounded late Friday on the Bill Alexander farm two miles south of Niangua. He was peppered with buckshot.

According to Sheriff E.I. Cunningham, Morris was wounded by Alexander after he went to the Alexander home and began hurling large rocks at the front of the house.

Morris, who reportedly had been causing disturbances in the neighborhood recently, was struck in the side, leg, shoulder and hand by a charge from a shotgun. He was treated by a Marshfield doctor.

Cunningham reported that the rocks smashed the front door of the Alexander home and also broke out a window. He said the rocks were the size of a 'half-gallon bucket.'

Cunningham said Troopers Stone and Turpin were called to the scene and brought Morris to Marshfield. He said that a sanity hearing for Morris is scheduled for January 3, in Magistrate Court. Morris is now in jail at Marshfield."

"Four Webster Countians were wounded Christmas night in a tavern about a mile east of Seymour.

Struck by rifle bullets were Frank Lynch, his wife Ruby, Calvin Rowe and Claude Box, all residents of the Seymour vicinity. Bill Blankenship, a Seymour man, was identified by Sheriff E.I. Cunningham as the gunman. Blankenship suffered head injuries in the incident when Lynch reportedly broke the rifle over his head.

Blankenship was taken to Springfield Baptist Hospital for treatment of head injuries.

Lynch was wounded three times in the arm, his wife was shot three times above the knee. Rowe was shot three times in the left leg below the knee and Box was slightly wounded in the thumb. The Lynch couple were taken to Springfield Baptist Hospital and later released.

Officers said Blankenship went to the tavern about 7:45 p.m. Christmas night and became angry after talking to some people in the place. He reportedly told them that he had a gun in his car and went outside and obtained it. He stepped back in the tavern and began shooting, hitting four of about 12 persons there. Lynch then wrested the gun from him and broke the .22 caliber automatic rifle over his head.

Blankenship was involved several months ago in a shooting when he was identified as a gunman who fired a shotgun blast at Dave Coots, former Seymour marshal. Felonious assault charges were filed and Blankenship was released on bond.

Blankenship was booked at Marshfield Saturday on a felonious assault charge."

January 8, 1953 "In the matter of alleged insanity of Roy Morris. Hearing held before Probate Judge Cline C. Herren Saturday, Jan. 3. Roy C. Miller appointed attorney for defendant and answer filed. Jury waived and trial by court. Judgment: Defendant is indigent insane. Ordered committed to State Hospital No. 3 at Nevada."

January 22, 1953 "Dwight David Eisenhower became the 33rd president of the United States Tuesday noon *[1/20]* in ceremonies that were heard by radio and seen by the largest television audience of any event in history....President Eisenhower, with a prayer on his lips, set for his administration a goal of peace with honor. He laid down for free men everywhere a challenge to join together against a world menace of communism....Private citizen Harry S Truman left Washington Tuesday night with Mrs. Truman for Independence, Mo., by train."

"The average national debt per person in the U.S. jumped tenfold during 20 years of Democratic rule, says House Speaker Martin (R-Mass).

In a statement Martin said a national debt of 21 billion dollars when President Franklin D. Roosevelt was inaugurated in 1933, has skyrocketed to $262,700,000,000. This is a rise from $162 to $1,697 on a per capita basis he said.

The Republican leader called it 'a staggering burden of debt to blight the hopes and dim the opportunities of generations yet unborn.'"

January 29, 1953 "Sheriff E.I. Cunningham, who was taken to Burge Hospital in Springfield Wednesday of last week *[1/21]*, was brought home Tuesday. *[1/27]* He underwent an operation Thursday and is recovering." *[No one I asked could recall what this surgery was.]*

[an ad] "We have been advised that one Springfield Television station will be on the air sometime in February. Western Auto has on display some 20 different sets from which to choose. May we urge you to select your New Admiral or Truetone immediately in order that it can be installed before the rush."

[During part of the writing of this book, all through 2003, the NBC affiliate—KY3—in Springfield, Missouri, was celebrating its 50th anniversary of being on the air.]

February 12, 1953 "The Producers Exchange was broken into again Sunday night. Entrance was made by the thief or thieves by breaking the glass in a back door. So far discovered is that only a small amount of change was taken.

The broken window was discovered Sunday night about 9:30 by night watchman Tom Nunn."

March 5, 1953 "Sheriff E.I. Cunningham arrested Billy Dean Ford, 22, wanted in California on forgery charges, Tuesday of last week at Seymour. Ford and his wife were visiting her folks there. Ford has been held in the jail here awaiting extradition papers to return him to Modesta, Calif.

According to Sheriff Cunningham there is a long story back of this arrest. Ford is charged with writing checks using the fictitious name of W. E. Wards on the Bank of America at Modesto in the amount of about $260, and the checks were passed by Orville Summers.

Recently Summers and his ex-wife, who had been in Oklahoma with her folks and Ford and his wife, who is only 16 years old, were arrested in Springfield after the robbery of a filling station and passing bad checks. They had managed to pay off and be released at Springfield, according to Sheriff Cunningham.

It was found that Summers was AWOL from the Navy and during that time of AWOL had joined the army, from which he was AWOL also."

March 12, 1953 "Officers cleaned up numerous small robberies of recent months Friday when three youths, two of them 12 years old and the other 13, admitted to entering several Marshfield business places and taking money.

Due to their age they will be taken before the juvenile division of the Circuit Court, and it is hoped that their apprehension will prevent their start in a life of crime. However, that will depend a great deal on their parents.

Friday morning it was discovered that two windows at the MAIL office had been broken and entry gained at one of them. Fingerprints on one of the windows disclosed it was small boys. $2 in nickels and about $2 in pennies were taken from a change box.

Sheriff E.I. Cunningham, Marshal Homer Alexander and a patrolman investigated. The Sheriff and city marshal immediately remembered seeing some boys loitering around the rear of a store building the night before and the Sheriff went to the school and called two of the boys out. He says they readily told about the robbery, as well as numerous others, and implicated a third youth. Only two of the three had entered the MAIL office building.

Other places the boys are said to have admitted robbing included: Producers Exchange several times; J.H. Robertson, Roy Meyer Filling Station.

The boys had buried the money taken from the MAIL office and went and dug part of it up. The two boys that entered the building had each told their parents that they were staying the night at the other boy's home. They had stayed in the school building."

[Darrell Letterman] "He'd *[Granddad Isam]* say, 'Okay, I gotta make my rounds' and he'd go around, I don't know who he talked to or who he didn't, but I know it was a bunch of kids, I'm just sure of that, and if somethin' went on, a robbery somewhere or somethin', he would make his rounds like that, and it wouldn't be very long 'til he went over and arrested somebody. I'm almost ten-to-one sure, because when the kids would come uptown they'd say, 'Hi Isam!', you know, across the street at him, and he'd say, 'Go to The Sweet Shop and getcha some ice cream' and I think that was his stool pigeons, they're the ones that told what went on in the county, that's my belief. I was sixteen when he died and up to then I was around. There was a lot of ice cream made in The Sweet Shop for some kids around Marshfield, let's put it thad-a-way. To this day I believe that, and my dad has even said, that's where he got his *deal* at."

[Jerry Letterman] "'Course, we all went, he always sent us to The Sweet Shop, we'd always go over there, that was the big treat for all of us. We pretty much got to do whatever we wanted when we was down there. All we'd have to do was walk in there and say we wanted a certain ice cream and they'd get it for us. Didn't have to pay; he'd always take care of that."

[Wilma Ryser] "My grandmother, May Rader, was Isam's half-sister. I guess one of the funniest things I remember was when my third son *[Dennis]* was born *[on March 13, 1953]* in the old Burge Hospital and Uncle Isam was Sheriff at the time. About midnight one night I heard the most awful racket out in the hall there ever was. They were arguing, the nurses and somebody, and finally I heard Uncle Isam say, 'By God, that's my niece and I'm goin' in and see her!' And it was *midnight*! And he came in to see me!

My kids all just loved him. That made their day if we came to Marshfield and Uncle Isam got a hold of them and aggravated them. He loved children."

April 2, 1953 "Officers in this area have been alerted for a man who slipped away from a state prison farm Monday night while serving a term for an assault on Webster County Sheriff E.I. Cunningham, during an unsuccessful escape attempt more than two years ago.

The man is identified as Kenneth Kile, 28, on state patrol reports, which describe him as being 5 feet, 9 inches tall, and weighing 190 pounds, having blue eyes and brown hair.

His father, K. K. Kiles, is said to live at Avilla, between here and Carthage.

Kile slipped away from Prison Farm Number Two near Jefferson City, sometime after 7 o'clock Monday night.

According to patrol records, Kile and a teen-age youth attacked the Webster County Sheriff in the Marshfield jail on November 26, 1950.

Cunningham was hospitalized for a time with severe lacerations inflicted by a hair tonic bottle in a sock.

He succeeded in keeping his gun away from the pair until his son and a state trooper came to his rescue.

Kile was held for car theft at the time. Records show he was sentenced to 15 years for felonious assault in January, 1951."

[Mary Lou Cunningham] "On that Kile story, I remember—Charley was in service—but I remember he *[Kile]* got out and Isam was just a little bit edgy, because he would lock the bedroom door."

[Charley Cunningham] "Dad had got word back that he *[Kile]* was going to kill Dad, 'cause Dad knocked him in the head up here after *Dad* got knocked in the head."

[Mary Lou] "Well, I had just heard that Kile was gonna be after him. And I just remember he was a little bit edgy about that. It just seemed like he was taking precautions because of Evie being in the courthouse. 'Cause she always took precautions with me if I went to the movie across the street. One of the city marshalls, like Homer Alexander, would always escort me back to my room in the courthouse. I would just stay if Isam needed me to help Evie in the jail or if I wanted to stay and go to a movie or something, instead of driving way back out in the country, I would do that. He was always very protective of me. Because it was a spooky place, at night, the courthouse."

[Charley] "I used to go in the south door all the time, by myself, of a night, in the wee hours of the morning. You could drop a pin and it would just ring all the way through. I wasn't ever scared there, unless, like Homer Alexander jumped out a couple times and scared the livin' daylights out of me."

April 9, 1953 "Eleven men were sent to Kansas City, Mo., on March 30, 1953, for their induction which covered the local board's March induction call, which included: Charles *[Charley]* Robert Cunningham, Marshfield."

April 16, 1953 "Board of Education Organizes with Ellsworth Haymes as President. Superintendent reported resignations effective at the end of this term...Harold Bell, after two years here as high school principal and one year as coach is returning to Indiana to enter business; Powell Edge plans to teach in another state; Wanda Edmondson is returning to school; Glendena Butler will live with her husband at Flemington when he is discharged from the army this summer; Marion Fillmer plans to stay at home with her pre-school age daughter...."

"Mr. and Mrs. Wilbur *[Red]* Cunningham and baby of Rockford, Ill., spent the weekend here visiting his parents, Sheriff and Mrs. E.I. Cunningham. They also visited Charles *[Charley]* Cunningham and Don Letterman at Fort Leonard Wood."

[Mary Lou Cunningham] "Charley served in the Korean war, from March, 1953 to March, 1955. When he stayed at Ft. Leonard Wood, he came home every weekend.
One time Isam drove Eva and me up to Ft. Leonard Wood to see Charley during training. Isam drove right up front next to the training area. I was thinking—'Oh my!' But that was Isam. He wanted to see what was going on. He was always that way."
[Charley served with the Military Police, once a friend of Isam's found out son Charley was in service at Ft. Leonard Wood. Charley found himself doing something very familiar, looking out for the Ft.

Leonard Wood soldiers on weekend leave, usually in Springfield, making sure they didn't get into trouble.]

April 23, 1953 "Two Alarms This Friday Will Warn People of 'Bombing'—Marshfield civilian defense officials are joining in the joint Army-Civil Defense Command Post Exercise for this 11-state area to be held this Friday, April 24.

Two alarms will probably be given here, the first, an alert, which will be three minutes of short blasts of the fire siren and whistles, and second, the all clear signal, which will be one long blast.

Sheriff E.I. Cunningham will receive the preliminary notice about 12:30 from Springfield, which will be known as the Yellow warning. The Director, R.W. Fyan, will be notified by the Sheriff. Then at 1:00 p.m. will come the Red warning, the alert, and the local civil defense organization will go into action.

The police, augmented by American legion and VFW organizations, will stop traffic. Veterans are asked to wear their caps.

The fire department will make a practice run.

The nurses will gather at the American Legion room in the courthouse.

The Boy Scouts will stand by for any duties assigned them.

There will also probably be a drill at the school.

Several local civil defense people will go to Springfield this Thursday afternoon for instruction, and a meeting of all those interested will be held here this Thursday evening at 7:45. All interested are invited to take part."

"'Back to God' parades on May Day as 'a counter move' to the anti-God demonstrations of the Communist parades on that date, have been urged upon all American Legion Posts in the State of Missouri....*[A]* resolution calls for bands playing 'Onward Christian Soldiers,' 'Battle Hymn of the Republic,' and 'God Bless America,' with groups carrying banners and placards reading, 'The word of God is the weapon most feared by the Communist,' 'Come to church on Sunday,' 'May Day is Back To God Day,' 'The family that prays together stays together' and other suitable slogans."

[an ad] "Why Send Your Insurance Money Away from Your Home County When You Can Have Just as Good Protection with the Farmers Mutual Fire Insurance Company of Webster County...Office in Court

House At Marshfield, Phone 33. John L. Alcorn, President. Elzie
L. Doyle, Sec.-Treas."

[Mitzi Hosmer] "Elzie was a little tiny bitty thing. Her eyes were a little
bit crossed. She really didn't look too much like Freda *[her daughter,
Freda Doyle Langston]* But she was a house-a-fire. Everybody would
pinch her 'behind,' just to hear her scream. Anywhere she was, they
just teased her to pieces! Because she reacted. She was just cute as
a button."

April 30, 1953 "The civil defense practice went off much as planned
Friday. To make it more realistic a bomb was exploded at the City
Park, but the direction of the wind prevented the sound being heard by
many in the city. The dynamite was donated by Bill Fipps.

Clarence Stadtler acted as a casualty, and looked the part. He
was rushed to the American Legion room where the nurses had
headquarters. Barber-Barto donated their ambulance service.

At the school, classes were instructed by their teachers what to
do in case of a bomb attack.

The fire department turned out in full force for their run.

A civilian defense meeting was held at the courthouse Tuesday
night where a film on communication was shown. Talks were made by
R.W. Fyan, Clyde Hargus, Warren Beck, Paul Langston and C.E.
Boulson.

It was decided to hold monthly meetings with pictures or
interesting programs each time. It was also decided to promote first aid
instruction for those connected with the civil defense."

....."Our 'Back To God' committee urges each citizen of our
town to display the American flag at his home and his place of business
this Friday *[5/1]* to signify that we are re-dedicating our lives for God
and country....Remember! Godless communism is our country's worst
enemy. 'Back To God' is our greatest hope for a lasting peace."

*[It wasn't until the next year, in 1954, that the U.S. Congress
would add "Under God" to the pledge of allegiance, in further defiance
of "Godless Communism."]*

May 7, 1953 "Congressman Dewey Short notified John Robert
Johnson, son of Mr. and Mrs. Warren Johnson, Tuesday that the local

youth had passed all tests and 'physical,' and has gained his appointment to the U.S. Naval Academy at Annapolis, Md."

May 14, 1953 "The Missouri Supreme Court Monday in Jefferson City upheld a 4-year prison term imposed against Herschel Burks for rape.

Burks was convicted in the Webster County Circuit Court of raping a 15-year-old girl and sentenced Feb. 6, 1952. The Supreme Court concluded the penalty was not too severe as to indicate the jury was prejudiced and ruled the conviction should stand.

He is being held here by Sheriff E.I. Cunningham for the marshal of the Supreme Court."

May 28, 1953 "Magistrate Court notes—May 21—State of Mo. vs. Loren Bledsoe, driving while intoxicated. Defendant arraigned. Defendant requests counsel. Hearing set for June 1. Bond fixed at $2000; commitment ordered....May 25—State of Mo. vs. Loren Bledsoe, careless and reckless driving. Defendant arraigned, opportunity to consult counsel offered and refused; pleas of guilty and fined $50. State of Mo. vs. Loren Bledsoe, driving while intoxicated. Dismissed at cost to defendant."

"Two young colored boys from Memphis, Tenn., were arrested at Thayer last week and returned to Sheriff E.I. Cunningham here. The youths, one 15 and the other [also] 15, had hitchhiked to Springfield, and were starting back to Memphis. When they got as far as Diggins, they are reported to have placed a tie across the rails, in order to stop a train and secure a ride.

Fortunately a freight train came along before a passenger, and ran upon the tie. The train was stopped before any cars were derailed, as the train was not moving fast. The boys got on the train, but were taken off at Thayer.

They said their mothers lived at Memphis, but that they had no fathers, just several brothers and sisters."

"Items From Correspondents...Haymes Chapel—Mary Lou McNabb, daughter of Mr. and Mrs. Ralph McNabb, Marshfield, Route l, and Pvt. Charles [Charley] Cunningham, Ft. Leonard Wood, were married Saturday, May 23, at 4 p.m. at the home of the officiating minister, Rev. Wilford Haymes. Mr. and Mrs. Jake Cunningham of

Marshfield, brother and sister-in-law of the groom, were the only attendants. A wedding trip is planned when Pvt. Cunningham receives his furlough. In the meantime the new Mrs. Cunningham is staying at the home of her parents...."

[During the writing of this book, Charley and Mary Lou celebrated their 50th wedding anniversary.]

June 4, 1953 "Jots From The Editor's Note Pad—...Talking about oleo and milk substitutes—the senior editor and his wife have been married 30 years, as of last month, and in all of these years they have never purchased a pound of oleo, nor had a can of filled milk in their home. They have never had a cow, but realizing the importance of the dairy industry to Webster County years ago, they never have thought it was saving any money to buy substitutes for butter and milk."

"With this issue, The MAIL celebrates its birthday and enters its 62nd year of publication.

The publishers cannot permit this date to pass without again expressing sincere appreciation to all of this newpapers' advertisers, subscribers, newswriters and friends for the co-operation, favors and friendship they have received over the years.

With the help of all its friends The MAIL has grown to be recognized as one of the best rural newspapers in Missouri, and we believe that it makes a good impression on all strangers and newcomers. We feel that this means much in building Webster County.

This issue also carries the announcement of the acquirement of ownership in The MAIL by the third generation of the Watters family. It is the hope of the senior editor that this ownership may go on down through the next generation and even thereafter.

Theron H. Watters became an apprentice on the MAIL force back in the 1890's, soon after this newspaper was started. He became a partner in the business in 1904, and later acquired full ownership. His children succeeded him in the business, and now two of his grandsons are entering into ownership.

They hope for the continued support and assistance of all readers, advertisers, reporters and friends of The MAIL and pledge their best efforts in working for what they believe to be for the best interests of Marshfield and Webster County."

"Sheriff E.I. Cunningham reports the solving of another series of robberies last week, when six youths were found involved. While two of the youths were 17 and 18, two others were 14, and one 13 and one only 4 years old.

Three of the boys were brothers, whose father has been in Indiana for some time, and who mother had apparently left them recently to join her husband. They had been stealing to get something to eat. The younger boys were brought here and placed under the orders of Judge Hawkins of the Circuit Court, who sent them to the county home. The older boys were placed under custody.

Among the articles taken were 4 cases of tomatoes from the Bob Blazor house, 5 quarts of oil said to have been stolen from Roy Fraker, a cut-off saw, tire and wheel from the stave mill, 10 gallons of gas from Elston Shannon, crosscut saw from Blazor's saw yard, axe from Perry Davis, and other canned goods and articles from other places.

The Sheriff, with Homer Alexander and Ellis Brown, had a puncture Tuesday evening of last week and while fixing it, stopped the car with five of the boys in it. The story then came from them as to what they had been doing."

[June 17, 1953 Workers rose in East Berlin, Germany, and Russian tanks mowed them down with machine gun fire.]

June 18, 1953 "Sheriff and Mrs. E.I. Cunningham, Mr. and Mrs. David *[Jake]* Cunningham visited Rockford, Ill., from Friday until Sunday with their son and brother, Wilbur *[Red]* Cunningham. They stopped in St. Louis Sunday evening to visit Mrs. Cunningham's uncle, Len Gray and wife.

The following story from the Rockford Register-Republic tells of an interesting event on the Cunningham's trip:

A spurious deputy sheriff got his comeuppance early today when he stopped the 'real McCoy' on his way to Loves Park from Missouri. Webster County Sheriff E.I. Cunningham of Marshfield, Mo., told Winnebago County authorities of being stopped about 1 a.m. by a man who represented himself as a deputy sheriff from this county. The Sheriff and party were just south of the Winnebago County line, in Ogle County, when they were halted by the self-styled deputy.

When the Missouri Sheriff, now serving his third term, asked for some identification, the stranger fumbled through his wallet, went back to his own car and drove off.

Cunningham noted the license number of the man's car and reported the incident to Winnebago authorities who traced the number.

State motor vehicle records revealed the license issued to a John Lapea, Chicago.

A warrant charging Lapea with impersonating a Winnebago County Sheriff will be issued today by Ogle County authorities on a complaint signed by Cunningham."

[Helen Cunningham] "Well, Jake and I took him. I think it was for a wedding, and we were going to Wilber's. And we were drivin' in the middle of the night, way in the middle of the night, and somebody with a blue light pulled us over. And he started to talkin' to us, and Isam pulled his gun out and laid it on his lap. And when we got on into Wilbur's, he called the police department. The blue light meant nothing! But we didn't know that. But Isam was ready to take care of him if he needed to!

Somebody pretending to be a law officer! He said something about 'hillbillies' and Isam said, 'By God, you're lookin' at one!' That sounds like him, doesn't it. And he had that gun in his lap."

"Plans are continuing for the annual Fourth of July Celebration and Homecoming to be held in Marshfield on The Square. The program committee, John Hosmer, chairman....Roy Miller, local attorney, will act as master of ceremonies at the program."

"Dr. Edward L. Clark, State Geologist, announced the release of four new topographic maps covering an area of approximately 250 square miles in the vicinity of Mansfield in Wright County and adjoining parts of Douglas and Webster counties....These maps cover some of the highest and most rugged parts of the Ozarks...."

"County News...Haymes Chapel—Pvt. And Mrs. Charles Cunningham were honored with a charivari and shower Saturday night, June 6, in the home of Mr. and Mrs. Marvin Updike. After the many gifts were opened and admired, treats were served the following guests:...E.I. Cunningham...."

[Many newlyweds during these times were honored with a charivari/shivaree, as evidenced by newspaper jottings. This one appeared to be very mild!]

June 25, 1953 "The Webster County Court was in session Monday. E.I. Cunningham, Sheriff, requests the County Court to purchase a 2-way radio for his car. The court refused his request.

Comes now Webster County officials and request a fan for each county office. The court refused this request...."

[Cline Herren, Jr.] "That was during the era where the judges wouldn't give Isam a two-way radio. They wouldn't spend the money for a two-way radio! Now if you can imagine that kind of a budget for a sheriff!

One of the judges wanted to take out all the telephones in the courthouse and put one on each floor. (Now, when I'm talking about the county judges, these are the *commissioners* now.) They wanted to take out all the phones and just put one phone on each floor! And they wanted to quit buying that coal. They wanted to take out a glass pane—an atrium—and put a wood stove in there, and everybody keep their own office warm, buy wood. Spur the local economy!

Now, if you could understand the budgetary problems...I don't guess there was any problem at all—you didn't *have* any budget!"

[Mary Lou Cunningham] "I helped there, too, especially when Charley was in the army. I was working in town then and lots of times Isam would ask me to stay and help out. Sometimes on my lunch hour I would go help.

It was always kind of funny. Isam would invite *anyone* to dinner. He didn't care who it was or what they had, he'd invite them to eat. It might even be the President of the United States. Sometimes Evie would say, 'I just don't have enough' so I'd say, 'Oh don't worry about me, I'll just go across the street.' But many times that happened to her. He'd just bring people in. Never a group but just someone who was around town."

"Jots From The Editor's Note Pad---....The last week of Spring which ended Sunday, June 21, set records for heat in Missouri and other parts of the United States. Many Webster County citizens said that the weather in Kansas and Oklahoma had escaped over into the Ozarks, and they wished it would go back home....The official toll of American battle losses in World War II is announced at 1,081,896 casualties, including 294,993 dead....To indicate the Communist strength in the United States one can note the big hullabaloo made at the execution of the two traitors, Ethel and Julius Rosenberg. It took 21 months after their conviction to carry out their execution. Now the communists plan to make martyrs of them. We wonder how long the Rosenbergs would have lasted in Russia had they been caught stealing atomic secrets in that country and sending them to the United States?"

"A new traffic code law will soon go into effect in Missouri, which generally puts Missouri in step with the recommended uniform code for all states.

Some of the features of the new code are: Changing of the arm signals drivers must use. When stopping you extend your arm below horizontal, when turning right you extend it above horizontal and when turning left you extend your arm straight out....The code goes into effect August 29...."

July 2, 1953 "NOTICE. Ordinance No. 19, Sec. 4 of Revised Ordinances of City of Marshfield, prohibits and makes it an offense to shoot firecrackers or fireworks of any kind on the Public Square or within 200 feet thereof. This is in effect at all times and will be enforced on July 4th. R.T. BRIDWELL, Mayor"

[July 4, 1953   Elvis Presley introduces Rock 'n Roll.]

July 9, 1953 "Jots From The Editor's Note Pad—It is reported that Sheriff Cunningham found a good way to solve the firecracker problem in the business section. He made six Boy Scouts deputies, giving them badges, and they handled the situation well. Of course they could not make arrests, but they gave warnings to other boys and they could report to officers any violators."

[Mildred Jarratt] "Now I remember Isam several years back. Friendly enough. But we were of different politics so we weren't with them a lot, you know. But that's all right.

He hated drunks! I remember that. Because he would walk the streets—like the 4th of July, times like that— to get 'em off the streets."

"The total number of passenger cars in use by consumers and business reached 44 million at the end of 1952, 50 per cent more than the previous peak reached in 1941, and almost double the number of cars on the road at the end of the war."

"Circuit Court Proceedings....State of Mo. vs. Ira Hyder, William Blankenship and Howard Davis, felonious assault. ..Application for change of venue on account of bias and prejudice of the inhabitants of Webster County filed and cause sent to Circuit Court of Hickory County...."

"Colonel Hugh H. Waggoner has announced plans to select the additional *[Missouri State Highway]* patrolmen authorized in the bill signed by Governor Phil M. Donnelly. The bill authorizes an increase of twenty-five patrolmen or a maximum of 320 members.... Applicants must be at least 21 years of age and under 33. The minimum height is 5 feet 8 inches without shoes, and the maximum is 6 feet 3 inches. The weight scale is slightly less than three pounds for each inch of height. The physical examination will be very rigid and similar to that for officer candidates in military service. A high school diploma or a certificate of equivalency from the State Department of Education is required. Applicants must also have been residents of the State of Missouri for the past three years...."

July 16, 1953 "Jots From The Editor's Note Pad---Some time back we stated that the Korean War is not over and at present there seems little chance of it being over....There will never be any getting along with the communists either in Russia or in this country. The sad part about it is that we have many pinks and so-called liberals who follow the communist line in this country, and a great uproar is made when Senator McCarthy or any other real American exposes them.

The danger at home is as great as overseas. We must face this fact."

"Oscar L. Carter, superintendent of schools of Webster County for the past 14 years, received notice Monday of his appointment as deputy director, United Savings Bonds Division of the Treasury Department. The appointment was under George Humphrey, Secretary of the Treasury, Washington....His job will be calling banks, industry and schools for U. S. Savings Bonds. The appointment of Mr. Carter's successor will be made by the governor for the unexpired term which ends July 1, 1955. It is reported that N.F. McKinley, Seymour superintendent of schools, has the endorsement of the Democrat Central committee for the appointment...."

"A special legislative committee started the big job of revision of Missouri's probate code Wednesday of last week....The committee agreed to meet monthly, starting August 12, and welcomed the aid of three men, who volunteered to help in the work *[including]* Cline C. Herren of Marshfield, president of the State Probate Judges' Association."

July 23, 1953 "The cafes in Marshfield and vicinity are cooperating with the 'Dairy Day' to be held in Marshfield Saturday, July 25, by featuring the maximum use of milk and milk products in their meals this day....The eating places who are cooperating in this program are as follows: Andrews Café, Marshfield Café, Spur, Joiners, Cross Road Café, Sweet Shop, Webster Hotel Café, Triangle Café, Blue Jay, Dairy Princess, Riggs Café, Illini Court Café."

[Talt Greer] "Probably about 1952 or '53, there was a little café, a motel, out there where the interstate runs now, where Wayne Biggs owns that land and has his horse motel, there was a little restaurant and motel called The Illini. There was five or six of us riding around The Square, looking for something to do. This friend of ours had just got out of the service and had all of his teeth pulled out, had false teeth. We went out to this café and Jim Lichtenberger and his wife ran the café.

Well, we got some old clothes from Jim's wife and we dressed this guy up to look like an old woman. We took him up on The Square and turned him loose up there, you know. We went off and kinda ignored him, let on like we weren't watchin' him.

He sashayed around The Square and then off down South Clay Street.

Isam and two of the highway patrol, they got to wonderin' about this old lady and they started checking, to find out where she went to. And probably about a half hour later they stopped us.

In the meantime we'd taken this guy back out to   Illini Court and took the clothes off. He really did look the part! Thin face, he'd pulled out his false teeth, just a little bonnet over his head.

And Isam asked us, 'Did you see that old lady?' And we said, 'Yeah, we saw her walking around out here but didn't pay much attention to her.'

He said, 'Well, we're trying to find out where she went to.'

We said, 'Well, the last we saw, she was going south down Clay Street there, toward the railroad tracks, and there was a slow train came through. She might have got on that train.'

And they spent quite a bit of time checkin' to see where that old lady came from."

"Jots From The Editor's Note Pad—The purpose of Webster County Dairy Day to be held here Saturday, July 25, is to call attention of everyone to the importance of dairying to this county, and to promote the sale of butter and other dairy products. The economic welfare of this county is built on the dairy industry....Every business firm in the county benefits directly from the sale of merchandise and services to the dairymen and to the employees of the plants handling cream and milk, and manufacturing them....People must be made to realize that the saving of a few cents in buying a substitute is really not a saving in the long run. If local prosperity is destroyed everyone will lose.

All must be made to realize that the prosperity of Webster County is based primarily on the dairy industry."

[Mary Lou Cunningham] "Betty Edwards *[Hyde]* and her sister *[Norma Edwards Bruce]* were in high school when the picture of her dad *[Oral 'Dog' Edwards, left above]* and Isam *[right above]* was taken at the Webster County fair. She thinks it probably was 1953. She said she and her sister were mortified at their dad doing that. She said that Isam was trying to marshal the fair and he got her dad on stage with him at the girlie show."

July 30, 1953 "Members of the Webster County draft board, under suspension from Washington, last Friday charged that 'militarists' in the state draft headquarters tried to make them enforce universal military training.

The board faces dismissal for deferring too many farm youths....John Hosmer, attorney hired by the board, said that until universal military training becomes the law, a draft board should continue to grant deferments justified by the existing law.

.... 'The state wants us to ignore farm deferments here in the largest dairy county in Missouri,' Hosmer said.

...The spokesman of the National Selective Service in Washington...pointed out that the law gives no absolute exemption to anyone but ministers, divinity students, and sole surviving sons....

No word has been received from General Hershey, National Draft Director as to his final decision on the dismissal of the Webster County Selective Service Board,...Atty. John Hosmer, attorney for the majority of the board, states that if the decision is adverse, an appeal will be made to President Eisenhower."

"The Korean War stopped Monday morning *[7/27]* at 7 a.m. our time, after the truce was signed the night before. Thus after 37 bloody months fighting, an uneasy truce, which does not mean peace, is agreed upon.

No public rejoicing or celebration in this country marked the end of fighting as in previous wars fought by the United States, because most people know that it does not end the so called cold war. Most people think it merely as a truce that may end at any time with more fighting in Korea or some other spot.

This is the first war the United States has lost, and at a cost of 25,000 dead, thousands still missing and over one hundred thousand wounded on the battlefields. The cost in money has run into the billions of dollars, and nothing has been decided.

There are those who rejoice—the people with sons, brothers or relatives in Korea that may now serve out their time and come home without being killed. However, the troops will be kept in Korea, the draft will continue and the United States must continue to be an armed camp until such time as the communists may be thrown out of the rule of Russia and China by revolution or other means."

"A large crowd, estimated at over 3500, was in Marshfield Saturday to attend Webster County Dairy Day. The main feature of the day was the longest parade ever held here....It is impossible to estimate the amount of milk, cream, cottage cheese, ice cream and other dairy products sold. Most stores report selling out their entire stock of many of these items....In the parade the rural people outnumbered the town people in making the parade the longest ever staged here...."

"Ellis O. Jackson, Marshfield abstracter, received word late Wednesday morning of his appointment *[by Governor Donnelly]* as Webster County Superintendent of Schools *[to finish the term of Oscar L. Carter]*. ...Jackson has a long background of school experience."

"All six members of the Webster County Selective Service Board 127 have been removed from office for 'failure to follow selective service regulations.' ...The Webster County board had deferred 39 farm boys, eligible for the draft. That meant...that eight percent of Missouri's farm deferments stem from that small rural county...."

August 20, 1953 "A Marshfield man last night spent an hour extricating a wallet from the pocket of a sleeping friend, spent the night in jail for his trouble, but today had his freedom—and his friend.

Officers called to the Union Bus Depot last night were met by employees who reported seeing Arnold E. Clark, 45, of Marshfield, work for about an hour before getting a billfold belonging to a traveling companion, Vern Comstock, 62, also of Marshfield, who was asleep on a bench in the bus station.

Clark readily admitted taking the billfold, which contained $26, and returned it to Comstock when an officer asked him about it.

Clark was booked for investigation, on Comstock's promise that he would return this morning to press charges.

During the night, however, Comstock had a change of heart.

He remembered, Comstock told Assistant Chief Sam Robards, how Clark was such a good neighbor last spring when Comstock was ill; how he cut and carried wood for Comstock.

Reunited in Robards' office, Clark assured his friend he was just keeping the billfold for him because it was about to fall from his pocket while he slept.

Just the same, Comstock warned him to leave his billfold alone from now on.

Clark couldn't find his bus ticket and officers urged Comstock to buy him one.

'No sir,' said Comstock firmly.

As they left the station together, Clark holding the door open for the older man, officers called to Comstock, 'You watch out for Arnold, now.'

'You think I need any caution about that?' asked Comstock.—From Springfield Leader Press, Tuesday, Aug. 18."

"Major Bowers, of the state selective service director's office at Jefferson City, came here Monday and took charge of the county selective service office....Major Bowers is reported to have had new locks placed on the doors of the office.

Up to this Wednesday no announcement has been made of the appointment of new board members to replace the former selective service board who were removed for 'failure to follow selective service regulations.' Four of the six members of the board have appealed to President Eisenhower for a hearing, after being refused a hearing by the national selective service office.

The former board members believe that the state selective service had been ignoring the law in refusing farm deferments in other counties, and believe that the facts should be brought out as to what is the law and how it should be administered."

September 3, 1953 "...The former Webster County board was removed last month for deferring too many farm boys, but when particulars were asked the charges had nothing to do with farm deferments...Among those named to the new board were Layne and Gaupp, both members of the ousted board. However, they were the only two members who did not join in a protest of the boards removal.

All five appointments have been approved by the President, [Col. R. T.] Finks said *[state director of selective service]*.

The four *[remaining ousted]* members who, by Attorney Hosmer, appealed for a hearing by President Eisenhower...thus far *[have]* been ignored."

September 17, 1953 "Four Marshfield youths ruined the truck patch of T.E.Vinyard west of Marshfield on Friday night. The youths raided the watermelon patch and completely ruined it. Tomatoes were also destroyed. The patch, heavily fertilized and tended this summer, was a promising crop for the 70-year-old farmer, when it was destroyed. The boys were watched raiding the patch, having a melon fight, then leaving. Early Saturday morning they were questioned by the Sheriff and Mr. Vinyard, and admitted the destruction. To the boys it may have been fun but to an elderly farmer, who had lost his summer's work and money, it was a heartbreaking situation."

[Willis Case] "Isam drove up down to my house once, was livin' in a big house on Jackson Street. He said, 'Is your son here, Mac Case?' I said yeah. He said, 'Tell him to come out here.' He took him up to the courthouse, him and the Brown boy.

He said to me, 'Old Man Vinyard been here and he said your boys got into his melon patch.'

So me and Ellis Brown went out to see the old man. Ellis Brown was a man run a sawmill. Old Man Vinyard said, to Mr. Brown and me, ' I woulda shot your boys if I could a seen 'em.'

Well, me and Brown told him, 'If you're going to carry a gun, you better have the guts to use it. And don't ever say that to us again.'

So Isam dismissed 'em. Old Man Vinyard wanted to have 'em arrested for tearin' up, for going in the watermelon patch, but Isam dismissed 'em. That's the only time I had a run-in with him in any way about the law.

Some of the people we've had for sheriff have actually helped some young people get through life. Isam was reasonable about some things."

September 24, 1953 "Magistrate Court—Sept. 21—State of Mo., Clarence Calvin Cantrell, citation against E.I. Cunningham; Judge Williard B. Leavitt presiding as special judge heretofore appointed by the Supreme Court of Missouri; John Hosmer appointed friend of the court; motion to dismiss filed and over-ruled; case set for hearing on Oct. 13, as attorneys for E.I. Cunningham desire to file a Writ of Prohibition in Circuit Court."*[This vague legal summary will all be explained soon.]*

[Cline Herren, Jr.] "Isam was told before the appearance in court, before the incident, to put the guy in jail. The problem was, Isam didn't know which one was supposed to be in charge in the court, I guess. *[The Judge or The Prosecutor]*. He *[Cantrell]* was drinking and the family came to take him home to milk. You know, you gotta get the cows milked!"

[Barbara Herren] "One other thing you need to remember: Marshfield was extremely political and politics would have played in this. Because John *[Hosmer]* was such a strong Democrat. You almost drew your line in the sand here on politics. Which side you were on, which your party was, made a difference."

[Mitzi Hosmer] "He was probably a second cousin of John's, this Cantrell. Probably *[John]* bent over backwards because a lot of them needed help. Ellsworth was the prosecutor and had told Isam, just off the cuff, that unless the charges had been filed, he didn't have to bring him to court for bond. Isam had called the prosecutor, *[Ellsworth]* Haymes. Ellsworth did it quickly, but later apologized for giving him the wrong advice.

But Isam was as stubborn as John was stubborn. So Isam would not do it. He would go to jail and stay there forever, because he thought he was right. He had asked Ellsworth. Once Ellsworth told Isam that he couldn't bring him up, he just stayed the course.

And then John always seemed to, liked to tweak Isam. And then, I think Isam at the same time, liked to do things to John. I mean, they just....

At first, John would always say he was a good Sheriff, never afraid to go out, you know. Then it got where it was kinda back and forth. So I think it ended up like a bad note.

John kept getting appointed prosecutor and it kept putting him against Isam."

October 1, 1953 "Dr. Edwin P. Hubble, 63, one of the nation's foremost astronomers and probably Marshfield's most noted son, died Monday *[9/28]* from the effects of a stroke, suffered at his home at San Marino, Calif...."

[from the Webster County Community Guide 2003-2004, presented and published by THE MARSHFIELD MAIL]
    "Marshfield's most famous resident was Edwin Hubble, who was born in a house on Third Street in November 1889. That home has since been torn down with another built in its place.

After graduating from Oxford in 1913 at age 23, Hubble experimented for a brief time as a high school Spanish teacher before giving in to his love for the heavens and signing on as a graduate student at Yerkes Observatory in Wisconsin. That is where Hubble began studying the nebulae that would eventually bring him world-wide fame.

In 1919 he accepted an offer from the prestigious Mount Wilson Observatory. There, Hubble proved that the universe was expanding, thus creating Hubble's Law: 'The farther away a galaxy is from earth, the faster it's racing away.'

This finding disproved an earlier theory by Albert Einstein. In 1931, Einstein visited Hubble to thank him for delivering him from folly.

After proving Einstein's theory incorrect, Hubble received nearly instant notoriety, and became the darling of the Hollywood crowd, befriending Charlie Chaplin, Helen Hayes, and William Randolph Hearst.

In honor of his contributions in the field of astronomy, Time magazine named Hubble as one of the top 100 scientists of the 20th century."

[During the writing of this book, there was concern that NASA didn't have the money to do necessary repairs to the Hubble Telescope, named for Edwin Hubble. A possible solution still remains: to let the Hubble Telescope continue to deteriorate and then blast it farewell, into space.]

December 3, 1953 "Mrs. Icie Mae Pope, instructor at Elkland High School, is one of about 100 Missouri high school counselors invited to attend the second annual invitational conference for counselors being presented at the University of Missouri, Dec. 9 and 10."

December 31, 1953—last issue of paper for the year.

[Sheriff Isam seems to have fallen off the face of the earth. I found nothing involving him in the MARSHFIELD MAIL issues since the September 24th contempt of court citation...and nothing more about it, either. Perhaps Sheriff Isam has been irreparably damaged, like the Hubble Telescope?]

Chapter Fourteen
1954

January 7, 1954 "County Court warrants issued:
E.I. Cunningham, Salary $212.90
Serving 2 notice warrants to Nevada and
mileage $34.00
Dec. expense $19.80
Board bill $305.25
Mileage $63.56"

[Looks as though Isam got a raise in salary.]

"The Mercury car belonging to Mrs. Louise Scott was stolen Sunday night *[1/3]* from beside her apartment on the north side of The Square. She left it there about 11:30, taking the keys out of it, but failing to lock the doors. She discovered it gone Monday morning and reported the loss to officers. Thus far the car has not been located."

January 14, 1954 "The Mercury car belonging to Mrs. Louise Scott, which was stolen from beside her apartment off the north side of The Square the night of January 3, was located Friday afternoon *[1/8]* at Cuba near a shoe factory. It apparently was not damaged. The thief or thieves had driven until it was about out of gas and parked it.

The night watchman at the factory, after seeing the car parked near the plant several days, became suspicious and notified the patrol. Thus the car was located."

"A Chicago welder taking a cross country trip with his wife and daughter was jailed for car theft Saturday after he left a Springfield service station without paying for gas.

Troopers began seeking a gray 1949 Ford club coupe after an attendant at Groves Service Station on Kearney Street complained the driver failed to pay him for about $3 worth of fuel Saturday night. A patrolman and Sheriff E.I. Cunningham halted the vehicle near Marshfield after it had doubled back from west to east, and the driver, Philip Kilan Raulerson, 24, of Chicago, was taken to the county jail here.

He later was transferred to the Greene county jail and his wife, Madeline Mary, was released. The couple had an 8-month-old daughter, Donna Lynn, with them.

Raulerson first claimed he bought the car from a hitchhiker and said he couldn't pay for the gas because he had been robbed in Sherman, Tex. However, a check on the vehicle, which had Texas license plates, disclosed it had been stolen at Bossier City, La.

Raulerson later admitted the theft and signed a waiver of extradition to be returned to Louisiana."

January 21, 1954 "Three youths were caught Friday morning by the Highway Patrol about 5 a.m. as they fled from the Kermit Lowery Café and Station which they had robbed, 7 miles north of Marshfield on Highway 66. They were William Hall, 17, Carl Spencer 18, and Edmond Harvel 18, all of Indianapolis, Ind.

They are held in jail here after waiving preliminary in Magistrate Court for action by the Circuit Court.

Kermit Lowery, owner of the café and station, next to his home on Highway 66, was awakened by the burglar alarm when the youths broke into his place of business. He quickly got his 30-30 rifle and as the boys drove on the highway he shot out one of the headlights.

He jumped into his car without even putting on his shoes and drove to Marshfield to secure the Highway Patrolman. The Patrol Headquarters at Springfield were notified and they started down the highway. They caught up with the wanted car west of Marshfield near the Guy Hyde place.

They found the car contained pennies, candy bars and loose packs of cigarettes which the boys were said to have admitted taking from the café. They also found that the boys had been delayed by driving off the highway and re-packing some of the stolen articles, which had caused a few minutes delay and enabled the patrolmen to catch their car so quickly after leaving Marshfield.

The car has been parked on the south side of the courthouse where it has been viewed by curious folks noting the bullet hole in the front light.

Sheriff Cunningham said he had to loan Mr. Lowery a pair of shoes after he came to Marshfield.

The boys were questioned by Springfield police regarding a glass breakage at a grocery store and service station on Kearney in Springfield. The young men deny any knowledge of the break-ins.

The manner in which Mr. Lowery took care of the robbery of his place of business should deter other such robberies in this county."

January 28, 1954 "Jots From The Editor's Note Pad….The Democrat 'left wingers' continue their campaign to sell this country on a depression, as they want socialism. If we have a depression the blame can be put on them. All signs point to a good year."

February 4, 1954 "A large crowd attended the Rogersville All-School Carnival held Friday, Jan. 29. The gross amount taken in was $877.50. After expenses were deducted, the net amount was $722.25…."

"Rogersville Wildcats played host to Strafford Tuesday, Feb. 2."

"Thieves broke into the Rogersville Schools' office Tuesday night *[2/2]* and took about $500 including about $55 March of Dimes money that had been contributed by the Rogersville school students.

As there was a basketball game at the school Tuesday night it is known that the robbery did not occur until after 11 p.m.

Entry was gained into the building by the breakage of a glass in a basement door. The door to the school's office was pried open with tools. The vault in the office was entered by drilling two holes and breaking the lock.

The highway patrol and Webster County officers were notified Wednesday morning and a deputy sheriff and the patrol made an investigation. The patrol believes that the robbery was done by professionals."

February 11, 1954 "Yellow 'No Passing' lines on Missouri highways, now centered in the driving lane, will be moved to a position four inches to the right of the pavement center stripe in the near future. The new location has been authorized by the State Highway Commission as another cooperative step toward providing uniform marking and signing for vehicle operators. Most other states place 'No Passing' zone lines near the pavement centerline….These yellow lines actually represent a barrier line announcing to a vehicle operator that he is entering a 'no-passing'zone. Such zones are established at hillcrests and on curves where passing must be restricted because of limited sight distance. Their sole purpose is to contribute to highway safety."

February 18, 1954 "The Garbage Can Café, target of thieves before, was rifled again late Saturday night, but the intruders were frightened away before they obtained much.

Webster County Sheriff E.I. Cunningham said a back window at the café, seven miles north of Marshfield on Highway 66, was broken between 11:39 p.m. and midnight Saturday.

Kermit Lowery, owner, who lives across the highway, flushed three youths from the café. When he turned his light on at his home the thieves ran and he did not see their car. They took some cigarettes and a small amount of change from the cash register.

Lowery, who shot a headlight out of a getaway car previously, didn't fire a shot this time and the thieves, unlike the other group—got away."

February 25, 1954 "Boy Scouts, this Friday and Saturday, will deliver envelopes to the homes of Marshfield. On these envelopes are printed some of the reasons why Marshfield should purchase and have the protection of a resuscitator. Fire Chief Clyde Hargus has stated the cost of the machine is $715."

March 4, 1954 "The people of this nation and the world were shocked Monday by the wild gunfire from guns of four Puerto Rican fanatics in the House of Representatives at Washington, D.C. Five Congressmen were shot....

The four assailants claimed to be connected with the group wanting independence for Puerto Rico, but Communist literature has been found in the apartment of one of them. They were in the gallery of the House of Representatives, when, without warning, they began pouring bullets into the floor where about 250 Congressmen were carrying on proceedings....

This attack is unprecedented, as nothing like this has ever happened before. Previously, visitors were warned against taking cameras either into the House or Senate, but there was no safeguard against concealed weapons. Steps are being taken to have tighter security regulations.

This group of terrorists is believed to be of the same group that made an attempt on the life of former President Truman. They represent a small group of Puerto Ricans, as all votes taken there for independence from the United State have shown that the vast majority in that country do not want independence, but want statehood status."

[During the writing of this book, terrorist attacks are considered the new type of war throughout the world. Security regulations are still being revised, especially in our nation's airports and large cities, since September 11, 2001.]

"The Annual Kite Flying Contest sponsored by the Barber-Barto Funeral Home will be held Sunday, April 4, weather permitting. Prizes will be awarded again this year and full details will be given in a later issue."

"Matters Before the Magistrate Court—February 26, 1954—State of Mo. vs. Clarence Calvin Cantrell, citation against E. I. Cunningham. Special prosecutor appointed."

"The third annual Independent Basketball tournament for over-age and exhausted former stars begins tonight, Wednesday, at the high school gymnasium here.

An added attraction this year is the first annual girls' independent tourney. These teams, four of them, will play men's rules....

Referees for the tourney will be Charles (Whistletooter) Hyde, Mac (Blind) Case and Chuck (Shorty) Robertson. The tournaments are being sponsored by the Marshfield Jaycees and proceeds will be donated to the school building fund."

"The State Historical Society of Missouri for the 17th straight year has the largest membership among state historical societies in the United States....Of the 6,000 members living in Missouri, St. Louis ranks first with 858, Kansas City second with 623, and Columbia third with 282."

March 11, 1954 "The case of Sheriff E.I. Cunningham of Webster County, who is seeking a temporary writ of prohibition to prevent Magistrate Judge Willard Leavitt of Polk County from proceeding with a contempt of court action against him, was argued in the Springfield Court of Appeals last Wednesday.

John Hosmer of Marshfield is special attorney for the state and Cunningham's attorneys are Roy C. Miller and Marion *[M.J.]* Huffman.

The case is an outgrowth of the Sheriff's refusal to take a prisoner into court before Judge Herren, sitting as a special magistrate, because according to Cunningham, there wasn't a warrant for the man's arrest.

Miller argued that Sheriff Cunningham believed he should not take the prisoner into court until a charge was filed. Hosmer contended that the Sheriff as an officer of the court could not fail to obey the court without showing contempt.

Among the entanglements of the case was the allegation that Hosmer had been contacted to serve as attorney for the prisoner.

After the hearing, at which Sheriff Cunningham was present, the appellate judges took the matter under advisement."

["Taking under advisement" means the judge isn't ready to give the decision at that time.]

[Cline Herren, Jr.] "I was still in high school, but there was a conflict there in the court. The family came in to get this *[Cantrell]* guy out of jail so he could go home and milk his cows, and I think Dad just called up on the phone and told Isam to let him out. Come down, do bail, whatever. And Isam refused to do it. And after that day was over, it was a bad day for everybody, because Isam had refused to do it, and so the judge held him in contempt of court. But he would not go ahead, as he could have, and would not hear the contempt charge.*[Judge Herren recused.]*

But when this was all over, actually, the prosecutor had told Isam not to let him out of jail. It was something that never should have happened, probably. But Isam did not know which one he should have answered to.

It became a circus. There was several of the churches in Marshfield had a caravan to Jefferson City. I don't know who you see in Jefferson City whenever you want to change a law, but it was headed up by churches. People went to Jefferson City to protest that the Sheriff had been held in contempt of court. Isam had a lot of people that liked him, and followed him. So it was not a good time. It was not a good time for Isam. It was not a good time for Dad. It was one of those things that happened, but it happened.

I went up and sat in on the thing when the judge heard that contempt case and he was another Magistrate and I think he was from Buffalo, I'd don't know. But it was kinda neat: he sat there sideways in the chair behind the bench, rolled cigarettes and smoked them the whole time. My dad recused. The judge was a little skinny white-haired guy. He never missed a word, I don't think.

Actually, that was one of the darker times and it caused a lot of hard feelings. But I think they still got along, because Dad would compliment the things that Isam would do, at home."

[Barbara Herren] "People had their opinions. Cline's mother had a club, and they made some comment, and she just got up and went home. She and Jo Shields were best friends and either Jo said something or...well, we called it psoriasis club but it's Sorosis Club. It's actually a national sorority. But there was kind of a split opinion on this, and rather than argue about it, Audrey [Herren] got up and went home and didn't go for two or three months, or something. Now *she* told me that. Everybody had an opinion and it was a strong one."

March 4, 1954 *Springfield Leader-Press*: "The case of the self-assured sheriff—Webster County's colorful Isom Cunningham, who defied a judge—was heard in Springfield Court of Appeals today, embellished by sallies of homespun wit.

Cunningham, a stalwart character who has gained much of his colorful reputation because of his vocabulary, is seeking a temporary writ of prohibition in appellate court to prevent Magistrate Judge Willard Leavitt of Polk County from proceeding with contempt of court proceedings against him.

The court took the case under advisement at 12:30 p.m. During its often-interrupted hearing, the sheriff, usually a man of many words, sat quietly in the courtroom, whittling on his nails with a huge pocketknife.

The contempt proceedings were brought against him last summer when Sheriff Cunningham infuriated Webster County Magistrate Cline C. Herren by refusing to bring a prisoner who was in jail, into magistrate court.

Attorney John Hosmer of Marshfield, special attorney for the state, acted out the little drama which occurred between Cunningham and Judge Herren in court here today. According to Hosmer, it went like this:

Judge Herren: 'Bring the prisoner into court.'

Sheriff Cunningham: 'I am not going to bring him down. There is no warrant for his arrest.'

Judge Herren: 'You don't need a warrant. The man is entitled to make bond and you ought to know it. So bring him down.'

Sheriff Cunningham: 'I am not going to bring him down.'

Judge Herren: 'Isom, that is an order of the court. Bring him down.'

Sheriff Cunningham: 'I am not going to bring him down.'

At this point Sheriff Cunningham, said Hosmer, walked out of court before contempt charges could be brought against him summarily.

Although Hosmer and the sheriff's two attorneys, Roy C. Miller and Marion Huffman, agreed that these were the facts which started the contempt charges, they violently disagreed as to who was right.

It was Hosmer's position that the sheriff, an officer of the court, could not fail to obey the court without showing contempt. Hosmer was also further entangled in the case because he had allegedly been contacted to serve as attorney for the prisoner, whom Cunningham refused to bring into the court to make bail.

It was the sheriff's position that the persons held in jail should make the request to be brought into court—and that there was no such request made. Furthermore, said attorney Miller, no one had told the sheriff that the prisoner wanted to make bail, and no one had informed him that Hosmer had come to see about making it.

When the magistrate ordered the sheriff to bring the prisoner down, the sheriff believed he should not do so until there was a charge filed, said Miller."*[Isam's name often was misspelled as Isom.]*

"Last week the plants which had been ordered from the Conservation Commission during the past winter were delivered to the extension office for distribution to the purchasers. Orders placed this year were heavy, particularly for the multiflora rose plants...."

"Classified Ads—LOST—One Sheep-Lined Air Force flying boot. If found phone 166 or 499W, Marshfield."

March 18, 1954 "A week ago Sunday night two robberies were reported in Seymour. The White Department Store in Seymour was broken into and more the $700 in merchandise was taken. Entry was gained by breaking through a rear door. An attempt was made to open a safe, but the thieves were unable to get into it. The combination was broken off. $40 to $50 worth of cigarettes and about $666 in other merchandise was taken.

The Seymour school building was robbed the same night. Entry was gained by breaking a window and prying the door open to the office. About $200 was taken from a locker in the office.

A week ago Friday night the Fordland Farmers Exchange was robbed again. Entry was made at the rear of the building. About $500 in merchandise was taken according to E.I. Cunningham, Sheriff.

The Marshfield Frisco Depot was broken into Tuesday night of last week, but it has not been determined if anything was taken.

Webster County officers are working on these robberies."

"Jots From The Editors Note Pad—It appears that 1954 may be the best business year in the history of this country—much to the consternation of those who have been prophets of gloom since the Republicans won the last election....

Editor and Mrs. T. Ballard Watters are on an extended trip through the Southland. They are viewing the historic and scenic wonders of Tennessee, Georgia and Florida.

The editor and Mrs. will undoubtedly see many wonderful things to talk about, but all-in-all the Ozarks contain the most beautiful country in the world."

"Mr. and Mrs. John Andrews, Jr., have sold the Sweet Shop in a deal completed last week. Miss Shirley Burchfield is the new owner."

March 25, 1954 "The Marshfield P.T.A. will present a minstrel show, the 'Dark Town Strutters' this Friday night, March 26.

The highly entertaining show will be held at the high school gymnasium with curtain time at 8:00 p.m.

Members of the black-face cast, all local talent, will be announced at the show...."

April 1, 1954 "Burglars broke into the MFA Exchange at Grovespring Monday night and drilled two holes into the safe, knocked the knob off, but failed to open it."

April 8, 1954 "Warren Beck of the Beck's Milky Way Dairy, was elected mayor of Marshfield Tuesday to succeed Ralph E. Bridwell. The vote was 90 to 63, which is a small percentage of the total number of voters...."

"Everett McNealy was elected mayor of Seymour Tuesday at the city election.

Unopposed for the post of [Seymour] city marshal was 'Pistol' Bill Silvey...."

April 15, 1954 "Mrs. E.I. Cunningham and son Charles and Mrs. Charles *[Charley and Mary Lou]* Cunningham, returned Monday from Rockford, Ill., where they had been on a few days' visit with their son and brother, Wilbur *[Red]* Cunningham and family. Mrs. Cunningham was getting acquainted with a new grandson, Dennis, born to Mr. and Mrs. Wilbur Cunningham five weeks ago.

Charles *[Charley]* Cunningham, who has been at Fort Leonard Wood, is leaving shortly on foreign assignment."

April 29, 1954 "...John Hosmer, program chairman *[of the Webster County Historical Society, at its second annual meeting at Andrews Cafe]* introduced panel members for the discussion of holding a Webster County Centennial;...The matter of growing beards and wearing old-time costumes, methods of securing historical data for the history, securing someone to write the history, whether the centennial should be held on March 3, the actual date of the organization of Webster County or later in the year, 1955, when weather might be more suitable, and many other items were discussed....It was decided that the Webster County Historical Society call a general mass meeting of people from all parts of the county....Atty. Hosmer called attention to the fact that dues of $1 per year are now due."

May 13, 1954 "An estimated 100 persons paid their respects to Mr. and Mrs. K. K. Kelley at their home in Fordland Sunday afternoon on the occasion of their 50th wedding anniversary. Friends were noted from Springfield, Ozark, Rogersville, Seymour, Marshfield, Fordland, and surrounding territory...."

[This suggests that the Webster County Coroner, K.K. Kelley, must have been around 70 years old. On May 28th, Ole Isam was about to turn 63 years old.]

"....Every person, man or woman, interested in celebrating the 100th anniversary of the founding of Webster County is urged to attend the mass meeting...to be held at the courthouse in Marshfield, due to its central location, starting at 7:30 p.m. June 11. If it is decided that the people of the county are really interested in holding a Centennial celebration, an organization will be perfected to take charge and arrange for the big event...."

"Cline Champion Herren, Jr., left Monday for the induction center in Kansas City. Three men will be sent for their physical examination May 24, two for physicals on June 1, and four men will be sent for induction June 28."

[Cline Herren, Jr.] "I was in the army from '54 to '56. I went to Europe. I went in, in May of '54.

Whenever I was in Germany, my dad would roll up *The MARSHFIELD MAIL,* after he got through with it, and send it to me. And where I was, there was a bunch of city boys there, and they kinda made fun of my news items anyway, so what I was doing, I was reading the *25 years ago* column and made it sound like it just happened."

"Thieves have been active around this section the past week. On Friday night thieves pried a lock off a side door of the McShane Service station, junction of Conway spur and Highway 66, and took six or seven hundred dollars worth of merchandise, including a car radio, table radio, two electric irons, 24 cartons of cigarettes, two dozen sun glasses and $5 in change.

Saturday night burglars broke in a back door of the Earl Ellis Service station at Seymour and took about $400 worth of tires, cigarettes, cigars, etc.

Also on Saturday night thieves broke a window at the Fordland Farmers Exchange and stole several pounds of coffee, electric fans, .22 shells and shotgun shells.

Over the weekend, safe burglars broke in and damaged the heavy aluminum doors at the Se-Ma-No *[Semour-Mansfield-Norwood]* Electric Co-op office at Mansfield. They then drilled holes beside the combination to open a cabinet-type safe from which $87.50 was stolen."

[May 17, 1954   The U.S. Supreme Court ruled in the Brown vs. Board of Education case—from Topeka, Kansas— that segregation in public schools is unconstitutional.]

May 20, 1954 "The highway patrolman residing at Lebanon arrested Robert Oliver Highland and recovered a car stolen in California on the highway Sunday. He stated he was going east in the car. The man was brought here because of lack of jail facilities at Lebanon.

Sheriff Cunningham states that Highland was released to U.S. Marshal Mosby and taken to Springfield where he will face charges in federal court."

"Arrests have been made in connection with the robbery of the Earl Ellis Service Station at Seymour recently. The sheriff of Jasper county arrested three persons at Carthage and they were brought here by Sheriff E.I. Cunningham under charges of burglary and larceny. Lloyd W. Eslinger was brought here May 13 by Sheriff Cunningham and on May 15 he brought Mrs. Edith Eslinger and Charley Leo Mitchell from Carthage. It is reported that some of the stolen goods were found at the Eslinger home and have been identified."

[Elzie Doyle will receive $39.20 next month for salary as deputy whenever a female prisoner is in jail, such as the above instance, or when females serve on a jury. She continues her job in the courthouse office of Farmers Mutual Insurance Company.]

May 27, 1954 "Russell Barber has acquired the interest of Mrs. Mary Barto in the Barber-Barto Funeral Home here, in a deal completed recently. The firm is now going under the name of the Barber Funeral Home.

Oral *[Dog]* Edwards will continue as manager and he states that there will be no change in the other personnel of the business here."

[Mary Lou Cunningham] "About 'Dog' *[Oral]* Edwards. When he was a young athlete he ran around the bases so fast, like a dog, that they nicknamed him 'Dog' while he was at Lebanon, and since he played against some from Marshfield, the name stayed with him when he moved here."

June 3, 1954 "...It was voted to hold the *[Marshfield High School Annual]* Alumni Banquet hereafter the Saturday night before Mother's Day each year, which will make it fall on a certain date thus enabling all graduates of MHS to plan ahead to attend...."

"Sheriff E.I. Cunningham took Eugene Stokes to the state penitentiary to begin serving a two-year term and Bobby Stogsdill to the Intermediate Reformatory at Algoa to begin serving four years in sentences for burglary and larceny."

June 10, 1954 "An international civil defense exercise will be held June 1 and 15, with all 48 states, U.S. territories and possessions and Canada participating, starting at 9 a.m. Monday, continuing for 24 hours. Simulated attacks are expected to be made on large cities.

According to R. W. Fyan, head of the local civil defense, participation here will be to open headquarters and be in readiness for contact by the State Control Center by some means of communication."

"Pfc. Charles *[Charley]* Cunningham writes his wife, Mary Lou (McNabb), that he has been stationed at Orleans, France with the Military Police company. He has been assigned to a baseball team, and will tour Germany and other countries."

[Mary Lou Cunningham] "Isam always liked his family so much, you know. When Charley went in service, I stayed with Isam and Eva once in a while. But I worked in the basement of the courthouse. *[in the ASCS office—Agricultural Stabilization Conservation Service]*

Every day Isam would go get the mail. If I had a letter from Charley, he would bring it to me, but he would stand over my shoulder—*he wanted to know what that letter said*—until I read that letter. He wanted to read that letter. And I've often thought about that. There was *no personal thing there.* When Charley would call, I'd *tell* him.

But it's because *[Isam]* was so excited. And the tears would roll down his face, you know, when he was reading these letters from Orleans, France, from Charley.

I always thought that was pretty neat that he wanted to be a part of that letter.

He didn't ask if he could read it, he just stood there.

I just think that was cute. *Now.*

At the time I wasn't too sure."

[Because Mary Lou lived with her parents in the country, while Charley was in the service, and they didn't receive their mail until 6 p.m or so, Charley sent her letters to Isam's post office box so she would get them sooner.]

[Todd Cunningham] "The men in my family are very emotional. They cry easily. It's true of my dad *[Charley]*, of Jake. What I've heard about my grandfather *[Isam]*, he didn't care what people thought. He was just himself."

[Board bill from Isam to the County Court this month is $554.40.

The jail seems to be full-to-overflowing most of the time now.]

June 17, 1954 "Sheriff E.I. Cunningham and Tom Nunn went to Harrison, Ark., Tuesday to bring Marvin 'Buck' Riley to the Webster County jail for appearance before Judge James P. Hawkins this Wednesday morning. He was brought back under forfeiture of his bond."

"Citizens from all the towns of the county, except Diggins, representing a great many organizations, were present at the mass meeting last Friday night at the courthouse....It was voted that Webster County hold a Centennial observance about the middle of 1955.....It was voted to elect a central or executive committee with one man and one woman from each town in the county...."

June 24, 1954 "News of our men in the service: Pfc. Don Letterman and Pfc. Charles Vestal, cousins and classmates, are now stationed in the same camp in Seoul, Korea."

July 1, 1954 "Several highway patrolmen, U.S. marshals, sheriffs and deputy sheriffs, assisted by a Seymour airman and a pack of coon dogs, worked together to capture two escapees from the Ava jail Saturday. The jail breakers were Robert Rhys Johns, 17, of New York state, and Robert Belton McCutcheon, 18, of Oklahoma City.

The youths fled from the jail Friday on foot and that night broke into a farm house about 1 1/2 miles northeast of Ava and took a .22 rifle and $6.50 in pennies.

About noon Saturday Fred Hosiner and men assisting him in cutting oats at his farm, Scott Kasliske, Johnny Todd and George Hosiner, saw the men come out of the brush. Fred followed them and saw them go through the fields and into a wooded area, while the other men notified officers.

Harold Owen, who operates a flying service at Seymour, took to the air for a search and soon located them. He flew in circles around the pair and then over the officers, to lead them. Paul Drybread, on whose farm the capture was made, turned loose his coon dogs, which the escaped youths thought were bloodhounds.

As the officers and the dogs advanced, the young men ran out of the woods and surrendered. They were taken back to the Douglas county jail.

The youths were being held for the FBI on charges of interstate transportation of a car stolen in Oklahoma City.

Officers assisting in the capture were: Sgt. Earl Barkley, Mt. Grove; Sgt. Warren Wallis, Springfield; Trooper Luke Holman of Ava; Trooper Don Turpin of Marshfield; Trooper F.E. *[Tony]* Stephens of Springfield, all of the Highway Patrol; W.E. Smith, Springfield; Sheriff E.I. Cunningham, Marshfield; Nightwatchman Harold Bakeman and Deputy Sheriff Lon Baker of Mansfield; C.W. Raines and Hal Onstott, U. S. Marshals, Joplin; Sheriff Prock and Deputy Gibbons of Ava; Ellis Davis and City Marshal Bill Silvey of Seymour."

[Highway Patrolman Tony Stephens] "There's   Isam Cunningham, me, and them two guys who escaped from the Douglas County jail. Don't remember their names. Over at Ava. Warren Wallis is back there, on the back row, another highway patrolman. You can just see his head. There's Bill Smith, there, to my right. Don't remember anyone else in the picture. Hell, they all gathered around for the picture! Just me and Isam caught 'em! Don't remember what year, early 50's. Just south of Seymour." *[photo courtesy of Tony Stephens]*

"Sunday, the sheriff at Buffalo was called and notified that a man was breaking into a house in Dallas County. The sheriff went to the place and found Ralph McNabb sitting on the porch. No one else was home.

McNabb ran and the sheriff overtook him in a cornfield and took a .38 gun and a knife from him. He was taken to the jail in Buffalo and turned over to Sheriff E.I. Cunningham Monday afternoon.

According to the Sheriff, Mr. McNabb had a blue army bag which was also searched. In it were found two $1,000 government bonds, two $100 government bonds, one $50 and one $25 government bond, five $500 postal savings bonds, five cents in money, and 43 government checks made out to him for $49.44 each which he had never cashed.

Sheriff Cunningham says that McNabb was shell-shocked in World War I, but after his release from the army it was thought he had recovered and he was appointed mail carrier at Elkland. He held this position for several years. However, about 15 or 18 years ago he apparently suffered a relapse, as he became a recluse. He never appeared in town any more and lived in a run-down place. When taken into custody he was dirty and his clothes were in tatters. His brother is said to have taken him food every week.

He is being held pending sanity hearing."

"A week ago Monday, Sheriff E.I. Cunningham was called to the Loren Kleier farm northeast of Seymour. He, with Deputy Ellis Davis and Sam Oxenreider, went down through the place and found a heifer that had been shot between the eyes that morning.

They went on and found Lloyd Manning, stepson of Oxenreider, about 40 yards from another heifer that had been freshly shot. Davis asked the young man for the .22 rifle he was carrying and then handed the gun back to him, after taking the shells out of it. The man loaded the gun again. The Sheriff asked for the gun, unloaded it and took the firing mechanism. Then the fight began. The Sheriff said it took an hour or more to subdue Manning.

Manning was taken to a doctor in Seymour, given a shot, and then placed in jail here."

[Warren Beck] "I was head of the 4th of July parade committee different times, and parade chairman. Every time during those 10 years or so he was Sheriff, you could count on him leadin' the parade, ridin' his horse carrying the American flag. And someone carried the Christian flag.

He was a big man so he demanded respect. Fourth of Julys, he roamed around through the crowd and you could see him head and shoulders above everybody else. Kept good order.

He was gruff, large, had the voice that went along with a large person."

July 15, 1954 "Mayor Warren Beck was prepared to preside at police court Monday, as Police Judge C. Tower had disqualified himself in the case on the docket Monday. The preparations of the mayor to assume the bench for the day were in vain; the defendant failed to appear."

[Police Judge is now called City Judge. The mayor still is next in line for this important law enforcement position.]

"Two Hammond, Indiana, youths were arrested Saturday by Patrolman Turpin, on charges of stealing a 1948 Ford belonging to Cletus Junior Cozark of Hammond on Thursday before. Raymond Nels Kempe, 17, and Elmer Charles Gregory, 17, were placed in custody of Sheriff Cunningham here.

Sheriff Cunningham says the youths admit the theft and he has received a telegram from Chief Martinsen, Hammond police chief, to hold the lads until they come for them. He said the Sheriff would also be contacted by the FBI. The Sheriff says the youths escaped the Indiana Boys School."

"June set a poor record in Webster County for traffic accidents, deaths and injuries in traffic accidents, according to the Missouri State Highway Patrol....June, with three deaths, marked up more deaths than the previous five months, in which a total of two deaths were caused by traffic accidents....The cause of the accidents in June, according to the Patrol, were as follows: 1 excessive speed, 1 following too closely, 2 on wrong side of road (not passing), 1 failure to signal, and 1 inattention or asleep."

July 22, 1954 "The record high for heat was registered here last Wednesday with a reading of 110 degrees at the Sho-Me plant. Old timers said it was the hottest they had ever seen, and broke the Springfield weather station records.

The tabulation by the Sho-Me Power Corporation shows that the temperatures reached 108 again on Sunday and has stayed all week above the 100 mark.

The continued drought and searing heat makes a dismal picture for grass, corn and other crops. But one of the worst features is the failure of springs, wells and other water supplies. Many farmers are hauling water for their stock. The heat has killed many chickens and even the birds are dying.

How long the conditions will continue is not known but it is hoped that a break may come soon. It is not too late for pasture growth if rain comes before too long."

[As of the writing of this book, these July 1954 record high temperatures still have not been broken. And no air-conditioning back then.]

July 29, 1954 "The people of Webster County are not whipped by the devastating three-year drought. Some of them thought about calling off the 17th Annual Webster County Fair because of the effects of the searing heat and lack of rain. However, at a meeting early this week, attended by farmers and businessmen of the county, it was decided unanimously to go ahead with plans for the fair and a Webster County Dairy Day. It was agreed by those present that the people of the County must learn to live with the drought....

According to Robert W. Fyan, president of the Webster County Fair Board, 'Webster County, the second largest dairy county in the state, can not afford to let down in the face of this calamitous drought. The 17th Annual Webster County Fair and Webster County Dairy Day will be bigger than ever before. And we kinda hope it rains us out,' said Fyan with a grin."

August 5, 1954 "President Eisenhower has designated 76 counties in Missouri as a disaster area due to the drought. Included are all counties in southwest Missouri, except Howell County, which has had rains when other sections did not...."

August 19, 1954 "A fire occurred about 5 a.m. Saturday morning at the home of Ralph Woofter on the west edge of Marshfield. No one was in the house at the time and there was no apparent reason for the fire to start.

Mr. Woofter has not been seen by anyone in Marshfield since the fire although Sheriff Cunningham has had a bulletin put on the radio. Mr. Woofter was visiting his six-year-old daughter in Springfield last Thursday and was seen in Marshfield on Friday afternoon at his home. Another report says he was near Phillipsburg a little after midnight and had commented that he could not sleep and was driving around. Anyone knowing the whereabouts of Mr. Woofter should contact Sheriff Cunningham at Marshfield.

An investigation of the fire was made by Fire Chief Clyde Hargus, Sheriff Cunningham and the Highway Patrol. The cause of the fire has not been determined. The fire started below the floor in the basement. The house was closed and the fire was contained in only two rooms. The heat and smoke damage was considerable. All the paint was blistered, and most clothing, drapes and furniture were damaged by the smoke.

A mystery surrounds the fire concerning the telephone; the phone was off the hook when firemen managed to get into the room. Sheriff Cunningham said it had been off the hook about 40 minutes when the alarm was turned in. Cunningham also stated the phone was in working order after the fire."

"Marion Jesse Huffman, 47-year-old Hartville attorney, sometimes called the political 'boss' of Wright county, was indicted for illegal possession of ballots by a grand jury at Hartville Tuesday afternoon along with three other prominent county Republicans—two of them county officials.

The two-weeks-old Wright County Grand Jury, ordered by Circuit Judge Joe Crain of Ozark, brought in all of the indictments for illegal possession of ballots, Garner Moody, county Prosecuting Attorney, said Tuesday night. John Pryor, Mountain Grove, is jury foreman. The jury reconvened Tuesday.

Indictments were brought against Huffman, Frank Little, Norwood, clerk of the Wright County Court; E. L. (Mooney) Colton, Hartville, county magistrate-probate judge and Chester Coday, a party worker and farmer in the Hartville area, according to Moody.

A complaint also was brought by the grand jury against Howard Coday of the Hartville area. The complaint was filed by the Wright County Prosecutor and charges Coday with illegal possession of ballots, according to Moody.

The five men were released on $2000 bond each and their trials will be scheduled for the October term of circuit court, Moody said.

Moody said the indictments are a result of the 1952 county primary election campaign. In the primary, Chester Coday was defeated for the post of committeeman from Hart Township. Howard Coday opposed Little in the primary for the circuit clerk post and was defeated by about 500 votes."

August 26, 1954 "The mystery of the disappearance of Ralph Woofter, after the fire at his home, remains unsolved. The Missouri Highway Patrol is on the lookout for Mr. Woofter. He was last known to be driving a 1951 or 1952 Chevrolet pick-up with his name imprinted on the left-hand side of the truck bed. Anyone knowing his whereabouts or has information that might locate Mr. Woofter should contact Sheriff Cunningham at Marshfield. No new information as to how the fire started has been discovered."

September 2, 1954 "Mac Case of the Marshfield Future Farmers of America is pictured with his Grand champion Jersey cow in both the Junior and Open shows at the State Fair at Sedalia...*[He will be]* showing in the Webster County Fair this Friday which promises to be a very good dairy cattle show."

"Mr. and Mrs. Wilbur *[Red]* Cunningham and children, Gail and Dennis, returned to their home at Rockford, Ill., Friday night of last week after spending a week with his parents, Sheriff and Mrs. E.I. Cunningham, and other relatives and friends."

[Gail Woody] "I was told that my grandfather was very proud of me, as I was the first grandchild born with the Cunningham name and my brother the first boy born with the Cunningham name.

I was only 3 when my grandfather died...The only memory I have is from the fall of 1954. I remember my small hand being held by a much larger hand, attached to a very large man. I was very happy. We were walking down some granite or marble steps. At the bottom of the steps was a large gumball machine. In my memory it must have been a foot or more in diameter. My grandfather bought me a gumball. I was so excited and happy. (My mom says it was probably the first gumball I'd ever had.)

Then I was picked up, held in the left arm way up high. Then we went out the doors to the outside.

I assume the building was the courthouse. I know I had the feeling of happiness and was not fearful of anything. I remember a booming voice talking to me, but not the words.

The gumball machine was like a magnet, drawing my eye, and the thought of getting something from it was thrilling."

September 9, 1954 "The Springfield Court of Appeals handed down a decision September 7 in favor of the court and against Sheriff E.I.

Cunningham. In denying the Sheriff's writ of prohibition, the Court said: 'Under the Supreme Court rule the Defendant Cantrell was entitled to make bond before the Judge of the Magistrate Court in Webster County, even though there had been no charge filed in any court.

'The Prosecuting Attorney who advised the realtor as to the law was mistaken. However, it is no defense for the Sheriff to say that he was mistaken as to the law. He is an officer of the court and it is his duty to obey the order of the court and his failure to do so impaired the respect due to its authority.

'The Sheriff in this instance tried to inform himself by phoning the Prosecuting Attorney to learn whether Cantrell was entitled to bond before a charge was filed. He was misinformed, but acted upon the advice. However, this is no justification for an officer of the court to refuse to obey the orders of the court.'

The decision was written by James C. McDowell, presiding judge. Attorneys for the Sheriff were M.J. Huffman of Hartville and Roy C. Miller. John Hosmer was attorney for the court."

"Henrietta Davis, colored, was brought here from Lebanon Saturday and placed in the custody of Sheriff E.I. Cunningham in the Webster County jail. She was convicted in the police court at Lebanon on charges of careless and reckless driving under the influence of alcohol. She was fined $250 and in default of payment of fine, sentenced to 90 days in jail."

September 16, 1954 "Jots From The Editor's Note Pad—A feature story by Joe Clayton concerning Sheriff E.I. Cunningham appeared in the *Springfield News & Leader* Sunday *[9/12]*, under the heading 'Webster County Sheriff Most Colorful in Ozarks, Good Old Isam: He's One in a Hundred.'

The article called Mr. Cunningham Mr. Law in the Ozarks, and told of his various experiences in the ten years he had been in office in bringing lawbreakers to justice. It also told of his mementos collected in his years of law enforcement and gave many of the events of his life.

Due to the length of the article The MAIL is not reprinting it, but as most people get the Springfield paper or can borrow it, the reprinting should not be necessary. The publishers offer congratulations to the Sheriff on this recognition."

[See Chapter One in this book for the entire feature story as it appeared in 1954. The photo is on this book's first page and dust jacket front . Reprinted with permission from Springfield News-Leader.]

[Cline Herren, Jr.] "I happened to actually have been in the courtroom on some occasions because we lived out in the country and Dad was crippled and so I'd come up and ride home with him after school. A lot of times I'd come in on some very interesting court deal going on. But I actually think Isam did a Herculean job. He measured up to the job that was for one or two people. And, you know, he'd deputize the Town Marshals, this sort of thing. But basically he was The Law. And he was the one they called and he was the one they expected to find people.

Isam would go out by himself, middle of the night. I don't think he was afraid of anything. And he would show up at times when people wouldn't expect anybody to catch them.

He went through some ordeals. Duke Petty robbing the Seymour Bank, the Essary killings up north of the county, the Mary Margaret Evans-Rainey thing, there was a lot of things that happened that were very unsavory, and as far as I know he did everything the way he should have.

He was good at catching people coming through, like a sixth sense. He could meet a car at night and, looking at the headlights, turn around and go back and stop them and arrest some feller. For some reason or another, Isam had that ability, he would catch people just passing through, and he wasn't out on the highway hardly at all, he had enough other stuff to do, but he was kind of unusual. If you realize the size of the county and you realize how much orneriness went on in certain areas of the county, and so forth, being Sheriff on the budget they were *[given]*...."

[Mary Bean Cunningham] "We lived next door to where we currently live *[in Springfield]* for a number of years, and I used to raise tulips. And, you know, they bloom onest a year. And if Evie and Isam come to see us or come to eat, he would pull a tulip and when I got to the door, he'd say, 'I brought you a flower!' Sometimes I could have...'cause, you know, they only bloom onest! But you knew what he was gonna do if they were in bloom! He was good. He was good.

Isam liked to come to my house. I tried to please him when they'd come in, and fix what he liked. He liked to come to my house because I made cherry pies and I used 'the bright red cherries.' And Grandma Evie couldn't stand it. She had to tell him I put red food color in there to make them red. And that's why he liked my cherry pie!

And he liked my baked sweet potatoes. I pre-cooked them, sliced them, and put them in the oven with some sugar and maybe some cream. But I don't remember the rest of how I made them.

And he did *not* like cooked onions! You know, like you have liver and onions, or onions on steak. No way. He would eat an onion, but don't ya cook it! One time he was at a restaurant down around The Square, George Barnes or somewhere, and he ordered Smothered Steak, or something that had onions all over it. They served it to him and he sent it back. They scraped off the onions, took it to him, he looked and sent it back again! He didn't want any cooked onions! He wanted a whole new steak, without the flavor of those cooked onions!"

[Wilma Ryser] "What I remember about Isam: the day he had all his teeth pulled, the highway patrolmen bought him a steak that night and he said he'd eat it. And he said if they'd awaited 'til the next day, he couldn't have eat it. But he ate it that first night! Because his teeth *[his gums]* were all numb at first. The day he had them pulled. The highway patrol dealt him a lot of grief, I think, but they had a lot of respect for him."

[Shirley Carrizales] "One thing that Granddad never wanted anyone to do was to make children afraid of him. That really upset him when people would say, 'There's the Sheriff and he'll getcha!' and he would walk over and say, 'No I won't, but you need to mind your mother.'"

[Don Letterman] "I don't know it for sure, but I actually think he sent more people home that he could have arrested, than he ever arrested. He told 'em, 'Just go on home, behave yourself.'"

[Tony Stephens] "He was something else, boy. You had to know him and work with him to really tell about him. He knew everybody in Webster County and all the surrounding counties. He knew every convict and anybody that done any problems.

We'd work a burglary and call Ole   Isam and Isam would say, 'You go and get so-and-so, he done that.' We'd go get so-and-so and he'd say, 'Yeah, I been there, I done that.'

He knew everybody, and what they were doin' and what they were *going* to be up to. That's the derndest guy I ever saw in my life. He really knew what was goin' on.

He was kinda hard to describe, really. You'd have to be around him a little bit to figure out what he was thinkin' and what he was gonna do.

We went in that Skyline Café over there in Seymour one time, me and Isam, and sit down to have our food, and everybody come by slappin' Ole Isam on the back and tellin' him what a good fella he was, and he'd get in there and wouldn't have time to eat his lunch! Things like that."

"Details concerning the robbery of the White Department Store and the school building at Seymour last March have been cleared up by statement of John Jerald Simpler and Bob Stogsdill....Simpler made a statement to Wichita officers at Wichita regarding the Seymour burglaries. Sheriff Cunningham states that the Wichita officers must be given full credit for their work in apprehending him.

Simpler's statement follows: '....After *[robbing White's Hardware Store]* we sat in the car until we were sure the marshal was asleep. Then we entered the schoolhouse through a window in the boys' rest room. We went straight to the principal's office. Bob knew the money was in a filing cabinet. The reason we went there on Sunday was because Bob knew that they kept money there to open the cafeteria. We got about $300—about one hundred in change....'

Stogsdill said he bought a car and was en route to Wichita, Kan., when he was caught just out of Marshfield. Stogsdill said they made ten break-ins on the route through New Mexico, Texas and Oklahoma. He said that Simpler pawned loot at Cheyenne, Wyo., Salt Lake City, Carson City, Nev., and Sacramento, Calif."

September 23, 1954 "Sheriff E.I. Cunningham reports the arrest of four men on the James River at Ira Farr ford last Friday. Ira Hyder, Wayne Stepp, Harm Henson and John Calvin are said to have been disturbing the neighborhood and they were picked up on a charge of vagrancy.

Monday Greene county officers came here and arrested the four on charges of stealing chickens in the nighttime. In addition they arrested Coy Miller, said to have been with them, on the same charge. They were taken to the Greene county jail in Springfield. All are Webster County men, except Harm Henson and John Calvin, who are from Ulysses, Kan.

Sheriff Cunningham reports the arrest on Tuesday of Art Snelson for receiving stolen chickens and cooking them at his place northwest of Seymour."

[Willis Case] "Some fellas come up from Ava. Ava was known to be kinda an outpost of just big, overgrown people that had fights and got drunk and all that stuff.

Isam said he got a call to come to Seymour. 'What was the trouble in Seymour?' I asked Isam. 'Well, they got out in the middle of the highway and spread their arms out wide like this and talked to all the traffic on highway 60. When I got over there, there was a bunch of them people from Ava over there.' I said, 'What did you do, Isam?' He said, 'I walked up to that boy that was standing in the middle of the road and took out my old blackjack and brought it right across his forehead.' He said, 'I fetched him down. 'Bout that time there's another'n come out of the car, about 7 foot tall.' And I said, 'What'd ya do to him, Isam?' He said, 'I took my old blackjack and I fetched him right acrost his body.' "

"On Monday, Sept. 13, someone stole a red and black key folder containing two locker keys, a truck key, a car key, driver's license and three $10 bills and four $1 bills belonging to Mrs. Irene Rader. They were taken out of her work case at the Blackwell Sale Barn.

Mrs. Rader is a poor woman but tries to help those in need and if the person who took the key folder were in need, she would have been glad to help them.

No charges have been filed as yet. As the keys and driver's license will do the one who took them no good, they should return them at least."

September 30, 1954 "One of the most bloody and most destructive prison riots in the history of this country took place at the state prison in Jefferson City last Wednesday. Four convicts were killed and 30 wounded. Four guards were incapacitated although not seriously harmed.

The loss in property damage from fires started is estimated from ten to fifteen million dollars. Among the buildings burned were the factories which gave employment to most of the prisoners. They are now idle.

Cause of the riot is said to have been the poor food and anger at parole board policies. State patrolmen and units of the National Guard were called to quell the riot.

If the rebellious prisoners had made an attempt to storm the walls of the prison when they first started the riot they might have been successful. Instead they made an ill-timed attempt to break into the administration building which was broken up by gunfire.

Jefferson City was panicked with the thought of a mob of 2600 maddened convicts running loose. Several families loaded their cars and left town. In nearly every home a loaded gun was ready."

["Missouri Highway Patrol History" as told by Bob Priddy in Across Our Wide Missouri, Vol. 2, 1984, pps. 150-152]

"On September 14, 1931, the law went into effect that created the Missouri Highway Patrol. The unions feared it. County sheriffs thought it might infringe on their authority. Some felt it would be centered on enforcement of prohibition. Regardless, it had become obvious by the mid-1920s and thirties that the number of automobiles and highways indicated that some kind of special law enforcement agency was required.

The movement for such an agency had begun seriously in 1923 but it was not until 1931 that two bills were introduced in the legislature—one providing for a state patrol, the other for a state police.

Organized labor opposed the concept of a state police, fearing the new agency would be used to break strikes, as had been done elsewhere. Labor didn't oppose a patrol that would have jurisdiction only over motor vehicle law enforcement, though. Some feared the troopers might wind up as keepers of county jails. Amendments took the unit out of politics, and by late April, the signature of Governor Caulfield had formally created the Missouri Highway Patrol.

....Missouri's first traffic safety program came through the patrol in 1935. A year later the patrol cars got shortwave radios. ....

In 1945, the year the war ended, patrolmen received their first pay raise. During the forties the patrol got its first superintendent promoted from within the ranks—Hugh Waggoner.

The Highway Patrol became airborne with a surplus army liaison plane, an L-5. In 1948 the patrol was sent in to take over the Boonville state training school because of trouble and dissension.

In 1954, during the prison riot, 265 troopers and 202 cars were sent to the capital city from throughout the state. Only fifty-five men were not sent in."

October 14, 1954 "Word has been received by Webster County Sheriff, E.I. Cunningham, as to the whereabouts of Ralph Woofter. Mr. Woofter was sought after his house was badly damaged by fire some time ago. Woofter's brother, Al Woofter, notified the Sheriff that Ralph Woofter is now in the state of Nevada. Later Mr. Woofter called the home in which his daughter is being cared for."

October 18, 1954 "State of Mo. vs. Wayne Stepp, Ira Hyder, Harm Henson, and John Calvin, vagrancy: dismissed."

"Chief of Police Troy Clelland of Springfield was here Monday investigating a case. Sheriff E.I. Cunningham introduced him to several around town as the police chief of the suburb of Marshfield. Some time ago the chief got a picture of the Webster County Sheriff and had the usual or rather unusual criminal description printed on it. The Sheriff took it in good nature, and keeps the picture to show his friends."

[Portions of a personal letter, dated October 31, 1954, to Charley Cunningham stationed in France, from Springfield Chief of Police Troy Cleland]
"Dear Charles:
Your letter of Oct 27 received, and while surprised, it was indeed a welcome one. I was in Marshfield twice lately and had quite a chat with your Father and Mother while there, naturally, asked of you and was assured by your Father you were doing mighty nicely for your self....They were really OK and I can assure you, no better folks ever lived...When back home, drive over—as your Father says, we are close by and attached to Marshfield for rations—We argue this over every time we meet you know.
Yes, Mr. Cunningham received a nice write up from Joe Clayton of paper here.*[see September 16, 1954 above]* I asked Joe to go over and give your Dad a nice one. I have been in law enforcement near 40 years and I have yet to meet an officer that I like more, think more of and trust as I do Sheriff Cunningham. He is one of the bestest I ever knew, and not only as an officer, but as a gentleman and good man any city would feel proud to call their very own. I believe Webster County feels the same way. I miss being in Marshfield as I used to be weekly, as I always stopped by when traveling east or returning home and saw him. Now we don't see one another so often. I have enjoyed many visits with your Dad and Mother and ate many meals with them, I miss them much....Be good and be careful. Clelands."

"Elzie Doyle of the Farmers Mutual Fire Ins. Co., left this Wednesday morning for Jefferson City to attend the annual convention of state Farm Mutuals, Wednesday, Thursday and Friday."

October 28, 1954 "Glory Hallelujah! It's raining again....The last month has shown a tremendous change in appearance of things. An unusual growth of grass, small grain and pastures promises feed for fall and winter. Flowers are blooming and people are happy with water in the springs and creeks."

"Next Tuesday is General Election Day....Anyone ill may vote an absentee ballot by calling their party officials, who will attend to getting their application and taking their ballot to them. Those not being in the county on Election Day may vote an absentee ballot. Be sure to vote next Tuesday or before."

November 4, 1954 "The Democrats and Republicans divided the offices in Webster County at the general election Tuesday with the Democrats carrying the county against Dewey in The Seventh District Congressional race,...In fact, most all races were close with Mrs. John C. Pope, Republican, for the state legislature, with the largest majority of any candidate on either side....The largest number of absentee ballots ever cast for this county await to be counted....John Hosmer defeated Ellsworth Haymes by 238 votes, for Prosecuting Attorney."

[Mitzi Hosmer] "John *[Hosmer]* and *[Ellsworth Haymes]* ran against each other for prosecutor. Ellsworth was so proper, did everything right. John did all these crazy things. Even when he was just being silly, I don't think Ellsworth could quite ever understand. Even when John was not being evil or vindictive, I think they were just so different. Things that tickled John or made him laugh, Ellsworth just couldn't see.

But after they had court here, the whole group would go down to Roy Miller's house and drink the rest of the afternoon. Judge Hawkins, Ellsworth, John, *[John]* Pope. And smoke cigarettes.

They were pillars of the community—Betty and Ellsworth Haymes. It took courage to go to AA, *[in later years]* both of them, in a small town. Ellsworth was a gentleman."

November 18, 1954 "Judge James Hawkins sustained a motion Tuesday of last week made by Prosecuting Attorney Garner L. Moody of Wright county to nolle prosequi indictments brought against M. J. Huffman, E.L. Colton, Frank Little and Chester Coday.

The motion was made by Mr. Moody during the recent term of circuit court and the decision was handed down last Tuesday by Judge Hawkins.

Moody said the judge's ruling dismisses the indictments and discharges the four men as defendants in the case.

They were charged with illegal possession of ballots in connection with the 1954 primary election in indictments returned by a Wright county grand jury last August."

[Philip Huffman] "That's an interesting thing. I have recalled being around there and it is difficult for me today because we have—and I don't want to say anything personally about any of these people, it's been going on for years—but when they had what they called The Courthouse Ring, and one guy named Watters, Ralph Watters, who was Ballard's brother I think, he raised cain constantly when he had the Mansfield newspaper. But the truth of the matter is, you probably didn't get elected unless those people were for you!

But it wasn't like everybody thought—accusations of all sorts of crooked stuff—none of that! I've been to the meetings. They met every week! Generally. At some point every Republican office holder, which was all of them at that time, they had beat one of their own or a Governor-appointed Democrat, for my whole life. And you would go around the deal, about any problems anybody knew, how was everything going. You were expected to run your office, and you were expected to run it straightforwardly and honestly and do your job. But if there were problems, then they'd all decide what to do about it. And the truth of the matter is, the public was perfectly happy with the government they had, as the election results would show every time they had one.

But those people that couldn't break it were really upset. And I've been the beneficiary of that changing somewhat over the years, for that very reason. But it wasn't just my dad. There were other people involved that were very good politicians."

"Magistrate Court—November 17—State of Mo. vs. Wilbur Marion Cunningham, driving while intoxicated. Preliminary held; defendant appears by attorney; defendant bound over to Circuit Court."

[Willis Case] "I heard *[Isam]* arrested one of his own boys once. He was making noise around The Square or something. That was Wilbur."

[Wilma Ryser] "Well, *[Isam]* didn't play favorites. If one of his children misbehaved, they got treated just like any other citizen. I don't know whether you've got this already, but Wilbur—we called him Red—he drank a little bit too much when he was in high school. Some of the kids talked to him and said, 'What will you do if your dad arrests you?' and he said, 'I-I-I guess, By God, I'll eat Ma's cookin'.' (He stuttered.) And the next weekend he got drunk, and he got to eat 'Ma's cookin'." *[in the jail!]*

[Helen Cunningham] "There was another Wilbur Cunningham in Springfield that made the paper a lot, but it wasn't *our* Wilbur. And *he* was *always* in trouble. I never heard of Wilbur in any kind of trouble after he moved to Illinois."

[Fran Steelman] "*[Wilbur]* was funny, a funny drunk. Just funny period. If he ever tried to be serious, he was still funny."

[Wilma] "I think everybody liked *[Wilbur]* and remembers him for the fun they had with him. I guess he's a lot like Uncle Isam."

[Fran] "*[Wilbur]* probably looked like *[Isam]* more than the others. He had the big nose."

[Mitzi Hosmer] "Isam didn't care whether it was his family or who the person was—which was to his credit—if they did something wrong, he was going to arrest them, he didn't care.

I think people thought when they called, they knew he would come. He was never afraid, he always took care of his calls."

"Thomas Gale Summers, 18, of Fort Wayne, Ind., and Norman David Howey, 15, of Muskegon, Mich., were stopped north of Marshfield November 7, by Trooper Turpin who shot into the back glass after a chase of a mile north from the junction of Highway 66 and Highway W.

The youths are charged with stealing a car in Michigan, leaving it at Pacific, and stealing a car there. They were spotted at Lebanon by Trooper Arnold, who had Trooper Turpin and Nightwatchman Tom Nunn head them off. When the youths saw the officers at Highway W, they turned off north and were stopped in about a mile.

The Sheriff of Franklin county, Union, came and took them to Union where they are charged with the car theft at Pacific."

"Thieves broke into the Marshfield school buildings Monday night by entering a back door and going through the furnace room of the main building and by unlocking a door of the cafeteria building. Evidently money was all the thieves were seeking.

Five rooms were entered by breaking the locks on the doors and one door was broken open. Also a Coke machine was broken open. It is estimated that the total amount taken was between $12 and $15 from the Coke machine, the superintendent's office, and one other room.

The school at Nixa was broken into the same night."

"It is most gratifying to the editors of this newspaper to learn that in an impartial analysis of this newspaper along with other weekly newspapers of the state, this publication has earned a rating of AAA and the designation of 'One of the Best Weekly Newspapers in America.'"

November 25, 1954 " Marshfield entered the spotlight of national attention when Thurman Priest, 48, of Grand Prairie, Tex., admitted slayer of his niece, 11-year-old Jeanette Earnest, of Fort Worth, Tex., was brought to Marshfield Tuesday evening from Lebanon, and placed in the jail here for safekeeping.

The body of the girl was found Sunday night about 9:45 in a densely wooded area four miles east of Lebanon after a 5-day hunt. She had been shot and showed signs of strangulation. Priest, picked up at Mt. Vernon, denied kidnapping the girl, but after long questioning began to admit certain things, leading the officers in a search in Oklahoma and other places. After the child's blood-soaked blouse was found hanging on a bridge railing in a culvert near Lebanon, Priest finally led the officers to the body. Search has been made in the Lebanon area for the gun.

Priest said he was in love with the child and that if he could not have her, no one else could. He claims he has been 'blacked out' and does not remember what happened.

Jeanette, whose mother is Mrs. Priest's sister, was abducted near her Fort Worth home last Tuesday afternoon while waiting for her mother near a self-service laundry. Priest had told his wife earlier that he planned to go to Ohio to look for work. The girl was last seen at a tourist court at Irving, Tex. A man, who registered as Priest and 'wife' checked into a tourist court at Baxter Springs, Kan., on Wednesday, but no one saw the girl.

It is said Priest checked in at a tourist court in Stanton, Mo., but it is said he stayed only long enough to shave and clean up. Later he checked into a tourist court at Mt. Vernon and called his wife. Mrs. Priest called the police and he was arrested on a kidnapping charge.

Arraignment was before the magistrate court in Lebanon Monday. Bail was denied and he was bound over to February term of circuit court. He was brought here by the sheriff of Laclede county and his wife about 7 p.m. Monday evening.

Reporters from all daily newspapers and news services have been here and at Lebanon following developments. The prisoner, a meek looking man of slight build, was being interviewed by reporters from various newspapers at the jail here this Wednesday. Among those coming here were his brother of Mt. Vernon, his daughter, Nancy 18, and a minister and his wife of Mt. Vernon.

Webster County officers, among troopers and officers from Greene, Laclede, Lawrence, and Jasper counties in the search for the child, were Sheriff E.I. Cunningham, Trooper Turpin and Marshal Homer Alexander. Ten carloads of officers were directed to the scene where the body was found by Priest.

The prisoner is being taken to Lebanon this Wednesday morning for the inquest over the body.

It is reported that the federal government may enter the case and charge him with violation of the Lindbergh Law."

[Gene Tinnin] "About the Jeanette Earnest murder. They call it Amber Alert now, but it was a national alert. Old Route 66. I saw a cloth along the side of the road. It was a blouse. Right by a culvert, where the banisters come right up. There came a report that they'd arrested him in Mount Vernon. I took the blouse to the police station and her family identified the blouse.

Thurman Priest called home from a motel in Mount Vernon. His wife asked, 'Where are you?' and he told her where he was. She called the police and told them. Vernon Smith of Mount Vernon, Lawrence County, arrested him instead of calling the patrol. When it became national news, he took Priest out of jail and took him to Joplin! So the press couldn't talk to him.

Sheriff Hendrix got involved in that, too. Sheriff Decker came along from Dallas, Texas. There wasn't much that took place in his county anyway. She was kidnapped in Fort Worth. He came up to Oklahoma and searching along, searching along, and he stopped when he found out where he was. And he went to Mount Vernon and got him out of jail!

I got a call that they were coming up with an officer convoy all the way from Dallas. Picked up officers in Joplin, Mount Vernon, Springfield, Marshfield, on up. They wanted to 'go back out there exactly where you found that blouse and search in that area.' And still, Decker had Priest in his Texas car, in custody! Terrible.

Well, we went out there, almost 13 miles, Priest said it was too far. So we went back, on top of Bear Creek Hill, about 4 miles east of Lebanon. The convoy went back to there and stopped. Sheriff Decker acted like he was in charge. He said, 'Priest said he thinks this is the place.' So we spread out, in a skirmish line as we called it in the army, and worked through the woods. And a detective from Joplin said, 'Here's the body!' And there she was. I believe she was lying face up. He shot her and it went through her and into the ground. Nobody thought about trying to recover that bullet. That night or the next morning I went out there and recovered the bullet, dug it out of the ground, a couple of inches.

The same day Gerald Grove, retired from the highway patrol, was a Lebanon policeman at that time, he walked, strolled just east of there, along the highway, and recovered the weapon on the opposite side of the highway. They called the coroner to come and take the body to the funeral home. And right away they wanted to perform the autopsy.

In the meantime, Decker, Bill Decker—I'll never forget that name as long as I live—he was out of his jurisdiction, out of his authority all the way, from A to Z. Wasn't even in his state! He had it in his mind to load up, extradite Priest back to Texas right there. And the young prosecutor of Laclede county was Eddie Mayfield, and he took charge and said, 'Mr. Decker, I believe you're out of your jurisdiction. Mr. Priest will remain in Sheriff [Neil] Brown's custody. The venue is right here in this county, not in your county down in Texas. So the best thing you could do is just get back in your car and drive to Texas.'

They put *[Priest]* in Marshfield for safekeeping and because Marshfield had the newest jail, better jail than Lebanon.

The prosecutor, the sheriff, and I stopped and talked to Glen Hendrix, the sheriff of Greene County. That particular trip down there, I had to bite my tongue. We had to pick up evidence...a fifth of whiskey, a rope."

"Thomas E. Whitecotton, who has been under fire since the disastrous prison riot in Jefferson City September 22, resigned Tuesday. The Governor accepted his resignation, but has not indicated who he will appoint to succeed Whitecotton.

In last year's legislative session the Republicans criticized the penal administration and charged Whitecotton with numerous administrative shortcomings. He denied that he had ever profited personally from his office."

December 2, 1954 "The job of house numbering in Marshfield, which has been long needed here, has been undertaken by Atty. Roy C. Miller....This project is being sponsored jointly by the City of Marshfield and the Marshfield Lions Club.

This is a big job requiring that each 20-foot frontage be measured on each street and given a number. The front door of a house will receive that number that falls on that frontage space....When completed this numbering of houses will meet the desire of the post office department in cities having city delivery of mail."

"Jefferson City, Nov. 29—Attorney General John M. Dalton today instituted quo warranto proceedings in the Missouri Supreme Court seeking ouster of Garner L. Moody as Prosecuting Attorney of Wright county.

The Attorney General's information in quo warranto charge Moody with 'gross misuse and abuse of discretionary powers' as prosecuting attorney."....*[most likely for dismissing charges against M.J. Huffman and others. See Nov.18, 1954.]*

December 9, 1954 "Seymour is one of 31 cities in Missouri that is being presented a plaque by the Automobile Club of Missouri to commemorate the 25th anniversary of the School Safety Patrols. The now famous Patrol Boy, with the white Sam Browne belt and badge first appeared on the street corners around these schools during the first year the Auto Club developed this life saving activity, 25 years ago.

It is interesting to note that the only field of traffic safety where the fatalities have been reduced is in the pedestrian group. Among the pedestrian group it is the children, age 4 to 14, who have shown the greatest reduction in deaths."

"Jean Paul Bradshaw of Springfield and Paul J. Dillard of Lebanon, were appointed by Circuit Judge Claude E. Curtis Monday at Lebanon as attorneys for Thurman Priest, 49, of Grand Prairie, Tex., held on a charge of having abducted and killed his 11-year-old niece, Jeannette Earnest of Fort Worth. Judge Curtis said the case would be called in the term of court starting February 1.

Bradshaw asked Judge Curtis as a matter of convenience that he transfer Priest to the Greene county jail in Springfield. Later Bradshaw said this may develop, though Priest was returned Monday evening to the Webster county jail in Marshfield.

When Priest was brought into court, Judge Curtis asked him if he had a lawyer and he said no. Thereupon the judge appointed Bradshaw and Dillard. They will serve without compensation."

[The position of a paid judge-appointed lawyer—now called Public Defender—became established January 1, 1973.]

"Pictured *[on the next page]* is Thurman Priest in his cell at the jail here, and Sheriff E. I. Cunningham, who is holding the confessed killer for Laclede County authorities.

Priest, 48, of Grand Prairie, Tex., faces a murder charge in the death of his 11-year-old niece, Jeanette Earnest, whose body was found in the woods east of Lebanon after an intensive search. Priest also faces federal charges under the Lindbergh Law, which also carries a death penalty.

A grand jury at Fort Worth, Tex., home of the murdered girl, may charge Priest this week with state kidnap charges, but it is doubtful if he will be tried on that charge as the Texas law only provides up to 25 years in prison for that offense."

December 16, 1954 "The body of a youth, later identified as Martin Buck of Margate, N.J., age 23, was found Friday morning about 7 o'clock in a ditch beside the country road that runs north from the foot of Northview Hill near Edwards Chapel about a mile north of Highway 66. ...The youth had been shot five times, under the chin, at his collarbone and three times down his side, all in a line. Three expended hulls appearing to be from a .32 automatic, were found in the road nearby....

It is believed by officers that Buck had picked up one or more hitchhikers on his road home, who shot him to death for his car and money. However, the car was found at Rolla Saturday....

Officers have stated that they believe Buck may have been shot while he was asleep in the back seat....

Oral *[Dog]* Edwards of the Barber Funeral Home, ...took the body to St. Louis Sunday. Cremation took place Monday...and the ashes were taken by the mother to New Jersey.

Coroner K.K. Kelley had an inquest Tuesday morning...in the circuit court room here. The jury brought in a verdict that Martin Buck came to his death by bullet wounds inflicted by a person or persons unknown."

"Two men and two women, one of the women accompanied by her two small children, were taken in custody late Sunday morning by Webster County Sheriff, E.I. Cunningham, and state troopers in connection with burglary of the Dick Beard store, known as the old Hans M. Rader store, northeast of Niangua, about midnight Saturday.

Sheriff Cunningham listed the four as Eugene Rhodes, 29, alias Bill Graham of Moab, Utah; Herbert Fitzgerald, 23, of Browning, Mont; Mrs. Barbara Weeks Terry, 25, of Colorado, and Mrs. Doris McCulmont, 25, also of Browning.

Rhodes, Fitzgerald and Mrs. Terry were booked at the Webster County jail for investigation of burglary and larceny and Mrs. McCulmont was permitted to remain at a residence here in order to care for her three-months-old son and a four-year-old daughter, Cunningham said....

The four were arrested about 12:30 a.m. Sunday at the home of Mrs. Terry's mother, Mrs. Anna Weeks, in Marshfield....

Cunningham said Mrs. Terry told him that she was a native of Marshfield who had been living in Colorado and that she and Mrs. McCulmont had left husbands to accompany Rhodes and Fitzgerald.

Rhodes told the Sheriff that he is an ex-convict and is wanted in Moab for house breaking. He and Mrs. Terry have admitted participation in the store burglary here, according to Cunningham.

Mrs. Terry had a Colorado driver's license under the name of Barbara Ann Phillips and a SS *[social security]* card under the name of Barbara Ann Terry.

After facing the burglary charges here they are wanted by Sheriff Seth Wright of Monticello, Utah, for robbery and car theft, also by the sheriff at Blair, Neb., and by the sheriff at Moab, Utah."

"Sheriff E.I. Cunningham was found guilty and fined $25 for contempt of court by Magistrate Judge Willard Leavitt of Bolivar here Tuesday afternoon. *[12/14]* The action resulted from the Sheriff refusing to bring a prisoner, Clarence Calvin Cantrell, before Magistrate Cline C. Herren on May 21, 1953.

Judge Leavitt delayed execution of the judgment until next Tuesday. It was understood that Jean Paul Bradshaw of Springfield, attorney for Sheriff Cunningham, could be present at that time.

Bradshaw had a case at Nevada *[Missouri]* and was unable to appear here this Tuesday. Attys. Roy C. Miller and Marion J. Huffman, representing the Sheriff tried to get a continuance because Bradshaw could not be here.

John Hosmer represented Judge Herren.

Judge Leavitt, in finding the Sheriff guilty, said he thought the issue had already been decided by the appellate court.

'My sympathies are with the Sheriff,' he said. 'He didn't know the law, but not knowing the law is no excuse.'

When the contempt case was first set before Judge Leavitt, Cunningham's attorneys asked the Springfield Court of Appeals for a writ of prohibition to prevent him from deciding the case. In an opinion by Judge A.P. Stone, Jr., the appeals court denied the writ.

At the announcement of the verdict Sheriff Cunningham said he was ready to go to jail and has indicated he would not pay the fine."

"Magistrate Court—December 10—State of Mo. vs. Clarence Calvin Cantrell. E. I. Cunningham, contempt. Application for continuance filed by E.I. Cunningham....

December 14—State of Mo. vs. Clarence Calvin Cantrell. E.I. Cunningham, contempt. Judge Willard Leavitt of Bolivar presiding. Motion for continuance overruled; trial by Court and E.I. Cunningham found guilty of contempt and is fined $25. Issuance of commitment ordered continued to December 21."

Springfield Daily News, December 20, 1954: "A potentially difficult situation could arise in Webster County in January when John Hosmer, often a foe of Sheriff E.I. Cunningham, takes over as prosecutor.

Hosmer and Cunningham will have to work together to enforce the law and both say they will do so.

'I'll expect Sheriff Cunningham to do his duty and I'll do mine,' said Hosmer.

'I'll do the best I can to do my duty, to enforce the law and to be a Sheriff the people can be proud of,' said Cunningham.

Hosmer was lawyer for the prisoner whom Sheriff Cunningham, in the contempt case, refused to bring before Judge Herren. Lawyers are few in Webster County and Hosmer later was named special prosecutor in the contempt case which he prosecuted vigorously.

At Cunningham's trial for contempt, Hosmer said the Sheriff, during the recent bitter political campaign, 'went around the county vilifying me.'"

[Peg Miller] "Did you know that all the time that John *[Hosmer]* was prosecutor, he and Isam didn't speak? They traded notes with Miller. He carried notes for them. Roy never said too much about it, it wasn't really my business. But he just said, 'You know, this is the craziest business: they won't speak to each other!'

Isam just hated John. I don't think John ever hated anybody in his life. He just kind of used people. He was such a rascal."

[Mitzi Hosmer] "Isam was always respectful to me."

December 23, 1954 "The question that had been on the lips of Webster County citizens since Tuesday of last week, whether Sheriff E. I. Cunningham would go to jail rather than pay a fine of $25 for contempt of court, has been settled. The Sheriff will not go to jail. Tuesday friends raised the money and paid the fine.

The person who delivered the money requested that his name not be given, according to Marion Corbett, clerk of the magistrate court. Magistrate Willard B. Leavitt, magistrate of Polk County, who last week assessed the fine against the Sheriff for having ignored the order of Webster County Magistrate, Cline C. Herren, said that this ends the case as far as he was concerned.

Sheriff Cunningham stated that he had made up his mind to go to jail because his lawyer had advised him to go to jail and to bring a writ of habeas corpus, as being the only way he could test the case out in the Supreme Court. He feels that he was in the right, as will be noted in his letter to the public printed in this issue.

Magistrate Herren, who originally brought the contempt case after the Sheriff had refused to bring before him Clarence Calvin Cantrell, a driver arrested by the highway patrol on May 21, 1953, said the case was ended as far as he was concerned.

The Sheriff in cross examination when the case was heard admitted that he had not informed Judge Herren that he had phoned the prosecuting attorney for advice, nor that the prisoner was intoxicated. Judge Herren states that if he had done so there would probably have been no contempt citation. He said he had agreed to a nominal fine of $1.00, but the Sheriff would not agree.

Judge Leavitt took the case after Judge Herren disqualified himself. Cunningham's attorneys then unsuccessfully sought a writ of prohibition in the Springfield Court of Appeals."

"To my friends:

As I don't know all who were involved in making up the money to pay my fine in the Magistrate court, I wanted to put this letter in the paper to express my appreciation and thanks to my loyal friends. I am very happy to have so many friends who were interested enough to do this. I thank each and every one. Also, I thank each and every one who came to me and offered his or her help. I feel the act of my friends is the highest honor paid to me since I have been Sheriff.

There are a few things about this case I want to point out to the people. In the first place, my attorneys told me that there was no way for me to appeal to a higher court from the decision of the Magistrate Court finding me in contempt. They told me the only way I could get a decision from a higher court was to go to jail and then bring a writ of habeas corpus to test whether my being in jail was legal. They told me there was no other way and I wanted a decision from the Supreme Court. That is the reason I was willing to go to jail.

Also, I wanted the people to know that my attorneys told me that I had no right to a trial by jury. I don't know why the law is that way, but they told me it was.

My lawyers were first notified on December 3 that my case was set for trial on December 14. Neither I nor my lawyers were ever consulted about the date nor invited to agree on a date. As a result, my trial was had without one of my attorneys being present even though I filed an affidavit stating he could not be at my trial because he was in court in another county in a jury case which had been set about 40 days before. Of course, the court records show these things.

When this thing all started, as I testified on my trial, I did what I thought was right—and what I would do again—and called the Prosecuting Attorney for advice. The reason I was interested was because no charges had been filed on the subject who had been arrested by the Highway Patrol and placed in jail about two hours earlier and he was in my opinion, highly intoxicated and I didn't think he should be turned loose in that condition for his own safety or the safety of the general public. Just shortly before Mr. Hosmer and Judge Herren called me to the Magistrate Courtroom around 7:30 in the evening with neither the Clerk of the Court nor the Prosecuting Attorney present, I had been in the prisoner's cell and he was passed-out and would not talk. It was under these conditions I was held in contempt for not trying to bring the prisoner into the Courtroom. However, I had not the least intent of being in contempt of Judge Herren.

They tell me the thing they are giving me a fine on is not a law passed by the Legislature, but a Rule adopted by the Supreme Court which I hadn't heard of and which every lawyer I've asked told me he didn't know about at that time. They say it only went into force in January before this happened in May.

Again, I wish to thank my friends. I had no intention of ever being in contempt and for that reason intended to go to jail so I could carry the case on to a higher court. My lawyers tell me now that there are no further steps which can be taken and if that is the situation, it is closed as far as I am concerned. I thought I was doing my duty when this all started and I shall keep on trying in the same way.

Respectfully,

E.I. Cunningham"

"A B-26 plane crashed near Good Spring community northeast of Niangua about 12:40 Sunday night which resulted in death for one National Guard officer....With the help of Sheriff E.I. Cunningham and a state patrolman, the body of Lt. Hilker was found near where the survivors had landed, at the edge of a wooded area, about a mile north of the plane...."

"Safe burglars obtained about $300 in classroom and activity funds at the Elkland High School Wednesday night of last week...

Thieves drilled into the safe combination and knocked it loose with a punch, the superintendent [Harvey Tucker] said, and no explosives were used...."

"Thieves broke into the Niangua school Saturday night taking over $200, Clyde Byrd, superintendent, reported. They forced open the front door, the office door, and drilled holes in the vault to gain entrance....Receipts from Friday night's basketball game, and various class and organization funds were taken...."

December 30, 1954 "Monday morning a week ago before daybreak a Guernsey heifer was taken from the A.J. Carter feed lot, north of the Spur. Sheriff E.I. Cunningham was notified and he and Mr. Carter found the heifer at the Richard Taylor home northwest of Marshfield. The Sheriff and Tom Nunn arrested Richard Taylor and Don Hartman on December 22 on a charge of stealing cattle.

They are reported to have admitted the theft and that they had taken the heifer to Springfield to sell her, but changed their mind and took her to the Taylor place.

They were arraigned in magistrate court and place under $2500 bond each. Hartman made bond."

"Miss Nancy Priest of Birmingham, Ala., came Friday to visit with her father, Thurman Priest, who is held in jail here for Laclede county authorities on charges of the murder of his niece. Two sisters of Priest, also of Birmingham, came Tuesday morning and are staying a day or two to visit with him."

[Mary Lou Cunningham] "Well, he kidnapped his niece. There was a manhunt from Texas to here. They found her down by Lebanon someplace. But they trailed him. Then they put him in jail here. And I became a friend of his daughter's, she'd come to visit."

"Mr. and Mrs. Commodore Smith and John Montgomery took Barbara Weeks Phillip to the penitentiary Friday to serve a two-year term."

Chapter Fifteen
1955

January 13, 1955 "The County Court decided to test the validity of the order of Circuit Judge James P. Hawkins made January 5, which provided the Sheriff appoint Mrs. Eva Alexander as a deputy to prepare food for prisoners.

The County Court issued a statement to The MAIL outlining its position. The gist of the statement is as follows:

On January 1, the County Court, in an attempt to save the taxpayers money, made an order fixing the compensation of the Sheriff at the 'actual and necessary cost' as provided by law. The court felt that the Sheriff was already compensated by salary for 'investigation, arrest, prosecution, custody, care, feeding, commitment and transportation' of prisoners, and that the board bill at the rate of $1.65 per day per person, which was ruled illegal by the state attorney-general, had been costing the county as high as $500 per month.

The Court had asked the Sheriff to present his actual grocery bills for audit by the Court, as provided by law.

On January 5, Circuit Judge James P. Hawkins signed an order providing the Sheriff with ten deputies, fixing their salaries as follows: Mrs. Elzie Doyle $25, per month (the same as heretofore); one deputy, Mrs. Eva Alexander, salary at $140 per month; three deputies to be compensated at rate of $5 per day when circuit court is in session, and when a jury is being used, and one deputy to be compensated at $5 per day when circuit court is in session. Also when the Sheriff deems it necessary to have the services of a deputy, he shall use said deputy in the performance of the Sheriff's official duties, and his compensation was set at $5 per day for days as are actually worked. (This is the same as previously allowed, except for Mrs. Alexander.)

The County Court also stated that the Sheriff's statutory salary is, in addition to fees which he can retain, $3,100 per year, plus up to $75 a month mileage, and in addition the County Court in the past has permitted the Sheriff and his family to live rent-free in the courthouse 'on the theory that this was extra compensation.'

The statute under which Judge Hawkins acted states that the Sheriff shall be entitled to the number of deputies and assistants as the judge shall deem necessary for the prompt and proper discharge of his duties 'relative to the enforcement of the criminal laws of the state, and according to the county court.' The law further provides that the judge shall in setting the number and compensation of such deputies, shall have proper regard for financial conditions of the county.'(Judge Hawkins states that there is no law stating that the Sheriff or his wife prepare the food for prisoners.)

The County Court's statement says that 'We feel that Webster County has been going into the red, protesting warrants and paying 6% interest early in every fiscal year, cannot afford this judge's order, and we have instructed the prosecuting attorney to test the validity of said order if it is possible.

The notice was signed by all three judges of the County Court."

[Something important to keep in mind from here on: the previous November elections resulted in four Democrats winning offices in what had been Republican Webster County. These Democrat victors include two of the three county judges: Presiding Judge Claude Whittenburg from Niangua, and Associate Judge from Eastern District Charles Silvey from Seymour.

The third Associate Judge, from Western District, is J.L. Uchtman of Fordland, the lone Republican, who ran against Isam in 1944's primary for sheriff. (See Chapter Four.)

Also, John Hosmer, elected Prosecuting Attorney, is Democrat.]

"Clarence Marion Hill, 43, and James Albert Fowler, 44, were arrested by Springfield police and turned over to Sheriff E.I. Cunningham of Webster County. They are charged with the robbery at the Elkland school building on the night of December 15. They are held in jail here under bonds of $3,000 each."

"Sheriff E.I. Cunningham reports the arrest on January 4 of Willard Denney at Seymour on charges of assault of the city marshal. He is serving a six-months jail sentence here."

"Mr. and Mrs. W. D. (Jake) Cunningham are the proud parents of a son born Saturday, Jan. 8, at Burge Hospital in Springfield. He weighed seven pounds eight ounces and has been named David Isom."

[Helen Cunningham] "When our first boy was born, we named him after him. David Isom. And he *[Isam]* came the first night. And of course it was way after visiting hours and they wasn't going to let him in, of course. And he said, 'I come here to see my grandson and I'm going to see him!' And he did!

And if he come by the house at night, don't matter when it was, if David was asleep, he'd pull him out, he was going to see that baby. He didn't care if I got him back to sleep or not!"

January 20, 1955 "Jots From The Editor's Note Pad—Judge James P. Hawkins informs The MAIL that even with the appointment by Sheriff E.I. Cunningham of Mrs. Eva Alexander as a deputy to cook for prisoners in jail here, the deputy hire by the Sheriff is approximately the same for Webster County as in the other counties in his judicial circuit, with the exception of Hickory county, which is much smaller in population.

Judge Hawkins also explained that a minor part of the cost of feeding prisoners was actually paid by the county. The board of all prisoners convicted on state charges are paid by the state, and when prisoners are sentenced to a fine and costs, the prisoner must pay his own board bill as part of the costs, unless he serves out his sentence. Thus, while the county pays the bill at the end of the month, the county is refunded when these costs are paid.

The judge commented that if feeding the prisoners had been costing the county $500 per month, with the board figured at $1.65 per day, the employment of a cook should save the county money."

"Law enforcement agencies of southwest Missouri are still attempting to solve the brutal and dastardly murder of 25-year-old Martin Buck, whose bullet-riddled body was found on a county road north of Northview Hill early the morning of Dec. 10.

The picture of the victim is being circulated in an attempt to ascertain if the discharged sailor was recognized by anyone as he journeyed east en route to his mother's home in New Jersey from his uncle's home in Santa Fe, N.M.

Sheriff E.I. Cunningham of Webster County and State Patrolmen assigned to the investigation are seeking to learn where Buck picked up the two hitchhikers believed to have been with him.

The theory on the hitchhikers results from the fact that Buck's new automobile was found abandoned on a street in Rolla and that two men bought bus tickets for Detroit about mid-morning Dec. 10.

The tickets have been traced to Detroit so authorities know that they were used. However, the users of the tickets did not go into the main terminal in St. Louis but instead were believed to have left the bus west of St. Louis and then re-boarded a later bus.

Persons in southwest Missouri who recall seeing Buck are asked to pass the information along to law enforcement agencies. Investigating officers feel that it will be useful to determine just where Buck was last seen alone and when he was first seen in the company of anyone after leaving Santa Fe.

The sailor was driving a 1955 cream and black Pontiac convertible he had purchased in Alameda, Calif., after his discharge from service on Nov. 22. His home was Margate City, N.J. The car was brought here and is being held by Sheriff Cunningham.

Officers hope to distribute the picture of Buck and the description of the two men who bought the tickets to Detroit, throughout Oklahoma, Kansas, western Texas and New Mexico.

The two alleged hitchhikers were described as both being in their 20's, one about 5-9 and dark complexioned and the other 5-3, heavy set and ruddy complexioned."

"A 14-year-old boy, residing north of Rogersville and who attends the Rogersville schools, admitted last week to Sheriff E.I. Cunningham, Trooper D.R. Turpin and to his father, that about 1:30 p.m. on January 9, he shot three Jersey heifers with a .22 cal.rifle, while he was out hunting.

The heifers belonged to Gaylord Yandell. Two of the heifers were killed and the other injured.

The prosecuting attorney has notified the Sheriff he will not file on the case unless Mr. Yandell desires it."

January 27, 1955 "Two youths, named Greer and Hilton, 14 and 17 years old, stole a 1953 Mercury at Wichita, Kan., Sunday night and wrecked it two miles east of Rogersville Monday morning. They turned it over but escaped injury.

Trooper Wilson was called and they were brought to the jail here. They finally admitted taking the car. The car was returned to the owner Tuesday.

The boys were turned over to Deputy Marshall R. H. Tucker and a Mr. Coon of Wichita by Sheriff Cunningham Tuesday night. The youths were said to be under parole at Wichita for car theft."

"Sheriff Gives His Side—To The Citizens Of Webster County: During the past few weeks many people have spoken to me regarding articles in the paper by the new County Court having to do with feeding of prisoners and with my deputy hire. For that reason I wish to make this statement regarding my position on these important matters.

In the first place, I wish to state that during the 10 years I have been sheriff, I have tried as best I knew to run the office in a legal way and as cheaply as I knew how. I have never had a full-time deputy although most of the sheriffs before me have. Also, in other nearby counties of about the same size as ours the sheriffs have one or more full-time deputies or jailers. I have worked many extra hours myself to save this cost.

Also, for the past 10 years my wife has given her services free to the county to cook for the prisoners. You will remember that when there was what seemed to be a big board bill, she has cooked all the meals without any pay from the county. When she has been sick or unable to fix them, as I have had an agreement with the old Court, I have stuck by it, and provided the meals without any extra cost to the County. She had not been doing any of the cooking for some time before the end of 1954 and has not done any since. However, the reason for this is not to try to cause extra expense to the County, but because she was—and still is—under the care of a doctor and not able to do it. She is not physically well enough to do the cooking.

The first of 1955, the County Court advised me that they desired to change the way I was being paid and asked me to submit the actual bills for the food bought, which I was glad to agree to do. I am planning on trying to do that in as accurate a way as I can.

As my wife was no longer able to fix the meals—and I have never had any lawyer to tell me the law ever required her to do so—I had the problem of getting them prepared. I am not a very good cook anyway and if I am to do my other duties such as investigating crimes, serving papers, taking prisoners to Jefferson City and many other duties which take me away from Marshfield, I can not count on being here at meal times. I think we all realize that when someone is placed in jail and confined, not only does the law require he be fed, but human decency would require it.

With that problem, the only solution I saw was for someone to be hired to do the fixing of the meals. I did considerable looking around for someone to do the work and selected the person who submitted the lowest bid. The lowest salary for which I was able to obtain anyone to come and cook three meals a day for seven days a week was $140.00 per month. I requested the Circuit Judge, Judge Hawkins, to approve the appointment of her as a deputy. Stating he felt it necessary to the enforcement of the criminal law that prisoners be fed, Judge Hawkins approved the appointment for the lowest bid I could get.

The statue under which I asked the judge to approve this deputy is Section 57.250 R.S. Mo., 1949, and reads in part as follows:

'The sheriff in counties of the third and fourth classes shall be entitled to such number of deputies and assistants, to be appointed by such official, with the approval of the judge of the circuit court, as such judge shall deem necessary for the prompt and proper discharge of his duties relative to the enforcement of the criminal laws of this state. The judge of the circuit court, in his order permitting the sheriff to appoint deputies or assistants, shall fix the compensation of such deputies or assistants.'

This is the first time I have asked for a full-time deputy in over 10 years as sheriff and would not now do it if I could see any way to avoid it.

It has been stated that the County is in a bad financial condition and the inference has, it seems to me, been made that the expenses of feeding the prisoners is the main cause of this bad financial condition. It is true that some months the board bill does seem to run pretty high. Of course, the sheriff has no control over how many are in jail except to arrest those who have been charged with a crime. I would like to explain that the taxpayers of this County do not have to bear all the expense that the Court reports show are paid to me for board. The County does pay me, but it receives back a considerable amount of this money. When anyone pays a fine and costs, the board bill is part of the costs. In many cases when Judge Hawkins has paroled someone, he has required as a condition of the parole that the board bill be paid as part of the costs in an effort to save the County money. In the great majority of felony cases, and always when someone is sentenced to the penitentiary, the State pays the County back for the board bill. As shown by the records in the Circuit and Magistrate Courts, during 1953 and 1954, a total of $1065.02 was assessed against defendants who plead guilty or were convicted. During the same time, the State repaid the County for board bills in felony cases a total of $2019.60, so that during that period, the County was reimbursed a total of $3084.62. To my knowledge the State has never complained about the amount of the board bill.

I hope this will explain somewhat my situation and if you feel I am being unreasonable I would appreciate your letting me know. Respectfully, E.I. Cunningham, Sheriff.

Adv."

February 3, 1955 "Due to fresh oil and wet blacktop on Highway A this side of Diggins, Robert F. Lea skidded Tuesday afternoon and his car overturned. Mr. Lea was not injured, but the car was badly damaged.

Mr. Lea saw a car ahead of him stopped in preparation of turning in a driveway with a car coming. He had plenty of time to stop, but when he put on his brakes the car began slipping and he was unable to get it under control."

[Robert F. Lea is Webster County's Collector of Revenue.]

"The Webster County Court, ignoring the recent order of Circuit Judge James P. Hawkins, Tuesday in approving and setting salaries of deputies for the Sheriff, refused to pay the deputy hire of Mrs. Eva Alexander as cook, reduced the pay of Mrs. Elzie Doyle from $25 per month to $3 for one-day court service, and the pay of Commodore Smith, deputy sheriff to $3 for one-day court service. The deputy sheriffs have been previously paid $5 per day for days they served.

As a result, the deputies appointed by Sheriff Cunningham, have or will resign, according to Sheriff Cunningham, leaving him with no deputies for Circuit Court next week.

The Court has set a rental of $50 per month for the Sheriff's living quarters in the courthouse, utilities, lights and heat. This order will be found in the County Court proceedings."

[Mitzi Hosmer] "I can kinda remember the county court was going to charge Isam and Eva to live in the courthouse.

When Charley lived there too, he used to clean the toilets out in the jail. He hated that he had to go and clean and mop the toilets out in the jail!"

"County Court *[notes]*—The Court 'finds that the reasonable and proper value of the rent, utilities, lights and heat of rooms at the southwest corner of the second floor of the Webster County Courthouse occupied by the sheriff as living quarters, is and has been for 10 years, $50 per month. That in performance of an agreement between the Webster County Court and previous sheriffs of Webster County, the rental of said quarters, utilities, lights and heat was provided without cost to the sheriff as extra compensation for feeding prisoners at the county jail as provided by Sec. 57.420 (R.S. Mo., 1949). That this agreement was for ten years performed by the present sheriff.

Therefore, it is ordered by the Webster County court that the sheriff pay the sum of $50 per month as rent, utilities, lights and heat, for said living quarters from and after 1st day of February, 1955, or perform his part of said agreement with this Court.'....

Report of E.I. Cunningham, sheriff, not approved."

[This is the first time I've read that the County Court did not approve Isam's report and pay him for the noted services he'd presented.]

"Attorneys for Thurman Priest, Grand Prairie, Tex., man accused in the killing of his niece, have asked Circuit Judge Claude E. Curtis of Lebanon for an order permitting him to be taken to St. Louis for a mental examination.

If Judge Curtis issues the order, it will be served on Sheriff E.I. Cunningham of Webster County, as Priest is now in jail at Marshfield.

Jean Paul Bradshaw of Springfield, one of the court-appointed attorneys for Priest, said he and Paul J. Dillard, the other attorney appointed by Judge Curtis, have asked Laclede county Prosecutor Joe Grossenheider to consider their request and agree to it.

Grossenheider, according to Bradshaw, has taken the matter under advisement and will probably let Priest's lawyers know sometime this week.

The mental examination, if permitted, would be made by Dr. A. B. Jones, nationally known neurologist at Washington University and Barnes Hospital in St. Louis.

Priest was arrested after the disappearance of his 11-year-old niece, Jeannette Earnest of Fort Worth, Tex. Later her body was found near Lebanon and Priest admitted he killed her.

The trial has been slated for the latter part of February at Lebanon."

February 10, 1955 "After hearing a request from John Hosmer, prosecuting attorney, representing the Webster County Court, for a review of his order of January 5, with regard to Sheriff E.I. Cunningham's deputies, Circuit Judge James P. Hawkins of Buffalo Monday ratified and affirmed his earlier order.

Judge Hawkins' earlier order authorized Sheriff Cunningham a total of 10 deputies to be used when needed, and specified what they were to receive.

The judge authorized the employment of Mrs. Elzie Doyle, who keeps the records in the Sheriff's office as a deputy at $25 a month.

He authorized the appointment of Mrs. Eva Alexander, who cooks at the county jail, as a deputy at $140 a month.

Judge Hawkins authorized the use of three deputies at $5 a day when Circuit Court is in session and a jury is being used. If Circuit Court is in session and there is no jury, one deputy at $5 a day is authorized.

Last week the County Court refused to pay the salaries of Mrs. Alexander and two other of Cunningham's deputies, while awaiting a review of the Circuit Judge's order.

At the hearing the prosecuting attorney called several witnesses, among them the following:

Wilma Casteel said she would accept the job of cooking for the county prisoners for $75 per month.

Mrs. Eva Alexander was questioned and said she had never been paid in excess of $22 per week for restaurant work where many were fed. She said there were four prisoners in jail at present.

Esley S. Trantham *[Webster County Treasurer]* testified that at the end of this fiscal year, 1954, he lacked $4,100 to pay all outstanding warrants, but he also explained that back taxes estimated on the county budget was about $15,000.

Judge Hawkins told the Sheriff that he could not tell the Sheriff who to employ as deputies, but that he should employ his deputies with the view of saving the county money. However, he reminded the Sheriff that he was elected by the people of the county, was responsible on his official bond for the acts and conduct of his deputies, and that he should employ deputies that he had confidence in and for whom he would be responsible. Sheriff Cunningham said he was satisfied with his present deputies.

The Judge is reported to have verbally notified the members of the County Court by attorneys that he would cite them for contempt of court if they did not pay the Sheriff's deputies."

"County Court *[notes]:* Clerk ordered to pay under protest the deputies and assistant of the Sheriff of Webster County, and the warrants to be marked under protest.

Eva Alexander......$118.73

Commodore Smith.....29.40

E. Doyle................26.40"

[Mitzi Hosmer] "He'd *[Isam]* go after them to get 'em! If anybody did anything, he was after them! He was ready to go in a minute. But he would get so mad at John, because John would dismiss cases right and left.

Isam said, 'I goes out and chases 'em down, catches 'em, and then John dismisses 'em!' He'd just get so mad 'cause he'd dismiss a whole group of the cases that he'd gone out and risked his life bringing them into court.

During the time when they were making little nasty comments, when Isam was probably thinking John wasn't doing his job, they were having these little tiffs. I think they had just gotten filled up with each other.

I just remember John coming home, telling that Isam coming down the steps *[at the courthouse]* had just *spit* in John's face. When he came home, he was so angry, when he came home his face was still white. I said, 'You did what you should. There's no use getting into it.' But John almost lost it. He was prosecuting attorney then.

Isam—everything was black and white. Somebody was drunk, he brought 'em in, he expected them to get the maximum. John would always say, 'Well, he's got a whole family to take care of. If he's in jail he's not making any money so he can't take care of his family.' He and Isam were just completely...John probably was too lenient."

[Jack Watters] "I always liked John Hosmer. He *worked* at being a character; he worked hard at that! And I think that was one of the fun things of growing up in this town is John Hosmer, because he was just....It was a shame they *[John and Isam]* did fall out, that's too bad, nothing can be done about it now. John then went on to be alienated from his family. That was just too bad. But that was part of this town, I guess."

February 17, 1955 "The Marshfield Blue Jays, playing perhaps their best game of the year, pulled a major upset Tuesday night by defeating Buffalo, 60-58, in an overtime battle here.

It was the first defeat in 20 straight Skyline league games for Buffalo stretching over a three-year period....."

Leon Jones with 20 and Mac Case with 18, paced the winning Jay attack...."

February 24, 1955 "The Webster County Bar elected Roy C. Miller probate judge and ex-officio magistrate Monday to serve during time Judge Cline C. Herren is confined to his home with a fractured knee cap, suffered in a car accident February 9. James Case served last week."

[Cline Herren, Jr.] "I was overseas when Dad had his wreck in '55. He was forced off the road and ended up hitting the end of the bridge there, on the James River. The guy that did it was coming right down the middle."

"Mac Case hit a field goal in the waning seconds to earn Marshfield a 59-57 victory over Niangua here last Friday night and kept the Blue Jays unbeaten in Altitude League action....Case led scorers with 23 points...."

"Circuit Court Proceedings...State of Mo. vs. Wilbur Marion Cunningham, driving while intoxicated. Amended information charging careless and reckless driving filed by special prosecutor; defendant waives formal arraignment and enters a plea of guilty. Punishment assessed as imprisonment in county jail for a term of one year. Ellsworth Haymes allowed a fee of $50 as special prosecutor and the same is taxed as costs herein. Application for a parole filed and sustained. Defendant placed on probation for one year under following conditions: (1) Pay all costs, including board bill and special prosecutor fees forthwith; (2) abstain completely from the use of intoxicants and 3.2% beer; (3) obey all laws...."

[This was from November 17, 1954, notice of Wilbur's arrest. Wilbur, often called "Red", was one of Sheriff Isam's sons.]

March 3, 1955 "County 100-Years-Old Today—Today, March 3, 1955, Webster County celebrates its 100th birthday. On March 3, 1855, the county was organized by Act of the Legislature.

In recognition of this date The MAIL is issuing a Centennial Edition, the largest newspaper ever printed in this county. This issue is devoted to the history of the county and some of the most important events over the past century...."

[Jack Watters] "The Centennial....That was a huge thing to have! Maybe the most planning of any single event that Marshfield ever had was that Centennial, in 1955."

[In this issue of the MAIL, the county's birthday was noted throughout with a special section divider, as shown below.]

---------**1855-1955**---------

"Thieves blew open the safe of the Fordland Farmers Exchange again Monday night and secured between $968 and $1000. The combination was broken off and explosives were used to blow off the safe door. The thieves took the stuff out of the safe into the rear of the building and sorted out the money from checks, leaving the checks on the floor.

Five cartons of cigarettes were also found missing. Entrance was gained by breaking in the north door. Sheriff E. I. Cunningham was called Tuesday morning about 7:15 and officers are still investigating."

---------**1855-1955**---------

"Sheriff E. I. Cunningham went to Alton Friday to bring back Bob Cowart of Thayer, who is charged with mortgaging ten head of cattle which he did not have to a Springfield bank. He moved about Christmas from here to Thayer."

---------**1855-1955**---------

"Sheriff E. I. Cunningham reports picking up Lawrence McFeeters of south of Marshfield Monday for the sheriff of Wright county on a felony warrant. He is charged with giving a check with no funds."

---------**1855-1955**---------

"Eva Hyde, formerly of Seymour, was arrested by the Greene county officers in Springfield last Thursday and was brought to the jail here Friday by Sheriff E. I. Cunningham. She is charged with passing a worthless check at the Seymour Farmers Exchange."

"Del Massey and his mother *[Rosie Mosby]* are the last of the colored people in Webster County. Back in 1856, the year after the organization of the county, there were 220 slaves. In 1860 the census listed 120 slaves. During the years after the Civil War there were as many as 175 colored people in Marshfield.

A Negro school was maintained and at one time there were two Negro churches, but in the last forty years the colored population has gradually decreased with the younger people going to the cities and the death of the older ones. The church and school were discontinued."

[Helen Cunningham] "Isam usually always took Thanksgiving dinner to Del Massey and his mother, or Christmas dinner. They would fix a plate and he'd take it down there to them."

[Fran Steelman] "Del Massey was the only black man I'd ever seen until I was in high school. Uncle Isam always had lots of compassion for Del Massey."

[Charley, just entering his teen years, practiced his baseball, played catch, with Del Massey on the courthouse yard after Charley and parents had moved there, though Del was much older than Charley.]
[Charley Cunningham] "He was a friend of my dad's. One time, when I was in high school, Del and another guy here in town got into it. This guy called Del a black SOB.

Del punched him in the eye (smack) just like that. And so the guy marched over to the courthouse and had a warrant issued to throw Del in jail. Well, they gave it to Homer Alexander—I believe it was Homer—or Charlie Ward, one. They wouldn't serve him, but they did go tell Del that they had a warrant for him.

Del says to 'em, he says 'Yep, I done it. But,' he says 'you're not taking me to jail.' This was long about the mid-afternoon. He says, 'I'll be sittin' at the south door *[of the courthouse]* and when Mr. Isam comes, if he wants to put me in jail, he can.'

Dad was in Seymour at the time and when he got back, Dad took him upstairs, fed him his supper, and sent him home.

And the guy was a businessman, too, that Del hit! But he's dead and gone. Two or three people saw Dad take him in the courthouse. Dad just fed him supper, waited 'til it got darker, sent him home."

March 17, 1955 "Dr. H.W. Young, assistant state veterinarian, made the following comments to Mayor *[Warren]* Beck this Tuesday afternoon.

430

'I just learned of the case of rabies in your city. I have been informed that this dog was running loose with other dogs in the vicinity.

This is just more proof of why the quarantine law reads, 'Dogs must be tethered or in confinement during the quarantine.'

The reason for the confinement is—the dog does not establish immunity the minute it is vaccinated. It takes about three weeks for immunity to establish itself after vaccination.

Every dog that has been playing, licking, eating or chewing the same bones, etc. has been exposed to rabies.

Further, that is why the state empowers officers of the law to destroy all dogs running at large during a quarantine. Even though it be vaccinated, since the quarantine, time enough has not elapsed for immunity to be established.

This child of your city was bitten by a dog that was not vaccinated. I would think the city would like to see every dog in its limits vaccinated and confined. Suppose it was any one child of any other family. They too, would then wish to see the law enforced.

Your laws are made and men are put in office to enforce them. If your city laws are not as good as the state law, it does not relieve you of enforcing the state law. Your marshal should familiarize himself with the rabies law. He should be required by you to carry them out.

Mayor Beck said, 'It has been disappointing that the co-operation of people in town has not been near what it should have been in the having vaccinated and confining of dogs. The city marshal has been disposing of several stray dogs and trying to catch and pen all loose dogs. Different owners of dogs are letting their dogs run loose because they don't care if the dog is picked up. These people are reminded that they should have the dog disposed of, if they don't think enough of it to have it vaccinated and confine it as the law requires, they should remember that they are liable for the actions of their dog.'

Mayor Beck told Dr. Young that he hopes to have the town close to 100% on vaccination and confinement of dogs within a few days. 'Extra help may have to be hired to help our city marshal, but we do not want any more incidents to happen like we had last week.'"

"Report has been received by Dr. C.R. Macdonnell from the Springfield laboratory of the State Division of Health that microscopic examination of the head of the dog submitted for rabies examination reveals the presence of Negri bodies which is evidence of rabies. The dog, which was owned by H.A. Guthrie, is reported to have bitten Tommy, son of Mr. and Mrs. Roy Beaver of Marshfield.

Tommy was placed under treatment March 12, on advice of Dr. D.D. Mottesheard, veterinarian."

[Doc Blinn] "Rabies? I did a bunch of those once-a-day for fourteen total shots. It was a poor vaccine but it was effective. Right in the belly. Fourteen of those, all around there. You finally got to where it was hard to find a place to put it, you know. The reaction? They'd swell up, get red, have pain.

We didn't have any antiphylactic reactions—when you have a sudden collapse, they lose consciousness, it becomes fatal. The treatment for that would have been to give them a shot of adrenalin.

The treatment—especially on little kids, they didn't have much of a belly to begin with, you know. Older people didn't like it either. 'Most every one of those spots would react, they'd be red, irritated spots. You'd put it in the fat, but still it was an uncomfortable situation.

I think the patients paid for that. I know the county didn't do it. It was only in a prophylactic measure, if somebody was exposed. You just didn't do it routinely! They either had to have a bite or be exposed in some way.

Seems like there was a ten-day period, that we had to get the shots started within ten days. So we tried to get the animal caught. 'Course, they usually had to kill it, because there was no other way to catch it; they were afraid of it! Then there was a test that could be run. And the vet sends a report—'possible rabid case, give the shots.' Oh, it was long, drawn out. Fourteen days. Consecutive days. Same time of the day, as much as possible.

When the vet examined the head of the dead animal, for the rabies disease, there was some sort of bodies that would occur in the brain as a result of the rabies organism. So they could tell fairly quickly. They just sectioned the brain and did microscopic examinations.

I know that was a period of time when we did a lot of them. Ordinarily there's not that many people exposed. Some years we didn't do any at all. But a lot of animals were found that year.

I hated to do it, especially with kids. Poor little guys. There was no easy way to do it."

"Dr. Don Mottesheard, local veterinarian, was elected president of the Marshfield Junior Chamber of Commerce at their annual election held Tuesday night. He succeeds Jack Watters...."

"Four traffic accidents were investigated by the State Highway Patrol in Webster County during February. One person was injured and property loss was $1,500.

Cause of the accidents were listed as: One did not have right-of-way; one was following too closely; two were inattention or sleep. In one accident a drinking driver was involved."

"Willis Case of Marshfield has been appointed campaign chairman for the April Cancer Crusade in Webster County and will head all activities of the drive for funds to support the program of the American Cancer Society in research, education and service....

'The 1955 campaign will begin April 11,' Mr. Case says, 'and all residents will have an opportunity to contribute to the fight against cancer in this year's state goal of $500,000.' "

March 24, 1955 "The Webster County Chapter of the Red Cross annual drive for memberships is now in its final stages. Marshfield...will probably go over its quota of $1,250, said Carl Young, this year's fund drive chairman."

"The reports for the current March of Dimes drive have all been filed, according to Ellis O. Jackson, county chairman....For the first time in some years the chapter will be able to pay all of their obligations and have a small bank balance."

"R.W. Fyan, chairman of Webster County Savings Bonds Committee, said Savings Bonds sales in the county...are much higher than last year."

[an ad] "Notice To All Foxhunters and All Dog Owners. A special meeting is being called for Saturday night, March 26, in the circuit court room at Marshfield to discuss the necessary steps to be taken to get the present quarantine lifted before the Heart of the Ozarks Meet in April.

All dog owners are invited and urged to be present at this public meeting.

HEART OF THE OZARKS FOX & WOLF HUNTERS ASSOCIATION.

Floyd W. Jones, President.

Roy C. Miller, Sec.-Treas.

John Wm. Brooks, Gen. Mgr."

[Philip Huffman] "All that rabies business. There was a doctor in Tennessee or Kentucky, named Johnson, who was a fox hunter, an M.D. with all the credentials, who had a standing reward, back then, of $10,000 for anyone that would show him a pathological case of rabies in a human being. And he never got called on it! Never. I'm not sure there's been a pathological case found by pathology today! But anyway, that was a debate amongst other things for years. There's been disease, and that hydrophobia, and whatever they talk about, but it was a *raging* debate back then, as to whether any such....They gave people those painful shots and all that stuff, and now the shots are not the least painful. It's not really a problem. They used to say that people would get that hydrophobia and die. The doctor *[named Johnson]* says that isn't what was wrong with those people. And he had a standing, huge reward for that time, for anyone who would show him a case where they had tested and actually found rabies in a human being. And they never did. I remember Dad *[M.J. Huffman]* coming to the meeting, when the Fox Hunt was threatened, and the quarantine seemed necessary."

"A two-way resuscitator has arrived here and will be placed on the fire truck to be ready for any emergency. According to Fire Chief Clyde Hargus, this unit is not quite as elaborate as the one that was on display here earlier, but can be added to make up a unit like that one. Funds were not available to buy the larger unit at this time. It is ready, he said, in any emergency for treating shock, drowning or in any case where respiration is needed."

[Webster Countians shared their money! Fund drives, led by the leaders of the community, were successful and often exceeded their goals. But money seemed less available for services not needed on a daily or personal basis, like Clyde's larger-sized emergency resuscitator. This resuscitator will show up soon at a critical time for Sheriff Isam.]

"Thieves burglarized Rogersville High School last Wednesday night, taking a mimeograph machine valued at $195 and a microscope worth $60. The thieves apparently gained entrance to the building through a side door. The door to the superintendent's office was locked and although it had been tampered with, the burglars were unable to enter. The mimeograph and microscope were taken from classrooms."

434

"An egg within an egg was found in the gathering of eggs by Mrs. E.W. Eaton, Route 1, Marshfield, several days ago. The unusual freak of nature was brought in to *[Carl]* Young's Market Monday and weighed over six ounces, with measurements each way of eight and nine inches.

The large outside egg was perfectly shaped, containing the yolk and white with the inner egg with shell of the same formation.

Mrs. Eaton has a flock of 65 Austra-Whites for family use. She expected to find one of her hens dead or ailing, but so far they are all in good condition."

March 31, 1955 "L. A. Rosner, state veterinarian, has proclaimed the end of the order requiring restraint and confinement of cats and dogs from running at large which is a part of the rabies quarantine measures that have been in effect here since February 19....Any dog or cat found running at large and not bearing a vaccination tag may be destroyed, according to ...Rosner."

[Just in time for the Fox Hunters Heart of the Ozarks Meet. Wonder if that March 26 meeting had any connection with this. Hmmm]

"OUR MEN IN SERVICES...Cpl. Charles R. Cunningham, son of Sheriff and Mrs. E.I. Cunningham, Marshfield, arrived home Saturday morning after receiving his honorable discharge from the U.S. Army. He served two years, the last year in Orleans, France, where he was attached to the Special Service branch. He distinguished himself in playing on basketball and baseball teams while in service. Cunningham flew to the U. S. from Orleans, arriving here Friday.

His wife, Mary Lou, has been living with her parents, Mr. and Mrs. Ralph McNabb, Route 1, Marshfield."

[Helen Cunningham] "At one time Evie had four of them in the service. Charley was after all the rest of 'em."

April 7, 1955 "Health officials, physician, school authorities and volunteers all over the county are planning and preparing for the polio vaccine program that may start this April. This planning is being done even though it won't be known until April 12 whether the Salk polio vaccine, given to 440,000 children last spring prevents paralytic polio...."

Word of current planning may give the impression that those in charge actually know the vaccine is effective. This is not the case. No one knows the answer yet."

"For the first time in the memory of many of the old timers here, the county is not furnishing living quarters to its sheriff. As a result of the county court requesting him to vacate the county courthouse, Sheriff and Mrs. E. I. Cunningham have moved to the place known as the Terry Property southeast of the square.

Robert Replogle was appointed last Wednesday deputy sheriff and jailer. He is staying at the jail at nights."

"Sheriff E. I. Cunningham, 65, was seriously injured last Friday evening *[4/1]* about 9:15 when his car smashed into the railroad embankment at the junction of Highway A with Highway 60 west of Diggins. The Sheriff was chasing a car and apparently was unable to make the turn onto Highway 60. He went over into the railroad right-of-way and smashed headlong.

The Sheriff was taken to Burge Hospital, Springfield, in a Bergman-Miller ambulance suffering from severe right eye injuries, a deep cut in his throat, a cut tongue and other cuts. Possibly the most severe injury was a smashed vertebrae in his back. Last reports from the hospital indicate he is 'holding his own.'

A short time before the accident the Sheriff, who was at Seymour, had been called to the home of Wm. Lineberger to investigate a robbery report. He was driving north on Highway A when he met the car, and turned around and gave chase. His car apparently skidded and careened across Highway 60 into the embankment. The car was badly damaged.

The party or parties the Sheriff was chasing is said to be known by the Sheriff, but no arrests have been made."

[Robin Rader] "The call to the Sheriff's office was about a robbery at my grandpa Will Lineberger's farm, on A Highway, that call when he had his wreck on 60 Highway.

Everybody knew what Will's habits were: the fact that he did not bank and he would have his money at the house. I think Will made it to town occasionally, and as these guys would sit and listen, they would begin to know what he did and when he did it. And so somewhere in the house there would have been money, but they knew that bib overall was the bank. When he got robbed, I don't remember him being injured in any way. 'Course, he was a rather tall man and he may have knocked him around a little bit but if he fell, he'd just grab it and be gone, 'cause I think there was probably a wad in there that he couldn't have put the button closed on.

I don't know if Grandpa knew who robbed him, but, as Isam said, he wouldn't say who it was. Who knows why?"

[Charley Cunningham] "When Dad was in the hospital, Bob Replogle took Dad's place. When Dad came back, Replogle stayed on as the first full-time paid deputy. Dad had asked for help before that.

Dad always had some 'card' deputies. He'd issue cards for deputy sheriffs, he'd deputize them. Like the county fair, he'd always have someone down there deputized.

About the car wreck—there was a robbery out here on A Highway. It was misting rain. I don't know what night it was, it was through the week. They'd robbed a man out here on James River, on the highway there. Mom got the call. She called Dad in Seymour. Dad came this way and met the car, recognized the car, 'cause they had a description. It was going towards Diggins. This is when the old highway was there, not four lane, just two lane. My dad missed the curve there at Diggins, went across it, went into the railroad tracks, and he was in the hospital eight or ten days, something like that. That was the only car wreck he ever had, and they always said it was because of the slick pavement because he tried to make the curve and it spun around on him. He was by himself. Most of the time he traveled by himself."

[Joe Arthur] "Isam's wreck happened on the south side. I *[with an ambulance]* wasn't involved in the wreck. They took care of it over there, at Seymour."

[Edna Cunningham] "When he had his wreck, we all came up. But they lived out of the courthouse then, you know, they lived down the street there."

[Willis Case] "He was after somebody, he run across the railroad tracks, and injured his throat, his breathing. I went to see him in the hospital. He said, 'They opened that up down there, and I'll tell you what, Willis Case, that was the best damn breath I ever took.'"

[Glen Wilson] "You know he had a wreck, west of Diggins, he was chasin' somebody, he went straight ahead instead of around the curve, up there on that embankment. Boy, it bunged him up real good. I went over to the hospital right after that accident. You know what he wanted me to do? He said, 'Glen, my feet hurt. Would you take my shoes off?' Well, sure, I took them off! He'd a done the same for me."

[Tony Stephens] "When Isam was in the hospital, whenever Bob Replogle needed anything, he'd call the Highway Patrol."

[Freda Langston] "He had a gold tooth, Isam did, right here *[one of the front two teeth]*. Somewhere in the roundup, he got his gold tooth knocked out, when he was chasin' that man. Somebody later on found it.

But, you know, Isam just hated people who stole things, he just hated a burglar, and I guess he was just bound and determined he was going to catch that fella and he got in that wreck."

[Mary Cunningham] "Now this Mildred! *[Isam's daughter]* She kinda...everybody needs to go *her* way. And she wouldn't let me in, when they had Isam over at the hospital, because I was pregnant with our son Gary. Didn't know it was Gary then, but that's what it turned out to be. She said that would mark the baby! And she wouldn't let me go in!

And they told me they could take their hand and put it in the hole in his throat.

I liked Isam and I wanted to go in and see him! But she wouldn't have it! 'You'll mark that baby!'"

[Shirley Letterman Carrizales] "After his accident, I wanted to find who he was chasing and take care of him myself! It was so sad to watch him suffer....it was really sad."

[Some people believed that James "Mutt" Casteel was the robber Isam was chasing, the same Casteel connected with Duke Petty's robbery November 12, 1947, of The Seymour Bank. However, Casteel was never arrested for the Lineberger robbery. No one was, most likely because there would have been no evidence, since it was cash that was stolen, and no witness, since Will Lineberger would say nothing.]

"A fair interest was shown in the city election Tuesday with some contest to enliven the voters....In a three-way race for city marshal, Joe Petet defeated Commodore Smith and Homer Alexander....Willis Case was elected to the school board....Ellis O. Jackson emerged as victor in the race for county superintendent of schools...."

April 14, 1955 "Before Sheriff E. I. Cunningham was hurt in a car accident on the evening of April 1 he had made arrangements for buying candy for distribution to the children here on Easter. Since he was in the hospital he made arrangements for Homer Alexander to pass out the Easter candy and miniature chickens Saturday afternoon at the courthouse lawn. The small children enjoyed the treat.

It is reported that Sheriff Cunningham continues to improve at Burge Hospital."

"A mad dog came to the D.B. Latimer home, Route 1, Elkland, last Wednesday, April 6, and fought with their dog. Burley followed the dog and killed it. He had Dr. Hartley send the head in for a rabies test. The report came back positive. The Latimers had their dog killed."

"Jots From The Editor's Note Pad—The County Court has advised The MAIL that the court did not place a rental charge against Sheriff E. I. Cunningham until after he had employed a cook to cook for the prisoners. The court also states that they offered to dismiss the rental charge on quarters occupied by the Sheriff in the courthouse, if he would fire the cook.

This statement was made as a result of the news item in last issue stating that for the first time in the memory of our older citizens the county is no longer furnishing living quarters for its sheriff."

[Helen Cunningham] "When Isam and Evie moved out of the courthouse, they lived in that big old house north of the Square. Charley and Mary Lou lived with them during that time. The house is gone now. It was on the street east of Crittendon."

"The biggest spring meet in America, The Heart of the Ozarks 6th annual Fox Hound Field Trials and Bench Show will be held in Marshfield next week....should be larger than last year, when about 600 dogs were entered...sponsored again this year by the school band...hopes to finish paying for their new uniforms with the proceeds...."

"Thieves raided Seymour last week, breaking into several places and taking more than $3500 in cash and merchandise. The week before the Ward Mackey grocery was broken into and some small change and several cartons of cigarettes were taken. Tuesday night of last week the White Department Store, Seymour Farmers Exchange and

Williams store were entered. The safe in White's Department Store was blown open, more than $1900 in cash stolen and an estimated $1000 to $1500 worth of merchandise taken, including guns, ammunition, hardware, clothing, luggage, and cigarettes.

L.S. Eddings, manager of the Farmers Exchange, reported between $900 and $1000 in cash was taken from a large safe and from a cash register. The amount of merchandise taken was not immediately determined, but may have run into several hundred dollars, with several tires and tubes stolen.

Willis Williams reported the safe in his store had been opened and more than $500 was taken. Some merchandise was also taken from this store.

Vern Anderson reported that an attempt was made to drill into the safe at the Anderson Motor Co., but the safe was not opened."

April 21, 1955 "Sheriff E. I. Cunningham, who was badly injured April 1, while chasing a robbery suspect south on Highway A, was brought home by ambulance from a Springfield hospital last Thursday afternoon. *[4/14]*

This Wednesday morning he reported that he was doing fine and was able to walk around some, although he will have to wear a cast for some time. He said he had received two or three hundred cards and many flowers since the accident. He told The MAIL that just as soon as he 'could get that corset off' he would be back on the job."

April 28, 1955 "The members of the Marshfield High School Band would like to take this opportunity to thank each individual and each organization that helped make the Heart of the Ozarks Fox Hunt a success this year.

The money they received together with the city band fund and a contribution from the Citizens State Bank, made it possible for them to complete payment on their new uniforms. Adv."

"Jots From The Editor's Note Pad—All of our reporters and readers should keep in mind that neighbors visiting each other, either during the week or on Sunday, is not news. Such items are not worth writing and not worth printing. Only when a fairly large group of neighbors get together for a dinner or community meeting is it news."

"Another Webster County school was burglarized Sunday night. The safe in the office of the Elkland school building was drilled and between $7 and $8 in change was taken. The job was done Sunday night because according to the Sheriff's office the janitor was in the building Sunday morning checking up and the robbery had not been done.

Supt. Harvey Tucker said a considerable amount of FFA funds was missed by the thieves. The office door was pried open with a pinch bar."

"Three of the state's four laboratory-confirmed cases of rabies in the week ending April 16, occurred in Webster and adjoining counties.

Greene county had a rabid cow; Laclede, a rabid skunk, and Webster a rabid dog during the week. The state's fourth case was in Atchison county, a rabid dog."

"The state has issued 25 subpoenas for the murder trial of Thurman Priest, charged with shooting his 11-year-old niece, Jeanette Earnest, which began Monday in Laclede County Circuit Court at Lebanon.

Priest, 48-year-old Grand Prairie, Tex., bookkeeper, was transferred to the Lebanon jail from the Webster County jail where he had been held since his arrest last November.

Among the state witnesses is Sheriff E. I. Cunningham.

Defense Attorneys Jean Paul Bradshaw and Paul Dillard declined to say what defense witnesses would be called."

[Gene Tinnin] "At the trial, Jean Paul Bradshaw was the defense attorney. He wept for the jury! Took his handkerchief out. Blew his nose. I was a witness at the trial."

"Some think professional burglars working in gangs have invaded the Ozarks region with so many break-ins unsolved. The tempo of burglaries has been picking up the past month. It has been estimated that about $100,000 in cash and merchandise has been stolen from stores, schools and banks in the Ozarks in the last seven months.

In the past month some towns have had several places broken into in one night which would indicate more than one gang working simultaneously, with several experienced safe-crackers along. One such unfortunate town was Miller. Another was Seymour, when on

April 5, the White Department Store, Farmers Exchange and Willis Williams stores were robbed of about $1,300 in cash and $800 in merchandise.

Other nearby robberies have been the Fair Grove school in September with $1,000 in cash and $400 worth of musical instruments taken; Strafford high school on March 3, $275 taken; Hokanson Store, Strafford, $600 in merchandise; The Fordland Farmers Exchange broken into more than once."

May 5, 1955 "J.E. Haymes, chairman of the Webster County Centennial Historical Committee, met with the Central committee and stated that arrangements had been made for printing the History of Webster County. Two thousand books have been ordered. The cost of publishing will require a sale price of $2. The books are expected to be ready for sale by June 1."

"Shown are the Marshfield Lions Club officers who were installed at the Marshfield Café on May 5, 1955. They are, from left, Hugh Bennett, vice president; Dean Walter, president; Ernie Vestal, secretary; J. Edward *[Doc]* Blinn, treasurer; Oral *[Dog]* Edwards, lion tamer; and Haskell Alexander, tail twister." Photo property of Thomas *[Dr. Tommy]* Macdonnell *[Note those Lions growing Centennial beards!]*

May 12, 1955 "The second polio vaccinations were given Friday and Tuesday to first and second grade school children in the schools of Webster County by Dr. C.R. Macdonnell and Dr. T. M. *[Tommy]* Macdonnell. The 405 vaccinated were as follows: Elkland 36, Niangua 42, Marshfield 151, Rogersville 45, Fordland 50, and Seymour 81....Those who wish to have the booster shot administered in seven or eight months can expect almost life-time immunity, according to local doctors. The cost of this additional shot must be paid privately."

[Doc Blinn] "About the first polio vaccine. The county nurse, she was a gem! We started doing clinics at all the schools. That's when we still had lots of country schools. They were at the stage when some of them were closing and they were coming into Marshfield or Niangua.

The county nurse would set up clinics and, gosh, we'd run them through.

It seems to me like once a month we'd have a clinic in the nurse's office, in the basement of the courthouse, and they'd bring the kids in, an hour or two. But that didn't keep us from doing the clinics at the schools. Some had forty or fifty. At the courthouse, there'd be several hundred! They'd be lined up. We did that for years."

"Eight traffic accidents in Webster County were investigated by the State Highway Patrol during April. Eight persons were injured and property loss was set at $3,545.

The causes of the accidents were shown as follows: 1 excessive speed, 4 did not have the right-of-way, 1 was following too closely, and 2 were caused by inattention or being asleep."

[I assume Isam's cause was determined to be excessive speed.]

May 19, 1955 "Atty. James Case was again elected by the Webster County Bar to serve as acting Probate Judge and Ex-officio Magistrate the first of last week. He will probably serve until Judge Cline C. Herren returns to his office. Judge Herren is recovering from injuries he suffered February 9, when his car struck the James River bridge abutment on Highway A.

Roy C. Miller has been acting as probate judge and judge of magistrate court in recent weeks."

"A thief or thieves broke into the Webster County Tractor & Implement Co. buildings Tuesday night by breaking a rear window.

The outer door of the safe was unlocked but the thief failed to gain entrance to the inner box.

The same night about $60 worth of copper wire is reported to have been stolen from Sho-Me Power Corporation.

Friday night two batteries were stolen from tractors belonging to the Marshfield Machinery Co. The tractors were stored outside the building."

May 26, 1955 "The Marshfield city board held a special meeting Friday evening *[5/20]* to discuss problems created when Joe Pettit was unable to take care of his police duties, for which he had been employed, due to ill health. The meeting was adjourned to Tuesday night *[5/24]* when an ordinance establishing a police force for Marshfield was presented and passed.

At present no new police officer has been appointed. Joe Pettit tendered his resignation as marshal because of ill health, at the meeting, but action on it was postponed until next regular meeting."

"Six of the confirmed cases of rabies to occur in Missouri the week ending May 14, were in Webster or adjoining counties, according to E. R. Price, veterinarian with the state department of public health. Laclede county had three cases, a cow, a dog and a fox; Webster and Greene counties each reported a rabid cow and Wright county had a rabid case. The only other laboratory confirmed case in the state was a cat in St. Louis."

"State of Mo., County of Webster vs. James Case, Robert F. Lea, Orven E. Davis, E. I. Cunningham, Walter Ray, Jr.

The above county officers are charged with appearing naked (face only) in and around the public courthouse, also with failing, refusing and neglecting to have hirsutical appendages.

Trial has been set for Thursday evening, June 9, at 8 p.m. in the Webster County courthouse....

The case against the defendants is being prepared carefully by Willis Case, persecuting attorney, assisted by Guy Dugan, Earl Shields and Ed Webb, special assistant persecutors...

Due to the prominence of the defendants there will be a 25 cent admission for the benefit of the Webster County Centennial.

Spectators are encouraged to wear their Centennial garb."

"Last Sunday *[5/22]* Sheriff Cunningham and his wife celebrated their birthdays, this week, by having 33 members of their family for dinner."*[Isam's birthday is May 28th; Eva's is May 25th.]*

"Jots From The Editor's Note Pad—What are you doing to make your Webster County Centennial a success?

Every Webster Countian should ask himself or herself that question, for it is their Centennial. No one citizen or group of citizens has a greater responsibility putting the Centennial over in a big way, than any other citizen or group. The same can be said for each town in the County. Each town or community has its share in this responsibility.

A great many have been doing something for the Centennial observance, men growing beards, other men paying for a shaving permit, women planning or making costumes, some acquiring oxen or old vehicles for use in the parade, some working on the various committees preparing for the Centennial, others taking their pageant parts.

Many have been writing their relatives or friends in distant parts telling them of the plans for the Centennial, others have been advertising the event in their clubs, activities, etc.

Much is being done, but there is a great deal more to do and every citizen, man, woman, or young person should feel his or her own personal responsibility in making the 100th year of Webster County a time to be remembered.

After all, it happens only once. None of us will be here for the 200th year. Let's make this a 'good 'un.'"

June 2, 1955 "Thurman Priest, 48, convicted slayer of his niece, Jeanette Earnest of Fort Worth, Tex., was sentenced to life imprisonment in the Missouri penitentiary by Judge William Kimberlin of Harrisonville Saturday at Lebanon. He had been held in jail here until his trial and then was taken to the Springfield jail.

The body of Jeanette Earnest was found in woods near Lebanon and the gun with which she was shot was also found by officers. Priest is said to have admitted the crime but later claimed he did not kill her. His attorneys, appointed by the state, made his defense on the basis of insanity."

"With tornadoes swirling over Kansas, Oklahoma, Texas and Missouri, and Weatherman Williford predicting tornadoes in this area, Webster County citizens were on the anxious seat last week. Having experienced several tornadoes in former years the natural fear of another such storm is always present...."

"...with nearly seven inches of rainfall in May everything looks lush, gardens are fine and crops look good. If the rains keep up, the grasshopper problem will be solved, and everything will 'look up' in this section."

"...Plans are being worked out for special sales on dairy products in all stores in Webster County on June 10. In order to make Webster County Dairy Day a success, all clubs, organizations, business firms, farmers and dairy industry people must co-operate."

"Two makers of oleomargarine were ordered by the Federal Trade commission May 28, in Washington, to stop using advertising which makes their products sound like butter. The cases were the first under a new law that prohibits use of dairy terms or association of ideas to imply that oleo is a dairy product...."

"Feeling that bias and prejudice of the judges (they all have whiskers or beards) might prevent them a fair trial, the five county officials charged with 'appearing naked (face only) in and around the courthouse, also with failing, refusing and neglecting to have hirsutical appendages,' may attempt to secure a change of venue....This maneuver is not likely to be successful, however, as the astute staff of persecutors headed by Willis Case, is meeting daily and sometimes hourly, to work up their case...."

"In a scene of quiet beauty, graves decorated with beautiful flowers and American flags, ex-servicemen under the leadership of the American Legion and Veterans of Foreign Wars posts here gathered at the flag pole in the Marshfield cemetery Monday morning to honor the soldier dead of all wars.

A large number of people, many of them from distant places, were present for the ceremonies...."

"L.H. Garst of the Webster County Telephone Co. has completed 40 years in Marshfield with the first of this June.....Each year more improvements have been made, until today the Webster County Telephone Co. is recognized as one of the best independent telephone systems in the state or elsewhere...."

[June 2, 1955] *[This picture, courtesy of Mary Bean Cunningham, shows all seven living children of Isam and Eva's.]*
"This was taken April 17, 1955, when all the boys were together for the first time in 15 years." Front row, left to right: Charles *[Charley]* 22, recently discharged from the army, now living in Marshfield; Mildred Letterman, 42; Mattie Letterman, 40; David *[Jake]* 29, Marshfield. Back row, left to right: Wilbur *[Red]* 26, Rockford, Ill; James *[Buster]* 37, of the Cunningham farm east of Niangua; Floyd *[Snooks]* 34, Springfield. *[Surely this reunion was caused by Isam's tragic accident.]*

June 9, 1955 "Bulletin: Law officers Sheriff Cunningham, Trooper Turpin and Deputy Sheriff Replogle have hired extra counsel. Sheriff Cunningham says, 'I will of course plead my own case, but will use a lawyer for technicalities.'....One of the defendants indicated that there was a possibility that someone might be 'sued for false arrest' when interviewed by a MALE reporter Tuesday.

Another rumor is that Willis Case, persecuting attorney, may dismiss charges against his uncle, James Case, 'because the older Case is the only one here that can prove that Webster County is 100 years old.' Cline C. Herren has been indicted to take Case's place....

Children and even babes in arms will be required to pay a 25 cent fee to see this infamous trial."

"Roger Thomas has been appointed city police by the Marshfield city board at a meeting last Friday evening. *[6/3]* Mr. Thomas began his duties the next morning.

The city board has instructed him to enforce the ordinances of the city and particularly the traffic situation. The board wants the public to know that something is being done to handle speeding on city streets and double parking. The city officials are anxious that the traffic into Marshfield is handled in such a way as to make everyone happy if possible."

"Sheriff E. I. Cunningham 'lost his corset' Tuesday at a Springfield hospital. The Sheriff was seriously injured in a car accident April 1, while chasing a suspect south of Route A. He failed to make the turn onto Highway 60. He spent two weeks in a hospital and has had a cast around his body since that time.

The doctor asked him if he wanted to keep the cast as a souvenir, but the Sheriff said he did not want to see it again."

"Carl Whitehurst, Bland Whittenburg and Mrs. Lois Clemens attended the funeral of Harry Nelson at the Rainey Chapel of the Ozarks last Thursday in Springfield. Mr. Nelson was their former neighbor."*[Here is the official name of Carmen and Rex Rainey's new funeral home business in Springfield.]*

"Some excellent entertainment has been arranged for the annual meeting of the Webster Electric cooperative to be held in the Marshfield school gymnasium this Friday, June 10, by Hugh Bennett, manager. On the program will be: The Marshfield Band in the morning. In the afternoon: Goo Goo Rutledge and Linnie Aleshire, radio artists of Springfield. Pat Hobson, acrobatic act. Mary Lou Fields, pantomime. A group of performers under direction of Miss Dorothy Leonard from the Walker School of the Dance. Door prizes will be awarded to members of the cooperative....Due to legal requirements and other matters, the date of the annual meeting of the cooperative has to be set about three months ahead of time. Some have complained that this meeting is in conflict of Dairy Day. This is no fault of the Webster Electric Cooperative, as when the committee met to set the date for Dairy Day they were informed that the annual meeting of the Cooperative would be June 10."

[Oh-oh].

"Thieves took an estimated $50 in cash and an undetermined quantity of merchandise from the Farmers Exchange at Niangua Saturday night.

Manager Raymond Chandler reported a window glass was broken near the lock to gain entry.

The $50 was taken from an open cash register in the grocery department. Chandler believes missing merchandise includes some cigarettes, watches, candy and clothing."

"The two most recent safe jobs in the Ozarks have been at Farmers Exchanges and although the pattern has been somewhat different, law enforcement agencies believe them to be the work of the much-wanted Crow-McCarthy gang.

Last Thursday night $990.50 was taken from the Exchange at Republic and 10 days before $750 was taken from the safe of the Exchange at Miller. The Republic safe was peeled and the Miller safe blown.

At neither was anything else taken. Law officers throughout the area believe that the Crow-McCarthy members still at large have stopped taking merchandise. The officers say they do not think the gang wants to be connected with anything that can be identified.

Two suspected members of the safe burglary ring, which faces some 21 warrants for seven individuals, are awaiting trial. They are Eugene Junior McCarthy, 29, and John Olin Mitchell, 29, facing trial on burglary and larceny charges in Webster County. McCarthy is in the Webster County jail and Mitchell in the Greene county jail.

The other five wanted in connection with the Webster County safe job at White's Department store in Seymour are the Crow brothers, Delbert Lee, 33, and Glen Eugene, 29; two other McCarthy boys, Donald M., 24 and Michael Larry, 26; and Harold Lee Rice, 27.

There are also seven warrants in Vernon county for the gang growing out of a safe job at Richards. The Crow brothers are wanted in Wright county for burglary at a Mansfield store and in Jasper county on charges of transporting stolen property.

Rice appears to be safe from any prosecution on the warrants calling for his apprehension since he has been in the California penitentiary since Jan. 19, several weeks before any of the crimes with which he is charged happened."

"Judge Cline C. Herren was in his office last Wednesday for the first time since he was injured in a car accident in February. He was forced from the roadway at the James River bridge south of Marshfield and suffered a broken leg.

He is being helped to his office from his car and the doctors have told him to stay off of his leg until the middle of July."

"Jots From the Editor's Note Pad—....Mr. Garst spent the first day of his 41st year last Wednesday, on further improvement of service by working on changing over the line north of Marshfield to dial. He says that within five years he will have to change over the entire Marshfield exchange to dial."

[Mildred Jarratt] "My dad *[Roy Tindle]* was so mad when you had to have a number with the phone company; he couldn't call and say, 'Operator, give me so and so.' He was so mad!

I've always had a telephone. And I'm 77 years old. My parents had telephones. But we had operators. You know, 'Number please!' Then you'd give them the number. Or a lot of people just said, 'Ring so-and-so.'"

[Celesta Davis] "Of course, Isam'd call the telephone office and tell us where they were going to be goin'. And if they got a call, we'd call them there. And the firemen and the doctors were the same way. If they had to leave their office, they'd call us and give us the number where they would be. We did lots of calls for funeral homes. Oral Edwards had the funeral home. Then Joe Arthur had it. He worked for Oral Edwards a long time.

They would just tell us operators direct. Of course, Ruby Jane Burchfield was in the *[front]* office, but when we'd get a call they'd tell us where they were going to be.

It was volunteer fire department, just like it is now, and when someone would call in a fire, we'd have to call all these volunteer fire people. So we were busy! That's the reason they went dial. We just got so busy. There were three of us on the board and we just couldn't take care of it all.

I worked with Betty Spriggs and Melba Young and Peggy Lehman and Donna Nickels and Ethel Hardy and Alyene Day. There were eleven of us. Most of the time there were three of us on, but sometimes just two. We had operators working twenty-four hours a day, seven days a week. Ethel Hardy stayed at night, most of the time. By herself. One of us worked, would stay until 8 or 9 at night. 'Course, you don't get many calls after that. She had a bed where she could sleep, close to the board, and she could answer the calls. She's gone now. Most of the operators are gone.

Isam would bring us gifts. We would get gifts at Christmas from the ones that we took their calls. I have several gifts from Dr. Blinn. We really loved him. He had an office on Washington Street, in fact he had a little hospital. He delivered babies all the time. Some of them were always bringing us cookies and different things. Isam wasn't the only one.

I went in at 7 and I'd work until noon. Sometimes I had a split shift. Then I'd go back at 1 and work until 4 or 5. Then on Sunday I'd go in early and work until 11. Then I'd go to church and then I'd go back in at 1.

Most of the time on Sunday afternoon we'd work alone, because there just weren't as many calls. And the girl that worked at night, she'd come early, at 5 or 6, Ethel Hardy. We weren't afraid when we were alone in the office, we always had it locked. The payphone was in the lobby. A lot of people didn't have phones. We could take a break whenever we needed to. We kept our own time. And if I didn't want to work today, I'd get some of the others to work in my place.

Mr. Garst was our boss and the owner. He owned it until he passed away.

I mean, he was a good boss. He was a friendly man. He was different. He didn't boss us or anything. 'Course, we had to be there, but if someone was there, it was all right if we had to be gone, we just had to find someone else to take our place.

He was in and out, he wasn't there all the time. And on Sunday—I don't know whether you know how the boards are or not—but we worked on one side of the board and the other side has all the wiring and everything. And he'd work over there on Sunday afternoon, and he'd talk to himself all the time, and we'd get so tickled. He'd be telling himself what to do. He was a good churchman. He did more for the town than almost anyone. Well, like giving the library.

When I was in the country we were on a rural line. Oh, I don't know how many was on it, but that was our entertainment! The main thing I remember—and I wouldn't tell you the names at all—but there were two women kinda fighting over a man and so one of them called the other one, one day, and they really got into it. I have a sister four years younger than I am and we had this old-time phone and we could both hear them, and we just had a heyday! And we knew both women, that was the thing that made it so interesting. Oh, and when I saw them next, I didn't let on I knew, they'd a killed me if I had of!

But after we went to dial, one lady we knew of—the phones didn't ring in other people's houses, you know—but she put her phone in a coffee can where, if anyone rang it would rattle enough she'd know someone was on it, and she'd go listen that way. But 'course, we wasn't supposed to listen. Of course! But we did. That was all the entertainment we had, out in the country! We didn't have television then. That was the good old days.

We were the emergency call, what we have with 9-1-1 now. We just had to call everyone. People would call, a lot of times they didn't know the number, they'd say, 'Celesta, call the Sheriff!' We had to memorize those numbers. We memorized a lot of them.

When I first started *[1950]*, Mr. Garst told Peggy Lehman, who was working with me then, he said, 'Now, when you aren't busy, you show Celesta around, show her how to do it.' So she started in, she said, 'Well, let's go around The Square.' She knew everyone's number around The Square and I thought, 'Ohhhh, I'll never learn those!' But you do, they just come to ya.

There was a list but you didn't have time to look them up. You just pretty well had to memorize them. At first I used a list.

We'd have dinners, once a month, the girls. We had a lot of fun.

Most people knew their number, for an ambulance, and would just give us their number. But if they didn't, just like in an emergency call now, everyone had a telephone book and they just didn't look up the number, it was easier to call us.

Children would call and say, 'Call my mother!' and we'd have to look their number up. It was interesting. I think I enjoyed that better than anything.

I worked six years at the phone company. From '50 to '55. I worked there until they went dial. I really enjoyed it.

We all lost our jobs and we hated it so much. They did away with all the operators. They just kept Ruby Jane in the office.

We weren't fired, we were laid off, we were out of a job. I didn't put in my application for Springfield, some of them did, but they never did hire any of them. I don't think our phone system was behind Springfield's, either. We knew about the changes. It took a long time for them to make the changes. They built a new building and everything."

"Large new 'Welcome to Missouri' signs will soon be greeting motorists as they cross state lines into Missouri on state highways...."

June 16, 1955 "On Saturday night, June 25, several Centennial beards from Webster County will be on the KYTV nation-wide television broadcast of Red Foley's Ozark Jubilee from the stage of the Jewel Theatre in Springfield...."

"Leniency was shown to the county officers at their trial last Thursday night. After the attorneys had challenged several jury panelists, the panel was reduced to 12. The persecution managed to take off the jury two jurists without beards, and one jurist with a fairly light beard. The defense managed to take off the panel three men with much beard covering.

The case of Sheriff E. I. Cunningham was brought before the court first. Delmar Massey was the persecution's first witness. Under cross-examination by the defense attorney, Ney Dugan, a question arose of whether Del had ever been a bronc buster for Sigel Dugan. Del's answer was that he had. And, 'for how long,' was asked. Del answered, 'About a minute.'

After much argument the case against the Sheriff was thrown out....

All the attorneys were fined 50 cents for talking and interrupting too much....

The big winner in this event was the Webster County Centennial. The receipts were $107.91.

The courtroom was packed and running over. Many of the women wore their Centennial dresses and men wore their hats.

John Dalton, Attorney General of the State of Missouri, was present to see that no one received any justice from the kangaroo court."

"Victor Sherer, 50, of Hartville, was taken into custody last Friday afternoon after a search by officers of several counties.

A search for Sherer began at 3:15 a.m. Friday, after the manager of the MFA Exchange at Grovespring, south of Lebanon, reported that the firm had been burglarized of a quantity of cash and merchandise. He told authorities he saw a car occupied by several men headed toward Niangua on a farm-to-market road.

A short time later a trooper came upon the suspected 1951 Ford near Niangua, but noticed it was only occupied by the driver. During a chase he fired twice at the vehicle with a revolver.

The driver tried to swerve onto a roadside park road south of Phillipsburg but was traveling too fast and his vehicle skidded to a halt. The trooper fired at the car with a shotgun, shattered the door glass on the driver's side and the windshield, but the man fled into a wooded area near a tourist court.

Officers from Greene, Webster, Laclede and Wright counties joined troopers in a search, augmented by a state patrol plane which hovered over the wooded site. At mid-afternoon, Laclede county Sheriff Neil Brown searched an old deserted house ten miles southwest of Lebanon, and found Sherer hiding inside.

The sheriff said Sherer admitted the Grovespring burglary, and insisted he was the only one involved.

Merchandise, $352 stolen from the store, burglary equipment and a pistol were found in the car he had abandoned earlier and Sherer had an additional $928 in his pockets, Brown said.

The sheriff searched the abandoned house—oldest in the Lebanon area and once used as a stopping place for a stage coach line which ran to Fort Scott, Kan.—after a farmer tipped officers that he saw a man enter the building during a rain. Brown and a volunteer searcher, Kermit Pruit of Lebanon, found Sherer hiding under straw in the place.

Springfield Police said Sherer recently had been staying at the Texas Hotel in Springfield. Sherer will be questioned about other robberies in this section."

"The Webster County Dairy Day and first installment of the County Centennial held in Seymour Friday was a big success, with a crowd estimated up to five thousand people. Many in the crowd were dressed in their Centennial finery...."

June 23, 1955 "Jots From The Editor's Note Pad—Indications point to the largest number of people being in Marshfield for the observance of the county's Centennial July 1, 2, 3, and 4, of any time in the city's history. A great many former citizens of this county plan to 'come home.'

....Only a few days remain to get ready. In this short time all lawns, vacant lots, streets and other places in the city should be cleaned up and rubbish removed. Everything possible should be done to leave a good impression on all visitors. It is the best advertisement that the people here can do to show that Marshfield is a clean city and a good place in which to live...."

"Mayor of Marshfield, Warren H. Beck, suggests that each citizen of Marshfield consider himself as a member of the Centennial decoration committee and do all they can between now and the first of July to make our town as clean and attractive as possible.

....In regard to weeds on right of ways, Mayor Beck said, 'We are sorry that the city does not have a labor force large enough or finances to mow everybody's ditches and right of ways every few days. The way I look at it, if each person would take care of the grass and weeds around his own place (which many of our property owners have enough personal and civic pride to do), it would be cheaper than paying taxes to have it all done. The city will continue to mow as many of the weeds, and as often, as it can.'

Mayor Beck also expressed a great concern for the apparent thoughtlessness of our citizens throwing trash out of vehicles as they travel up and down our streets and highways...."

"The History of Webster County, as ordered by the Webster County Centennial Committee, has been printed and is now available. The History was edited by Floy Watters George and is well done...."

[Jack Watters] "Floy Watters George's book is more of a compilation, her work is, than it is a book that she wrote. She did write a lot of that, worked on that all during the Centennial and had it ready for sale at the Centennial time. "

June 30, 1955 "Three men were fined here Monday morning in the court of E. E. Manning, city police judge, on charges of being drunk on the street. The arrests were made by Roger Thomas, city police, Saturday evening...."

[David Cunningham] "When I turned 16 and started driving, there was one city policeman, Roger Thomas. Heard of him? And I don't know what his role was in the 40's and 50's. He knew Grandpa, was probably about Grandpa's age. He was a really old city policeman. And if I was missing a stop sign or going too fast, I never got a ticket. I got pulled over and lectured: '*Your* grandpa would be *so* disappointed in you! If *he* knew you were out here *this* hour of the night, going *this* fast...' Long lecture, every one starting out, '*Your* grandpa would be ...' He never gave me a ticket for speeding or anything.

One time he was telling me a story about how Grandpa and the State Highway Patrolmen would shoot beer cans along the side of the road, or pop bottles or whatever. Apparently a lot of them did that with him, and Grandpa always won! Shoot cans out the window of the patrol car, and Grandpa never lost. 'And the secret was,' Roger Thomas said, 'he had *me* loading his pistol shells with *buckshot*.' He had special ammo he carried with him when he rode with the troopers! And Roger Thomas said that he loaded the buckshot in the pistol cartridges so he would have those with him when he went out with the troopers. Roger Thomas finally said he was the one who loaded the shot in the pistol. And I would believe that, 'cause I've heard that, about them shooting, from all the boys, from all of Dad's *[Jake's]* brothers, how he would do that with the troopers, shoot cans on the roadside, as they were on their way to a call or something, or going to court somewhere else. Times have changed!"

"Mr. and Mrs. Floyd *[Snooks]* Cunningham of Springfield announce the birth of a son, Gary Lee, on June 18 at 12:25 a.m. in St. John's hospital. He weighted 8 pounds and 10 ounces. The Cunninghams now have two sons, and Gary Lee is the 12th grandchild for Sheriff and Mrs. E. I. Cunningham."

"Jots From The Editor's Note Pad—Heading the parade Monday will be the Sheriffs of Webster County in 1855 and 1955. The sheriff of 1855 will have saddle bags which were owned by Moses Lineberger of south of Marshfield. Mr. Lineberger drowned in James River at Bell Ford about 60 years ago during high water. He was the father of Will Lineberger."

[A reminder: Will Lineberger was the man robbed the night of Isam's tragic wreck, April 1st.]

"An old log cabin belonging to Del Massey has been moved from the southwest corner of the city to the north side of the square.

Del was born in this old cabin. He, with Marshfield Boy Scouts, are building a mud chimney and getting the cabin in shape.

It will be used during the Centennial as a stand from which souvenirs of the Centennial will be sold."

"....The Mayor, together with the city police court, the county Sheriff and prosecuting attorney, made the following statement:

'We, all, are anxious to see that proper law and order is kept in Marshfield, during the celebration—not only for safety measures, but to leave a good impression upon those people who are visitors—as well as our own good and satisfaction. Parents are reminded and requested that, they are responsible for the actions of their children—and so, should properly instruct their children about obeying the city ordinances appertaining to the purchase and shooting of Fireworks.

All juveniles found guilty of law violations will be bound over to the Juvenile Division of the Circuit Court.'"

"Rabies cases in Missouri continue to be centered around Webster County. Four out of nine laboratory-confirmed rabies cases reported to the state veterinarian during the week ending June 18, were in the Ozarks, with Webster and Wright counties each reporting a rabid cow, Laclede county reporting a rabid dog and Jasper county a rabid fox."

July 7, 1955 "Jots From The Editor's Note Pad—The story of the Centennial Celebration in Marshfield is hard to cover in a news story as it was so large and had so many different parts. In addition to the main program which filled four days from Friday until Monday night, there were reunions at churches, schools and families which brought hundreds of people....It has been amusing to note the many different estimates as to the crowd here on the Fourth. It was so large that it was amazing and defied making any definite estimate. The senior editor placed his estimate at 30,000 and considers that a conservative guess....With a few minor exceptions all Webster County people worked cooperatively to make the celebration of Webster County's 100th birthday a success. In a few spots envy and spitefulness showed its ugly head, but on the whole everyone worked together with friendliness and good will. The result was a fine success. It shows what cooperation can do...."*[No details about the "envy and spitefulness".]*

"...There were many horse-drawn floats, horseback riders. Many said they did not know there were so many horses left in Webster County....The four-day Centennial program was the biggest thing ever attempted in the entertainment line here. And the wonderful thing about it was that there were no disturbances of any kind. Sheriff Cunningham, reporting for the law enforcement officers, said there were no drunks and not a single thing to mar the peace of the celebration."

"...On Sunday a county-wide singing convention drew a large crowd to the court yard in the afternoon. In the evening the 200-member choir directed by Lyman Mooney, drew a crowd estimated at more than 1500 people to the park. The singers were from all towns and communities in the county. After the 45-minute singing program, ministers with more than 30 years service were introduced and then other ministers were asked to go up and be presented. Warren Johnson was master of ceremonies of this and other events during the Centennial program...."

[Warren Johnson] "I kept trying to get on a Centennial committee. They kept sayin' no. So just before the Centennial they said, 'We want you as Master of Ceremonies.' I talked from 8 o'clock that morning until 12 o'clock that night. By the time I was through, *I talked like this [hoarse].* It would have been a lot easier to be on a committee!"

[Edna Cunningham] "We got a picture of the 4th of July, the Centennial...that he rode that horse.
And he got off of that and he was all...water runnin' out of his mouth...he wasn't well *then.*
Didn't he die the next day? No? Well, I knowed it wasn't very long after that parade.
Somebody said when he got off the horse he was spent bad."
[This photo, shown on the next page, was taken by Dr. C.R. Macdonnell]

July 14, 1955 "An 11-year-old Niangua youth drowned in the Osage River near Niangua about 10:30 a.m. Sunday, when he jumped from a bridge into water which was over his head. The youth did not know how to swim.

Norris Eugene Deckard, who had entered the water with his mother and two sisters at Kilburn Bridge, five miles east of Niangua, could not be revived by the efforts of Oral Edwards, Clyde Hargus of Marshfield and others who used a resuscitator without success for two hours after the body was recovered...."

July 21, 1955 "Jots From The Editor's Note Pad—...With the cleaning up of The Square after the celebration, the beards worn by Webster County men have also had a clean-up, and with few exceptions they have mostly disappeared. However, a few are still wearing a mustache."

July 28, 1955 "Sheriff E. I. Cunningham reports bogus check writers have been busy around here to the loss of several Webster County business firms.

Held in jail is Ermell Ginger of Springfield, charged with forging a check and cashing it at the Bay Shoe Store in Seymour and one for $36.26, the same amount, at the Seymour Farmers Exchange.

The Sheriff stated that a hold order has been given Dade county authorities for Norman Dean Cardwell, alias Norman Cagle, also of Springfield, who is being held in jail at Greenfield. Cardwell (or Cagle) is charged with cashing a forged check in amount of $36.26 at the Davis Shoe Store here and one for the same amount at the Producers Exchange. It will be noted that all the four above mentioned checks are for the same amount, and were claimed to have been for work in the hay.

A younger brother of Cardwell, Ray Clinton Cardwell, who has been in Oklahoma, but who had been back in Springfield for a week or so, is also said to be confined in the jail at Greenfield for passing bad checks at Bolivar and Clinton."

"The number of bogus checks being passed seems to be increasing to the loss of many merchants. The newspapers are filled with stories of such crimes and many worthless checks are not even reported.

Business people are cautioned, when cashing checks to be suspicious of anyone offering a check made out for more than the amount of the purchase, except when they are doing business with someone that they know. Also it is only good policy to identify anyone offering a check in payment of merchandise."

[Mildred Jarratt] "The one time that Jack went to *[Isam]*, we had taken a check in the afternoon written on a pastor here. And you know how you just don't feel right? You just have an inkling that something's wrong? And I don't remember if I took the check or if Jack did, I don't remember. But anyway, I said, 'Well, I'm just going to find out!' because I knew the pastor, he was a Methodist preacher. And I went back and called the pastor. Told him who I was, that I had taken the check written to a certain person...I can't remember the name now...and that he was a magazine salesman. And I was wondering if he *[the pastor]* wrote a check to him *[the magazine salesman]*. And the pastor said, 'Yes, I did.' And I said, 'Well, I just wondered, because it was...so much, and I don't remember the amount, but it was less than $50 but bigger than what I thought it should be, for a magazine, and especially just a salesman coming through town.'

And so, he *[the pastor]* said, 'No, that isn't right.' He said, 'What do you mean?'

And I said, 'Well, I have the check right here.'

And he said, 'How did he get a check?'

Well, at that time you could go into the bank and pick up a counter check. And at that time we didn't have our names on checks, we *all* had blank checks. Back then, I don't think we even had our bank numbers on the checks.

And that's what he *[the magazine salesman]* had done. And then he had copied the name off. And there were several from the bank! What he did, he somehow forged the signature. And he was smart enough to know the people in town would know that was a Methodist minister. And whenever he pulled that out, they'd go, 'Yeah, I know him.' He would buy something, some clothing, with some change going to him. The check was made out to him, for a magazine. He would endorse the check

But anyway, Jack went to   *[Isam]* 'cause it hadn't been very long, I caught it pretty quick. And he told Isam what had happened. And Isam said, 'I bet he's already out of town. But we'll go to Springfield.' He said, 'He's probably in Springfield. I know there's a couple of hotels where those kind of people kinda hang out at. We'll go up there and see if we can see him.'

And Isam went with Jack that night. And I was scared to death! I knew he was with Isam and I knew Isam had a gun. But I still was scared to death, because you don't know what those people are gonna do! And it was about 1:30 or 2 *[a.m.]* when he came home and they never did see him, they didn't get to see him.

Jack said when they first went in this one hotel, a couple of men that was sitting over in the corner, got up and left. He figures if they were his buddies, they went to find him, to tell him not to come in. But *[Jack]* didn't *know* that, that's just what he thought.

But that's the only time I know of we ever asked help from Isam. But he was very willing to help and tried hard to find him. Because he was mad, too."

"The Webster County Selective Service Board has received notice that this county will not be called upon for any men for induction or for physical examination during August…Two men will go as volunteers during September.

In view of the improved world situation, it is possible that young men registering now may not have to enter the service.

However, they are still required to register within five days after they become 18 years of age."

"Fire struck twice within a short period of time last week in Marshfield....The residence was owned by Beulah Haggard, who resides in the first house north of the destroyed home. She says that a house will be built back on the same location.

When asked if she had any insurance, Beulah said that was nobody's business....

While the city truck was still at the *[Haggard]* fire, fire broke out in the Paul Langston home....the fire was brought quickly under control after the firemen arrived....Langston said that he had 'some' insurance."

[Elzie Doyle's daughter, Freda, is married to Paul. A reminder: Elzie works at the Farmers Mutual Insurance office in the courthouse, in addition to being Isam's deputy sheriff.]

"As the firetruck arrived at the Langston fire, the rural truck stood by. Water from the rural truck was used in the final stages of the fire. Although this was one of the few times that both trucks have been used, the need for both trucks in Marshfield is evident."

[Fire Chief Clyde Hargus seems always to be justifying his equipment, perhaps in fear of its otherwise being taken away and considered extravagant.]

August 4, 1955

[Helen Cunningham] "The night he had his heart attack, I remember they called us. We were in bed. I don't know how I got my clothes on so fast. I don't think they took him to the hospital. He died.

And that's another time Charley conked out. When Isam died. They *[Charley and Mary Lou Cunningham]* weren't home. They had gone to somewhere, Joe Arthur's or somebody's, partying, you know, visiting. And when they called me...*[Charley]* wasn't much help. Maybe you'd better not put that in."

[Joe Arthur] "*[When Isam died]* Charley and Mary Lou were visiting us. We lived out on Maple Street at the time. We got the call and I had to tell them, which is not a pleasant thing to do. Somebody called. I don't remember who."

[Billie Arthur] "Mary Lou was trying to take care of Charley so he wouldn't faint, but I can't remember whether he did or not. It was a hard time for all of us."

[Ruby Hargus] "And when he got hurt, chasing that burglar, and then later when he died, Jake called Clyde. They had ordered a resuscitator for the fire department. Jake called Clyde and Clyde went up to the fire department and got that and they took him to the hospital and they tried to use the resuscitator but he died."

[Joe Arthur] "Clyde Hargus was the fire chief, Oral Edwards was the assistant, and, 'course, Haskill Alexander also helped *[with the resuscitator and Isam, after the heart attack].*

Eva, she did real well. She could handle things pretty well. She had her own style about everything. She was just in the background."

[Edna Cunningham] "They called us and we went up. I don't think he was dead when they called, but he was dead when we got there. We were milkin' or anyhow it happened right along that time of the evening, you know. And we had to quit everything.

I never will forget that I had washed my hair, and had it rolled up in rollers, and here we went! Didn't have time to take it down! I don't know whether we'd finished milking or whether we just let it go, but we got in the car and left as soon as they called us.

We knowed he'd been sick, you know, 'cause he'd been in this wreck. We knew he wasn't too well. Buster worried about him after that wreck. "

[Fred Letterman] "And I can remember comin' out and Mom *[Mildred]* was sittin' on the front porch cryin' and Dad told me that they'd called and said Grandpa had died. That's about all I can remember. That was the start of my third grade. I was in the house, it was at night."

"HEART ATTACK TAKES LIFE
OF SHERIFF E.I. CUNNINGHAM, 65.
Popular Officer Dies Sunday; Businesses Close For Funeral

"Sheriff E. I. Cunningham, one of the Ozarks' most colorful and popular law enforcement officers, died unexpectedly at his home here Sunday evening *[7/31]* from a heart attack.

The Webster County Sheriff had been severely injured in April in an auto accident, but believed to have recovered fully. It is believed, however, that his injuries constituted a strain on his heart.

Sheriff Cunningham, who was 65, had been summoned to investigate a minor accident at the south side of Marshfield at 5 p.m. Sunday, and later complained of weariness, but decided he was not ill enough to call a doctor.

A short time later, he attempted to rise from a chair at his home, but collapsed to the floor, and Barber Funeral Home attendants were summoned. They administered oxygen and a heart stimulant, but the Sheriff lived only a few minutes after their arrival.

Following his election to office in 1945, Cunningham soon became one of the best-known sheriffs in the midwest, colorful and individualistic. He was elected to three consecutive terms after failing in two earlier tries for office.

Cunningham was proud of the fact that he knew 'almost every inch' of his county, and was able to spot and track down criminals almost as soon as they set foot in the county. He set a remarkable record of law enforcement in many instances.

Among the more notorious criminals with whom he tangled was Louis (Duke) Petty who in the 1920's robbed the Niangua Bank and surrendered after a gun battle. Arrested for parole violation in 1947, Petty broke out of the Lawrence county jail and was captured by the FBI and Cunningham at a Webster County farmhouse.

Among the tragedies Cunningham investigated during his term of office was the killing of four members of the Shockley family near Conway in 1951. A 23-year-old youth, Kenneth Essary, was given multiple life sentences.

The Sheriff narrowly escaped death several times—once when he was beaten severely by two men who attempted to break out of the jail at Marshfield. The accident in which Cunningham was seriously injured a few months ago occurred as he was chasing a car occupied by a man suspected of robbing a farmer.

As the Sheriff's patrol car reached the junction of Highway A with Highway 60 it skidded across the highway, crashed up a railroad embankment. Cunningham was hospitalized several weeks with a back fractured, punctured eye, and other injuries. He lost a considerable amount of blood from a slashed throat and never had recovered his normal weight since then.

During his hospitalization, the Sheriff—tears in his eyes—remarked on the wealth of flowers sent him by friends and observed:

'I didn't know that many people cared—and here I haven't even died yet.'

He was a native of Webster County.

His most recent major appearance in a crime case was in connection with a hearing for Thurman Priest, accused of slaying his 11-year-old Texas niece near Lebanon. Priest was held in jail here for some time.

Sheriff Cunningham brought a great deal of publicity to Webster County by the news articles in newspapers over the United States and in stories written for detective magazines. Stories in several magazines were published about the Priest case, Rainey case, Essary case and others.

The son of James Cunningham, a county judge who also operated a canning factory, sawmill and farm at various times, Sheriff Cunningham was born at Susanna, seven miles east of Niangua, May 28, 1890. *[1891?]* In later years, Cunningham acquired much of the land which formerly belonged to his family 'to keep it in the family.' He was named for Isham H. Cunningham, one-time Webster County recorder, but the Sheriff decided to drop the H from his name because folks didn't pronounce it.

He was married to a neighborhood sweetheart, Eva Randolph, Feb. 8, 1911, and after living in Oklahoma a brief time they returned to Webster County.

Surviving in addition to his wife are two daughter, Mrs. Mattie Letterman, who lives north of Springfield, and Mildred Letterman of Springfield; five sons, Charles of Marshfield, James of near Niangua, Floyd of Springfield, David of Marshfield and Wilbur of Loves Park, Ill.; two brothers, Fred of Springfield and Jodie of Bakersfield, Calif.; three half-sisters, Mrs. Hulda Duncan of Ardmore, Okla.; Mrs. Ida and May Rader, both of Niangua; 13 grandchildren and one great-grandchild.

Funeral services were held at the Barber Chapel this Wednesday afternoon at 1 p.m. A second service was held at 3 p.m. at Prospect Church, east of Niangua, where burial will take place. Most all business firms and offices in Marshfield were closed during the funeral hours....

Pallbearers were Jake Burchfield, L.T. Melton, Dave Roper, Roy C. Miller, Clyde Hargus, and Oral Edwards. Honorary pallbearers: Sheriff Clay Hodges, Ozark; Sheriff Neal Brown, Lebanon; Sheriff Glenn Hendrix, Springfield; Sheriff James Baker, Hartville; Bryan

Miller, Guy Hyde, Tom Farr, Marion Huffman. Highway Patrolmen Troopers Glenn Wilson, Don Turpin, Tony Stephens, Dill Mumford, Warren Wallace, Gene Tinnin, Jack Waters and Sgt Claude Arnold. Judge James P. Hawkins, Charles Kensinger, Murray Thompson, Clyde King, Orven Davis, Hobart Guthrie, Hermon Pearce and Willis Case."

[Darrell Letterman] "Hendrix was the Sheriff in Greene county, Missouri, and so was Pierpont and some of 'em, and I have had a chance to talk to them—just, you know, as a youngster, but—anyway, they had the most respect for [Granddad] Isam Cunningham as a Sheriff, as a police department could have. He was well liked by patrol and all law enforcements."

[Shirley Carrizales] " I think the thing that really brought to me exactly how wonderful [Granddad] was, is, at his funeral when the troopers came in, saluted, clicked their heels, and showed so much respect for him, and the place was overflowing, couldn't even get all the flowers in, they were everywhere, but I was so impressed with the way his fellow law enforcements paid tribute to him, from other states as well."

[A double line of Ozarks peace officers flanked the casket as it was brought down the steps of the funeral home after the services. Many of them were honorary pallbearers. One officer attending estimated that there must have been at least 75 present or former peace officers at the funeral. All had known the Sheriff or worked with him at one time or another.

A convoy of more than 100 cars made the trip over country roads to the Prospect Cemetery east of Niangua where Isam Cunningham was laid to rest about 5 p.m. in the family lot which was shaded by a small elm tree.

It was the first time in the memory of Marshfield's old-timers that there had been four ministers conducting a funeral.]

[Joe Arthur] "Isam's funeral service was one of the biggest funerals we had ever had in the funeral home at that time. It had the most flowers, way over a hundred flowers, sprays.

Very hot. We did the burial in Prospect. Isam and Oral Edwards were good friends.

We had people standing and backed up out on the street, it was such a large crowd."

[Mary Lou Cunningham] "Betty [Edwards Hyde, Oral Edwards' daughter] was just 16 when Isam died and had just got her driver's license. There was so many flowers, she had to drive one of the vehicles and was scared to death she would get lost on the way to the burial site at Prospect *[Cemetery]*."

[Glen Wilson] "I got up to the funeral home, just off The Square, right before they were supposed to start. They were full, I mean *full* full. Some big guy scooted over. I got to lookin' around. There were cars in the lot: Cadillacs, Model A Fords—back that far—junky cars. Then you looked at the people. There were some women in there with fur coats on and there were some men in there with bib overalls on. No kiddin', there wasn't just his group. The whole world liked Isam; they were there to pay their respects."

[Raymond Day] "This ole feller come in about the time the war *[WWII]* was over, from Chicago. He was a retired barber out of Chicago. He come down in here on a visit and he liked this country so well, he bought a little service station, out on 66, which was the main highway then. He got along with all the neighbors and everything, he was pretty high strung, but he was a good ole feller. He put him in a little counter there and got to sellin' beer.

When Isam got in the wreck, got hurt, then died, some boys come down there and this ole feller that owned the station heard one of 'em make a remark about them celebrating Isam's death. And he run 'em out! He was from Chicago but he run 'em out!

M.B. Pace. His name was Mervin Brice but he didn't like that name so he went by M.B. That was down about three miles south of Conway, where the old tank pond used to be. Where the train used to stop and take in water. The trains ran on steam and had to have water.

He was a good ole feller. You think him being from Chicago, been up there all his life, that he wouldn't pay much attention to somebody celebratin' a deal like that. But he liked Isam and he knowed he kept law and order. The day of the funeral is when they was down there. The afternoon of the funeral. They was in their early 20's and needed a talkin' to, like I said Isam talked to me. They weren't bad kids.

To me, it was like not standing up when the flag went by."

"The Webster County Court, in session Monday, ordered a special election to be held Tuesday, Aug. 30, for the purpose of filling the vacancy in the office of Sheriff of Webster County, said vacancy caused by the death of E. I. Cunningham July 31.

Reports of Don Davis, circuit clerk and recorder, Orven E. Davis, county clerk, and E. I. Cunningham, Sheriff, for July, approved.

The court ordered county bills paid."

"August 30 is the date set by the Webster County Court for holding a special election for the office of Sheriff of this county, which office is to be filled because of the death of Sheriff E. I. Cunningham Sunday evening. The court acted Monday morning. The law requires that an election be held within 30 days after the death of a sheriff.

The County Court has the power to appoint an acting sheriff to fill the office until a sheriff can be elected. Until the court acts, Coroner K.K. Kelley of Fordland, who succeeded to the office on the death of Mr. Cunningham, will continue to be the sheriff.

Mr. Kelley appointed Robert Replogle deputy sheriff. Replogle has been serving as deputy under Mr. Cunningham.

Beginning Monday morning there has been conjecture as to who would be candidates for the office to serve the rest of this year and next year. Several possible candidates have been mentioned from each party.

The party committees will meet and name candidates. The Republican committee will meet Friday night and the Democrat committee will meet on Monday night."

"Jots From The Editor's Note Pad—Although Sheriff E. I. Cunningham had not looked well since his accident in April, his passing was not expected. Many think that he should not have attempted to return to his duties as soon as he did.

But Sheriff Cunningham was a most conscientious officer. He may have had his faults—what person does not—but no one could say that he did not try to do the best job he knew how as Sheriff. He made himself go when he was really not able.

No matter what blocks were placed in his way toward bringing law offenders to justice, he would not give up. He just went ahead and did the best he could. He will surely be missed."

[Philip Huffman] "I thought that Isam, maybe, was controversial, but I'm not sure exactly whether it was about the malaprops and whether people thought he wasn't *[educated]*...but as far as I know, he wanted to do what was right and he was pretty hard-headed about it. I think he got more effective prosecutions that a lot of other people.

I think that Isam was an excellent law enforcement man, as far as I know. He did it his own way and he was not polished. But he intended to enforce the law! And people thought that he was mean, but as far as I know he wasn't, really. When my dad *[M.J. Huffman]* presented, he could ask him anything and he would tell him the absolute truth about how it happened and what he knew about it. That was not uncommon among sheriffs in this area back then. I don't know whether it's uncommon today.

That's what I remember about him. He was not unlike Clay Hodges who was the sheriff in Christian County; Jim Baker, who was the sheriff in Wright County."

[Darrell Letterman] "After he got in to the Sheriff's department, he was pretty much of a changed person to where, you know, he respected Law and he worked at it and tried to see two sides of a story and make it work the best he could. I think he was pretty fair in all his stuff, whether he sent 'em in or maybe let'em go, you know, and say 'Okay, this is your last chance'. He knew when and when not to be real harsh and stuff, so, I think that was the reason he was well respected by all the law enforcement, because he just had a knack of, you know like they was talkin' about goin' into that Shockley deal, he had a knack of bein' able to talk to someone whether he had a gun or not, so that was a rare individual. I was just proud he was my grandfather."

"A great many of the MAIL's reporters have expressed sympathy....These have been omitted with the view of using this column to express the love and deep feeling felt by the reporters and staff of The MAIL, and to speak for the people of Webster County in extending words of sympathy at this sad hour."

Filed Aug 8, 1955
THE DIVISION OF HEALTH OF MISSOURI
STANDARD CERTIFICATE OF DEATH

Place of Death: *Webster* **County City or Town**: *Marshfield* **Length of Stay (in this place)**: *10 yrs.* **Was Deceased Ever in U.S. Armed Forces?** *No* **Disease or Condition Directly Leading to Death**: *Coronary Occlusion, Acute* **Interval Between Onset and Death**: *one hour* **Antecedent Causes**: *Coronary Arteriosclerosis, 2-3 years* **Autopsy**: *no*

I hereby certify that I attended the deceased from about 1953 to July 31, 1955, that I last saw the deceased alive on July 31, 1955, and

*that death occurred at 10:00 P.M., from the causes and on the date
stated above. [7-31-1955]*
Signature*: C.R. Macdonnell, M.D., Marshfield, Mo.* **Date Signed***: 8-2-
55* **Burial***: 8-3-1955* **Cemetery***: Prospect* **Location***: Webster Co., Mo*
Funeral Director's Signature*: R.W. Barber, Marshfield, Mo*

"Clyde Hargus, Marshfield fire chief, was in Columbia
Tuesday, Wednesday and Thursday of last week attending the Missouri
Firemen's conference....He said it was the best meeting he had ever
attended."

August 11, 1955 "The Democrat Central Committee of Webster
County met at the courthouse Monday night and nominated Clyde
Hargus of Marshfield as candidate for sheriff to fill the vacancy caused
by the death of E. I. Cunningham. The special election will be August
30.

Mr. Hargus, who has operated the Marshfield Café for the past
eight years, is 44 years old. He was born near Marshfield. He served six
years as guard at the Intermediate Reformatory and six years as plant
guard at Weldon Spring ordinance plant near St. Charles, before going
into the café business.

This will be his first campaign for public office.

The Democrat Committee is reported to have had the names of
three candidates before it, Mr. Hargus, Lester Garton and Roger
Thomas. The first ballot was divided evenly between them. It required
ten ballots to reach a majority. After Mr. Thomas withdrew the final
vote is said to have been 13 to 12."

"Floyd (Tiny) Owen of Elkland was nominated for sheriff at a
meeting of Republican Central Committee of Webster County held at
the courthouse Friday evening. All 32 committeemen and
committeewomen were present in person or by proxy. Owen received
20 out of 30 votes cast....

Mr. Owen is 38 years old, a farmer and is Republican
committeeman in Jackson township. He has never held public office.

The unexpired term will run until January 1, 1957. Next year,
the office is one to be filled at the general election.

With the passing of Mr. Cunningham, Coroner K. K. Kelley of
Fordland automatically became sheriff until the county court should
appoint a sheriff. The county court waited until Tuesday and appointed

Clyde Hargus who had become the Democrat nominee the night before."

"The Webster County Court, in session Tuesday, appointed Clyde Hargus to the office of sheriff of Webster County, to serve until his successor is duly elected and qualified...."

[Ruby Hargus] "I didn't get to join much, have a social life, but someway Clyde kept up. He loved people. He belonged to everything.
Clyde had been a night watchman too, besides the restaurant, and he had experience. He went with Isam a lot. That's why they appointed Clyde to fill in after Isam died. Then he ran for the election but the Republicans were in and Clyde was a Democrat. I was hoping he didn't get it, because I worried about it when he had that. But he wanted it."

[an ad] "To The Voters: ...I have never held any elective office, but served for about two years as a deputy under Sheriff Cunningham....I solicit your vote and call upon me any time I can help. Floyd (Tiny) Owen"

August 25, 1955 "The special election to select the new sheriff of Webster County will be held next Tuesday, August 30. It became necessary to hold an election when Sheriff E. I. Cunningham died July 31. The law requires that an election be held within 30 days.
The candidates have been nominated by their party committees. Floyd (Tiny) Owen, farmer, of the Elkland community is the Republican nominee.
Clyde (Skeeter) Hargus, Marshfield businessman, is the Democrat nominee. They have been making active campaigns in the short time that they had.
The special election will be carried on in the same manner and at the voting places in each of the 16 county precincts as are general elections. Absentee votes are being cast just the same as in regular elections."

September 1, 1955 "Floyd 'Tiny' Owen Wins Hot Race for Sheriff....More than half of the voters of the county turned out Tuesday to elect a successor to E. I. Cunningham....
Hargus 1,901   Owen 2,229 Majority---328

The absentee votes are to be counted this Thursday *[9/1]* starting at 9 a.m.....

Mr. Owen, who is 6 feet 4 inches tall and weights 275 lbs., will take charge of the office as soon as the official results are determined and he can qualify....

Mr. Hargus made a good race and says that while he is disappointed, he did his best and has no regrets."

September 8, 1955 "As of 11 o'clock this Wednesday morning *[9/7]* Webster County has a new sheriff. Floyd (Tiny) Owen was sworn in by County Clerk Orven E. Davis after Mr. Owen's bond had been approved by Judge James P. Hawkins. Mr. Hawkins came to Marshfield for that purpose.

Sheriff Owen announced that for the present Bob Replogle would be his deputy and that Mrs. Replogle had agreed to cook for the prisoners at the rate of $1.50 per day.

Mr. Owen moved his family to Marshfield Tuesday to what is known as the David Jones house, on old Highway 66 just north of Lilley-Calton Motor Co."

September 29, 1955 "The eyes and ears of the nation have been focused on a Denver hospital since Saturday when it was learned that President Eisenhower had suffered a heart attack early that day. Optimism is gaining since he has passed the crucial 72-hour mark, and if complications do not set in within the next nine days, doctors say he will recover....

Government will go on during his illness with little or no friction. He has prepared Vice-President Nixon, 'just in case,' by having him sit-in on all important decisions in government. He has organized the executive branch of the government by picking strong cabinet members and letting them handle their departments. Ike does not believe in 'one-man shows.'"

October 13, 1955 "Thieves blew the safe in the Niangua Farmers Exchange Monday night, taking all cash on hand, which was estimated to be between three and four thousand dollars....Sheriff Floyd Owen and the highway patrolmen checked over the scene Tuesday morning and are making an investigation."

[The nickname 'Tiny' has been dropped from Sheriff Owen's name from here on.]

November 24, 1955 "Wave of Burglaries Over County—The theft of four heifers from a Webster County farm was reported to Sheriff Floyd Owen of Marshfield Monday.

W. T. Triplett, Route 3, Rogersville, said he missed the cattle Monday and presumed they had been stolen. They weighed about 750 pounds each and two were white roan, the other two red roan.

The information was relayed to the state patrol and Greene county sheriff's office.

Sheriff Owen reports that Tuesday another cow was reported stolen from Bernard Curry, Route 2, Niangua. He thinks it was taken the last two or three days.

The service station operated by O.E. Hutchinson at the west side of town was broken into Monday night. He reports about $30 taken.

Thirty dollars in silver was reported stolen from Lynch's Tavern near Fordland Sunday night. Thieves broke in the front door."

December 1, 1955 "Haymes Chapel News...Mr. and Mrs. Ralph McNabb entertained at dinner on Thanksgiving for Mrs. E. I. Cunningham *[Eva]* and Mrs. and Mrs. Charley Cunningham of Marshfield and J.R. McNabb of Springfield...."

[pictured above: Eva Randolph Cunningham]

[Mary Lou Cunningham] "Edna says that Eva always held her hands and arms similar to the picture. I called her Evie and after talking with both Helen and Edna *[two other daughters-in-law]*, that is what most people that knew her well called her. Charley says both. Interesting that Edna said for some reason she called her Miss Cunningham a lot of the time, and I have heard her call her this many times and still does at times. She doesn't know why."

[Mitzi Hosmer] "Where Isam was all business, I always felt like Eva was what gave the kids their goodness. She had a softness and a sweetness about her. She was a big lady, heavy. To somebody's credit, though, all of their children were great kids.

She always had an apron on, a dress. She had her hair pulled back. Kind of neat looking. She never looked like she belonged to Isam. Soft spoken. Maternal."

[David Cunningham] "But *[Grandma]* was always quiet. I don't remember her talking very much about anything. I don't remember her talking about life on the farm or life in the courthouse. But what I remember about Grandma—Grandma was big. I remember she was about 210 pounds. She was a big woman. She was tall but she was really big. One of those big laps to sit in, you know. We have these pictures. When she was young she was real pretty!"

December 8, 1955 "Thurman Priest, convicted at Lebanon last spring of the murder of his 11-year-old niece, Jeanette Earnest of Fort Worth, Tex., has suffered a heart attack, according to a report from Fort Worth. Priest was held in jail here while awaiting trial at Lebanon.

Because of the heart attack, he will be too ill to stand trial January 30 in federal court for kidnapping, a Fort Worth doctor said, terming his condition 'critical.'

Priest was sent to the Missouri penitentiary for the murder, but was recently removed to Fort Worth to face the federal charge.

Priest has been at the U.S. Public Health Service Hospital in Fort Worth, where he was sent a month ago for mental test.

According to U.S. Attorney Heard Floore, there has been no change in plans for the trial and he still intends to ask for the death penalty."

December 15, 1955 "Matters Before The Magistrate Court—December 19, 1955...Eva Cunningham, Exec. vs. Zeke Silkey, et al, replevin. Continued to December 30."

[David Cunningham] "There weren't really any big family battles between the seven of them. And usually with that many kids, and only one farm to be inherited, and all the other stuff that goes along....There might have been some feelings here or there that weren't right, but, you know, they'd always get together, and always have a good time, and there didn't seem to be any big battles they couldn't live with. That's kinda remarkable, I think, for families."

December 29, 1955 "Webster County officers and the Patrol were called to Fordland Monday evening to investigate a break-in at the Fordland Farmers Exchange....

Monday night or early Tuesday morning the cash register was rifled and a large safe at the Elkland Farmers Exchange was hauled off...."

"Circuit Court Proceedings...Dave Coots vs. Bonnie Payton and D. Wayne Rowland, d-b-a <u>The Seymour Citizen,</u> damages. Motion for continuance considered and sustained. Case set for February 7, at 9 a.m."

[J. C. Cunningham] "All mine *[memories about Grandpa Isam]* are good, what I know, but I'm sure there's gonna be some bad ones that come out, but like Charley said, that's just part of life."

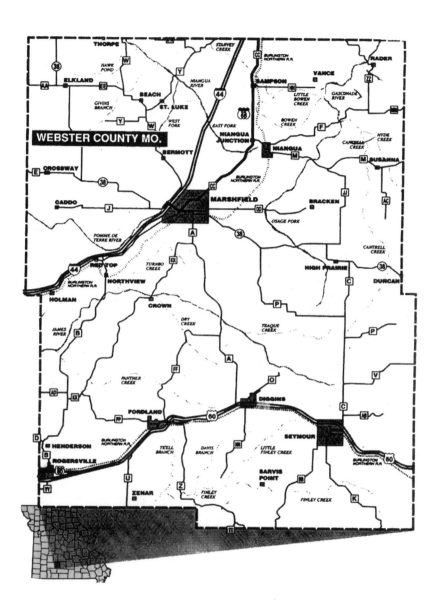

WEBSTER COUNTY MO.

[Gene Tinnin] "On September 19, 1956, on Route 66 in Laclede County, I was shot four times. Every year on the anniversary of that day, I celebrate the fact I am still alive. I retired as a Captain in the Missouri State Highway Patrol on July 15, 1982."*[photo and Missouri U S 66 logo courtesy of Gene Tinnin]*

Chapter Sixteen
An Epilogue: After 1955

Janet Sue Letterman Aday... "I took a videotape of my mother *[Mattie Cunningham Letterman]* telling about memories she had of her family. But I may have chosen a bad time, and perhaps waited too long, because some of her memories weren't clear."

Billie Galbraith Arthur... "I don't know when they *[funeral homes]* got out of the ambulance business and starting handling that through the county. Joe started working there in 1951 and he did that, ambulance service and everything, until the county took them over. We *both* did it. Sometimes I'd go by myself! Oh yes! Because *everybody* had to do it!

I became a legal secretary for Ellsworth Haymes. It was during the time after *[their son]* Randy was born *[in 1956]*. And I was typing up a petition and it said, 'The petitioner prays the court' and I put 'The petitioner praise the court' and Cline Herren called me up and thanked me for the compliment, and I think Roy Miller and Ellsworth had a few laughs over it.

Now I'm Administrative Assistant to the General Manager at Sho-Me Power. I've been there for forty years. From 1969 until now. Full time. *And* the funeral home! We was in the funeral business forty-six years. We probably got out in '97.

We've lived here in Marshfield all our lives."

Joe Arthur... "'Course, Billie and I, we're both licensed EMTs. We had to go through all that school *[Emergency Medical Training]* and all that stuff, get our license, to keep operation.

Everybody had to work at the funeral home. You had to do everything there is. You're janitor, plumber, embalmer, everything! I had to go to school and got my license in embalming.

We bought a fourth interest, in 1979, and then we bought a half interest in '83 or '84, and then we bought it all, maybe in the latter '80s. Then in 1987 we sold it but I stayed on and ran it for ten years. Arthur Chapel.

She'd *[Billie]* take vacations and help me on funerals, just like for an hour or two, then we'd get to the cemetery and she'd come back to work and I'd stay and finish up.

The Shockley Fire! *[the 1986 fire that killed five of Joe and Mary Shockley's grandchildren.]* We took care of their children, we went down and picked them up and everything. I went on the ambulance call. We went down to the house when it was still burning. We helped dig them out, get them out. That was a sad sad thing.

I *still* can *see* these things.

I still work! I'm going to work Saturday and Sunday. I work down at Branson at Track 4. This will be my seventh year. I sell tickets for miniature golf. They have two golf courses and go-carts and that sort of thing. There's five tracks. We're just right below Whitewater, on the left side, as you go down.

We just lost our mother a month ago. She was 96."

Warren Beck... "Jerry Yarborough was in jail, and Davis allegedly beat him up. John Hosmer filed charges against the Highway Patrolman Davis. Davis was transferred to another area, but was later killed in a wreck at West Plains. This really changed John Hosmer, because Hosmer lost the case.

I was in the milk business for 35 years. That was a long time ago. I've lost a lot of those memories."

[Warren Beck died during the writing of this book, on September 22, 2004, at the age of 85. I attended his funeral.]

(J.E.) Doc Blinn... "We had a few in Lions Club who were out a little way into the county, but it was mostly businessmen. 'Course, there were no women. Twelve, thirteen years ago they first started inviting women in. I've been president five different times. We were not very good at keeping the membership built up, bringing in new people. We all got gray-haired, old, and weren't putting new ones in from the bottom. I said, during one of my terms as president, I said, 'One thing we are going to do: we are going to open this club up to women! This is ridiculous. There are a whole slew of them out there who would make really good members.' Well, they took to it right away.

In Missouri, even today, most of the coroners are funeral directors. There aren't requirements for coroner except you be of age and resident of the county for at least six months of the year.

I didn't interact back then with the coroner at all, but I've been the coroner here for the past fifteen years. I took it a couple of years before I retired. They never did call me on things like that. Dog Edwards was a funeral director and a coroner back then for a long time. He really didn't know much about being a coroner.

When Dog Edwards took over—I got to looking back at the books when I took over—there were three or four years that he'd have only three or four cases he'd put in his book. If he had something that he didn't know what to do—he didn't know how to fill out a death certificate or anything—he'd come down to me or he'd ask me to come up to the funeral home and look at the body, and I'd do that, and then I'd make a diagnosis for him and I'd sign the death certificate. No, he wasn't illiterate, but he just didn't know how to fill out the paperwork.

About Coroner's Inquests, we don't do much of them anymore. Most of the time it really isn't necessary to do it. It's run something like a court case, but it's much more relaxed. The jurors can question the witnesses, if they want to, and the prosecutor helps out with it, with the questioning. I'd do some questioning. It has some rules and regulations but they're relaxed, not like a court case. Actually, it is done if there is some question about what the cause of death was.

The coroner can order an autopsy if he wants to. It was a little more difficult to order an autopsy back then, but the coroner can order an autopsy without having anybody else have anything to do with it. 'Course we have a forensic pathologist do the autopsies.

There still aren't a lot done. It costs over a thousand dollars—$1200 to $1500—the autopsy, plus lab work plus x-rays. The county pays for it. I'm not adverse to ordering an autopsy, but I feel that most of the time I know what the situation is and it wouldn't serve any purpose except to give the pathologist a good fee. We do from two to four or five a year."

Patsy Shockley Browning... *[about Kenneth Essary and the Shockley family murders]* "I don't even remember where we lived, but I *do* remember every night, for *ever* it seemed like, I dreamed I was hidin' in the corner between the wall and the piano—and I think I'd asked Bill where the piano set, evidently I knew—and I would be dreaming I was hiding there, because I thought someone was tryin' to kill me. But maybe I was thinking of that guy, maybe, I don't know. I used to have that dream *all* the time. But I do not remember *anything.*"

Shirley Letterman Carrizales..."I think we can say that the seed that Granddad *[Isam]* planted in his law enforcement years has made hundreds and hundreds of people better persons, and I can't think of one family member that's ever had a run-in with the law. We've all learned respect from him and I think he planted this seed and it spread and grew."

Willis Case... "They asked me to run for sheriff once, when Isam died. Said you can get to be sheriff without leavin' your front yard. But I said 'I try and spend my time makin' friends and you don't make friends in the sheriff's office. You don't necessarily lose them but you don't make them.'"

[Willis's wife, Ruby Hoover Case, died during the writing of this book, on July 5, 2003. I attended her funeral. Then on August 2, 2004—one year later—Willis died, at age 94. I attended his funeral.]

(Charles) **Charley Cunningham**..."I was elected Webster County Circuit Clerk and Recorder from 1966-1974.

May Vestal is the oldest on my mom's side—she'll be 98 in May [2004]. Grace *[Cunningham]* Hickman is the oldest on my dad's. She's 96."

David Isom Cunningham..."I'm David Isom Cunningham. Currently living in the Austin, Texas area. Pflugerville. Small town outside of Austin.

The spelling, Isom? That's how Dad *[Jake]* thought Isam spelled his name. But it appears it's Isam and when he dropped the 'h'....and his old records and some things from the courthouse, I have some in Texas, and I've actually found one place...he always uses initials—'E.I.'— when he signed, but I actually have one document that he signed 'Isam.' And that's really only in the last year or so that I discovered, that that really and truly was how he spelled it. 'Cause everyone just saw his initials. On his tombstone it says 'Isam' also.

The only one of Isam's brothers or sisters that I knew well would have been his half sister which we called Aunt May. May Rader. That would be Wilma's *[Thomas Ryser]* grandmother. How he *[Isam]* gave her that place down there, on the backside of the farm, to live. Because her husband died real, real young. And she spent 60 years a single woman after her husband died. Wilma said that house was there before she moved into it, that it was on the Cunningham farm, on the dirt road behind where that old store building is today, and how they fixed the house up. He fixed it up enough for her to stay there forever. Didn't have indoor water or anything, plumbing, whenever I remember going down there as a kid.

Last year at Christmas we were at a cousin's Christmas gathering, and one of the boys that's my age, Gary Letterman, we were all sitting around after lunch, and he says, 'You know, it still carries a lot of weight when you mention you're Isam Cunningham's grandson, around this town, with some of the old timers, the people who have been around here forever, the old families, it's a good thing to be Isam's grandson—Gary would be his *great* grandson. It wasn't 'Are you Jake's or Charley's or Buster's?' but 'Which one of *Isam's grandkids* are you?'

I don't know what kind of records and stuff existed but I kinda got the impression that when Grandpa was out of being Sheriff, that everything got boxed up and went with him. 'Cause we had stuff in our basement for years that came out of the Sheriff's department. It didn't stay with the courthouse. The bullets that were pulled out of the bodies of the Shockleys...we had them wrapped up in newspaper and in a shoebox in the basement, until the late '60s and Dad finally cleaned out a lot of that stuff, threw it away. He said, 'I'm not going to give these to somebody's family!' And they weren't the shell casings; they were the lead bullets. I understood that some of the guns that were confiscated from criminals, Isam would box them up and take them home. And I just kinda had the impression that whenever Grandpa left the office they took everything and there was no repository for county records of the department.

I've got the pistol that Isam carried. That's the only gun that I know that he ever really owned.

To me Grandma seemed quiet. She didn't talk a lot. I don't remember her watching TV or anything. I don't remember a TV being in her house. But it wasn't long after I remember that they had to have someone living with her. You [his mother, Helen] got home from a vacation or something, went across the street first to check on her, and she wasn't there. She'd had a stroke.

And I remember at Dad's funeral—William David, 'Jake'—the preacher got the crowd to laugh a couple of times. 'Might not have agreed with what he said but you all knew where he stood on everything, didn't ya?' And everybody laughed, got a chuckle. About my dad, at the tomb. So that's very...you know...you can see...it was said about *his* father [Isam], in the paper, when he passed away, and I remember that from *my* dad's service.

Apparently Grandma Evie, even before Isam died, Dad had to take her to the burial places. It took a whole day.

Good Hope Cemetery, that would be Isam's grandma. Then you go down the creek to Osage Cemetery and it would be Isam's mom. And you go further down to Prospect and you would get Isam's dad and his first wife. His second wife, Alice, is buried up the creek here at Osage Cemetery. Grandma Alice. The group we're out of, his second wife, is not buried directly across from him. She's buried at Osage Cemetery, by her *first* husband. So between that, and...on Evie's side you've got Shaddy and Eureka and Rader areas where they were all from, to catch all those old cemeteries. Shaddy Cemetery, just south of Grovespring in Wright County. Just off Highway 5, in Grovespring. So that's where Grandma Evie's side all came from."

Edna Henderson Cunningham... "Buster was the kind of guy that liked to work, liked to make money, and then he'd like to rest. We didn't do a lot of goin'. After Isam died, he said to his mother, if she didn't wanna sell [the farm to him], we would just have to buy another place. We weren't gonna just stay there and just work all the time and not own it. We wanted to do what we wanted to do, and have the money. It wasn't much more than a year after Isam died that we bought it.

We sold the farm...let's see...well, I've been here 28 years, will be, in July. Now what would that be? I should know. We moved here in '74. We lived there six or seven years before we bought it. We lived there 31 years. Milked cows and farmed.

See, the doctor told him he'd have to sell. We had a herd of cows, fifty cows, I don't know what all. He told him he just couldn't do it. And he didn't want *me* to be left there. I mean, you know. He lived eight years after we moved here [to Marshfield].

The trade school built this house. We knew we was gonna have to sell the farm, so we kept watchin' it. It took them quite a while to build and we'd come up here. And then, see, they put it up on a bid, see, you bid for it. So we put our bid in, you put your bid in, I don't know if they still do it or not, but that's the way we done it, up here to the school someplace. And this lady that was working there told me one day....

When I come to town, I would come to town oftener than Buster because my mother and sister lived up here, you know, I'd go up to see about them and do things, and he'd tell me, he'd say, 'Now while you're up there, see if anybody has put their name down to get that place!' so I'd go in, down at the schoolhouse, and I knowed this woman that was workin' there, Warren Beck's wife was workin' there at the school, and the clerk said, 'Well, I think you've got you a house!' And I said, 'Well, we're a hopin' so.'

Well, the first thing we knew, then, the Halls had put *their* bid in on it, you know. So when we come to bid it off that night, we had a certain night to come, Buster said, 'Well, I don't know whether we'll get it or not.' And *we* sat there, and the Halls. And there was her and him and the daughter. And they sat down here and we sat here. So we bid back and forth. And Mrs. Hall said to him, turned around and says, 'Well, do you think that's enough?' And he says, 'I think that's far enough!' Well, then we got the last bid so we got it. And Buster says, 'I thought pretty soon we was going to have to quit, too!' That's how we got it.

I never will forget that one of the board members or somebody, when they got it sold, Buster said, 'What do I do about the money, about payin' for it?' Well, the guy said, 'Oh, go get 'em all in quarters, Buster.'

I'll be here 28 years this summer. Twenty years by myself. I'm about ready to give up! I'm not able to do things, you know. I like to keep the yard pretty, and I like to keep the house up and have repairs and work done, and shoot, I'm just not able to do anything. I'm just not.

Whatever I've said, it's that a way or I wouldn't have told it."

Helen Jones Cunningham…"After Duke Petty got out of prison, after Isam died and Evie lived across the road there, Jake loaded his dad's pistol. And he kept it loaded until Evie was gone. Isam was the one who found him out here east of town, out on High Prairie somewhere, after he robbed the Seymour Bank. I remember Jake loaded that pistol and kept it loaded. Now our son David has his pistol. He took it home with him *[to Texas]*, had it all cleaned up, and put it away for safekeepin'.

Jake was with her *[Eva]* when she died. He'd always went by on Fridays to see her. He got in about noon from his route, you know. He was a coffee man. Quinn's Coffee. She died while he was there. 'Course, she got to the point where they had to feed her with a tube from, I guess, the stroke. But she lived across the road from us, pretty much, until she had to go in the rest home."

(John Calvin) J.C. Cunningham…"You know, I've got law enforcement on both sides of my family. My wife's dad was in law enforcement. *[Tom Martin.]* He's heard a lot about him *[Isam]*. 'Course, he didn't know him, either. He come here after Grandpa was gone, but he's heard an awful lot of good things about him. He *[Isam]* was well-respected around here. And I heard Mom said how good he was with teenagers. Before I was even dating Debbie *[J.C.'s wife]*, her dad was the same way. He sent my friend home several times, took him home. Just pulled him over, locked his car up, and took him home. We'd see him on the interstate, we'd slow down 'cause we knew who it was. To me, from hearing about Grandpa, it just looked, I just thought to myself, they're about the same type, that's how Grandpa probably was. Like Tom Martin.

Mom's got the blackjack. I supposedly have the nightstick, but Charley and Mom said they never remembered him carrying it. But Willis Case brought it to me one night and he said it was Grandpa's. But they don't ever recall him even carrying one. But Willis said it was Grandpa's, so as far as I'm concerned, it was Grandpa's.

You know, we're *[the Cunninghams]* all like that, though *[hard-headed, strong-willed]*. Everybody knows where we stand. They might not like it but, seriously, we all are, at one point or another. My boys can vouch for that. They don't agree with it, but they know where I stand.

But it's hard to go to the south side of the county, you know, that thing *[Isam's wreck April 1, 1955]* with Grandpa there. That intersection of 60 and A highway. You look right and that's it. I'm sure it's a little different now."

Mary Bean Cunningham..."When my mother passed away, we still have a shoe box full of pictures. She knew, but there's nothing on the back. So I have set down and on pictures like this, there's a *story* on the back!

I was so young. I didn't pay attention.

If you've got anything at home, like these pictures, go home and write on the back of them! People forget!

I like history. I didn't like it in school but I liked it later. And cemeteries."

Mary Lou McNabb Cunningham... "I served [*was elected*] as Treasurer of Webster County from January 1, 1991 to December 31, 1998."

Todd Cunningham..."Every one of the children had a personality and I think I knew every one of the kids. *[Grandpa Isam and Grandma Eva's children]*

For instance, living here in this house, we had down the street my Uncle Buster. His wife Edna, my aunt, is still living. The oldest boy, Buster, was probably closest in height to Isam, about 6' 4". Tall, thin guy who was an infantryman in Germany. He used to live at the farmhouse that they had down in Niangua. I'd love to go back there.

The oldest boy, Buster, was probably the calmest—not that any of them were outlandish or wild or anything—he had this ability while sitting around of just being calm. He could get irritated and wound up like anyone else, but the stories he would tell about growing up on the farm and things about the war. He was the only uncle of all the boys who went to war that I could get to tell about World War II.

The other uncle, Jake, was the other uncle I saw the most. Very firm opinions, stubborn, but loved him to death. You would see this man, my Uncle Jake, who likes to take charge, to get people to do what he wants. But any time you'd get him to talk about his dad, he'd just smile, laugh. I don't recall ever hearing him complain.

It seems to be the vogue for kids my age to complain about how their parents traumatized them. But all the kids had a reverence for both their parents. They worked hard. They're always fond of telling stories about how contrary he was, and what a kidder Isam was, a responsible kidder.*[not mean]*

All the kids talk with somewhat reverence of their parents. Not the worshipping where people that you miss who are long gone, you start to think that they were perfect and you hold them up as the ideal. I'm sure they did some of that. But they talked with a great deal of respect and affection, which is kind of amazing coming from a big family in which kids are spread out so apart in years to where some kids didn't really know the others as well because they were already out of the house by the time they had entered their teenage years.

I've heard the phrase that 'you're typical Cunningham.' I have to be careful explaining because I have some of the same traits. The phrase usually means you're being stubborn, hard-headed, pushing through your opinion. Does that mean that Evie or Isam were like that? I have no idea. But it's usually meant in reference to all the brothers. 'I told you so, I knew this, I hold this opinion.' Very opinioned group of siblings. I'm talking about my dad *[Charley]* and his siblings. As family stories go, my dad and Jake and Floyd tell stories about Wilbur being pretty quick to pick up a fight as a teenager. Kind of a forceful, get hot. Jake was very solid and firm on his opinions. He wouldn't relinquish saying he was wrong 'til he had to sometimes. I think my dad is one of the milder ones with his opinions.

I heard stories that Wilbur was left in jail by his dad.

I always heard that Evie had quiet power, that she didn't say much.

A trait that I know would have been a trait of Isam's, and that I think my dad has the disease or the affliction probably the worst of all the brothers, is being a people-person to the extreme that family trips, when I was younger, he would go out of his way— we were traveling through Texas and we went out of our way in Waco to hunt up an old army buddy he hadn't talked to in twenty or thirty years. To just hunt him up, to drop by on Sunday! He's done that all my life. You could sit him down next to someone from China and he would try to figure out some way to make it six degrees of separation or less. 'I know somebody who knows somebody you know.' My dad has this phenomenal memory, which I did not inherit, of the ability to remember names, places associated with people, what they do, who they're related to, what kind of kids, all this kind of stuff. He's just got a memory for this kind of stuff. I think it's incredible. Absolutely incredible. The people-person aspect, being sociable, likes to know everything that's going on socially, has a very good memory for what people have done, who they're associated with, all of that.

I've always had the impression that Isam was the same way.

I've heard stories about people swearing that Isam could see a car driving down the street, read the license plate, and know that it doesn't belong in his county. I've always heard stories about how he had a memory like that. How he knew people so much, about where they were going, that for minor offenses he would chase people and show up where they were going, and catch them.

Another trait: responsibility toward family, making sure the kids do well. Not the absent-father syndrome.

About Susanna...when I was growing up, Uncle Buster and Aunt Edna lived there. Usually on Sundays we went out there, for lunch. Two dogs—Toby, a friendly farm dog—would jump up on me. You'd come through a side porch, Aunt Edna would be making stuff, Uncle Buster would be there. I never went upstairs, wasn't allowed. Went out to the barn. Mice. Cats. I went to a creek, about a quarter of a mile from the house, caught crawfish. The front living room was dim but that orange-yellow light of a hot, hot, hot Ozark summer day, you could taste the dust. It was interesting. I wasn't bored, not anxious to get out of it. That was Susanna, the family home that Dad grew up in.

Buster farmed it while I was a kid. Sold it to Schooleys. After they moved here, down the street, I used to walk two houses down or ride my bike. Almost any summer day they'd be out in the yard. Aunt Edna would want to get me something to drink. Buster would talk about World War II. It was fun. Older people that I enjoyed visiting when I was a kid.

Edna is alive. I don't get to see her as much as I'd like. I miss Buster. I miss Jake. I'd be asleep on the couch and someone would bust right in the door. 'Hey!' That's Jake.

I had an experience in the courthouse when I was young. My dad was County Clerk, Recorder. I spent time in there after school. Had been taken on numerous tours of the courthouse by my father, when he showed me where his bedroom had been.

There was always the sense that my dad couldn't do anything that Isam didn't know about.

I don't want to call myself an ancestor worshipper, but there are pictures on the wall, typical pictures of family, and I miss the older people in my life who I had in my life as a kid.

I'm trying to decide which one of the siblings looked the most like [Grandpa Isam]. I guess it's a toss-up between Jake and my dad.

I'd give anything to have some sort of time machine. I think I'd just go back and spy because I'd hate to pop out in the middle of, to find out, that these people weren't who I thought they were.

I'm a radiologist, a physician....I have to know all of pathology, I have to know what surgeons do, I have to know what internists are thinking. I live in a suburb of Minneapolis, Medina. I actually work in St. Cloud, which is about an hour away. The reason why I live there is because of friends.

I don't know if it's unique to myself...I went to medical school in Kansas City and there were a few times, either because of the rotations I was on or because of the studies and the stress, that I needed some calming effect. And I have the habit, however strange it is, of wanting to be near my ancestors, so I would come to the Marshfield Cemetery where my mother's parents are now buried. She had one brother, one uncle on that side, who had lived far away and I always felt close...to one uncle on her side, that's all there was.

There were several on Dad's side. It seemed to me that going there, I was thinking thoughts that meant a lot. And so Prospect Cemetery, up on top of that hill, I made several trips unbeknownst to my parents, I'd stand up there and scream, ask for help.

One time in medical school I'd come down to stay with my sister—I'd been on general surgery call—I'm so used to it now I could literally see someone blown apart and I wouldn't bat an eye—but there was a well-muscled seventeen or eighteen-year-old black man who'd been shot with a shotgun and who was dead on arrival in the emergency room and it was the first time I saw someone enter a chest cavity in less than ten seconds. Sure enough, the heart had sprung a leak from the shot going through and the chest was just pouring out blood. I was so disturbed by seeing that kid having died, for whatever reason, whether he was a bad kid or a good kid it didn't matter, but seeing something that awful, after being up all that night and the next day, I still had been awake for thirty some hours and I drove—intending for my sister's—but I came down here and actually stopped by my uncle's grave, my mother's brother's grave.

Every time I come home, if I have my own vehicle, I will disappear and go alone to the cemetery."

Celesta Keeler Davis... "After I went out of there *[Garst Telephone Company]*, my sister-in-law and me had a children's shop. On the north side *[of The Square in Marshfield]*. Called Tots to Teens. Until I retired, five or six years later. I sold the store to Bea Rader and they kept the name the same. We sold a jillion Buster Brown things. We didn't really compete with Jarratt's. They had suits and things. We had more for children, for babies. *[Jaratts]* had a really nice store. They were really good.

I was up at the courthouse quite a bit because my husband, Orven Davis, was County Clerk, for twenty-six years. He was elected six terms, beginning in '48. In fact, he worked until the doctor told him he couldn't work anymore. He always had really good deputies; they were more like secretaries. He was there twenty-six years and he only had three. He was good to them and they were good to him.

His health...my husband had stomach ulcers forever and they'd hemorrhage, you know. Then he finally ran into cancer and that's what he died with, stomach cancer. I had it also. They removed 40% of my stomach.

Mary Margaret Evans—she died just recently, you know. I knew her well.

Ethel Hardy, Ruby Jane, they're gone now. I'm 89."

[The Keeler and Davis nieces and nephews invited the public—via an ad in The MARSHFIELD MAIL— to celebrate "Our Aunt Celesta Davis' 90th birthday at the Marshfield United Methodist Church on Feb.22, 2004", during the writing of this book.]

Raymond Day... "You know, when the country *[USA]* had its two-hundred-year celebration? *[1976]* Those plates that were made for it? They weren't even made in the U.S.!"

Kenneth Essary...*Essary, given a multiple life term for the murders of the Shockley family on April 3, 1951, died March 17, 1986, in the state penitentiary at Fulton, Missouri and was buried at Long View Cemetery in Jefferson City, Missouri, in Lot 429, Space 10. There is no marker on his grave.*

Oliver Evans..."I drove for MFA for 7 or 8 years. Then for MFA Oil Co. for about that many years. Then when Marshfield Steel moved down here, I worked over there for 11 years. I retired from the MFA Plant Division in '82. I worked for the telephone company a little while, as a lineman.

[When he was Night Watchman] I always figured if someone was up that time of the night, they was up to no good. Marshfield Police still does that. In the '60s my wife was operated on. My son was driving a truck. He come in that night. They lived down on Jackson Street. He called his wife to come after him. They had two little girls and she didn't want to take them little kids, it was one or 2 o'clock at night. So she called down here and wanted the wife and me to stay with the girls while she was gone.

I was comin' home, up Jackson Street, and turned up there by Blinn Clinic, and just as I had got turned around going down Washington Street, a car pulled in behind me, almost on my bumper. The town had just done some sewer work on Washington Street and I was dodgin' them holes 'cause every time I'd hit one, my wife would pretty near get torn apart, her surgery and all. So we got out to the city limits and my wife said, 'I wish that feller would go on around,' and about that time he throwed his light on. He said 'I saw you a comin' up the street and you was weavin' a little.' I told him about my wife. I was glad he stopped me. He thought I was drunk 'cause I was weavin' around all that sewer work."

[During the writing of this book, the sewers and water lines were again torn up all over Marshfield, for months and months.]

Alberta Scott Fraker..."Gene *[Fraker, her now-deceased husband]* had some good Republican people who insisted he run for Sheriff—it was Bill Fellin and Miller, Roy Miller—and he was getting some real pains in his legs from standing on the concrete all those years, beating on the tires, at the service station.

Gene was first elected Sheriff *[of Webster County]* in '68, but took office in '69. We had a two-way radio in the house! We didn't get much sleep for a few years. He went out in '88. Retired. Gene never did get beat."

Marsha Cunningham Gorman..."I'm 47 years old. Just turned it. I live in Round Rock, Texas, which is just outside of Austin. We live within a four-mile radius of each other *[referring to her brother David Isom Cunningham]*. And I did not know Grandpa at all. But I wish I had.

I remember Grandma Evie's sandwiches. Mustard and catsup sandwiches."

Paula Case Greer..."It just came to me: it seems to me when Isam was Sheriff, that everything was under control. I remember thinking that, when I was a teenager, a kid, that Isam had everything under control. Feeling good about it, feeling safe, 'cause Isam was Sheriff."

Talt Greer... "No, I don't think they ever found out we'd played this trick. There's two or three around that would remember this. No, we never did tell. I'd rather not tell the other guys' names who were in on it, we always had a lot a family around here."

Ruby Childress Hargus..."I was never able to go back to the restaurant. He *[her husband, Clyde]* was upset. He gave it away. The Style Shop is there now. That had been a café there ever since the town was there.

Mitzi *[Hosmer]* was such a good person, you know. She had these babies so fast. I babysat for her once in a while after we got out of the restaurant and everything.

After we got out of the restaurant business, that's when Clyde started working for the state. He tested scales, weights and measures. Then he got real sick and had to go to Mount Vernon *[in Missouri, a special hospital for tuberculosis]* for a year."

Barbara Dugan Herren... "I worked for Roy Miller for years. He wasn't good on his feet. He was very good at preparation and in research. He finally got smart enough to pull in another attorney to do court work. He even went to Springfield and practiced with him a little bit; Roy had an office in Springfield for a while and here, too, and that was the guy. Miller would start getting red and you could tell, if you were the other attorney, you could just read him like a book and you were just looking for a place to stab because you were going to be able to do it!

Marion Corbett called Judge Herren The Old Bear. See, I worked for Roy when his dad [Cline, Jr.'s] was Judge. 'Course, that was before Cline and I got married. I always enjoyed going in because the Judge always had a really quick wit and a good sense of humor. But Marion would call him The Old Bear. Very lovingly. 'The Old Bear's gone home.' 'The Old Bear can't do this.' Marion was his secretary. Never married, I don't guess. A beautiful woman. Her work was perfect. She was a very stylish dresser. Very career.

Billie Arthur went to work for Ellsworth [Haymes] and was just learning. And she typed from dictation, 'Ellsworth <u>praise</u> the court' instead of '<u>prays</u> the court' and 'course the Judge showed everybody that and said, 'Now, that's the respect they ought to have for the court, they ought to <u>praise</u> the court!' So Billie kind of got her feet wet with the Judge on that!

But Cline's dad was very well respected and very well liked and very fair, very just. He always made them clean up and cut their hair."

Cline Herren, Jr. ... "It was a long time ago, it was in the pre-hippie time, long about '56. Brought in this guy. Dirty and long hair and smelly. Dad told the sheriff, probably Tiny Owens, 'Take him up to the jail and let him clean himself up before he comes into court, and shave.' And this guy said, 'You can't make me shave!' And Dad said, 'No, I can't make you shave, but if you want to be in the favor of the court, you'll shave!' You couldn't get by with that today, I don't think.

Dad died in office. In March of '66. John Hosmer was appointed.

I did not know that Dad sold real estate and whenever they were cleaning out the old round-top desks at The MARSHFIELD MAIL, when Watters sold it, they brought over some business cards. That's when I got one about 'Lawyer in Springfield.'

About 15 years ago, the senior Lonnie Wilson told me—the Lonnie Wilson who's gone now—that he'd bought a house from my dad.

The county started auctioning off things, you know, and I own the bench that used to be the judge's bench."

Grace Cunningham Hickman... "I drove 'til I was 94. I run into the church up here and I said, 'Well, the Lord's a tryin' to tell me something,' so I just quit. It was pure carelessness. I went to turn the corner and I'd tucked my seat belt, I couldn't turn in my car to back out my driveway, with my seat belt. So I backed out and got started to the corner, I drew up my seat belt and pulled it, and as I turned that corner I dropped it, and it caught in one of them spokes in my steering wheel and jerked me right in to the church. I know it wasn't my fault, but it was *stupid* not to fasten my seat belt before I turned the corner, and I thought, 'Well, if you can't think any better than that...and you're gone and hit the church house', I thought the Lord was warnin' me!

I run into Jake's wife—I call him David but everybody else calls him Jake—the last time Danny took me to the cemetery. She recognized me. Two of her sons were with her. I really like her. When I go, I don't get out of the car. I can't walk on the grass anymore. Danny will take me and he goes through that gate right down there at the bottom, and he drives right around and Dad and Mother's grave is right there....One thing never dawned on my dad, that all his kids wouldn' t be buried at Prospect!

I've give up all my freedom. You can't be independent when you aren't able!

I said to my doctor when I was out there, I said, 'Do you have a pill for old age? You've got a pill for everything else!' She said, 'No, and if they did, I'd take it!'

I go all the time and I eat like a pig and I sleep good. I like to eat out. Not too much TV. I watch 'Walker Texas Rangers' on Sunday, but some of these new shows I just can't get interested in 'em. Sometimes there'll be a movie on [Channel] 15. I watched a movie the other night with Bruce Willis and a little boy. Now *that* was good. But this modern stuff I just don't go for.

Charley, you look more like Uncle Isam than any of the rest of 'em. You're the *baby* of the Cunningham clan, and I'm the *oldest. Alive*, I mean. *Just barely.*"

(Melba) Mitzi Hosmer..."I think John [Hosmer]...I think he started out wanting to do the right thing, you know, as he saw it, maybe not like everybody else saw it. But then, sometimes I think about how it all ended where he just did so many things I never would have dreamed of, before we got divorced. In the '60s...'61 or '62... when he went through the patrol case, that's when our life just went upside down. John was Prosecutor. Bill Davis, one of the troopers...Oh, I heard that day in and day out. Then after all that, he got so bitter. I think he had too high expectations, of what he wanted to achieve.

It was like, then he became where he wanted to   *get even.* Before then...his mother held grudges. He didn't want to even discuss holding a grudge. He said, 'I don't want *my* children to be that way!'

And then he became exactly like his mother. Although she usually held grudges over *petty* things.

John wasn't like that for the first few years. But I think his mother had a big influence. I think he wouldn't dare do what he did *[while she was alive]*. She died in '57. Then in '62, the trooper thing, and little by little.... *[John]* died in '78.

Judge Childress called me up. I told Ruby Hargus and Clyde, I said, you know John was supposed to give me money, but he didn't give me any money. I had seven kids at home, I told Ruby, 'I've got to get a job!' She told Judge Childress *[her brother]* and he called me up and said, 'You want to come to work tomorrow?'

John was mad at Judge Childress for hiring me. He said he had hired a felon! Because at that time when I got my job, *[John]* was still Public Defender and I asked Tom McGuire *[an attorney in Springfield]* what I should do. He said, 'He's not going to send you any money. Has the check always come to the bank?' I said, 'Yes.' He said, 'Open up your account and put half of it in your account, just exactly half.' That's exactly what I did. It was $1300 a month, so I wrote myself a check for $650, put it in my account. John said I was a felon because I was taking his money and using it. He came and yelled at Judge Childress while in court. He said, 'I'm going to take out an ad in the Springfield newspaper and say, Judge Childress Hires Felon!' I was just shaking all over! Not for me, but for Judge Childress. He just sat there.

John never really ever was physically abusive to me.

Judge Cline Herren. He had a great sense humor. Yes, he was crippled. This is a funny story about him. Remember Old Judge Scott? Ted Scott? He had big bushy eyebrows. We had a 30th Judicial Circuit Bar Meeting. I was sitting by Judge Herren, across the way was Icie Mae Pope, Judge Ted Scott was master of ceremonies, calling the meeting to order. Judge Herren was sitting right here, by me.

Judge Scott is kind of looking around like he's wanting something *[to tap on the table, like a gavel]*, to get everybody's attention. So somebody finally gives him a pencil. And Icie Mae meanwhile is going through her purse and she says, 'Oh, you already *have* a pecker!' She said that to Ted Scott! And Judge Herren was sitting beside me, he could barely get up and get on his crutches and get out of there because he was ready to die, he was exploding. And Ted Scott, had those big thick eyebrows—he just raised an eyebrow as if to say, 'Oh!' Everybody just went nuts! And Icie Mae, she never knew, she was just as sweet and naïve. It just broke everything up!"

Philip S. Huffman..."You learn things over the years—and this is a true aside—there was a guy named Williams who was the prosecutor down in Tulsa, Oklahoma, who used to lecture us when I first became prosecutor and tell us about closing arguments. They'd bring him up to our statewide prosecutors' meeting. Was his first name Ron? I cannot remember. But anyway, he would tell you about cases. And after telling one of his stories, he pointed his finger to all the state prosecutors of Missouri and say, 'Remember, folks, if The Son-of-a Bitch deserved to die, you've got the hardest case to make you ever had in your entire life!' *[to get a verdict of guilty from a jury]* He was right, you know.

Jim Baker was sheriff of Wright County for thirty years. Until the '70s. And he was quite a guy.

You could write a whole book about John Hosmer! Hosmer was something else. Colorful! Melba put up with a lot. Dad was good friends with both of them.*[John Hosmer and Mitzi Hosmer]*

Tom Eagleton became the Attorney General, and, of course, he and Hosmer had one thing somewhat in common and that was the love of good bourbon. Eagleton had lots of problems. But he filed a *quo warranto*, to oust Hosmer from office *[as Prosecuting Attorney]*. And that was over a trooper named Bill Davis. I think that's what he filed.

And this is one of the funniest Hosmer stories you'll ever want to hear. They were at the law school picnic at the University of Missouri in Columbia. Eagleton was up ahead of Hosmer, and Hosmer *hated* him after he filed the *quo warranto, personally* hated him. And Eagleton had gotten in trouble and the rumor was that they had taken him from his office in a straitjacket to an institution, while he was Attorney General. He later became U.S. senator. Anyway, Hosmer was given to stuff like this—that is, talking loud where he could be heard when he didn't need to be.

He said, 'There's Tom Eagleton! They say he's his own worst enemy!' —standing in line up there at the law school picnic, loud enough to be heard two counties over— 'Not, by god, as long as John Hosmer's alive!'

You see, much of this I have learned later, because I was born in '43. I was twelve years old when Isam died and I remember it was a big deal, when he was no longer in office. I have talked to my father any number of times about all this.

My dad called them Mugwumps. The bird that sits on the fence with its heinie on one side and its nose on the other. My dad wouldn't have anything to do with people who said they were Republican and then voted the other ticket.

What's happened in our county: we may have some Democrats in office but they run on the Republican ticket. And I have no patience with it. And that has been very very disturbing to people and it's caused them not to like me, I think. Well, I was Chairman of the Republican Party and there was a law—and it's still probably law—that if you have a primary election, actually the *party* is running the primary.

Now, the Clerk runs it but the party has some input into it and names its judges. And, for years, you could appoint the group of poll watchers. Well, what the poll watchers were there for was to watch and see if a known Democrat came in to vote in a Republican primary. Whereupon, you would ask the *[election]* judge, say, 'He's a known Democrat. Swear him!' And what 'swear him' meant was, before you let him vote in a Republican primary, he would put his hand on the Bible and raise his hand and solemnly swear to support the entire Republican ticket in the general election before he got to vote in the primary.

And when I started to wanting to do that, a bunch of our committee members 'went south' on me! Members of the Republican Central Committee! Because their relatives are Democrats and are voting in the primary for *them*, and stuff like that. And they said, 'You can't do that. That would disenfranchise them!' and I said, 'That's fine. It doesn't disenfranchise them, because they can vote in the general election, but they don't need to be voting in our primary!'

Because one of these days we'll have Democrats elected in the general election. And we will. My dad told me it would happen. If we couldn't do something about it. And he saw we were not going to be able to, before he died *[in February 1983]*."

(Mary Rosamond) Sally Day Hyde…"My husband *[Bill]* graduated from Rolla and we lived in Minnesota. Sixty-five miles north of Duluth. Ninety-eight miles from the Canadian border. We were right straight north, if you draw a straight line from here *[Marshfield]* to where we lived in Minnesota, it went right straight in to International Falls. Fort Francis, which is a little old place. We lived in Virginia *[Minnesota]* just about the whole time.

Wilbur *[Cunningham]* and his wife *[Eldeen]* came through to see me one time. They were going into Canada on vacation and they stopped one morning in the town of Virginia.

The first or second year I was there we had 128 inches of snow. Lived there thirty-eight years. We just learned to live with it. No, I did not teach in Minnesota. Then we moved back to Springfield."*[Sally Hyde died on October 11, 2004, just before this book was published. Her obituary said her husband Bill had died August 4, 2004.]*

Helen Jackson… "We moved into Marshfield 53 years ago. In 1950. I've never been married. I moved here with my daddy and mother. They retired. Sold the farm.

I was the first woman to work at Welch Manufacturing. I worked at Welch factory for 33 years. Right behind Ramey's *[in Marshfield]*. They shut down. I run a drill press the whole time I was there. From 8 to 3:30. Had a half hour for lunch. After work I'd mow the yard. If they had a school activity I went. Church activities. I still have church activities. I've been on the food committee for 30 years. I work for the Historical Society two days a month.

I'm 83 years old. Probably nobody else you interviewed knowed Isam the way I knowed him."

Mildred Tindle Jarratt... "Oren *[Cardwell]* just kept the rent at...you won't believe this...at $100 a month, for years and years and years. But that helped us get started. '52 to '92. I closed *[Jarratt's Men and Boys Store]* in '92.

I think being close to the courthouse helped our business. I know when Carl Young made his splash out there *[on the Spur]* with all the buildings and everything, he just thought sure that Jack and I needed to move out there. And Jack said, we talked about it, we thought it was a good location, but he says, 'Now how are we going to operate two stores the hours that need to be open, need to be serviced? And if you have to hire that much more help, are you going to be any further ahead?' As I said, he was the thinker. I just did a lot of the work. I *bossed*, but he *thought*. (I *was* bossy!)

I think most of them who went in out there were new people.

Drumright Hardware was next to us on the north. And Webster Hotel was on the south. Across the street was Johnny Andrews Café. And John Rainer's Aluminum Window Store where he did window repairs, and they had a laundry in the back of it. And Western Auto was across the street. And then the Phone Company. And then Mary's Variety Store. That's it. We had a pretty good business draw there, the people who were there.

We had salesmen that would call on us at the store, but we would go to Kansas City to market. We went to Dallas a couple of times to market and that's a great place to go if you want to be wined and dined. I mean, that's what they do. But that wasn't our object of going to market. Our object was to walk the floors and see what's new and see if we thought it was going to work here or not, and know what to do.

I'll never forget the first time we went to market and I saw pink shirts for men. Now go back, that's quite a ways back. That's in the 60's. They'd set up in the big ballroom, in Kansas City, usually at one of the big hotels. They'd had maybe two or three floors, different booths. I'd see the pink shirts and say under my breath, 'Look at that pink shirt.' We'd walk on to the next booth. Pink shirts. We went back up to the room and Jack says, 'What's your feelings about all this?' And I said, 'Oh, I just don't believe pink shirts will go in Marshfield.' And Jack said, 'I think with everyone showing them, we better buy pink shirts.' We did. They sold! He was good!

We had one front window broken out, before Jack died in '83. We got a call from the sheriff's office. It might have been Fraker. They said, 'We understand from a person that came up to the sheriff's office that you have a front window broken out.' So we jumped up and dressed and went up there and, sure enough, we did. And the only thing we could miss was a real nice silkey bright colored shirt I had put in the window that day to draw attention. I said, 'OK, Jack, that did the job!'

You know, I saw that boy go to school in that shirt! I didn't say anything, not for a shirt. I didn't jump him or say anything to him. He wouldn't look in the window. He'd go down toward school looking the other way. I'm always surprised when someone does something like that, but it didn't really surprise me that this boy took it. We have people that aren't very good to take care of it. They don't want to believe their children would do anything wrong. That was the only time we had a robbery.

I had some shoplifting. I realized it twice. I caught them by walking right up to them. We had a glass case by the front window that we kept our billfolds and things in. After school one afternoon there was three boys that came in. I knew them all. See, that was the thing, you knew everybody! So, they were looking around, and that glass case, if you moved the back of it, it kind of clicked, click, clicked. I heard that click. And they were talking, you know, and I heard that click. So I just walked up there and stood in front and looked over. This boy looked up at me and saw, and, boy, his hands went back and...he was going to take a billfold, it's what he was getting ready to do. He said, 'They're nice.' And I said, 'Yes, they are.' But then I had some socks disappear that I didn't know about, and we had a belt that everybody liked and some of them would disappear. And that's too minor to report. If you can catch them and make them think about what they're doing, it's better than doing anything else. If it had been anything bigger....

You know the last thing Jack did before he died? He was measuring Mac Case's slacks. It was the 23rd day of December and we were busy. Erma—Mrs. Price—had left and gone to lunch, and Jack and I was trying to wait on everybody in every direction. And I thought, 'What in the world is wrong with him? He's been down there pinning those pant legs for no tellin' how long.' And I kept looking at him and waiting on somebody and looking. And when he got through, he walked over and sat down on the chair, you know that old folding chair that sat there, and I said, 'What's wrong?' And he said, 'I don't know but there's something wrong.' And he said, 'Call the clinic,' and I did, and Dr. Bareis was there. And Jack said, 'I'm going out,' and I said, 'Let me go with you' and he said, 'No! You stay here and take care of the store.' That's the last words he ever spoke to me. He drove out there, they called the ambulance, sent him to Springfield. When I got up there, but he had already...they had done an angiogram. He had gone out again and they were working with him, trying to revive him. He died of a heart attack. He was 63. Not very old. I was pretty upset for a while.

Jack died in 1983. Jerry *[their son]* joined me not very long after Jack died. He was in the state of Washington working. Just all of a sudden he called one night and said, 'Mom, I've got to come home.' I said, 'What's wrong?' He said, 'I've got to help you.' So he came home. And he was good, but he couldn't stay in. He couldn't be confined to that. He just couldn't do it. He was good! He could buy well and he could display good. He could have been a little more mellow with some of the customers. I tried to work something out with him. I'd say, 'OK, you open these three days and I'll open the other three.' Well, he was on the fire department and if there was a call, I'd go to the store and there was a sign, 'Gone to fire. Be back.' Locked up. Tighter than a jug. He was dedicated to it! Now we have the paramedics. Then we didn't have any. They were just starting when Jerry was here.

It's just not his nature. If you knew him you'd understand. 'Cause he's just swish, swish, swish! He went and lived in St. Louis and worked with HAZMAT *[Hazardous Materials]* team. He did well. He was well trained.

I was getting tired and old.

I didn't sell the store, I closed it out. I would have sold it and I had several inquiries. But a lot of the inquiries were not financially able to buy out the store and we had friends in Kansas that had sold their store 'on time'. We used to go to market in Kansas City and we would visit with them because it was in a town that was small and we had similar problems and things. And they had sold their store and the people had paid so much and then they were to pay on it. And she said, 'Be careful what you do because we got took. They had sold all the merchandise and had nothing to pay us with.'

Dr. O.L. Cardwell's estate still owned the building—he'd had the dentist office in the old Webster Hotel there. The business was mine to sell but not the building. It was much easier to get out from under it. It was easy to close it out because you could reduce stuff along and people were really interested in buying something.

And you know, to this day I am still surprised that, after Jack died, that maybe, I didn't have someone try to rob me, when I closed the store, 'cause I'd go around to the bank and drive, and I've often wondered, 'How did I get by all those years carrying money at 5:30 when it got dark?' Now John Bradstein, he worked for me after school, he would always go over and sit by the bank until I got there and put it in. Then he'd go on home. We tried to figure out something to deter. But I'm still surprised. Then I got to where I'd send John around to get my car, from behind, and bring it to the front, so all I had to walk was from the front door to the car.

I was as careful as I could be, but I'm still surprised that someone didn't try to rob me. But nobody did, that I know of. And I don't think we had any money taken out of the store. If we did, it was very little.

We had a drawer, we didn't have a cash register. We didn't lock it. We had sales slips and we knew how much money was in there, how much we needed to balance. Every night we balanced. We didn't go home until we balanced."

Warren Johnson…"My dad was 92 or 93 when he died. I don't think the job of sheriff hurt my dad.

I traveled for Sho-Me for 25 years.

I carried a tape recorder for years with Sho-Me, and you'd be amazed at the number of people who just wouldn't talk 'in front of that thing.' But I love my voice; that's why I'm so gabby.

I sang tenor in a quartet, a pretty good quartet, and we sang mainly for funerals. Over a thousand funerals!"

Mary Ellen Shockley Kilburn… "Robert and Juanita *[Schultz]* was a packin', to move to Lebanon, and I took my grandson over there, to see the house. She said, 'Is there any place else you wanna go?' and I said, 'No.' We went upstairs, downstairs. We went in every room. I told my grandson…you know…what happened, and she said, 'You can come anytime you want, it don't make any difference what time of day it is.'

I've always wondered, we've all wondered, how we'd a turned out if we still had a mom and dad. Maybe we wouldn't be living as close as we are.

But I've learned a lot from my losses in life. I lost my mom and dad at 10, and when I was 20 I got slapped again! I was left with two little girls to try to raise my husband got killed in California. And I was left with two little girls so I come back to 'Missourah'. My boyfriend I went with before I married my first husband found me again and we've been married for almost 42 years, and we have a son together and he's the only father my girls know. Don't you ever tell either one of those girls that's not their dad; they'll fight you over it real quick! They *know*, of course. My life changed a lot just from losing Mom and Dad, but it changed a lot more after J.H. got killed and I married the right guy. So, yeah, I learned a lot.

In the beginning, you do *[feel that it's too much, it's not fair]*, but then I turned around and said, 'Hey! I've been where they're at, [but] they've got one left! I didn't have one left, I've got to be there for 'em.' And when J.D. asked me to get married, I said, 'I can't marry you! I have two little girls to raise.' And he said, ' But I can help you.' And he has!

From the time Mom and Dad got killed, I'd say for at least ten to fifteen years, you could just say Shockley, and they'd say, 'Oh! I knew these people!' and they'd start tellin' ya and then they'd stop and they'd say, 'Uh oh, you're one of 'em.' I mean, the name Shockley just stuck.

And then, it was 1986—wasn't it, Jimmy?—that Joe Shockley, my dad's baby brother, he lost five grandchildren in a house fire. They lived just up the hill from 'em there. That brought home some memories. The night it happened my son came home, we didn't live far from there, and he said, 'Mom, Dad, get up! I see a big fire. Let's go see about it.' And we went over there and my uncle *[Joe]* was in the hospital at the time, 'cause I'd just talked to Aunt Mary on the phone, and the fire department was there, and Larry King come up and said, 'Oh J.D., it's bad.' He said, 'Bill's lost five kids in the fire tonight. The helicopter's takin' Bill and Eileen to the hospital.' And that kinda brought back the Shockley name and all, that kinda took it back to when it happened to us."

Daniel Max Knust..."When Gene *[Fraker]* was sheriff, he used to come down and talk to me *[Judge Knust]* 'bout every day.

And he was tellin' about a burglary down at the Seymour Apple Orchards. He was explaining that they had these apples in these crates and the crates had some type of red paint or powder or something on them that would come off on your hands when you lifted them, probably some type of cheap paint like whitewash. Anyway, someone had noticed there was someone in the warehouse that shouldn't be and they pulled up and caught these guys outside and noticed someone had broken the lock and they had this red stuff on their hands where they'd been movin' the crates and probably going to load them into their truck, and that was extremely incriminating. And Gene said, 'It's kinda like Isam used to say,' and Gene kinda grinned, he said, 'We caught them with the red on their hands!'

From that point on, catching somebody red-handed in Webster County became Isamized.

Around the courthouse we still refer to the sirens as syringes, occasionally, because of Isam."

Freda Doyle Langston... "I was the first woman ever elected City Judge in Marshfield. They used to call it Police Judge. For eight years. Claude Lewis was the mayor and they came to me to run.

I was deputy five or six years: for Lefty Davidson and for Fraker. Sometimes—I'm ashamed to say this—sometimes when I'd be in church, I felt like some of them women I knew had been in trouble would be eyein' me, because I knew what they had done. I felt kind of funny. I think they were eyein' me because they wondered, 'Is she tellin' stuff on me?' But, you know, when you're deputized you take an oath that you won't talk.

Kid, when I was workin' with the sheriff's office there was so many women would come in to swear out papers on their husbands for beatin' them up, and they'd be black and blue. And every time, I never knew of one, that didn't come in before they had him in court and withdraw their complaint. It used to, their husband was just about all they had to depend on for a livin', but nowadays they all have jobs of their own and they don't have to take all that stuff, and that's why they have these homes for the battered women and children.

My husband *[Paul]* worked for Burchfield Mills for thirty-three years, until he retired. He was a supervisor there. Paul died five years ago. Mama's *[Elzie Doyle]* been dead 39 years. She died from cancer. I sat many a time beggin' her to go to the doctor. She wouldn't go. So finally she had to go to the hospital, and she didn't come back.

There's not too many of us left, honey, I'm 88 years old. I've got a good mind but, with this back trouble, I can't get out like I did."

Fredrick Isom Letterman... "I liked Evie. I don't know how i can describe her. Best I could remember, she lived across there from Jake. We'd go down there to see her and she'd always be sittin' in some kind of a rockin' chair, or a big ole chair, she'd always be sittin' there in it. And she had this woman that took care of her, that got to stealin' her money and stuff. They had a lady hired to take care of her, an older lady, and she got to stealin' stuff and they got rid of her. Then I can remember they brought her up to Springfield, had to put her in a rest home. Mom *[Mildred]* would go over there, and they hadn't changed her sheets, or something like that, you know. It was kinda depressing. I didn't go over there much. All I can do is remember how she was in that little white house across from Jake. And she was just settin' in there, and she'd talk. You'd talk to her. I don't even remember what....'Course, I was so little then, I didn't even think about talkin' to somebody. I was wantin' to run around and play, you know. I remember goin' to see her there a lot.

Mother and Dad's favorite thing in the world to do was to go to Silver Dollar City *[near Branson]*. And they had season tickets and they wouldn't buy nothin'. 'Cause they'd go down there and they'd sit in the square and watch people go by. Wouldn't ride nothin'. Wouldn't go to the shows. Just go down and set and watch people. And they'd say, 'Well, we saw so and so down there today and....'"

Thomas Dwaine Letterman... "I remember Grandma Eva in the nursing home, and I didn't like that at all.

I remember the stubbornness was a Cunningham thing. My mom *[Mattie]* didn't forget what you'd done wrong. When we got too old for her to whip, she'd come up to us a couple weeks later and whup us, say it was for what we did a few weeks earlier. She didn't forget! But she had to catch us off guard, 'cause we got too big.

I've driven a delivery truck for Nabisco for 28 years, here in Springfield. It's a distribution center. I used to deliver to Marshfield when Carl Young had his store there, and he knew I was Isam's grandson. He'd talk to me about that.

My mom said Isam wouldn't let her go to high school, so she went two years to eighth grade, so she could stay in school. She took eighth grade twice.

My mom had that Cunningham nose, for sure."

(Margaret Elizabeth McFall) Peg Miller..."Roy Miller...he was a character. He loved it all. He loved the courthouse business. He liked the intrigue of it all. The political thing. Courthouse politics. He and M.J. *[Huffman]*, they were arms around it all. He was an organizational person. I've forgotten how much he was in things. He was Prosecuting Attorney for a long time. He was City Attorney for Seymour, for a while. He was for Marshfield, too.

Roy was a fun person. Very much a fun person. He liked parties. Jolly. They would go somewhere after court, to somebody's house, and drink whiskey. Cline *[Herren]* of course was the 'Magic' Judge. *[an Isam-ism, explained in Chapter One]*

Roy and I started Webster County Abstract. Barbara Herren was his secretary, and we sold it to her.

He died in '71. He had cancer. He hurt, kind of down in his side. They couldn't find out what it was. They didn't have MRI and a lot of things they have now. After several months of being miserable, he had surgery. They found it was in the pleura. The pain was from nerves, called intercostal nerves. There wasn't much they could do about it.

He was 53 when he died, would have been 54 in about two weeks. Dave was off in the navy. Sarah and her husband flew back from Brussels. Marge was in high school. Sarah—she reads medical stuff—always thought it was the kind of cancer that was linked with asbestos. Roy was on a ship in the navy, for four years, that was filled with asbestos. Crawling with asbestos.

The women back then...I would have loved to work part time. But it was sort of stigmatized. Really. You supported your wife. Man's work. And there was woman's work. I worked at the office the entire time during tax season. He did all kinds of tax work, *[the lawyers]* all did. The farmers would bring in their stuff in a paper sack. All of their milk checks. They were weekly!

After Roy's death, I ran for and was elected State Representative.

The good old boys reigned supreme down in Webster County when I was there. But I came back and cast the deciding vote for the Equal Rights Amendment. I sponsored the bill! It passed 164 to 83. I knew what I'd get hit with from Webster County and I did. I had to have a blind phone number for a while.

After four years of trying to find something, *[U.S. Senator]* Kit Bond called and asked me to be a lobbyist for him. I also lobbied eight years for *[U.S. Representative]* Roy *[Blunt]*.

I left Marshfield, finally, in the early 80's *[and she now lives in Jefferson City]*. I was on Kit Bond's staff, his second term as governor.

I'm 80. I never was one to be able to remember word by word a conversation that I had, the way some people can, and I always really feel that most of those people lie a lot. They just make it up."

Mary Lee Day Peck..."That *[the Shockley grandchildren]* fire was probably in the mid-80's. My daughter was the first one over there. She saw the fire from the back door and she went, 'Oh! That's got to be over on the other road, the Bowen Road,' and she jumped in the car and went over there and they were trying to get some of these children out.

Eileen, the mother of them, is with our *[Niangua]* Fire Department and a First Responder; we're on the board together and she still has these awful scars, on her arms, they're just horribly scarred. I think they had three more children since they lost the five."

Bill Rader... "Another thing that I think is interesting, and I think it's all because of my Great Grandmother Alice...now she married, and she and Jim Cunningham had these children, and there's a big history, especially in Isam's family, of heart attack. Lots of it. To begin with, Alice's first husband died when they hadn't been married too long, rather young. And they'd had two children, my grandmother *[Ida]* and her brother Estell. You take the Cunninghams. Isam's children, many of them have heart conditions, circulatory problems. So did Alice's children. Her son died of a heart condition. My father died of a heart condition. My uncle Hugh died of a stroke. My aunt Beulah died of a stroke-like thing. So I guess she spread this throughout the land, because there's a lot of connections to circulatory...the whole connection, with the heart condition, seems to be with her.

Buster died of a heart condition. Floyd *[Snooks]* has heart problems."

Jane Hyde Rader... "We lived over the last twenty years in the south St. Louis area, Hillsboro was our address, we lived in the country. But I think the twenty years we lived there we went to one or two funerals. We moved down here *[Marshfield]* and it's a funeral every week! 'Cause it will be somebody that we knew or...I see people who knew my parents, every once in a while, and that always makes me feel good. But we're gettin' up there, the older generation. Bill's comin' up on eighty; he doesn't want to talk about it!"

Robin Lineberger Rader... "Will *[Lineberger]* never believed in taxes or banks and so when it came time that he passed, boy, did they get taxes out of his estate.

He had a nephew that would come from California to here, and he would take his Uncle Will down to the bank and he'd sign everything into *his [the nephew's]* name. And I doubt if his taillights got down to the corner before my dad would take Will down and change it all back into his *[Will's]* name. I think now, 'All the paperwork you caused those *[bank]* people!' My dad would change it all back to my grandpa's name, because Dad was the guardian.

Grandpa *[Will Lineberger]* died November 13, 1959, in Portland, Oregon. We took him with us when we moved out there in '58."

Jack I. Rainey... "Shoot. I'll tell ya now, the phone don't hardly ring twice 'til it gets answered. I'm sure that's a throwback to *[his growing up in Rainey Funeral Home]*...when the phone rang, it was the most important thing there was, because it was either a death or an accident or somebody needing attention."

Maxine "Toots" Shockley Replogle... *[Maxine's husband, Glenn Replogle, died during the writing of this book, on June 29, 2003. I* *attended his funeral. After Glenn's death, three times during the next six months, I conducted Shockley group interviews.]*

"Well, just since Glenn's passed away, Joe come to me that day and he said, 'I want to tell you somethin,' he said, 'I thought the world of your dad *[the murdered Bill Shockley].*' He said, 'If I needed advice I'd go to him and he'd tell me what to do and what I needed to know.' That was Dad's youngest brother and he told me that at my door, within the last month."

Fred Rost... "I'll tell ya, there's lots of things that's happened around here the last 70 years, it's a sight on earth!"

[Fred's wife, Velma McElwain Rost, died during the writing of this book, on March 28, 2004. I attended her funeral.]

Wilma Thomas Ryser..."Buster and Edna had the big sale, when they sold the farm down there. Before Evie died. They had somebody come stay with Evie for a long time, but then they had to put her in the rest home, in Springfield.

And we lived...the Christian parsonage was between us and Jake, out here on Washington. So I visited Aunt Evie, I guess, more when we lived in town across the street from 'em, than I ever did in my younger life.

She'd sit and talk and tell things that had happened. I'd give anything if I'd had a tape recorder to tape hers and my grandfather's and my daddy's tales. She was a very nice lady, as far as I know. I don't remember her ever talkin' about anybody or anything. Just more or less went along with the flow."

Bill Shockley..."The administrator *[of the estate]* was Ellsworth Haymes. We dealt with him for years until we finally closed out. And he did a real good job. It finally closed out in '63 or '64. Most of the money was used. Very little left. Less than a hundred dollars to each one of them was left. Most of the estate was used up.

Kenneth Essary wrote me a letter from prison but the court decided that I didn't get to see it."

Don Shockley..."Course, I only did it four years...but what we'd do, I can remember. We would walk over from our house, we'd meet Jack's kids, you walk up and there'd be *[Joe and Mary's]* kids, and from there we had a ball. We'd meet other kids, and by the time we'd get to school we'd have half the school. In fact, one year at Reed School, I think there was fifty some kids and over thirty-five were first cousins. That's right, I remember!

One time I was drivin' through Louisiana and I seen a mailbox that had Shockley so I went in and introduced myself, and I told them I was from Missouri, and they asked me if I knew the Shockley family that was murdered and I told them that was *my* family."

Jim Shockley ..."In 1961, I got laid off from McDonnell *[Aircraft]* and we moved down here for a summer. And Glenn *[Replogle]* had a gravel business and I kinda worked for him at that time and then during that period of time I got called back.

We were getting ready to move back to St. Louis...and we had talked about this...as we went through life, I thought that since I was an adult and they had given all their life to us, that I should be able to contribute something. And Billy, his family was getting rather, well, it wasn't *big,* but it was just my turn, it was time for me to do something. And, anyhow, we talked it over, and Bob and Carol—who was living with him *[Bill]* at the time, the two youngest ones—moved with us back to the St. Louis area. We lived in Westfield at the time.

And Bob was in the sixth grade and Carol was in the eighth, I believe. And they stayed with us until he graduated out of high school and she graduated and got married. They were both good kids when they were with us. And Juanita *[Jim's wife]*, she was every bit as much a mother to them as Glenn *[Maxine's husband]* and Lorene *[Bill's wife]* had been *[dad and mother]*. She was willing to do her part, and anyway, I've always appreciated that.

And I don't want any praise for it or anything, but when they come with us, we thought we could probably go to Child Aid or whatever and get some kind of help with 'em. And we started to do that and we talked about it and we decided we wouldn't do anything, we'd just forget it, and whatever we had, we had, and if we couldn't make it, if we got to the point we couldn't make it, we'd get help somewhere.

But it never did get to that point. We had some rough times but Juanita was a good manager during all that time. And we made it just fine. But anyhow, Bob got drafted and after that he never did come back home. He was out on his own at that point in time.

Carol got married and she had three kids. Unfortunately, when she was 42 years old she contracted cancer, lung cancer. She found out that she had lung cancer in February, I believe it was, and in six weeks from the day she found out she was diagnosed with cancer, she passed away. She passed away on April the Fifth, and...had her funeral on the same day that they had Mom and Dad's funeral. April 5th.

She was a wonderful girl.

One thing that they *[Bill and Maxine]* both done, that I can say about them, is they provided us with something *they* didn't have: a place to come home to.

You know, after that all happened, we were orphans and *they* were *too*. But *we* had a home to go back to, after we grew up and left home, but *they* didn't have that. They were kind enough and good enough to give the rest of us—I'm talking about myself and Mary Ellen and Don and Patsy and Bob and Carol—they gave us a home to come back to.

And that's important in life, is to know you belong somewhere. And they provided that for all of us, even though neither one of them had the luxury of being able to go home to anyone except mother-in-law and father-in-law, which, they were good folks too but there's still something missing with that.

One thing that Juanita reminded me of, that I know that the other kids have appreciated down through the years: we sold the farm to Robert and Juanita Schultz, and they almost got to the point where they seemed like family to us, because we could go back down there and they would invite us in the house, and we just...they wanted us to treat it just like it was home. And you could almost *feel* at home when you went back to see them.

I think one of the things that kinda helped *me* as I went through life: I would hear other kids talkin' about their parents, talkin' about their 'Old Man' or 'Old Lady' and say bad things about 'em, and, you know, ours was gone and they were *anything* I wanted them to be! I always figured that mine was not like that, and I never ever seen any proof that they were any different than that! And I could make 'em be anything I wanted 'em to be, and I didn't bad-mouth my mom and dad. In my mind, they were ideal."

Joe Shockley..."Some people told me that his older sister went and seen him *[Kenneth Essary, in prison]* just pretty regular, and said she was the only one of his family that they could ever get to go at all. And I know a few years back, before he died, they said one of the officials up at the state prison called one of his brothers and asked if it was all right if they released Kenneth and let him come back down to where *he* was at and he said, 'No sir!' he said, 'he had no reason whatsoever for doin' what he done,' he said, 'and we don't know, he might decide to do that again.' He said, 'He's where he belongs, just let him stay.' He wouldn't even talk to him. I heard about him dying *[in prison]*.

I was born in 1919, Mary was born in 1923. We were married when she was 15 and I was 20. If we make it 'til July 8th *[2004]* we'll celebrate our 65th anniversary."

[On July 11, 2004, I attended a 65th anniversary party in Conway for Joe and Mary Shockley, given by their family.]

Mary Martin Shockley… "Since it's all over with, Jimmy Lee has told us that him and Don would take the *[bath]* tub upstairs and they would rub the floor, to get the water dirty you know. Wouldn't even get in the tub theirselves! Do you remember that, Don?"

(Mary Francis) Fran Thomas Steelman… "Evie was always very good to me, but not in a lovey-dovey sort of way. 'Course, *our* mother wasn't either! We just wasn't raised that way. And then I married a Southerner! I've lived with it long enough now, I just hug like the rest of them. But it's very different from what we were raised into.

After I graduated from high school, in '50, I got married and left here. So I've been gone longer than I lived here. California, Illinois, Kentucky, Canada, then Alabama. I lived in California when my husband was in service. We had one child. Then we went back to Illinois when he got out and I lived there 17 years and had three children *[total]*. Then we moved to Kentucky and I had two more boys. Then I moved from Kentucky to Canada with four children and an eight-month-old baby. I lived there for a year. Then to Alabama. I've been there about 34 years. I've been there longer than I lived any other place. My husband was born there. He's a native. He was from Huntsville, Alabama. I live about 47 miles from Huntsville."

(Francis E.) Tony Stephens… "I retired from Missouri State Highway Patrol Troop D in 1979."

May Cain Vestal… "I married brothers. Herbert first, the oldest. He died in '83. Then Herman, in '91 or '92, and he lived for eleven years.

My first husband didn't like parades, but my second husband, his brother, liked parades."

Jack Watters…"The Lions Club was *the* Chamber of Commerce. There was no Rotary Club or no Optimist Club or no Chamber of Commerce. I don't think I got into the Lions Club until 1960 or so, after I'd run out of time in the Junior Chamber of Commerce, the Jaycees as we called it. Others may have been members of both, some were, but that didn't seem to work very well. The Lions Club had the elder statesmen, you might say, of the town. They were the people who made it happen, they made things move.

There was a closeness of Marshfield merchants back then that I don't detect now. But that's probably because we have downtown, The Square in Marshfield, and then we have The Spur. We have two things. And then we have businesses scattered everywhere along Highway 38, going east a little bit. Business is done a little bit differently now. It's good! And I think Marshfield fared very well, as far as the business part. You always have a worry that if Niangua went downhill, and Fordland went downhill, are we next? But I don't think so. I think we're close enough to Springfield that we'll have a certain number of people back and forth that will do a lot of shopping.

We *[The MARSHFIELD MAIL]* built a new location in 1967 and went to offset printing. Dad died in 1976. Ed Webb also owned a little, four or five percent. Then Floy *[Watters George]* died in 1984 and so the Watters family, Warren and I, sold *The MARSHFIELD MAIL* in 1985 to Gordon Nordquist."

David Young…"The *[Beach]* store is torn down now. But that house is still there. My grandfather's house was across the street and was just torn down four months ago.

I have served *[been elected]* as Webster County Collector for two terms."

Cathy Cunningham Youngblood… "I did not know my grandfather *[Isam]* so everything I can tell you are stories I have heard. And most I hear about are, oh, just his personality and the way he handled things.

When I was working at Cox *[Hospital, in Springfield],* I was there for 16 years and there wasn't one year that I know of that went by without running into *somebody*—obviously, especially before I got married and I would have Cunningham on my name tag—that always had to bring up, you know, if I was related to anybody in Marshfield, then it would always go back to if I, well, 'Did your family know of Isam Cunningham?'

And I heard many, many stories—which I cannot recall to this day—but they were…it was always good to hear, and a lot of times I would just sit down on the bed and listen to them, because there were numerous stories to tell."

AFTERWORD: From the Author

Isam Cunningham was an ordinary person who began to confront extraordinary challenges. Facing the vague Communist menace and the possibility of a bomb being dropped on his Webster County were secondary to his routine dealings with drunks, robbers, and murderers.

Was Isam Cunningham a hero? Most people who are viewed as heroes will humbly state that they only did what they had to do, didn't think too much at the time about being afraid, and went on with their lives after they did the reputed, glorious deed or deeds. We don't know what Isam would have been like after he was no longer sheriff, because of his untimely death, but we do know while in office that he was so vigilant, always available and on call, that he slept in his clothes.

Theodore H. White explains, in his 1978 biography <u>In Search of History,</u> that learned historians speak of The Law of Unintended Consequences: simple day-by-day actions that turn history into drama. I have discovered this drama, which I choose to call an epic, with the stories I've heard and read and researched, all during Isam's ten years as Sheriff.

What I began, a writing-down of the beloved stories about Ole Isam, became so much more.

I'm convinced that none of these people who loved or argued or drank or shot guns or voted could have envisioned that what they did, created unintended consequences that *still* ripple through Webster County—and throughout the world, for that matter.

Furthermore, I have seen myself, my family, my friends, my neighbors, and my politicians in these stories.

Bob Priddy published some of his radio essays in two volumes, both called <u>Across Our Wide Missouri.</u> In the 1982 Foreword to Volume 1, he explains:

"History is the blood and sweat, tears and smiles of real people—our ancestors socially, politically, and geographically. Whatever they were, we are. Whatever possibilities for greatness or failure they had within them exist within us. Realizing that and understanding those things about the people who shaped our past, we should be better able to shape our present and future."

Missouri journalist Jim Hamilton editorialized in July 2003: "We've altered the Ozarks unintentionally in many cases. Multiflora rose is likely the best example of good intentions gone awry...." Yet, during the ten years when Isam was Sheriff, many positive changes occurred, among other told and untold attributes: the polio vaccine, a new national highway system, electricity to rural areas, television, and a country unified against Communism.

In Webster County, Missouri, 1945 to 1955 brought highway patrol being based in the county seat of Marshfield, a city police force being created in Marshfield, a historical society being established. A sheriff serving more than one term and women serving for the first time on a jury resulted from a new Missouri state constitution that included many other changes.

But most of all, *When Isam Was Sheriff* is the story of how a common man dreamed of being sheriff and then became one, not only in name but in the hearts of his people. It's the story of how an average family survived a great tragedy. It's also the story of how a small community adjusted to post-World War II changes. It's a lot of little stories that make up a big story.

Webster County was a microcosm of rural America in the middle of the 20th century and, because of that, it needs to be remembered and understood as a part of who many of us were and are and who we might become.

Timeline of Major Events

1945 Isam sworn in as Sheriff/ Smith sworn in as P.A./ Burks jailbreak attempt/ WWII ends/ Hewson jailbreak attempt/Tom Cantrell murdered

1946 Blinn begins practice in M'fld/ New MO constitution takes effect/ Women serve as jurors for first time

1947 Miller sworn in as P.A./ Petty arrested/ Petty escapes/ Petty robs Seymour Bank/ Petty captured

1948 Judge Jackson slain/Gregory-Miller jailbreak/ Hosmer passes MO Bar/ Huffman files for Circuit Judge/ Hawkins elected Circuit Judge/ Pres.Truman's train stops in M'fld

1949 Miller sworn in as P.A./ "Aunt Ruth" Caldwell robbed/ Evans becomes M'fld's 1st full-time night watchman/ Carmen Rainey attacked by Mary Margaret Evans/ Carmen divorces Rex Rainey

1950 Mary Margaret Evans trial and conviction/ Carmen remarries Rex/ Evans resigns/ Smith named night watchman/ US enters Korean War/ Coots begins as Seymour City Marshal/ Bledsoe kills wife/ Kile-Clark assault Isam in jailbreak attempt/ Pope elected State Representative

1951 Hosmer sworn in as P.A./ Coots fired/ Shockleys murdered/ Rex Rainey acquitted/ Essary sentenced

1952 Web. Co. Historical Society founded/ Hosmer runs for Congress/ New section of Route 66 bypasses M'fld,Straf.,Conway,Niangua/ Watters wins nom. for Sec. of State/ Two hwy. patrolmen stationed in M'field

1953 Haymes sworn in as P.A./Eisenhower becomes US Pres./First TV in Web. Co./Kile escapes state prison/Back-to-God parades/Web. Co.'s Selective Service Board removed/End of Korean War/Isam sued for contempt of court/Hubble dies

1954 Congress adds "under God" to pledge of allegiance/ Brown vs. Bd. of Education/ Jeff.City prison riot/ Priest murders niece/Hitchhikers murder young N.J. driver/Isam fined for contempt

1955 Hosmer sworn in as P.A./ Web. Co. hires a cook for jail/ Isam and Eva move out of courthouse/ Web. Co.'s 100th birthday/ Rabies outbreak/ Polio vaccine/ Replogle first full-time deputy and jailer/ Isam's car crash/ Priest trial/ Web. Co. begins to get dial phones/ M'fld. City Police Force started/ Web. Co's Centennial Celebration/ Isam dies of heart attack/ Owen elected sheriff/ Pres. Eisenhower has heart attack/ Priest has heart attack

HOW TO ORDER:

<u>TELEPHONE ORDERS</u>:
          CALL 417-859-6061

<u>EMAIL ORDERS</u>:
          knust@fidnet.com

<u>POSTAL ORDERS</u>:
          BIRCH CREEK PUBLISHING
          P.O. BOX 777
          MARSHFIELD, MO
              65706-0777

<u>COST</u>: $29.00 (includes
          applicable sales tax)
        [postage and packaging for
        mail order: additional $5.00
        per book within the US]